Handbook of
Couples Therapy

Handbook of Couples Therapy

Edited by

Michele Harway

WILEY

John Wiley & Sons, Inc.

For general information on our other products and services please contact our Customer Care Department within the United States at (800) 762-2974, outside the United States at (317) 572-3993 or fax (317) 572-4002.

Wiley also publishes its books in a variety of electronic formats. Some content that appears in print may not be available in electronic books. For more information about Wiley products, visit our web site at www.wiley.com.

Library of Congress Cataloging-in-Publication Data:

Handbook of couples therapy / edited by Michele Harway.
    p. cm.
  Includes bibliographical references.
  ISBN 0-471-44408-1 (cloth: alk. paper)
  1. Marital psychotherapy—Handbooks, manuals, etc.   I. Harway, Michele.
  RC488.5.H3263 2005
  616.89'1562—dc22

                                2004042252

Printed in the United States of America.

10 9 8 7 6 5 4 3 2 1

Acknowledgments

COMPLETING A VOLUME like this is accompanied by a variety of feelings. The main one is relief at being able to take the manuscript off my desk, although knowing how busy I get, my desk will probably stay clean for a grand total of about 50 seconds. Closely following the relief is the sense of gratitude that I feel toward a myriad of people who were involved in helping me complete this project. I first want to thank Dr. Florence Kaslow who encouraged me to develop this edited volume and who was instrumental in convincing Wiley to publish it. Dr. Kaslow has always been a wonderful role model and professional cheerleader for me.

The staff of John Wiley & Sons, particularly Isabel Pratt and Peggy Alexander (who stepped in when the original editor changed positions), are much appreciated.

During the time I was developing the concept behind the book and inviting chapter authors, I was going through a difficult professional transition and I want to thank all of my friends at the Phillips Graduate Institute who were my sounding boards and dear, "family members." I won't mention you all by name, but I think you know who you are, and I hope you know that I care about you deeply.

Since joining the faculty at Antioch University, Santa Barbara, I have found a wonderfully supportive group of colleagues and new friends. I want to particularly thank Dr. Catherine Radecki-Bush who tolerated my brief moments of insanity as I completed this task. Cathy also was helpful to me in my work by asking me to teach a class on couples therapy, knowing perhaps that preparing for the class would crystallize some important relevant ideas.

Finally, I would like to thank the many couples I have been honored to work with clinically over the years. I have learned so much from you!

And to my husband Bruce Antman who has always maintained that any relationship is salvageable as long as both members of the couple are willing to do whatever it takes to make it work, I say, "I agree."

MICHELE HARWAY, PhD

Contents

About the Contributors

Donald W. Adams, PhD, earned his doctorate in clinical psychology from Duke University. After three years as director of Children's Service in a rural North Carolina Mental Health Center and another three years as director of Psychological Services at Dorothea Dix Hospital Inpatient Adolescent Treatment Program, he began, in 1981, full time private practice in Cary, North Carolina. Dr. Adams specialized in play therapy and taught seminars and conducted conference workshops on child psychotherapy in the 1980s. His practice has been consistently oriented toward the healthy adjustment of children and families. He has been active in the North Carolina Psychological Association and served as president in 1995/1996. He and his wife, Jo, a psychiatric nurse specialist, were trained in PAIRS in 1993. He refocused much of his professional energy toward treating troubled relationships and teaching relationship skills. He has taught many aspects of PAIRS and has been active in developing and refining PAIRS programs. He is currently the vice president of the PAIRS Foundation and serves on the executive board and steering committee of PAIRS. Dr. Adams co-authored a chapter on sensuality and sexuality in *Building Intimate Relationships.*

James F. Alexander, PhD, is the progenitor (with B. V. Parsons) of functional family therapy (FFT), a nationally and internationally acclaimed and empirically demonstrated intervention model for juvenile delinquents, oppositional and conduct-disordered youth, and substance abusing youth. Since 1968, he has been on the faculty at the University of Utah. He is the 2001 recipient of the Distinguished Award for Lifetime Contributions to Family Therapy Research of the American Association for Marriage and Family Therapy. Dr. Alexander is the author of over 90 chapters and refereed journal articles, two books, and over 150 convention presentations and academic colloquia. He has also presented at over 300 national and international clinical training workshops.

Daniel J. Alonzo, MA, is a member of the core faculty at Phillips Graduate Institute in Encino, California. He is a member of the Society for the Scientific

Study of Sexuality (SSSS) and has presented papers at the SSSS Western Regional Conferences and the Los Angeles SSSS Chapter. He is also a member of the American Association of Sex Educators, Counselors, and Therapists (AASECT), and he is an AASECT Certified Sex Therapist. In addition, he is an American Association for Marriage and Family Therapy Approved Supervisor and a California Association of Marriage and Family Therapy Certified Supervisor, providing supervision, training, workshops, and consultation with mental health agencies in the Los Angeles area. He has been a California Licensed Marriage and Family Therapist for more than 13 years, specializing in sexual minority mental health, couple therapy, and working with same-sex couples.

Brent Bradley, PhD, is assistant professor of counseling and director of the marriage and family therapy track in the Graduate Counseling Department at Indiana Wesleyan University. He received his doctorate in Marriage and Family Therapy from Fuller Seminary School of Psychology in 2001. He is a clinical member of the American Association for Marriage and Family Therapy. Dr. Bradley has published original research in emotionally focused couples therapy (EFT), and actively researches, writes, and presents the approach.

Stephen Cheung, PsyD, is an interim core faculty of clinical psychology at Antioch University in Los Angeles. He is teaching Brief Therapy, Family Therapy, Group Therapy, and Psychological Testing. Before he joined Antioch University in 2004, Dr. Cheung had been a program director and clinical psychologist at Asian Pacific Counseling and Treatment Centers (APCTC) in Los Angeles coordinating and supervising their children and adult programs for 12 years. For almost three decades, he has been providing short-term and longer-term psychotherapy to a wide variety of clients. He has specialized in: Eating, Substance-related, Personality, Mood, and Anxiety Disorders; grief therapy; and psychological testing. Since 1996, he has been teaching at Phillips Graduate Institute, California State University at Los Angeles, and Pepperdine University. He has also been presenting training in strategic and solution-focused brief therapy, an integrated treatment approach to eating disorders, and psychotheray with childhood abuse survivors in local, national, and international mental health conferences.

Kahni Clements received her BA in psychology from the University of California at Los Angeles. She is currently a graduate student in clinical psychology at Indiana University-Bloomington. Her research interests are relationship violence and couples communication interactions.

Yolanda de Varela, PhD Candidate, is a clinical psychologist with a master's degree in educational psychology and is completing her doctorate. She has been president of the Panamanian Psychological Association, a founding member of the International Institute of Object Relations Therapy, and director of the Panama Satellite Program of IIORT. She is author and co-author of many articles on object relations and on couples therapy.

Coreen Farris received her BA in psychology from Brandeis University. She is a graduate student in clinical psychology at Indiana University-Bloomington. Her research interests are in substance use and aggression.

Ellen Faulk, MA, is a faculty member at Phillips Graduate Institute in Encino, California. She is a member of the California Association of Marriage and Family Therapists, the American Association for Marriage and Family Therapy, and a student member of the American Psychological Association. Ms. Faulk provides training, workshops, and consultation for mental health providers on working with adult survivors of sexual abuse. She has been a consultant to the Los Angeles Police Department and the Los Angeles Federal Bureau of Investigation. Ms. Faulk is a practicing marriage and family therapist specializing in traumatized populations.

Lori H. Gordon, PhD, is founder/president/training director of the PAIRS Foundation, Inc. and serves as chief executive officer of the executive board. She conducts a private clinical practice through the Family Relations Institute, Falls Church, Virginia, and consults through Tequesta Consulting Services, Ltd. in Fort Lauderdale, Florida. She is the author of three popular books: *Love Knots, Passage to Intimacy,* and *If You Really Loved Me.* She is also co-author of two professional articles on the PAIRS program as well as a range of professional training curricula, articles, and materials. She continues to develop relationship programs through the PAIRS Foundation that are designed to sustain healthy marriages and stable families. Dr. Gordon trains health care professionals and selected public worldwide to teach the range of PAIRS programs.

Michele Harway, PhD, ABPP, is a member of the core faculty in the Psychology Department at Antioch University, Santa Barbara. She is also a member of the consulting faculty at the Fielding Graduate Institute and she maintains a private practice in Westlake Village, California. Dr. Harway has written and presented extensively on domestic violence, trauma survival, gender, and family issues. She is the author or editor of eight books including *Treating the Changing Family: Handling Normative and Unusual Events* and *Spouse Abuse: Assessing & Treating Battered Women, Batterers, and Their Children (Second Edition).* Active in governance of the American Psychological Association (APA), she is past-president of the Division of Family Psychology and current treasurer of the Society for the Study of Men and Masculinity. She is a fellow of three divisions of APA and is also a board-certified family psychologist (ABPP).

Amy Holtzworth-Munroe, PhD, is a professor of psychology at Indiana University, Bloomington. She received her doctorate in clinical psychology from the University of Washington. For almost 20 years, she has conducted research on the problem of husband violence, comparing the social skills of violent and nonviolent husbands and examining the marital interactions of violent couples. Her more recent research focuses on subtypes of male batterers. She has led batterer treatment groups and worked with a local domestic violence task force to set up a batterers' treatment program. Dr. Holtzworth-Munroe teaches a couples therapy practicum for graduate students. She is past associate editor of *Journal of Consulting and Clinical Psychology* and *Cognitive Therapy and Research* and a past member of NIH grant review panels in the area of family violence.

Susan M. Johnson, PhD, is professor of psychology and psychiatry at Ottawa University and director of the Ottawa Couple and Family Institute. She received her doctorate in counseling psychology from the University of British Columbia. She is a registered psychologist in the province of Ontario, Canada, and a member of the editorial board of the *Journal of Marital and Family Therapy,* the *Journal of Couple and Relationship Therapy,* and the *Journal of Family Psychology.* She is one of the originators and the main proponent of emotionally focused couples therapy, now one of the best validated couples' approaches in North America.

Florence W. Kaslow, PhD, ABPP, is in independent practice as a psychologist, coach, family business consultant, and mediator in Palm Beach County, Florida. She is also director of the Florida Couples and Family Institute; an adjunct professor of medical psychology, Department of Psychiatry at Duke University Medical School in Durham, North Carolina; and a visiting professor of psychology at Florida Institute of Technology in Melbourne, Florida. Dr. Kaslow is board certified in clinical, family, and forensic psychology from the American Board of Professional Psychology (ABPP), and in sexology from the American Board of Clinical Sexology. Dr. Kaslow is a fellow of Divisions 12, 29, 41, 42, 43, and 46 of the American Psychological Association, the American Association for Marriage and Family Therapy (AAMFT), and other organizations. She has edited, authored, or co-authored 19 books and has contributed chapters to more than 50 other books. Over 150 of her articles have been published in professional journals here and abroad. She is also on the editorial boards of numerous journals in psychology and family psychology. Dr. Kaslow has received numerous honors in psychology, family psychology, and international psychology.

Charley Lang, MA, MFT, has a private practice in Los Angeles. He also teaches Narrative Therapy at Antioch University, Los Angeles, and supervises the mental health staff at the AIDS Service Center in Pasadena. He produced and directed the award-winning documentary films *Live to Tell:*

The First Gay and Lesbian Prom in America, Battle for the Tiara, and *Gay Cops: Pride Behind the Badge.*

Linda Morano Lower, MS, MA, LMFT, holds masters degrees in both marriage and family therapy and ascetical theology from California Lutheran University and Fordham University, respectively. She has been in private practice as a marriage and family therapist for 17 years in Camarillo and Westlake Village, and she specializes in working with couples at all stages of their life cycles. Linda lives in Camarillo, California, where, with her therapist husband, she is parenting two teen-aged daughters.

Don-David Lusterman, PhD, is the author of *Infidelity: A Survival Guide* and co-editor of *Casebook for Integrating Family Therapy: An Ecosystemic Approach* and *Integrating Family Therapy: Handbook of Family Psychology and Systems Theory* as well as several other books, book chapters, and articles. He also serves as consulting editor for the *Journal of Family Psychology* and is on the editorial board of *The American Journal of Family Therapy.* He founded the program in family counseling at Hofstra University in 1973 and served as its coordinator until 1980. He was also the founding executive director of the American Board of Family Psychology (now part of the American Board of Professional Psychology) and holds an ABPP Diplomate in family psychology. He is a fellow of APA's divisions of Family Psychology, Psychotherapy, Independent Practice, Media Psychology, and Men and Masculinity. He is also a fellow and approved supervisor for the American Association for Marriage and Family Therapy. He is a charter member of the American Family Therapy Academy on whose board he also serves. Dr. Lusterman is in private practice in Baldwin, New York.

C. Haydee Mas, PhD, did her undergraduate work at the University of Michigan and her graduate studies in clinical psychology at the University of Utah where she was chairperson of the graduate student minority committee. Her research interests and publications have focused on therapist-client communication styles, FFT process studies, support systems in abusive families, as well as family communication and attributional styles in families with an adolescent. She is currently in private practice working with couples and families with adolescents and children, and she conducts therapy in Spanish with bilingual and bicultural clients and families.

Susan H. McDaniel, PhD, is professor of psychiatry and family medicine, director of the Division of Family Programs and the Wynne Center for Family Research in Psychiatry, and associate chair of the Department of Family Medicine at the University of Rochester School of Medicine and Dentistry in Rochester, New York. She has many publications in the areas of medical family therapy, family-oriented primary care, and supervision and consultation. Her special areas of interest are family dynamics and genetic testing, somatization, and gender and health. She is a frequent speaker at meetings of both health and mental health professionals. Dr. McDaniel is co-editor, with Thomas Campbell, MD, of the multidisciplinary journal, *Families, Systems and Health,* and serves on many other journal boards. She co-authored or co-edited the following books: *Systems Consultation, Family-Oriented Primary Care, Medical Family Therapy, Integrating Family Therapy, Counseling Families with Chronic Illness, The Shared Experience of Illness, Integrating Family Therapy,* and the *Casebook for Integrating Family Therapy.* Some books have been translated into several languages; an additional volume is exclusively in German.

Dr. McDaniel was chair of the Commission on Accreditation for Marriage and Family Therapy Education in 1998, president of the Division of Family Psychology of the American Psychological Association (APA) in 1999, and chair of the APA Publications and Communications Board in 2002. Dr. McDaniel was recognized by the APA as the 1995 Family Psychologist of the Year. In 1998, she was the first psychologist to be a fellow in the Public Health Service Primary Care Policy Fellowship. She also won the Postdoctoral Academic Mentoring Award from her medical school in 1998, and in 2000 she received the award for Innovative Contributions to Family Therapy from the American Family Therapy Academy.

William C. Nichols, EdD, ABPP, is a marital and family therapist and diplomate in clinical psychology, a fellow, clinical member, and approved supervisor of the AAMFT; a charter member of both the American Family Therapy Academy and the International Family Therapy Association (IFTA); and a fellow of both the American Psychological Association and the American Psychological Society. He was in full-time private practice for nearly 25 years and taught and supervised postdoctoral, doctoral, and masters' students in MFT programs and postdegree professionals for 35 years at Florida State University, the Merrill-Palmer Institute, and elsewhere. Founder and first editor of the *Journal of Marital and Family Therapy,* he also edited *Family Relations,* and currently edits *Contemporary Family Therapy.* He has written or edited eight MFT and therapy books, conceptualized and launched MFT accreditation, wrote the first model licensing laws, co-wrote the national licensing examination, and chaired a state licensing board for seven years. He has been president of the AAMFT, IFTA, and the National Council on Family Relations.

Roberta L. Nutt, PhD, ABPP, is the founder and director of the counseling psychology doctoral program that emphasizes family psychology and women's/gender issues at Texas Women's University. She is co-author of the "Division 17 Principles Concerning the Counseling/Psychotherapy of Women: Rationale and Implementation" and *Bridging Separate Gender Worlds: Why Men and Women Clash and How Therapists Can Bring Them Together.* Dr. Nutt has written and presented extensively on gender and family issues, served in a number of leadership roles in psychology including president of the Family Psychology Division of APA and held offices in both the women's and men's divisions. She holds the ABPP diplomate in family psychology. She is currently co-chairing an APA Interdivisional Task Force developing new guidelines for psychological practice with girls and women.

Terence Patterson, EdD, ABPP, is professor and director of the doctoral program in counseling psychology at the University of San Francisco. He is a licensed psychologist and is board certified in family psychology with the American Board of Professional Psychology. His specialties are family psychology, ethical issues, and theoretical orientation in psychotherapy. He is on the boards of a number of professional journals and has authored Vol. II (*Cognitive-Behavioral*) of the *Comprehensive Handbook of Psychotherapy,* and the *Couple & Family Clinical Documentation Sourcebook.* Dr. Patterson has served as president of the Division of Family Psychology of the American Psychological Association and is a fellow of APA.

Thomas H. Peake, PhD, ABPP, is professor and associate dean for the School of Psychology at Florida Institute of Technology (Melbourne), and adjunct professor in the Department of Aging and Mental Health of the Florida Institute of Mental Health of the University of South Florida (Tampa). Licensed in Virginia, Michigan, Florida, and chartered in Great Britain, he has practiced clinical, health, and family psychology for over 15 years. He is a diplomate (ABPP) in both clinical and health psychology and is an approved supervisor for AAMFT. Dr. Peake's publication and practice areas include books and articles on brief psychotherapies, clinical training and supervision, couples therapy, medical/health psychology, healthy aging, and a book *Cinema and Life Development: Healing Lives and Training Therapists.*

Patricia Pitta, PhD, ABPP, is a board-certified family psychologist. She received her doctorate from Fordham University and completed postdoctoral training in family therapy at the Center for Family Learning, Ryebrook, New York. In addition, she holds a degree in pastoral formation which enables her to integrate spirituality with psychology. For the past 10 years, Dr. Pitta has been a professor of psychology in the doctoral and postdoctoral training programs at St. John's University. As developer of Integrative Healing Family Therapy, Dr. Pitta has published many articles about the theory and its applications. She has also produced a video entitled "Parenting Your Elderly Parents" (published by APA Publications) and is the author of a marital therapy manual (published by Division 42 of APA).

Joy K. Rice, PhD, is clinical professor of psychiatry and Emerita Professor of Educational Policy and Women's Studies at the University of Wisconsin–Madison. She also maintains an active psychotherapy practice with Psychiatric Services in Madison. Her research activity includes more than 100 national and international presentations and publications on family change, poverty, and mental health. *Living through Divorce: A Developmental Approach to Divorce Therapy*, written with Dr. David Rice, was honored as a Book-of-the-Month selection.

Active in international psychology, Dr. Rice is secretary of the International Council of Psychologists, chair elect of the APA Committee on International Relations in Psychology, and president elect of APA Division 52, International Psychology. She has received numerous awards and honors for her research and social policy work on behalf of disadvantaged families and women nationally and internationally. She is a recipient of the Educational Press Association Distinguished Achievement Award, a fellow of the American Psychological Association, and is listed in Who's Who of Women and the World's Who's Who of Women.

Lynne V. Rosen, LCSW, is core faculty and director of the Post Modern Therapy Training Program at Phillips Graduate Institute in Encino, California. She is interested in collaborative education and integrating her passion and commitment to diversity and social justice in training and teaching contexts. Ms. Rosen is co-founder of Women's Project Los Angeles (WPLA), a community-based project focused on social constructionist and feminist ideas. WPLA utilizes innovative forms of dialogue in order to bring forward new perspectives and possibilities that can lead to meaningful change in women's lives. She maintains a private practice and has a long-standing interest in working with women who are taking their lives back from eating problems, abuse, and trauma and in working with couples and families.

David E. Scharff, MD, is a psychiatrist and psychoanalyst. He is co-director of the International Psychotherapy Institute, Washington, DC. Dr. Scharff is clinical professor of psychiatry at Georgetown University and at the Uniformed Services University of the Health Sciences. He is author, co-author, and editor of 15 books including *Object Relations Couples Therapy* and *Object Relations Individual Therapy*.

Ilene Serlin, PhD, ADTR, is a licensed psychologist and a registered dance/movement therapist. Dr. Serlin is a fellow of the American Psychological Association, past president of Division 32 of APA, council representative from Division 32, and has served on the editorial boards of *The Arts in Psychotherapy, Journal of the American Dance Therapy Association,* and the *Journal of Humanistic Psychology*. She has taught at Saybrook Graduate School and Research Institute, UCLA, Antioch University, and Alliant Graduate School. She has consulted and worked with clergy, and is the author of: *Therapy with a Borderline Nun, A Psycho-spiritual Body Approach to a Residential Treatment of Catholic Religious,* and *The Last Temptation of Christ*.

She is currently in private practice in San Francisco and Sonoma County, California.

Louise Bordeaux Silverstein, PhD, is associate professor at the Ferkauf Graduate School of Psychology at Yeshiva University, Bronx, New York, where she has taught courses in family therapy and the social construction of gender since 1992. Dr. Silverstein is a past president of the American Psychological Association's Division of Family Psychology. She is co-founder, with Dr. Carl Auerbach, of the Yeshiva University Fatherhood Project, a qualitative research study of fathering from a multicultural perspective. Dr. Silverstein's publications focus on fathering, feminist theory, and the social construction of gender. She is the co-editor (with Thelma Jean Goodrich) of *Feminist Family Therapy: Empowerment and Social Location* and co-author with Carl F. Auerbach of *An Introduction to Coding and Analyzing Data in Qualitative Research.* Dr. Silverstein is a family therapist in private practice in Brooklyn, New York.

Sally D. Stabb, PhD, is a licensed psychologist and associate professor of counseling psychology at Texas Woman's University. Her research interests include women's issues, emotion, couples, and multiculturalism. Dr. Stabb teaches courses in process and outcome research, qualitative research methods, psychotherapy theories, professional issues, and practicum.

Mark Stanton, PhD, ABPP, is professor of psychology and chair of the Department of Graduate Psychology at Azusa Pacific University. He is a diplomate in family psychology, American Board of Professional Psychology, and a licensed psychologist in the state of California. He is the editor of *The Family Psychologist* and 2005 president of the Division of Family Psychology of the American Psychological Association.

Angela E. Steep, PsyD, is a postdoctoral fellow in primary care at the University of Oklahoma Health Sciences Center. She did her internship at the Medical College of Virginia, graduate work at Florida Institute of Technology, and her undergraduate work at the University of North Carolina at Chapel Hill. Particular areas of interest include mind-body medicine, medical/health psychology, primary care psychology, and motivational interviewing.

Robin Rose Temple, MA, MSW, CAC II, is a master teacher and trainer for the PAIRS Foundation, where she has been teaching for eight years. She holds post-master's certification from the Gestalt Institute of Denver and the Family Therapy Training Center of Colorado, which recently awarded her the Alumnus of the Year Award for her work teaching PAIRS in the Front Range of Colorado. She is also certified as a Colorado addictions counselor and contributing author to the book *Bridging Intimate Relation-ships*. Ms. Temple has been working with families for 25 years. She is a de-voted mother of three, and she is passionate about healing relationships of all sorts. It is in her own marriage that she has learned the most about being part of a couple.

William H. Watson, PhD, is associate professor of psychiatry (psychology) and neurology at the University of Rochester School of Medicine and Dentistry/Strong Memorial Hospital. He is senior training faculty of the Family Therapy Training Program and is the family psychology consultant to the Strong Epilepsy Center. Areas of interest include spirituality in psy-chotherapy, family systems in the workplace, couples therapy, and a family systems understanding of mind/body problems.

CHAPTER 1

Setting the Stage for Working with Couples

Michele Harway

I N THE FAIRY TALE, the Prince and Cinderella fall in love, get married, and live happily ever after. Our culture abounds with similar stories. In each case, the story seems to end at the moment of commitment and we are seldom privy to the adjustments that the couples must make in beginning a life together. And yet, the adjustment must be great or more couples would succeed in celebrating their Golden Wedding Anniversary (Kreider & Fields, 2002, based on U.S. Census data, cite only 5% of married couples reach at least their 50th anniversary). The same authors report 10% of married couples divorcing within 5 years of marriage and 20% of married couples divorcing within 10 years of marriage. There are no parallel figures for same-gender couples or cohabiting couples. But clearly the track record is not good.

Some professionals (Nichols, Chapter 3) suggest that the first year of marriage (or of living together) is actually the most difficult year of a relationship. This makes sense: Even when the couple has a similar cultural background, they have grown up in different families, whose daily living habits may differ on the most mundane issue (how to put the roll of toilet paper on the holder) to the somewhat more important issues (who is responsible for what tasks in the home). These two individuals may have different expectations of a relationship and different values on a wide variety of subtle and not-so-subtle topics. The differences may multiply when, in addition, the two come from different cultural groups. Faced with the complexities of ironing out those differences and the lack of support from the culture at large, it is not surprising that many couples simply give up. Some, however, seek out psychotherapy, often as a last-ditch effort.

This book focuses on couples therapy and the interventions that mental health professionals implement in helping couples develop the tools to make a successful dyad.

Yet, many psychotherapists begin seeing couples without extensive training in how to do couples work. The intention of this book is to fill in those gaps in mental health professionals' repertoire.

While much of this book focuses on heterosexual couples (often married), many of the issues we consider affect same-gender couples, as well as heterosexual cohabiting couples. Because there are issues with which same-gender couples struggle that are unique to their relationships, we have included a chapter that specifically addresses these couples. Recognizing that cultural issues are very powerful determinants of couple interaction, we have woven cultural issues into each chapter rather than having a separate chapter on this topic.

We have considered work with couples from three perspectives: a developmental one, a theoretical one, and a situational one. Section I of this book looks at couples at different stages of the life cycle, since clearly different issues affect them at each stage and distinct therapeutic approaches to working with them are appropriate. We have used McGoldrick's life cycle stages (loosely construed) to guide us in our choices. Accordingly, Section I begins with couples at the premarital stage (Chapter 2). Gordon, Temple, and Adams describe PAIRS, a premarital counseling curriculum, extensively designed to include a multiplicity of interventions to assist couples as they enter a committed relationship. In Chapter 3, Nichols thoroughly explores the first years of commitment. He includes a discussion of the nature of marriage, cohabitation, and commitment; an overview of the tasks of the family cycle; and issues related to psychotherapy with couples in the early stages of the life cycle. Lower (Chapter 4) considers the difficult life transition to parenthood and the adjustments that confront couples with young children. In Chapter 5, Mas and Alexander explore the four essential features of treatment based on clinical, research, and theoretical literature as applied to families with adolescents. Highlighting the multiplicity of differences that such families may bring into the therapy room, these authors focus on cultural diversity issues. Completing the part on life cycle stages, Peake and Steep (Chapter 6) examine novel ways to intervene with older couples capitalizing on their lived experience and using popular films and other resources as adjuncts to psychotherapy.

Section II of the book focuses on different theoretical approaches to working with couples. Silverstein (Chapter 7) considers the application of Bowen family systems theory to work with couples and provides a supportive feminist critique of the theory. In Chapter 8, Patterson argues that common conceptualizations of cognitive-behavioral approaches to couples therapy do not always provide an adequate integration of these two traditions. Focusing on the separate foundations of behavioral approaches on the one hand, and cognitive theories on the other, Patterson provides an understanding of the melding of these two traditions into cognitive-behavioral couples therapy. Scharff and de Varela (Chapter 9) describe how object relations therapy would be applied to couples. Shifting from more traditional approaches of working with couples to postmodern thinking, Rosen and Lang (Chapter 10) introduce key aspects of doing narrative therapy with couples. In the first of several integrative approaches to working with couples, Bradley and Johnson (Chapter 11) present emotionally-focused therapy, an integration of collaborative client-centered, gestalt, systems approaches, constructivist thinking, and understandings derived from attachment theory and the empirical literature. Cheung (Chapter 12) proposes the integration of strategic family therapy and solution-focused approaches to working with couples. In Chapter 13, Pitta describes integrative healing couples therapy that uses psychodynamic, behavioral, communication, and systemic theories in understanding the couple's functioning. Concluding this part, Nutt (Chapter 14) describes feminist and contextual approaches to working with couples.

Section III approaches couples' interventions from the perspective of common presentations in therapy. Thus, Watson and McDaniel (Chapter 15) describe the work with couples who are confronting medical concerns. The interface of the biological and the emotional provide the framework for their work in medical settings. In Chapter 16, Harway and Faulk consider how a history of sexual abuse in one member of the couple may affect the overall couple's functioning and may lead to difficult therapeutic concerns. A common concern in couples therapy is the existence of physical violence. Holtzworth-Munroe, Clements, and Farris (Chapter 17) discuss the implications of intervening with these types of couples. Addiction is another difficult issue that couples bring with them into therapy. Stanton (Chapter 18) reviews key elements of couples therapy for the treatment of addictive behaviors. Infidelity is said to affect a large number of couples and presents particular challenges. In Chapter 19, Lusterman explores issues related to working with couples who have been touched by infidelity and proposes an effective model for intervention. Psychotherapists are often uncomfortable with exploring spiritual issues in therapy. Yet, spiritual and religious differences, like other forms of cultural difference, contribute to some couples' dissatisfaction with their relationship. Serlin (Chapter 20) considers how to interweave spiritual concerns in the course of psychotherapy. While couples comprised of two same-sex partners share many of the same issues as heterosexual partners, Alonzo (Chapter 21) describes some unique issues for gay or lesbian couples. Kaslow (Chapter 22) examines the impact of socioeconomic factors on couples' functioning and describes some approaches to working with money issues in therapy.

Not all couples presenting for psychotherapy are there to improve the couple's bond. Some couples initiate therapy to provide a smoother transition to divorce, while other couples initiate therapy in the hopes of saving their relationship but ultimately decide instead to focus on marital dissolution. Rice (Chapter 23) considers special issues in working with divorcing couples.

Finally, while many of the chapters interweave empirical information with clinical information, in Chapter 24, we consider what the research has to tell us about the nature of couples functioning and the effectiveness of our interventions. Stabb reviews both the literature on well-functioning and dysfunctional couples and research that elucidates what is useful in couples therapy interventions. Chapter 25 summarizes the multiplicity of threads that have been developed in the many outstanding contributions to this volume.

Couples therapy can be challenging work. Nonetheless, since couples and families provide the major building blocks of our society, the work that we do in shoring up the foundations has impact beyond those we touch directly. As we know from systems theories, the concentric circles of involvement of the individuals who comprise our families and couples, within the larger context of our communities and cultures, makes our impact ricochet from its point of impact to the entire pond. As such, couples therapists have the possibility of being change agents at a much wider scale than they may have believed. Good training in doing couples work thus becomes critical.

REFERENCE

Kreider, R. M., & Fields, J. M. (2002, February). *Number, timing and duration of marriages and divorces: 1996* (Current population reports). Washington, DC: U.S. Department of Commerce, U.S. Census Bureau.

SECTION I

LIFE CYCLE STAGES

CHAPTER 2

Premarital Counseling from the PAIRS Perspective

Lori H. Gordon, Robin Rose Temple, and Donald W. Adams

THE PREMARITAL COUPLE treads a challenging path between falling in love and solidifying a commitment. Premarital couples seek professional help to prevent or to understand and resolve relationship difficulties that may have arisen even before marriage. The status and circumstances of premarital couples seeking help vary from the young-and-inexperienced to the previously married (with or without children) to long-term cohabiters who have not committed to marriage. The premarital couple is wise to be cautious. Statistics tell us that the likelihood they will find happiness and longevity in marriage is despairingly low whereas 90% of couples married during the years 1945 to 1949 made it to their 10-year anniversary. Forty years later, barely 70% of those married during the years 1985 to 1989 celebrated a decade of wedded bliss—and the statistics continue to decrease (Fleming, 2003).

Premarital couples seek assurance that they can create a lifelong intimate partnership. Each partner needs accurate concepts, conducive attitudes, technical knowledge and skills, and practiced competencies to sustain a loving relationship. As in ballroom dancing, the couple relationship gains best through co-learning, by acquiring and practicing these intimate relationship skills together. The couple needs to acquire high levels of skill to continue dancing lovingly in the face of changing family life with its unrelenting and often discouraging economic, domestic, and parental responsibilities. The counselor, who wishes to effectively offer such knowledge and skills to couples, needs to undertake relevant professional training. Such training is not yet established in most graduate clinical programs.

ABOUT PRACTICAL APPLICATION OF INTIMATE RELATIONSHIP SKILLS

Practical Application of Intimate Relationship Skills (PAIRS) is a curriculum for intimate relationship skills training. PAIRS grew from the ashes of marital disaster. The creator and developer of PAIRS (co-author Lori Gordon), on the demise of her own 17-year marriage, set out to find missing answers. PAIRS is drawn from many emerging humanizing interpersonal therapies of the second half of the twentieth century (Satir, Casriel, Bach, Sager, Brandon, Framo, Bowen, Wynne, Perls, Guerney, Brandon, Zilbergeld, etc.). PAIRS has evolved over 30 years. Gordon has refined the keys to intimacy and shaped and polished the training exercises needed to create deep personal transformative learning by relationship partners.

PAIRS has been experienced by tens of thousands of couples, many who were on the brink of divorce (DeMaria, 1998); and by tens of thousands of individuals, wanting to develop skills to prevent a repeat of the devastation of relationship breakup. Gordon's self-help book for couples and individuals, *Passage to Intimacy* (1993), presents the main ideas and exercises of PAIRS that can be learned at home and practiced outside the classroom. Incisive descriptions and thoughtful discussions by PAIRS Master Teachers, a review of research about PAIRS, and critical issues such as the PAIRS Ethics Code for teachers are brought together in *Building Intimate Relationships: Bridging Treatment, Education and Enrichment through the PAIRS Program* (DeMaria & Hannah, 2003). The PAIRS experience significantly increases relationship satisfaction, sustainable love, and commitment.

A central tenet of PAIRS is that *sustained intimacy is required to maintain a lasting marriage.* When intimacy, the deep emotional experience of loving connection, is lost, the ground the marriage is built on becomes shaky. Good will is then lost and the desire (and ability) to solve problems, overcome obstacles, and persist in the face of fear and uncertainty, quickly erodes. With its emphasis on intimacy, PAIRS goes to the heart and the heat of the matter. Once couples learn to create, re-create, and sustain intimacy, many premarital and marital issues, such as commitment, cooperation, fidelity, and creative management of differences, are much more quickly resolved.

PAIRS is designed to (1) realign attitudes and beliefs about love and relationships and about marriage and family life; (2) train and evolve each partner's self-knowledge, emotional literacy, and emotional efficacy; and (3) change ineffective behaviors that diminish intimacy by teaching those behaviors and skills that increase intimacy and relationship enhancement. The PAIRS curriculum is a theory-based, cohesive, orchestrated body of concepts and practical activities that is a powerful technology for change. PAIRS has, thus far, proven effective in every population, including disadvantaged youth, middle and high schools, foreign cultures, entire families, business groups, faith-based adult education, separated and divorcing couples, premarital couples, and devitalized couples in marital doldrums.

GOALS AND OBJECTIVES OF PREMARITAL COUNSELING FROM THE PAIRS PERSPECTIVE

The PAIRS trained professional (PTP) translates the PAIRS concepts and tools found in the 120-hour experiential PAIRS Relationship Mastery Course into an effective counseling approach that is titled OFFICE PAIRS. A PTP is a licensed mental health professional who has been trained in the PAIRS professional training program. PTPs have had more than 100 hours of direct experience with the PAIRS concepts and training exercises. During their training, PTPs personally experience the full range of PAIRS exercises, usually with their partners. After training, most PTPs teach, practice, and internalize the PAIRS concepts and tools. In OFFICE PAIRS, the PTP personally and directly helps the couple learn PAIRS competencies, practice them under an experienced eye, and apply them outside the office and obtain feedback on their "homework."

When working with a premarital couple, the PTP holds in heart and mind an awareness of what is necessary to be an effective partner as well as those skills, attitudes, and strategies couples need to assure an ongoing satisfying relationship, conducive to family permanence. These competencies focus on three areas: (1) emotional literacy; (2) conjoint partner skills for building and maintaining intimacy; and (3) practical knowledge, strategies, and attitudes for sustaining positive marriage and family life. Tables 2.1, 2.2, and 2.3 list these competencies.

The PTP holds these competencies in heart and mind as a standard for what is needed to sustain couple satisfaction. When couples seek counseling, the PTP notes which of these competencies are missing and develops priorities and strategies for offering knowledge and training in what is needed. Effectively addressing what is missing with interventions, new understandings, and the teaching of new skills, especially for the premarital couple, can prevent years of confusion, misery, and probable later family disintegration. Without training in new competencies, the couple cannot advance far. During the early romantic "illusion" stage of a relationship, moments of hurt, misunderstanding, noting differences, or use of power often trigger doubts and fears about the relationship. Those couples in early relationships coming for counseling are typically experiencing challenges to illusions of perfect fit and unconditional love. This is the optimal time to develop the knowledge, skills, and strategies needed to build a solid relationship rather than an illusory one.

Table 2.1
PAIRS Competencies: Emotional Literacy

1. Comfortable with the names and manifestations of the five basic emotions, i.e., pain, fear, anger, love, and joy. Identifies and expresses these emotions and can listen empathically to them.

2. Recognizes defensive *overreactions* as emotional allergies based on painful memories. Takes responsibility to reduce, control, and change inappropriate responses.

3. Recognizes being emotionally open vs. emotionally closed. When feeling attacked, threatened, or denied, evaluates reality by checking out speaker's meaning and intent, rather than assuming and reacting defensively via rationalizing-explaining-justifying, withdrawing, avoiding, or fighting back.

4. Expresses pain, fear, and anger without attacking or blaming.

5. Listens without interjecting self-concerns. Creates and maintains emotional safety for others.

6. Uses anger constructively to assert self, set limits, define boundaries, and effectively solve problems. Expresses anger appropriately and safely to release suppressed emotions.

7. Believes in one's own value. Feels lovable and good enough without having to be perfect. Accepts having healthy needs and actively pursues getting them met, including the biological needs for physical closeness and emotional openness in an intimate relationship.

8. Experiences and expresses emotions of a type and at an intensity that appropriately fits and that sustains action in accord with one's purpose, intention, and circumstances (emotional efficacy).

Table 2.2
PAIRS Competencies: Conjoint Couple Skills to Create and Maintain Intimacy

1. Confide in one another regularly with emotional openness and empathic listening.

2. Complain to one another regularly (without attacking) including requests for change. Can listen to complaints without defensiveness.

3. Resolve differences and conflicts by seeking to *learn* rather than to prevail. Use fair fighting that involves confiding, empathic listening, complaining with requests for change, and contracting, effective win-win solutions, all without manipulation and dirty fighting.

4. Agree on areas of autonomy, areas of consultation, and areas of mutually shared ownership and decision making.

5. Clarify hidden assumptions and unspoken expectations to minimize misperception and misunderstanding.

6. Help one another heal pains and disappointments, resolve emotional allergies, and clarify hidden assumptions. Conjointly heal and resolve emotional allergy infinity loops.

7. Meet basic needs for sensuality, appropriate sexuality, physical closeness, bonding, and intellectual and emotional sharing with one another.

8. Follow clear, equal, negotiated boundaries regarding what is private and not shared with others outside the relationship.

9. Initiate change when the status quo (division of roles, responsibilities, and privileges) is not satisfactory. Follow through on negotiated changes.

Table 2.3
PAIRS Competencies: Attitudes and Strategies for
Successful Long-Term Relationships

1. Affirm the essential role of regular bonding with an abundance of physical closeness and emotional openness to sustain intimacy. Satisfactorily blend sensuality, sexuality, and bonding in marriage.

2. Choose play, pleasure, recreation, creativity, and humor for the relationship to balance the necessary duties and hard work required to maintain the relationship, home, family, and economic security.

3. Express important hurt, fear, or irritation directly to each other in words, asking to be heard and understood with empathy. Recognize that what is left *unsaid* in a relationship is often more harmful than what is said.

4. Seek forgiveness for hurts inflicted in the relationship by taking responsibility for transgressions, repairing and restoring damages, and expressing regret for pain experienced by partner. Partner, in believing the pain is understood, feels assured that transgressions will not easily reoccur, restores trust and forgives. Let go of grudges and choose to forgive.

5. Give up being right. Invite and express diversity. Welcome differences as sources of vigor, perspective, and healthy growth of a relationship. Choose to learn from each other.

6. Choose trust, truth, mutual respect, and fidelity as the foundation of a lasting, loving relationship.

7. Extend goodwill and positive intent. Do what is pleasing and satisfying to partner. Choose to engage in caring behaviors. Be a good leader or a good follower as each fits.

8. Know each other's pleasure and pain buttons. Refrain from triggering negative reactions.

9. Develop a strong sense of "we." Have intentional rituals, customs, and styles that create a unique relationship and family identity.

10. Encourage connecting to friends and community to assure each has adequate autonomy, independence, and breathing room. Balance the intense closeness and needful interdependence that is at the center of a permanent passionate relationship.

11. Maintain active connections with extended family and other couples and families to provide community, perspective, and support for the relationship and family.

12. Regularly express gratitude, appreciations, blessings, wishes, hopes, and dreams. Positive expressions focus couple and family on desire, fulfillment, and happiness, rather than on victimization, deprivation, scarcity, outrage, or despair.

THE PAIRS PREMARITAL ASSESSMENT

The format Gordon developed for the PAIRS premarital assessment begins with a two-hour *joint interview* with couples to explore their history together, establish the context of their relationship, and set initial goals and plans for the assessment. It involves questions such as:

- How did you meet?
- What drew you together?

- What made you decide to commit to this relationship?
- What are family responses and reactions to this relationship and your reactions to each other's families?
- What are you seeking from this counseling?
- What are your questions of the counselor?
- What are your vocations and how does your work and work communication styles affect your relationship particularly during times of stress.

This longer session is needed to grasp the fabric and playing field of the relationship. The 50-minute hour simply cannot build the trust, connectedness, and collaboration needed for this initial inquiry.

Next schedule two-hour *individual interviews* with *each* partner: This time provides an opportunity to discuss what might be uncomfortable to share in a joint session. These sessions gather the individual social and emotional histories—family conditioning, early beginnings, models from the parental marriage, sibling relationships, decisions and experiences regarding love, trust, caring, criticism, competition, power, communication styles, and marital role expectations, including their hopes for the future as well as fears. Beliefs, expectations, experiences, and life decisions that might affect the couple's relationship are tracked, including invisible loyalties, changes through time in previous relationships, a history of previous marriages or engagements and what led to their dissolution, children, job changes, communication and power impasses, disappointments and how they were handled, and personal hopes and dreams. The individual sessions generate an attitude of openness and growing curiosity on the part of each participant about unique histories, and the conditioning each has brought to the relationship including how differing styles and expectations may mesh or clash. These individual sessions open windows to new understandings that have not previously been realized or considered.

Next, a two-hour *joint interview* for feedback is scheduled. The PTP inquires about and carefully listens to new thoughts or questions that may have arisen from their exploration of issues. The PTP then reviews pertinent data that has been collected and offers specific significant relationship concepts and skills as applicable, such as the PAIRS Dialogue Guide, a communication tool for complaining without blaming. Or a listening skill. Or an exercise designed to uncover mind reading. Or hidden expectations that in PAIRS are called *Love Knots*, such as, "If you loved me, you would know . . ." A nonblaming attitude is maintained throughout. Humor, as appropriate, is often included along with pertinent wisdom and insights. The PTP relabels and reframes many past behaviors and intentions, pointing out how blame is often not the issue. The PTP demonstrates how enormous misunderstandings have often arisen from a lack of information, which if asked for and then given, would clarify misperceptions and hidden assumptions.

In this joint session and, if needed, in one additional joint session, the PTP provides possible explanations of issues that have become tangled or difficult in the relationship. The PTP then discusses formats for acquiring specific relationship knowledge, relationship skills, or specific competencies for emotional literacy. These formats might include PAIRS courses and/or OFFICE PAIRS counseling sessions. These suggestions may also include books to read, specific exercises to practice, and brief workshops to attend that have proven to be effective.

MORE ABOUT RECOMMENDATIONS

Very often PTPs recommend and encourage premarital couples to participate in the four-month PAIRS Relationship Mastery Course developed for the specific purpose of practicing, improving, and sustaining healthy marriage relationships. This semester-long course is recommended because it not only fully addresses relationship fundamentals, it also addresses emotional literacy, understanding one's history and oneself, as well as advanced topics such as pleasure (sensuality and sexuality) and relationship reconstruction.

Alternatively, when appropriate and available, the PTP may recommend that the premarital couple attend one of the shorter PAIRS programs. These include the one-day PAIRS JumpStart, If You Really Love Me . . . , and the Jewish, Catholic, or Christian PrePAIRS programs; the two-day Passage to Intimacy Workshop; or the three-day Christian PAIRS or PAIRS First programs. The PAIRS website, www.pairs.com, provides descriptions, schedules, and location information about these programs. The short programs contain a careful selection of pieces from the full PAIRS curriculum tailored to specific target groups. Most of the short courses begin with understanding the PAIRS Relationship Road Map, learning basic communication and confiding skills as well as how to complain constructively to effect helpful change. Each program adds further PAIRS pieces that are appropriate for its purpose. The PrePAIRS and PAIRS First programs were originally designed for couples in the early years of relationship commitment. These courses are highly appropriate for premarital couples seeking to strengthen their relationship through learning intimate relationship fundamentals.

The premarital couple with moderately high ego strengths, emotional literacy, and openness to learning often finds that the 6- to 10-hour assessment, by itself with the new insights and brief but specific skills and concepts offered, is sufficient to gain renewed confidence in the relationship and in plans to marry. The PTP may also recommend one of the shorter PAIRS workshops to provide elaboration, practice, and consolidation of the new concepts, skills, and strategies that have been developed in the assessment. An invitation is issued for them to return when need arises in the future, indicating the PTP's interest and availability as well as the normal inevitability of the need for continuing attention to the work of a relationship.

For the majority of premarital couples (considering that about half of all marriages end in divorce) and especially for those who are emotionally illiterate, ignorant about successful relationships, and unskilled at intimacy, PTPs routinely recommend the 120-hour Relationship Mastery Course. This program affords the breadth, depth, time, and practice needed to change destructive attitudes and behaviors. This Mastery Course is recommended for those who already have complex issues, are possibly in mutual allergy, may be embarking on a second or third marriage, or are on the verge of breakup but not ready to give up. Typically, the PTP will remain available to the assessment couple for evening 90-minute office sessions to oversee extra practice with the PAIRS skills *during* their participation in the course, and then again *after* the course for any "RePAIRS" that may be needed to refresh the concepts, practice the tools, or help the couple get quickly unstuck should they again become negatively entangled.

When a course or workshop is not immediately available, the PTP may counsel premarital couples in need of more training via OFFICE PAIRS until they can participate in a PAIRS program. The PTP selects concepts, exercises, and experiences thought to be most cogent to their missing competencies and then teaches these in a series of 90-minute sessions. In locations where there are no available PAIRS courses or workshops and when a couple cannot travel to one in another location, the PTP may contract to lead the couple through the content of one of the shorter PAIRS curriculums in a defined series of 90-minute sessions. When engaging a PAIRS curriculum, each purchases a participant's handbook for the selected course and a copy of *The Passage to Intimacy* book, which provides a deeper presentation of the ideas, skills, or attitudes under study. In such OFFICE PAIRS activities, couples receive homework assignments and are expected to practice daily the skills they are learning. OFFICE PAIRS is not undertaken lightly. Teaching these skills is usually easier and more natural in a group setting than in the office.

THE PAIRS RELATIONSHIP MASTERY COURSE

The full PAIRS curriculum is divided into six main sections:

1. Communication and problem solving;
2. Clarifying assumptions;
3. My history and unique self;
4. Emotional reeducation, emotional literacy, and bonding;
5. Pleasure—sensuality and sexuality; and
6. Contracting—clarifying expectations.

The following summary highlights specific PAIRS exercises and key concepts in italic.

COMMUNICATION AND PROBLEM SOLVING

PAIRS begins with a presentation of the *Relationship Roadmap,* the basic PAIRS model of how relationships succeed or become stuck and fail. Couples learn of the essential role of *confiding* in intimacy and then how to listen and speak in ways that deepen their level of confiding. They are taught the *Daily Temperature Reading,* in which they are expected to confide in one another each day sharing Appreciations, New Information, Puzzles, Complaints with Request for Change, and Wishes, Hopes, and Dreams. Participants then read and practice Virginia Satir's (1988) *The New Peoplemaking* and discover how the style one uses can be a far greater problem than the actual issue under discussion. When stressed and communicating in stress styles (Blaming, Placating, Computing, and Distracting), the underlying problem goes unresolved.

Couples are then taught the *Leveling Style of Communication* practiced in the congruent position (face to face, hands in hands), which is a foundation for the subsequent confiding work in the course. They cultivate the skill to slow down communication using *Empathic Shared Meaning,* taking turns being the speaker and the listener with feedback to assure understanding. They next learn how to confide a negative reaction to their partner's behavior all the way through in safety using the PAIRS *Dialogue Guide.* The Dialogue Guide leads the speaker through a sequence of 18 "I-Statement" sentence stems regarding this negative reaction. Maintaining eye contact, holding hands while they speak, giving verbatim feedback, and not answering the complaint or introjecting defensiveness helps couples to stay connected to one another and avoid misunderstandings. They discover how to speak so that the other person really wants to listen, and how to listen with empathy so that the other feels deeply heard and understood.

One of the many paradoxes of PAIRS is how direct and skillful engagement of conflict builds greater closeness, trust, and confidence in the relationship. Couples are taught safe and structured ways to move into the intense emotion regarding a conflict as a first step toward resolving an issue. The *Emotional Jug* is one of the core metaphors of PAIRS. When emotions are cut off or suppressed, it is as if they are poured into a jug and stopped up with a cork—a cork that becomes the "stiff upper lip" of indifference. Partners are taught how to safely remove the cork and "blow their lid." An initial expression of anger quickly gives way to more vulnerable feelings like fear, pain, or grief, which is followed by relief and then gratitude for their partners' listening and acceptance. This process can occur relatively quickly when couples master the tools and are not fearful of each other's emotions. By learning how to express fully one's fear, pain, and anger in safe and nondestructive ways, and to do so in the arms of their beloved, and/or with the support of peers, the bond between intimate partners powerfully deepens. The *Emptying the Jug Exercise* is also taught as a prenegotiation release and as an emotional confiding tool that may be used like the Daily Temperature Reading.

The PAIRS anger and conflict management tools were adapted largely from the work of George Bach (Bach & Wyden, 1969). They include the *Anger Rituals* (the *Haircut*, and the *Vesuvius*) in which one partner asks permission of the other to vent in a time-limited fashion with as much intensity as is present. The Anger Rituals help to contain anger in those who explode or speak caustically *and* to give permission to be angry and assertive to those who rarely allow themselves to do this. Once suppressed emotions around an issue are released, couples can then productively engage the *Fair Fight for Change*, another Bach ritual adapted by PAIRS for use as a structured negotiation. Here, couples learn to fight for the relationship, rather than against their partner. Peer couple coaches guide the partners through the fight format, prohibit dirty fighting, and enable reflective evaluation of the partners' emerging healthy fight styles. Peer coaches learn as much about the Fair Fight process when coaching as they do when negotiating their own issues. Through a *Shared Art Exercise* in class and *Follow-the-Leader Dates* as homework, issues related to power and control, leadership and followership, flexibility versus rigidity of power roles, as well as the impact of unspoken assumptions are all brought to the surface and examined. Couples discover that they can remain connected while disagreeing and that they can grow closer through successfully addressing their differences. A potent sense of "we," a sense of shared competence, higher self-esteem, and greater generosity and goodwill ensue from safely and successfully finding a real, mutually satisfying, win-win solution to conflict.

CLARIFYING ASSUMPTIONS

Partners' expectations of one another, conscious or unconscious, are largely formed by long-past experiences. Unspoken assumptions and hidden expectations lead to great misunderstanding. A *Mind Reading* tool is taught for respectfully checking out assumptions rather than proceeding without knowing what is true for the partner or with mind reading without permission. To help couples become more aware of their hidden assumptions, Gordon catalogued the common *Love Knots*, or unexamined beliefs, that sabotage intimate relationships. (See *If You* Really *Loved Me . . .*, Gordon, 1996.) Couples learn to recognize knots and to untangle them so that they lose their power to sabotage the relationship.

MY HISTORY AND UNIQUE SELF

A study of family systems, through psychodramas enacting *Family Systems Factories* and what happens with the addition of children (*Dyad-Triad*) leads into the study of each person's own family of origin. *Genograms*, a three-generation family map, allows exploration of influences in the family of origin and reveals the invisible rules, scripts, and loyalties that may be affecting current relationship. Participants also revisit their personal history through *Guided Visualizations* and *Intensive Journaling* to discover the impact of early messages and past decisions, especially regarding love, adequacy, and worth. They uncover their *Revolving Ledgers,* the emotional bills of debts owed from the past that, as they walk through the revolving door of life, they hand to whomever is there. Participants identify intense over-reactions to relatively minor behaviors of their partner that indicate the presence of *Emotional Allergies* (another concept unique to PAIRS). These allergies are acute sensitivities to whatever now reminds a person of pain or threats from the past. Allergic responses are accompanied in the present by protective reactions (ideas and emotions) and protective behaviors that were used to manage the pain long ago.

Tools for healing allergies and past painful experience include the *Healing the Ledger Exercise* and the *Museum Tour of Past Hurts and Disappointments.* Here, partners confide previous painful or frightening experiences to one another. This confiding helps the listener to understand and have more compassion for the partner, and it helps the speaker to express pain safely to a comforting, validating, and supportive partner. Partners are shown how to hold each other in a nurturing way, while they are expressing and releasing old pain. Participants may use the *Letting Go of Grudges Letter* as a journaling and/or confiding tool, for finding relief and freedom in working through grudges (hurts held in angry resentment to protect from risking being hurt again). Through these experiences, participants clear up misunderstandings of one another by reclaiming their personal history rather than continuing to project and blame their partner. They reconnect with suppressed early experiences and decisions that have been interfering with their ability to trust or be intimate with their partner. Partners also learn they can help to heal instead of hurt one another.

Couples also find that *Emotional Allergy Infinity Loops* underlie many of their unresolved conflicts. Such a loop occurs when a person's behavior *triggers* an emotionally allergic reaction in his or her partner. The partner's allergic reaction then triggers an allergic reaction in the first partner, whose reactive behavior then retriggers the second, and so on, ad infinitum. In the throes of an Emotional Allergy Infinity Loop, each partner often re-experiences the worst pains of childhood and the helpless reactions of a small child. Typically each feels, "if it is like this, then I cannot be here!" Each forgets to see his or her partner as a friend and experiences the partner instead as the enemy. Each becomes lost in a reactive state of believing the worst about self and partner and of using primitive protective actions. Devastating distance can grow.

Couples now develop concepts and a language to understand and explain what they are experiencing when they are conjointly in the grip of such emotional intensity. As participants begin to understand and discuss their Love Knots, Early Scripts and Decisions, Ledgers, Grudges, Emotional Allergies, and Emotional Allergy Infinity Loops, they become capable of taking responsibility for their own reactions, rather than blaming the other.

Couples are helped to strategize together to devise "emergency exit ramps" from their loops and to work together to escape those slippery slopes. Through empathy for the partner's "child responses" and revision of beliefs about the meaning of the partner's behavior, the Emotional Allergy Infinity Loop can be transformed into a *Loop of Vulnerability and Empathy* (LOVE).

To help see their unique self and inherent personality differences, participants rate themselves on the Meyers-Briggs type indicator (Kiersey-Bates). Through the use of exercises to illuminate the differences between the poles of the four basic personality preference scales, couples begin to see how many of their disagreements and conflicts are better understood as differing styles of decision making, problem solving, information gathering, and style of interaction. Differences, which had appeared to be threatening and perceived as personal attacks, can now be reframed as temperament differences. This often allows individuals to accept their own preferences and styles, and helps couples approach their personality differences with a sense of humor and even with compassion, instead of frustration, resentment, or fear. Additionally, couples begin to appreciate how their differences can be complementary in accomplishing life tasks together.

Participants also learn the "PARTS of Self," a system of classifying and understanding the various aspects of their own unique personality. Drawn from the work of Virginia Satir, participants learn to identify and give meaningful names to their subpersonalities, usually names of renowned figures in culture, history, or literature. Disowned or suppressed PARTS of a person's psyche tend to act outside of a person's control. Coming to know and discover the positive value in each PART of Self allows each person to better coordinate, utilize, and, if necessary, transform these PARTS so that they are acting in harmony with personal goals and life choices. Their PARTS can be perceived as resources. In a series of PARTS parties, classmates act out the PARTS of one individual, and later the PARTS of a couple. The PARTS party players help individuals or couples discover new and more creative combinations of PARTS that the couple can use in conflict and stress or even romance. Following these PARTS parties, individuals and couples explore their own inner cast of characters and experiment with ways to rearrange the PARTS they tend to use the most. In doing so, they discover how to better use all their resources and uncover new possibilities for interactions with their partners that are more harmonious and productive.

EMOTIONAL REEDUCATION, EMOTIONAL LITERACY, AND BONDING

PAIRS dives even more deeply into emotion via the *PAIRS Bonding Weekend Workshop*. PAIRS adapted the New Identity Process (Casriel, 1972) to the couple orientation of PAIRS, calling it *Bonding Work*. Casriel, a renowned specialist in the treatment of drug and alcohol addiction in therapeutic communities, originally developed this expressive process to treat character disorders. Paul MacLean's (1973) *A Triune Concept of the*

Brain and Behavior is presented as a model to understand emotional memory that, when activated, does not know time and place and is experienced as reoccurring now. Participants learn several different positions for holding their partner while he or she is expressing intense emotions. Participants learn how to progress from less intense emotions to more intense expression, to the reexperiencing of emotions in full measure. In this intense emotionally open state, emotional reeducation can occur. Once individuals have emptied old pain, they become open to receive positive, comforting, and affirming messages about themselves from their partners and the group. When ready, they are assisted in construction affirmations of their own value, rights, and entitlements. They replace old or toxic choices with new, healthy attitudes and decisions.

During this process, couples develop deep empathy and compassion for one another. They discover that, not only can they handle their partners' intense emotions, but they can also offer their partner comfort through holding and touch when they are in pain. Over the course of this weekend, participants commonly lose their fear of both their own and their partners' emotional intensity. They experience directly and observe in others how an intimate relationship generates intense emotions about bonding, belonging, needing one another, never leaving, and being loved for oneself. They learn that the expression of these powerfully intense emotions cements their bond at the deepest of levels and can restore passion to their relationship.

The culmination of this workshop is the *Death and Loss* experience in which participants enact saying goodbye to their deceased loved one. They are led to speak what would need to be expressed to say goodbye. Music and the use of carefully chosen sentence stems make this an emotionally charged and deeply meaningful exercise for partners. They experience the depth of their bond in the "experience" of losing one another through death. This exercise also allows communication about the meaning of their lives together. Rest-of-life *wish-baskets* are shared between partners.

PLEASURE—SENSUALITY AND SEXUALITY

Couples explore how they can expand the range of pleasure that they share together. PAIRS recognizes three special biological needs (sources of pleasure) that require physical touch met by the married couple: *Sensuality, Sexuality,* and *Bonding.* The *Pleasure Weekend Workshop* is devoted to removing barriers to pleasure and enhancing skills and understandings that enable couples greater pleasure, joy, and fun through stimulation of the senses, touch, and physical closeness. Same gender groups explore: (1) early experiences and messages that have impacted one's development as a sensual and sexual being; (2) playful exploration of gender differences in romantic turn ons and turn offs; and (3) sexual saboteurs and stereotypes, myths, and fallacies about sex. Cross-gender conversations and guided visualizations about early experiences with sex development help generate more empathic understanding between partners and more acceptance for their biologically based differences.

Sprinkled throughout the weekend are exercises designed to open the five senses, as well as *guided massages* where couples practice giving and receiving pleasuring touch with feedback. The *Guided Face Caress* and *Foot Massage* are among the most enjoyable moments of the entire PAIRS program.

Along with these sensual exercises, an explicit film on lovemaking is shown that re-focuses the couple on intimacy and pleasure, and helps to relieve performance anxieties. Participants fill out detailed and explicit inventories to help identify romantic, sensual, and sexual preferences, dissatisfactions, and wishes for change. Couples are guided through a safe process in which they share their pleasure inventories with each other and discuss their reactions and feedback. Often, a lack of communication or a buildup of resentment or fear of hurting or embarrassing one another has blocked giving and receiving pleasure freely. Sensual and sexual pleasure dates (McCarthy & McCarthy, 1990), which are assigned for homework, give couples permission to experiment in new and creative ways with both giving and receiving pleasure. Couples usually leave the weekend with a renewed sense of hope and excitement about their sex life, and frequently describe breakthroughs in the following weeks from having been able to enjoy each other based on leveling about their physical and sexual needs and preferences.

The roots of *jealousy*—the downside of natural sexual possessivness—are examined. Participants are shown how the *Web of Jealousy*, comprised of fear, shame, pain, guilt, and rage, negatively affects self-esteem and trust. Jealous reactive behaviors to stem the pain and control outcomes often make matters worse, creating a *Jealousy Infinity Loop*. Through a *Jealousy Journaling Exercise* with guided discussions with partner, couples come to understand one another's jealous reactions and vulnerabilities to jealous reactions. Betrayal and love triangles are discussed. The essential steps to prevent jealousy are presented using guidelines developed by Shirley Glass (2003).

CONTRACTING—CLARIFYING EXPECTATIONS

Based on Clifford Sager's work (1976), the PAIRS curriculum culminates in an integration and application of all the tools and concepts learned in the proceeding months toward a revised *relationship contract*. To prepare for the *Contracting Weekend*, the *Powergram* (Stuart, 1980) is examined as a model for understanding how power is shared and decisions are made in each relationship. Using this model, couples address where and how to change the division of power and responsibilities so that both are satisfied with their degree of input, influence, and responsibility, and areas of autonomy in decision making. Couples use the *Museum Tour of Past Decisions,* to review and learn from past decisions about which there may remain a residue of resentment or hurt.

Participants extensively journal to clarify expectations and needs in their relationship. They examine all areas of life—work and career, leisure time, money, housework, children, in-laws, religious observances, sexuality—and rank areas of importance or dissatisfaction in order of urgency. Couples also identify their core expectations or *Walking Issues*—the ones that are nonnegotiable. Couples work together to make a priority list of those issues they agree need adjustment through negotiation. They are coached in *Contracting Sessions* by other couples using the *Fair Fight for Change* as the basic structure for contracting. They also use any of the other tools they have learned in PAIRS.

Through contracting, couples discover that seemingly impossible differences can be bridged with goodwill, hard work, and support. They now possess the self-awareness and necessary skills to continue this recontracting work after the course on an on-going basis at home using the full range of skills in their *PAIRS Tool Kit.* Issues that have not yet been resolved are identified and prioritized for homework, and couples have a network of peer coaches on whom they can draw if they need assistance. Lifetime friendships are commonly forged in the group, and there is a profound sense of trust and community that group members enjoy. It is typical for class groups to continue to meet on a regular basis and continue to provide a network of support to one another. They form a caring community. Some groups have met for many years following the *Relationship Mastery Course.*

In contrast to individual growth activities, such as individual counseling or therapy, PAIRS highlights the importance of the *couple* as a crucible from which healing, personal growth, and the development of higher capacities can emerge. Thus, sustained intimacy and pleasure are assured and the relationship becomes a lasting source of authentic love, mutual respect, and trust between two growing and evolving partners. Premarital couples in PAIRS courses find enormous support from veteran couples. They acquire mentors, role models, support figures, and (for the younger premarital couples) new surrogate mothers and fathers to support them and reparent them toward successful marriage. Couples considering a second marriage find opportunities to explore what went wrong for each earlier and take responsibility for their part so that the old maladaptive patterns do not reemerge in their new relationship. Many divorced individuals who take PAIRS as singles have vowed never to reenter another relationship until they understand what happened and acquire the skills to assure a different outcome the next time around. PAIRS training provides the strongest opportunity for the newly committing couple to acquire the skills, concepts, understandings, self-knowledge, and strategies for building deep intimacy and assuring a lasting, healthy marriage.

PREVENTIVE MAINTENANCE PROGRAMS

At the close of the semester program, participants often wish to continue their group learning and practice in a preventive maintenance format.

They often request monthly meetings with the support of their PAIRS instructor or the PTP. Requests from class groups often include a desire for periodic weekend workshops, usually once or twice a year. Repeating the Bonding Weekend Workshop is most often requested because it helps to maintain access to the core emotional openness needed for bonding and intimacy.

A PAIRS Three-Year Preventive Maintenance Program is under development for graduates to sustain their strong foundation for loving, healthy marriage and family relationships. This program provides opportunities for those who have had PAIRS experiences (including premarital assessment and OFFICE PAIRS) to refresh and practice a wide range of skills, such as the Fair Fight for Change with Peer Coaches, PARTS Parties, Dialogue Guides, Daily Temperature Readings, and Genograms. Options in this program include continuing monthly three-hour classes, periodic six-month one-session check-ups, and twice-yearly day-long seminars. Fees for this program vary by the options chosen by each couple. Based on years of experience conducting PAIRS programs, relationships clearly benefit from a psychoeducational program in knowledge and skills in building and sustaining intimacy in relationships and this benefit can be sustained with regular preventive support.

SUMMARY

PAIRS premarital counseling and training offers premarital couples rich resources that will enhance not only their intimate relationship but also enrich and emotionally deepen their personal and family lives. Research documents that the PAIRS experience results in achieving far higher levels of self-worth, emotional literacy, emotional maturity, and relationship satisfaction. Love and community are well documented to be potent healing powers that create longer, healthier, more joyful lives (Ornish, 1990). This chapter presented premarital assessment, counseling, training sequences, and preventive support from the PAIRS perspective, as applications of a powerful technology for healing, building, strengthening, and sustaining healthy marital and family relationships.

The PAIRS technology is available to train counselors and through them their clients in how to build lasting, satisfying, healthy, successful relationships. With successful lifelong marriages, there will be healthier children and reduced suffering in successive generations. It is the profound hope of the PAIRS network of leaders and trained professionals that PAIRS, as an educational and counseling resource, will become an essential part of the training for all those who provide therapy, counsel, assist, and train couples, particularly premarital couples. This knowledge base needs to be culturally incorporated as a universally expected foundation for every new couple considering a permanent commitment to building a lasting, stable marriage and healthy family life together.

APPENDIX: RESOURCES USED TO DEVELOP PAIRS

Adams, T. M. (1987). *Living from the inside out.* New Orleans, LA: Self published.

Assagioli, R., & Servan-Schreiber, C. (1974) *A higher view of the man-woman problem: SYNTHESIS I—The Realization of the self.* Redwood City, CA.

Bach, G., & Torbet, L. (1983). *The inner enemy.* New York: William Morrow.

Bach, G., & Torbet, L. (1982). *A time for caring: How to enrich your life through an interest and pleasure of others.* New York: Delacorte Press.

Bach, G., & Wyden, P. (1968). *The intimate enemy.* New York: Avon Books.

Barbach, L. (1982). *For each other: Sharing sexual intimacy.* New York: Doubleday.

Barbach, L. G. (1975). *For yourself: The fulfillment of female sexuality.* New York: Doubleday.

Benton, W. (1943). *This is my beloved.* New York: Alfred A. Knopf.

Berg, L., & Street, R. (1962). *Sex: Methods and manners.* New York: McFadden Books.

Berne, E. (1964). *Games people play: The psychology of human relationships.* New York: Random House.

Boszormenyi-Nagy, I., & Spark, G. (1984). *Invisible loyalties.* New York: Brunner/Mazel.

Bowen, M. (1985). *Family therapy in clinical practice.* Rowman & Littlefield.

Bradshaw, J. (1988). *Healing the shame that binds.* Deerfield Beach, FL: Health Communications.

Bradshaw, J. (1990). *Homecoming: Reclaiming and championing your inner child.* New York: Bantam.

Branden, N. (1983). *If you could hear what i cannot say.* New York: Bantam.

Branden, N. (1983). *Honoring the self: The psychology of confidence and respect.* New York: Bantam.

Branden, N. (1969). *The psychology of self-esteem.* New York: Bantam.

Buber, M. (1958). *I & thou.* New York: Charles Scribner's Sons.

Casriel, D. (1972). *A scream away from happiness.* New York: Grosset & Dunlap.

De Beauvoir, S. (1952). *The second sex.* New York: Alfred A. Knopf.

DeMaria, R. (1998). *Satisfaction, couple type, divorce potential, attachment patterns, and romantic and sexual satisfaction of married couples who participated in marriage enrichment program.* Unpublished Doctoral Dissertation, Bryn Mawr College, Bryn Mawr, Pennsylvania.

DeMaria, R., & Hannah, M. (Eds.). (2003). *Building intimate relationships: Bridging treatment, education and enrichment through the pairs program.* New York: Brunner-Routledge.

DeMaria, R. Weeks, G., & Hof, L. (1999). *Focused genograms.* Taylor & Francis.

Dinkmeyer, D., & Jon C. (1984). *Training in marriage enrichment.* Circle Pines, MN: American Guidance Service.

Durana, C. (1994). The use of bonding and emotional expressiveness in the PAIRS training: A psychoeducational approach for couples. *Journal of Family Psychotherapy, 5*(2), 65–81.

Durana, C. (1996). A longitudinal evaluation of the effectiveness of the PAIRS psychoeducational program for couples. *Family Therapy, 23*(1), 11–36.

Firestone, R. (1985). *The fantasy bond.* New York: The Glendon Association/Human Sciences Press.

Forward, S. (1986). *Men who hate women and the women who love them.* New York: Bantam.

Friday, N. (1985). *Jealousy.* New York: William Morrow and Co.

Friday, N. (1973). *My secret garden.* New York: Simon & Schuster.

Fromm, E. (1956). *The art of loving.* New York: Bantam.

Gaylin, W. (1986). *Rediscovering love.* New York: Viking Penguin.

Gibran, K. (1982). *The prophet.* New York: Alfred A. Knopf.

Gibran, K. (1967). *A tear and a smile.* New York: Alfred A. Knopf.

Glass, S. (2003). *Not just friends: protect your relationship from infidelity and heal the trauma of betrayal.* New York: Free Press.

Goleman, D. (1995). *Emotional intelligence.* New York: Bantam Books.

Gordon, L. H. (1996). *If you really loved me . . .* Palo Alto, CA: Science & Behavior Books.

Gordon, L. H. (1990). *Love knots: A laundry list of marital mishaps, marital knots, etc.* New York: Dell.

Gordon, L. H. (1993). *Passage to intimacy.* New York: Simon & Schuster.

Gottman, J., et al. (1976). *A couples' guide to communication.* Champaign, IL: Research Press.

Gottman, John. (1999). *The seven principles for making marriage work.* New York: Crown Publishers.

Gottman, J. (1994). *Why marriages succeed or fail.* New York: Simon & Schuster.

Gould, R. (1978). *Transformations: Growth and change in adult life.* New York: Simon & Schuster.

Goulding, R., & Goulding, M. (1979). *Changing lives through redecision therapy.* New York: Brunner/Mazel.

Gray, J. (1980). *What you feel, you can heal.* Santa Monica, CA: Heart Publishing.

Haley, A. (1976). *Roots: The saga of an american family.* New York: Doubleday.

Harris, T. (1967). *I'm ok, you're ok.* New York: Harper & Row.

Hendrix, H. (1988). *Getting the love you want.* New York: Harper & Row.

Herberg, W. (1956). *The writings of martin buber.* Cleveland, OH: World Publishing.

Heschel, A. J. (1955). *God in search of man: A philosophy of Judaism.* New York: Farrar, Straus & Cudahy.

Hooper, A. (1988). *Massage and loving.* New York: Henry Holt and Company.

Janov, A. (1971). *The anatomy of mental illness.* New York: G. P. Putnam & Sons.

Janov, A. (1970). *The primal scream.* New York: Dell.

Janov, A. (1980). *Prisoners of pain: Unlocking the power of the mind to end suffering.* Garden City, NY: Doubleday.

Kahn, M., & Lewis, K. (1988). *Siblings in therapy.* New York: W. W. Norton.

Keyes, Jr., K. (1990). *The power of unconditional love.* Coos Bay, OR: Love Live Books.

Kiersey, D., & Bates, M. (1978). *Please understand me.* Del Mar, CA: Prometheus Nemesis Book Company.

Kushner, H. (1986). *When all you've ever wanted isn't enough: The search for a life that matters.* New York: Summit Books.

Lair, J., & Lechler, W. (1980). *I exist, i need, i'm entitled.* New York: Doubleday.

Lerner, H. G. (1989). *The dance of intimacy: A woman's guide to courageous acts of change in key relationship.* New York: HarperCollins.

Lidell, L., et al. (1984). *The book of massage.* New York: Simon & Schuster.

Liebman, J. L. (1946). *Peace of mind.* New York: Simon & Schuster.

Liedloff, J. (1977). *The continuum concept.* New York: Warner Books.

Love, P., & Robinson, J. (1994). *Hot monogamy.* New York: Dutton.

Lynch, J. J. (1938). *The language of the heart: The body's response to human dialogue.* New York: Basic Books.

MacLean, P. D. (1964). *Man & his animal brains: Modern medicine.*

MacLean, P. D. (1973). *A triune concept of the brain and behavior.* Toronto, Canada: University of Toronto Press.

Masters, R., & Houston, J. (1972). *Mind games: The guide to inner space.* New York: Viking.

McCain, E., & Shannon, D. (1985). *The two step.* New York: Grove Press.

McCarthy, B., & McCarthy, E. (1990). *Couple sexual awareness: Building sexual happiness.* New York: Carroll & Graf Publishers.

McGoldrick, M., & Gerson, R. (1985). *Genograms in family assessment.* New York: W. W. Norton.

Miller, A. (1981). *Prisoners of childhood.* New York: Basic Books.

Miller, S., et al. (1982). *Straight talk.* New York: Rawson Associates.

Missildine, W. H. (1988). *Your inner child of the past.* New York: Pocket Books.

Montague, A. (1986). *Touching* (3rd ed.). New York: Harper & Row.

Napier, A. Y. (1988). *The fragile bond.* New York: Harper & Row.

Napier, A. Y., & Whitaker, C. A. (1978). *The family crucible.* New York: Harper & Row.

Nerin, W. F. (1986). *Family reconstruction: Long day's journey into light.* New York: W. W. Norton.

Ornish, D. (1990). *Dr. Dean Ornish's program for reversing heart disease.* New York: Random House.

Paul, J. & Paul, M. (1989). *From conflict to caring: An in-depth program for creating loving relationships.* Minneapolis, MN: CompCare Publishers.

Pearsall, P. (1996). *The pleasure prescription.* Alameda, CA: Hunter House.

Peck, S. (1978). *The road less traveled.* New York: Touchstone Books.

Pelletier, K. R. (1977). *Mind as healer, mind as slayer: A holistic approach to preventing stress disorders.* New York: Dell.

Pert, C. (1997). *Molecules of emotion: Why you feel the way you feel.* New York: Simon & Schuster.

Pittman, F. (1998). *Grow up! How taking responsibility can make you a happy adult.* Golden Books.

Pittman, F. (1989). *Private lies: Infidelity and the betrayal of intimacy.* New York: W.W. Norton.

Progoff, I. (1975). *At a journal workshop.* New York: Dialogue House Library.

Progoff, I. (1959). *Depth psychology and modern man*. New York: McGraw-Hill.

Progoff, I. (1985). *The dynamics of hope*. New York: Dialogue House Library.

Progoff, I. (1980). *The practice of process meditation*. New York: Dialogue House Library.

Rado, S. (1969). *Adaptational psychodynamics: Motivation and control*. New York: Science House.

Rich, P. (1990). *Pamper your partner: An illustrated guide to soothing and relaxing your mate with the sensual healing arts*. New York: Simon & Schuster.

Richardson, R. (1984). *Family ties that bind*. British Columbia, Canada: Self-Counsel Press.

Rosenstein, N. (1990). *The unbroken chain*. New York: CIS Publishers.

Sager, C. J. (1976). *Marriage contracts and couples therapy: Hidden forces in intimate relationships*. New York: Brunner/Mazel.

Sager, C., & Hunt, B. (1979). *Intimate partners: Hidden patterns in love relationships*. New York: McGraw-Hill.

Saint-Exupery, A., de. (1943). *The little prince*. New York: Harcourt, Brace & Company.

Satir, V. (1967). *Conjoint family therapy*. Palo Alto, CA: Science and Behavior Books.

Satir, V. (1984). *Master series videotapes on intimate relationship skills*. Falls Church, VA: PAIRS Foundation, Ltd.

Satir, V. (1988). *The new peoplemaking*. Palo Alto, CA: Science and Behavior Books.

Satir, V. (1975). *Self esteem*. Berkley, CA: Celestial Arts.

Satir, V. (1978). *Your many faces*. Berkley, CA: Celestial Arts.

Satir, V., & Baldwin, M. (1983). *Step by step: A guide to creating change for families*. Polo Alto, CA: Science and Behavior Books.

Scarf, M. (1987). *Intimate partners, patterns in love and marriage*. New York: Random House.

Scarf, M. (1980). *Unfinished business: Pressure points in the lives of women*. New York: Doubleday.

Schnarch, D. (1997). *Passionate marriage: Sex, love and intimacy in emotionally committed relationships*. New York: Norton.

Sheehy, G. (1982). *Pathfinders: Overcoming the crises of adult life and finding your own path to well-being*. New York: Bantam.

Siegel, B. S. (1989). *Peace, love & healing*. New York: Harper & Row.

Sotile, W., & Sotile, M. (1998). *The super-couple syndrome*. New York: Wiley.

Steiner, C. M. (1990). *The scripts people live*. New York: Grove/Atlantic.

Stone, H., & Winkelman, S. (1989). *Embracing each other: Relationship as teacher, healer, and guide*. San Rafael, CA: New World Library.

Stuart, R. (1980). *Helping couples change: A social learning approach to marital therapy*. New York: Guilford Press.

Tannen, D. (1990). *You just don't understand*. New York: William Morrow.

Viorst, J. (1986). *Necessary losses*. New York: Simon & Schuster.

Warner, S. J. (1966). *Self-realization and self-defeat*. New York: Grove Press.

Weigert, E. (1970). *The courage to love*. New Haven, CT: Yale University Press.

Whitfield, C. (1990). *A gift to myself*. Deerfield Beach, FL: Health Communications.

Whitfield, C. (1987). *Healing the child within.* Deerfield Beach, FL: Health Communications.

Wile, D. B. (1988). *After the honeymoon: How conflict can improve your relationship.* New York: Wiley.

Zilbergeld, B. (1978). *Male sexuality.* New York: Bantam.

Zukov, G. (1990). *The seat of the soul.* New York: Simon & Schuster.

REFERENCES

Bach, G. R., & Wyden, P. (1969). *The intimate enemy: How to fight fair in love and marriage.* New York: Morrow.

Casriel, D. (1972). *A scream away from happiness.* New York: Grosset & Dunlap.

DeMaria, R. (1998). *Satisfaction, couple type, divorce potential, attachment patterns, and romantic and sexual satisfaction of married couples who participated in marriage enrichment program.* Unpublished doctoral dissertation, Bryn Mawr College, Bryn Mawr, Pennsylvania.

DeMaria, R., & Hannah, M. (Eds.). (2003). *Building intimate relationships: Bridging treatment, eduction and enrichment through the Pairs program.* New York: Brunner-Routledge.

Glass, S. (2003). *Not just friends: Protect your relationship from infidelity and heal the trauma of betrayal.* New York: Free Press.

Gordon, L. (1993). *Passage to intimacy.* New York: Simon & Schuster.

Gordon, L. (1996). *If you really loved me . . .* Palo Alto, CA: Science and Behavior Books.

MacLean, P. (1973). *A triune concept of the brain and behavior.* Toronto, Ontario, Canada: University of Toronto Press.

McCarthy, B., & McCarthy, E. (1990). *Couple sexual awareness: Building sexual happiness.* New York: Carroll and Graf.

Ornish, D. (1990). *Dr. Dean Ornish's program for reversing heart disease.* New York: Random House.

Sager, C. (1976). *Marriage contracts and couple therapy.* New York: Brunner/Mazel.

Satir, V. (1988). *The new peoplemaking.* Palo Alto, CA: Science and Behavior Books.

Stuart, R. (1980). *Helping couples change: A social learning approach to marital therapy.* New York: Guilford Press.

CHAPTER 3

The First Years of
Marital Commitment

William C. Nichols

MARITAL COMMITMENT AND the treatment of couples who are in their first marriage are the focus of this chapter. In American society, this refers mainly to couples who are in their twenties, or in some instances, in their early thirties, who have not been married previously. Couples in later stages of marriage and gay or lesbian couples are the subject matter of subsequent chapters.

What do we need to know to work therapeutically with couples in their early years of committed relationships? We need to understand, in the broadest terms, the nature of marriage, cohabitation, and commitment in such relationships.

The next section delineates the nature of marriage, cohabitation, and commitment. Following that is a brief review of family development and the concepts of individual and marital life cycles—with some reference to family life cycles and the central tasks of those cycles as they pertain to first marriage—and the commitment process; and integrative marital therapy, involving object relations, system theory, and cognitive behavioral constructs. Clinical illustrations of how interventions are made with couples and individuals requesting marital therapy are then presented. Because not all couples have difficulties with all parts of early marital adjustment, illustrations are taken from a variety of cases. Next, reference is made to some issues typically found in therapy with mainstream White American couples and couples from other ethnic, racial, and religious backgrounds. The majority of extant research literature deals with differences between White Americans and African American or Hispanic couples. A brief summary is provided in the final section.

THE NATURE OF MARRIAGE,
COHABITATION, AND COMMITMENT

THE NATURE OF MARRIAGE

Marriage is a complex relationship. Napier has succinctly stated, "Marriage involves learning to be both separate and together, learning to allocate power, learning to play and to work together, and [for some] perhaps the greatest challenge of all, learning to rear another generation" (2000, p. 145). There are varied and contradictory needs to be satisfied in marriage. Lewin expressed it decades ago as follows:

> Manifold needs are generally expected to be satisfied in and through marriage . . . failure to fulfill one of these functions may leave important needs unsatisfied, and result in a high and permanent level of tension in the group life.
>
> Which of these needs are dominant, which are fully satisfied, and which are not at all satisfied, depend upon the personality of the marriage partners, and upon the setting in which the particular marriage group lives. (Lewin, 1948, pp. 90–91)

Marriage Is an Intimate Relationship   It is a different kind of intimacy from the close relationship one may enjoy with a parent. A distinction made by Kantor and Lehr (1975) is helpful in understanding some of the essential differences between the dependency relationship we are involved in with our parents during our formative years and the intimacy in a healthy, adult relationship with a spouse. They distinguish between intimacy and nurturance, defining intimacy as a condition of mutual emotional and often intense closeness among peers. Nurturance, instead of being a two-directional emotional exchange, "implies a primarily unidirectional flow of affect" (Kantor & Lehr, 1975, p. 47).

As with other parts of marriage, workable, appropriate intimacy is not easily attainted. Persons may have different "social distances":

> Willingness to marry is considered a symptom of desire for the least social distance. Indeed, marriage means the willingness to share activities and situations that otherwise are kept strictly private. Married life includes permanent physical proximity brought to a climax in the sex relationship. (Lewin, 1948, pp. 88–89)

Marriage Is a Voluntary Relationship   Marriage in the contemporary United States, Canada, and much of the Western world involves essentially free choice of mate. Marriage is the lone voluntary family relationship (Napier, 1988; Nichols, 1988, 1996, 2000). As such, it is the most fragile of family relationships (Napier, 1988). This fragility is found not only in the attainment and maintenance of intimacy but also in the maintenance of the structure of the marriage. Most people marry in the United States, but for recent marriages, nearly half eventually may end in divorce, according to projections by Kreider and Fields (2001). Bramlett and Mosher (2001) report that one-fifth of first marriages end within five years.

The first year or so long has been identified by demographers as the most difficult time of adjustment in marriage. Divorce may come a few years later in the marriages in which there is early breakup, but the actual breakup tends to reflect conflict that began in the earliest stages and that did not secure adequate resolution. Kreider and Fields (2001) found that first marriages that end in divorce last seven or eight years, on average, and the median duration of all marriages that end in divorce is almost eight years. Hence, we need to give close attention to the early stage of marriage in order to engage in effective preventive and corrective therapeutic interventions.

Marriage Is Changing   The proportion of people's lives in the United States spent in marriage declined in the last half of the tumultuous twentieth century, but most adults (about five-sixths of all men and seven-eighths of all women; Schoen & Standish, 2000) continue to marry and to spend most of their lives in committed relationships. We have tended to marry later, however, and to divorce more frequently than earlier generations.

THE NATURE OF COHABITATION

Cohabitation, or living together without marriage, is an increasingly popular pattern; it grew some tenfold in the last four decades of the twentieth century, according to U.S. Bureau of the Census statistics. The rising rates of cohabitation have largely offset decreasing rates of marriage (Bramlett & Mosher, 2001; Bumpass, Sweet, & Cherlin, 1991; Cherlin, 1992; Schoen & Danish, 2001). More than half the couples marrying today have lived together before marriage (Teachman & Polonko, 1990). Does this mean that cohabitation is a permanent replacement for marriage?

Cohabitation as an Alternative to Marriage   This is a pattern adopted by a minority of cohabitors. Rather than permanently replacing marriage, cohabiting tends to be a short-term arrangement for most couples. Only about one-tenth of heterosexual cohabiting couples live in a long-term relationship that does not end in marriage. For about half, the relationship lasts approximately two years, at which time they terminate their relationship or marry. Overall, around 40% of these relationships end without marriage (Bumpass et al., 1991).

Cohabitors have told clinicians and researchers that they think that living together provides a better way to genuinely get to know your partner than traditional dating and that cohabitation is a preferred way for testing compatibility and the relationship. Recent research in several countries including the United States, Canada, New Zealand, and Sweden has thrown these beliefs into question (Axinn & Thornton, 1992; Bennett, Klimas, & Bloom, 1988; Thomson & Colella, 1992). Some authorities, like Rodriguez (1998) flatly conclude that cohabitation prior to marriage does not necessarily lead to better marriages.

Other research findings include:

- Couples who cohabit before marriage reported poorer communication and greater marital conflict than married couples who had never cohabited (Thomason & Colella, 1992).
- Premarital cohabitors have demonstrated significantly lower marital quality and significantly higher risk of marital dissolution (DeMaris & Rao, 1992).
- Premarital cohabitors in several countries, including the United States, Canada, Sweden, and New Zealand, have divorce rates that run 50% to 100% higher than noncohabitors (Axinn & Thornton, 1992).
- One finding, which would seem to have rather explicit implications for commitment, is that following a relationship breakup, cohabitors were much more likely to return to their parents' home for an extended stay than those who had married, that is, 20% as opposed to 2% of the married. Goldscheider, Thornton, and Young-DeMarco concluded: "it is difficult to argue that cohabitors resemble married people" (1993, p. 695).

Cohabitation as a Brief Prelude to Marriage   This pattern involves couples who intend to get married and who live together for a few months prior to actually entering into marriage. The majority of cohabitators who plan to marry are engaged in relationships similar to those of married persons (Rodriguez, 1998). When no children are involved and the partners have not cohabited previously, the negative effects found in the first pattern are not strongly present in research findings (Popenoe & Whitehead, 1999).

NATURE OF COMMITMENT

It is vitally important to understand the nature of commitment and the role it plays in close relationships and in marriage in particular. Marital commitment is defined here as the degree to which a person intends to remain in the marital relationship.

Commitment Is Different from Attachment   Attachment has been described as involving the symbolic bonds that emerge between two persons because of shared beliefs, values, meaning, and identity (Eckstein, Leventhal, Bentley, & Kelley, 1999). One can be strongly attached to being married and to the maintenance of the status quo without being emotionally and faithfully committed to one's spouse and sharing in a reciprocal and mutually fulfilling relationship. Examples may be found in marriages in which a man is bound to marriage by the security and social status of having a wife and children while maintaining a mistress on the side with whom he shares an emotionally meaningful relationship.

Commitment Is Different from Marital Satisfaction   Jones, Adams, and Berry (1995) pointed out that commitment and marital satisfaction are conceptually different phenomena when they developed and tested marital satisfaction and commitment scales. Satisfaction was defined as the degree to which one expresses happiness and satisfaction with the marital dyad or with the partner.

Commitment Has Multiple Features   Johnson, Caughlin, and Huston (1999) have described marital commitment as providing personal, moral, and structural reasons for staying married.

Commitment Is Central to Marital Stability and Success   Clinical observation and study of experiences with hundreds of couples highlight the importance of commitment in the formation and stability of a workable and satisfying marriage (Nichols, 1988; Nichols & Everett, 1986). Among the elements that seem to influence fear of marriage and/or certain avoidant patterns associated with marital commitment are fear about loss of identity, fear of loss of control, financial fears, and fears about accepting adult responsibility (Curtis, 1994).

Hence, we need to know what the issues are for couples attempting to make a strong commitment and to form a serious relationship. What factors enter into forming a workable relationship? What factors mitigate against getting off on the right foot in entering into the marriage or coupling?

REVIEW OF EXISTING THEORETICAL AND EMPIRICAL INFORMATION

We need to understand as best we can, and to help clients understand and accept, the factors and expectations that affect their desires and behaviors during the period of their early relationship and commitment.

CHOICE OF MATE

Mate selection in American society, as noted, is a relatively open process in which two young persons decide whom they will wed. Unlike some societies in which there is little or no choice, American marriages typically are not arranged by the families of the bride and groom. Contextual factors such as race, religion, education, propinquity, and socioeconomic status tend to influence heavily the field of eligibles (Hollingshead, 1950) among whom one fishes for a mate in this voluntary quest, but in the final analysis one selects a partner on essentially psychological grounds (Nichols, 1978). Personal dynamics and interpersonal interaction (N. Murstein, 1976) provide the final, major push behind selecting a mate in our voluntary selection process.

Within the realm of psychological and emotional choice of a mate, two different patterns have been posited: need complementarity, which stems from the work of Sigmund Freud (Bowen, 1966; Dicks, 1967; Kubie, 1956; Sager, 1976; Winch, 1958), and need similarity (B. I. Murstein, 1961; and others). Framo (1980) sought to reconcile these conflicting opinions, indicating that both ideas may be accurate, depending on the depth and length of inference one makes regarding mate selection.

Object relations play a major role in selecting a mate and engaging in family and marital interaction (Dicks, 1967; Fairbairn, 1952; Framo, 1970; Nichols, 1988, 1996; Nichols & Everett, 1986; Scharff & Scharff, 1991). "Object relation theorists generally agree that the process of relating and the internalized residues of the early experiences, as developed subsequently, provide the basis for later intimate relationships" (Nichols, 1996, p. 29). Space limitations prevent a description and discussion of object relations and the important object relations processes that affect mate selection and marital interaction, specifically splitting, projective identification, introjection, projection, and collusion. (See Nichols, 1996, pp. 26–35, for a brief summary of object relations in mate selection and marital interaction, and pp. 21–56 for a framework for an integrative psychodynamic, behavioral, and systems approach to marital and family therapy. See also Scharff & de Varela, Chapter 9, this volume.)

Models of relationships (Nichols, 1988, 1996; Nichols & Everett, 1986; Skynner, 1976) are a special kind of object relations, which stem from what we absorb from exposure to marriage relationships, primarily in our family of origin, while growing up. We internalize a model of each parent, a model of the affective interaction between spouses, and a model of our parents as a system (Davis, 1983; Skynner, 1976). These models contain more than "simply images of what marriage looks like; they also contain a strong emotional feeling about what marriage is supposed to be" (Nichols, 1988, p. 11). These models exist partly in our conscious awareness and partly outside awareness.

Differential Background Experiences for the Genders   John Gottman (1994) contends that our "upbringing couldn't be a worse training ground for a successful marriage" (p. 140), pointing out that "boys and girls grow up in parallel universes where emotional roles generally are different. This may be when the trouble between the sexes begins" (p. 140). [They] ". . . tend to have very different emotional communication styles from early on. . . . Usually, boys care most about *the game,* while girls care most about *the relationships* between the players" (p. 141).

LIFE CYCLES

Individual, marital, and family life (transgenerational) cycles are all involved in a cogwheeling fashion in the stage of life with which we are dealing during the early marital commitment phase. These cycles, including their specific tasks, are discussed in detail in Nichols (1996) and in *The Handbook of Family Development and Intervention* (Nichols, Pace-Nichols, Becvar, & Napier, 2000).

There are at least two basic approaches to the use of developmental stages in viewing family pathology. One is that family pathology comes from a combination of life-stage events plus external circumstances (Duvall, 1957, 1977; Haley, 1973). Another, based more explicitly on clinical work, "suggests that pathology emerges as a function of the continuation of the family system itself, and that the developmental stage simply colors its expression or defines the nature of its symptoms" (p. 32, Fisher, 1977).

CLINICAL ADAPTATIONS OF THE FAMILY LIFE CYCLE

Marriage is concerned with moving from a dependency relationship with one's parents to a peer relationship with one's spouse. This is the major focus of the marital relationship in large, dynamic terms. Adaptations of family life cycle and marital cycle stages to clinical work are discussed next.

Haley (1973) presented six stages in the family life cycle in describing Milton H. Erickson's therapeutic work, starting with the courtship period of the young adult and moving through to retirement and old age. The implicit assumption that symptoms appear when there is a dislocation or disruption in the life cycle of a family has been retained by some mainstream family therapists.

Solomon's (1973) five-stage clinically oriented framework included developmental tasks. Two tasks were proposed for Stage 1 (the marriage): ending the primary ties with one's parents and redirecting one's energies from the family of origin into the marriage.

Barnhill and Longo (1980) basically kept the stages from Evelyn Millis Duvall's (1957) pioneering framework, but strongly emphasized the transitions from one stage to the next stage. The key issues for the partners in the transition to Stage 1 (commitment) are similar to those of Solomon, breaking away from their respective families of origin and forming attachments to their new partner (and subsequently to the family they form).

Carter and McGoldrick (1980a, 1980b, 1988, 1999) have offered a six-stage schema that begins with young adults who have left their family of origin but have not started a new family. They emphasize the combination of individual, family, and social perspectives, multiculturalism, and multicontextualism and provide exceedingly practical illustrations of the use of these constructs in clinical work.

Nichols and Everett (1986) and Nichols (1988, 1996) introduced a four-stage developmental-clinical framework for use with intact families. Rather than a stage in its own right, they regard departing from one's family of origin as more of a process, which usually begins with the increasing differentiation of self in late adolescence and is advanced when one enters into a marital relationship. Rather than simply emphasizing the tasks involved in making transitions from one stage to another, this approach follows Duvall in holding that special attention needs to be given to adequate completion of the developmental expectations and to tasks within stages.

MARITAL LIFE CYCLE

The core internal relationship tasks of marital couples described by Nichols (1988, 1996) apply to couples in this mating and marriage phase as discussed next:

- *Commitment* refers to how and to what extent the partners value the marital relationship and their intentions pertaining to its maintenance and continuation. Commitment here pertains to developing an initial commitment between the partners.
- *Caring* is the kind of emotional attachment that ties the partners together. This term is used in explorations with clients instead of the ambiguous term "love," particularly when there is any question about the clarity of their meaning when they talk about their emotional ties. Gottman (1994) calls "love and respect" the basic marital ingredients (p. 64) of marriage success. Caring in this stage involves determining whether there is sufficient and appropriate caring to warrant marriage.
- *Communication* is the ability to share meanings, verbally and nonverbally/symbolically. Communication is not viewed as a panacea, but rather as a tool for effectuating the relationship and working on strengthening it. Here, it refers to the initial construction of a shared universe of discourse and establishing workable patterns of communication.
- *Conflict and compromise* is the extent the partners are able to recognize and deal with the disagreements and hurts that are inevitable in any intimate and lasting relationship. The importance of this set of abilities has been stated by Gottman (1994, p. 28), as follows: "If there's any one lesson I have learned from my years of research, it is that a lasting marriage results from a couple's ability to resolve the conflicts that are inevitable in any relationship." During this stage, the task pertains to beginning to learn how to effect compromise and resolve conflicts.
- *Contract* is the set of expectations and explicit, implied, or presumed agreements held by the partners. Sager (1976) has described these expectations and agreements as existing on three levels, (1) conscious and verbalized, (2) conscious but not verbalized, or (3) outside awareness

levels. For couples in this stage, this task is concerned with working to explore and clarify expectations and to resolve conflicts. Two tasks for this stage include separating from families of origin and developing a couple identity and establishing a mutually satisfying affectional-sexual relationship.

SOME PSYCHOLOGICAL TASKS OF EARLY MARRIAGE

Judith Wallerstein (Wallerstein & Blakeslee, 1995), from a longitudinal study of 50 happy marriages, identified some psychological tasks of marriage; those that are relevant to this chapter include consolidating separation (from one's family of origin); establishing new connections (social, emotional); establishing the marital identity; establishing the sexual identity of the couple; and establishing the marriage as a zone of safety.

SOME CASE ILLUSTRATIONS

Couples asking for therapeutic help early in their marriage have been relatively rare in my nearly 40 years of practice. Typically, couples are reluctant to seek professional assistance in the first few weeks or even months unless florid pathology has emerged or other dramatic changes have erupted. Often, they have been too embarrassed about encountering unexpected problems and their inability to handle things for themselves to contact a professional. Parenthetically, my experience as a psychologist and marital and family therapist has been that the majority of the small number of couples who presented prior to marriage for premarital counseling came in because one of the individuals had serious doubts about continuing with the marriage plans. In some instances, one had already decided that he or she wanted out of the relationship and was seeking outside assistance in making the break. (This is probably somewhat different from the situation faced by ministers, priests, and rabbis, where institutional cultures form a set of expectations for premarital contact between marrying couples and officiating clergy.)

There are a limited number of procedures for assessing the marital relationship. These include verbal reports, therapist observation of interaction, and standardized testing. My approach generally involves seeing both partners together, giving them the opportunity to tell their story and then react to therapist interventions. The initial conjoint interview frequently is interrupted by seeing the partners separately for a few minutes when I give each partner the opportunity to "talk about anything that you have not mentioned that is important" and to "go back to anything that was mentioned that we didn't go into adequately." Along with dealing with whatever the clients bring up in the session, assessment also involves looking for symptoms and problematic issues that affect the clients' relationship and, in some instances, cause them individual difficulties. Assessment and intervention proceed concurrently.

THE COMMITMENT ISSUE

Exploring the question of whether the partners have adequate commitment to one another and to being married needs to be done early in the therapist's contact with them. How willing are they to work on the relationship? Sometimes, it is not possible to get a firm handle on their commitment until after marital therapy has begun and they have tried to change. Some suggestions for exploring commitment issues include the following steps, which must, of course, be adapted to the particular couple one is seeing:

- Based on what they say and do, explore with the couple their feelings and assess their motivation as well as possible. What are the relational or object relations capabilities of each partner, including the level of maturity in their choice of the other person, their need for him or her, and the ability to give emotionally to the partner?
- Ask them where they stand in their commitments (as best they can tell at the present time). This can be done with them together or in individual sessions, depending on the therapist's judgment regarding possible contraindications to either approach. (See Nichols, 1996, for typical patterns with regard to commitment and possible contraindications to using individual sessions and/or a conjoint meeting for obtaining such information.)
- Share with them your impressions of where they seem to be in their commitments and where they seem to be heading. This can include as much straightforward explanation of your assessment of the commitment as the mates seem able to absorb. Secure their reactions to those impressions and the analysis of them and their situation.
- Test the emotional boundaries of their relationship and tickle their defenses in the manner of Nathan Ackerman (1958) by raising in a casual or serious manner issues that would challenge the status quo.
- Observe what they do after they have been given any observations or recommendations regarding needs (which can include practical steps) and any other therapeutic interventions have been made.

THE OTHER "Cs" AND INTERVENTIONS

Similar explorations regarding Caring, Communication, Conflict/Compromise, and Contracts can be made, and appropriate actions can be taken. Among other important things are the boundary, power, and intimacy/closeness dimensions of the marriage. What are the boundaries—that is, who is included in the marital relationship? What is being excluded from the relationship and assigned to others? Who and what are intruding into the marriage? How is power dealt with in the relationship? How do the partners tolerate or respond to the needs and desires of each other for intimate contact and closeness (Nichols, 1988)? Following examination of the presenting complaint of the clients and examination of how they are functioning in accordance with the five "Cs," exploration is made of what keeps them jointly and individually from fulfilling the marital tasks.

Sometimes, the actions of one or both partners are so transparent that it is clear from the outset that adequate commitment is missing.

CASE STUDY

Albert, for example, met Janet while he was on an extended work assignment in her small hometown. She pushed for marriage from early in their contact. They scheduled their wedding for shortly after Albert completed the assignment, and they began their married life in the large city where his corporate employer was located. Within a few weeks, according to Albert, Janet threw a switch and cut off all forms of intimacy, and began staying out of their apartment until late at night following completion of her work day as a secretary. Bewildered, he finally sought out a therapist and tried to get Janet to go with him to "work on our marriage." She went once and indicated clearly that she did not wish to work on the marriage. It emerged that the pair had a faulty contract, that Janet had no commitment to Albert, had viewed marriage to him as a way to get out of the hick town in which she had been reared, and had begun secretly creating a separate life and circle of friends for herself from the outset of the marriage. They separated and divorced within a few months. Subsequent individual therapeutic work with Albert consisted of helping him to deal with the pain of the loss and the disillusionment and feelings of betrayal.

Working with family-of-origin issues can be quite productive, particularly with regard to conflict and "contracts"—the sets of expectations regarding the marital relationship held by the partners.

CASE STUDY

Hope and Jeremy, for example, soon after marriage encountered difficulties because from her point of view Jeremy expected too much of her. On the other hand, Jeremy complained that there were (figuratively) "too many people living in our home; it's like her family has chains on her." Exploration revealed that Hope feared she would lose her family of origin if she did not do what they wanted. She felt responsible for her parents. She reported that her mother, a nurse who loved money, had given up her career and income to stay home and "devote her entire life to her children." Her father "worked all the time and was never home." Hope's parents gave the couple "a lot of money." Hope had become parentified and was carrying a sense of responsibility for her mother because "there really isn't much of a marriage and she [the mother] doesn't get much out of life." Clinical work was aimed at effecting a compromise between Hope's reluctance to lessen her family-of-origin ties and Jeremy's desires to cut off contact with her family entirely. The therapist worked with the couple to obtain a compromise by creating a workable middle ground in which each partner's concerns could begin to be met in a reasonable, satisfying way. A couple of sessions with Hope and her family of origin (Nichols, 2003) paved the way for Hope to begin gradually letting go of her role as parentified child, as she learned that her parents were willing and able to function without her caring for her mother and that reciprocally they could lessen their hold on her. Concurrently, Jeremy and Hope began to work on making their marriage central and their home their own territory.

What else needs to be looked for and attended to in clinical work with couples who genuinely seek assistance? There are a variety of possibilities. One more example of clinical work follows.

CASE STUDY

Amy was the pursuer and Carl the pursued in the emotional and sexual relationship of a newly married young professional couple. Things seemed to go smoothly in their sexual activity until they reached the stage of sex play and coital activity. Then, Carl frequently would lose his erection or ejaculate prematurely. Sexual experience was rarely satisfying for either mate. With careful support and explanation, both were given the task of monitoring their thoughts and feelings as they started foreplay and intercourse, "so that we can understand what the blocks are." It became apparent to them that Carl was the one who pulled out of the sexual cycle, Amy's behaviors being basically reactive to his actions. Carl would get "anxious" if he got close or if Amy began the foreplay. In response to the question "Can you remember other times when you felt similarly?" Carl recalled his reactions to being rejected by his first girlfriend, which he associated with their petting and sexual activity. This experience, coupled with other losses, had made him highly sensitive to possible losses and anxious about getting close and intimate with females. As he worked through some of his residual rejection fears, Amy relinquished some of the tension that had been pervading her approach to her husband. A contract was agreed to in which Carl would approach Amy for foreplay with the understanding that she would not reject him; roles would be reversed on alternate nights; and they would discuss their pleasures and concerns. With some support, they soon moved to a point where they could report disappearance of the dysfunction.

CONSIDERATION OF ETHNIC
DIVERSITY ISSUES

In some sense, all of our clients have a different background from ours, even if they were reared in the same country, state, and neighborhood.

Determinants of personality—constitutional, group membership, role, and idiosyncratic experiential—have been discussed elsewhere (Nichols, 1996; Nichols & Everett, 1986). Ethnic background is one of the important determinants of personality and behavior. It deserves the same kind of attention that other factors require if we are to work sensitively and effectively with human beings. What are the general values and expected behaviors held by those in their group and its culture? The areas of couple interaction—the "Cs"—tend to be present for much of humankind but are colored by the values, beliefs, and behaviors peculiar to one's social and cultural group.

Essentially, working with marital couples appears to be done most effectively when we acquire information about marriage and family development in their ethnic settings from the study of general values and expected roles within their ethnic group. One of the best general sources for learning about ethnicity and marital and family therapy in North America is McGoldrick, Giordano, and Pearce's (1996) edited work, *Ethnicity and Family Therapy*. Excellent material for understanding and working with new American families who have come to the United States from India, Hispanic countries, Russia, Taiwan, northwestern Europe, and southwest Asia (Hmong families) appears in Gates et al. (2000) in the *Handbook of Family Development and Intervention*. More general sources consist of scattered articles in therapy journals and work in cultural anthropology and family sociology.

Such materials form a useful background, but also need to be accompanied by a genuine respect for the clients and a willingness to ask them to explain to us what marriage and marital behaviors are expected in their families and ethnic group. A frank acknowledgment about what we do not understand and need to comprehend and the genuine request by the therapist to "help me understand" are the sine qua non for such work.

SUMMARY

This chapter summarizes the nature of marriage, cohabitation, and commitment, noting research that distinguishes between the different, stronger commitment that seems to prevail in marriages versus cohabitation. A brief description of American mate selection, marital life cycle, five tasks of marital couples focused on early marriages, ethnic diversity issues, and some clinical illustrations are given.

REFERENCES

Ackerman, N. W. (1958). *The psychodynamics of family life*. New York: Basic Books.

Axinn, W. G., & Thornton, A. (1992). The relationship between cohabitation and divorce: Selectivity or causal influence? *Demography, 29,* 357–374.

Barnhill, L. R., & Longo, D. (1980). Fixation and regression in the family life cycle. In J. G. Howells (Ed.), *Advances in family psychiatry* (Vol. 2, pp. 51–64). New York: International Universities Press.

Bennett, N. G., Klimas, A. B., & Bloom, D. E. (1988). Commitment and the modern union: Assessing the link between premarital cohabitation and subsequent marital stability. *American Sociological Review, 53,* 127–138.

Bowen, M. (1966). The use of theory in family therapy. *Comprehensive Psychiatry, 7,* 345–374.

Bramlett, M. D., & Mosher, W. D. (2001). *First marriage dissolution, divorce, and re-marriage: United States* (Advanced data from vital and health statistics, no. 323). Hyattsville, MD: National Center for Health Statistics.

Bumpass, L. L., Sweet, J. A., & Cherlin, A. (1991). The role of cohabitation in de-clining rates of marriage. *Journal of Marriage and the Family, 53,* 913–927.

Carter, E. A., & McGoldrick, M. (Eds.). (1980a). *The family life cycle: A framework for family therapy.* New York: Gardner Press.

Carter, E. A., & McGoldrick, M. (1980b). The family life cycle and family therapy: An overview. In E. A. Carter & M. McGoldrick (Eds.), *The family life cycle: A framework for family therapy* (pp. 3–20). New York: Gardner Press.

Carter, E. A., & McGoldrick, M. (Eds.). (1988). *The changing family life cycle: A framework for family therapy* (2nd ed.). New York: Gardner Press.

Carter, E. A., & McGoldrick, M. (Eds.). (1999). *The expanded family life cycle: A framework for family therapy* (3rd ed.). Boston: Allyn & Bacon.

Cherlin, A. J. (1992). *Marriage, divorce, remarriage.* Cambridge, MA: Harvard University Press.

Curtis, J. M. (1994). Factors related to fear of marriage. *Psychological Reports, 74,* 859–863.

Davis, W. S. (1983). *A test of the predictability of collusion, ambivalence, and idealization in the mate selection process.* Unpublished doctoral dissertation, Florida State University, Tallahassee.

DeMaris, A., & Rao, K. V. (1992). Premarital cohabitation and subsequent marital stability in the United States: A reassessment. *Journal of Marriage and the Family, 54,* 178–190.

Dicks, H. V. (1967). *Marital tensions.* New York: Basic Books.

Duvall, E. M. (1957). *Family development.* Philadelphia: Lippincott.

Duvall, E. M. (1977). *Family development* (4th ed.). Philadelphia: Lippincott.

Eckstein, D., Leventhal, M., Bentley, S., & Kelley, S. A. (1999). Relationships as a "three legged sack." *Family Journal: Counseling and Therapy for Couples and Fami-lies, 7,* 399–405.

Fairbairn, W. R. D. (1952). *Psycho-analytic studies of the personality.* London: Rout-ledge & Kegan Paul.

Fisher, L. (1977). On the classification of families. *Archives of General Psychiatry, 34.* (Reprinted from *Advances in general psychiatry,* Vol. 1, pp. 27–52, J. G. How-ells, Ed., 1979, New York: International Universities Press)

Framo, J. L. (1970). Symptoms from a family transactional viewpoint. In N. W. Ackerman (Ed.), Family therapy in transition. *International Psychiatric Clinics, 7*(4), 125–171.

Framo, J. L. (1980). Marriage and family therapy: Issues and initial interview techniques. In M. Andolfi & I. Zwerling (Eds.), *Dimensions of family therapy* (pp. 49–71). New York: Guilford Press.

Gates, R. D., de Esnaola, S. A., Kroupin, G., Stewart, C. C., van Dulmen, M., Xiong, B., et al. (2000). Diversity of new American families: Guidelines for therapists. In W. C. Nichols, M. A. Pace-Nichols, D. S. Becvar, & A. Y. Napier (Eds.), *Handbook of family development and intervention* (pp. 299–322). New York: Wiley.

Goldscheider, F., Thornton, A., & Young-Demarch, L. (1993). A portrait of the nest-leaving process in early adulthood. *Demography, 30* 694–699.

Gottman, J. (1994). *Why marriages succeed or fail: What you can learn from the breakthrough research to make your marriage last.* New York: Simon & Schuster.

Haley, J. (1973). *Uncommon therapy: The psychiatric techniques of Milton H. Erickson, M.D.* New York: Norton.

Hollingshead, A. B. (1950). Cultural factors in the selection of marriage mates. *American Sociological Review, 15,* 619–627.

Howells, J. G. (1975). *Principles of family psychiatry.* New York: Brunner/Mazel.

Johnson, M. P., Caughlin, J. P., & Huston, T. L. (1999). The tripartite nature of marital commitment: Personal, moral, and structural reasons to stay married. *Journal of Marriage and the Family, 61,* 160–177.

Jones, W. H., Adams, J. M., & Berry, J. O. (1995). A psychometric exploration of marital satisfaction and commitment. *Journal of Social Behavior and Personality, 10,* 923–932.

Kantor, D., & Lehr, W. (1975). *Inside the family.* New York: HarperColophon.

Kreider, R. M., & Fields, J. M. (2001). *Number, timing and duration of marriages and divorces: Fall 1996* (Current population reports, pp. 70–80). Washington, DC: U.S. Census Bureau.

Kubie, L. (1956). Psychoanalysis and marriage. In V. Eisenstein (Ed.), *Neurotic interaction in marriage* (pp. 10–43). New York: Basic Books.

Lewin, K. (1948). The background of conflict in marriage. In K. Lewin (Ed.), *Resolving social conflicts* (pp. 84–102). New York: Harper & Row.

McGoldrick, M., Giordano, J., & Pearce, J. K. (Eds.). (1996). *Ethnicity and family therapy* (2nd ed.). New York: Guilford Press.

Murstein, B. I. (1961). The complementary needs hypothesis in newlyweds and middle-aged married couples. *Journal of Abnormal and Social Psychology, 63,* 194–197.

Murstein, N. (1976). The stimulus-value-role theory of marital choice. In H. Grunebaum & J. Christ (Eds.), *Contemporary marriage: Structure, dynamics, and therapy* (pp. 165–186). Boston: Little, Brown.

Napier, A. Y. (1988). *The fragile bond.* New York: HarperCollins.

Napier, A. Y. (2000). Making a marriage. In W. C. Nichols, M. A. Pace-Nichols, D. S. Becvar, & A. Y. Napier (Eds.), *Handbook of family development and intervention* (pp. 145–170). New York: Wiley.

Nichols, W. C. (1978). The marriage relationship. *Family Coordinator, 27,* 185–181.

Nichols, W. C. (1988). *Marital therapy: An integrative approach.* New York: Guilford Press.

Nichols, W. C. (1996). *Treating people in families: An integrative framework.* New York: Guilford Press.

Nichols, W. C. (2000). Integrative marital therapy. In F. M. Dattilio & L. J. Bevilacqua (Eds.), *Comparative treatments for relationship dysfunctions* (pp. 171–188). New York: Springer.

Nichols, W. C. (2003). Family-of-origin treatment. In T. L. Sexton, G. Weeks, & M. Robbins (Eds.), *Handbook of family therapy* (Vol. 3, pp. 83–100). New York: Brunner/Routledge.

Nichols, W. C., & Everett, C. A. (1986). *Systemic family therapy: An integrative approach.* New York: Guilford Press.

Nichols, W. C., Pace-Nichols, M. A., Becvar, D. S., & Napier, A. Y. (Eds.). (2000). *Handbook of family development and intervention.* New York: Wiley.

Popenoe, D., & Whitehead, B. (1999). *Should we live together? What young adults need to know about cohabitation before marriage.* New Brunswick, NJ: The National Marriage Project.

Rodriguez, H. (1998, May). *Cohabitation: A snapshot.* Center for Law and Social Policy. Retrieved April 26, 2003, from www.clasp.org.

Sager, C. J. (1976). *Marriage contracts and couple therapy.* New York: Brunner/Mazel.

Scharff, D. E., & Scharff, J. S. (1991). *Object relations in couple therapy.* Northvale, NJ: Aronson.

Schoen, R. J., & Danish, N. (2001). The retrenchment of marriage: Results from marital status life tables for the United States, 1995. *Population and Development Review, 27,* 553–563.

Schoen, R., & Standish, N. (2000). *The footprints of cohabitation: Results from marital status life tables for the US 1995* (Working Paper No. 00-12). University Park: Pennsylvania State University, Population Research Institute. Retrieved January 13, 2003.

Skynner, A. C. R. (1981). An open-systems, group-analytic approach to family therapy. In A. S. Gurman & D. P. Kniskern (Eds.), *Handbook of family therapy* (pp. 39–84). New York: Brunner/Mazel.

Solomon, M. A. (1973). A developmental-conceptual premise for family therapy. *Family Process, 12,* 179–186.

Teachman, J. D., & Polonko, K. A. (1990). Cohabitation and marital stability in the United States. *Social Forces, 69,* 207–220.

Thomson, E., & Colella, U. (1992). Cohabitation and marital stability: Quality or commitment? *Journal of Marriage and the Family, 54,* 259–267.

Wallerstein, J., & Blakeslee, S. (1995). *The good marriage: How and why love lasts.* Boston: Ticknor & Fields/Houghton Mifflin.

Winch, R. F. (1958). *Mate selection.* New York: Harper & Row.

CHAPTER 4

Couples with Young Children

Linda Morano Lower

COUNSELING COUPLES WITH YOUNG CHILDREN

AMONG LIFE CYCLE transitions, few are as difficult or complex as that of spouse to parent. The changes required to accommodate a new family member impact every aspect of the marital relationship. The emotional focus shifts from an individual's needs and that of one's spouse to another. Finances are reapportioned, leisure time is curtailed, family relationships are realigned, and physical and emotional resources are stretched. Research has shown that marital satisfaction declines within the first year after the birth of a child (Bradt, 1989). Couples are overwhelmed by the amount of work involved in caring for a child, and most couples revert to stereotypical roles within one year of the child's birth. Quality of sexual activity declines, and communication suffers (Gottman & Notarius, 2002). It is during the transition to parenthood that couples report the highest divorce rates and the most difficulty with marriage (Carter & McGoldrick, 1999). Becoming a parent puts both men and women at risk for individual and marital distress (Cox, Paley, Burchinal, & Payne, 1999), and recent studies cite both men and women at increased risk for depression (Cowan, Cowan, Heming, & Miller, 1991).

Recent studies supporting the perception of a decrease in marital satisfaction after parenthood (Cowan & Cowan, 1992) confirm that the dissatisfaction crosses ethnic lines. Both White and African American spouses report lower marital happiness and more frequent conflict after the transition than before (Crohan, 1996).

With couples experiencing such significant quality-of-life declines during the parenting years, attention must be directed to the problematic elements of the transition, with therapeutic interventions directed toward both relieving stress and strengthening the marital bond. This chapter explores many of the concerns of first-time parents and couples with young children: expectations, returning to work, sex and intimacy, in-laws, leisure time, and communication. It also discusses an early-intervention model aimed toward diminishing marital dissatisfaction in first-time parents.

For the purposes of this chapter, we will consider a couple, married once, who together are the biological parents of all children in the family, although this scenario seems less and less likely with the preponderance of blended families.

MARITAL EXPECTATIONS

Couples enter counseling because of the real or perceived pain of one or both partners. Since women are frequently the emotional caretakers of the relationship, it is often the woman who is first aware of disruption in the relationship following the birth of a child and seeks assistance. She is also the one whose life is impacted most directly by childbirth, both physiologically and emotionally. When counseling couples who are either transitioning to parenthood or adding more children to the family, it is important to help them verbalize their expectations of the changing relationship and of each other. They need a mutual acknowledgment that established patterns will need to be adapted and roles renegotiated.

Experience from the original family strongly influences an individual's parenting style and affects decisions such as which parent will be the primary caregiver and nurturer, whether or not the wife works outside the home, the level of paternal involvement, and the emotional closeness or distance of extended family members, especially grandparents. Too often, couples operate from unspoken expectations, with a new mother perhaps anticipating that her husband will be the hands-on father of her childhood memory, while the new father plans to relegate to his wife all childcare and homemaking duties. Mark and Angie had such a problem with unexpressed expectations.

Angie and Mark had agreed that Angie would stay home for at least six months following the birth of their child, Amy. However, when Mark announced that he was extending his own parental leave by several weeks, without pay, to share fully in this important family event, Angie became agitated and fearful. Her own father had never heard of parental leave and left all child raising to her mother. Money, or the lack of it, was always an issue in her home, and the family had to make sacrifices to survive on her father's modest income. Mark's decision to take leave without pay and be a hands-on dad aroused fearful memories in Angie of financial hardship and concerns regarding her adequacy as a parent, since she believed Mark now looked to her as the expert in matters of childcare. Their constant bickering and Angie's anxiety brought them into counseling, lamenting the loss of closeness at what they had hoped would be the "happiest time of their lives."

Feelings of inadequacy and insecurity in caring for a newborn are common to many first-time parents, as are the feelings of anxiety associated with change. In Angie's case, her new responsibilities aroused old memories and fears of financial instability. She was also burdened by the unfounded belief that Mark expected her to be the expert.

When the expectations of each partner were explored in therapy, Angie shared her assumption that Mark was looking to her for childcare expertise. She also shared her discomfort with having Mark at home after the initial settling in period, since it would soon become obvious to him how little she really knew about caring for their newborn. Mark, on the other hand, looked forward to his time at home as an opportunity to bond with their child and learn with his wife how to be parents. He was surprised to learn of Angie's expectation that she be the expert.

Initially, neither Angie nor Mark was able to directly verbalize fears and insecurities to each other. They learned basic communication skills, and with the help of their therapist, each was able to express and acknowledge insecurities about their new roles. They recognized that neither was the expert and developed a plan to participate together in infant-care classes immediately, and parenting classes as their child developed. They were encouraged to expand their circle of friends to include other couples with infants and young children. They learned problem-solving skills to help them resolve parenting and relationship issues as they arose.

Some additional time in therapy was used to explore Angie's unresolved fears around the couple's finances. The couple was instructed to prepare an annual household budget together, giving them a clear picture of their financial needs and resources, and to make whatever adjustments were necessary to live within their means. This exercise concretized their financial picture and made them partners in finding solutions. Having specific knowledge of their family finances and actively participating in developing a budget and brainstorming necessary changes alleviated Angie's fear of the unknown, a significant factor in her childhood experience of financial hardship. Finally, the couple was instructed to prioritize their relationship by planning a weekly date night. To eliminate the financial burden of such an assignment, they were instructed to be creative beyond the typical movie night or dinner out and spend no more than five dollars. This added an element of fun and creativity and encouraged dates such as walks along the beach and picnics in the park.

Marriage partners bring individual skills into the marriage and develop couple skills that impact their ability to parent effectively. On an individual level, one's ability to be flexible, to adapt to change, assume new responsibilities, and defer personal satisfaction to attend to another are all qualities that bode well for the new parent.

Couples acquire a style and identity in the early days before children that characterizes their relationship. Those who have bonded too tightly may have difficulty expanding to include a child, and those so loosely connected may find it challenging to reorganize around a new member. Rigidly structured relationships with clearly defined roles are especially challenged when a new baby arrives, but among the most important skills couples bring to the childbearing years is their ability to problem solve.

When a new baby enters the family circle, there is a decided shift in attention from the spouse to the newborn. New parents are often unprepared for the complexity of feelings they experience. Although having positive feelings toward their child, anger and resentment may simultaneously be directed at their partner. Fatigue from many sleepless nights, insecurity in handling the numerous childcare tasks, unmet expectations, and the loss of the undivided attention from one's spouse all contribute to the confusion and turmoil young parents experience. The ground rules have changed, and although old patterns of relating are not always accessible, new patterns have not yet been clearly established (Wolfson & DeLuca, 1981). The history of how well they solve problems together influences how likely they are to make adjustments and compromises required in reorganizing their lives (Cox et al., 1999).

RETURNING TO WORK

When both partners are employed prior to a child's birth, the assumption is often made that the mother will return to her former employment after maternity leave. This decision is sometimes determined purely by economics. Some couples may choose not to alter their lifestyle and make the adjustments necessary to live on a single salary, while others are simply unable to survive on one income. Even when there is a choice as to whether or not the wife returns to work, the decision is often influenced by the availability of adequate childcare.

In earlier times, when our society was less mobile, extended families offered a ready supply of babysitters, and mothers could reliably leave their infant in the care of a family member with little or no cost involved. With families increasingly living at greater distances from one another, this is not always an option. With the older generation living longer and healthier lives, extended family members who are geographically accessible are choosing to pursue their own personal or career interests rather than become full-time babysitters. Couples are forced to go outside the family circle for childcare and assess their comfort with a paid caregiver, understanding that the hired help may in fact hear their child's first word or witness his first step.

Full-time parenting and nurturing versus the stimulation of childcare opportunities has been argued for decades by vocal advocates in support of their positions. But the decision often comes down not to what others say, but to the mother's choice of what works best for her and her family. Some women cannot imagine leaving their children in the care of another during these early years, while others are unwilling to remain home full-time with an infant, no matter how engaging its personality.

When the mother has decided to return to work after finding suitable childcare, there is still the inevitable sick child or emergency. Although spouses agree in theory that their careers are of equal importance, there inevitably arises the question of which spouse leaves work to retrieve a sick child or who remains home when communicable childhood illnesses prevent the child from attending the childcare center. The decision is often based on which spouse's income is higher or whose employment offers the greatest potential for growth. Employers may pay lip service to the family-friendly workplace, but are less likely to promote the employee who prioritizes family over long hours and high productivity (Bradt, 1989). Additionally, contemporary society does not universally esteem mothers who forgo careers in order to parent full time. By applauding the hardworking father and devaluing the stay-at-home mom, there seems little in modern America that supports couples' efforts to prioritize family life.

SEX AND INTIMACY

Sexual intimacy is the emotional barometer of a relationship, and most couples are eager to return to their prechildbirth sexual activity after the customary six-week postnatal visit. But sex, like most activities after the birth of a baby, usually requires some adaptation, accommodation, and patience.

Although women, in theory, may be eager for the physical affection and intimacy of sex, physiological and emotional issues may interfere, at least initially. Sex may be simply physically uncomfortable for her still-healing body, especially if there has been the added complication of caesarian surgery. Fatigue from lack of sleep and the stress of a demanding new role may diminish sexual desire. A postnatal body that bears little resemblance to the prepregnancy one may engender negative feelings regarding self-image. Nursing mothers may experience themselves as one giant milk bottle, on call day and night for a demanding infant. Sex may feel like just another obligation.

Men, too, have to contend with the mixed emotions they experience at this time, perhaps conflicting feelings about their wife's body being both a source of sexual pleasure and nourishment for their child. When the wife is a neutral or even unwilling sexual partner, the husband's feelings of being rejected or inadequate can result in emotional distancing.

Couples who anticipate resuming their former sexual activity and reinvesting in the we-ness of their relationship are often unprepared for the period of adjustment required. Sex can represent yet another area of their lives where they are struggling to regain control and reestablish former patterns. A husband who is already somewhat of an observer of the special connection between mother and child can be isolated further by a wife with little energy or interest in sex. A woman who feels less than sexually attractive to her partner may wonder at her own diminished desire for sex. The resulting emotional distancing reinforces their worst fears about life ever returning to normal.

Although postnatal difficulties with sexual adjustment are common to many couples, they are rarely talked about. Candid communication between husbands and wives about their own vulnerabilities, especially in the area of sex, can greatly reduce marital stress. Although this phase generally passes without outside intervention, it is a cause of much concern among young parents.

As newborns age and family size increases, couple intimacy is an ongoing problem. Growing children leave parents little time or opportunity to be alone together. The ongoing challenge for parents is to prioritize their marriage while caring for and nurturing children. During these child-rearing years, it is easy for couples to develop completely separate lives, giving rise to the statistics of high divorce rates and an increase in extra-marital affairs. The common expression describing these years is that "men marry their work and women marry the children."

Without special attention to the marriage, partners become so involved in the children's activities and their parenting roles that they forget they are lovers. The busyness of child raising easily distracts partners from their primary relationship, with couples falling into a routine that focuses on roles not relationships. Constant activity masks serious relationship issues that are never recognized or attended to, simply because no one has the time to notice.

Mary Ellen and Matt were typical of the young families in their upscale neighborhood. Matt was an executive with a large firm and worked long hours. Mary Ellen gave up her position as an office manager with a medical supply company when the first of their three children was born. Two others followed in rapid order, and as they grew, she involved herself with their scout troops, school projects, and athletic teams. Her role as soccer mom ended abruptly when an automobile accident sidelined her activities. Recuperating at home for six weeks, she relied on neighbors to shuttle her children to and from school and practice. Matt's attentiveness during her recuperation reminded her of their former relationship, before her absorption with the children and his long hours at the office distanced them from each other. Mary Ellen and Matt began spending evenings catching up and actively making plans to reprioritize their marriage.

It took an automobile accident for Mary Ellen and Matt to recognize what they had almost lost in their relationship. For many couples, the child-raising years pass all too quickly. When children grow and begin to leave home, some partners hardly recognize each other. Spouses who have not prioritized their marriage while raising their families are often faced with the daunting task of rebuilding their relationship in midlife.

IN-LAWS

Although members of the extended family may be a source of tangible and emotional support in times of difficulty, they are often the cause of conflict in families with young children. Most couples occasionally disagree on which set of grandparents gets priority visiting rights and whose parents are spoiling the grandchildren. More often, the issues center on well-intentioned but problematic intrusion when it comes to child-raising philosophies. These suggestions are frequently couched in terms that imply that the listener "turned out all right so I must have known what I was doing."

Young couples need to find their own way with child-raising techniques, using all the resources at their disposal. Childcare practices have changed, and what may have been acceptable in grandma's day may no longer be the way things are done. A case in point is the common practice in past decades of laying infants on their stomachs when putting them in cribs, fearing they would choke if placed on their backs. It is commonly accepted today that infants are far more likely to smother on their stomachs since they lack the neck muscles to lift or turn their heads.

Partners who have not sufficiently separated from their family of origin court serious interference from well-meaning but intrusive parents. The early years of the marriage (usually before the children arrive), provide the opportunity for a couple to bond and present themselves as a unit to their families and society, free from unwanted interference. If individuals see themselves as members of their original family first and a spouse to their husband or wife second, the relationship is in serious jeopardy. The new bride who threatens to go home to mother at the first sign of difficulty or the son who is always needed at home to mediate the ongoing arguments of his parents, a role he filled growing up, has never completely separated from the original family.

Consider Ron who was the oldest of three boys in a family dominated by an alcoholic father. Early on, it was clear that mom was unable to cope with dad's drinking but was unwilling to issue an ultimatum that might include divorce. After dad's drinking bouts, it was Ron whom mom depended on to take care of dad. Ron became the surrogate parent who stayed up late waiting for dad and calling his boss the next day if he was unable to go to work. It was Ron who kept the family secret for many years, even from his younger siblings. In later years, as each of the children in turn left home and dad's drinking bouts lasted for days instead of hours, Ron remained the enabler.

Ron's wife, Cindy, initially accepted this arrangement, touched by Ron's concern for his father. After their daughter was born, however, she found herself increasingly alone and lonely caring for their child. Ron's frequent absences from home put a strain on their marriage. Ron and Cindy entered therapy when Cindy issued an ultimatum that Ron must choose between caring for his dad and prioritizing his wife and child.

Ron's failure to separate from his family of origin by essentially remaining the caretaker of his alcoholic father and the enabler in the alcoholic system threatens to derail his own marriage. His failure to appropriately separate from his original family prevents him from bonding totally with his wife and establishing his marriage as his primary relationship. Intervention with this couple must include education about the alcoholic family system and Ron's ongoing role as enabler. As he appropriately, though belatedly, separates from his original family, Ron needs a strategy for responding to his mother's frantic pleas for help, one that includes placing responsibility on dad for his drinking and its consequences. Ron and Cindy can then begin to repair the damage to their own marriage.

There is no one-size-fits-all approach when helping couples determine the direction of their lives and the degree of parental involvement. A young woman in therapy complained about her mother-in-law's determination to provide ethnic dishes from her native India at all the traditional holidays, even when the celebrations were hosted by the son and daughter-in-law. The young wife felt that her best efforts at entertaining were discounted while the extended family exclaimed over the native dishes. She was alarmed that her children were beginning to assimilate some of the basic Hindi phrases of their grandparents' native tongue and spoke of visiting India one day.

Although it would seem to many that this young woman is blessed with the opportunity to understand and experience her husband's heritage close-up and expose their children to widely different cultures, the experience brings out her own insecurities. Although there are obvious benefits from learning to cook her husband's favorite dishes and encouraging their children's exploration of their paternal heritage, it is ultimately the couple, not the therapist, who determines which cultural assimilations are appropriate for them.

LEISURE TIME

As important as leisure time is for the couple's relationship, it is often first to be forfeited in the time crunch of busy families with young children. Social circles narrow as couples spend less time with their childless friends and substantially more time with parents of similarly aged children, recognizing that only other parents can truly understand their frantic pace and last-minute cancellations. Changes of plans and cranky kids are acceptable to other parents, who have had similar experiences and know how to be flexible. Little time is left for quiet romantic evenings, as intimate dinners are replaced by soccer team pizza parties and parents' night at school.

As children grow, helping them develop their interests and talents is a high priority. Although parental involvement is critical in nurturing healthy children, without careful planning, little time remains for couples to regenerate and relax away from the constant demands of a busy family. But by failing to find a balance between their needs and their children's, husbands and wives place a tremendous strain on their marriage and risk disengaging from each other. When communication is limited to planning children's activities and coordinating schedules, it is easy to lose sight of the loving relationship that preceded the children. The solution lies not in dismissing the need to spend adult time together or lamenting the fact that children absorb all available time and energy, but in creating new patterns of togetherness and balancing couple time with family time. Although much of the spontaneity of earlier years may be unavailable to a couple who are raising young children, with creative planning and prioritizing, it is possible to create opportunities for leisure-time activities.

Therapists can offer stressed couples a few practical suggestions when they seem unable to find time or money to prioritize their relationship.

Trading childcare with another couple gives each couple a night out. Babysitting cooperatives are another form of sharing childcare that allows couples to bank babysitting credit by working at the coop. Cooperatives are fairly easy to start if one does not already exist. Couples can be encouraged to schedule midday dates, when children are in school. And one couple recently scheduled a short road trip complete with a VCR-equipped, rented van and Disney videos for their preschool-aged children. Although using an electronic babysitter is not recommended as a steady diet, it provided this couple with hours of almost uninterrupted conversation, a luxury they had almost forgotten existed.

The overextended family is a variation on the theme of couples who have little or no adult time. Parents can easily fall into the trap of believing their children will grow up deprived or otherwise inadequate unless they are afforded every possible extracurricular opportunity. The new phenomenon of overextended and stressed-out kids is starting to attract the attention of school counselors and mental health professionals. Couples with no time for each other should be encouraged to reexamine their commitments and priorities, for the sake of their relationship and the well-being of their families.

COMMUNICATION

Marriage is a long conversation, so marry a friend.

—Anonymous

Effective communication is identified in many marriage guides and by most practitioners as the single most important skill necessary for a lasting marriage (Fischer & Hart, 1991; Markham, Stanley, & Blumberg, 1994). Couples who communicate effectively have the ability to affirm each other, listen and respond nondefensively to the needs of their spouse, stay focused on the issues at hand when the inevitable misunderstandings occur and communicate negative feelings in a nondestructive manner. With so much emphasis on effective communication in both academic and corporate settings, therapists may be tempted to assume that these skills are widely known and commonly practiced. Unfortunately, among distressed couples, this is rarely the case. Many couples who seek marital therapy demonstrate an amazing lack of basic communication skills. Moreover, unless a distressed couple learns the appropriate skills, they are bequeathing to their children the same dysfunctional communication style.

The initial interview offers an opportunity to evaluate couples' communication skills. As they tell their story, they reenact their interpersonal style in the therapist's office: interrupting, mind reading, blaming, defending, generalizing, defocusing, and on and on. One simple intervention is to state that only one spouse may have the floor at a time, or simply put, no interrupting. Also, it is helpful to encourage the silent partner to engage in active listening and reflect back what has been said before taking a turn to speak. This simple intervention allows the therapy to continue while making subtle inroads into the dysfunctional communication style. It is far more effective to introduce small, positive changes in the context of therapy than to attempt to teach an abridged version of Communication 101.

Beyond the obvious intent of allowing each partner time to speak and be listened to, the purpose of effective communication is to encourage partners to reach out to each other at a far deeper level than in the past. Keeping communication at a superficial level is what they have become accustomed to. Using new communication skills involves risk: sharing insecurities and vulnerabilities, listening to the emotion beneath the words, and sharing profoundly in the joys and struggles that are part of life. It is also important to encourage couples to find time daily to check in with each other on a feeling level, not just coordinate schedules, plan meals, or handle a myriad of details required in keeping a family running. This simple but significant commitment communicates a deep level of caring and concern. It connects couples emotionally on a regular basis, sharing the good feelings and preventing the negative ones from being buried, only to emerge more forcefully later on.

CONFLICT RESOLUTION

A universal fact of married life is that all couples have problems, and some are more skilled than others in resolving them. The more skilled in communicating, the more willing to share feelings and risk vulnerability, the more nondefensive each partner is or becomes, the greater the likelihood the couple will satisfactorily resolve conflicts.

Couples with children resist, in many cases, the temptation to quarrel in front of them. Although this is commendable, and certainly children should never be subjected to screaming matches or physical violence, it conveys an inaccurate message. Parents occasionally disagree. Children who have never witnessed a minor squabble between parents, and more importantly, its subsequent resolution, develop the unrealistic expectation that adults never fight. This is a serious misconception. The first disagreement with their spouse at some future date will portend a tragedy of monumental proportion. It is far wiser for children to recognize that minor disagreements do occur now and then, and learn from their parents the appropriate conflict-resolution skills.

Couples draw closer together through honestly facing the differences in their relationship and working together to find satisfactory solutions. When the same issue arises repeatedly, clearly there is another issue underneath the symptom. A wife who is distressed over finding her husband's carelessly discarded dirty clothing strewn about the house may be upset about something more than living with a sloppy husband. Sometimes it is necessary to look for the issue underneath the issue when the same fight keeps occurring. When conflicts do arise, there are basic rules regarding conflict resolution and fair fighting that partners should observe:

1. Clarify the precise issue and state it simply.
2. Set aside time, away from children, when there will not be interruptions. Couples may have to literally make an appointment to disagree.
3. Limit the discussion to the agreed on topic.
4. No interrupting.
5. Use "I" statements and avoid blaming behavior.
6. Practice nondefensive behaviors.
7. When both partners have spoken and been heard, brainstorm possible solutions.
8. Continue to work until a solution acceptable to both partners is found.
9. If additional time is needed, another period can be set aside to continue working toward a solution. Agreeing to disagree may be an acceptable solution.

POSITIVE FEEDBACK AND GRATITUDE

In the busy-ness of parenting young children, couples can focus on the difficulties and lose sight of all that is positive in the marriage. One way to affirm and provide positive feedback is to specifically express gratitude for all the partner has done that day, for the spouse, the children, even the routine tasks (Fischer & Hart, 1991). This has an amazing power to enhance the relationship and assure couples of their mutual love and support.

PREVENTION

Although there have been at least 15 longitudinal studies conducted on the transition to parenthood (Gottman et al., 2002), the only readily available prevention intervention model is the Cowans' study in Berkeley, California. The study was comprised of 96 couples, 72 of whom were expecting a child, and 24 not having decided to begin a family at the time the study began (Cowan & Cowan, 1992). The researchers recruited couples in their sixth month of pregnancy and followed them through three months postpartum, meeting weekly with a professionally trained couple for 24 weeks. The goal was to assist couples in making sense of the changes in their lives and making small changes that would be satisfactory to both of them (Cowan & Cowan, n.d.). Their results, with group participants reporting greater satisfaction with the marriage after the first year following the birth of the first child than the control group, suggests that early intervention groups offer some promise in assisting couples through the difficult transition to parenthood.

Prevention intervention groups like the one described previously offer a supportive network for couples in the same life cycle transition, providing them with opportunities to discuss and normalize their experiences while learning skills to deescalate stressful situations. Although groups of this nature undoubtedly already exist, their widespread availability, perhaps as an adjunct to prepared childbirth classes, could make them accessible to more couples.

CASE STUDY

Ted and Emily were each 34 years old, had been married for five years, and were parents of an 8-month-old daughter, Sarah. When they first married, they were interested in having children, but, although not actively trying to prevent pregnancy, were making no particular effort to start a family. Once they decided the time was right, they were unable to conceive as quickly as they anticipated, raising fertility concerns. They were seriously investigating testing, which Emily's doctor had been recommending for some time, when Emily learned she was pregnant. Although Emily experienced more fatigue than she expected throughout the nine months, the pregnancy was uneventful. Both she and Ted attended childbirth classes and made plans to share the baby's care and household tasks, since both intended to resume their careers.

Ted worked as an accounting manager for a mid-sized electronics firm. He enjoyed his work but often put in 12-hour days and was frequently called after hours and during the weekends for emergencies. He and Emily had been discussing his desire to return to school part-time to work toward his master's degree in Business Administration with a view to earning his CPA. He felt this would open up many more career opportunities within larger firms or perhaps lead to opening his own accounting business. When they learned they were expecting a child, those discussions were temporarily halted.

Emily had graduated from college with a degree in English but with her basic knowledge of computers and excellent writing skills, she found employment writing user manuals for a software firm. She enjoyed her position and her colleagues but arranged with her company to work from home for six months after her maternity leave ended. This would give her the advantage of remaining home with her baby while still retaining a position she enjoyed and that paid well. Her employers had some doubts about this arrangement but liked Emily and did not want to risk losing a good employee. Although they were not a particularly innovative company, they were willing to try the arrangement, at least temporarily. Although Emily had no long-term career plans, she had vague ideas of pursuing an advanced degree at some future date. For the time being, she was content with her current position, which seemed compatible with their lifestyle and parenting goals.

Emily came from a loving and supportive family, and was the youngest of three children. Her older brothers lived in neighboring cities and were both busy with their families and careers. Being the only girl, Emily was close to her mother. The family was still recovering from the death of her father, who had been killed in an automobile accident a year earlier. Although Emily missed him terribly, she was grieving appropriately and was accepting the loss.

Ted had been raised by adoptive parents after having been born to a teenage mother. He had been raised as an only child and had a good relationship with his parents. He and his father had embarked on many do-it-yourself projects and enjoyed working together on the weekends. Ted had known about his birth mother from a young age but had made only passing attempts to locate her. With Sarah's birth, finding his birth mother had become an obsession with him. His parents had always encouraged his search, but since they had adopted him through an agency that sealed birth records, the search would be complicated, but not impossible.

After Sarah's arrival, Ted stayed home for two weeks to get acquainted with the baby and assist with childcare. Emily's mom had been invited as well but was asked to time her arrival after Ted returned to work. This gave Ted and Emily uninterrupted time to bond with their child and the opportunity to make some adjustments at home. Although Emily's mom was careful about asking which tasks Emily wanted done and not interfering with Ted and Emily's way of doing things, her presence in the home seemed particularly irritating to Ted. Prior to the baby's arrival, he had a good relationship with his mother-in-law so he was surprised by his own reaction.

The months following Sarah's arrival were difficult for both Ted and Emily. They were overwhelmed by all the work involved in caring for a new baby and seemed to always be behind on basic household chores. Ted would come home to dirty dishes and piles of laundry, and complained that with all the time Emily had at home, these simple tasks should be completed.

Although originally looking forward to working from home, Emily was unhappy when the arrangement actually allowed her little time to complete her projects. Sarah's constant interruptions and distractions left Emily feeling unproductive in her work and neglectful of the baby. She had decided to end the arrangement and return to her office, since she missed her colleagues and was not enjoying working from home as she had hoped.

Ted had begun spending more and more time at work, finding it stressful to come home to a cranky baby, a tired wife, and a disorganized house. He began taking on more projects with his dad and seemed never to be home. When he was home, he willingly helped with the baby but only occasionally with basic household tasks. He spent his free time doing computer searches through agencies that assisted adoptees in locating their birth parents. Emily was feeling angry, neglected, and unloved. Whenever she attempted to discuss her feelings with Ted, he became angry and defensive, blaming her for the untidy house, after which he withdrew into a stony silence. They came into therapy when Emily started thinking seriously about a divorce.

Ted and Emily are experiencing problems typical of many first-time parents. A new baby has disrupted their lives, and they are struggling to find a balance between their needs and Sarah's. They have not yet established the routines that enable their household to function smoothly, and they miss the intimate moments of the past. Additionally, Emily is unhappy with her decision to work at home and feeling unproductive in her career and neglectful and incompetent as a mother. Ted expected Emily to simultaneously juggle household tasks, child care, and her career in her usual efficient manner, and is feeling a bit jealous of her time at home. Also, Sarah's birth has triggered unanticipated feelings of grief and loss. While he recognizes that his early years were spent with loving, adoptive parents, his own idealization of family life with the birth mother he has never known contrasts sharply with the present reality. Both Emily and Ted are having difficulty accessing their complex feelings and are pushing each other away at the time they most desire closeness.

Ted and Emily could benefit from emotionally focused therapy (EFT), a thorough discussion of which is found in Chapter 11 of this text. "EFT," in the words of Susan Johnson, "is an effective, short-term approach to modifying distressed couples' constricted interaction patterns and emotional responses and fostering the development of a secure emotional bond" (Johnson, 1999, p. 13). The brief summary that follows highlights in very general terms the interventions and goals of EFT. It is not meant to be a thorough analysis of the therapeutic process.

What makes Ted and Emily excellent candidates for EFT is the fact that they have a basically stable marriage and are experiencing a life cycle change. They are struggling to redefine their relationship, but the marriage is absent of any significant trauma. In attachment terms, Emily is uncertain of Ted's unconditional commitment to her. Her attempts to emotionally connect with Ted are met with defensiveness and emotional and physical withdrawal, which only reinforces Emily's insecurities during a time when she is juggling three roles somewhat unsuccessfully.

It is essential that both Ted and Emily feel validated and affirmed in their emotional experience as they struggle to redefine their relationship.

The therapist assists them in clarifying the emotions that underlie their interactions. Ted's envy of Emily's time with their baby, his disappointment at the disrupted and untidy household, and his experience of loss in never having known his birth mother can be reframed as his desire to spend more time with Emily and Sarah. Emily's feelings of inadequacy and loneliness, as well as her experience of being overwhelmed in her new roles are normalized as the therapist builds an alliance with each spouse. Using the techniques of Emotionally Focused Therapy—heightening, interpreting, tracking, reflecting, reframing, and restructuring, the clinician clarifies their experiences and provides new meaning for their interaction patterns in the context of their attachment needs. The therapist encourages a new understanding of their current behavior and assists them in shaping new responses and a more emotionally focused dialogue.

The therapist encourages Ted to talk about what he experiences when he comes home to a tired wife, disorganized household, and cranky baby. He can only state that "this was not what I expected, and she has all the time in the world. She should be able to handle it." The therapist encourages him to further explore his expectations and he acknowledges that he had the perfect household in mind, in part because he had always imagined his own perfect home whenever he thought of his birth mother. He had created an ideal that Emily had failed to live up to. He further acknowledges that he is jealous and resentful because he has so little time with Sarah. He is encouraged to share his feelings with Emily.

The therapist reframes their differences in terms of both wanting more time with each other but unable to ask for what they need. The therapist normalizes the conflicting feelings that often accompany a major life transition, and Ted and Emily are encouraged to dialogue in a more meaningful way. Emily acknowledges her feelings of inadequacy as a mother and her ambivalence about returning to work.

Emily begins to soften and feel less isolated when the therapist points out that Ted's distancing is not due to lack of love for her and Sarah, but in being overwhelmed with the negative feelings he felt guilty expressing. When his idealized household did not materialize as he'd always imagined, he began to look to his roots for consolation. He began his search for his birth mother in earnest, in the hope that she would live up to his expectations since Emily had not. He also recognized that seeing the close bond between mother and daughter aroused in him intense feelings of loss for the birth mother he had never known. Recognizing how important it was to him to pursue his search, Emily encouraged his effort to locate her.

Ted and Emily sought to further involve Ted's parents and Emily's mother and brothers in their lives, recognizing that they had isolated themselves from the extended family and were feeling cutoff. They took steps to invite family members for informal visits, often finding fix-it projects in their own home for Ted and his dad to tackle. Both grandmothers offered to babysit now and again, giving the new parents an occasional night out.

As the weeks progressed, Emily decided that although she loved her job and wanted to continue working, she was unwilling to spend so much time away from Sarah. She arranged to work part time and found satisfactory childcare near her home. Ted and Emily were still adjusting to the change, but were welcoming the balance this new schedule brought to their lives.

Both agreed that Ted's plan to return to school was a good one, but chose to delay it for at least one year. At that time, Sarah would be almost two, and Emily would consider working full-time, allowing Ted the opportunity to cut back on his hours and start school.

SUMMARY

Research has shown that the transition from partners to parents is one of the most stressful of the life cycle changes and one for which most couples are inadequately prepared. Couples report being overwhelmed with the amount of work a new baby requires, exhaustion from sleepless nights, a decline in the quality of sex, both positive and negative feelings toward their baby and each other, disorganized households, little leisure time, and lack of affordable childcare if the mother chooses to return to work. Our increasingly mobile society denies many couples the emotional support previously provided by extended family. Few businesses provide a family-friendly workplace or offer on-site child care.

Two indicators of a couple's ability to weather this transition successfully are their ability to problem solve and communicate effectively. Although there are few opportunities for couples to prepare for this transition other than the sink or swim approach after the baby arrives, the prevention group described earlier offers some preliminary positive results.

Prevention groups attempt to offset the early parenthood turmoil and assist couples with the transition by meeting weekly from late pregnancy through the early postpartum months. Couples learn how to deescalate stressful situations and make sense of the changes they are experiencing by meeting regularly with other new parents. Listening to couples struggle with similar issues provides hope and reassurance that one's experiences are not unique. Initial results are promising, since participants reported less dissatisfaction with their lives in the first year following the birth of their child than those in the control group.

Counseling couples with young children requires an understanding of the upheaval the transition to parenthood occasions in the lives of most new parents and knowledge of therapeutic interventions enabling them to access the conflicting emotions of this challenging period while working to strengthen the couple bond. The goal of the therapist is to recognize the level of their distress, help them make sense of their experiences and conflicting emotions, provide them with the tools needed to connect emotionally during the transition, and instill hope in the possibility of being intimate partners as well as parents.

REFERENCES

Bradt, J. O. (1989). Becoming parents: Families with young children. In B. Carter & M. McGoldrick (Eds.), *The changing family life cycle: A framework for family therapy* (2nd ed., pp. 235–254). Boston: Allyn & Bacon.

Carter, B., & McGoldrick, M. (Eds.). (1999). *The expanded family life cycle: Individual, family and social perspectives* (3rd ed.). Boston: Allyn & Bacon.

Cowan, C. P., & Cowan, P. A. (1992). *When partners become parents.* New York: Basic Books.

Cowan, C. P., & Cowan, P. A. (n.d.). *Preventive interventions for couples with young children* (Brief report from Two Family Intervention Studies: The Becoming-a-Family and the Schoolchildren-and-their-Families Projects). Retrieved May 8, 2003, from http://www.biu.ac.il/SOC/peleg/pub/e-preventative.rtf.

Cowan, C. P., Cowan, P. A., Heming, G., & Miller, N. B. (1991). Becoming a family: Marriage, parenting and child development. In P. A. Cowan & E. M. Hetherington (Eds.), *Family transitions* (pp. 79–109). Hillsdale, NJ: Erlbaum.

Cox, M. J., Paley, B., Burchinal, M., & Payne, C. C. (1999). Marital perceptions and interactions across the transition to parenthood. *Journal of Marriage and the Family, 61*(3), 611–625.

Crohan, S. E. (1996). Marital quality and conflict across transition to parenthood in African American and White couples. *Journal of Marriage and the Family, 58*(4), 933–943.

Fischer, K. R., & Hart, T. N. (1991). *Promises to keep.* New York: Paulist Press.

Gottman, J. M., & Notarius, C. I. (2002). Marital research in the 20th century and a research agenda for the 21st century. *Family Process, 41*(12), 159–198.

Johnson, S. M. (1999). Emotionally focused couple therapy: Straight to the heart. In J. M. Donovan (Ed.), *Short term couple therapy* (pp. 13–42). New York: Guilford Press.

Markham, H., Stanley, S., & Blumberg, S. L. (1994). *Fighting for your marriage.* San Francisco: Jossey-Bass.

Wolfson, R. M., & DeLuca, V. (1981). *Couples with children.* New York: Warner Books.

CHAPTER 5

Couples with Adolescents

C. Haydee Mas and James F. Alexander

WHY A CHAPTER on couples with adolescents? How different are they from couples with younger children? As a conceptual as well as clinical issue, are the differences between couples with adolescents and couples with younger children primarily quantitative (e.g., adolescents are taller, heavier, have more education, and eat more!) or are they qualitative? These changes often seem to be discontinuous ("All of a sudden she is taller than I am!"), and involve such fundamental shifts in relationships (e.g., from parents as the authority figures to adolescents asserting equal power in terms of physical strength, and a movement from primarily dependent to much more autonomous) that they can involve major changes in relational dynamics. Particularly for parents who have relied heavily on position or information superiority in order to influence their children's behavior, such shifts can create major crises. In addition, relational bonds, which are known to be major risk factors (when negative) or protective factors (when positive) for positive adolescent functioning characteristically change, as peers become increasingly important and the emancipation process begins. For some couples, these changes are ones of degree (respect, closeness, and trust are less positive than with younger children) and are manageable. In other families, they are of such magnitude that they also become qualitative or categorical (i.e., positive to quite negative).

In this chapter, we address both the quantitative/dimensional differences, as well as the more dramatic categorical/qualitative differences that accompany adolescence, but we tend to highlight the latter, because they more often present to the clinician for treatment. For example, many families report greater parenting stress with adolescents than with younger children, but in blended or stepfamilies the differences seem more dramatic, difficult to manage, and more likely to result in clinical levels of adolescent dysfunction.

In addressing the topic of couples with adolescents, we also face the challenge of honoring individual differences while at the same time describing uniformities within a given developmental range, a culture, or a family structure. This represents the same challenge that authors face when writing a chapter about any particular therapy model, about a particular ethnic group, or about alternative lifestyles. To what extent do we consider individual differences, and to what extent is it appropriate to generalize to the entire group? Generalizing our assertions to a group, which often can appear as an externally imposed descriptive uniformity, can be quite dangerous. In fact, as a field we now understand, and in fact embrace, notions of diversity and uniqueness both between and within cultures, family forms, and orientations. We appreciate the concept that any social unit (family, couple, neighborhood) can only be understood from within in ways that reflect if not represent the unique experience of the members. Thus, although as authors we could construct a generic image of couples with adolescents and a particular trajectory of adolescent development, such constructions would undermine the very foundations of current conceptual approaches to couple and family work.

This issue of uniqueness versus generality extends also to the therapists seeing couples with adolescents. We therapists represent greater heterogeneity than is often apparent in descriptions of professional training programs regarding which credentialing agencies and state licensing bodies tend to emphasize common (core) beliefs and competencies rather than the diversity. Training to uniform standards often ill serves clinicians who enter practice in diverse contexts (e.g., private practice versus social service agency), funding streams (Medicare, private insurance, various HMO structures, other federal- or state-funded programs), and treatment populations. Many of our traditional mental health training programs, for example, still center on interventions that involve certain levels of intellectual capacity, motivation to change, and value systems about what "family" and various roles therein "should be." However, in experience across more than 100 nationally and internationally certified Functional Family Therapy (FFT) sites (Sexton, Alexander, & Mease, 2003), therapists and families differ immensely from each other. Some communities represent considerable multicultural diversity; for example, in one south Florida agency, our clients and therapists represent the following cultures: African American, third-generation Cuban American, first-generation Central American, Haitian/Creole speaking, and a small number of Anglo families. In other communities, FFT therapists represent and clinically treat almost no diversity (e.g., in several sites the great majority of the families are African American, and in other sites the clinicians and clients are predominantly Anglo American). Finally, some sites are seen as relatively homogeneous by external funders (e.g., the Southeast Asia Community

Center), but participants see themselves as representing very diverse cultures (Korean, Hmong, Cambodian, various different dialects representing China, etc.). Finally, diversity rather than uniformity also reflects many of the family forms and structures we see. Even in a cohort of adolescents who are more or less in similar developmental stages, some are living with a couple that represents their birth parents, some with a stepparent, some with a couple that represents a parent and grandparent who share (comfortably or dysfunctionally) parenting roles, some are adopted, and some live in temporary or longer term foster homes.

Although it is important to consider these myriad variations, we cannot discuss couples with adolescents in a way that ignores commonalities that do exist. It does little good to adopt the totally transactional or contextualist perspective (e.g., Altman & Rogoff, 1987) that does not recognize nomothetic and context-independent general tendencies that transcend individual differences within various groupings. For example, not all representatives of a religious belief system share identical spiritual beliefs, but as a group one can identify general differences, which can inform the clinician preparing to work with a couple who self-identifies as Muslim as opposed to couples who self-identify as Orthodox Jewish, Christian, Japanese Buddhist, or couples not professing any particular theological orientation. Case examples can be compelling and informative, but much of our theoretical, empirical, and experiential base for the field is founded (whether we like it or not) on fairly homogeneous groups, or groups that are treated as though they are homogeneous at the expense of recognizing and honoring their individual differences.

In addressing the chapter content (couples with adolescents), we had a choice to struggle with these ubiquitous tensions (e.g., nomothetic-ideographic and categorical-individual difference) as representing a dilemma, or to embrace it as a dialectic that we savor (Alexander & Sexton, 2002). Dialectic (from the *American Heritage Dictionary*) is defined as "The Hegelian process of change whereby an ideational entity (thesis) is transformed into its opposite (antithesis) and preserved and fulfilled by it, the combination of the two being resolved in a higher form of truth (synthesis)."

We cannot aspire to accomplishing such a goal, but the rationale of "savoring the dialectic" forces us as a field beyond some of the polarizations that often stagnate rather than enhance our ability to help couples with adolescents who are dysfunctional or in great pain. Thus, at the risk of seeming conceptually inconsistent, in this chapter, we have attempted to discuss both generic trends and issues, but frequently identify context-specific issues, especially in clinical examples.

To do so we present five *essential features* of treatment, which are based on clinical, research, and theoretical literature. These features also represent our own diversity (e.g., in background, gender, and culture) and extensive clinical experience (over 55 years between the two authors) in couple and family-based intervention with diverse and often multiproblem couples

with adolescents. Finally, the principles draw heavily on the widely disseminated, evidence-based mature clinical model identified as functional
family therapy (FFT; see Alexander & Sexton, 2002; Sexton & Alexander,
2003).

One principle that will receive particular attention includes respecting
diversity and basing all interventions on cultural competence. That principle will be introduced immediately in our first orienting case example.

CASE STUDY

Miguel and Angela had been together for 25 years. They entered the treatment process by virtue of Miguel Sr.'s calling a local clinic because of concerns regarding his son's (Miguel Jr.) truancy and depression during the
previous several months. Miguel Jr. was a 15-year-old bilingual (his father
was also bilingual but not his mother) adolescent who had grown up in the
United States. Their insurance company referred the family to a bilingual
and bicultural therapist. The parents were able to afford therapy (but with
limitations) because of medical insurance provided through Angela's work.
Both parents and Miguel Jr. came in for the first session. All three family
members presented with a host of problems and concerns.

During the first session the following information emerged: Miguel Jr.
began missing school several months prior to the referral, often remaining
in bed until 2:00 P.M. and refusing to go out afternoons and evenings. He
rarely smiled and was described by his parents as tearful daily. Angela had
been raised in Mexico and knew little English. She worked full time as a
clerk and also was struggling with depressive symptoms. Angela had a long
history of depression apparently related to abuse as a child. She had experienced physical problems the previous year, resulting in surgery, and it
was at this time that Miguel Jr. began staying home to take care of her.
Miguel Sr., also bilingual, had difficulties with substance abuse and depression. Prior to the referral to the author, Miguel Jr. had been seen by a
psychiatrist and had begun an antidepressant medication regimen, which
he reported was not having any noticeable positive effect. Miguel Sr. also
had been referred to a substance abuse treatment program, which he described as unsuccessful as well. He described being unable to cope well
with his memories of severe abuse as a child and had started using heroin
as a young adult to cope with his depression and emotional pain. He was
unemployed, and the family was having financial difficulties because of
his heroin and methadone dependency. In addition, he had been recently
diagnosed with hepatitis.

Despite the pattern of emotional distress in both parents, Angela and
Miguel entered the therapy process asking the therapist to "fix" Miguel Jr.
In the process, they also asserted that they were considering separation or
divorce. Angela had been given the responsibility to make that decision,
since her husband expressed feeling like such a "complete failure" with

"little to offer to the family." Furthermore, Angela repeatedly expressed being extremely tired and worried that her husband's problems were causing her son's symptoms. Her financial responsibilities, marital conflict, and now her son's truancy likely overwhelmed her.

ESSENTIAL FEATURES OF EFFECTIVE INTERVENTION

We chose this case because of the overwhelming number of issues and symptoms presented during the first therapy session. Such cases often are considered to be at very high risk for dropout or failure given the histories (plural) of physical/sexual abuse, drug abuse, and ongoing (but not particularly effective) prescribed medication treatment. Other factors often cited include the family's minority status in a dominant culture, the economic issues surrounding them almost like a blanket of oppression, and their isolation from extended-family resources. As noted above, it may be difficult to generalize from this couple to another couple who would be considered mainstream if not privileged, who have considerable resources and no history of abuse, and yet who also experience emotional and behavioral problems with their child (truancy and depression), and who are considering divorce. However, processes that can be generalized are the essential features of intervention such as respectfulness and matching, the integration of a strength and a risk factor perspective, goals and techniques that are phase-based, and the emphasis on a balanced alliance with all family members, which involves an *unwillingness* on the part of the therapist to take sides or to force an agenda on this family or a particular family member. It also should be noted that if this case had been seen by the second author (an older Anglo male) rather than the senior author (a younger bilingual female), the dynamics of change would reflect the very same core factors, but they would have to unfold in a very different manner, which would be totally contingent (Sexton & Alexander, 2002) on the family.

ESSENTIAL FEATURE 1: RESPECTFULNESS

At the outset, we must make a distinction that may seem minor, but which is critical, and perhaps only tangentially captured in the distinction between *respect* and *respectfulness*. Asking therapists to *respect* all clients can be very challenging and even inappropriate, especially in cases (like those we see often) where one or more family members have physically, emotionally, and sometimes even sexually abused other family members or people outside the family. Some of these family members enter treatment defensive and resistant, and sometimes even offering no sense of remorse or desire to change. "Respecting" such people from the very beginning of the very first session, especially when recipients of the abuse are present in the room, is difficult (to say the least) and to many clinicians not even defensible. However, generating an atmosphere of "re-spectfulness," or working relentlessly to develop respect (Alexander & Sexton, 2002), is both possible and essential if the therapeutic process is to begin in a way that maximizes positive outcomes for all family members. Respectfulness is a complex process, involving an attitude on the part of the therapist, a belief system that *all* the family members in the room have the potential for dignity and positive growth (no matter how the individ-uals present at the outset), a set of specific therapeutic interventions, and understanding the dynamics of the family sitting with us in the room (whether it be the clinic, the emergency room, the waiting room at the detox center, or in their home). This need for respectfulness of the fam-ily's right to access community resources and effective interventions is not always foremost in a marital/family therapist clinical practice. Thera-pists need to become multiculturally educated and market themselves as such to begin to offer ethnically diverse families access to effective in-terventions given that one out of six individuals in the United States is foreign-born and that one out of four individuals is the offspring of immi-grants (Falicov, 2003).

ESSENTIAL FEATURE 2: UNDERSTANDING

Understanding, at the level of the therapist's observations but also at the level of the family members' phenomenology, involves three domains:

1. *Culture and diversity*
2. *Developmental aspects* of adolescence and the parent(s)/parent figures involved
3. Dynamics of the family's *relational functioning*

With respect to culture and diversity, therapists working with any eth-nically diverse population can, and we would argue, must enhance their therapeutic effectiveness by developing cultural competence. *Cultural com-petence* is defined as thinking and behaving that enables members of one culture/ethnic group to work effectively with members of another (Samantrai, 2003). More specifically this process entails the therapist ac-cepting and respecting the client's cultural differences and then adapting one's practice to become more relevant to the client. Furthermore, thera-pists need to develop a self-awareness of how they perceive others and of any judgments they may be making regarding their differences. In addi-tion, therapists need to make an extra effort to develop trust and coopera-tion with ethnically diverse clients who might come to therapy suspicious about the prominent culture. Cultural competence is especially critical in psychotherapy with couples and families, since culture influences all aspects of individual and family life and parent-child relationships (Samantrai, 2003).

Children and adolescents from families of ethnic minorities are one of the largest growing segments of the U.S. population (Aponte, Rivers, & Wohl, 1995). A number of studies have shown a higher rate of dropping out from therapy than Anglo clients after the first session. Dropout rates can be significantly altered by the client-therapist relationship. The mental health system has often not responded to the needs of ethnic minorities. As therapists, we need to address what techniques and what conditions are most therapeutically effective with ethnically diverse populations.

As mentioned in the beginning of this chapter, it is important not to overgeneralize regarding the relationship between the therapist and the ethnically diverse couple, but to tease apart the more specific factors that facilitate this therapeutic relationship. The degree of acculturation of the client, language fluency, diagnostic validity, symptom expression, and the client's worldview have all been found to be significant influences on therapeutic effectiveness (Aponte et al., 1995). As therapists, we need to be sensitive to centicultural bias where criteria defined and validated in one culture are used to determine psychological disorder in another culture. The interaction between culture and symptom expression needs to be carefully understood so as not to label a normative expression of a particular emotion in one culture as dysfunctional because of its current expression among professionals of a different culture (Falicov, 2003). For example, couples with an adolescent might find it perfectly acceptable and common in their culture to vent their emotions in a loud, prolonged, and frequent manner as a reflection of their involvement with and caring for that teenager, but be labeled by a therapist as a highly conflicted family. Furthermore, the therapist needs to engage the couple and adolescent in compatible expectations for change (matching-to-sample mentioned earlier) since this collaboration can contribute to reducing recidivism rates.

As therapists, it becomes our clinical responsibility to explore how our constructs and paradigms are seen by those from other cultures (Aponte et al., 1995). Potential resistance can then be recognized early on and addressed by either reframing the therapist's behavior for the couple or by changing the treatment goals or the interventions for achieving certain goals. One generalization found in the literature that can be helpful in developing effective interventions is the importance of extended family members within a variety of ethnic groups. Integrating relatives of the couple in interventions can likely reduce resistance and help in generalizing behavioral and interactional changes after termination. Another important generalization related to ethnically diverse clients is the grief and loss inherent with relocation from another culture and country (Falicov, 2003). A thorough assessment needs to occur early in therapy regarding the specific losses that each individual may be experiencing and how he or she is coping with those losses.

In summary, the cultural context from which a couple with an adolescent is operating has to be understood by the therapist. The couple's definition of normative functioning and symptomotology needs to be carefully explored, and treatment goals need to be determined jointly by the therapist and client. A genuine acceptance of the couple's ethnic background needs to occur and an awareness of any biases that a therapist may be bringing into the therapeutic process.

The second dimension of understanding is that of *developmental processes.* With respect to this chapter topic, adolescence is an especially volatile and emotionally intense time because of the tasks inherent (identity development and separation from parents' values) in this particular stage. A parent, parent figure, or parents who have been disciplining and communicating with their children in relatively consistent ways throughout the elementary-age years find that these previously effective approaches may no longer work. This can leave the couple experiencing confusion, frustration, and anger. The couple is tested to support each other and work as a team in parenting their adolescent or to criticize each other for their ineffectiveness and to displace feelings toward the adolescent onto the spouse. Furthermore, with adolescence being the last childhood stage before the adolescent leaves the couple, success during this stage can launch the couple into the next stage on more solid ground as opposed to leaving them feeling alienated, criticized, and without reason for staying together once the children leave home.

The third major component of understanding relevant to our case example is that of the dynamics of *relational functioning,* that is, the pattern of family behaviors with respect to autonomy/connectedness and hierarchy. Therapists need to clearly understand how each of the dyadic relational patterns affects these critical aspects of family behavior, and especially how they relate to symptoms (Alexander & Parsons, 1982; Alexander, Pugh, Parsons, & Sexton, 2000; Barton & Alexander, 1981; Sexton & Alexander, 2003). Referring back to our case example, it was necessary to understand the impact of Miguel Jr.'s truancy and depression regarding his contact/distance with each parent, as well as how his behavior problems impact the marital dyad. With this specific case, Miguel's truancy seemed to *function* to bring more contact between him and his father as they argue over his missing school, but the father's drug involvement and depression *functioned* to distance the father from his son. At the same time, Miguel Jr.'s behavior problems also *functioned* to bring the couple closer together, as the parents tried to understand his refusal to go to school and to identify possible solutions to help their son attend school. With respect to Miguel Jr. and his mother, the relational functions were not as immediately clear, but it appeared that Angela's illness represented a context in which Miguel Jr. reestablished more contact/closeness with his mother (via caretaking), but as her immediate physical problem abated, his development of symptoms served to continue more of a closeness function than would have been possible had he gone back to school. Thus, although the literature often articulates emancipation as an inevitable mandate for adolescents, in this family it appeared that in fact the adolescent's behavior problems facilitated more relational closeness, not less. These relational dynamics represent the organizing focus of change (Sexton & Alexander, 2003), and they point out why intervention must be individualized rather than based on some generic truth of a developmental phase, a family structure, or an ethnic stereotype.

Two levels of relational assessment comprise the clinical assessment domain. The first consists of stable sequences of behavior in the family. These sequences help the therapist understand how problems experienced by the family are embedded in a few common behavior patterns. The second, or functional, level of clinical assessment leads the family therapist to understand how these relational patterns contribute to adaptive and legitimate relational outcomes—first within the family and then outside the family. These are reflected in where everyone is when the dust settles (Barton & Alexander, 1981), and consist of two dimensions of interpersonal relationship: relatedness and hierarchy (Alexander & Parsons, 1982; Sexton & Alexander, 2002, 2003).

Relatedness (distance/autonomy and closeness) is characterized not by physical location but on the functional interdependency within the relationship compared to other important relationships (Alexander & Parsons, 1982; Sexton & Alexander, 2003, 2004). People who are close have high degrees of psychological interdependency, even if the behavioral patterns that represent this interconnectedness are aversive and full of unhappiness. Those with more distant relatedness functions have little interdependency, and often appear walled off. A mixture of both, identified as midpointing, reflects a mixture of both autonomy and interdependency, as in a parent who is committed to work (thereby having to create a pattern of separation from a child for many hours each week) yet also high connection (ensuring that during nonwork hours high connection is possible, and even during working hours the child can experience continued connection in terms of phone calls from the parent, etc.).

Hierarchy is the one-up one-down characteristics of the relationship. The one-up position is one in which the level of influence is high compared to another person, while the one-down is one in which there is low influence based on position or role. A symmetrical position is one where both members of the couple allow coequal influence of the other based on their roles as mates (e.g., both one-up, both one-down, both a similar configuration between these extremes). The FFT position is that most solutions in couples having conflict with adolescents is to attempt to create some "ideal" hierarchy pattern, such parents are symmetrical with one another and both in a one-up power position with the child. In contrast, FFT asserts that influence in relationships can often come by means of positive relational functioning and strong positive affective bonds, and not just by means of instituting a shift in power. This is especially the case in families and even cultures where establishing certain relational patterns based on someone's "deal" (such as symmetrical hierarchy in parents) may run dramatically in the face of individual and even cultural norms with respect to role hierarchies. It often is also the case that certain physical (e.g., a single parent who suffered a stroke) or existing behavioral symptom patterns (parental drug use) prevent invoking a hierarchical relationship in order to positively affect the adolescent. In our case example, the adolescent's positive behavior changes preceded, rather than followed, the father's stopping drug use and resuming a functionally hierarchical role. Instead, through positive engagement and motivation, which were based on respectfulness and cultural sensitivity, the therapist was able to enlist the father in positive parenting that was relationally, rather than hierarchically, based. Such an approach is quite different from many treatment strategies in multiproblem families, but has been associated with dramatic positive outcomes in multicultural contexts with high-risk families (U.S. Department of Health and Human Services, Surgeon General's report, 2001).

ESSENTIAL FEATURE 3: POSITIVE CHANGE IS A PHASIC PROCESS

Many, if not most, professionals and textbooks describe different intervention models in terms of particular techniques (challenging false beliefs, circular questioning, motivational interviewing, assertions training, reframing, etc.) or philosophical stances (solution-focused, narrative-based, social learning, etc.). However, in practice, both underlying epistemological orientations and specific techniques unfold over time and in an interactive process that is based on a relationship between the therapist (or at times therapists) and a couple or family. With rare exceptions (e.g., interactive DVD or Web-based consultation), therapists and individuals, couples, groups, or families interact face to face. This interaction is guided by both the family members and the therapist; the latter pursuing phase-based goals and techniques that follow certain developmental trajectories. In the case of the authors, the phasic, developmental, relational trajectory of working with families is guided by FFT (Alexander & Parsons, 1982; Alexander et al., 2000; Barton & Alexander, 1981; Sexton & Alexander, 2002). FFT includes three major phases (Engagement and Motivation, Behavior Change, and Generalization) and a specific assessment philosophy (relational assessment of functions) that guides the therapist in all three phases.

Engagement and Motivation Phase   Engagement represents involvement of all relevant family members from the beginning of intervention in a manner that will help them become interested in taking part in and accepting therapy. Often, one or more family members enter the therapy context not wishing to be there—or even actively opposing involvement—so the responsibility for engagement often falls upon the therapist. To accomplish this goal, we have found that many of the core features of individual therapy are in fact contraindicated in couples or family work.

Motivation is the second major goal of this phase. It involves the development of hope, which includes a shared belief among all family members that problems can change, that the therapist and therapy can help promote those changes, and that all family members are to be a part of the change process.

For engagement and motivation to occur, members of couples and families experience rapid changes in the experience of interpersonal behaviors between themselves and other family members, especially with respect to blaming and other negative interactions. This changed experience does not represent long-term interactive change; instead, it is an example of concrete new (but transient) patterns that family members attribute to the therapeutic process and that motivate them to return in order to develop the skills that can maintain the new patterns. In other words, engagement and motivation are immediate goals, which normally are attained in the first one-to-three session (or not at all) and which must be accomplished before specific out-of-the-therapy-room behavior changes can be successfully initiated. With high-risk couples and families, especially with one or more unmotivated members, the engagement and motivation process cannot be initiated in the traditional private practice format (e.g., weekly sessions). Usually, with high-risk couples and families, the first few sessions are closely bunched in order to initiate and capture a new momentum that can counteract the older (but very powerful) maladaptive inertia couples and families bring to the clinical situation.

For many family-based intervention approaches, including FFT, the process (not technique, but process) of reframing is emphasized during the engagement and motivation phase. However, in-session research, based on actual clinical interventions (e.g., Robbins, Alexander, & Turner, 2000), demonstrates that reframing on average occurs 10% to 15% of the time, and as a result therapists must also undertake additional interventions that serve to reduce blaming and negativity, create a balanced alliance (Robbins, Turner, Alexander, & Perez, 2003), and facilitate a movement from an individual problem focus to a couple/family focus. Interestingly, many of the techniques (prompting in response to negativity, empathy for one person, and commenting on or reflecting the negativity) are seen as basic (or core) features of individual therapy, and yet are often counterproductive in couple and family work. Stated bluntly, most couple and family therapists articulate some aspect of a systemic belief system, yet many still rely heavily on techniques developed in and for individual therapy. Clinical data from multiple community sites representing great diversity of therapists and families suggest that failing to adhere to a family-based (versus individual) philosophy and set of techniques is associated with considerably poorer outcomes, such as continued drug abuse and other problems of conduct in high-risk families (Barnoski, 2002). Thus, rather than relying on individually oriented interventions, successful FFT therapists rely, in addition to reframing, on sequencing without blaming, asking strength-based questions rather than pointing out dysfunction, and avoiding taking sides or blaming any individual at the expense of a balanced alliance.

For example, the parents were blaming and critical of Miguel Jr.'s refusal to go to school and his general social withdrawal. These behaviors were reframed as his mutual grieving at his parent's early childhood abuse and their subsequent inability to function more adaptively in current social situations. Initially, staying home served to directly support his mother after the surgery, thus contributing to the daily functioning of the household.

Behavior Change Phase   The primary goal of the behavior change phase is to use the momentum created in the engagement and motivation phase as a base for helping the family increase their ability to competently perform a myriad of tasks that contribute to successful couple and family functioning. The behavior change phase involves a focus on specific changes in behaviors, and involves such strategies as improved communication skills, problem solving, redirecting a range of thinking errors, negotiation skills with respect to limits and rules, and conflict management (Sexton & Alexander, 2002). This is accomplished by developing an individualized change plan that targets the risk and protective factors evident in the couple or family and achieves those goals using the unique relational pathways to change that fit the family. Specific behavior change interventions commonly used in FFT can be found in various sources (Alexander et al., 2000; Barton & Alexander, 1981; Morris, Alexander, & Waldron, 1988).

During this phase, the respectfulness of diversity is evident. Although the targets of a behavior change plan are somewhat common (e.g., communication, parenting, problem solving) the implementation of changes is unique to each couple and family relational system. Implementation of behavior change is unique because the paths to behavior change are through the relational functions and patterns of the individual family. The goal is to increase competent performance of, for example, parenting, but in a way that matches the relational functions of that particular parent and adolescent.

The targeted changes are implemented both within sessions and through assigned family tasks that are accomplished between sessions. As behavior change sessions progress, the therapist may model new skills, ask the family to practice, or provide guidance in the successful accomplishment of these new behaviors. Through therapeutic directives, the therapist may structure activities that the family practices. The implementation of these changes draws on many of the typical technical aids that help to increase the likelihood of success in changing behaviors. For example, communication might be enhanced through message boards, reminders, and other methods.

Reviewing the functions of our case example, father and son were in a primarily distant relationship, with a little contact achieved with the school truancy. Once Miguel Jr. returned to school, we made his father responsible for providing his son with the behavioral reward for school attendance, which consisted of driving his son once or twice a week to play cards at a game store. In addition, Miguel Jr. and his mother continued some contact through the joint babysitting of his niece and nephew. Third, Miguel Jr.'s need to help take care of his family was accomplished by his attending an alternative high school program that was afternoons only. Thus, he provided day care for his sister's children in the morning and was paid for his help.

Generalization Phase   In the generalization phase, the focus of attention turns from changing current patterns of couple or family functioning to anticipating the future and helping the couple utilize multiple systems to maintain and enhance the positive changes within the family. There are three primary goals in this phase. First, the therapist helps the family extend the changes into similar family situations. Second, he or she helps through relapse prevention techniques to develop an expectation that things will get worse, but can get better again, in order to build confidence that the newly acquired skills will work in different situations over time. Finally, the therapist supports change, ensuring that as many community resources as possible are available to, and supportive of, the couple and family. In general, long-term change is accomplished when the family is helped to use their own skills to obtain these changes with the guidance of the therapist. Miguel's enrollment in a school program that gave him time to support his family during the day increased the chances of his staying in school and thus graduating from high school. Furthermore, Miguel's sister and father were instructed to take Miguel Jr. to weekly teen basketball games to help reduce his depressive symptoms and to help him develop positive peer relationships. His sister was supported to find a job and enroll in a community college class but to continue living at home and help the family financially by paying for some of the food and transporting her mother to medical appointments and on errands.

In order to support the changes made by families, therapists must attend to multiple systems (e.g., extended family, peer, and cultural context). These systems provide valuable resources to help the family maintain the positive trajectory developed during therapy or defend against powerful negative influences that the therapist must anticipate and work to minimize. This is best accomplished when undertaken with an appreciation of the relational system of the family, and it can be matched to available resources (Alexander et al., 2000).

ESSENTIAL FEATURE 4: ALLIANCE AND HOPE-BASED MOTIVATION

Couples who display resistance in therapy experience little behavior and relationship changes, even though they come to therapy wanting to change dysfunctional patterns and behavior. FFT has specifically addressed this problem by developing and describing interventions and strategies to reduce this resistance, creating clients' motivation for change, and thus improving their success rate with difficult-to-treat couples and families. One key feature to motivating a couple is forming a strong alliance between the therapist and couple early in therapy and throughout the therapeutic relationship (Robbins et al., 2003; Sexton & Alexander, 2003). This positive alliance is critical to establish between family members as well. Key qualities of this alliance include helping the couple experience a sense of hope, expectation of change, and a sense of control and responsibility. Sexton and Alexander go on to describe therapeutic motivation, which is an incentive to action that results in new and adaptive behavior and relationship patterns.

At the point of intake with our case example, the therapist identified the immediate therapeutic goals as first engaging the family, creating a sense of hope, and reducing individual members' defensiveness before the end of the first session. These tasks have been found to significantly reduce early dropout rates from therapy (Alexander & Barton, 1995). The therapist recognized that she must be sensitive and responsive to issues of culture, gender, developmental stage, and mental health issues, and she needed to provide intervention in a manner that was appropriate to the economic, cultural, and motivational realities of these family members. Long-term intervention with individual members, residential treatment, medication, or many other wraparound services simply would not be available, affordable, or even culturally *sensitive* with respect to this family. Furthermore, this family had experienced failure with therapy and would likely be cautious and skeptical of standard interventions. The therapist also noted that although secondary education system, juvenile justice system, or division of family services system involvement was a potential reality, at the point of referral there were no mandated activities or consequences for nonparticipation. As a result, the therapist adopted the Family First perspective of Functional Family Therapy (Alexander & Sexton, 2002). Specifically, the Family First perspective orients the therapist to engaging and motivating all family members together, in a balanced manner that avoids taking sides, and to conceptualizing the treatment focus as enhancing the relational processes *within* the family before shifting the focus to outside the family.

A balanced alliance is needed when working with couples and families (Robbins et al., 2003). This alliance occurs when the therapist has established a positive working relationship with all the family members in therapy. An intervention that supports this balanced alliance occurs when the therapist uses reframing to address the problem or negative behaviors (as defined by the couple or family) brought to therapy by the couple. In FFT, reframing occurs at several different levels, in that this intervention can change the clients' emotional reaction to other family members in a more emotionally positive direction, motivation, intent of behavior, and responsibility for the behavior (Sexton & Alexander, 2003). Most importantly, reframing can change the affective atmosphere between couples and the therapist. Reframes establish alternative cognitions and attributional perspectives that create different meaning for past negative and painful events and behaviors in the family history. This newer and more positive meaning then reduces the negative affect between couples and their adolescents, allowing more neutral and positive affect to surface. Effective reframes also link family members' behaviors to the referral problem so that each family member shares responsibility in more adaptive future interaction patterns.

A successful reframe will include the three steps of validation of the client perspective, reattribution of that perspective that is both relational and positively charged, and eliciting client feedback about this new reattribution (Sexton & Alexander, 2003). Validation of the client must delicately balance respect, support, and understanding for that client's experience, without alienating or blaming anyone else in the family. In our case example, Miguel Jr.'s school truancy was reframed as his way of feeling powerful in helping the family by caretaking his mother after surgery. His depression and withdrawn behavior were ways of grieving for his parent's pain from past abuse and his way of protecting himself from perpetrators in society. Miguel Sr.'s substance abuse was reframed as a way to dim the pain of his own abuse, allowing him to parent both his children with love and protection, and without physical or sexual abuse in their home.

Finally, although the family's ethnicity and culture were critical to address when engaging the family, we do not believe that it is inevitably necessary that the therapist's ethnicity be similar to that of the family. Instead the therapist's qualities that seem to be more influential are an awareness of the power structure within the family (because of their culture), the therapist's respect of cultural norms with respect to relating with the different spouses, and taking into account both their and the therapist's gender (Falicov, 2003). Therapists who are not familiar with values and norms relevant to the couple's ethnicity need to take the time to have the family teach him or her critical family norms. For example, in this family the father as the head of the family is expected to have ultimate decision-making power, yet his substance abuse and depression were internal issues that contradicted this cultural mandate. A therapist falling into the trap of treating him as a drug addict or abuse victim and becoming an ally with the mother or the son would be deepening the father's sense of failure and poor self-efficacy. The therapist needed to be particularly sensitive to this issue, because even without taking sides there was a risk that she would be seen as doing so, simply as a function of her gender. The therapist instead needed to relate to the father as the expert of his family, asking for his opinion and help. She offered more respect and fewer directives than would have been appropriate for a male therapist. She also allied more closely with him than with other family members because his past substance abuse therapy experience had likely left him feeling blamed and responsible for the family's stress and difficulties. She felt that a therapeutic alliance might be most difficult to form with him. In addition, the therapist would need to work especially hard to reframe (Alexander & Parsons, 1982; Alexander et al., 2000) the father's symptoms to the rest of the family before they changed their attitude and behaviors toward him.

ESSENTIAL FEATURE 5: OBTAINABLE CHANGE GOALS THAT MATCH THE FAMILY'S CULTURE, CAPACITIES, RESOURCES, AND RELATIONAL DYNAMICS

Once a couple or family is successfully engaged and motivated, the specific goals that are identified for change are carefully chosen by the therapist and couple. Targets of change need to be meaningful for the couple and directly tied to the previous reframes as adaptive ways to accomplish the intentions of the family members. Furthermore, these goals need to be realistically obtainable behavioral changes and have lasting impact on the family (Sexton & Alexander, 2003). These outcome goals must fit the couple's values, culture, and capabilities. The goals targeted for change must fit the couple's definition of health as well. Last, the goals need to meet the same interpersonal functions of different dyads that the maladaptive patterns were meeting.

In our case example, in addition to the referred male (Miguel Jr.), Miguel Sr. and Angela were parents of an older 26-year-old married daughter, Maria, who was living with them because her husband had left her and their two children, and moved out of the state. Expecting the daughter to move out on her own with her two children would violate the importance of extended-family support in this culture and would likely be resisted by the parents as well as by the daughter. However, goals that were jointly supported by the family were those of Maria finding work in order to help herself and her parents' financial situation, and having different family members available to help with the childcare of her children. Many couple or family therapists would label these goals as enabling, codependent, and maladaptive. These goals were also compatible with this adult child's eventually moving out, but only in a time frame that was comfortable and adaptive for *this* family.

At this point in therapy, the healing resources of the family were elicited and used to establish more adaptive interactional patterns. It also became important to be sensitive to the multicultural couple's integration into the mainstream culture when identifying goals for the family. Falicov (1993) discusses that acculturating too quickly into the current culture can increase emotional distress on the family. What might be more therapeutic and adaptive for the couple is to empower the family in their interactions with the dominant culture and community (Falicov, 2003) by providing them with relevant community resources and specific guidance regarding effective ways to impact these systems. In addition, the therapist needs to help the family create and utilize as many supports (friends, family, church, and hobbies) as are available to serve as current and future protective factors.

SUMMARY

When couples with adolescent children present to the clinician, the individual or relationship that is symptomatic will strongly determine what system or subsystem is targeted in therapy. Couples coming into therapy where they have identified the adolescent as the problem are, with rare exceptions, best treated with a family therapy such as FFT, with the guardians and often other youth in the family involved in treatment. This sometimes will also include extended family members who have a major role in the family functioning. Furthermore, therapy that initially targets the family may evolve to several couple-only sessions later in treatment, when marital issues become the focus in treatment. However, if a couple with an adolescent child or children presents for treatment for marital issues, then meeting with the couple is most desirable, following the same phases and principles described earlier but with a narrower focus, primarily on the couple. Note also that some couples might include grandparent-parent relationships, dating relationships, and of course committed same-sex relationships where at least one partner has an adolescent.

Issues that will likely need to be addressed may commonly include parenting as a team, effective communication, problem solving, blended families (of various forms), and how to meet each other's relational and intimacy needs (Gottman & Silver, 1999). These issues are qualitatively similar to those of couples with children of different ages. One issue that is a qualitative jump from children of other ages is the distribution of power between the parents and the adolescent, whether or not the adolescent's behavior is problematic. Couples may be facing an adolescent who feels that her parents no longer need to control or influence her and who asserts her independence on a regular basis, though not necessarily with clinical problems. This couple would need to have each of their parenting expectations considered by the therapist, who (following the phasic FFT model) would work with the parents with respect to positive parenting in a manner that involves appropriate expectations for the adolescent, and parental influence that is effective and also appropriate for the developmental status of the adolescent.

At another extreme, a couple with an adolescent who was having difficulty emancipating and working on adolescent goals of identity definition and separating from parental values and beliefs would need help on how to support their teenager to feel emotionally safe enough to reach out more into the adolescent subculture. The peer group is another qualitative jump from children of other ages. Relationships with peers are the primary relationships for many adolescents, even when family members had previously been the center of their relationships. Couples need to define how much peer influence they feel comfortable with their adolescent experiencing and may need the therapist's help with setting appropriate boundaries for their teenager's time, activities, and freedom spent with peers.

Last, as parents feel a sense of success with the rules, responsibilities, and freedoms allowed for their teenagers, they are likely to find themselves with extra time and energy that had previously been directed to parenting. A couple who has resolved conflict or issues regarding their adolescent can allow themselves to develop other areas of their lives. Parents can then face and make clearer decisions about what directions they may need or want to pursue at this point in their lives. For many couples, this may include redis- covering passion in the marriage, spending time in joint activities or hob- bies, or pursuing individual psychological and/or professional goals that were delayed. Conversely, members of the couple may decide to undertake new growth that represents increasing individuation within the couple, but in ways that are productive for both members. Such decisions are not the therapist's to dictate, but therapists can become trusted resources for the couple as they move beyond a problem focus to a new developmental era of their own.

REFERENCES

Alexander, J. F., & Barton, C. (1995). Family therapy research. In R. H. Mikesell, D.-D. Lusterman, & S. H. McDaniel (Eds.), *Family psychology and systems therapy: A handbook* (pp. 199–215). Washington, DC: American Psychological Association.

Alexander, J. F., & Parsons, B. V. (1982). *Functional family therapy.* Monterey, CA: Brooks/Cole.

Alexander, J. F., Pugh, C., Parsons, B. V., & Sexton, T. L. (2000). Functional family therapy. In D. S. Elliott (Series Ed.), *Blueprints for violence prevention* (2nd ed., Book 3). Boulder: University of Colorado, Institute of Behavioral Science, Cen- ter for the Study and Prevention of Violence.

Alexander, J. F., & Sexton, T. L. (2002). Functional family therapy: A model for treat- ing high-risk acting-out youth. In F. W. Kaslow (Editor-in-Chief) & J. Lebow (Vol. Ed.), *Comprehensive handbook of psychotherapy: Vol. 4. Integrative/eclectic* (pp. 111–132). New York: Wiley.

Altman, A., & Rogoff, B. (1987). Handbook of environmental psychology. In D. Stokols & I. Altman (Eds.), *World views in psychology: Trait, interactional, or- ganismic, and transactional perspectives* (pp. 7–40). New York: Wiley.

Aponte, J. F., Rivers, R. Y., & Wohl, J. (1995). *Psychological interventions and cultural diversity.* Needham Heights, MA: Allyn & Bacon.

Barnoski, R. (2002). *Washington state's implementation of functional family therapy for juvenile offenders: Preliminary findings.* Seattle: Washington State Institute for Public Police. Available from www.wsipp.wa.gov.

Barton, C., & Alexander, J. F. (1981). Functional family therapy. In A. S. Gurman & D. P. Kniskern (Ed.), *Handbook of family therapy* (pp. 403–443). New York: Brunner/Mazel.

Falicov, C. J. (1993, Spring). Continuity and change: Lessons from immigrant families. *American Family Therapy Newsletter,* 30–34.

Falicov, C. J. (2003). Culture in family therapy: New variations on a fundamental theme. In T. Sexton, G. R. Weeks, & M. S. Robbins (Eds.), *Handbook of family therapy* (pp. 37–55). New York: Brunner-Routledge.

Gottman, J. M., & Silver, N. (1999). *The seven principles for making marriage work.* New York: Crown.

Morris, S. B., Alexander, J. F., & Waldron, H. (1988). Functional family therapy. In R. H. Faloon (Ed.), *Handbook of behavioral family therapy* (pp. 107–127). New York: Guilford Press.

Robbins, M. S., Alexander, J. F., & Turner, C. W. (2000). Disrupting defensive family interactions in family therapy with delinquent youth. *Journal of Family Psychology, 14*(4), 688–701.

Robbins, M. S., Turner, C. W., Alexander, J. F., & Perez, G. A. (2003). Alliance and dropout in family therapy with drug using adolescents: Individual and systemic effects. *Journal of Family Psychology, 17*(4), 534–544.

Samuntrai, K. (2003). *Culturally competent public child welfare practices.* Pacific Grove, CA: Brooks/Cole.

Sexton, T. L., & Alexander, J. F. (2002). Functional family therapy for at-risk adolescents and their families. In F. Kaslow (Editor-in-Chief) & T. Patterson (Vol. Ed.), *Comprehensive handbook of psychotherapy: Vol. 2. Cognitive-behavioral approaches* (pp. 117–140). New York: Wiley.

Sexton, T. L., & Alexander, J. F. (2003). Functional family therapy: A mature clinical model. In T. Sexton, G. Weeks, & M. Robbins (Eds.), *Handbook of family therapy* (pp. 323–348). New York: Brunner-Routledge.

Sexton, T. L., Alexander, J. F., & Mease, A. C. (2003). Level of evidence for the models and mechanisms of therapeutic change in couple and family therapy. In M. Lambert (Ed.), *Handbook of psychotherapy and behavior change* (pp. 590–646). Hoboken, NJ: Wiley.

U.S. Department of Health and Human Services. (2001). *Youth violence: A report of the surgeon general.* Rockville, MD: U.S. Department of Health and Human Services, Centers for Disease Control and Prevention, National Center for Injury Prevention and Control; Substance Abuse and Mental Health Services Administration, Center for Mental Health Services; and National Institutes of Health, National Institute of Mental Health.

CHAPTER 6

Therapy with Older Couples: Love Stories—The Good, the Bad, and the Movies

Thomas H. Peake and Angela E. Steep

> O wad some Pow'r the gifte gie us
> to see oursels as other see us.
>
> —Robert Burns

THE AUTHORS HAVE had enlightening experiences working with families and couples. We have also been able to work with an interesting array of older couples. Therapists will find older couples a rich source of knowledge. These same people are also a source of conundrums and solutions in navigating life and love.

A useful principle in working with seniors is that they may be challenged by three dimensions. These challenges include psychological (psyche), medical (soma), and generative (or spirit) issues. Another important consideration is the concept of a person's life story, or the story of a family or couple.

A wise cultural psychologist, G. S. Howard (1991), suggests that a person's identity may be thought of as a life story. Psychological or physical illness may be thought of as a person's life story that has gone awry. And psychotherapy can be viewed as an exercise in life story repair. A person's life history, current focus, and future can be reconsidered, retold, reframed, and renewed. This same principle fits well when counseling couples. Couples create their own love story. As the relationship evolves beyond the romantic first stage of love, problems can appear. Therapy may help them revise or reform their relationship.

Sharon Kaufman is a psychologist who works in medical and rehabilitation settings. She has written an excellent book called *The Ageless Self* (1986), which gives valuable guidelines on how to understand people and the difference between a clinical history and a life story. One strategy she emphasizes (in improving people's lives) is the concept of the *minimal interference principle.* This principle says that a good therapist (who works with individuals, families, or couples) listens to a life story (or life episodes) in a personal way. The wise therapist needs to understand:

- Who they have been
- Who they feel they are now
- How they have navigated their life's journey
- Who they have become in their relationship

Kaufman also developed an interview format that emphasizes a *life story* in contrast to a *clinical history.* The life story is a personal perspective and overview of one's life. The life story may be a better reflection of the self than a clinical conceptualization. An accurate and humane combination of a history and a life story works well.

The nature of intimacy is a crucial dimension in working with older couples. A crucial principle is that *intimacy is a balance of control and vulnerability* in a *committed relationship.* Both partners need to influence the relationship; to be able to get their own needs met, yet still sustain a climate where it is safe to be vulnerable. Intimacy is a balance of commitment, influence, and the safety to make one's needs known and honored. This intimacy is not a pseudo-mutuality, however. A poignant quote by George Bernard Shaw suggests, "If two people agree on everything, one of them is unnecessary."

It is also helpful to consider the notion of a creative relationship. The psychologist Rollo May in *The Courage to Create* (1975), suggested that creativity in art, literature, and music is also a balance of form and passion. Loving relationships must balance form and passion (guided by sincere commitment) in order for a relationship to stay vital. When counseling couples, relationships may need change if a relationship has become stagnant. At other junctures, life's challenges and changes (e.g., financial problems, medical troubles, or lost relationships) call for stabilization and recommitment. Form and passion help us understand and plan the task and scope of therapy. Does the couple need change—or integration?

In a way, relationships (or movies that portray them) are another example of Rollo May's notion (1975) that creativity is a balance of form and passion. This balance can be in art, literature, cinema, or human relations. Growth often means reconfiguring a work of art. The fascinating parallel is that relationships (like art) are a balance of passion, form, and commitment. The form of a loving relationship, and the ingredients of commitment and passion, parallel the core of creativity. Each person in a loving relationship contributes to make the couple vital as well as committed.

The life stages explained by Erik Erikson (1982) can also guide our ability to promote needed changes and relevant topics, which older couples can use to foster continued growth and intimacy. Once again, this principle of growth, commitment, and passion provides a background in which both people continue to shape and influence the relationship.

Other experts on life stages have built on Erikson's work to give more insight into ways women's development may vary from men's. Ruth Josselson (1987) described *pathways to identity development in women.* Building on her earlier explanations, Josselson and Lieblich (1993) have described the *narrative study of lives.* In addition, they offer techniques on how to listen to, and understand people's life stories. The fabric of these life stories merge (or sometimes collide) in loving relationships.

Loving relationships go through stages of development. They go through periods of integration and stabilization. However, as relationships evolve, they go through periods of tension, which can lead to change or accommodation. Unfortunately, sometimes the losses or stressors lead to separation or divorce. The tough task for an artist, a couple, or a therapist is knowing when to stabilize and when to change. With older couples this may involve the evolution (or in bad times, devolution) of their relationship.

THERAPY APPLICATION, UNDERCURRENTS, AND STRATEGIES

What considerations are important for therapists working with older adults? We train so that we may better understand our clients. We work to grasp their weaknesses and build on their strengths. The therapist must appreciate potential *blind spots* that can hamper solutions. Older adults have much to tell us as we help them navigate both their past and future. Addressing a couple's hopes and fears is crucial.

"What are your expectations of love, communication, and making a relationship work?" These questions are a good place to begin. Add the request of "What have been your experiences—good and bad—in past relations?" Learn how they have navigated earlier life stages. The couple's individual or shared history of life challenges, losses, and growth are important to address. We only want to make the changes that are needed, while building on past strengths.

One definition of emotional health is "to love well, work well, play well . . . and to expect well" (integrating some thoughts from Sigmund Freud and Gerald Caplan, the father of preventive psychiatry). A couple saw this quote in the author's office and asked, "How's one success out of three?" If we have success in one of the three dimensions, the others may follow.

Therapists with older adults must also understand health care systems, insurance configurations, and interaction of medical problems with psychological and spiritual dimensions. The reader is encouraged to read *Setting Limits: Medical Goals in an Aging Society* (Callahan, 1995). Callahan clarifies the forces that shape ethics (or lack thereof) and policy in health care. Therapists for senior couples must also understand Medicare and other insurance realities. Aging issues and medical problems can certainly challenge couples of any age, but perhaps more so with older adults.

FAMILIES OF ORIGIN AND DEVELOPMENTAL STAGES

Among the important therapists and researchers in life span development are Mike Kerr and Murray Bowen (1988). These therapists and educators are well known for looking at *family of origin* influences across the generations. This perspective takes into consideration the *expectations, comfort zones,* and *styles of relating* in couples. The authors say that our capacity for intimacy comes from the models that we have experienced. Our ability to be close, yet maintain our own identity, is a gift influenced by the family from which we came. Healthy individuation allows people to love without losing their identity. To have *roots and wings* is a more lyrical way to describe the balance. Healthy ways of loving (without smothering) and encouraging (without abandoning) can forecast how well we may enjoy our later years.

A healthy family models intimacy and independence. Family of origin work is a rich dimension to pursue with older couples. Creating an atmosphere of safety where each person can examine his or her own expectations is crucial. Therapists can create an atmosphere of interest, hope, and safety to explore each person's background. Older couples simply have had more time to try their luck or skill.

Laura Giat Roberto is an excellent resource on the topic of family lineage. Her book *Transgenerational Family Therapies* (1992) illustrates how to balance each partner's experience by using practical guidance in the use of genograms or "systemic maps." This history can provide a collaborative approach on how these people understand their strengths, but also perhaps their blind spots or expectations about what is a healthy couple and a healthy climate. Family of origin, genograms, and other techniques make Roberto's book an excellent tool for both novice and experienced therapists.

Also, in *Intimate Partners: Patterns in Love & Marriage,* Maggie Scarf (1988) provides great insight into predictable stages in love and relationships. Her wisdom applies to couples of any age. Scarf is not a therapist, but she has interviewed, observed, and researched the ebbs, tides, and eddies of protean relations. She drew from the Family Institute of Westchester, the Smith College of Social Work, and the Yale Psychiatric Institute. She interviewed countless couples, practicing therapists, and clinical researchers. The result is an infinitely readable and helpful book.

Couples tend to resurrect unresolved dilemmas and patterns (smuggled from their family of origins) in current relations. These patterns have more layers when this marriage is not their first. Resources that can help the family or couple and the therapist might include:

- *Genograms.* Exploring family of origin themes in a nonthreatening way.
- *Recollections.* Prior relationships (or prior history together) plus what attracted the couple to each other in the beginning.
- *Examinations.* Of strategies that help or hinder conflict resolution. Plus honoring hopes and fears.
- *Histories.* Of endings and beginnings, are extremely valuable to see what issues may linger . . . unfinished. What themes have closure and what unfinished topics complicate intimacy.

The afterthought in this section is that census reports suggest there is a shortage of men in the senior ages. Women tend to live longer than men. We have no solution for this at present, but forecasting the disparity may lead to other creative therapies. Some women patients have even suggested that sharing men may be a solution. Other women, however, disagree.

In an upcoming book, *Cinema and Life Development: Healing Lives and Training Therapists* (Peake, 2004), popular movies are used to help understand the normal life stages laid out by Erikson (1982), Gilligan (1982), Viorst (1986), Pittman (1989), Scarf (1988), Napier and Whitaker (1988), and others. The principles from their work can inform and energize therapy with older couples.

Popular movies can help us understand the dilemmas and conundrums couples encounter. In that respect, movies are a rich venue to practice: conceptualization, treatment planning, and applied strategies that improve relationships. Movies can be an entree to talk with elders who may be more resistant to therapy. Psychotherapy may not be consistent with the era or worldview in which they grew up.

There are many examples from movies that can inform and improve therapy with older couples. These are good movies. The films were not developed to train therapists, but were made to entertain and clarify life. Consequently, the richness of the films makes them a good place to practice discernment. The silver screen makes the issues real and enriches our appreciation of life span development and life challenges. Focusing on life changes and life enrichment can improve senior couples lives. Movies can provide perspective and clarity and help treat tough issues. Television also provides funny and ironic models for relationships (e.g., *Everybody Loves Raymond, All in the Family, The Jeffersons, The Golden Girls, Bill Cosby, The Huxtables*). Thank goodness for a sense of humor.

Some valuable movies are previewed in this chapter. These stories show problems and universal themes. The reader may enjoy adding to this list. Often, people benefit by seeing someone else's conundrums from a distance. Couples are able to make wonderful suggestions for the characters in the movies, although that same couple or family may be too close to solve their own dilemma.

A sampling of relevant movie options include:

- *The Trip to Bountiful* (Geraldine Page and Rebecca De Mornay)
- *The Last of His Tribe* (Graham Greene and John Voight)
- *Used People* (Shirley MacLaine, Kathy Bates, and Marcello Mastroianni)
- *Fried Green Tomatoes* (Kathy Bates, Jessica Tandy, and Mary Stuart Masterson)
- *Wrestling Ernest Hemingway* (Robert Duvall, Richard Harris, and Piper Laurie)
- *Cocoon* (Hume Cronyn, Wilford Brimley, Maureen Stapleton, and Jessica Tandy)
- *On Golden Pond* (Henry Fonda, Jane Fonda, and Katharine Hepburn)
- *Nobody's Fool* (Paul Newman and Jessica Tandy)
- *Grumpy Old Men* (Jack Lemmon, Walter Matthau, and Ann-Margret)
- *A Gathering of Old Men* (Louis Gossett Jr., Richard Widmark, and Holly Hunter; based on the novel by Ernest J. Gaines)
- *A Walk in the Clouds* (Anthony Quinn, Keanu Reeves, and Aitana Sanchez-Gijon)
- *Steel Magnolias* (Shirley MacLaine, Olympia Dukakis, Sally Fields, Dolly Parton, and Julia Roberts)
- *Parenthood* (Steve Martin, Mary Steenbergen, Jason Robards, and Keanu Reeves)
- *Twilight Zone—Montage* (excerpt on retirement home)
- *Driving Miss Daisy* (Jessica Tandy and Morgan Freeman)
- *The Shadow Box* (Joanne Woodward, Christopher Plummer, and Valerie Harper)
- *To Dance with the White Dog* (Jessica Tandy and Hume Cronyn)
- *Nothing in Common* (Tom Hanks and Jackie Gleason)
- *War of the Roses* (Michael Douglas, Kathleen Turner, and Danny DeVito; a good one to scare people regarding divorce)
- *The Witches of Eastwick* (Jack Nicholson, Cher, Susan Sarandon, and Michelle Pfeiffer)
- *Terms of Endearment* (Shirley MacLaine, Jack Nicholson, and Debra Winger)
- *Home for the Holidays* (Holly Hunter, Anne Bancroft, and Robert Downey Jr.)

Themes, patterns, or dynamics in these movies offer the chance to commiserate, laugh, or cry at the situation and to suggest solutions. The solutions are clearer when viewed from a safe emotional distance. The above movies have worked well in training therapists. The authors have used them in doctoral courses for psychologists and family therapists. Whenever the course is taught, the students regale us with additional movies they want to add. The format has also been effective with more experienced therapists as a vehicle to understand dynamics and plan therapeutic strategies.

With older adults, it is not unusual that the partners have one or more previous marriages, following divorce or death of a spouse. We will consider some movie examples that portray challenges older couples may encounter. These themes may include the couple themselves, with other tugs such as their children or their families of origin.

Used People (1992) is a funny and memorable example to try out therapy options on families that would drive any therapist crazy. The main characters include Shirley MacLaine, Marcello Mastroianni, Kathy Bates, and a cast of unforgettable family members. The Italians collide with the Jews after MacLaine's first husband dies and Mastroianni's character appears at the wake to pay his respects. He intimates that he met MacLaine's husband at a time when the husband was about to leave his wife because she focused too much on her duties and grown children. MacLaine and her family were shocked that the charming Italian asked her to go out on a coffee date.

The ensuing collision of three-generations of Jews and Italians contrasting ethnic prototypes (in 1960s Brooklyn) is hysterically funny. The movie is a rich venue to address older couples' constellation of prior marriage leftovers. The cast of characters and ethnic types are hilarious (even lampooning therapists). Laughter leads to insight, and insight provides cross-generational appreciation and reconnection.

Fried Green Tomatoes is a wonderful book by Fanny Flagg (1991) and a funny and powerful movie. Flagg looks at women across generations, in different loving relations, in changing roles, and from every angle. The meaning of Erik Erikson's stages of life are given vitality, anguish, plus a human heart and soul wrapped in a strange irony. The movie spans three generations. The examples of couples show a rainbow of options from hate and despair to love and redemption. The laughs are full throated, with everything from religion to marriage, nursing homes, southern males and females, consciousness-raising, and a killer recipe for barbecue. People do not sleep through this movie.

The Trip to Bountiful (1985) is a bittersweet but powerful movie about Carrie "Mother" Watts, who lives with her grown son and daughter-in-law in a too-small apartment in Houston during World War II. It is one the best examples of Kaufman's notion of understanding life stories in contrast to a clinical history. Carrie wants desperately to go back to her childhood home and small community of Bountiful, south of Galveston. She sneaks off and takes a memorable bus ride, on which she sits by a young woman. The two share their life stories. The power of this telling and listening process can energize therapy with older couples.

Listening to those we love can strengthen any relation and help understand past and current hopes and fears. The actresses (Geraldine Page and

Rebecca De Mornay) provide a memorable experience of putting lives in perspective and demonstrate the meaning of *generativity*.

An excellent book on generativity is *The Care of the Soul* (Moore, 1992). Moore, a Jungian analyst, provides perspective on spirituality in every day life. Erik Erikson's (1982) work on life span challenge and growth, also gives a rich model for "generativity," and each person's personal trip to Bountiful. The two ladies in the movie on the bus to Bountiful show the value of hearing and affirming all of our experiences.

Terms of Endearment (1983) is a movie about finding love in midlife, communication problems, dealing with an adult child's death, and deceiving someone you love. In it, Shirley MacLaine and Jack Nicholson have a fling. He's an alcoholic former astronaut, and her daughter is dying. The couple and family interaction provide great examples of bad communication and confusion about what people want (or think they want) in relationships. The movie does have redemptive moments with lots of laughs along with the tears.

War of the Roses (1989) is a movie not soon forgotten. Living in a love-hate relationship, a couple (Michael Douglas and Kathleen Turner) come to define themselves by their possessions. They are further fueled by a greedy lawyer (Danny DeVito). It is said, "some people's role in life is to serve as a bad example." This movie is the best bad example in memory.

Home for the Holidays (1995) is a frantic saga of a dysfunctional family and their Thanksgiving holiday reconnection. Addictions, denial, narcissism, and old-fashioned looniness all make an appearance. The characters are extreme examples of almost any psychological variant. The movie provides many laughs, the healing power of recognition, and puts problems in perspective. One couple this writer/therapist saw in therapy said, "This movie makes our conflicts seem minor . . . we can do much better than that crew!" Anne Bancroft, Robert Downey Jr., Holly Hunter, and Geraldine Chaplin create quite an ensemble. There is, however, a sense of acceptance in even this wacky family. And the musical score is very good.

In *Grumpy Old Men* (1993), Jack Lemmon, Walter Matthau, and Ann-Margret provide laughs in a more enduring version of a buddy movie for boys who don't grow up. Burgess Meredith is the prototypical dirty old man. Entertaining and also valuable in seeing exaggerated styles lampooned, so that even the most thick-headed male gets the message, the movie is close to vaudeville in its broad humor.

Many people feel that life is set, but that same life can fall apart. *Kramer vs. Kramer* (1979), a movie based on divorce and a custody war, captures the heartbreak of breaking up no matter when it happens. The wounds from these battles often endure for decades.

In *Cocoon* (1985), senior citizens discover a fountain of youth, but get some surprises when they meet the aliens who share the same source. The movie is entertaining, but it also shows the dynamics of one of the older men who (when sexually revitalized) returns to his philandering ways. It provides many laughs and a powerful fantasy.

In *On Golden Pond* (1981), Chelsea (Jane Fonda) has never been close to her father, Norman (Henry Fonda). Chelsea treads cautiously as she tries to make a connection with the man who never listened or praised. Chelsea's mother Ethel (Katharine Hepburn) shows how she learned to connect with him, but that approach cannot work with the daughter. A combination of changes develop when Chelsea and her new beau (a dentist, whom Norman goads and insults) leave his son for Ethel and Norman to look after. Ostensibly, the movie paralleled Henry and Jane's real-life struggles. This is another film rich for discussion and training therapists.

In *To Dance with the White Dog* (1993), Robert Samuel Peek (Hume Cronyn) is a pecan grower who has been married to Cora (Jessica Tandy) for 57 years when she dies. Their daughters try to help, intervene, and to take care of their father. They do more fussing and clashing than helping. Sam's outlook veers to loneliness until he befriends a stray white dog that no one else can see. His dialogues have some insight into loss and preserving relationship memories and loyalty (what the psychodynamic therapists call object relations). The movie shows a touching connection of personal hope in an unusual example of mourning and preserving love.

Moving on, an important perspective in looking at couples' interactions may be the quote, *"Some things are too important to be taken seriously."* There is a great deal that is serious in helping couples gain, grieve, or regain healthy intimacy in their relationship.

On the other hand, consider some humor on sex and love:

It's okay to laugh in the bedroom as long as you don't point.

—Will Durst

Instead of getting married again, I'm going to find a woman I don't like and give her a house.

—Louis Grizzard

Oysters are supposed to enhance your sexual performance, but they don't work for me. Maybe I put them on too soon.

After making love I said to my girl, "was that good for you too?" and she said "I don't think this was good for anybody."

—Gary Shandling

And from the queen of candor on sex and relationships:

Too much of a good thing can be wonderful.

I used to be snow white, but I drifted.

I generally avoid temptation unless I can't resist it.

When choosing between two evils, I always like to take the one I've never tried before.

—Mae West

RELATIONSHIP AND GENDER THEMES FROM DIFFERENT ERAS

Several valuable resources can enlighten us about life, people, and love stories.

Betty Friedan has long been a standard-bearer for women's (and men's) rights. Friedan has expanded and raised our consciousness for 40 years. Her book, *The Fountain of Age;* describes "intimacy beyond the dreams of youth." Some self-disclosure from her presents a positive vision of love and maturity.

Nancy Peske and Beverly West have written a funny and insightful book using popular movies to capture the ups and downs of relationships. A short sampling of their approach should open some minds and mouths with laughter.

Then, family psychiatrist, Frank Pittman (who writes a column for the *Family Therapy Networker* magazine) examines popular movies and the vicissitudes of lives in transition, stagnation, tragedy, and health. His lively and insightful columns probe, decipher, and guide couples and the therapists who treat them.

Betty Friedan in *The Fountain of Age* (1993, pp. 254–255), talks about women's relationships and intimacy, "beyond the dreams of youth." Her powerful musings include this one:

> I had a dream: In my house, propped up against a wall, pushed out of the way, was something quite large, all wrapped up in a rug. Like a mummy. "What is wrapped up in that rug?" . . .
>
>   There was a woman in the rug and she was still alive! She was brandishing a knife in her hand. I had wrapped her in that rug, and she was going to kill me if I didn't let her out. How could I let her out without her exploding with rage? And I felt the pain of my own yearning.

Love sustains and defines the years of our growth toward maturity. Love is essential to the continued affirmation of the person's self. An extra 25 to 30 years of life have been opened to us in this century. Friedan goes on to ask whether the problem is really that men die too young, seek younger women, and most women are therefore doomed to lives alone or lives without intimacy. Her suggestion is that the problem is not a sexual imbalance, but the fear and denial of age; which reaches its high water mark in sex. Many women and men (married, widowed, single, divorced) fail to move past the youthful sexual measures (with their masks, fears, and shames). Friedan suggests that there is an intimacy that can only be possible in age.

Make no mistake. She does not denounce the sexual, but uncovers the possibilities of a deeper connection.

Friedan argues convincingly that this is new territory, but a territory with much to recommend it. She also references Butler and Lewis (1988) who write about their research on love and sex after 60. The findings are uplifting.

In the vein of women's themes, there is an entertaining and enlightening popular book: *Cinematherapy: The Girl's Guide to Movies for Every Mood* (1999). Just as a sample of their humor, enjoy Nancy Peske and Beverly West's chapter headings on such timeless topics as:

1. Vacillating Between Weeping & Homicidal Rage: PMS Movies
2. He's a Jerk, But He's Sooo Cute!
3. But He Has Such Potential, and I Know He Can Change
4. Going Postal! Working Girl Blues
5. I Know She's My Mom, But She Drives Me Nuts!
6. Someday Has Come and Gone and My Prince Still Hasn't Shown Up
7. When Women Were Women and Men Were Nervous
8. Nobody Understands Me Like You Do, Girlfriend
9. Hell Hath No Fury: Dumped and Out-for-Blood Movies
10. I'm Gonna Eat Some Worms: Martyr Movies
11. My Heart Belongs to Daddy: Father Issue Movies
12. I Am Woman, Hear Me Roar
13. When Men Were Men and Women Were Wicked

Recently, the TV network OXYGEN (which offers themes of particular interest to women) has given Peske and West a regular program to keep current on movies of interest. Their book provides fun homework assignments for couples therapy. The authors discuss countless movie recommendations to capture themes, dreams, and nightmares. Laughter saves the day.

Frank Pittman is a highly respected family psychiatrist, and a writer on families and the nature of men and their possibilities and peculiarities. One of his books is *Private Lies: Infidelity and the Betrayal of Intimacy* (1989). Maggie Scarf in her review called it "delightfully readable, compassionate, and awfully funny at the same time." Pittman is also a regular contributor to a professional periodical with a popular readership. The magazine for its formative years was called the *Family Therapy Networker*, and more recently: the *Psychotherapy Networker*. His column is *The Screening Room*.

A sampling of Pittman's reviews shows keen insight into a wide range of issues in society, families, couples, and gender contrasts. Some of his perspectives and movie reviews fit well in working with couples of any age. The venue of the silver screen has rarely been explained so well in showing us our themes and blunders, strivings, and self-deceptions, but also the possibilities and paths of loving couples.

One of Pittman's columns "Rebels Without a Clue" (*Family Therapy Networker,* August, 1995), compared Marlon Brando, James Dean, Montgomery Clift, and Paul Newman. He saw each of them as alienated in their own lives and adept at portraying that experience in powerful films that shaped our culture. Each of them apparently grew up in middle-class, middle America. But each struggled with his own version of alienation.

Brando, diagnosed with Attention Deficit Disorder and labeled "uneducable," was said to wander around unbathed, seeking love and food for his unquenchable appetites. His movies included *The Last Tango in Paris, A Streetcar Named Desire, The Wild One, On the Waterfront, Guys & Dolls, Mutiny on the Bounty, The Young Lions,* and his later roles as *The Godfather.* Then Brando played the heart of darkness himself in the role of Colonel Kurtz in *Apocalypse Now.*

James Dean and Montgomery Clift didn't last so long. Dean the rebel, remains an icon of adolescent romance and angst in *Rebel Without a Cause.* Clift was tortured by acceptable norms for relationships in his era. He received enduring support from Elizabeth Taylor during his career.

Pittman felt Paul Newman somehow escaped the alienation that took the others in rocky directions. Newman became the poster boy for cockiness. Since Pittman's article, Newman won an Academy Award for his character in the movie *Nobody's Fool.*

He plays a handyman who reconnects with his adult son, his grandson, and his ability to give and get love in a blue-collar smart aleck fashion. Newman has also dealt with the death of a son, countless cinematic successes, and an enduring marriage. He even created salad dressings.

What these male movie stars portrayed for us was not the healthiest model for couples and relationships. On the other hand, Elizabeth Taylor and Greta Garbo did not offer the greatest models of women in relationships either. Older couples we see may have these icons in their memory bank. These same couples may have better solutions than any movie stars.

PERSPECTIVE IN REWRITING LOVE STORIES

On a more applied note: Another useful book on couples is *The Dance Away Lover* (Goldstein, Larner, Zuckerman, & Goldstein, 1977). This book is particularly valuable in helping people understand the predictable stages in relationships. The concept of *The Dance Away Lover* accounts for a person's "interpersonal valence." Each person brings a special attraction to the relationship, which helps in the beginning. However, this quality is not so helpful as the relationship moves past the glow of the first stage in love.

The therapist working with older couples (as with any couple) must strike a balance of joining couples in a way that helps collaboration, yet can be forceful and clear when difficult issues must be addressed. Goldstein et al. (1977) in their entertaining book *The Dance Away Lover,* believe the qualities that attract us romantically in the first stage of a relationship often become the ones that annoy us and cause conflict as the relationship evolves.

The *first stage* shows up in popular music, movies, and hero worship in our culture. Beauty, humor, perceived success, sex, and a host of other qualities often win the day. However, the luster usually does not last. This romantic stage is worshipped in most popular music.

The *second stage* involves the realizations that a relationship gets tougher when the qualities that attract us to another become the same ones that annoy us or cause conflict. The romantic first stage of love seeks excitement, rapture, and immersion in another. The cute or enthralling qualities that attract at the start become annoyances. Some of our students (when introduced to the concept of Stage 1 as worshipped in popular music) jokingly suggest that the second stage may be more like country and western songs where "somebody does somebody wrong." For example, the outgoing personality who charms a party may not do well in a sustained relationship.

The *third stage* is when couples often split or seek therapy. Does the conflict or flagging romance mean the relationship is not a true one? Actually, this stage is an opportunity to explore what is each partner's responsibility for foiling continued love and growth. Then, the couple may reform and balance a mature appreciation of commitment and responsibility to strengthen the relationship. With older couples, there can be a lot of baggage. The *third stage* is the time when reality arrives. If there is a real commitment, this is when both partners take stock of their own foibles, irritating habits, or unfinished business. Each person in the couple can work to enrich their relationship, by knowing their blind spots, and their strengths. A new chapter can be written for their love and commitment.

Some of the funny dyads the authors describe include:

The Dance-Away Lover, The Anxious Ingenue, The Disarmer, The Provider, The Prizewinner, The Fragile, The Pleaser, The Victim, The Ragabash and The Tough-Fragile.

The stages are elaborated along with perspectives on sex, affairs, and risks of splitting up. The book offers an entertaining yet informative way of looking at enduring patterns. Couples of any age seem to resonate with the insight provided by this model. They like the book and grasp the predictable emotional undertow that the therapist authors describe in funny, yet clear examples. Let us consider an example to anchor the theory.

The therapy with a senior couple, Bob and Helen, may help clarify the process of forming and reforming each of their identities, as well as revising the story of their relationship together.

Bob and Helen had been married for more than 25 years. Together, they have an adult son, daughter-in-law, and grandchild. Bob was referred to the treating psychologist by his neurologist. Bob came with symptoms of agitated depression, a strong conviction that he needed a divorce in order to get relief from various frustrations, and an unnamed anger that was currently haunting him. The referral from the physician also asked to consider whether there was a dementing neurological disease. Bob was an interesting, proud, and intelligent man. At the same time, he was opinionated but possessed a redeeming sense of humor. He usually could get a new perspective on himself in response to firm confrontation. Bob had a number of successes in his adult life. He was a military officer in the Second World War. He carried a strong part of his identity in the traditional pride and rigors of standing up for what he believed in. After his retirement from the military, he was able to make the transition into civilian life as an engineer involved in the NASA space program. Now in retirement, he and his wife are financially stable and comfortable, but his ego engine runs high. He has to offer his opinion on every topic. At times, he shared with the therapist articles he had written on topics from revamping the IRS to a touching and insightful look at his experience with prostate cancer and surgery.

Bob had been married before. There was little contact with his ex-wife, but his sons who lived three hours away were a low-level stressor or anxiety for him. He often second-guessed himself on how he raised the boys and what he might be able to do now to redirect them.

Several years ago, he was hospitalized for depression and significant mood swings. He said his previous psychological treatment was most beneficial, and he talked with high regard for the psychiatrist who had managed his medication and therapy.

Bob related, in bits and pieces, the story of his years growing up. He was raised by a demanding and emotionally withholding mother (in his view). He felt that she never gave him the praise or affirmation that he dearly sought. He vacillated between being angry at the mother who raised him and the father who was not around to do so. In Bob's recollection, he learned not to dwell on the sadness, but rather made it the strongest motivator of his life. He was prone to sharing stories of his struggles and successes in the marines where he learned that challenge, determination, and commitment to beliefs were the "secrets to a successful life." He liked a good fight and never missed an opportunity to challenge the therapist and laugh uproariously when the therapist came back forcefully. He was comfortable with a confrontational approach, which allowed the therapist to point out how Bob contributed to marital conflicts. He said he liked it when the therapist called him a "horse's ass" when he was one.

Through neuropsychological testing, we were able to rule out a dementing process. That is, his difficulties in memory and cognition were more related to his agitated depression. The consulting neurologist prescribed antidepressant medication, which helped greatly. The therapy relationship was solidly created, and before too long Bob was receptive to bringing in his wife Helen.

Helen was a delightful woman 12 years younger than Bob. They had been married for more than a quarter of a century and they had an adult son living not far away from them. Helen was a recently retired teacher who was an educational administrator in the last part of her formal working years. By listening to Bob's boasting and accompanying complaining about Helen's career, the therapist discovered that Helen was highly regarded as an educator. She was the prototype of an inspiring teacher. Families (across two generations) would return to visit and share with her the influence she had on their lives.

Helen was afraid Bob would present a slanted perspective on their marriage and his condition. She had developed some ways to contend with his forceful bravado as well as the insecurities that motivated him. In retirement, he no longer had officer's rank or an engineer's status. Clearly, she cared deeply for him, but Helen had her own recent medical difficulties. These included breast and ovarian cancer. Her cancer had been in remission for over three years, but the fear of a possible return was never completely removed. In some ways, Helen saw Bob's current angry depressed state as possibly a re-occurrence of the depression that hospitalized him years before. Helen was unsure whether to view his current condition with sympathy (because it followed his operation for prostate cancer) or with protective anger that his maladies were simply selfish and petty.

Helen had a circle of caring and supportive women friends. She often talked about how, without their support, she probably would have sent Bob packing in recent years. Bob frequently criticized Helen by rehashing how she allowed the school system to take advantage of her ("she wasn't tough enough") in the past. He told her to stand on her own and not overfocus on relationships with her friends. He was jealous. Bob's repeated solution to situations was to get tougher. Helen was frustrated with her conflicting needs to nurture and be sympathetic to him, against the need to be defended lest he steamroll her. Usually, the subtlety eluded him, so the therapist often adopted a confronting and salty style of interacting with him. He liked a good fight. Unfortunately, that sometimes seemed to be his idea of intimacy.

As the therapy progressed (interspersing individual sessions with couples counseling), we were able to clarify the core fears and hopes that propelled each of them. Together, we were able to recognize each of their styles for trying to get their needs met, and the ways their stories collided. Through some irony and humor, we were able to caricature their defensive styles and fears, while at the same time validating their needs as healthy and meetable.

We also reflected on the serious cancer-related illnesses they were both surviving. In spite of their conflict, there was a history of supporting and caring for each other during these illnesses. They protected one another, and they told stories of the cancer support groups (formal and informal) who had helped them through the toughest times. Part of their healing stories included shared anger at health professionals who had been insensitive, obstructive, or even iatrogenic during the diagnostic, treatment, or recovery phases. They were able to translate their shared anger and sadness into helpful suggestions about how the process could be rehumanized. Helen drew on her traditional religious values and beliefs for strength. In contrast, Bob's spirituality is best characterized as a kind of rage-at-the-moon agnosticism. This was tempered by his testimonial to the benefit he derived from his cancer support group.

Like most couples who have known each other for a long time, they were skilled at naming their partner's irritating ways of relating. Each of them could describe and label provocative (if not sinister) motives that the other might have for not fighting fairly. At times, each of them would be extremely defensive and unwilling to compromise or make concessions to the other. However, we were able to clarify an important principle: Intimacy in a healthy relationship is a balance of the need for *control* in the relationship (being an equal partner who exerts an appropriate assertive influence), against the need for *vulnerability* (receiving caring and closeness in a safe emotional climate).

After one of Bob's tirades, Helen protectively moved back into her shell, and we took time to clarify the pattern. Helen reported that each time there was one of these explosions, Bob would come around and be apologetic. However, she was too vulnerable and defensive to trust his sincerity. He was oblivious to the way his anger made her more defensive. A valuable funny quote was useful in clarifying this pattern to them: "The lion and the lamb will lie down together and the lamb won't get much sleep." Another metaphor that they warmed to is the notion of getting your back scratched. This is a simple, straightforward, and useful metaphor. The therapist asked them what they would need to do to get their backs scratched. This analogy for the process can be used without a lot of memory baggage that triggers certain hurts and fights in a couple's history.

The back-scratching metaphor allows people to consider what communication steps are needed to clearly express one's needs, wishes, and preferences, thereby sustaining communication in a way that encourages (rather than criticizes) each person to ask for help. Too often, talking has broken down to the point where the only communication is to tell the other person how bad he or she is at sensing and meeting your needs. The analogy helps defuse blaming by rethinking the process and clarifying steps to get one's needs met. The metaphor also clarifies how each person's defensive strategy can almost guarantee that no one gets his or her back thoroughly scratched. The metaphor also has a sexual undercurrent, which can remain subtle at a time in therapy when explicitly addressing the sexual theme only heightens fear, anger, and conflict. Bob and Helen liked the process so well that they eventually brought the therapist a wooden back scratcher as a symbol of their appreciation and the rediscovery of their mutual caring, intimacy, and shared sense of humor.

This example incorporates central qualities we have stressed. There is an appreciation of the individual and family developmental landscapes and how they blend or collide. The therapist conveyed a sensitivity to their losses and their history of change. Then a conflictual pattern was described with humor to defuse fear and anger. This was followed by developing a strategy to regain support from each other. This was done by showing how each person's conflicting needs for control and vulnerability were keeping them apart. They were able to reclaim their intimacy; their ability to scratch each other's back.

THEMES IN RELATIONSHIPS AND CREATIVE LIVING

We have made recommendations about the essential skills and perspective that help therapists work well with older couples. We feel that the essential ingredients are:

- Integrity conveyed to the patients
- Knowledge of the universal challenges older adults face
- Enthusiastic commitment to working with older couples

We hope this chapter helps therapists merge the skills of honoring people's life stories, grasping core dynamics, and a fostering of healthy loving relationships. An appreciation for family systems principles is essential. The other task is to create a safe environment to think, cry, and laugh out loud. We collaborate with couples to build on past strengths and grow from life challenges. These skills and perspectives accompany a maturing life and maturing couples.

We close with some quotable ironies:

You don't marry one person; you marry three:

1. The person you think they are,
2. The person they are, and
3. The person they are going to become as the result of being married to you.

—Richard Needham

In every couple's relationship each person wants to grow the other one up! That really means we want to shape our partner to better meet our needs.

—Gus Napier

Happiness is having a large, loving, caring, close-knit family in another city.

—George Burns

A model for conceptualizing individuals or couples we treat appears in Table 6.1. The model helps focus on the dimension(s) most likely to foster change as quickly as possible.

Table 6.1
Case Conceptualization with Older Couples

Presenting Problems
Couples' views
Therapist's view
Developmental Backdrop
Individual
Current Family
Family of Origin
Physical/Medical Related Factors
Life Change and Relevant Stressors
Fun Activities
Core Dynamics
Coping Resources/Limitations
Relational
Cognitive
Affective
Behavioral
Existential
Etiological Core Pattern(s)
Implications for Prognosis and Treatment Strategies
Short-Term and Long-Term Goals

Therapists need to understand the hopes and fears of each person in any couple they treat. By helping them define their conflict, their fears, and their goals, the couple can renew their love.

Psychotherapy has much to offer older couples and families. Conversely, older couples broaden the scope of family therapists' skills. These folks may teach us that love grows into late life and beyond. Old dogs learn, apply, and invent new tricks to keep love alive for generations.

REFERENCES AND RESOURCES

Note: References with asterisks are additional readings.

Bateson, G. (1972). *Steps to an ecology of mind.* New York: Ballantine Books.

Bowen, M. (1978). *Family therapy in clinical practice.* Northvale, NJ: Aronson.

Butler, N., & Lewis, M. L. (1988). *Love and sex after 60* (pp. 1–7). New York: Harper & Row.

Callahan, D. (1995). *Setting limits: Medical goals in an aging society.* New York: Norton.

*Carlson, M. B. (1991). *Creative aging: A meaning-making perspective.* New York: Norton.

*Carter, E., & McGoldrick, M. (Eds.). (1988). *The changing family life cycle.* New York: Gardner Press.

*Chinen, A. (1989). *In the ever after: Fairy tales for the second half of life.* Wilmette, Il: Chiron.

*DiGiovanna, A. G. (2000). *Human aging: The biological perspective.* New York: McGraw-Hill.

*Dychtwald, K. (1999). *Healthy aging: Challenges and solutions.* Gaithersburg, MD: Aspen.

*Epston, D., & White, M. (1975). *Literate means to therapeutic ends.* Adelaide, South Australia: Dulwitch Centre.

*Erikson, E. (1980). *Identity and the life cycle.* New York: Norton.

*Erikson, E. (1982). *The life cycle completed.* New York: Norton.

*Ford, G. (2000). *Treasures of the silver screen.* Nashville, TN: Highlands.

Friedan, B. (1993). *The fountain of age.* New York: Simon & Schuster.

Gilligan, C. (1983). *In a different voice.* Cambridge, MA: Harvard Press.

Goldstein, D., Larner, K., Zuckerman, S., & Goldstein, H. (1977). *The dance away lover: And other roles we play in love, sex and marriage.* New York: Ballantine Books.

Howard, G. S. (1991). Culture tales: A narrative approach to thinking, cultural psychology and psychotherapy. *American Psychologist, 46,* 187–197.

Josselson, R. (1987). *Finding herself.* San Francisco: Jossey-Bass.

Josselson, R., & Lieblich, A. (1993). *The narrative study of lives.* Thousand Oaks, CA: Sage.

Kaufman, S. (1986). *The ageless self: Sources of meaning in late life.* New York: Median.

Kerr, M. E., & Bowen, M. (1988). *Family evaluation.* New York: Norton.

*Knight, B. (1996). *Psychotherapy with older adults.* Thousand Oaks, CA: Sage.

May, R. (1975). *The courage to create.* New York: Norton.

Moore, T. (1992). *Care of the soul.* New York: HarperCollins.

Napier, A. Y., & Whitaker, C. (1988). *The family crucible.* New York: Harper & Row.

*O'Hanlon Hudson, P., & O'Hanlon, W. H. (1993). *Rewriting love stories: Brief marital therapy.* New York: Norton.

*Peake, T. H. (1998). *Healthy aging, healthy treatment: Telling stories.* Westport, CT: Greenwood-Praeger.

Peake, T. H. (2004). *Cinema and life development: Healing lives and training therapists.* Westport CT: Greenwood-Praeger.

Peske, L., & West, B. (1999). *Cinematherapy: The girls guide to movies for every mood.* New York: Dell Trade Paperback.

Pittman, F. (1989). *Private lies: Infidelity and the betrayal of intimacy.* New York: Norton.

Pittman, F. (August 1995). The Screening Room. Review of "Rebels without a Clue," *Family Therapy Networker.*

Prest, L., & Keller, T. (1993). Spirituality and family therapy: Myths and metaphors. *Journal of Family Therapy, 19,* 137–148.

Roberto, L. G. (1992). *Transgenerational family therapies.* New York: Guilford Press.

Scarf, M. (1988). *Intimate partners: Patterns in love and marriage.* New York: Ballantine Books.

*Dr. Seuss. (1986). *You're only old once.* New York: Random House.

*Solomon, G. (1995). *The motion picture prescription.* Santa Rosa, CA: Aslan.

*Viney, L. (1993). *Life stories: Personal construct therapy with the elderly.* New York: Wiley.

Viorst, J. (1986). *Necessary losses.* New York: Ballantine Books.

THEORETICAL PERSPECTIVES ON WORKING WITH COUPLES

CHAPTER 7

Bowen Family Systems Theory as Feminist Therapy

Louise Bordeaux Silverstein

Bowen family systems theory was originally developed by Murray Bowen, in the 1970s (Anonymous, 1972; Bowen, 1978). In the late 1980s, this theoretical model was repeatedly criticized by feminist therapists as overvaluing personality characteristics associated with traditional masculine gender role socialization and undervaluing characteristics associated with feminine socialization.

This critique is more than two decades old. Why resurrect this controversy now? As Thelma Jean Goodrich has wryly noted, "This just in: Women still oppressed" (Goodrich, 2003, p. 4). Women suffer discrimination and violence in both the public world and the private world of the family. The subject of this chapter is the private world of the heterosexual couple, a world in which gendered inequality in power continues to construct the lives of most couples.

From my point of view, the dismissal of Bowen theory by feminist therapists represents a missed opportunity. Feminist theory has articulated how power inequities are embedded in gender roles. Bowen theory has provided a blueprint for effective change in families. The Bowen concept of differentiation of self is particularly well-suited for helping women change because it advocates finding a balance between one's need for defining a unique self, while at the same time remaining emotionally connected to significant others. Thus, combining feminist theory and Bowen theory enhances the power of each, and generates an effective model for feminist family therapy.

In the first section of this chapter, I present a brief outline of the Bowen theory. I correct some misconceptions, and then expand on what I see as an accurate feminist critique. I then outline the advantages of a feminist-informed Bowen model for therapeutic change in working with women and men from a feminist perspective. The final section presents two clinical case examples that demonstrate how this combined theoretical perspective can be implemented with actual couples.

FEMINIST CRITIQUES OF BOWEN THEORY

THE EARLY CRITIQUE

In the 1980s, feminists (Bograd, 1986; Goldner, 1989; Lerner, 1988; Leupnitz, 1988) charged that the concept of differentiation of self defined the healthy adult in terms of personality characteristics usually associated with the traditional masculine gender role, that is, emotional separation, rational thinking, and being-for-self. Correspondingly, Bowen theory was understood to devalue traditional feminine gender role characteristics, such as psychological connectedness, emotional expressiveness, and being-for-others.

This reading of Bowen theory does not accurately reflect the concept of differentiation of self. Bowen theory (Kerr & Bowen, 1988) posits that two biologically based life forces, *togetherness* and *individuality*, propel all life forms. For human beings, the togetherness life force reflects a need to be emotionally close to others, to be approved of, and to feel that one belongs to a group. The individuality life force, in contrast, represents a need to be a unique organism, unlike others, with psychological space between oneself and others. *Differentiation* is the *balance* that each individual achieves between these two competing life forces. An individual who has achieved a relatively high level of differentiation of self can maintain a more or less equal balance of gratifying both individuality and togetherness needs.

Because human beings are born in a physiologically immature state and remain helpless for a very long time afterward, humans are dependent for their survival on the efforts of others. Until a human being becomes capable of economic independence, togetherness needs remain paramount. This imbalance in favor of togetherness needs leads most individuals to spend the rest of their lives struggling to increase their ability to define a self in response to the individuality life force. For this reason, much of Bowen therapy focuses on increasing the power of the individuality life force in the process of self-definition. However, the goal of this emphasis on individuality is to achieve a more equal balance between the two life forces, not to emphasize the individuality life force at the expense of the togetherness force.

It is helpful to imagine an old-fashioned scale. One side of the scale represents individuality needs, the other togetherness needs. Until adolescence or early adulthood, the scale is severely weighted toward the togetherness force. Each of us is strongly influenced by what our family and friends think are the appropriate ways to organize our lives, regardless of our personal preferences. An individual could spend the rest of her life trying to develop an authentic self that was not unduly influenced by the desires of her family, and never quite achieve an equal balance between the two sides of the scale.

Without a solid grounding in the theoretical relations between the togetherness and individuality life forces, a reader could interpret this emphasis on individuality as an emphasis on autonomy and separation. However, autonomy and separation are not concepts in Bowen theory. Differentiation of self reflects the ability to define authentic life goals without needing the approval of one's family, *while at the same time* remaining in active emotional contact with them. The goal for both men and women would be to define a self that expresses our need for individuality, while at the same time, acknowledging our continuing need for togetherness. Thus, the critique that Bowen theory idealizes emotional separateness and masculine gender role values is not accurate.

A MORE ACCURATE CRITIQUE

Bowen theory, like all traditional (i.e., prefeminist) theories of psychotherapy, failed to acknowledge the relation between the larger sociocultural context and both symptomatology and therapeutic change. Bowen's original theory, in its acceptance of our culture's binary definition of gender, failed to acknowledge the ways in which this binary system automatically encouraged men and women to give up self.

Similarly, Bowen theory does not address the concept of power (Bograd, 1986). Bowen theory does not acknowledge that husbands and wives have differing amounts of power and therefore differ in their flexibility, both to initiate change and to resist the system's pressure not to change. It is these two aspects of Bowen theory—its failure to address both the ways in which gender roles encourage women and men to give up self and the inequalities between men and women within patriarchal culture—that limit its sensitivity to feminist goals.

Traditional gender roles can be seen as examples of cultural prescriptions that are transmitted unconsciously through the multigenerational transmission process. The traditional feminine gender role prescribes that women become facilitating environments for others, rather than defining and pursuing personal goals that are not related to family roles. The more modern feminine gender role prescribes that women do it all. A woman can now have personal goals, primarily work-related goals, but if she is a wife and mother, she still must remain a facilitating environment for her husband and children.

Masculine gender role prescriptions socialize men to focus on achievement in the world of paid employment and to deny their need for intimacy and closeness. The more modern masculine role prescribes that men must be nurturing fathers, even while they remain the primary providers for their families. However, this continuing focus on economic provision keeps men away from their families and makes intimate relationships with their children exceedingly difficult.

It is especially interesting that Bowen did not understand the function of gender roles in family systems, because he was extremely clear about the function of sibling positions. Bowen integrated Walter Toman's (1961) research on sibling position into family systems theory. Toman suggested that certain fixed personality characteristics were determined by an individual's place in the sibling configuration of their family. For example, Toman found that oldest children tend to be overly responsible, naturally accepting responsibility for what needs to be done. A youngest child, in contrast, tends to assume that others will get things done and that he will be taken care of.

The concept of functioning sibling position predicted that people from different classes, races, and cultures would have certain personality characteristics in common if they shared the same sibling position within their families of origin. Family systems theory assumes that as long as one individual performs certain functions, other individuals will not perform those functions.

Similarly, feminist theory argues that gender socialization in childhood prepares men and women to assume the functional positions of wife/mother or husband/father. Women overdevelop personality characteristics that are appropriate for functioning in the private world of the family (i.e., a high capacity for emotional closeness, a focus on caretaking). Men overdevelop personality characteristics (i.e., emotional distance, instrumental thinking, competitiveness) that enhance functioning in the public world of work. The family is the emotional milieu within which cultural expectations about gender roles are transmitted. Thus, gender must be integrated into family systems theory.

In terms of the invisibility of power within Bowen theory, again its absence is especially interesting, because the theory is clear about power differentials between parents and adolescents. From a Bowen family systems perspective, it is often advantageous to work with only one person in a family. However, this is never done with adolescents. Therapy would encourage the adolescent to begin to change her behavior. Bowen theory assumes that change on the part of one person within the system automatically and inevitably generates pressure within the system to encourage that person to change back into the old way of doing things. Because adolescents are not economically self-supporting, they are seen as not having enough power to withstand the family's demand to change back. Although Bowen family systems therapy is often practiced with only one member of the family in the room, therapy with an adolescent alone is never recommended. Within this framework, power is acknowledged as being linked to generation, but not to gender.

If we consider the economic context of full-time wives, however, they certainly are not economically independent. Given the continuing pay differential between women and men in general ($0.73 for every $1.00), even wives who work often have much less economic power than their husbands (U.S. Census Bureau, 2001). Feminist family therapists (Bograd, 1986; Goldner, 1989; Lerner, 1988) have pointed out that these economic inequalities generate corresponding power inequalities between husbands and wives.

In addition to the absence of gender in Bowen theory, there was also an absence of sensitivity to issues of race and class. Drawing attention to the impact of institutionalized racism on marital relations in African American families, Elaine Pinderhughes (1986) characterized Black women as holding a nodal position in which the stresses of racism and gender coalesce. Cognizant of the struggles of their fathers, brothers, and sons, many Black women tend to give up self rather than negotiate for their own interests, and thereby add to the burden of their husbands, domestic partners, or sons. Thus, institutionalized racism exacerbates gender socialization by increasing the pressure on Black women to give up self in the family.

Again, it is interesting that Bowen did not address issues of race and power within Black families, because he was so clear about how Black families were used to manage the anxiety of the White majority in U.S. society. In his concept of the "societal projection process," Bowen (1978) proposed that all nondominant groups, but particularly African Americans and individuals labeled mentally ill, become the object of "benevolent" help by members of society. This help serves to keep the recipients in an inferior position, effectively institutionalizing their marginal status. Keeping certain members of society in an inferior position relieves the anxiety of others by reassuring them that they are superior to the marginalized group.

Bowen theory's failure to address the inequalities of power between wives and husbands in both White and Black families represents serious limitations to its usefulness in helping families change. However, if these issues of race, gender, and economic power are addressed, Bowen theory has the potential to be extremely helpful.

INTEGRATING FEMINIST THEORY AND BOWEN FAMILY SYSTEMS THEORY

Many issues that couples struggle with are systemic rather than personal. For example, the cultural process of gender socialization sets the stage for women to assume the majority of the responsibility for childcare and housework by constructing women as primary caretakers and men as primary providers. Patriarchy creates economic inequalities that further reinforce the traditional division of labor. For Whites, women's lower earnings predispose wives, rather than husbands, to limit paid employment at the birth of the first child. For Blacks, men's lower rates of paid employment discourage marriage, leaving large numbers of Black women to struggle as single mothers, and large numbers of Black men to be isolated from their children.

For married couples, the male power and privilege that derives from male dominance constructs a sense of entitlement in men. This entitlement denies the unfairness of leaving their wives with more than 50% of the household responsibility, even when she shoulders almost 50% of the financial responsibility. In the Black community, the unfavorable ratio of eligible men to women too often discourages long-term commitment and responsibility within intimate heterosexual relationships. Although these marital dilemmas are actually systemic problems, they are experienced as personal insults and betrayals.

The question that confronts marital therapists is the following:

> In the context of these social forces that stress long-term relationships, is there a way to work with couples to mitigate the impact of these negative systemic influences, so that their decisions might be based more on personal preferences, rather than on emotional reactivity to systemic pressures?

Most couples get into trouble because each person is trying to get the other person to change. "Why won't he help me get the kids ready in the morning?" "Why doesn't she appreciate everything I do for the family?" "Why won't he marry me?" "Why is she always on my case?" As anxiety increases, most of us automatically focus on blaming someone else. "Why is she so critical of everything I do?" "How can he be so selfish?"

John Gottman (1998) has described how this reciprocal process of criticism and blame can be toxic to marriages. As we think about our unhappiness, we become experts at analyzing what our partner is doing that makes us unhappy, or what she or he is not doing that would make us happy. It is infinitely more difficult for us to see what *we* are doing that contributes to our being stuck.

Yet, anyone who has lived in a family knows that, in the context of emotional conflict, people do not willingly change simply because someone else wants them to do so. The more we try to pressure others to change, often the more entrenched they become in their position. At times, the other person may change in response to emotional pressure, but the change is usually accompanied by resentment that is subsequently expressed, either overtly or covertly. The content of the battle may change, but the process of relationship conflict continues.

The solution to this dilemma in Bowen's terms is to focus on the self, rather than on the other. However, because of power differences, women often have less flexibility to initiate change. They often risk punishment if they take direct action that displeases others. Given the likelihood of punishment, women often resort to using power indirectly. Lerner (1985, 1988) described some of the ways that women try to exert indirect power: by sexual withdrawal, emotional manipulation, and overinvestment in children. Even when these efforts are successful, they do not lead to the establishment of personal life goals for the woman.

In general, most women do not know how to use the power that they have, nor do they know how to obtain more power. By exhorting women to take the focus off the other and place it on self, Bowen therapy encourages women to think directly about what they want, to use the power that they have, and to develop a life plan for achieving their goals.

The Bowen concept of the systemic change-back reaction also helps women anticipate the resistance that their personal changes will provoke.

The change-back reaction predicts that whenever one person in a system changes, other people in the system will pressure that person to change back to the way she was prior to upsetting the equilibrium. This is true even when changes are perceived as positive. The change-back reaction does not emanate only from others. The person who is changing often becomes anxious about the change and may change back even without pressure from others. If these systemic reactions are predicted and planned for, women are less likely to capitulate to efforts to get them to return to their former way of being.

Another advantage of Bowen theory is the idea that, when conflict in a marital couple is high, conjoint therapy is often not helpful. Bowen family systems therapy is often practiced with only one member of the family in the room. Because women are socialized to adapt to emotional pressure from others, being in the physical presence of her spouse or children may undermine a woman's efforts to define a more differentiated self. Women often have difficulty distinguishing between being selfish and focusing on self. Thus, working alone in therapy can enhance the change process.

Feminist theory deconstructs the larger cultural pressures and outlines the pitfalls that power inequalities will generate if the couple begins the change process. Bowen theory provides a road map for negotiating the inevitable potholes and speed bumps that are encountered as relationship patterns change. This combination provides the opportunity for each member of the couple to change in a way that can repair the relationship, or end the relationship with a minimal amount of stress.

Not all clients choose to change in a way that sustains the relationship. Preserving relationships is not the goal of feminist-informed Bowen therapy. The goal is to help each person define a more authentic self. If at least one person in the couple makes progress in this regard, the total amount of chronic anxiety in the couple decreases, and the prospects for positive change increase. Next, I present examples of the way this process works.

CLINICAL APPLICATIONS OF A FEMINIST-INFORMED BOWEN THEORY

THE UNEQUAL BURDEN

Before presenting a case example, I present the larger systemic context within which the conflict over the unequal burden occurs. For White, middle-class, dual-earner, married couples, one of the most common sources of marital complaints is the husband's failure to share responsibility equitably for childcare and housework. Hochschild (1989) identified this as a major source of marital stress in 1989, and more recent studies have illustrated that this conflict continues to stress married couples with children (e.g., Deutsch, 1999; Dienhart, 1998). Although women now contribute substantially (on average, 40% of total family income in U.S. households) to family financial stability, men have yet to contribute equitably to childcare and household management. Overall, estimates suggest that father involvement is proportionately between 25% to 54% of mother's involvement (Pleck, 1997), depending on family structure and socioeconomic group.

Using qualitative interviews, Dienhart (1998) studied 18 White, middle-class, highly educated couples with young children ages 2 to 6 who lived in Ontario, Canada, and southern California. Both members of the couples agreed that they shared parenting equally. However, despite the couples' explicit and persistent attempts at equality, Dienhart noted obstacles to shared parenting. These included institutional rigidity (workplace practices such as a chilly climate for fathers who took family leave), and gender entitlements (such as mothers wanting to be the primary caregiver, and fathers taking time for leisure activities). Overall, Dienhart reported that couples resisted talking about conflict.

In another qualitative study, Deutsch (1999) interviewed 30 White, mostly Christian couples, whom she divided into several categories according to self-report data: equal sharers, potential equal sharers, 60% to 40% sharing couples, 75% to 25% sharing couples, and alternating-shift couples. Couples who shared parenting equally tended to be comprised of women who felt confident and entitled to equality. These couples negotiated ways to share responsibilities by dividing tasks.

In contrast, unequal sharers included fathers that Deutsch designated "helpers," "sharers," or "slackers." In these families, women were ambivalent about what they wanted at home. Their traditional side wanted to take care of the home and family, while their more progressive side felt that tasks in the home should be more equally divided. The men in these homes felt entitled to their wives' domestic services.

Deutsch outlined some of the ways men got out of doing household work in homes with unequal parenting. Techniques included passive resistance (just say nothing), incompetence (it always ends up being a disaster), praise ("but you're better at it than I am"), different standards ("I just don't care about cleanliness the way you do"), and denial ("I'm better than my father was").

In my clinical practice, I have found a recurring pattern of emerging marital conflict. It is common for women to deny their resentment about the unequal burden when the children are very young (i.e., when the youngest is less than age 3). At this juncture in the family life cycle, the women feel so dependent on their husbands for both economic and psychological stability that they cannot allow themselves to feel angry about the unfair balance of work.

However, as the children get older (especially when the youngest is age 4 to 6 and in a full day of school), the wives begin to think about going back to work, or have already returned to work part-time. They begin to try to negotiate a more equitable sharing of the childcare/housework burden. All too often, the husbands, overwhelmed by their financial responsibility as the primary (or sole) breadwinner, feel entitled to reject the demand to share childcare and especially housework. They resist their wives' demands and begin to feel resentful: "No matter what I do, it's never enough." Many husbands withdraw into stony silence.

After some period of time locked in this power struggle, many marriages break apart. Wives often become exhausted by the struggle. One client said recently, "It seems easier to get a divorce than to get my husband to do things at home." Husbands feel unappreciated and betrayed: "I don't understand why she's complaining, I do so much more than any of the other fathers we know." At this point, many couples enter marital therapy, but it is often too late to save the marriage. The wife feels deeply betrayed because her husband has been unwilling to treat her fairly, and the husband has often retreated into an angry emotional cut-off. One or both may have begun an affair in an effort to find someone to value and appreciate them.

CASE STUDY*

This is precisely the context in which J. M. and Rose entered therapy. They had been married for 15 years and had two children, ages 11 and 6. Both of them had started out with careers, but Rose had been the one to decrease her involvement in paid work in order to take care of the children. She had been working part-time during the past 10 years. When their second child was 4, she went to work full-time. Rose still assumed responsibility for much of the childcare and all of the executive functions of running a household.

In the past two years, she had been feeling more exhausted and resentful. "I have 175 things on my list, and he has 2." Her husband had a theoretical commitment to gender equality and fairness. However, he was exhausted from a very stressful job. Because his income was more than twice as much as hers, he felt entitled not to assume an equal burden in the household. "When you make as much money as I do, I'll make dinner twice a week."

Rose felt very hurt by his attitude. It contrasted with the affection and love they had for each other. J. M. was an exemplary husband in many ways. He supported her active involvement in her career, and never complained when she needed to work late or travel. He was an involved father, much more involved than either of their fathers had been. Still, she found his attitude about money incredibly disrespectful. "Why doesn't he value all of the unpaid work I do looking after the kids and keeping the household running?"

Feeling betrayed and helpless to change things, she transformed her hurt into anger and attacked J. M. as a selfish, callous husband. Her clear understanding of the feminist issues allowed her to analyze accurately how J. M.'s exercise of male power and privilege was unraveling their marriage. However, this intellectual understanding did not provide her with a strategy for

*The demographic information (e.g., marital status, sex, and number of children) of the couples discussed in this chapter has been changed to maintain confidentiality.

change. Her feminist commentary made J. M. even less empathic to her, because he did not want to see himself as enacting male privilege.

Through the process of "coaching," the Bowen metaphor for therapy, Rose came to the realization that trying to change her husband was actually disempowering her. Her nagging and complaining was not effective in motivating him to do more. However, she did have the power to change her own behavior. She decided that an effective strategy to deal with her fatigue and resentment was to do less childcare and housework, rather than trying to get J. M. to do more.

Rose began this process of reining in her overfunctioning by dispensing with some household tasks. One of her big complaints was that J. M. did not feel obliged to participate in cleaning up after meals. She decided to tackle a simple task: clearing the table on weekend mornings. Every weekend, J. M. would get up from the table, leaving the dishes where they were. Rose experienced this behavior as disrespectful. She felt as if he were treating her like a maid, acting as if he were entitled to her cleaning services. She decided that she would stop clearing the table after breakfast on weekend mornings.

This decision was difficult for her because being a good housekeeper was part of her identity as a woman. When other parents came over to pick up or drop off their children for play dates, she did not want them to see a dining room table full of dirty dishes. Her husband, in contrast, did not have any of his identity tied up in the way the house looked.

Rose realized that she could either work hard to have a neat house and be angry with her husband because he wasn't participating in keeping it that way, or she could have a messy house and be less angry with her husband. She decided to develop what she called "hysterical blindness" about the dirty dishes. She trained herself not to notice whether the table was cleared and not to care if guests arrived and saw dirty dishes on the table.

Taking this small, positive action made Rose feel better. She no longer angrily cleared the table, setting a negative emotional atmosphere for the entire day. Interestingly, the dishes would stay on the table until it was time for the next meal. At that time, J. M. would notice the dishes, and together they would clear the table and set it for the next meal. This pattern continued for several months. Finally, J. M. began to notice that the dirty dishes were being left on the table. "Gosh, the table's a mess! Why are these dishes still here!" He began to initiate clearing the table immediately after meals.

I have come to think of this model as "doing less is really doing more." Doing less of what one doesn't want to do will actually do more to help a relationship. Although her strategy was going well in terms of housework, doing less in terms of childcare was a much more difficult choice for Rose. Rose had spent much of her childhood feeling neglected by her own mother. She was very invested in being a better mother than her mother had been. Thus, she was driven to overfunction in the parenting arena, by both external gender role expectations and internal family dynamics.

After careful consideration, she decided to take going to the dentist off her list. She asked J. M. to take responsibility for this task. As usual, he cordially agreed and then promptly forgot about it. Rose had chosen the dentist because she knew that, with fluorine in the water system, the risk of tooth decay was small. She thought that, even if her husband did not accomplish this, she would be able to resist stepping in and doing it. J. M. finally got around to taking the children to the dentist two years later, after numerous reminders from their daughter (an overresponsible woman in the making), "Dad, I really need to go to the dentist!"

In this model, Rose had to engage in a tremendous amount of internal and relationship work. From a feminist perspective, one must ask, "Is it worth it?" Many women may prefer to live alone or with other women rather than to work this hard to create a satisfactory relationship. For some women, living with a man, even in the context of patriarchy, has more advantages than disadvantages. For others, living with a member of the dominant group is too costly.

In the example of the dishes, J. M. did finally change his behavior as Rose had hoped. However, that often does not happen. His failure to take the children to the dentist is a common result. Rose had to be prepared to accept the no-change outcome in her spouse. She had to be motivated to change *for herself alone,* that is, to avoid feeling angry and resentful, and to stop overfunctioning. As Rose continued to decrease her overfunctioning, her level of chronic anxiety also decreased, and she began to feel better. She revised the balance of work versus family responsibilities, and began to devote more time and energy to her career. This gave her a great deal of satisfaction, and her mood improved as well. The changes she initiated helped her define a more authentic and gratifying self.

From a feminist and clinical perspective, it is important to consider whether J. M. also made changes. Bowen theory predicts that, because all behavior is reciprocal, when one member of a couple defines a more robust self and decreases her level of chronic anxiety, the level of chronic anxiety in the couple decreases. It therefore becomes likely that the partner will increase his level of differentiation as well. In the context of Rose's improved sense of self, J. M. decided that his career was too stressful. He restructured his professional life to be much less demanding. He quit his job in the Manhattan corporate world and began working out of their home. This resulted in a significant decrease in his income, but it allowed him to spend much more time at home with the children.

Although he really enjoyed spending more time with the children, and being less stressed in general, J. M. had difficulty making peace with being a less successful provider for his family. Given traditional masculine gender role socialization, being a good husband and father meant providing the highest level of income possible. Yet, J. M. realized that providing a high income meant that he saw little of his children, and was often too tired and too irritable to enjoy them when he was with them. This is the dilemma for many contemporary fathers. How can they fulfill the mandate of being both a good provider and a nurturing father? The former requires long hours away from home, and the latter requires long hours at home. Ultimately, J. M. decided that being there for his family was more important than making more money.

Both members of this couple readjusted their gendered identities. Rose gave up overfunctioning at home in an attempt to be the perfect wife and mother. J. M. gave up overfunctioning at work in an attempt to be the ultimate good provider. J. M. did not accept as much responsibility for childcare and housework as Rose wanted. Rose did not appreciate J. M. as much as he thought she should. However, they each created a more authentic self, decreased their chronic anxiety, and lessened their marital conflict. Not every couple has such a happy ending. Even for J. M. and Rose, the process has not ended. They continue to negotiate just about everything.

I want to underscore the point that working on self from a feminist (or profeminist in the case of men) perspective can create the *opportunity* for the other to change, but does not *guarantee* that he or she will. In my experience, the partner who refuses to change is most often the man. This makes sense because we live in a male-dominant society. The person with the most power has the least motivation to change. I have also seen a few couples in which it has been the wife who refused to change. However, in most couples when the man makes progress in defining a more authentic self, the woman uses that opportunity to do the same, and the conflict in the couple decreases.

THE UNFAVORABLE MARRIAGE MARKET

Before discussing the next case example, I present the cultural context for African American families. During slavery, White slave owners routinely disrupted African American families by raping and impregnating slave women and by selling members of the same family separately. Similarly, during Reconstruction and continuing to the present, White middle-class men have controlled local economic and labor systems, severely limiting employment opportunities for African American men (Burton & Snyder, 1998). Contemporary under investment in inner city neighborhoods has resulted in impoverished cultural institutions, poor educational and job opportunities, especially for men, and social problems such as the drug culture with its ensuing high rates of incarceration and homicide. Given the under investment in these neighborhoods, large numbers of African American men have difficulty finding and maintaining jobs (Jarrett, Roy, & Burton, 2002).

All kinds of economic studies, including time series and cross-sectional and longitudinal analyses find that poor male job opportunities are associated with low marriage and high nonmarital fertility (Sigle-Rushton & Garfinkel, 2002). Employment for African American women has remained stable because low-paying domestic positions, such as babysitter or house-hold worker, have remained plentiful. From a woman's perspective, this gender difference in economic viability renders the available pool of African American men unattractive as marriage partners.

Other factors contributing to the low numbers of marriageable men are the high rates of incarceration and death among young African American men. Without an adequate education, many African American men have few employment choices. Many ultimately become involved in the alternative economy of drugs or gambling. This involvement leads to early death and imprisonment.

Few men can navigate this system successfully. Thus, the ratio of desirable men to women gives African American men a decided advantage. The operational sex ratio (OSR) influences the bargaining position of each sex, and thus the mating (marriage) market (Marlowe, 2002). With many attractive women to choose from, many men refuse to make the long-term commitment of marriage, preferring serial cohabitation. Within relationships, this unfavorable ratio provides men with a significant degree of power, because both partners know that if he is dissatisfied, he has many available alternatives, whereas she has few.

CASE STUDY

Linda and Lance are an example of how these socioeconomic forces play out in the context of personal relationships. Linda had been in two long-term relationships before meeting Lance. Her first partner left her for another woman when their son was two months old. She was "rescued" by Richard, who married her and accepted responsibility for her son. Richard and Linda had a tumultuous marriage of 12 years. Richard was frequently unemployed, used cocaine, was involved with other women, and was abusive to Linda. During these years, they had two daughters. Throughout this period, Linda worked continuously as a bank teller, went to community college at night, and managed the household and the children. For several years, her mother lived with them, providing some measure of childcare, although she abused alcohol and suffered from serious depressive episodes.

When her second child was 3, Linda came into therapy, feeling depressed and discouraged about her marriage. Richard came to one session, but refused further treatment. Over the course of several years, Linda came sporadically to therapy. She worked on her relationship with her father, her mother, and many of her siblings and stepsiblings. She made a great deal of progress improving her relationships with family members, entered college, and completed her associate's degree.

However, although she complained about her marriage, she was unsuccessful in either improving it or leaving it. She would periodically throw Richard out. He would spend several weeks at his mother's house, or with another woman, but would always come back to Linda. Although she "knew she shouldn't," she would always take him back. In general, he was a loving, if somewhat remote, father to the children. Linda felt that having him around was better than being a single mother, as her mother had been.

When her youngest daughter was 10 years old, Linda became involved in an extramarital affair with an older man. Lance owned a home and had a steady job. She saw him for about a year and finally moved in with him, taking her youngest child with her. Richard moved to Florida, taking the two older children, and the couple got a divorce.

For the first time in her life, Linda had a man who was emotionally supportive and financially responsible. She went back to college and luxuriated in her new stability. Over the next two years, Lance kept promising that they would get married soon. Marriage was a very symbolic act for Linda. After her abandonment by her first partner and her years of instability with Richard, she wanted the commitment of a marriage. Her parents had never been married, and she felt that had contributed to the failure of their relationship that occurred she was 3 years old.

Lance, in contrast, found every excuse to delay getting married. In therapy, Linda reported trying to get Lance to change. She alternated between berating him and seducing him. At one point, it seemed that Lance would capitulate, but with an undercurrent of anger and resentment.

We worked on the dangers of forcing someone to do what he really did not want to do. At that point, Linda decided to focus on herself instead of trying to change Lance. She decided that if he really was not willing to get married, she would prefer to break up the relationship. She calmly told him of her decision, and began to search for an apartment. It took her several months to find an apartment that she could afford. They lived together amicably during this time, although Linda was quite sad. When moving day came, she asked Lance to help her move, and he did.

Linda moved into her apartment and continued to see Lance from time to time, but refused to have a sexual relationship with him. After three months, Lance suggested that they get married. He realized that he wanted the relationship more than he wanted to avoid marriage. He bought her an engagement ring, they threw an engagement party together, and planned a family wedding. Five years later, they are happily married, and contemplating retirement.

This case illustrates, not only the power of focusing on self, but also the importance of action rather than words. Linda had talked and talked about how important marriage was to her, but Lance was not able to respond until she changed her behavior. As long as she was willing to continue living with him, he was not forced to address her needs. Once she changed her behavior, he responded.

The power of behavior over words is a rule of relationships that is often difficult to implement. It was really hard for Linda to look for an apartment, buy furniture, and actually move in. She wanted Lance to do what she wanted, simply out of his love for her. However, most of us change in response to behavior, not words.

It is important to note that behavior change cannot be designed as an attempt to manipulate the other to change. If we act simply as a way of pressuring the other, it will be doomed to failure. Our partner will realize that our action is a ploy, and resistance will emerge, either immediately or over time. We must be convinced that changing our own behavior is a better life choice than remaining locked in a continual struggle to get the other to change, or in a situation that we feel is unacceptable.

We must be totally prepared to accept the possibility that our partner will choose *not* to change. Our behavior shift creates the opportunity for the other to change, but is not a guarantee. Linda had decided that she preferred to live separately, rather than to feel resentful about not being married. Paradoxically, it is this complete shift away from trying to change the other that increases the probability that the other might actually choose change rather than resistance.

SUMMARY

In this chapter, I have shown how Bowen family systems theory, with its emphasis on defining an authentic self, is particularly useful for achieving feminist goals. Bowen theory's focus on the self encourages one to embrace the power needed in order to achieve self-definition. This focus on defining an authentic self and embracing the power to do so is the perfect antidote to feminine gender role socialization.

REFERENCES

Anonymous. (1972). On the differentiation of self. In J. Framo (Ed.), *A dialogue between family researchers and family therapists* (pp. 111–172). New York: Springer.

Bograd, M. (1986). A feminist examination of family therapy: What is women's place? *Women and Therapy, 5,* 95–106.

Bowen, M. (1978). *Family therapy in clinical practice.* New York: Aronson.

Burton, L. M., & Snyder, A. R. (1998). The invisible man revisited: Comments on the life course, history, and men's roles in American families. In A. Booth & A. C. Crouter (Eds.), *Men in families* (pp. 31–39). Mahwah, NJ: Erlbaum.

Deutsch, F. M. (1999). *Halving it all: How equally shared parenting works.* Cambridge, MA: Harvard University Press.

Dienhart, A. (1998). *Reshaping fatherhood: The social construction of shared parenting.* Thousand Oaks, CA: Sage.

Goldner, V. (1989). Generation and gender: Normative and covert hierarchies. *Family Process, 21,* 17–31.

Goldner, V. (1991). Feminism and systemic practice: Two critical traditions in transition. *Journal of Family Therapy, l,* 95–104.

Goodrich, T. J. (2003). A feminist family therapist's work is never done. In L. B. Silverstein & T. J. Goodrich (Eds.), *Feminist family therapy: Empowerment in social context* (p. 4). Washington, DC: American Psychological Association.

Gottman, J. M. (1998). Toward a process model of men in marriages and families. In A. Booth & A. C. Crouter (Eds.), *Men in families* (pp. 149–192). Mahwah, NJ: Erlbaum.

Hochschild, A. (1989). *The second shift.* New York: Viking.

Jarrett, R. L., Roy, K. M., & Burton, L. M. (2002). Fathers in the "Hood": Insights from qualitative research on low-income African American men. In C. S. Tamis-LeMonda & N. Cabrera (Eds.), *Handbook of father involvement: Multidisciplinary perspectives* (pp. 211–248). Mahwah, NJ: Erlbaum.

Kerr, M. E., & Bowen, M. (1988). *Family evaluation.* New York: Norton.

Lerner, H. G. (1985). *The dance of anger.* New York: Harper & Row.

Lerner, H. G. (1988). Is family systems theory really systemic? A feminist communication. In L. Braverman (Ed.), *A guide to feminist family therapy* (pp. 47–63). New York: Harrington Park Press.

Leupnitz, D. (1988). *The family interpreted: Psychoanalysis, feminism, and family therapy.* New York: Basic Books.

Marlowe, F. (2002). Evolutionary perspectives. In C. S. Tamis-LeMonda & N. Cabrera (Eds.), *Handbook of father involvement: Multidisciplinary perspectives* (pp. 303–307). Mahwah, NJ: Erlbaum.

Pinderhughes, E. (1986). Minority women: A nodal position in the functioning of the social system. In M. Ault-Riche (Ed.), *Women and family therapy* (pp. 51–63). Rockville, MD: Appen Systems.

Pleck, J. H. (1997). Paternal involvement: Levels, sources, and consequences. In M. Lamb (Ed.), *The role of the father in child development* (3rd ed., pp. 66–103). New York: Wiley.

Sigle-Rushton, W., & Garfinkel, I. (2002). The effects of welfare, child support, and labor markets on father involvement. In C. S. Tamis-LeMonda & N. Cabrera (Eds.), *Handbook of father involvement: Multidisciplinary perspectives* (pp. 409–429). Mahwah, NJ: Erlbaum.

Toman, W. (1961). *Family constellation.* New York: Springer.

U.S. Bureau of the Census. (2001). *Current population reports P60–213: Money income in the United States 2000.* Washington, DC: Author.

CHAPTER 8

Cognitive Behavioral
Couple Therapy

Terence Patterson

I N PRESENTING THE essence of *cognitive behavioral couple therapy* (CBCT), it would be presumptuous to attempt to improve upon the many excellent articulations of the theories and methods currently in the literature (e.g., Bussod & Jacobson, 1983; Datilio, 1989; Epstein & Baucom, 2002; Gottman, 2002; Jacobson & Margolin, 1979; Stuart, 1980; Weiss & Perry, 2002; Whisman & Weinstock, 2002). The focus of this chapter is to identify the origins and practices specific to each key realm: the cognitive and the behavioral. The underlying premise of this discussion is that CBCT is not a singular model; it draws upon psychodynamic constructs as well as cognitive and behavioral principles and may also incorporate humanistic approaches. Thus, CBCT effectively spans the theoretical spectrum as it is commonly practiced and can be an extremely valuable integrative approach to use with a variety of problems and populations.

Without a clear understanding of the components of CBCT in regard to its foundations in major theories and methods, CBCT can become a haphazard approach that is indistinguishable from other models and become diminished in its effectiveness. For example, if psychodynamic constructs are emphasized in CBCT to the exclusion of cognitive restructuring, outcomes may be less than desired. Similarly, excessive attention to attributions (Fincham & Bradbury, 1993) may result in a low priority on needed behavior exchange skills; this is the risk involved with integrative models that attempt to incorporate too much. Therefore, CBCT integrates various

The expert assistance of Jennifer Henley, MA, in the preparation of this chapter is greatly appreciated.

aspects of functioning. Before any clinical theory or technique is applied, a functional assessment (Epstein, 1986) should be conducted to guide treatment planning.

It is beyond the scope of this chapter to conduct a meta-analysis of research in the field, but it is clear that there is more empirical support for this approach than for any other theoretical model (e.g., Bradbury & Fincham, 1987; Epstein & Jackson, 1978; Hahlweg & Markman, 1988; Jacobson, 1984; Jacobson & Follette, 1985; Jacobson, Follette, & Pagel, 1986; Jacobson, Follette, Revenstorf, et al., 1984; Jacobson, Schmaling, & Holtzworth-Munroe, 1987; Waring, Stalker, Carver, & Gitta, 1991; Wills, Faitler, & Snyder, 1987). The overall results show robust improvements in outcome on a number of variables, particularly and predictably for behavioral dysfunction in relationships. However, the field has generally moved away from research comparing CBCT with other models on global outcomes, such as satisfaction and quality of the relationship, and is attending more to process variables, such as the effect of specific interventions on target populations and problems, and is emphasizing the inclusion of enhanced and integrative techniques and concepts. A lively, significant debate took place over an extended period in the early 1990s concerning outcomes comparing behavioral and insight-oriented marital therapies. Many studies at that time questioned whether the manualized protocols that were used were distinctive from one another (there was much overlap between them), and whether outcomes (e.g., rates of divorce after treatment) were valid indicators of treatment success (Jacobson, 1991; Snyder, Wills, & Grady-Fletcher, 1991).

A comment is in order here about the current use of the term *cognitive-behavioral*. Over the past decade, it has become the most common response of students and clinicians in identifying their theoretical orientation. It is unclear whether these respondents are truly familiar with and trained in cognitive and behavior theory and intervention science, whether they mean they attend to thoughts and behaviors in addition to insight and transference, or whether they are merely identifying the model currently in vogue. As always, *competence* is the key to ethical and clinical integrity, and the objective of this chapter is to assist practitioners in understanding both cognitive and behavioral foundations so that they may implement them effectively. Numerous theorists, including Kelly and Halford (1995), have elucidated the elements of CBCT, and the following sections will attempt to further clarify its basic cognitive and behavioral foundations.

This chapter highlights the cognitive and behavioral foundations of CBCT, especially for the nonbehavioral practitioner. The wide range of problems and clients treated by CBCT are discussed, and key principles are illustrated in the case discussion. The main objective is for all clinicians who integrate cognitive and behavioral principles into their work to do so in an informed manner, and to apply those principles as competently as possible so that the best client outcomes can be achieved.

BEHAVIORAL FOUNDATIONS

Although behavioral principles have been known and applied for most of the past century in fields ranging from organizational development to education, it wasn't until the 1970s that behavior therapy became a distinct stream in outpatient psychotherapy. Previously, behavior therapy had been used extensively in residential settings and to some extent in outpatient practice for specific behavioral disorders, such as phobias (Wolpe, 1990). Four areas of behaviorism are especially pertinent to the emergence of mainstream behavior therapy: *classical conditioning, operant conditioning, social learning theory,* and *cognitive science.* (For a more detailed review of the fundamentals of behavior therapy, see Wolpe, 1990.)

Regarding couples, the first modality to emerge was *behavioral marital therapy,* based on the social learning approach of Bandura (1977). Jacobson and Margolin (1979) wrote the first comprehensive text on this model, and it was expanded in a later volume by Jacobson and Holtzworth-Munroe (1986). They identified its components as communication, problem solving, and behavior exchange. Stuart (1969) had written an earlier article on operant conditioning principles applied to marital therapy, and followed it with a book (Stuart, 1980) detailing a social learning model. Although substantially revised, and to some extent currently disregarded in the behavioral field, the three basic elements of communication, problem solving, and behavior exchange remain, in this author's opinion, the lynchpins or the sine qua non of effective intervention with couples.

The behavior therapies have often been characterized as being cold and sterile, and have been criticized for not including essential elements of relationship, such as love, sex, caring, and affection, as targets for assessment and intervention. Indeed, these and other dimensions have not been adequately emphasized in research-based, technical descriptions of CBCT, and this lack has contributed to the negative stereotyping of behavioral approaches. In reality, most CBCT practitioners do not ignore these basic factors in conducting a functional assessment and in focusing on the total context of relationships as part of treatment planning. An example is Stuart's (1980) emphasis on *caring days,* in which partners each devote days to doing specific activities requested by the other.

Other additions to the basic model that belie the stereotype of CBCT have gained widespread recognition. First is the importance of *acceptance* and *commitment,* which can be observed and operationalized behaviorally, treated as cognitions, or remain as constructs, depending on one's philosophical inclination. Jones, Christensen, and Jacobson (2000) describe this model as *integrative behavioral couple therapy* and emphasize the aspect of facilitating acceptance by one partner of the other's specific behavior, rather than attempting to change it. Commitment reflects willingness to put forth the necessary effort to make the relationship succeed. Hayes, Pankey, Gifford, Batten, and Quiñones (2002) called the model acceptance and commitment therapy (ACT) and apply it to numerous disorders. They state:

> ACT amplifies the scope of traditional classical and operant conditioning to the extent that it becomes a truly integrative operant approach. Historical criticisms such as the lack of attention to the nature of the relationship, the need for flexibility, the importance of cognition and affect, and the utility of openness to experience are thoroughly addressed and empirically substantiated in ACT. (p. 348)

Another model of couple therapy that belies the cold, technical label is not exclusively cognitive-behavioral and incorporates some of its methods is *emotion-focused therapy* (Greenberg & Johnson, 1988; Johnson, 2004; see also Bradley & Johnson, Chapter 11, this volume). It stresses emotional intensity between couples, has been used extensively in couples work, and has a significant amount of empirical support. Margolin (1987) has also described a focused approach to emotions using CBCT. Another form of CBCT, known as *enhanced CBCT* (Epstein & Baucom, 2002; Halford, Sanders, & Behrens, 1993) encompasses the full range of dyadic functioning, including personal characteristics, past history, and the total context of the couple's environment. All of the foregoing approaches give appropriate emphasis to the emotional, relationship, and historical aspects of CBCT.

In examining these seminal works and recent enhancements, it is possible to identify what is essential in cognitive behavioral couple therapy, which is sometimes drawn from other models and is often integrated into them.

First, all interactional therapists work with communication. Satir (1972), in her classic *Peoplemaking* described communicators in dysfunctional relationships as *placators, blamers, distractors,* and *computers.* Her approach and that of some other humanistic therapists has been identified as a communication-interactional approach. Gordon (1976), neither a behaviorist nor a psychotherapist, identified *I-messages* (congruent feeling-tone communications sent by a parent to a child) as an effective model for clear communication. *You-messages* are often blaming, ineffective, and hostile in tone. Couple therapists have extended these typologies to communication training with couples, both from a preventive and clinical perspective. All are based on social learning principles and characterized by clarity, congruence (verbal and nonverbal), and effectiveness. Emmelkamp and colleagues (1988) differentiate between the effects of communication training and cognitive therapy alone.

Behaviorists have described and systematized communication procedures and components in detail. Gottman (1979) described the elements of marital interaction, indicating that the intent of the sender of a message needs to be congruent with the actual impact on the receiver. Jacobson and Margolin (1979) identified communication training/retraining as necessary to couple therapy and specified a program of skill training, feedback, instructions, and behavioral rehearsal. Elements include empathy, assertiveness, cues, and role reversal. Gottman's (2002) multidimensional approach is based on decades of research, including his early work on communication and micro-analysis of thousands of videotaped discussions by couples. His approach incorporates essential behavioral foundations that focus on "start-ups" and utilize repair techniques in conversations that go awry. Girodo, Stein, and Dotzenroth (1980) and Hahlweg, Revenstorf, and Schindler (1984) also described early models of communication skills training in couple therapy.

The second critical behavioral element of *problem solving* addresses the dysfunctional pattern of aversive control that is often present in clinical couples (Baucom, 1982; Jacobson & Margolin, 1979; Johnson & Greenberg, 1985). By first elucidating the pattern and then teaching strategies of negotiation and compromise, problem solving modifies the pattern of negative exchanges in which one partner typically dominates the other verbally and behaviorally. An essential quid pro quo emerges from this process, in which partners begin to feel that they are able to get as much from the relationship as they give, a concept first introduced by Lederer and Jackson (1968). New problem-solving skills, coupled with effective communication, also serve a preventive function by obviating either future escalation of negative exchanges or a spinning out of control that entrenches dysfunctional patterns and resentment. The *setting* and *attitude* of problem solving is critical. The steps are detailed by Jacobson and Margolin (1979) as follows: (1) begin with something positive, (2) be specific, (3) express personal feelings directly, (4) be brief, (5) define only one problem at a time, (6) paraphrase the other's statements, (7) avoid inferences—discuss only what is factual, (8) focus on solutions, (9) emphasize mutuality and compromise, and (10) reach agreement before closing discussions.

The third fundamental behavioral element, *behavior exchange*, is integral to communication and problem solving. When communication becomes clear, direct, and congruent, and the mutual sense of reciprocity involved in the quid pro quo (a push for equity) emerges, a *contingency plan* or *contract* is developed (Jacobson & Margolin, 1979). It is a written agreement that relationship-enhancing behaviors will occur, along with rewards and built-in corrections to ensure compliance. One valuable component is the use of the Premack Principle (cf. Danaher, 1974), in which a high-probability behavior is performed only after another behavior that a partner desires is accomplished (e.g., Roberta goes to work in the morning *only after* she kisses Jack goodbye, as he had requested). Similar to communication and problem solving, behavior exchange incorporates systematic behavior therapy elements and involves the commonsense notion that individuals do not contribute freely to a relationship in which they do not feel they are receiving what they need in proportion to what they are giving. Thus, a comprehensive, methodical approach to open communication, compromise, and mutual exchange is the foundation of the behavioral underpinnings to relationship enhancement and to modification of dysfunctional interactions.

COGNITIVE UNDERPINNINGS

We now turn to the cognitive realm of CBCT in order to identify more clearly those elements that have developed from behavior therapy.

From a radical behavioral perspective, thoughts and feelings are viewed as aspects of private behaviors, and all aspects of functioning are seen as behaviors to be operationalized (Skinner, 1989). Cognitivists, however, generally view thoughts and behaviors as separate from each other. It is unclear whether this philosophical disparity was responsible for the later arrival of cognitive therapy as a major model or whether the field of psychotherapy was reluctant to integrate cognitive and behavioral elements, perhaps due to their technical nature. It is abundantly clear, however, that therapists have embraced the role of cognitions as elements for assessment and intervention, particularly in the past decade. Although the matter of cognitions as private behaviors or independent phenomena (Skinner, 1989) might be dismissed by some as insignificant, it is important to consider how these aspects affect assessment and treatment planning. One formulation of this issue is articulated by T. E. Patterson (1998), who recommended that the *etiology* and *objectives* of treatment should be factors in determining the essentials of a therapeutic approach. With this perspective, behavior therapy views learning as the essence of problems, and the objective is simply to modify behavior.

The social learning elements of communication, problem solving, and behavior exchange, which were described earlier in the passages on behavioral foundations, also contain cognitive components. As observable, measurable behaviors, they come into play when working in a cognitive mode as well, when CBCT clinicians across the spectrum focus upon partners' general views regarding relationships, expectations during the pair-bonding process, and attributions toward the other over time. Object relations theory surfaces when family-of-origin dynamics are examined as part of the need-fulfilling expectations partners have of their mates. These are clearly cognitions, and although they may be philosophically based on unconscious motivation in object relations theory, cognitivists explain these elements in terms of social learning and attribution theories. Simply stated, we learn from observing and experiencing interactions in relationships, and we base our expectations of others on these interactions. Partners in a relationship therefore assume that the other person will interact in certain ways based not just on superficial impressions, but on past experiences with relationships. They communicate, collaborate (or not), and generally interact based on these attributions and interactions.

The research of Baucom, Epstein, Sayers, and Sher (1987) clearly delineates five cognitive aspects of CBCT: selective attention, attributions, expectancies, assumptions, and standards. Attention refers to relationship-relevant events; the reasons a person believes his or her partner acts a certain way account for attributions; predictions for the future based on attributions are expectancies; one's beliefs about the way one's relationship works are assumptions; and standards refer to a partner's beliefs about the way things should be in the relationship. These cognitive variables are assessed through self and partner reports, observation, and interviews. The essence of cognitive intervention is *cognitive restructuring* of these five elements, typically with the integration of the behavioral components of communication and problem solving. However, the overall effects of cognitions as an addition to marital therapy remain inconclusive. Baucom and Lester (1986) concluded that when comparing behavioral marital therapy (BMT) with cognitive restructuring, and later comparing both BMT and cognitive restructuring with emotional expressiveness training (EET; Baucom, Sayers, & Sher, 1990), there were few significant differences to the overall effectivenesss of treatment when cognitive restructuring itself was added.

COGNITIVE-BEHAVIORAL INTEGRATION

The question arises in considering integration and emphasis of cognitive or behavioral elements, *What really is CBCT* (Baucom & Epstein, 1991)? Adhering to fundamental behavioral principles, a solid CBCT approach would begin with a functional assessment of the target problem and the contingencies that support it. It may be irrelevant whether one initially emphasizes thoughts or only includes them while focusing primarily on behaviors, as long as the intervention is tied to the target behaviors and modified as data emerges. A cognitivist who discovers that the initial focus on attributions has not resulted in change would then shift to modifying behaviors in the most effective way. Similarly, a behaviorist who included thoughts only incidentally might emphasize them to the extent that they influence target behaviors. In this fashion, an integrated approach would be appropriate, and the dispute over definitions and the primacy of cognitions or behaviors could be avoided.

But what of the clinician who uses some cognitive-behavioral approaches, but is not grounded in either cognitive or behavioral principles? As suggested in the introduction, although the majority of therapists use some form of behavioral technique, there is danger in applying them inappropriately or inadequately. For example, most couple therapists assign some activity for clients to engage in outside of therapy, whether it is as simple as keeping a journal or as potentially complex as using thought-stopping. The latter is a technique grounded in behavior analysis and covert sensitization and, if applied inadequately, can be futile and frustrating for all. The task of keeping a journal can be very simple, but clinicians should be aware of effective compliance-monitoring methods and the consequences of losing credibility if they do not follow up on assignments given to clients.

Similarly, consider the concept of *caring days,* mentioned earlier as a behavioral approach (Stuart, 1980). Many couple therapists prescribe the simple assignment of "doing something nice for your partner." Done effectively, this is a task based on an operant social learning model and involves assessment, collaboration, approximation, behavior exchange, and evaluation. From a cognitive perspective, it may be impossible to begin the discussion of doing things for each other without a thorough exploration of one or both partner's attribution of ulterior motives whenever a favor is done for them or of lingering resentment over real or imagined hurt. The simple assignment of doing something nice without integration of the relevant cognitive and behavioral principles may backfire and result in unintended consequences, such as clients dropping out of treatment.

Thus, a combined approach necessitates grounding in foundational principles, as does true *integrationism.* Psychotherapy integration (Goldfried & Castonguay, 1992) advocates grounding in the fundamental principles and methods to be included in an integrative model, rather than assembling bits and pieces accumulated through brief exposures. The latter approach, *eclecticism,* is often a wide rather than a deep methodology and can reflect knowing a little about a lot but very little about any one thing. As mentioned earlier, this style cannot only be ineffective but also frustrating and at times may result in inadvertent negative outcomes. Therefore, clinicians of all theoretical orientations are urged to become familiar with the principles and objectives underlying CBCT and to integrate them appropriately and systematically.

PROBLEMS AND DISORDERS TREATED

Besides addressing couple problems in communication, problem solving, behavior exchange, and cognitive restructuring, CBCT has been applied extensively to the treatment of couples and families with substance abuse, juvenile delinquency, depression, and health-related issues. In addition to describing work in these areas, treatment-planning decisions are also discussed in the following section.

G. R. Patterson (1982) was one of the earliest to describe a behavioral family approach to juvenile delinquency. He identified interactions used by couples intended to decrease negativity and to increase the positive affective climate in the family. Thus, attention to the types of couple interactions that pertain to overall family climate may be an effective means of creating a family atmosphere more conducive to clear communication and problem solving and may directly affect behaviors such as delinquency. Using a functional family therapy (FFT) model, Alexander and Parsons (1973) and Sexton and Alexander (2003; see also Mas & Alexander, Chapter 5, this volume) also apply behavioral methods to couples and families who have adolescents involved in delinquent behavior.

Depression has been identified extensively as a factor in the assessment and treatment of couple disorders under a CBCT model (Addis & Jacobson, 1991; Beach, Sandeen, & O'Leary, 1990; Dobson, Jacobson, & Victor, 1988; Follette & Jacobson, 1988; Gotlib & Beach, 1995; Jacobson, 1984; Scott, 1990; Teichman, Bar-El, Shor, & Elizur, 1998; Waring et al., 1988). Controversy exists regarding the etiology and sequence of depression in couples and whether the depression or the couple disorder is primary (i.e., which came first, which causes which, and which should receive emphasis). Jacobson, Dobson, Fruzettti, Schmaling, and Salusky (1991) found clinical samples with depressed individuals who were not dissatisfied with their marriages, and in these cases behavioral couple therapy was no more effective than other treatments for depression. Thus, it appears that couple dissatisfaction does affect depression, and couple therapy should be used in these cases to consolidate and extend the gains made in individual treatment (Alexander & Barton, 1995).

Numerous theorists and clinicians have identified approaches to substance abuse using CBCT methods (Fals-Stewart, Birchler, & O'Farrell, 1996; Noel & McCrady, 1993; Zweben, Pearlman, & Li, 1988, and O'Farrell, Choquette, & Henry, 1998). Approaches range from one partner observing the treatment of the abusing or addictive individual and using standard CBCT interventions with both partners, to involving extended community and family systems. In similar fashion, chronic pain (McGrath & Goodman, 1998), anxiety (Craske & Zoellner, 1995), and medical illness such as cancer (Carlson, Bultz, Speca, & St. Pierre, 2000) have been the focus of CBCT interventions, and a wide range of interventions have been used that are similar to those indicated above for substance abuse. Lichtenstein (1991) has described a method for using CBCT with couples who have children with disabilities.

There is nearly universal agreement among clinicians of various theoretical orientations that family involvement of some type is useful for most cultural groups in the treatment of a variety of psychological or medical disorders, and it appears that directive CBCT-type interventions are very commonly used, although not always comprehensively or systematically. In addition, CBCT methods such as homework assignments may seem intuitive, but they become effective therapeutic tools when they are applied methodically and in the appropriate context. Even more complex procedures such as systematic desensitization and paradoxical intervention can be taught to paraprofessionals and seasoned therapists alike, but perhaps the most important factor in applying CBCT methods to diverse problems is for clinicians is to use structured, precise interventions in order to increase their effectiveness.

ETHICAL CONSIDERATIONS

Couple therapy in general, and especially CBCT, raises particular ethical issues for clinicians. As indicated earlier, it is difficult to conceive of effective couple therapy that does not include some focus on communication, problem solving, behavior exchange, and exploration of attributions between partners. In addition, all forms of psychotherapy involve some potential risks, and the active, direct nature of CBCT requires special attention in order to attenuate any adverse consequences.

First, couple therapy may directly focus on aspects of difference and conflict between partners, at least in the short term. For example, highlighting unspoken expectations and attributions based on fantasies or previous relationships may initially contribute to dissonance for a couple. Second, clarifying communication may bring to light personal characteristics, behaviors, beliefs, and other realities that are aversive to the other partner. Third, behavioral rehearsal may inadvertently escalate conflict outside of sessions and result in precipitous action by one or both partners. Fourth, the specificity and distinctiveness of CBCT methods may lead a couple to assume incorrectly that they are being advised to follow a particular course in their relationship (e.g., to spend some time apart during their vacation). In the end, CBCT methods may be so direct that a couple might identify a particular intervention that they feel has led to the dissolution of their relationship. Therapists who use CBCT techniques need to be fully informed of the principles and methods that underlie them because of the potential consequences of inadequate or improper use. Clinicians must be trained to apply them systematically. Assessment, preparation, collaboration, and timing are key to effective implementation.

Similar to the ethical considerations in other forms of couple therapy, "change of format" issues as identified by Gottlieb (1995) are important considerations in CBCT. These include decisions about whether to interview partners separately; how much time to focus on an individual disorder; and disclosure of secrets, referrals, and decisions about whether to conduct couple, individual, family, or group therapy, or to refer for other specialty treatment. CBCT clinicians, by virtue of using systematic functional assessment and treatment planning, are more likely to make these types of decisions early in the process of consultation with a couple, and to formulate a specific clinical direction. This type of formulation is grounded in the empirical foundations of CBCT and ultimately enhances its ethical validity, but it may also result in misunderstanding if not presented clearly and thoroughly to couples. For a more extensive discussion on the ethical implications of cognitive-behavior therapy, refer to T. E. Patterson and Gottlieb, 2002.

Many of the aspects of CBCT focused on to this point are highlighted in the following case study.

CASE STUDY

The following case represents a couple from my clinical practice, with selected aspects modified to protect confidentiality. It was chosen because it involves a middle-of-the-road couple who are unhappy but not severely dysfunctional. They face fairly common twenty-first-century stressors. The assessment and treatment methods are typical of those I use and teach. The cognitive and behavioral elements discussed earlier are applied in this case.

BACKGROUND

José and Indira are 45 and 42 years old, respectively, have been together for 20 years, and have been married for 18 years. They have two children, Elena, 16, and Roberto, 13. José grew up in Arizona, where his parents have lived since emigrating from Mexico when he was 2 years old. Indira was born in India, and her parents have lived in northern California (near José and Indira's current home) since she was 5 years old. Both partners have college degrees and work full-time outside the home.

The couple sought treatment, saying that "things just aren't working" between them. Their lives are so busy that routine household chores barely get done; they rarely see their two children; and they feel they have lost intimacy as a couple. Their children are doing well enough, although Indira believes her daughter "is growing up too fast," and José is concerned about some of his son's friends. They feel like business partners rather than lovers, and their sex life is infrequent and routine. They visit each other's extended families periodically, but rarely have time for socializing with other couples or families.

José complains that Indira's family of origin tried to interfere and impose their traditional views on them and that he has assumed most of the household chores because Indira has been working long hours since her career began progressing. He also says that although she is a loving mother, she rarely has any time to do things for the children. The partners are abrupt and irritable with each other and rarely discuss what is happening between them directly. A colleague of José's recommended a problem-focused couple therapist.

ASSESSMENT

Preliminary   I was contacted and explained that I specialized in CBCT, with emphasis on the behavioral or action-oriented methods. I sent José and Indira each copies of the Couples Pre-Counseling Inventory (CPCI; Stuart & Jacobson, 1987), which each was asked to complete and bring to the first session. When they arrived, I scanned the inventories briefly before seeing the couple. I explained my informed consent form and theoretical approach and procedures, including fees, confidentiality, recordkeeping, and methods for contacting me. I then indicated that after the first session, I would complete a thorough review of their background information and inventory data, interview each of them separately, and then bring them back together in a third session for further assessment and feedback. I carefully told them that although it appeared at this point that I could assist them effectively, a contract for ongoing therapy would not be made with them until the end of the third session when a thorough assessment had been accomplished.

Findings   Upon briefly scanning the inventory, I noted discrepancies of 3 or more points on the CPCI (on a scale of 5) between Indira's and José's respective ratings on 4 out of 11 general sections: General and Specific Happiness, Communication, Sexual Adjustment, and Division of Home, Child Care, and Work Responsibilities. Because the theme of their initial comments focused on communication, I inquired further and found that the couple had never developed a method for discussing major issues (positive or negative) between them. During the early years of their relationship, they were head-over-heels in love with each other; they had few responsibilities and lots of time; and things went well for them. As they devoted more time to their careers and had children, they drifted into a routine that became increasingly difficult to manage. The discrepancies on their Happiness, Communication, Sexual Adjustment, and Home and Work Sections responses clearly reflected these difficulties. The computerized report and my analysis of the overall information provided by the couple confirmed these four aspects as major targets for treatment.

Individual interviews were conducted back-to-back during an extended second session, and I focused on briefly assessing José and Indira as individuals. Developmental, family, and health history were discussed in an attempt to evaluate individual strengths and deficits and to screen for major disorders. Primary emphasis was placed on determining each partner's acceptance of the other and commitment to the relationship—a major component added to CBCT by Jones et al. (2000). Both partners indicated that they were committed to their relationship and to working on their current difficulties. They had grown to accept each other's differences and truly liked each other, although humor and light moments had become infrequent in recent years. José stated that family was first and foremost for him, and he was uncomfortable knowing that Indira placed equal priority on her career. Neither had any major secrets relating to outside relationships, finances, past history, or any disorder that could interfere with improving their relationship.

At the end of the third session, I presented the following to Indira and José:

- Developmentally, their relationship began with excitement and intensity and progressed well during times of low stress.
- As their lives became busier and they took on more responsibilities, their basic affection and commitment to each other allowed them to function effectively for the most part, but as stresses and responsibilities increased, problems often remained unsolved, and their vitality and communication as a couple decreased.

- Their implicit expectation was that their earlier free and easy style would carry them through times that demanded greater planning, clearer communication, negotiation skills, and free time for themselves as a couple. As the stress increased, so did their sense of not getting what they needed from the relationship. Although each had successfully individuated from their respective family of origin, the pressure for Indira to be a traditional homemaker and for José to assert himself as head of the household, and their overloaded schedules weighed on them and resulted in some guilt, repression of feelings, and isolation from other dual-career couples.
- Their difficulties focused mainly on their General and Specific Happiness, Communication, Sexual Adjustment, and Home and Family Responsibilities (as identified on the CPCI), and these issues were compounded by the discrepancy in their respective perceptions of these areas.
- Their basic acceptance of each other, energy to work on their difficulties, and commitment to each other indicated strong potential for progressing to a more satisfying level in their relationship.

COGNITIVE-BEHAVIORAL FORMULATION

Based on the problems presented by this couple, an exploration of cognitive elements was essential. Unspoken assumptions and expectations were resulting in dysfunctional interactions and resentment, and I could not assume that acceptance and commitment levels were adequate at their current stage of development. They were also deficient in their knowledge and practice of communication, problem solving, and behavior exchange. Psycho-education and skill acquisition in these areas was essential. Thus, activation of more satisfying behaviors appeared to be contingent upon cognitive intervention, and both areas were emphasized in the treatment plan presented to the couple.

INTERVENTION

Contracting   During the fourth session, I proposed the following to Indira and José in the form of a written contract based on my assessment:

1. Weekly conjoint sessions of 75 minutes, initially for six more weeks followed by a mutual evaluation of progress and an option for renewal
2. The treatment would focus on:
   a. The partners' perceptions of their early relationship and style of relating and their expectations for dealing with children, home, work, and family
   b. Discussion and rehearsal of clear communication concepts and methods

    c. Discussion and rehearsal of effective problem-solving techniques
    d. Discussion and evaluation of the importance of both partners having the sense that they are receiving and giving equitably in the relationship
    e. Determination of each partner's ability to accept differences in the other and maintain a consistent sense of commitment
    f. In-session and at-home exercises, including some reading and videos on the concepts and skills they were working on
    g. Sessions at home where they would discuss their concerns about their children individually with each child and together as a family

Discussion of this treatment plan continued during the fourth session, and the couple and therapist signed it and began to implement it.

Progress   The first treatment session (end of number 4) and the subsequent one (number 5) focused on the cognitive aspects of initial perceptions and expectations about the relationship. The couple was animated in discussing how they met and were so excited about each other, and believed that the glow they felt would carry them through everything. They acknowledged that they assumed incorrectly that they did not need to plan their time more carefully; work on clear, direct communication; or develop negotiating skills. Their refrain was (commonly heard among clinical couples) "Why should we have to work so hard on our relationship?"

Sessions 6 and 7 involved my brief explanation of the principles of clear communication, including a handout on "I-messages" (Gordon, 1976). The concepts of empathy and listening skills, the difference between feeling and thinking, and assertiveness were also discussed (cf. Jacobson & Margolin, 1979). This was followed by behavioral rehearsal and role reversal, and as the couple took well to these ideas and techniques, they were urged to practice them during the week, including a 30- to 45-minute session consisting of only "feeling talk" and active listening.

During the eighth session, the feeling tone between Indira and José was notably more vital and positive. When I mentioned this, they responded that they realized that by facing their difficulties and working on them, they could move ahead and have more realistic expectations of each other. Consequently, their resentment and irritation with each other was decreasing. The session then moved from communication to problem solving. They identified and prioritized key problem areas and agreed to work on them one at a time.

The first area to be addressed was their concerns about their children. In the ninth session, they acknowledged their different perceptions regarding Elena and Roberto, but concluded that each of their perceptions were valid, and the couple could work with each other in addressing them. Because José felt strongly about Roberto's choice of friends and Indira was most concerned about Elena's "precociousness," they both agreed to have individual discussions with the child each was most concerned about and then to discuss the results as a couple. As it turned out, Indira was satisfied with Elena's comments and assurance that she was not in danger and knew her limits. José was less confident about Roberto's descriptions of his activities with his friends, and Indira agreed that the three of them would speak together. Essentially, a mutually supportive process for problem solving was created, and they proceeded to work on their sexual relationship and division of home responsibilities for six additional sessions following the end of the contract, bringing the total to 15.

As the treatment reached conclusion, the issue of behavior exchange, or quid pro quo, was highlighted as a means of integrating the cognitive, communication, and problem-solving dimensions. By progressing sequentially through these areas, Indira and José each came to feel that their partner was truly as invested in the relationship as they were. I pointed out that this sense of equity is essential to maintaining goodwill in the relationship, and for accepting differences and strengthening commitment. Further, I explained that at any moment, the balance of responsibility may be 80%/20% when one partner shoulders most of the responsibilities while the other is ill, has extra work commitments, or may be caring for an aging parent. Such an imbalance requires open discussion and negotiation, with a clear sense that the balance of responsibility will be more nearly equal when the stresses of the 20% partner decrease. With this sense of equal behavior exchange, clear communication, and good problem-solving skills, all aspects of a relationship can remain functional and satisfactory over time.

CASE ANALYSIS

In many respects, José and Indira are typical of couples who met each other at a relatively young age and who remain together for decades. They were very excited about each other and had a free and easy relationship until their lives became more complex. The idea of working on their relationship never occurred to them. There was some remote pressure from Indira's family and some culturally based expectations, although these were mediated by educational and geographic factors. Mostly, they are a typical middle-class, middle-aged, dual-career couple with predictable stressors. A general problem assessment indicated a lack of fundamental relationship skills. Their relationship needed routine maintenance.

Initially, an open discussion between Indira and José was needed to clarify their perceptions and feelings about their relationship. Numerous assumptions had evolved over the years, and because they were unspoken, they led to misperception, confusion, and irritation. As these became explicit, it was important for both partners to state their reactions of acceptance and commitment (or lack of them) to each other regarding major issues. This is an important cognitive process in understanding attitudes and attributions, and partners usually develop a more positive view of each other as a result. As the couple acknowledged their lack of direct communication, their tension began to ease and they began to feel better about each other. This shift might have been seen as a sort of spontaneous remission. It was important for the therapist to reinforce this change, while remaining focused on the key areas they needed to address systematically as a couple. Although cognitive behavioral clinicians acknowledge the significance of problem awareness and feeling tone, improvement in these areas is not sufficient for therapeutic effectiveness. Without sufficient attention to skill acquisition in the identified areas, the problems are likely to remain unresolved and the couple remains unequipped to deal successfully with similar matters in the future. Thus, the behavioral contract was presented to them at the end of the third session in order to obtain their explicit agreement to work on these issues.

Behaviorally, the couple needed to acquire the skills of first-person, assertive, effective, and functional communication, negotiation, and behavior exchange. Their educational level, pragmatism, and commitment enabled them to acknowledge their problems, accept each other's influence (Gottman, 2002), acquire skills relatively easily, and prioritize their schedules to be more in line with their values. Specific focus on the allocation of household and family tasks allowed them to rectify the inequity that had been occurring and to balance activities among family members. It was necessary for the misunderstanding and irritation between them to decrease before addressing sexual activity more intensely. At that point, I could renegotiate with them to assess their sexual relationship in greater detail, and to focus on this aspect with them or to refer them to a specialist. This was also true of devoting attention to any problems involving their children that may require a referral; it should not be assumed that the couple's initial request for treatment would include specialized interventions within the course of couple therapy. Although recommendations for referral for specialized treatment should be made very clear, a couple always has the right to accept or reject them.

As mentioned above under treatment formulation, the assessment of this couple indicated the need for a balance between cognitive and behavioral interventions, which were often intertwined. Without systematic assessment, this dual-focused goal would not have emerged clearly, and unfocused interventions would not have addressed the relevant aspects adequately. The therapist's awareness of assessment, developmental, and cultural issues, and ability to build rapport and implement targeted techniques enabled the couple to make significant improvements in their relationship. The approach illustrated in this case should be useful for all who employ CBCT methods in their work with couples.

SUMMARY AND IMPLICATIONS FOR THE FUTURE

The premise of this chapter is that cognitive and behavioral interventions are used in nearly every active form of couple therapy, and an attempt has been made to delineate the distinct components that are specific to the cognitive and behavioral realms. At the same time, it is clear that CBCT integrates aspects of other models and, as is true of psychotherapy in general, these integrative elements are not always clearly identified as to their origin. The more that clinicians are able to identify the foundations of specific interventions and constructs, the better they are able to grasp the best context and most comprehensive methods for applying them.

Although there is evidence that both behavioral and cognitive techniques are effective for specific problems that appear in couple therapy (e.g., communication, role expectations, and inequity), there is little empirical confirmation that the addition of cognitive components (such as restructuring) results in significantly better outcomes, as mentioned previously in this chapter. However, because most areas of psychotherapy outcome research remain equivocal at best, there is no reason to exclude cognitive or other techniques that may enhance compliance, produce greater understanding, and appear to be positive from both the couple's and therapist's perspectives. An intensive review of past experiences, attention to the therapist-client relationship, or a focus on spiritual concerns may be included in treatment from an intuitive or practical viewpoint, even though these are not a formal aspect of CBCT tradition. A caveat is that techniques need to be selected thoughtfully, and not contraindicated (e.g., dream analysis or deterministic attributions would be considered incongruent with a CBCT model). Treatment approaches always need to be based on assessment and carefully matched with client needs and expectations.

Random eclecticism has been decried both in this chapter and elsewhere, and *integration* is being promoted widely. Although an informed use of techniques from various models can be logically assimilated into a solid theoretical framework, true integration of seemingly disparate theories is a more difficult matter. A solid grounding in diverse theoretical models *and* techniques is essential for successful integration to occur. Novice clinicians in particular are advised to develop competence before using a theoretically integrated model.

Because of its wide range of techniques and pragmatic foundations, CBCT can be used for many types of issues presented in couple therapy, and it is effective for clients who vary greatly by culture, presenting problem, sexual orientation, age, setting, disability, and other factors. The empirical basis for CBCT provides ethical grounding for its diverse methods. However, because of the complexity that is often involved in using CBCT techniques appropriately, clinicians are advised to be skilled in applying them. Continuing education, reading, and supervision can assist in developing competence for ethical, effective practice. Therapists need to be open to using a systematic approach in order for CBCT to be successful.

The future appears to be bright for CBCT. A large number of therapists from all disciplines identify themselves as cognitive behavioral. Training programs and continuing education are increasingly emphasizing CBCT methods. It is clear that CBCT is highly adaptable to short-term and managed-care models as well, and extensive, ongoing CBCT research will continue to demonstrate its applicability to clients, insurers, and clinicians. Psychotherapy integration is also a growing trend, and the natural appeal of blending theories and techniques will undoubtedly persist and increasingly be validated by research. It is hoped that these trends will be accompanied by recognition by all in the psychotherapy field of the need for a complete understanding and thorough training in the foundations of cognitivism, behaviorism, and other relevant integrative approaches.

REFERENCES

Addis, M. E., & Jacobson, N. S. (1991). Integration of cognitive therapy and behavioral marital therapy for depression. *Journal of Psychotherapy Integration, 1,* 249–264.

Alexander, J. F., & Barton, C. (1995). Family therapy research. In R. H. Mikesell, D.-D. Lusterman, & S. H. McDaniel (Eds.), *Integrating family therapy: Handbook of family psychology and systems therapy* (pp. 199–215). Washington, DC: American Psychological Association.

Alexander, J. F., & Parsons, B. V. (1973). Short-term behavior interventions with delinquent families: Impact on family process and recidivism. *Journal of Abnormal Psychology, 81,* 219–225.

Bandura, A. (1977). *A social learning theory.* Englewood Cliffs, NJ: Prentice-Hall.

Baucom, D. H. (1982). A comparison of behavioral contracting and problem solving/communications training in behavioral marital therapy. *Behavior Therapy, 13,* 162–174.

Baucom, D. H., & Epstein, N. (1991). Will the real cognitive behavioral marital therapy please stand up? *Journal of Family Psychology, 4,* 394–401.

Baucom, D. H., Epstein, N., Sayers, S. L., & Sher, T. G. (1987). The role of cognitions in marital relationships: Definitional, methodological, and conceptual issues. *Journal of Consulting and Clinical Psychology, 57,* 31–38.

Baucom, D. H., & Lester, G. W. (1986). The usefulness of cognitive restructuring as an adjunct to behavioral marital therapy. *Behavior Therapy, 17,* 385–403.

Baucom, D. H., Sayers, S. L., & Sher, T. G. (1990). Supplementing behavioral marital therapy with cognitive restructuring and emotional expressiveness training: An outcome investigation. *Journal of Consulting and Clinical Psychology, 58,* 636–645.

Beach, S. R. M., Sandeen, E. E., & O'Leary, K. D. (1990). *Depression in marriage.* New York: Guilford Press.

Bradbury, T. N., & Fincham, F. D. (1987). Assessing the effects of behavioral marital therapy: Assumptions and measurement strategies. *Clinical Psychology Review, 7,* 525–538.

Bussod, N., & Jacobson, N. S. (1983). Cognitive behavioral marital therapy. *Counseling Psychologist, 11,* 57–63.

Carlson, L. E., Bultz, B. D., Speca, M. & St. Pierre, M. (2000). Partners of cancer patients: Part II. Current psychosocial interventions and suggestions for improvement. *Journal of Psychosocial Oncology, 18*(3), 33–43.

Craske, M. G., & Zoellner, L. A. (1995). Anxiety disorders: The role of marital therapy. In N. S. Jacobson & A. S. Gurman (Eds.), *Clinical handbook of marital therapy* (pp. 394–410). New York: Guilford Press.

Danaher, B. G. (1974). Theoretical foundations and clinical applications of the premack principle: Review and critique. *Behavior Therapy, 5*, 307–324.

Dattilio, F. M. (1989). A guide to cognitive marital therapy. In P. A. Keller & S. R. Heyman (Eds.), *Innovations in clinical practice: A source book* (Vol. 8, pp. 27–42). Sarasota, FL: Professional Resource Exchange.

Dobson, K. S., Jacobson, N. S., & Victor, J. (1988). Integration of cognitive therapy and behavioral marital therapy. In J. F. Clarkin, C. I., Haas, C. L. Glick, & I. D. Glick, (Eds.), *Affective disorders and the family: Assessment and treatment* (pp. 53–88). New York: Guilford Press.

Emmelkamp, P. M. G., Van-Linden-Van-den-Heuvell, C., Ruphan, M., Sanderman, R., Scholing, A., et al. (1988). Cognitive and behavioral interventions: A comparative evaluation with clinically distressed couples. *Journal of Family Psychology, 1*, 365–377.

Epstein, N. B. (1986). Cognitive marital therapy: Multi-level assessment and intervention. *Journal of Rational Emotive Therapy, 4*, 68–81.

Epstein, N. B., & Baucom, D. H. (2002). *Enhanced cognitive-behavioral therapy for couples: A contextual approach.* Washington, DC: American Psychological Association.

Epstein, N. B., & Jackson, E. (1978). An outcome study of short-term communication training with married couples. *Journal of Consulting and Clinical Psychology, 46*, 207–121.

Fals-Stewart, W., Birchler, G. R., & O'Farrell, T. J. (1996). Behavioral couple therapy for male substance-abusing patients: Effects on relationship adjustment and drug-using behavior. *Journal of Consulting and Clinical Psychology, 64*(5), 959–972.

Fincham, F. D., & Bradbury, T. N. (1993). Marital satisfaction, depression, and attributions. A longitudinal analysis. *Journal of Personality and Social Psychology, 64*, 442–452.

Follette, W. C., & Jacobson, N. S. (1988). Behavioral marital therapy in the treatment of depressive disorders. In I. R. H. Falloon (Ed.), *Handbook of behavioral family therapy* (pp. 257–284). New York: Guilford Press.

Girodo, M., Stein, S. J., & Dotzenroth, S. E. (1980). The effects of communication skills training and contracting on marital relations. *Behavioral Engineering, 6*, 61–76.

Goldfried, M. R., & Castonguay, L. G. (1992). The future of psychotherapy integration. *Psychotherapy, 29*(1), 4–10.

Gordon, T. (1976). *Parent effectiveness training: Workbook.* Solana Beach, CA: Effectiveness Training Associates.

Gotlib, I. H., & Beach, S. R. H. (1995). A marital/family discord model of depression: Implications of therapeutic intervention. In N. S. Jacobson & A. S. Gurman (Eds.), *Clinical handbook of marital therapy* (pp. 411–436). New York: Guilford Press.

Gottlieb, M. C. (1995). Ethical issues in change of format and live supervision. In R. H. Mikesell, D.-D. Lusterman, & S. H. McDaniel (Eds.), *Integrating family therapy: Handbook of family psychology and systems therapy* (pp. 561–570). Washington, DC: American Psychological Association.

Gottman, J. M. (1979). *Marital interaction: Experimental investigations.* New York: Academic Press.

Gottman, J. M. (2002). A multidimensional approach to couples. In T. Patterson (Ed.), *Comprehensive handbook of psychotherapy: Vol. 2. Cognitive-behavioral approaches* (pp. 355–372). New York: Wiley.

Greenberg, L. S., & Johnson, S. M. (1988). *Emotion-focused therapy for couples.* New York: Guilford Press.

Hahlweg, K., & Markman, H. J. (1988). Effectiveness of behavioral marital therapy: Empirical status of behavioral techniques in preventing and alleviating marital distress. *Journal of Consulting and Clinical Psychology, 56,* 440–447.

Hahlweg, K., Revenstorf, D., & Schindler, L. (1984). Effects of behavioral marital therapy on couples' communication and problem-solving skills. *Journal of Consulting and Clinical Psychology, 52,* 553–566.

Halford, W. K., Sanders, M. R., & Behrens, B. C. (1993). A comparison of the generalization of behavioral marital therapy and enhanced behavioral marital therapy. *Journal of Consulting and Clinical Psychology, 61,* 51–60.

Hayes, S. C., Pankey, J., Gifford, E. V., Batten, S. V., & Quiñones, R. (2002). Acceptance and commitment therapy in experiential avoidance disorders. In T. Patterson (Ed.), *Comprehensive handbook of psychotherapy: Vol. 2. Cognitive-behavioral approaches* (pp. 319–351). New York: Wiley.

Jacobson, N. S. (1984). A component analysis of behavioral marital therapy: The relative effectiveness of behavior exchange and communication/problem solving training. *Journal of Consulting and Clinical Psychology, 52*(2), 295–305.

Jacobson, N. S. (1991). Behavioral versus insight-oriented marital therapy: Labels can be misleading. *Journal of Consulting and Clinical Psychology, 59,* 142–145.

Jacobson, N. S., Dobson, K., Fruzettti, A. E., Schmaling, K. B., & Salusky, S. (1991). Marital therapy as a treatment for depression. *Journal of Consulting and Clinical Psychology, 59,* 547–557.

Jacobson, N. S., & Follette, W. C. (1985). Clinical significance of improvement resulting from two behavioral marital therapy components. *Behavior Therapy, 16,* 249–262.

Jacobson, N. S., Follette, W. C., & Pagel, M. (1986). Predicting who will benefit from behavioral marital therapy. *Journal of Consulting and Clinical Psychology, 54,* 518–522.

Jacobson, N. S., Follette, W. C., Revenstorf, D., Baucom, D. H., Hahlweg, K., & Margolin, G. (1984). Variability in outcome and clinical significance of behavioral marital therapy: A reanalysis of outcome data. *Journal of Consulting and Clinical Psychology, 52,* 497–504.

Jacobson, N. S., & Holtzworth-Munroe, A. (1986). Marital therapy: A social learning/cognitive perspective. In N. S. Jacobson & A. S. Gurman (Eds.), *Clinical handbook of marital therapy* (pp. 29–70). New York: Guilford Press.

Jacobson, N. S., & Margolin, G. (1979). *Marital therapy.* New York: Brunner/Mazel.

Jacobson, N. S., Schmaling, K. B., & Holtzworth-Munroe, A. (1987). Component analysis of behavioral marital therapy: 2-year follow-up and prediction of relapse. *Journal of Marital and Family Therapy, 13,* 187–195.

Johnson, S. M. (2004). *Attachment processes in couple and family therapy.* New York: Guilford Press.

Johnson, S. M., & Greenberg, L. S. (1985). Differential effects of experiential and problem-solving interventions in resolving marital conflict. *Journal of Consulting and Clinical Psychology, 53,* 175–184.

Jones, J., Christensen, A., & Jacobson, N. (2000). Integrative behavioral couple therapy. In F. M. Dattilio & L. J. Bevilacqua (Eds.), *Comparative treatments for relationship dysfunction: Springer series on comparative treatments for psychological disorders* (pp. 186–209). New York: Springer.

Kelly, A. B., & Halford, W. K. (1995). The generalisation of cognitive behavioural marital therapy in behavioural, cognitive and physiological domains. *Behavioural and Cognitive Psychotherapy, 23,* 381–398.

Lederer, W. J., & Jackson, D. D. (1968). *Mirages of marriage.* New York: Norton.

Lichtenstein, J. F. (1991). Support for couples with children with disabilities: Behavioral marital therapy treatment. *Dissertation Abstracts International, 51,* 3385.

Margolin, G. (1987). Marital therapy: A cognitive-behavioral-affective approach. In N. S. Jacobson (Ed.), *Psychotherapists in clinical practice: Cognitive and behavioral perspectives* (pp. 232–285). New York: Guilford Press.

McGrath, P. J., & Goodman, J. E. (1998). Pain in childhood. In P. J. Graham (Ed.), *Cognitive-behaviour therapy for children and families* (pp. 143–155). New York: Cambridge University Press.

Noel, N. E., & McCrady, B. S. (1993). Alcohol focused spouse involvement with behavioral marital therapy. In T. J. O'Farrell (Ed.), *Treating alcohol problems: Marital and family interventions* (pp. 210–235). New York: Guilford Press.

O'Farrell, T. J., Choquette, K. A., & Henry, S. G. (1998). Couples relapse prevention sessions after behavioral marital therapy for male alcoholics: Outcomes during the three years after starting treatment. *Journal of Studies on Alcohol, 59,* 357–370.

Patterson, G. R. (1982). *Coercive family processes.* Eugene, OR: Castalia.

Patterson, T. E. (1998). Theoretical unity and technical eclecticism: Pathways to coherence in family therapy. *American Journal of Family Therapy, 25*(2), 97–109.

Patterson, T. E., & Gottlieb, M. C. (2002). Ethical issues. In T. Patterson (Ed.), *Comprehensive handbook of psychotherapy: Vol. 2. Cognitive-behavioral approaches* (pp. 587–610). New York: Wiley.

Satir, V. M. (1972). *Peoplemaking.* Palo Alto, CA: Science and Behavior Books.

Scott, M. (1990). Tackling depression: Cognitive therapy and cognitive behavioural marital therapy. In W. Dryden & M. Scott (Eds.), *An introduction to cognitive-behaviour therapy: Theory and applications* (pp. 19–30). Loughton, England: Gale Centre.

Sexton, T. L., & Alexander, J. F. (2003). A mature clinical model for working with at-risk adolescents and their families. In T. L. Sexton, G. R. Weeks, & M. S.

Robbins (Eds.), *Handbook of family therapy* (pp. 323–350). New York: Brunner-Routledge.

Skinner, B. F. (1989). The origins of cognitive thought. *American Psychologist, 44*(1), 13–18.

Snyder, D. K., Wills, R. M., & Grady-Fletcher, A. (1991). Long-term effectiveness of behavioral versus insight-oriented marital therapy: A 4-year follow-up study. *Journal of Consulting and Clinical Psychology, 59,* 138–141.

Stuart, R. B. (1969). Operant interpersonal treatment of marital discord. *Journal of Consulting and Clinical Psychology, 33,* 675–682.

Stuart, R. B. (1980). *Helping couples change: A social learning approach to marital therapy.* New York: Guilford Press.

Stuart, R. B., & Jacobson, B. (1987). *Couple's pre-counseling inventory* Champaign, IL: Research Press.

Teichman, Y., Bar-El, Z., Shor, H., & Elizur, A. (1998). Changes in cognitions, emotions, and behaviors in depressed patients and their spouses following marital cognitive therapy, traditional cognitive therapy, pharmacotherapy, and no intervention. *Journal of Psychotherapy Integration, 8,* 27–53.

Waring, E. M., Chamberlaine, C. H., McCrank, E. W., Stalker, C. A., et al. (1988). Dysthymia: A randomized study of cognitive marital therapy and antidepressants. *Canadian Journal of Psychiatry, 33,* 96–99.

Waring, E. M., Stalker, C. A., Carver, C. M., & Gitta, M. Z. (1991). Waiting list controlled trial of cognitive marital therapy in severe marital discord. *Journal of Marital and Family Therapy, 17,* 243–256.

Weiss, R. L., & Perry, B. A. (2002). Behavioral couples therapy. In T. Patterson (Ed.), *Comprehensive handbook of psychotherapy: Vol. 2. Cognitive-behavioral approaches* (pp. 395–419). New York: Wiley.

Whisman, M. A., & Weinstock, L. M. (2002). Cognitive therapy with couples. In T. Patterson (Ed.), *Comprehensive handbook of couple therapy: Vol. 2. Cognitive-behavioral approaches* (pp. 373–394). New York: Wiley.

Wills, R. M., Faitler, S. L., & Snyder, D. K. (1987). Distinctiveness of behavioral versus insight-oriented marital therapy: An empirical analysis. *Journal of Consulting and Clinical Psychology, 55,* 685–690.

Wolpe, J. (1990). *The practice of behavior therapy* (4th ed.). New York: Pergamon Press.

Zweben, A., Pearlman, S., & Li, S. (1988). A comparison of brief advice and conjoint therapy in the treatment of alcohol abuse: The results of the marital systems study. *British Journal of Addiction, 18,* 899–916.

CHAPTER 9

Object Relations Couple Therapy

David E. Scharff and Yolanda de Varela

Object relations couple therapy integrates in-depth individual dynamics with a systemic understanding of couples and the larger family. It stresses the intergenerational origins of development and the centrality of relationships. The couple has an overarching relational personality unique to that pair that also contributes to the evolution of each individual. Their relationship is also in a systemic relationship to the larger family that includes children or aging parents and extends to the social groups in which the couple and family exist. We believe this way of thinking provides the most in-depth way of understanding—and of intervening with—couples, both within the larger ecological situations in which they live and in resonance with individual issues.

Object relations therapy is centered on the relationship between the partners, considering both their patterns of interaction and the contributions of each individual. We focus on helping the couple achieve the level of function appropriate to their stage in life (e.g., newlyweds, new parents, retirement) and the intimacy that they seek—rather than on symptom relief alone.

Object relations theory builds on the work of Ronald Fairbairn (1952), a Scottish psychoanalyst who modified analytic theories of development from the drive-centered, linear thinking of Freud and created a cybernetic view of psychic structure with internal parts in dynamic relation in line with the general systems theory developing in the late 1950s. He proposed that the need for relationships is most important to children and adults, rather than gratification as Freud had proposed. The child, centered on its relationship with its mother (or other primary caretaker), inevitably experiences dissatisfaction because no mother can be perfectly attuned. The infant internalizes (or introjects) the image of the mother in order to get control of the pain of rejection, but now experiences similar hurt inside that resembles the external relationship. Then the child performs a second set of defensive mental functions, splitting off the painful part of the mother (not the mother herself, but an internal image that is now the internal object of the infant's longing, love, hate, or interest). Once this painful internal object is split off from the main core object, it is repressed, put out of central awareness as too painful to be kept in consciousness. Splitting and repression continue unconsciously, powered by the main core of the self known as the *central ego*. However, it is not possible to repress just the object. A part of the self that is in internal relationship to the painful part-object is also split off and repressed, and the relationship between self part and object part is marked and given meaning by the affects that characterize it, in this case, the affects of pain, anger, sorrow, and frustration. This constitutes the rejecting internal object relationship.

At the other end of the continuum is what Fairbairn called "the need exciting object relationship," or "exciting object" for short. The mother who overstimulates, overfeeds, anxiously hovers, or is sexually seductive evokes in the infant unsatisfiable, painful neediness. The infant takes in, splits off, and represses an image of its experience of this tantalizing mother, and splits off the part of the self that longs for her, constructing an internal relationship marked affectively by unrequited longing, unsatisfiable desire, and frustration.

These two classes of unconscious object relationships (exciting and rejecting) feel bad to the child. The more conscious relationship between the central ego and its ideal (or good-enough object) is characterized by fuller, acceptable feelings stemming from satisfiable desire and acceptable limits in relationships.

These six internal structures (Figure 9.1) are the parts of a dynamic organization. The anti-libidinal object constellation attacks and secondarily represses the libidinal (desiring) constellation as it presses to be reconnected with the central ego. That means it is easier to hate someone than to long for them in a situation that will never give satisfaction. Some couples fight so fiercely that we wonder why they stay together. They do so because their unsatisfiable libidinal longing for each other is further buried from awareness by an attack by the anti-libidinal or rejecting ego. Likewise, a sugary-sweet, cloying couple can leave therapists feeling annoyed when they use libidinal, exciting relationships to further disguise the rejecting anti-libidinal system. Figure 9.1 provides an overview of Fairbairn's theory of psychic structure and its internal dynamic quality.

CASE STUDY

Dennis, 38, called asking for an urgent appointment with me [Y. de Varela] because his marriage was about to end in divorce after eight years. Christie, 37, was fed up with his verbal abuse, and now Dennis had pushed her. Dennis was scared Christie had gotten mad enough to walk out.

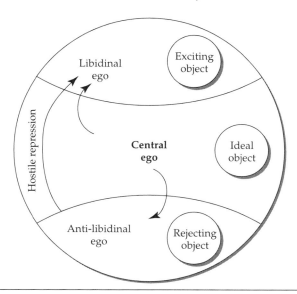

Figure 9.1 Fairbairn's Model of Psychic Organization. The central ego in relation to the ideal object is in conscious interaction with the caretaker (or spouse). The central ego represses the split-off libidinal and anti-libidinal aspects of its experience of others along with corresponding parts of the ego and accompanying affects that remain unconscious. The libidinal system is further repressed by the anti-libidinal system. © 1982 David Scharff. Used with permission.

Christie represents alternately both the exciting and fearful internal object for Dennis as he craves and then attacks her. Dennis represents an internal rejecting object for Christie. She longs for him, but immediately experiences him as a persecutory object and rejects him. Their relationship reproduces individual internal issues in their interaction, producing a joint personality that is fearfully dominated by their shared rejecting object relations.

A THEORY OF UNCONSCIOUS COMMUNICATION

To make an object relations theory of individual development applicable to conjoint therapy, we need a theory of unconscious communication. Melanie Klein (1946/1975), a London analyst born in Germany, coined the term *projective identification* for the way a person evacuates part of his mind into another person's mind in order to rid himself of excessive anger or other unacceptable, dangerous elements. We now believe that all persons in intimate relationships use projective identification not only to protect themselves, but also to communicate in depth (J. S. Scharff, 1992). An infant puts unthought feelings, needs, and fears into its mother through facial and bodily gestures, vocal intonation, and subtle eye movements. The mother takes in these communications through *introjective identification*—through resonance with her own internal object organization, thereby joining with the infant's experience. Her past experience of distress, fear, or happiness lets her understand the infant's experience. The experience of getting to know each other occurs through endless iterations of these cycles of projective and introjective identification, which go on in both directions: The mother also puts her anxieties about being a mother into the infant, who identifies with them and if things are going well, projects back reassurance. In infancy, the quality of these interactions is the major component in determining the security of the infant's attachment to the parents (Fonagy, Gergely, Jurist, & Target, 2003). In adulthood, the mutuality of these cycles is equally important and more reciprocal. Couples engage continuously in cycles of projective and introjective identification that are by nature largely profoundly unconscious. Therapy makes these matters more conscious so that a couple has new choices about how to relate.

Figure 9.2 shows the cycle of projective and introjective identification between a mother and infant that could equally be between spouses. The infant unconsciously seeks an exciting object identification with the mother, for example by crying for more to eat. In the figure, the mother shakes off the identification—identifying instead with the experience of rejection her refusal brings. Rejecting the infant's excess neediness results in the infant's enlarging the rejecting object constellation.

CASE STUDY

Dennis comes from a prominent family whose secret is his mother's illegitimacy. Raised by her father, she refused to acknowledge her mother. Dennis grew up longing for this exiled grandmother, because his mother rejected her mother-in-law, too. Dennis unconsciously experienced his mother's hatred as reliving her repressed longings for her own mother. The unexpressed longing hidden beneath her hatred came through as though it were his longing for the mother she could not be.

Christie was the youngest of three girls. Her parents, married to others, met in a celebrated, scandalous affair. Disinherited and banned socially, they escaped to Europe where their first child was born before they could get divorces. Years later, they married while Christie's mother was carrying her.

In a system of mutual projective identification, the couple replays both kinds of repressed bad objects described by Fairbairn, living out in their relationship both the longing and rejection they absorbed from their parents during painful childhoods, nourished in emotionally impoverished families.

HOLDING AND CONTAINMENT

The mother-infant relationship is marked by two processes central to couple therapy. The first, psychological *holding,* is analogous to the way a parent holds a child in an "arms around" attitude to provide for safety, growth, and development. We call this the *contextual relationship.* Within this envelope of safety, the parent offers herself in a focused eye-to-eye relationship

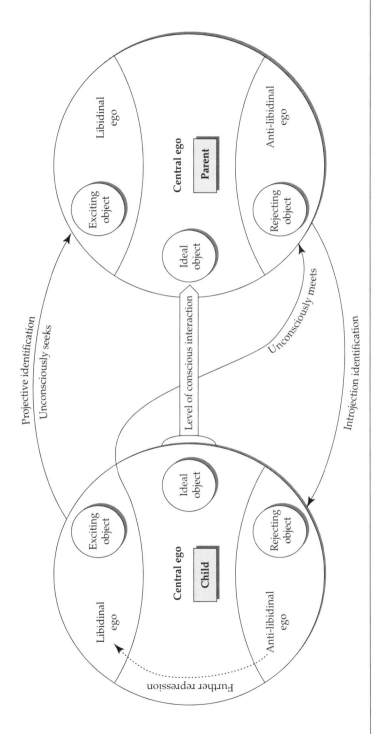

Figure 9.2 The Action of Projective and Introjective Identification. The mechanism here is the interaction of the child's projective and introjective identifications with the parent as the child meets frustration, unrequited yearning, or trauma. (The same situation could apply to two adult partners.) The diagram depicts the child longing to have his needs met and identifying with similar trends in the parent via projective identification. The child meeting with rejection identifies with the frustration of the parent's own anti-libidinal system via introjective identification. In an internal reaction to this frustration, the libidinal system is further repressed by the renewed force of the child's anti-libidinal system. © 1982 David Scharff. Used with permission.

that is subjectively I-to-I, that is, a direct communication of the intimate couple's inner feelings and inner worlds. The mother is also the object of the child's love, hate, and interest, and he uses her to fashion his world of internal objects in the *direct* or *focused relationship*. As the infant spends less time in the parent's arms, a space opens between infant and parent that we call the "transitional space" because it mediates between inner and outer world of both parent and child—between the parent and the child, and between the contextual and focused aspects of the relationship (D. E. Scharff & Scharff, 1991; Winnicott, 1951/1975). Figure 9.3 illustrates a conceptual basis for our use of transference and countertransference in couple therapy.

CASE STUDY

Dennis and Christie's holding capacity is severely compromised. In the first three years of weekly treatment, progress was slow, largely because they

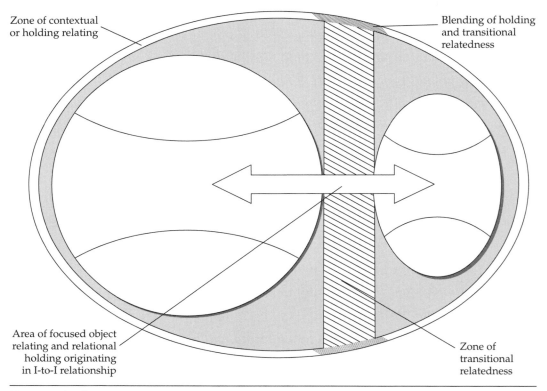

Figure 9.3   Contextual Holding, the Transitional Space, and Focused Relating. Focused (or centered or I-to-I) relating occurs in and across the transitional space. The transitional space is in contact with both contextual relating and focused relating, and is also the zone with blends of the two. © 1991 D. Scharff and J. S. Scharff. Used with permission.

could not hold themselves psychologically. It was difficult for me to get in a word, as they spilled out details of dreadful interactions without thinking about or analyzing the consequences for each other.

They only slowly allowed me to demonstrate their mutual projective identifications, and their individual defenses and anxieties. I said, "Dennis, I have come to feel that when you shout at Christie, you are secretly feeling she has rejected and wounded you. If you understood and said that, she might be more sympathetic." Christie nodded vigorously.

This interpretation produced relief from their shared persecutory objects, and, as if waking from a trance, they began to see each other differently. The problem was that I now became an exciting object who represented the hope that now tantalized them because it seemed unattainable. All possibility seemed to reside in me, not in their own potential for understanding. A shift to twice weekly therapy improved the holding. They started to bring dreams and to begin attempts at analysis.

A concept closely related to holding is *containment* (Bion, 1970) in which the parent accepts the child's projective identifications unconsciously and allows them to resonate with her own internal object relations, understanding them intuitively through her added maturity and tolerance of anxiety. Bion called this unconscious process, the parent's *reverie*. Then the parent feeds the altered mental contents back to the child, through her own projective identification, and the child experiences mental growth. Similarly, therapists constantly have to tolerate couples' fears. Often, we do this through conscious thinking, but mostly it happens through unconscious resonance and understanding. In the growth of the individual, containment occurs through continuous, mutual cycles of projective and introjective identification, forming the basis of the child's mental growth while the parent also matures. The child's mind itself is therefore a product of personal interaction. In neurobiology, Schore (2003a; 2003b) has described the *entrainment* of unconscious cycles of communication between infants' and mothers' right brains (where emotion is processed) that predominates in interaction during the first 18 months of life. The rapid reading of facial gestures, vocalization, and shifts of body position are decoded instantaneously as parent and child read each other's emotional states. These processes are below the level of conscious understanding, happening rapidly and continuously. They color everything else that happens, in infancy and throughout life. Couples provide unconscious containment for each other while also relating consciously. In therapy, we also receive constant signals from the couples we see, most importantly affective signals we process unconsciously as we make unconscious understanding conscious, first to ourselves, then with couples, using our reverie to make things thinkable (which means to give verbal and emotional meaning to experience) that were previously unthinkable because they were rooted in early experience, in their bodies, or too frightening.

CASE STUDY

Dennis came to a session upset at Christie's unladylike dancing and love for ethnic music. What kind of example is she giving to their oldest daughter—who, by the way, is more feminine than Christie.

I see the humiliation in Christie's face as she screams that she is tired of this abuse.

Dennis appeals to me, "Look how she's, like, crazy. Please calm her down." He has no conscious awareness that his own anxiety has fueled hers. It is only when she shouts at him that he becomes anxious, but then thinks it arises only in reaction to her.

I feel invaded by their anger, not understanding (in identification with Christie's confusion) what it is Dennis wants from her. It seems to me that her dancing is a spontaneous expression of vitality that he attacks, scared of the sensuality others admire. The thought comes to me that he is carrying an identification with his own mother, scared of people finding out about his family's sexual past. Identifying unconsciously with his mother, he projects this hated identification into Christie, thereby trying to control the sexually exciting object part of his self in her. On her side, Christie feels rejected and humiliated through identification with her mother. Between them, they share a need to protect many painful internalized objects. Once I processed this myself, I was able to give an explanation for their behavior. It immediately brought more insight to the sessions.

Henry Dicks (1967) began the process of putting together an in-depth psychology of interaction by combining the ideas of Fairbairn on the relational organization of mind with Klein's theory of projective identification. Adding the ideas of Winnicott and Bion has augmented the theoretical support for this approach.

Developments in attachment theory (Bowlby, 1979; Clulow, 2000; Fonagy et al., 2003) augment the ways we describe the bond between infants and parents, and between couples. The classification of infants' attachment to their mothers is based on a research procedure called the "strange situation" in which the infant's response to separation from its mother is coded by looking at the infant's behavior when the mother returns. Infants are classed as (1) secure (goes to mother, may protest, but uses her well); (2) ambivalently insecure (alternates clinging and angry protest); (3) distancing-insecure (walks away from mother, avoids her); or (4) disoriented and disorganized (darts away from the mother, then toward her, looks at her furtively and looks away, a pattern that shows fear in response to her (Ainsworth, Blehar, Waters, & Wall, 1978; Main & Solomon, 1986).

Main and her colleague (Main & Goldwyn, 1991) described adult attachment styles in a similar way using a structured interview about the person's development and family. The interviewers coded the style of language in the narrative, not the content of the story of development. The best predictor of an infant's attachment style is the attachment classification of the parent, even done before the infant's birth, giving our first research evidence of intergenerational transmission of internal object relations. Attachment styles are mediated by each person's internal object set. Fonagy and coworkers (2003) studied how mothers teach infants to "mentalize" experience, to grow understanding of other persons' mental states facilitated or hampered by the attachment process. Similarly, adult couples are either secure in a relationship of mutual understanding, or are impeded by their insecure attachment status, a situation studied clinically by research on attachment in couple therapy (Clulow, 2000).

CASE STUDY

Christie and Dennis's attachment styles are expressed during Christie's yearly visit to her family in Europe. Prior to her trip, they become abusive to each other and threaten each other with divorce. Dennis's attachment is ambivalent-insecure. He could never separate from his mother because of his concern for her depression and emotional deadness. He often tried to anger her to bring her to life. Now he relates similarly to Christie, requiring satisfaction of his needs instantly. When she often fails, he angrily distances from her. Then he cannot tolerate being away from her, but he makes sure she understands that he is never satisfied with her. Thus, he recreates the unsatisfying relationship to his depressed inner mother. Failing to understand this impact on Christie, he remains childishly centered on the rejection for himself, even though he triggers the very rejection he fears. He has a limited capacity to reflect both on her state of mind and his own.

When we turn to Christie, we see that her happy early childhood was abruptly destroyed when her father got into serious debt. The continual threat of being thrown out of their house, and the way her father failed to pay the bills meant they were not so much poor as irresponsible. When the parents seemed withdrawn from the children in their preoccupation with themselves, Christie learned to do for herself. Her style of attachment corresponds to the distancing-insecure classification, although other insecure patterns of clinging and fearful types alternate with times she feels more secure. When things are difficult, she does not allow herself to feel need, but walks away from situations she interprets as rejecting. When Dennis tries to engage her through angry blaming, she often turns her back, leaving him more frustrated and seeking to cling to her.

SEXUALITY

Sexuality plays a central role in the "psychosomatic partnership" that ties psychological relating to bodily intimacy in adolescent and adult love relations (D. E. Scharff, 1982/1998). Marital therapists need a working knowledge of the role of physical sexuality in adolescence, in partner choice, and in the maintenance or breakdown of marriage, and of the ways children both draw on the parents' sexual bond and impinge on it. For many couples, a specific focus on sexual difficulty requires the therapist to switch to sex therapy herself or refer to a colleague. We recommend all therapists learn about the development and dynamics of sexuality (Kaplan, 1974; Levine, Risen, & Althof, 2003; D. E. Scharff, 1982; D. E. Scharff & Scharff, 1991).

CASE STUDY

When Dennis and Christie are on good terms, they enjoy sex. But when Christie refuses, Dennis often talks about other attractive women. Christie reacts by further distancing herself.

Christie says she does not like oral sex, which Dennis pushes for. He does not understand her refusal, since she sometimes suggests it. She says she does it to please him, but she resents it, as when he surprises her by suddenly forcing her to try oral sex.

Dennis's desires have stimulated her suppressed memories of pornography, focused on oral sex, left around the house by her father while she was growing up. Combined with the painful memories of her mother's social ostracism, she feels like a prostitute when Dennis requests oral sex.

Discussion of the family history of these matters led to increased understanding and an enhanced capacity to differentiate their situation from the one with Christie's father. She decided that she could tolerate performing oral sex on him during intercourse but not his doing it to her. With my help, he was able to understand why and move to a position of feeling they could have a good sexual life without it.

When we see couples from varying ethnic and cultural backgrounds, we look for similarities of pattern extending from the culture, to the social groups it contains—the extended family group, the nuclear family, the couple, and the individual. We look to the couple to inform us about the cultural differences that reside in them, and to work with us toward understanding those matters as much as toward understanding their individual and couple dynamics. This is true with couples of any ethnicity so long as we understand that we must let their experience penetrate us, and open ourselves to sharing their in-depth experience in order to let our therapeutic reverie help all couples with culturally saturated projective identifications and interactions.

CLINICAL TECHNIQUE

We have many functions in mind while working with couples, but relatively few specific techniques. Object relations theory is principally a way of working together with couples toward understanding and growth. The major functions are:

1. *Management of the space within a frame.* We do not tell a couple what to do, but work to maintain a psychological space analogous to the environmental provision the parent offers the child for safety and space to grow. To this end, we offer regularity of boundaries and conditions, the fee, times of meeting, length of sessions, and other logistical matters that frame a psychological space within which we work.

Initially, it was difficult to hold Dennis. Even though a steady frame of work had been established through setting up regular appointments, and beginning and ending on time, his anxious insecurity was expressed by his frequent urgent phone calls to me, trying to stay past the end of the sessions, and, sometimes, even appearing at my office between sessions. Slowly, he internalized the regularity and continuity of the appointments and adapted to the frame I offered.

2. *Management of the environment.* Within the frame, we do not tell patients what to do, where to sit, whether to face each other, or what to say. We ask them to work with us in an environment in which unspeakable things can be voiced and there is growing tolerance for difficult matters. It is up to us to manage the holding environment—analogous to the parents' environmental provision—and then to work toward the understanding that is the analog of the parents' in-depth understanding. We also want to assess the couple's developmental level of function, in order to see deficits or whether they cling to old dysfunctional patterns out of fear of change and growth. Developmental levels will change over time, and often will oscillate within a session.

At first, it seemed that Dennis had more difficulty dealing with emotion than Christie. He was frightened of expressing sadness, and it was easier, for both of them to fight than to cry. But as the sessions evolved, it was Dennis who first started to bring scraps of his own history. In one session, he broke down crying. He immediately stopped, hiding his tears. Christie laughed at him for crying. Containing my own feelings about her reaction, I tried to make sense of it in such a way that both could feel contained. The incident was a defensive replay of early experience. Being the only boy, Dennis was expected to behave like a strong, emotionless man. His family made fun of his tears. Christie's seemingly heartless reaction came from fear. In the session, she had suddenly seen in Dennis her father's vulnerability. To avoid the danger of an unreliable man, she laughed to distance herself from danger.

3. *We demonstrate our ways of working.* We encourage communication and tolerant listening toward deepening understanding that is the couple's equivalent of reverie. We want our own reverie and that of each partner to be a receptive space for each partner to speak and be heard. We do not ask for genograms or a set history, but look for object relations histories of the therapeutic moment. What was it like growing up when certain issues are stirred up? For instance, if a couple argues about one keeping the other waiting, we ask what it was like for each of them growing up around this issue. That way we get a living history connected to the session's here-and-now. We value slips

of the tongue as clues to unexpressed ambivalence, just as in individual therapy. We ask for dreams from both partners, and ask the dreamer and the other partner not "What does the dream mean?" but to unpack the condensed dream images. Dreams belong to the couple and to the therapy process itself.

Christie's defensive facade was unmasked by working on recurrent dreams. In them, she was falling from an airplane, looking desperately for something to hang on to. In one dream, her mother was falling with her. We came to see that these dreams represented the anxiety that led to her distancing behavior that gave Dennis, too, the feeling of not having someone to hang on to.

4. *Tracking the affect.* Within each session, we follow the fluctuations in emotion to let us know when we are in the territory of an excited or rejecting repressed relationship and to note defensive shifts between differing organizations accompanied by heightened anger, sadness, fear, or arousal.

Christie's intense anger was the frequent clue to her more painful longing for her father. Her chronic difficulty working through losses led her to busy caretaking of others to avoid her own sadness. I pointed out this maneuver frequently before she began to recognize it herself.

5. *Noticing bodily signals.* Some of the most profound or traumatic issues are only sensed by observation of somatic cues, either in the couple or at times, because of projective identification, in the therapist. Noting when one of the partners is ill, has muscle soreness, is sleepy—or noting comparable things in the therapist's response during sessions—can lead to deeply buried issues.

Christie uses an IUD and therefore has bloody spotting between periods. She does not want more children, but does not want a tubal ligation. She wants Dennis to have a vasectomy. Dennis refuses, being clear about the body-damage anxiety it stirs up in him. She has the same fear. She refuses surgery because, if they got divorced, he could have more children, but she could not.

Meanwhile, her bleeding is an excuse to curtail intercourse. Dennis says she is punishing him. She answers that he knows what he has to do. Here we see how the undercutting of each other expands concretely from affects and verbal communication to the physical arena.

6. *We give feedback in many ways, an activity we generally group under the category of making interpretations.* We give support or advice because sometimes couples can take advantage of it, particularly parenting advice. But these are not the engines that drive object relations therapy. All our activities are aimed at improving the couple's capacity for thinking cognitively and emotionally. At the simple end, we observe things the couple has not observed, link two or more events that belong together, or underscore something they have observed but not given much weight. In the more complex levels of understanding and explanation, we construct narrative hypotheses of their development that have contributed to patterns in which they are stuck, interpret bodily symptoms and messages in terms of the memories they

encode, and develop a picture of the unconscious assumptions that power conscious behaviors. Finally, we work from their transferences to each other and as a couple, to the shared transference to us, in order to understand underlying unconscious issues.

Christie's periodic visits to her two sisters in Europe are always a cause for fighting. Dennis starts thinking that she prefers to be with them, that maybe they will go out at night to some bar or dancing with their friends, while he is at home with the children and the bills. He says Christie's sisters try to convince her she would be better off without him. For many years, to avoid an extended fight, Christie worsened the situation by waiting until a week before her trip to announce it. After a while, they agree on some conditions for these trips, although Dennis still gets upset.

I link these situations, and help them see how these trips remind him of his sisters ruthless teasing of him as his father's favorite. In response, he hid in his room doing his homework. Now he imagines Christie plotting against him with her sisters, leaving him alone again, doing his own homework.

Nonanalytic therapists criticize object relations therapists for relying on interpretation that is too focused on emotions and too weak an instrument to achieve change. For us, interpretation is the analog to the way a parent speaks and behaves to convey to an infant that he or she is working to understand. While the parent does not always get things right, the process of working together toward understanding builds a relationship of mutual concern and signifies continuing containment. In therapy, showing the couple that we are working with them cements our alliance, encourages them to work, and facilitates the unconscious right-brain resonance that carries the emotional side of the work.

7. *Transference and countertransference form the central guidance mechanism of our work.* When patients communicate aspects of their inner experience concerning both their individual object relations sets and the issues about environmental holding, we call this *transference*. With couples, we focus mostly on the contextual issues that convey the way the couple cannot provide holding for each other adequate to their needs as a group of two. This is communicated to us through our own introjective identification, which we feel as our countertransference—that is, the whole range of feelings and thoughts experienced in relation to the couple. Some of these will feel benign, but the ones that give us the most important clues will feel painfully exciting or rejecting. Training, supervision, and experience help therapists develop a baseline for understanding nuances in meaning of internal responses to couples, but even the most experienced therapist will have to surrender to the process of allowing painful countertransferences to understand couples' experiences from inside a shared situation. For this reason, interpretation from the experience of countertransference of the couple's transferences in the here-and-now of the therapeutic session forms our most powerful tool. Constant monitoring of countertransference also acts as a global positioning system that informs our understanding in other areas.

Dennis had a dream: Coming home after work, he finds Christie with another man whom he beats up. Next, he is outside the house, walking around the neighborhood with me. I tell them he has to ask Christie for an explanation instead of jumping to conclusions. He regains control and feels better.

I tell them the dream portrays the way in which they both use me to ward off bad objects: I help Dennis avoid the threat of being ignored and abandoned (like his mother), or envied for what he has (like his father). I help Christie with the threat of being the unfaithful woman (like her mother), or sexually depraved (like her father).

Usually during sessions, I feel I have two children who need mothering. Christie expresses the rejecting object constellation, often threatening to leave therapy, but I do not feel animosity because she looks at me with intense longing. Dennis expresses the other side, wanting to stay in therapy— the longing of the exciting object constellation. I feel that they want me as the mother they both longed for, but this interferes with therapy because they cannot get better if they want to keep me. I interpreted this in a moving session. They agreed and began to discuss this legacy of early unfulfilled needs.

8. *Working through.* Object relations offers an in-depth, long-term approach for couples, who typically see a therapist for months to years. Some come only for one session or a few times and derive considerable benefit. Some come for "serial brief therapy," perhaps 3 to 12 sessions at a time, returning several times over the years. The therapist is trained to think in depth, but that training can be applied in either long- or short-term work (Stadter & Scharff, 2000).

When we have the opportunity to work with a couple over a longer period of time, from a few months to two or more years, we strive to help them "work through" their issues. This process mirrors the natural processes of growth, circling to cover overlapping territory again and again, each time using slightly different ways of addressing problem areas from different angles, contributing slowly to building new patterns with more adaptability. The human need for this kind of growth process makes long-term therapy a more beneficial process than most short-term interventions. Short-term therapy is as effective as long-term therapy in those challenges to a couple that derail them from a normally healthy adjustment—sudden illness, loss of a job, death of a child, or developmental crises (marriage, a birth) that challenge them in ways for which they are unprepared. Then a short intervention may get them back on track so that their normally adaptive skills take hold again.

Both Dennis and Christie were strongly in the grip of their bad, rejecting, and exciting internal objects. In those moments when they were able to see each other differently, they felt lucky to have each other, but too often the potential space collapsed and they went back to criticizing and complaining. They needed to mourn the losses in their lives over and over, before they could accept their own family as good enough.

9. *Working with loss and termination.* Object relations therapists see loss as the most frequent issue derailing development: losses in the early life of one or both partners, or in their shared life, as in the case of loss of a child or in previous divorces (J. S. Scharff & Scharff, 1994). Clinically, an opportunity to mourn comes in the separations and reunions that are intrinsic to the ending of each session. This rhythm prepares couples for the loss of the therapy and therapist at the end of therapy. Studying the anxiety of ending sessions and mourning these losses—which are often felt in the transference-countertransference exchange—is a major focus of our work, leading to the work of termination of therapy that centers on using the opportunity to review the course of therapy and the anxiety of proceeding in life without the therapist as guide.

Over the years, Dennis and Christie made many changes in the way they related. They considerably lessened their abusive behavior, and threats of divorce rarely came up. Dennis tolerates Christie's taking the yearly trip to her family, and she has been good in sticking to their agreements. They increasingly express tenderness, and Dennis is more empathic about Christie's sexual preferences.

During the termination phase, they worked on re-owning their projective identifications. In the face of anxiety about going on alone, Christie fell back on holding Dennis responsible for derivatives of the corrupt sexual activities of her father and the dismissive attitude of the high society. Dennis fell back on holding Christie responsible for his renewed insecurities and anxieties, and renewed demands that she have everything ready at home, waiting for him to arrive, so that without me, he did not risk finding in her once again the neglectful mother who fails to take care of him. Reviewing these symptoms, which recalled the beginning of our work, allowed them to mourn termination of the therapy itself and to achieve a sad but satisfying termination.

SUMMARY

A couple's relationship is central to both nuclear and extended family organization, the place where individual issues come to poignant focus and the foundation stone for the entire human relational system. It draws on the history of each partner to create something new from which they both draw sustenance. Difficulties in their relationship pose formidable obstacles to their continued development and to offering a secure base for the next generation and the wider family.

Clinically, we draw on the ways relationships are played out in the session to inform our work. Therapy is vitalized by the ways the therapeutic relationship parallels the couple's relationship as they recreate their difficulties in the transference-countertransference interaction. We depend most on our growing understanding derived in this way, but we also use other tools—focusing variously on a living history of the couple's internal objects as it explains times of heightened affect in sessions, examining the couple's sexuality, making use of their dreams, establishing links between issues and events that the couple has been unable to link. The multiple losses suffered by most couples warrant special attention. All of these factors combine to give object relations couple therapy poignancy and efficacy.

REFERENCES

Ainsworth, M. D. S., Blehar, M. C., Waters, E., & Wall, S. (1978). *Patterns of attachment: A psychological study of the strange situation.* Hillsdale, NJ: Erlbaum.

Bion, W. R. D. (1970.) *Attention and interpretation.* London: Heinemann.

Bowlby, J. (1979). *The making and breaking of affectional bonds.* London: Tavistock.

Clulow, C. (2000). *Adult attachment and couple psychotherapy.* London: Brunner-Routledge.

Dicks, H. V. (1967). *Marital tensions.* London: Routledge & Kegan Paul.

Fairbairn, W. R. D. (1952). *Psychoanalytic studies of the personality.* London: Routledge.

Fonagy, P., Gergely, G., Jurist, E., & Target, M. (2003). *Affect regulation, metallization, and the development of the self.* New York: Other Press.

Kaplan, H. S. (1974). *The new sex therapy.* New York: Quadrangle Books.

Klein, M. (1975). Notes on some schizoid mechanisms. In *Envy and Gratitude and Other Works3* (pp. 1–24). London: Hogarth Press (Original work published 1946).

Levine, S. J., Risen, C. B., & Althof, S. E. (2003). *Handbook of clinical sexuality for mental health professionals.* New York: Brunner-Routledge.

Main, M., & Goldwyn, R. (1991). *Adult Attachment Classification System* (Version 5). Berkeley: University of California.

Main, M., & Solomon, J. (1986). Discovery of an insecure/disorganized/disoriented attachment pattern. In T. B. Brazelton & M. W. Yogman (Eds.), *Affective development in infancy* (pp. 95–124). Norwood, NJ: Ablex.

Scharff, D. E. (1998). *The sexual relationship.* Northvale, NJ: Aronson. (Original work published 1982)

Scharff, D. E., & Scharff, J. S. (1991). *Object relations couple therapy.* Northvale, NJ: Aronson.

Scharff, J. S. (1992). *Projective and Introjective Identification and the use of the therapist's self.* Northvale, NJ: Aronson.

Scharff, J. S., & Scharff, D. E. (1994). *Object relations therapy of physical and sexual trauma.* Northvale, NJ: Aronson.

Schore, A. N. (2003a). *Affect dysregulation and disorders of the self.* New York: Norton.

Schore, A. N. (2003b). *Affect regulation and the repair of the self.* New York: Norton.

Stadter, M., & Scharff, D. E. (2000). Object relations brief therapy. In J. Carlson & L. Sperry (Eds.), *Brief therapy with individuals and couples* (pp. 191–219). Phoenix, AZ: Zeig, Tucker & Theisen.

Winnicott, D. W. (1975). Transitional objects and transitional phenomena. In *Through pediatrics to psychoanalysis* (pp. 229–242). London: Hogarth. (Original work published 1951)

CHAPTER 10

Narrative Therapy with Couples: Promoting Liberation from Constraining Influences

Lynne V. Rosen and Charley Lang

Because she was a genius and a visionary . . . because she knew that everyone, every single person, is the hero of his or her own epic story.

—Michael Cunningham, on choosing Virginia Wolf as a subject for his Pulitzer Prize–winning novel, *The Hours* (Cunningham, 2002).

THE ORCHESTRA BEGINS. In the first movement, we strain to hear the themes unfold. The composer's intentions seem clearly defined. The second movement takes us to places we have not been before. The themes develop in unpredictable ways that could not have been revealed until this part of the journey. We move through different landscapes, unsure of where we are heading. Perhaps this feels a bit unsettling, because it is hard to integrate new discoveries with what has come before. The third movement arrives. Hearing familiar threads from the beginning of the journey provides comfort, but something is different.

The story is now more richly described, made possible by the willingness to risk moving through unfamiliar places. The listener is moved and excited by what has been constructed and can only imagine what can become possible.

When couples come into therapy, the stories and themes about their relationship unfold. Their stories no longer fit with the original intentions with which they entered into partnership. Couples talk about feeling trapped in the repetition of themes that no longer carry them forward. They have been taught by the culture what the second movement should look like, but the joining of their notes creates dissonance. Familiar with the notes of the other, they stop listening for subtle differences, become attached to a dominant sound, and lose the richness of what could be made possible by the unique contributions of the other.

Like the composer, one can write music or a script as a solitary endeavor. One can be positioned as the listener and make meaning of the themes that unfold. The members of the orchestra each make a unique contribution, but they must collaborate to create music that sings. How can couples collaborate in creating their own symphony? How do we create a context for people to speak and listen in ways that will span differences and make their lives richer? This chapter explores ways in which we seek to assist couples in learning to honor the differences of each unique sound and the complexity of joining their notes in constructing music that is pleasing to the ear of each listener. What are the assumptions that we make as therapists in this work with couples? What assumptions do we carry about what couples can look like and about the therapeutic relationship? How do we, as clinicians and academicians, address in the therapy room the effects of power relations and the politics of gender, race, class, ethnicity, and sexual orientation?

Narrative therapy is influenced by the tenets of feminism, social constructionism, and cultural anthropology. Understanding that power relations and discourses (sociocultural beliefs, ideas, rules, and values) shape and define how people make meaning of their lived experiences opens new options for couples to move forward in their lives. In addition to turning a critical eye on the real effects of societal discourses, therapists, as part of the culture, turn a critical eye on therapy practices. We evaluate our position in condoning or challenging how taken-for-granted societal "truths" and practices of power may inadvertently contribute to the problems that bring couples into therapy.

EXPLORING JULIE'S AND CARLO'S EXPERIENCES THROUGH A NARRATIVE LENS

Letter writing is a practice that narrative therapists sometimes use to document a couple's achievements, skills of living, and resources. Questions in these therapeutic letters engage the couple in continued dialogue and reflection about their preferences and hopes for their relationship. The following letter was written after a first session.

Dear Julie and Carlo,

I want to be transparent about some of the ideas that influence my thinking so that you can judge my knowledge and determine whether you want to be in conversation with me. I believe that couples entering therapy are on a path of becoming. I walk beside others exploring how stories, ideas, and beliefs in the culture shape the direction of that path. Sometimes, these stories no longer fit with the couple's lived experiences. I am interested in ways of talking that will help you construct the texture, color, and design of the path you want to be on.

Julie, you told me about your experience in your previous couple therapy. You said that after sessions, you felt as if you were the problem. You also described leaving therapy feeling depressed, hopeless, and riddled with guilt and self-blame. When we began therapy, you were clear that you did not need to delve deeply into the history of abuses in your life. Instead, you wanted to find a way to live differently in the present. I wonder what "living differently" would look like? When you decided to seek out a different experience, despite your previous therapist's objections, was that action in support of your desire to live differently? I wonder what it means to refuse to participate in conversations that others think you should be having? Is there a history of your refusing such invitations in the past?

Carlo, would you consider yourself an ally of Julie's in support of diminishing the power of guilt and self-blame in your relationship? Is this, in fact, a step in the direction of living differently? Do you have your own ideas of what "living differently" would look like in your relationship with Julie?

I am curious about the hopes and intentions you each had for your relationship when you entered into this marriage. Were these intentions made explicit? Have your intentions changed during the course of the past year? What do you want this relationship to stand for, now and in the future?

I am struck by the clarity with which you both express hope for what might be possible in exploring a different kind of therapy conversation. I'm wondering how you've been able to keep this sense of clarity safe from the grip of guilt and blaming practices. I also wonder what other territories in your relationship you have managed to keep safe from these forces.

Yours in partnership-building practices,

Lynne

This letter highlights practices that support the assumptions and intentions that guide narrative therapists. What was your experience reading this letter? What captured your attention? What did this inquiry make visible about the therapist's stance in regard to problems, the couple, and the therapy relationship? Consider how these questions positioned couples as experts in their lives, contextualized problematic relational practices and ideas, invited the couple to evaluate the real effects of these practices on their lives and relationships, and opened space for Julie and Carlo to explore preferred ways of relating. The following sections address the philosophical underpinnings that give rise to this kind of inquiry.

THEORY THAT GUIDES NARRATIVE THERAPY

The postmodern argument is not against various schools of therapy, only against their posture of authoritative truth.

—Kenneth Gergen, 1992, p. 57

Narrative therapy, cofounded by Michael White and David Epston, steps outside a tradition that is familiar to us all, a tradition of knowing. Traditionally, expert knowledge and theories of systemic analysis have informed our understanding of couples, problems, and therapy relationships.

Narrative practices follow a different tradition, a hermeneutic one. This tradition is less interested in digging for dominant/core truths about who couples are and seeks instead to understand how social interactions shape the way couples make sense of themselves, their relationships, and the world around them (White & Epston, 1990). The meanings that are derived from these interactions prescribe the range of possibilities for action. These actions can take the form of either relationship-promoting or relationship-restraining practices.

SOCIOPOLITICAL CONTEXT AND DISCOURSE

To the narrative therapist, context is everything. Therapeutic inquiry seeks to deconstruct discourses and the institutions that promote them. These discourses create social realities that often keep problematic relational patterns alive (White, 1991).

Terry and Shawn enter therapy with a very thin description of their relationship (Geertz, 1973; White, 1991). Terry is "too emotional" and Shawn is "distanced and shut down." This relationship-restraining story has the couple caught in a repetitive cycle of blaming each other for what's wrong in their relationship. By eliciting the messages that Shawn received in his training as a young adult, he identifies the following discourse: *"If a woman cries, it's my fault."* Instead of locating the problem within Shawn, we turn an evaluative eye on this discourse and how it shapes Shawn's understanding of gender relationships. In so doing, space is opened for Shawn to evaluate the real effects of this discourse on his life, and he's invited to choose whether or not these beliefs serve his own preferences for his relationship. At the same time, Terry is invited to consider renegotiating other discourses that may be constraining to the couple, and she identifies this one: *"Emotion equals weakness."* Through this process of expanding the couple's options, Terry and Shawn begin exploring alternative descriptions of themselves as a couple and find themselves on the path to relationship-promoting practices.

LANGUAGE MATTERS

Another important contribution of nonstructuralist thinking to narrative work is the "linguistic turn" in philosophy. As poignantly expressed by

Wittgenstein, "The limits of my language are the limits of my world" (1963). Burr (1995), referring to the writings of Saussure regarding the structure of language, explains that language transcends mere *descriptions* of words that describe the world and actively *constructs* and *constitutes* reality. The meaning of a word does not exist in the word itself, but in the relationship between the word and the context of its location. A couple who have been described as "dysfunctional," for example, will use this description to make sense of their experiences. They will tend to select out experiences in their lives that fit into this constructed story of dysfunction. Language has the power to either liberate or marginalize.

IDENTITY AND SELF

Postmodern therapies depart from the conceptualization of the self as fixed and located inside an individual and instead view identity as socially constructed and negotiated within the context of community (Burr, 1995). Identities are seen as fluid, containing a multiplicity of selves. Different selves are likely to come forward in different contexts. Rather than positioning couples as objects of our understanding and therapeutic gaze, couples remain in the subject position as we seek to understand *their* intentions and meanings. "We are not self-contained and autonomous 'personalities' but relational beings whose feelings and behavior are shaped in an on-going way through our interactions with other people in particular social environments" (Johnson, 1997, p. 62).

Narrative practice resists any notion of labeling couples with terms such as "enmeshed" or "combative," because these narrow descriptions obscure the multistoried identity that we seek to reveal in couple relationships. In this excerpt, the therapist invites the couple to evaluate the idea of *being enmeshed:*

"You mentioned 'being enmeshed.' What is your understanding of this word? Where did this idea come from?"

"If I were to teach another couple how to become enmeshed, what would I instruct them to do?"

"Does this idea of 'being enmeshed' make it difficult for you as a couple to create new ways of relating (outside of this description)?"

"I wonder if there have been times when the term 'enmeshed' did not capture your experience of being a couple? Is there a story you could share that might reflect this?"

White (1995, 2001) distinguishes between structuralist definitions of identity based on the understanding of *internal* states (personalities, motives, drives, nature, essence), and nonstructuralist definitions of identity based on the understanding of *intentional* states (preferences, hopes, values, commitments, purposes). Prior to the proliferation of psychological theories used to help individuals and couples make sense of their lived experiences, people relied on the knowledge, customs, practices, and beliefs of their local culture. Folk psychology focused on how people negotiated their lives and actions according to their intentions. White (1995) has exemplified how inquiry that connects people's everyday actions to their intentional states also creates movement in their own preferred directions. By maintaining clients in the subject position, they have the power to actively negotiate and mediate their own lives.

Informed by Bateson's theory of restraint and negative explanation, White (1986) postulates that couples stand in one place, not because they don't want to stand in a preferable place, but because they are restrained from doing so. By subscribing to the social constructionist view that multiple realities exist simultaneously, narrative therapists believe that as the social (and dialogic) landscapes shift, alternative understandings, perceptions, and ways of relating become possible. The following sections aim to demonstrate how narrative conversations create bridges to alternative stories that support couples' preferences for whom they want to become.

NARRATIVE PRACTICES IN ACTION

Every time we ask a question, we're generating a possible version of life.

—David Epston, 1995, pp. 70–74 (as cited in
Cowley & Springer, 1995)

Postmodern therapies view couples as full of possibility, rather than pathology. Narrative therapy uses the metaphor of *story* to understand and enrich partners' lives and relationships. Stories consist of events, linked in sequence, over time, according to a plot (Morgan, 2000; White & Epston, 1990).

Following are some of the practices that assist couples in separating from restraining influences on their relationships and in renegotiating those relationships in ways that are meaningful to them. We prefer the term *practices* rather than techniques, because practices can coexist in a manner that is fluid, not rigidly sequenced, and respectful of the couple's pace.

LISTENING TO THE PROBLEM STORY

Couples generally enter therapy with a problem-saturated story about what is not working effectively in their relationship (White & Epston, 1990). We shift our focus from the description of the problem story to capturing the meaning that the couple has given to these events. We listen discursively for themes and metaphors that speak to constraining forces in couples' lives. This sets the stage for challenging taken-for-granted truths about the problem.

EXTERNALIZING THE PROBLEM

As narrative therapists, we are interested in naming and externalizing problems that couples struggle with, thereby separating each partner's identity from the problem. "This approach does not see the person as the problem but rather the internalization of certain ideas about the self which circulate within a given culture" (Elliot, 1998, p. 45). Externalizing conversations help to assuage blaming practices, challenge limiting ways of being, and create distance from problematic ways of relating so that couples can create alternatives. The language used in naming problems comes directly from the partners consulting with the therapist. The following questions illustrate how the therapist and couple can engage in an externalizing conversation:

> "You mentioned feeling guilty. Would Guilt be a good name for the problem that has you avoiding each other at home?"

> "If you thought of this problem as a person or thing that was interfering in your relationship, what might you call it?"

> "What does Conflict have you thinking about your partner?"

> "Would that experience be an example of what you describe as the isolating effects of Discrimination?"

EXPOSING THE PROBLEM STORY AND ITS EFFECTS

Once externalized, we seek to explore the details of how the problem affects the lives of the partners in consultation. Here, we invite inquiry into the knowledge that each partner carries about how the problem first gained access to their relationship and how it has managed to gain control over time. We are looking for specific examples of the problem's real effects and the methods it uses to exert its influence. Mapping events through time is necessary to help couples perceive differences that may lead to new possibilities for action (Bateson, 1972), as evidenced by the following questions:

> "What is the earliest recollection you have of Defensiveness infiltrating your relationship?"

> "How does Overwhelm have you feeling about yourself, your partnership, and your hopes for the future?"

> "Does Insecurity have allies that it calls on to help do its work in your relationship? Who or what are they?"

> "Could we write down some of the rules that Chaos is trying to have you follow?"

EVALUATING THE REAL EFFECTS OF THE PROBLEM

When internalized problems are located outside of partners, and the personal, emotional, physical, and spiritual costs of problems are made visible, couples are invited into renegotiating their relationship with the problem. Will they continue to submit to the requirements of problematic practices or do they want to take a different stance? The following questions aim to help couples evaluate the real effects of problems that are influencing their relationship:

> "Is it acceptable that Suspicion has co-opted your relationship in this way?"
>
> "Is the impact of Uncertainty helpful at this juncture?"
>
> "Is Mistrust useful to hold on to as you consider taking this next step?"
>
> "What does Betrayal have you thinking about each other?"

JUSTIFYING THEIR POSITION

Couples are asked to justify their stance by helping us understand why they have chosen to take a position (relative to the problem). What often emerges are glimpses of what matters most to couples. This provides an opening for therapists to explore new perspectives and hopes for helping the couple to move forward with their relationship, as seen by the following questions:

> "Can you tell me a story that illustrates why this problem of Withdrawal is important to you? What has it been stealing from your relationship?"
>
> "What is your stance in relation to this problem of Obsession?"
>
> "What position would you like me to take regarding your relationship with Addiction?"
>
> "Why are Jealousy's requirements no longer acceptable to you?"

IDENTIFYING UNIQUE EXPERIENCES

In chronicling the historical effects of the problem, we stay attuned for any events, plans, thoughts, dreams, feelings, or qualities that contradict the problem story (Bird, 2000). By exploring the history and effects of these unique experiences, we reconnect the couple to resources that often have become dormant due to the escalating strength of the problem. Through this dialogue, couples sometimes name the emerging, alternative story. The following questions seek to make visible unique experiences that contradict problematic ways of relating:

> "I understand that Sorrow is currently in the driver's seat for your relationship. Was there ever a time when it was more in the back seat? What was different then?"

"Can you tell me of a recent experience in which the two of you managed to get the upper hand on Manipulation? How did you do that? What would you call this quality that enabled you to sidestep Manipulation's influence?"

"You mentioned that Depression hasn't managed to take over your experience of each other sexually. How do you account for that?"

"If an Abuse-dominated lifestyle wasn't ruling your relationship, what kind of lifestyle would be there instead?"

CONSTRUCTING THE ALTERNATIVE STORY

In identifying the couple's resources and preferences, we invite them to re-describe themselves and their relationship according to this new information. How do these new descriptions alter the stories the couple holds about their partnership? We also look for evidence of experiences, intentions, and people that support the couple's new path. Identifying this evidence from the past and imagining how it might evolve into the future adds density to the emerging story, as evidenced by the following questions:

"You mentioned Collaboration as a recent re-discovery. Is Collaboration more indicative of your preferred way of relating with your partner?"

"Do these new developments inspire any new directions for your relationship?"

"Who from the past would not be surprised by your reengagement with Excitement?"

"If you were to continue nurturing Respectful Listening in the coming week, what might that look like?"

INVITING THE EXPANSION OF COMMUNITY

We attempt to situate this new preferred story within the context of community by inviting other members from the couple's life to join in the witnessing and acknowledgment of the unfolding story. This may take the form of letter writing or having outside members of the couple's community participate in a therapy session. We also create *communities of support* by inviting others to share their past successes (in taking their lives back from certain problems) with couples currently struggling with similar problems. The following questions invite the couple to consider ways of expanding their community of support:

"Would you be interested in hearing about strategies that other couples have used in coping with Suicide?"

"Who in your community would be most excited about your new plans to pursue Adoption?"

"If you were to break the cycle of Violence, what would this make possible for your children in the future?"

"You talked about the Safety you felt with your grandmother. What were some of the ingredients for creating Safety in that relationship? What would your grandmother say about the qualities you brought to her life? If you could carry your grandmother with you as you risk having this conversation with Bill, what difference might that make?"

CREATING A CONTEXT FOR DIALOGUE

Truth is not born nor is it found inside the head of an individual person, it is born between people collectively searching for the truth, in the process of their dialogic interaction.

—Mikhail Bahktin (as cited in Morson & Emerson, 1990, p. 60)

Practicing narrative therapy for over a decade has helped to highlight the usefulness of working on the front end to create a context for couples to speak and listen differently. What is required of partners to speak and listen from a different position? Partners often come into our offices engaged in monologue or in ways of relating that restrain genuine listening. Clinical theories tend to focus on improving speaking skills, while paying less attention to forces that restrain the listening process.

Like the construction of music, dialogue exists in a space that allows for the participation of many voices. This requires openness to expressions from the other, which transports the conversation to a place it hasn't been before. When restraints to listening dominate, new perspectives are not integrated into the conversations. One partner might be forming a rebuttal while the other partner is speaking. Or one might be fitting the partner's expressions into a framework that's congruent with one's own beliefs, ideas, and assumptions. Conversations can open space and generate possibilities or close down space and limit options for moving the dialogue forward (Chasin et al., 1996).

Following are examples of how some of the ideas used by the Public Conversation Project in their work fostering dialogue between polarized groups around divisive issues (Chasin et al., 1996) can be applied to working with couples. Concepts from the Winslade and Monk (2001) text on narrative mediation are also reflected in the following practices.

In the first session, the conversation makes room right at the start for a broader context of understanding the partners present, in this case, Lisa and Ian. We begin by inquiring about what the couple imagines might move their relationship forward, underscoring our interest in the many orchestral instruments capable of contributing to the richness of their music:

What is your hope for what therapy will be able to provide for your relationship?

The question itself assumes a direction of possibility for the couple, which is distinctly different from the question: *What is the problem?*

STRUCTURE OF THE THERAPY CONVERSATION

Out of respect for the subjective experiences and stories that Lisa and Ian have about their relationship, they are each invited to participate in a one-on-one interview with the therapist. It is explained that while one partner speaks, the other will be asked to witness this interview from a listening position. The listener may be asked to notice anything that captures the attention, is new information, or which may be surprising to hear. The purpose of this structure is to encourage reflective listening while discouraging interrupting or forming rebuttals while others are speaking.

When multiple issues are discussed in a first session, couples are asked to take a few minutes and think about what might be most useful to discuss first. It is sometimes helpful for couples at this juncture to consider naming the project that they will be addressing. This invites partners into some agreement as to the joint project that will be constructed in the space between them. Lisa and Ian decided to work on restoring Calmness to their relationship:

> "You both talked about missing the presence of Calmness in your relationship. If you were to invite more Calmness into your interactions, what might that look like?"

> "You mentioned that running has helped ground you in Calmness in the past. How might your participation in running nurture Calmness in your relationship today?"

In addition, when first sessions are overtaken by hostile ways of relating, the following question used by Public Conversation Project facilitators can be useful in inviting reflection on the qualities each partner wants to bring into the room:

> Given the different social positions you occupy: partners, parents, friends . . . and given how you show up in these respective contexts, what aspects of yourself do you want to bring forward in our conversations (and what ways of relating do you want to leave behind) that would promote your hopes for moving your relationship forward? (Roth & Stains, 2002)

After the initial consultation with Lisa and Ian revealed the presence of Violence in their marriage, the following questions were sent to them via e-mail, inviting reflection on what they wanted their marriage to stand for:

"You stated that you didn't want Violence to be a part of your relationship. Is this a recent decision? Do you prefer to handle disagreement in other ways? In *any* circumstance?"

"You mentioned your preference for having a relationship based on Respect. Would you prefer that your partner stay with you out of Respect or out of Fear?"

"Do you want a marriage in which you enjoy each other's company or tolerate each other's company?" (Jenkins, 1990, p. 72)

Questions seek to support partners in their commitment to the process of actively changing in preferred directions.

STRUCTURED REFLECTION

In a world that has been overtaken by speed and capitalism, partners often don't take the time to genuinely listen to each other. Creating time for structured listening helps to slow down the process and encourage partners to think carefully about what they want to express.

THE PAUSE

Couples often appreciate identifying the pause as a powerful tool that encourages reflection and serves as a precursor to creating new possibilities for action, as evidenced by the following:

"I'm wondering if you'd each be willing to take a moment and reflect on what you've heard before responding to your partner's statement?"

KINDS OF TALKING

Early in our conversations with couples, we ask what would be different if we were to talk in ways that were useful in moving their relationship forward:

"What are the intentions, hopes, and values that you would like your relationship to stand for?"

Couples have described their stance by referencing stories about Equality, Justice, Respect, Love, Integrity, and Safety:

"You both talked about missing the presence of Fun in your relationship. How might experiences of Fun support your project of Connection?"

BOTH/AND CONVERSATIONS

Are partners interested in having conversations of influence that will support the "rightness" of one perspective, or are they interested in having conversations of understanding? What would be useful? Here the couple is invited to identify constraints that may inhibit their listening skills:

"What might get in the way of your listening with an open ear and body?"

When there is a difference, couples tend to get recruited into a binary position of either/or thinking. Narrative practices support the holding of two different perspectives simultaneously.

REFLECTION VERSUS REACTION

Positioning one partner as listener as the other partner speaks highlights subtle differences that might become obscured in debate-style conversations. This structure also guards against one voice becoming too dominant in the session. The following questions illustrate how the therapist invites reflection:

"Has the pattern of Interruption helped or hindered your hopes of understanding each other differently?"

"What kind of agreement between the two of you might help dispel the negative effects of Interruption?"

CURIOSITY

We explore with partners what it would mean to listen from a stance of genuine curiosity:

"Is there a kind of Generosity that goes along with your willingness to hear your partner's story?"

ASSUMPTIONS THAT GUIDE NARRATIVE PRACTICES

There are no resistant clients, only inflexible therapists.

—R. Bandler and J. Grindler
(as cited in Walter & Peller, 1975, p. 23)

Every therapeutic conversation carries assumptions about problems, people, and the therapeutic relationship. By being mindful of the assumptions that underlie our work as narrative therapists, we reinforce our clients' sense of choice, empowerment, and personal agency. Following are some of the assumptions we carry in our work with couples.

Assumptions about Problems

- *It's not a "Who," it's a "What."* The couple (or partner) is not the problem, the problem (or constraining force) is the problem. Since problems are viewed as external to couples, we look for nouns that name problems, rather than adjectives that describe partners (as problematic). So, rather than viewing Marci and/or Max as "codependent," we'd be more inclined to see them "struggling with the effects of Codependency."
- *Problems reside in the "shoulds" and "supposed to's."* Using a social-constructionist lens in our work, we remain curious about whether statements beginning with "I should . . ." are actually of value to the couple. Examples of social constructs and possibly problematic discourses are the following: Religion (*I should not be gay*), Media (*I should have a partner*), Patriarchy (*I should have sex when my partner wants to*). Couples are continually recruited into evaluating themselves against dominant norms. If they don't conform to these norms, couples often experience themselves as failures.
- *There is no such thing as a too small unique exception.* It is not uncommon for couples to speak of exceptions to their problems as small or insignificant: *"It was just that one time,"* or *"It only lasted about five seconds."* There is no such thing as a too small exception. Every unique exception is a piece of gold, waiting to be grown (from 1 time to 2, from 5 seconds to 10) into alternative stories.
- *Problems can be multifaceted.* In the same way that we refrain from totalizing descriptions of couples, we resist totalizing descriptions of what the couple defines as problematic. "Are there aspects of Fear that might actually be useful to you, for example, in alerting you to unsafe situations?"
- *Problems are maintained by discourses embedded in power relations.* Beliefs and ideas keep certain problems alive. We turn a critical eye on ways in which the culture privileges certain belief systems over others, impacting couples and the ways in which they view their relationships.

Assumptions about Couples

- *The Partners are the experts.* We don't presume to be experts on the lives of couples who consult with us. We view each couple as unique and individual, and resist any ideas of holding them up to a normative standard of what constitutes a healthy couple.
- *Couples are inherently resourceful.* Oftentimes, a couple's resources have been obscured by the strength of the problem. It is our job as narrative

therapists to reconnect the couple to the resources that support their preferred ways of relating in partnership.

- *Power is an intrinsic part of all partnerships.* We seek to make visible the dynamics of power in partner relationships, addressing all of its sources. By naming taken-for-granted truths embedded in power relations, we invite couples to research the effects of power imbalance on their relationship.

  "Are you wanting the kind of relationship where your partner adopts all of your ideas, or do you see value in her having ideas of her own?"

- *Couples carry assumptions about each other.* We question the assumptions that partners carry about their relationship and each other. One person's unexpressed ideas about being a man/partner/lover/parent/provider are not necessarily the same as his or her partner's.

- *The style of relating is more important than the content.* Can partners agree to disagree, or is there a polarized, debate-style manner of seeing differences, as in "either I win or you win"?

  "Does your current style of resolving differences make it more or less likely that you could resolve future differences?"

  "What are your intentions for the conversation as you attempt to manage differences? What are you hoping will happen?"

  "Do you like the self you present as you attempt to resolve differences? Do you like your partner's self? Which of your selves would you prefer to bring into these interactions?"

Assumptions about the Therapeutic Relationship

- *The direction of therapy is a shared responsibility.* We aim to create a space where couples feel they have the right to evaluate the usefulness of our questions:

  "Does one of these questions capture your attention? Are we having the kind of conversation you want to be having today? Are there other questions you would like me to be asking?"

- *It's not my job to know, it's my job to wonder.* Assuming a genuinely curious stance requires the therapist to ask questions from a place of not knowing, free of interpretations. We are less interested in how we make meaning of the couple's experience, and more interested in how the couple makes meaning of their own experience.

- *Transparency pushes against the power imbalance inherent in the therapy relationship.* Therapists share their own beliefs, assumptions, and experiences related to the therapy conversation, so that couples can situate and judge the therapist's biases in deciding what is useful for them. Therapy is seen as a real relationship, not a symbolic one. We are willing to share the impact that therapeutic conversations have on our lives, acknowledging the recursive quality of dialogue.

- *Professional language and knowledge have real effects on how couples' lives unfold.* Our language constructs how couples come to see themselves. We consider our position of power and the weight given to our professional knowledge. Narrative therapists collaborate with couples around diagnosis and correspondence with others, keeping them in the position of co-authors of the stories that get circulated. In professional, academic, and supervisory settings, narrative therapists aim to speak about couples as if they were present in the room. This adherence to respectful practice invites generative conversations and shapes the lens that others use in viewing couples. If you're looking for Resourcefulness in couples, you're more likely to find it.

DISCOURSE AND DECONSTRUCTION

Until lions have their own historians, tales of hunting will always
glorify the hunter.

—African proverb

Derrida (1978) calls attention to the background assumptions that enable our stories to make sense. What creates the context for problems to appear? Understanding Michel Foucault's concept of *modern power* opens up new understandings of how oppressive practices and self-subjugation operate. Power is distributed unequally among members in the culture, privileging the voices of some while marginalizing the voices of others (Foucault, 1979, 1980). White and Epston (1990) describe how Foucault used the prison architectural structure designed by Jeremy Bentham in the eighteenth century as a metaphor to speak about the operation of modern power in our cultural and historical landscape.

The *Panopticon* was a structure designed to house prisoners that made it possible to achieve the greatest degree of social control. A round building surrounding a courtyard housed prisoners in individual cells, isolating them from their fellow inmates. A tall tower stood in the middle of the courtyard, from which guards could see into every cell. The guards, however, were never visible to the inmates. In exploring the effects of this over time, Foucault describes how *the gaze* of the guards would recruit the prisoners into modifying or policing their own behaviors, acting as if they were always being watched. In the context of social or relational isolation, partners practice self-surveillance and self-regulation based on socially constructed norms. When this form of power remains invisible to couples, its effects can be insidious (Foucault, 1979; White, 1991).

Narrative therapists listen for oppressive (often invisible) discourses that influence a couple's relationship. Once identified, therapeutic inquiry deconstructs the assumptions and beliefs that support the taken-for-granted status of the discourse. When an oppressive discourse is made visible, couples are invited to renegotiate their position within that discourse or to choose an alternate discourse that is less restrictive. By refusing to comply with a marginalizing discourse, couples are challenging the status quo and promoting social justice in the larger community.

Suzanne and Pete come to therapy concerned about Suzanne's eating disorder. Anorexia had successfully recruited Suzanne into self-subjugating practices of self-starvation, excessive exercise, rigid rules regarding eating, and continual practices of measuring up. The meaning she has constructed of the events in her life is that she is a "mess," unable to handle the stressors in her life and "codependent." Pete describes Suzanne as "overemotional" and "dramatic."

By locating Anorexia in the social context rather than in Suzanne, therapeutic questions focus on mapping the effects of Anorexia's requirements on Suzanne and on her relationship to Pete. By unveiling the tricks Anorexia uses and the cultural discourses that keep it alive, Suzanne and Pete are able to join forces in reclaiming their relationship from the problem's grip. Suzanne enlists Pete's support in resisting Anorexia's attempts to undermine her efforts, and as a result, she is no longer silenced by Secrecy and Shame. In the following, Pete and Suzanne are invited to consider the sociocultural influences that have supported Anorexia:

> "Suzanne, how do you think Anorexia gets women to participate in self-shrinkage and diminishment? Does Anorexia make certain promises to you?"

> "Pete, do you think our culture makes enough room for women's voices? Who do you think benefits from Anorexia's uncanny ability to silence women?"

> "Are there ideas in our culture that you think are worth refusing to ingest? What are they?"

> "How does Anorexia recruit men into encouraging 'measuring up' practices for women?"

> "Is the expression of emotion less valued in our culture than other forms of expression?"

As members of the culture, therapists also live within dominant discourses that shape therapy practices. How do we challenge practices that position us as "agents of social control" (Foucault, 1979)? Narrative therapists turn a critical eye on practices that might inadvertently maintain dominant ideologies by supporting certain groups over others (Freedman & Combs, 1996; Madigan, 1993). Although it is not possible to completely flatten the hierarchy inherent in the therapeutic relationship, we remain vigilant about using our power in support of client agency and empowerment.

DIVERSITY AND SOCIAL JUSTICE

I urge each one of us here to reach down into that deep place of
knowledge . . . and touch that terror and loathing of any difference
that lives there. See whose face it wears. Then the personal as the
political can begin to illuminate all our choices.

—Audre Lorde, 1984, p. 113

All therapy conversations are multicultural. Whether we are talking about
a couple, two religious groups, or two nations, narrative practice is interested in how people handle the process of differing. Do conversations
around difference create space for many perspectives, or do they quiet the
voices that stand outside the dominant view? How do cultural discourses
influence the ways in which a couple handles day-to-day dilemmas?

Western society privileges productivity and gives power to individuals
and groups based on binary positions; educated/uneducated, rich/poor,
white/person of color, heterosexual/gay, thin/large, young/old, able-
bodied/disabled (Cushman, 1995). Dominant and privileged groups develop exaggerated entitlements that lead to abuses of power and the ongoing oppression of less-dominant groups (Winslade & Monk, 2001).

Narrative therapists challenge discourses related to race, class, gender,
sexual orientation, age, and mental and physical ability. The following examples illustrate the deconstruction of any oppressive discourse.

GENDER

A culture that gives men resources to succeed in a capitalist society may
have the effect of objectifying women in relationships. Through this lens,
questions would aim to make the effects of this structure visible for couples to evaluate:

"I am wondering what society has taught you about 'being a man' in relationship to women."

"Are there aspects of Control (as a result of these lessons) that have
been beneficial to you? How has Control affected your partner and
your relationship?"

"You've talked about some negative effects of Domination on your relationship. Where did this training come from? Did your father receive similar training?"

"Was there ever a male figure in your life who showed up differently, or
outside of these particular specifications for being a man?"

Through deconstructive inquiry of the practices, contradictions, and effects
of gender on both men and their partners, couples can reevaluate their preferences for the kind of relationship they want to be in. Narrative therapists

also explore the effects of power relations between themselves and the couple, and may reflect on the following questions:

> "Does the therapy room create enough room for women's voices?"

> "Which discourses does a female therapist have to challenge in order to address Patriarchy in the room with a male client?"

> "Do therapists challenge Mother-blaming or Absent-father discourses?"

> "Do biases and assumptions recruit therapists into aligning themselves with one partner over another?"

CLASS

The powerful influences of class are often not discussed in therapeutic conversations. As far back as the Elizabethan Poor Laws, one's status in society was commensurate with one's ability to work and produce. Not only do ideas of Productivity and Worth continue to impact modern day couple relationships, but they also impact the therapist's relationship with the couple. Are couples that are marginalized by discourses of class able to choose a direction for themselves, or is the path largely being chosen for them? The following question invites the couple to consider the impact of class on the therapeutic relationship:

> "I'm wondering how I might be alerted to the possibility that our class differences could be affecting our therapy conversations?"

FRAMEWORKS

Narrative therapy also unpacks broader constructs that impact couple relationships. For example, bell hooks (2000) examines cultural discourses related to the concept of love. Do we have a shared understanding of this construct? Media and culture support notions of romantic love and the assumption that love is a feeling. When lived experiences don't fit the resulting norms and expectations, couples conclude (or are told) that something in them, or in their relationship, is "dysfunctional":

> "Instead of defining Love as a feeling, what difference would it make if Love were something that was demonstrated through acts of Care, Responsibility, Respect, and Commitment?"

> "Can you think of any ways that conventional definitions of Love might surreptitiously support economic agendas and power relations in partnership?"

When we challenge discourse, privilege, and entitlement positions, we are promoting ways of relating that extend beyond the couple and into the social and political arena.

SUMMARY

I dwell in Possibility
A fairer House then prose,
More numerous of windows—
Superior—for doors

—Emily Dickinson, No. 657
(as cited in Winslade & Monk, 2001)

Narrative therapy is based on a philosophy and worldview, not on a methodology. It is less interested in supporting the rightness of any theory and more interested in remaining open to new ideas and possibilities that can lead to more meaningful change in the lives of couples.

This chapter highlights the usefulness of externalization, discourse analysis, and challenging power relations in partnerships. Even though this worldview maintains that we always operate within discourses, Foucault underscores the point that we become more effective as therapists by supporting couples in consciously choosing some discourses over others.

It is the belief of narrative therapists that exposing discourses and depoliticizing problems help to promote social change. Change occurs through making discourses visible, contextualizing and externalizing problems, and inviting couples to evaluate positions of power. Narrative practices challenge *power-over* relationships that become so taken for granted that they go unchallenged. By not exposing problematic discourses, are we not in effect silently colluding with their oppressive effects? Challenging what is dominant requires us to leave the safety of knowing the outcome or the direction of change. The intention of narrative conversations is to liberate clients, not to educate or impose the therapist's predetermined knowledge, agenda, or belief on them.

Change occurs in the relational space constructed between people. Therapists are rigorous in being accountable for the real effects of the questions they ask, as well as the influence of their own assumptions on the conversation, the direction of therapy, and how couples come to see themselves.

Throughout our therapeutic conversations, notes come together to make new chords. Sometimes the chord is flat, sometimes sharp. The differences in tone create a richness that undulates across time. The notes are brought together not for their sameness, but for their collaborative uniqueness. Some individual notes may take turns being louder than others, but if one note dominates, the others lose their value in adding to the complexity of the sound. Immersed in the process of creating new music, couples who consult with us sometimes strain to hear their new song. And when the work is transformative, what they realize, through the exploration of intentions, reflections, dialogue, and practices, is that they are already singing.

REFERENCES

Bandler, R., & Grindler, J. (1975). *Patterns of the hypnotic techniques of Milton H. Erickson, M.D. (Vol. 1).* Cupertino, CA: Meta.

Bateson, G. (1972). *Steps to an ecology of mind.* New York: Ballantine Books.

Bird, J. (2000). *The heart's narrative.* Auckland, New Zealand: Edge Press.

Burr, V. (1995). *An introduction to social constructionism.* London: Routledge.

Chasin, R., Herzig, M., Roth, S., Chasin, L., Becker, C., & Stains, R. (1996). From diatribe to dialogue on divisive issues: Approaches drawn from family therapy. *Mediation Quarterly, 13*(4), 323–344.

Cowley, G., & Springen, K. (1995, April 17). Rewriting life stories. *Newsweek,* 70–74.

Cunningham, M. (2002). *The hours* [Motion picture]. United States: Paramount Pictures.

Cushman, P. (1995). *Constructing the self, constructing America: A cultural history of psychotherapy.* New York: Addison-Wesley.

Derrida, J. (1978). *Writing and difference.* Chicago: University of Chicago Press.

Elliot, H. (1998). Engendering distinctions. In S. Madigan & A. Law (Eds.), *Praxis: Situating discourse, feminism and politics in narrative therapies* (pp. 35–61). Vancouver, British Columbia, Canada: Cardigan Press.

Foucault, M. (1979). *Discipline and punish: The birth of the prison.* Middlesex, England: Peregrine Books.

Foucault, M. (1980). *Power/knowledge: Selected interviews and other writings.* New York: Pantheon Books.

Freedman, J., & Combs, G. (1996). *The social construction of preferred realities.* New York: Norton.

Geertz, C. (1973). Thick description: Toward an interpretative theory of the culture. In C. Geertz (Ed.), *The interpretation of cultures.* New York: Basic Books.

Gergen, K. (1992, November/December). The postmodern adventure. *Family Therapy Networker,* 52, 56–57.

hooks, b. (2000). *All about love: New visions.* New York: Perennial.

Jenkins, A. (1990). *Invitations to responsibility: The therapeutic engagement of men who are violent and abusive.* Adelaide, Australia: Dulwich Centre.

Johnson, A. (1997). *The gender knot: Unraveling our patriarchal legacy.* Philadelphia: Temple University Press.

Lorde, A. (1984). *Sister outsider: Essays and speeches.* Freedom, CA: Crossing Press.

Madigan, S. (1993). Questions about questions: Situating the therapist questions in the presence of the family. *Dulwich Centre Newsletter, 3,* 41–52.

Morgan, A. (2000). *What is narrative therapy?* Adelaide, Australia: Dulwich Centre.

Morson, G., & Emerson, C. (1990). *Creation of prosaics.* Palo Alto, CA: Stanford University Press.

Roth, S., & Stains, R. (2002). *The power of dialogue: Constructive conversations on divisive issues* (Public Conversations Project, Watertown, MA. Training conducted at the Western Justice Center, Pasadena, CA).

White, M. (1986). Negative explanation, restraint and double description: A template for family therapy. *Family Process, 25,* 169–184.

White, M. (1991). Deconstruction and therapy. *Dulwich Centre Newsletter, 3,* 21–40. (Reprinted in D. Epston & M. White, 1992, *Experience, contradiction, narrative and imagination,* Adelaide, Australia: Dulwich Centre)

White, M. (1995). The narrative perspective in therapy. In M. White (Ed.), *Reauthoring lives, interviews and essays* (pp. 11–40). Adelaide, Australia: Dulwich Centre.

White, M. (2001). Folk psychology and narrative practice. *Dulwich Centre Journal, 2,* 1–37.

White, M., & Epston, D. (1990). *Narrative means to therapeutic ends.* New York: Norton.

Winslade, J., & Monk, G. (2001). *Narrative mediation.* San Francisco: Jossey-Bass.

Wittgenstein, L. (1963). *Philosophical investigations* (D. E. Linge, Trans.). Berkeley: University of California Press.

CHAPTER 11

EFT: An Integrative Contemporary Approach

Brent Bradley and Susan M. Johnson

THE COUPLE ALTERNATED between glaring at each other and staring straight ahead, each glare singeing with white heat. "If you want to go play golf on a Saturday and leave me home all alone, that's fine, do it," Rosie said in a stern, yet slightly pained voice that belied her actual words. "It's a golf tournament," Rusty replied. "You know I like golf. I tried to tell you about this ahead of time to make sure it was okay and everything." "I said it was okay!" Rosie angrily shot back, and then looked down to the floor with tears in her eyes. Rusty sighed, shrugged his shoulders, and looked away from his wife. "Fine. Whatever," he added with intense anger.

Rosie, 28, and Rusty, 34, are a Caucasian couple who have been married one year. Both have children from previous relationships living with them. The presenting problem was "intense fighting," and both partners talked of "anger problems." The fights started about 18 months ago. Rosie has full custody of her 8-year-old son, and Rusty has his 9-year-old daughter from a previous marriage for six months at a time. This couple immediately described a fighting cycle of Rosie attacking, Rusty defending, and then withdrawing. They reported being ashamed at the intensity of some of these fights. Rusty had once kicked a dent in the car, and each reported screaming at the other. After these fights, the couple did not speak for up to three days, and Rusty would sleep in the guest bedroom. One night Rosie got so angry that she spent the night in her car in the garage. Typically, after three days, they reported getting so exhausted that one of them would give up, and the other would be receptive. The arguments, however, were never resolved, and this vicious cycle quickly came around again, getting "worse each time." Rusty, in particular, reported a strong desire to win these fights, and to be right. They had attended previous counseling from their pastor, who then referred them for professional therapy. Segments of their therapy will be used to illustrate the clinical application of emotionally focused therapy (EFT) and how it fits in the current field of couples therapy.

THE CHANGING FIELD OF COUPLES THERAPY

The field of couple and family therapy is signaling its readiness to move into a less-radical postmodernism and develop in an integrative direction (Johnson, 2003b; Johnson & Lebow, 2000; Linares, 2001). Linares describes how the stage is set for a shift into an ultramodern family therapy, one that expands the systemic field and leads to both new achievements and new adherents. Johnson describes how a revolution is occurring in the field and how couple therapy is coming of age. She lists common integrative elements of contemporary approaches (Johnson & Denton, 2002). Scholars stress that contemporary approaches must move beyond a bag of tricks mentality (Liddle et al., 2000) and provide empirical support for their effectiveness, recognizing that therapy is both an art and a science (Crane, Wampler, Sprenkle, Sandberg, & Hovestadt, 2002; Sprenkle, 2002). Absent from these observations are the messianic tendencies that in the past have been part of the couple and family therapy field (Johnson, 2001). In contrast to the next new way of thinking mentality, these authors describe a field desiring to use knowledge from expanding areas of psychology and break bread with other treatment approaches and disciplines historically viewed as existing outside of MFT circles.

EFT (Greenberg & Johnson, 1988; Johnson, 1996) fits with the present zeitgeist of the field in that it's well suited for integration and cross-fertilization with other therapy approaches and academic disciplines because it is essentially integrative. In EFT, collaborative client-centered, gestalt, and systemic approaches are intertwined with constructivist thinking, a passion and commitment to research, and a vision of love relationships best captured in attachment theory. The focus on the regulating role of emotion and attachment needs and fears allows the EFT therapist to address universal elements of couple relationships, while the humanistic stance and focus on the process of interaction finds it sensitive to unique individual differences.

Since its inception 17 years ago, EFT has emphasized how emotional bonds are of primary concern in conceptualizing and creating change in intimate relationships (Johnson, 1986). Emotion is viewed in EFT as an adaptive relational action tendency—a natural part of systems theory (Johnson, 1998). EFT has established itself as an empirically validated approach to couple therapy (Baucom, Shoham, Mueser, Daiuto, & Stickle, 1998; Johnson, Hunsley, Greenberg, & Schindler, 1999) and has demonstrated efficacy apart from the originators of the approach (Denton, Burleson, Clark, Rodriguez, & Hobbs, 2000). Recognized as one of only about five empirically supported

(EST) marital and family treatment approaches, EFT is a meta-analytically supported treatment (MAST; Sprenkle, 2002). The targets of the EFT change processes and the theory of relatedness are also supported by empirical research (Gottman, 1994; Simpson, Rholes, & Phillips, 1996). In terms of outcome, a meta-analysis of the four most rigorous EFT outcome studies yielded a 70% to 73% recovery rate for relationship distress and a 90% significant improvement over controls (Johnson et al., 1999). Positive changes made in treatment also appear to be stable with little evidence of relapse (Clothier, Manion, Gordon-Walker, & Johnson, 2002).

EFT continues to evolve and expand, as evidenced in the newer constructs of attachment injuries (Johnson, Makinen, & Millikin, 2001) and the outlining of key therapist interventions utilized in softening change events (B. A. Bradley & Furrow, 2004). There is a growing base of treatment applications with diverse populations such as families with a bulimic child (Johnson, Maddeaux, & Blouin, 1998), couples suffering from trauma (Johnson, 2002), depression (Dessaulles, Johnson, & Denton, 2003; Whiffen & Johnson, 1998), and chronic illness such as heart disease (Kowal, Johnson, & Lee, 2003), older (M. J. Bradley & Palmer, 2003) and gay couples (Josephson, 2003). EFT's collaborative and affirming stance makes it particularly well suited to value the spiritual beliefs of clients and families (B. A. Bradley, 2001). An individual version of EFT has been repeatedly tested (Elliott & Greenberg, 2001). In addition, EFT is used with families (EFFT: Johnson, 1996). Keiley (2002) reports the usefulness of EFT with incarcerated adolescents and their parents. The approach has also been integrated within feminist (Vatcher & Bogo, 2001) and life-cycle (Dankoski, 2001) perspectives.

With the couple in the vignette, EFT is specific enough to help the therapist see through the smoke of such a hot session to pinpoint relationship-defining elements and focus the therapist on key issues and processes. In this chapter, we offer a snapshot of an ever-evolving approach to couple therapy that we call emotionally focused therapy. We highlight the specifics of the approach and try to take the reader in-session as the couple begins to share moments of happiness and despair.

EMOTIONALLY FOCUSED COUPLES THERAPY

Essentially, EFT offers a brief systemic approach to changing distressed couples' rigid interaction patterns and emotional responses and enhancing the development of a secure bond (Johnson, 1996; Johnson & Denton, 2002). This approach targets absorbing affect states that organize stuck patterns of interaction in distressed relationships (Gottman, Driver, & Tabares, 2002; Heavey, Christensen, & Malamuth, 1995). These patterns become self-reinforcing, often taking the form of critical pursuit followed by distance and defensiveness; EFT combines an experiential, intrapsychic focus on inner experience with a systemic focus on cyclical interactional responses and ensuing patterns. It is a constructivist approach in which clients are seen as the experts on their experience. Key elements of experience, such as attachment needs and fears, are unfolded and crystallized in therapy sessions. Clients are not labeled or pathologized. Rather, they are viewed as struggling with problems arising from a particular social context that would likely be just as problematic for the therapist to deal with if she found herself there (Neimeyer, 1993).

To achieve these goals, EFT integrates key elements of client-centered therapy (e.g., Rogers, 1951) with general systems theory principles (von Bertalanffy, 1956) as seen in structural family therapy techniques (Minuchin & Fishman, 1981). Attachment theory (Bowlby, 1969, 1988) provides EFT with a developmental nonpathologizing theoretical context for understanding the importance of emotional bonds, interdependency, and adult love and intimacy. A brief overview of principles from these theories that have impacted EFT follows.

SYSTEMS THEORY ROOTS

Systems theory places an emphasis on the power of present interactions, especially patterned sequences and feedback loops, to direct and prohibit individual behavior (Watzlawick, Beavin, & Jackson, 1967). Systemic therapists make in-session process assessments based on present sequences of interactional behavior. The therapist is active and directive, using such interventions as reframing and creating enactments between family members (Butler & Gardner, 2003). The systemic therapist uses shifts in intensity to modify current problematic patterns within the family. This is done not only with the words chosen, but also with changes in tone, volume, and pacing (Minuchin & Fishman, 1981).

Although sharing in these historic systemic principles, the EFT focus on emotion and the inclusion of the concept of self differs from pure systemic models. The idea of emotion, often thought of as a "within" phenomenon, being a leading or organizing element in interactional cycles is not addressed in traditional versions of systems theory. The field is increasingly recognizing that an understanding of emotional processing and a focus on self as defined in key interactions can be integrated into systems theory (Johnson, 1998; Linares, 2001; Nichols, 1987). Early systems theorists tended to rely heavily on mechanistic concepts, such as homeostasis. Von Bertalanffy himself hated this application, believing it reduced a living organism to the level of a robotic machine (Nichols & Schwartz, 2003). Therefore, EFT views emotion as a primary signaling system that organizes key interactions in couple and family systems.

EXPERIENTIAL ROOTS

Greenberg and Johnson, coauthors of EFT, are trained in the humanistic experiential perspective as outlined by Rogers (1951) and Perls, Hefferline, and Goldman (1951). In experiential therapy, clients are led to experience, become aware of, and *process* their emotions. Emotions are seen as powerful, healthy, informative, and organizational (Johnson, 1996). The disowning of emotion and needs is viewed as problematic. Human beings are viewed as generally healthy and oriented toward growth with healthy needs and desires.

In EFT, emotions are viewed as *relational action tendencies* forming a basis of social connectedness and constantly giving us signals about the nature of our social bonds (Greenberg & Paivio, 1997; Johnson, 1996). Emotion orients partners to their own needs, organizes responses and attachment behaviors, and activates core cognitions concerning self, other, and the very nature of relationships. It is also the primary signaling system in relationship-defining interactions (Johnson, 1998). Expressions of affect pull for particular responses from others and are central in organizing interactions. As one spouse, for example, angrily insists that his partner has neglected him repeatedly, his partner braces and withdraws in self-protection. Later, however, when he moves through his anger and accesses emotions involving being hurt, and his fear that he no longer really matters to his spouse, his partner is drawn toward him.

ATTACHMENT THEORY

Attachment theory (Bowlby, 1969, 1988; Johnson, 2003a) provides a theory of healthy and unhealthy functioning, a way of answering the whys behind couple conflicts. The EFT therapist perceives symptoms of marital distress as distorted expressions of normal attachment-related emotion (Johnson, 1986). The experiential focus on affect and the systemic focus on interpersonal patterns are understood within an attachment context of separation distress and an insecure bond. In attachment terms, a bond refers to an emotional tie, that is, a set of attachment behaviors to create and manage proximity to the attachment figure and regulate emotion. The accessibility and responsiveness of attachment figures are necessary to a feeling of personal security. Separation anxiety and efforts to cope with it are believed to occur in both infant-caregiver relationships and in romantic adult relationships (Hazan & Shaver, 1987, 1994).

Attachment theory offers a much-needed theory of adult love relationships (Roberts, 1992). It is a systemic theory of development that has been studied extensively with families and couples across many forms of psychopathology and approaches to psychotherapy (Bartholomew & Perlman, 1994; Cassidy & Shaver, 1999). Bowlby believed in the power of social interactions to organize and define inner and outer realities. Human beings naturally seek love and connection from other human beings—that is how we flourish and that is how we know who we are. This love sustains us and offers us a safe haven or a secure base from which to explore the world. Attachment theory depathologizes dependency in adults and sees autonomy and connection as two sides of the same coin. In attachment contexts, a couple that is fiercely fighting in session is in reality fighting for a sense of safety and security with each other. Recent research demonstrates that a "turning towards" and soothing behaviors are the basis for friendship, passion, and great sex (Gottman et al., 2002). Attachment theorists suggest that sexual behavior connects adult partners, as holding connects parent and child (Hazan & Zeifman, 1994). Adult attachment research has demonstrated that secure relationships display higher levels of trust, intimacy, satisfaction, and better communication practices (Cassidy & Shaver, 1999; Johnson & Whiffen, 2003).

Process of Change

The EFT process of change has been delineated into nine steps, contained in three stages and change events (Johnson, 1996). An explanation of the interventions, stages, steps, change events, and interventions in EFT follows. A case example of a couple treated in the approach is illustrated within each of these corresponding stages. Therapy excerpts with identified interventions are included to exemplify clinical application within each stage across the overall process that is EFT.

STAGE 1: CYCLE DE-ESCALATION

Step 1: Assessment. Creating an alliance and identifying the relational conflict issues between spouses from an attachment perspective.

In EFT the client is the *relationship*. Initiating and maintaining a collaborative alliance in which each spouse experiences being sensitively listened to, understood, empathized with, and not blamed is essential. The therapist assesses positive and negative cycles of interaction, attachment insecurities, longings, and needs, which often underlie intense negative cycles of interaction in initial sessions. The therapist also assesses for factors that preclude the use of EFT, such as ongoing abuse or violence. The assessment phase of EFT is discussed in detail in the literature (Johnson, 1996).

Step 2: Identify the negative interactional cycle that maintains attachment insecurity and distress.

In Step 2, the therapeutic focus narrows, and the therapist must help the couple slow down and recognize their interactional patterns. Like the structural therapist, the EFT therapist allows the couple to reenter their negative cycle, often by focusing on a recent argument. The therapist persists in getting a blow-by-blow account, as if she were listening to a live event broadcast on the radio. This is focused explicitly on who does what and when, then who does what and when, then . . . , and so on. As each spouse gives the reenactment, the therapist is often taking notes of the cycle and reflecting it back by checking in with each spouse. The therapist puts the cycle into an attachment context by reflecting how each spouse ends up in separation distress, becoming absorbed in angry protest, and feelings of helplessness and isolation.

Step 3: Access the primary/unacknowledged emotions underlying each partner's interactional position.

In Step 3, secondary reactive emotions such as anger, frustration, bitterness, feelings associated with depression, or distance, are reflected and validated as couples initially recount them, but they are not emphasized. The underlying primary, or more vulnerable emotions, such as sadness, fear, and shame, are emphasized in therapist reflections. The therapist must, however, often go through secondary emotions, such as frustration or helpless numbing, to elicit a more nuanced awareness of more primary emotions. As a husband, for example, tells of withdrawing from his wife, the therapist reflects his secondary anger. When he subsequently relates, however, that he moves away from her because he feels "overwhelmed" and there is "no way out"—this is reflected with emphasis. A typical tracking intervention is "Let me be sure I am hearing you right, Rusty. She is asking you for answers. You experience this as (therapist slightly raises voice) 'Answer me!' You go silent. And then you experience her behavior as 'Bam! Bam! Answer me!' At that point, so much has been said that you don't know where or how to start answering. Inside, you feel . . . overwhelmed? It's like, 'This is just too much. I can't deal with all of this.' If it continues, you sometimes yell 'Stop!' Is this how it goes for you? Is that close?" The therapist would then move into accessing the primary emotions underlying feelings of being overwhelmed. "Could you please help me understand what it's like for you to feel so overwhelmed, like there is no way out?"

Step 4: Reframe the problem in terms of the negative cycle, the primary emotions, and the unmet attachment needs so that the cycle is viewed as the key relationship problem.

The therapist has a real sense of the problematic cycle now and repeatedly reframes distress in terms of the cycle, thus removing the focus of blame from any one partner: "There just seem to be these arguments that you guys get into. You've told me of it over and over again. It's like it has an energy all of its own. This cycle is powerful." The therapist emphasizes the problem in terms of circular causality and moves this cycle from an inner, and perhaps unclear phenomenon, to something outside and malleable. Together, the couple now sees their cycle, which has the effect of externalizing the problem (White & Epston, 1989).

The therapist further expands on the significance of the cycle from within an attachment context by reflecting how the aftermath of the negative cycle leaves partners alone and disconnected from each other. Feelings of loneliness, failure, and despair are pitted against what the couple really wants, which is safety, companionship, and connection. Steps 1 through 4 lead to cycle de-escalation, the first change event in EFT. Couples who have de-escalated their cycle typically spend much less time in their more reactive secondary emotions, are more cheerful, helpful, and have a real understanding of their cycle in its totality (behaviors, stances taken, reactive and underlying emotions). They still fight, but less often, and report being able to exit from the cycle and rediscovering activities they mutually enjoy.

The cycle must de-escalate before moving into Steps 5 through 7. Partners will not take the emotional risks necessary for the emotional restructuring in the next stage of EFT unless there has been cycle de-escalation. The couple is then prepared to enter Stages 2 and 3 of the approach in which a new, positive cycle is created that promotes attachment security—a second-order change.

STAGE 2: RESTRUCTURING INTERACTIONAL POSITIONS

Step 5: Promote an experiential identification of disowned or marginalized attachment needs and fears and aspects of self.

Step 6: Promote acceptance by each partner of the other's emerging experience.

Step 7: Facilitate the expression of needs and wants to restructure the interaction, based on new understandings, and create bonding events.

Steps 5 through 7 should be processed with the withdrawing and more-placating spouse *before* deeply engaging the more-attacking spouse in this process. If this is not done and the more-attacking partner is encouraged to take significant risks that the withdrawer cannot respond to, the couple may relapse and lose their ability to de-escalate negative interactions. Step 5 is the most individually oriented step in the EFT process. The therapist explores the intrapsychic processing of attachment-related affect with more experiential detail. The sense of underlying failure and helplessness, for example, previously recognized by a more-withdrawing spouse such as Rusty, may now become the focus of therapy. Concepts of views of other and self, often as unlovable or incompetent, emerge as partners touch and organize painful emotions. As each partner further explores attachment-related affect, new meaning emerges that grounds and mobilizes them for action. As the withdrawer experiences his sense of failure in his marriage, for example, he often becomes sad. He begins to grieve that he is not the husband he wants to be. As this primary emotion of sadness is further processed, he often touches a real sense of loneliness and his need for a more secure connection. His awareness of his longing and fears begins to help him assert his needs and change his way of engaging his partner.

The following excerpt highlights the beginning of withdrawer reengagement in Step 5:

THERAPIST: Rusty, before you talked about how after you guys had gotten into your cycle a little, at some point you felt as if you got "kicked in the stomach," was that the wording you used (Tracking and Reflecting Interactions)?

RUSTY: Yeah, that's it. It's like we are fighting at this one level, and that's bad enough, but then, bam, she will say something that just hits me hard, like getting kicked in the stomach.

THERAPIST: Right. And at that point, in the past, the wall just immediately came up. Once that happened, you got angry and sometimes fought back for a while, but most often ended up getting the heck out of there (Reframing Behavior in Context of the Cycle).

RUSTY: Oh yeah. Once that happened, I wasn't going to stand around and seek reconciliation. That was it. That hurts too much (shakes his head slightly and casts his gaze down slightly).

THERAPIST: (slowing pace) It's just so painful when that "kick" comes. I see now that it's like you are going there, you kind of look toward the floor and have this expression on your face like you are reentering it (Reflecting Underlying Emotion). Help me understand what it's like for you to be "kicked in the stomach?" It's like you're trying to do the cycle differently, you're trying to find a way to beat this thing, and wham, there it is. What happens inside for you (Evocative Responding)?

RUSTY: It's just terrible (looking down, slightly shaking his head). Like I said, it feels like I have just been kicked in the stomach. Here I am, once again trying to solve things, or trying to do something different to derail this thing, and, just like that, it's over. Once that happens, the wall comes up, or I fight back like crazy.

THERAPIST: The impact Rosie has on you is enormous. When you experience her as coming at you with full guns blazing, you try to dodge the bullets, but when they hit dead center, you're saying, "That's it. That just hurts too much. I am outta here" (Reflecting Primary Emotion within Context of the Cycle). Is that kind of how it goes for you (Evocative Responding)?

RUSTY: That's exactly how it goes for me. I try to dodge as many as I can, hoping to stop the firing, but when they hit center, the armor comes out, and the wall goes up.

THERAPIST: So, it's like you are there trying to connect with your wife, trying to find a peaceful resolution, but you end up running for cover.

RUSTY: That's right. It's the exact opposite of what I am trying to accomplish. I go in with a peace treaty. I come out wounded, angry, and out of range.

THERAPIST: The sense I get, and help me here if I am off, is (slow and with emphasis). "Oh no, here it is again. I try and try to connect, or please my wife, and once again I miss the mark. Once again, I go into this cycle, and I can't make it better. No matter what I do I lose" (Heightening).

RUSTY: (with emphasis) Yeah! I can't get it, or do it right.

THERAPIST: (still slow) What's that like for you, *to try and try and try,* only to feel as if you've messed it up again (Evocative Responding)?

RUSTY: Failure (very quickly and very definitely, looking right at the therapist).

THERAPIST: (slowly and softly) Right. And you say that with such clarity.

RUSTY: Because that's what it is. I have failed again. I can't get it right.

THERAPIST: It's like, "I can't win. I've tried everything I know, and yet in the end I still measure up as a failure as a husband" (Heightening).

RUSTY: That's right. That's how I feel. I've failed.

THERAPIST: That's tough Rusty. That's a tough place to be. It sounds like you not only feel like a failure, but that you wind up feeling like you've failed *and* are all alone. You're alone in that sense of failure as a husband. Would you please, right now, begin to share with Rosie what this is like for you? You've done it with me, I'd like for you to talk with Rosie some about this (Restructuring and Shaping Interactions: Enacting New Behaviors Based on New Emotional Responses).

In Step 6, the therapist processes the above event with the opposite partner. The therapist emphasizes the reframe of the other's stance in terms of underlying and vulnerable emotions that pull for comfort and connection. Reframes, Reflections, and Evocative Questions, such as "What is it like sitting here right now hearing from your husband how he feels like he is failing?" are common. The therapist helps this spouse integrate her own emerging primary emotions that have been pricked while witnessing Step 5 with his or her partner. Processing these emerging emotional action tendencies prepares this partner to hear and respond soothingly in Step 7, where the once-withdrawn partner will be asked to risk and reach for acceptance and comfort.

Step 7 in many ways is the most crucial step in EFT. Continuing the theme of withdrawer reengagement, as the primary attachment emotions identified in Step 5 are more fully processed, the associated action tendencies propel the partner toward asserting attachment needs for connection and security. Typically, the therapist initiates an enactment in which the engaging partner states quite clearly his desire for a new kind of connection. This is a Stage 4 enactment characterized by intensity and attentiveness to affect, focus on attachment needs and wants, mutual responsiveness and empathy, with therapist mainly as observer and consultant (Butler & Gardner, 2003). Rusty was able to articulate his attachment hurts and fears from a deeper level as:

"I just am tired of running, tired of being afraid."

"Let the cards fall. I'll deal with it. I'm just tired of being scared."

"That fear is still there, it's just smaller. I know she will get angry, but now I know that she really is hurt underneath that anger, and that we'll make it through."

The process continues as the therapist helps Rusty confide with his spouse:

"I hate it when we fight. It kills me. I want to keep that connection with you."

"I need for you to back off from your anger some. I need for you to give me a chance."

Rosie states that it is scary for her too, but that she likes what is happening: "On the one hand I feel really sad for him, but on the other it's really good to know" (Looking at Rusty). "It's really good to know that you want this to work so deeply. I don't ever see this other side of you. I need to see it."

The next part of the process, now that Rusty is emotionally engaged, is to initiate Steps 5 through 7 with Rosie and complete a blamer-softening event. A softening event happens when a previously hostile/critical spouse asks from a position of vulnerability for reassurance, comfort, or some other attachment need to be met. The blaming spouse is able to disclose vulnerable aspects of self, and the withdrawn partner responds acceptingly. A softening represents a shift in the negative interaction cycle toward increased accessibility and responsiveness. The blamer-softening event has been found to be crucial in successful EFT (Johnson & Greenberg, 1988). B. A. Bradley and Furrow (2004) recently discovered six distinct therapist thematic foci shifts and specific interventions in Step 7 of EFT during the softening process.

For Rosie, key aspects of the softening process were anchored in a negative view of self. Fears of not being good enough or perfect, and of feeling deficient, were explored. The therapist empathized, reflected, and heightened these fears. Rosie was encouraged to make a Softening Reach to her husband from a vulnerable position, asking him for attachment needs of acceptance and comfort to be met. Key moments in the softening process for Rosie and Rusty were the following:

- In Step 5, Rosie wept as she expressed the burden and shame associated with always needing to "have everything together" and "be perfect." The therapist empathized with, reflected, and heightened this sense of burden, and helped Rosie begin to share with her spouse how afraid and plagued she feels trying to meet her own impossible standard.
- In Step 6, the therapist supported Rusty, who spoke of feeling sad for Rosie, and yet "relieved." "I can relate to someone who makes mistakes," Rusty explained. "Because I make mistakes too."

In Step 7, the therapist further heightened and expanded Rosie's fears of not achieving perfection, which evolved into a view of self as deficient, and a deep-seated fear that underneath it all she might not be what Rusty really wanted. "Who would want someone as screwed up as me?" she cried.

- The therapist reflected slowly and softly, "He's right there, and he does want you. In fact, he's just said that it's that afraid and unsure part that he wants the most. He wants to comfort you. Can you let him? Can you tell him now how afraid you are to show this part to him? Can you begin to ask him for acceptance . . . for reassurance . . . right now?"
- Rosie was able to risk a Softening Reach: "It's so scary for me. I mean, I know that you will be there, but I am just so afraid . . . I just need you not to think I am yuckie, or messed up. I need you to sometimes just hold me when I feel this way."
- The therapist aided Rusty in articulating and responding with acceptance and comfort toward his wife. Rusty very softly told Rosie that he would never leave her, and that "I want you just the way you are. Imperfect. Like me."

STAGE 3: CONSOLIDATION/INTEGRATION

Step 8: Facilitate the emergence of new solutions to old problems.

Step 9: Consolidate new positions and cycles of attachment behavior.

In Stage 3, the therapist reviews the accomplishments of the couple by highlighting the initial negative interactional cycle and contrasting it with the new positive interactional cycle. The couple often brings in a recent example of how they interacted positively and supported each other in some area that previously would have been toxic. The therapist praises the couple and helps them to own a narrative of how they have repaved the bond between them. She continues to reflect each partner's behavior in attachment terms of mutual accessibility and responsiveness. The therapist thus helps the couple further consolidate the newly acquired and still-forming secure base between them.

Ultimately, EFT offers the couple therapist a clear conceptualization of couple relationships that fits with recent research on marital distress and adult attachment. The targets of the change process are clear, and the process of intervention has been delineated, manualized, and tested. Finally, EFT appears to get at the heart of distress in close relationships and to be applicable to many different kinds of couples. This integrative contemporary approach is part of the new revolution in couple therapy, in which the terrain and repair of adult relationships is no longer a mystery but a charted domain where the couple therapist can guide and support couples in their struggle for a more secure bond.

REFERENCES

Bartholomew, K., & Perlman, D. (1994). *Attachment processes in adulthood: Advances in personal relationships* (Vol. 5). London: Jessica Kingsley.

Baucom, D., Shoham, V., Mueser, K., Daiuto, A., & Stickle, T. (1998). Empirically supported couple and family interventions for marital distress and mental health problems. *Journal of Consulting and Clinical Psychology, 66,* 53–88.

Bowlby, J. (1969). *Attachment and loss: Volume I. Attachment.* New York: Basic Books.

Bowlby, J. (1988). *A secure base.* New York: Basic Books.

Bradley, B. A. (2001). An intimate look into emotionally focused therapy: An interview with Susan M. Johnson. *Marriage and Family: A Christian Journal, 4,* 117–124.

Bradley, B. A., & Furrow, J. (2004). *Toward a mini-theory of the blamer softening event: Tracking the moment-by-moment process.* Manuscript submitted for publication.

Bradley, M. J., & Palmer, G. (2003). Attachment in later life: Implications for intervention with older adults. In S. M. Johnson & V. Whiffen (Eds.), *Attachment processes in couple and family therapy* (pp. 281–299). New York: Guilford Press.

Butler, M. H., & Gardner, B. C. (2003). Adapting enactments to couple reactivity: Five developmental stages. *Journal of Marital and Family Therapy, 29,* 311–327.

Cassidy, J., & Shaver, P. (1999). *Handbook of attachment: Theory, research and clinical applications.* New York: Guilford Press.

Clothier, P. F., Manion, I., Gordon-Walker, J., & Johnson, S. M. (2002). Emotionally focused interventions for couples with chronically ill children: A two year follow-up. *Journal of Marital and Family Therapy, 28,* 391–398.

Crane, D. R., Wampler, K. S., Sprenkle, D. H., Sandberg, J. G., & Hovestadt, A. J. (2002). The scientist-practitioner model in marriage and family therapy doctoral programs. *Journal of Marital and Family Therapy, 28,* 75–83.

Dankoski, M. E. (2001). Pulling on the heart strings: An emotionally focused approach to family life cycle transitions. *Journal of Marital and Family Therapy, 27,* 177–187.

Denton, W. H., Burleson, B. R., Clark, T. E., Rodriguez, C. P., & Hobbs, B. V. (2000). A randomized trial of emotion focused therapy for couples in a training clinic. *Journal of Marital and Family Therapy, 26,* 65–78.

Dessaulles, A., Johnson, S. M., & Denton, W. H. (2003). Emotion-focused therapy for couples in the treatment of depression: A pilot study. *American Journal of Family Therapy, 31,* 345–353.

Elliott, R., & Greenberg, L. S. (2001). Process-experiential psychotherapy. In D. J. Cain (Ed.), *Humanistic psychotherapies: Handbook of research and practice* (pp. 279–306). Washington, DC: American Psychological Association.

Gottman, J. M. (1994). *What predicts divorce?* Hillsdale, NJ: Erlbaum.

Gottman, J. M., Driver, J., & Tabares, A. (2002). Building the sound marital house: An empirically derived couple therapy. In A. S. Gurman & N. S. Jacobson (Eds.), *Clinical handbook of couple therapy* (pp. 373–399). New York: Guilford Press.

Greenberg, L. S., & Johnson, S. M. (1988). *Emotionally focused therapy for couples.* New York: Guilford Press.

Greenberg, L. S., & Paivio, S. (1997). *Working with emotions in psychotherapy.* New York: Guilford Press.

Hazan, C., & Shaver, P. (1987). Conceptualizing romantic love as an attachment process. *Journal of Personality and Social Psychology, 52,* 511–524.

Hazan, C., & Shaver, P. (1994). Attachment in an organizational framework for research on close relationships: Target article. *Psychological Inquiry, 5,* 1–22.

Hazan, C., & Zeifman, D. (1994). Sex and the psychological tether. In K. Bartholomew & D. Perlman (Eds.), *Attachment processes in adulthood* (pp. 151–180). London: Jessica Kingsley.

Heavey, C. L., Christrensen, A., & Malamuth, N. M. (1995). The longitudinal impact of demand and withdrawal during marital conflict. *Journal of Consulting and Clinical Psychology, 63,* 797–801.

Johnson, S. M. (1986). Bonds or bargains: Relationship paradigms and their significance for marital therapy. *Journal of Marital and Family Therapy, 12,* 259–267.

Johnson, S. M. (1996). *The practice of emotionally focused marital therapy: Creating connection.* New York: Brunner/Mazel.

Johnson, S. M. (1998). Listening to the music: Emotion as a natural part of systems theory. *Journal of Systemic Therapies, 17,* 1–17.

Johnson, S. M. (2001). Family therapy saves the planet: Messianic tendencies in the family systems literature. *Journal of Marital and Family Therapy, 27,* 3–11.

Johnson, S. M. (2002). *Emotionally focused couple therapy with trauma survivors: Strengthening attachment bonds.* New York: Guilford Press.

Johnson, S. M. (2003a). Introduction to attachment: A therapists guide to primary relationships and their renewal. In S. M. Johnson & V. Whiffen (Eds.), *Attachment processes in couple and family therapy* (pp. 3–17). New York: Guilford Press.

Johnson, S. M. (2003b). The revolution in couple therapy: A practitioner-scientist perspective. *Journal of Marital and Family Therapy, 29,* 365–384.

Johnson, S. M., & Denton, W. (2002). Emotionally focused couple therapy: Creating secure connections. In A. S. Gurman & N. S. Jacobson (Eds.), *Clinical handbook of couple therapy* (pp. 221–250). New York: Guilford Press.

Johnson, S. M., & Greenberg, L. S. (1988). Relating process to outcome in marital therapy. *Journal of Marital and Family Therapy, 14,* 175–183.

Johnson, S. M., Hunsley, J., Greenberg, L., & Schindler, D. (1999). Emotionally focused couple therapy: Status and challenges. *Clinical Psychology: Science and Practice, 6,* 67–79.

Johnson, S. M., & Lebow, J. (2000). The "Coming of age" of couple therapy: A decade review. *Journal of Marital and Family Therapy, 26,* 23–38.

Johnson, S. M., Maddeaux, C., & Blouin, J. (1998). Emotionally focused family therapy for bulimia: Changing attachment patterns. *Psychotherapy, 35,* 238–247.

Johnson, S. M., Makinen, J., & Millikin, J. (2001). Attachment injuries in couple relationships: A new perspective on impasses in couple therapy. *Journal of Marital and Family Therapy, 27,* 145–155.

Johnson, S. M., & Whiffen, V. (Eds.). (2003). *Attachment processes in couple and family therapy.* New York: Guilford Press.

Josephson, G. (2003). Using an attachment based intervention with same sex couples. In S. M. Johnson & V. Whiffen (Eds.), *Attachment processes in couple and family therapy* (pp. 300–320). New York: Guilford Press.

Keiley, M. K. (2002). The development and implementation of an affect regulation and attachment intervention for incarcerated adolescents and their parents. *Counseling and Therapy for Couples and Families, 10,* 177–189.

Kowal, J., Johnson, S. M., & Lee, A. (2003). Chronic illness in couples: A case for emotionally focused therapy. *Journal of Marital and Family Therapy, 29,* 299–310.

Liddle, H. A., Rowe, C., Diamond, G. M., Sessa, F. M., Schmidt, S., & Ettinger, D. (2000). Towards a developmental family therapy: The clinical utility of research on adolescence. *Journal of Marital and Family Therapy, 26,* 485–500.

Linares, J. L. (2001). Does history end with postmodernism? Toward an ultra-modern family therapy. *Family Process, 40,* 401–421.

Minuchin, S., & Fishman, H. C. (1981). *Techniques of family therapy.* Cambridge, MA: Harvard University Press.

Neimeyer, R. (1993). An appraisal of constructivist psychotherapies. *Journal of Consulting and Clinical Psychology, 61,* 221–234.

Nichols, M. P. (1987). *The self in the system.* New York: Brunner/Mazel.

Nichols, M. P., & Schwartz, R. C. (2003). *Family therapy: Concepts and methods.* Boston: Allyn & Bacon.

Perls, F., Hefferline, R., & Goldman, P. (1951). *Gestalt therapy.* New York: Dell.

Roberts, T. W. (1992). Sexual attraction and romantic love: Forgotten variables in marital therapy. *Journal of Marital and Family Therapy, 18,* 357–364.

Rogers, C. R. (1951). *Client-centered therapy.* Boston: Houghton-Mifflin.

Simpson, J. A., Rholes, W. S., & Phillips, D. (1996). Conflict in close relationships: An attachment perspective. *Journal of Personality and Social Psychology, 71,* 899–914.

Sprenkle, D. H. (2002). Editor's introduction. In D. H. Sprenkle (Ed.), *Effectiveness research in marriage and family therapy* (pp. 9–25). Alexandria, VA: American Association for Marriage and Family Therapy.

Vatcher, C. A., & Bogo, M. (2001). The feminist/emotionally focused therapy practice model: An integrated approach for couple therapy. *Journal of Marital and Family Therapy, 27,* 69–84.

von Bertalanffy, L. (1956). General system theory. *General Systems Yearbook, 1,* 1–10.

Watzlawick, P., Beavin, J., & Jackson, D. (1967). *Pragmatics of human communication.* New York: Norton.

Whiffen, V., & Johnson, S. M. (1998). An attachment theory framework for the treatment of childbearing depression. *Clinical Psychology: Science and Practice, 5,* 478–493.

White, M., & Epston, D. (1989). *Literate means to therapeutic ends.* Adelaide, Australia: Dulwich Centre.

CHAPTER 12

Strategic and Solution-Focused Couples Therapy

Stephen Cheung

C OUPLES THERAPY IS very complex. Couples therapy must be sensitive to and simultaneously address a myriad of variables, such as the first person's unique life challenges, personal developmental stage, and interpersonal style vis-à-vis those of the second person; the couple's collective challenges; the couple's progress in their developmental life cycle; the interaction between the couple; and the interaction between the first person and/or the second person with another outside the couple relationship. These variables all impact the couples and the way they perceive their problems and their resources to solve their problems (Berg & de Shazer, 1993; Berg & Miller, 1992; Carter & McGoldrick, 1999; Haley, 1973, 1987, 1990, 1996; Madanes, 1981, 1990, 1991; O'Hanlon & Weiner-Davis, 1989). From the inception of psychotherapy until recently, many therapists had a one-size-fits-all mentality toward couples therapy and individual therapy in general. In other words, therapists tended to believe that one kind of therapy would be suitable for all couples and that one type of therapy would adequately address all problems between these couples. However, in the twenty-first century, therapists, informed by modern and postmodern schools of therapy, are more humble and realistic, and have rejected the one-size-fits-all approach. Instead, they realize their own limitations and those of their favorite therapy approaches (Cheung, 2001; Corey, 2004; Ivey, D'Andrea, Ivey, & Simek-Morgan, 2002; Prochaska & Norcross, 2003). They further respect the phenomenal world of the individual and trust his or her ability to solve problems. In this zeitgeist, this chapter presents strategic and solution-focused couples therapy (SSCT) and discusses how SSCT can be beneficially applied to couples. SSCT selectively integrates principles from two therapy approaches: namely, strategic couples therapy (SCT) and solution-focused therapy (SFT).

A brief review of the existing theoretical and clinical literature on SCT is first described. Next comes a brief review of the existing theoretical and clinical literature on SFT. The methodology of SSCT that selectively integrates principles of SCT and techniques of SFT is then presented. After that, the methodology of SSCT is applied to a specific case to illustrate how it is utilized to address problems presenting in a couple. Last, the chapter explores how cultural and ethnic sensitivity in the application of SSCT can lead to beneficial results.

REVIEW OF THEORETICAL AND CLINICAL LITERATURE

SCT is based on Milton Erickson's Strategic Therapy. The most prominent proponents of SCT are Jay Haley and Cloe Madanes.

Underlying Assumptions and Key Concepts   Haley and Madanes concur with Erickson's emphasis on tolerance of the idiosyncrasies of the individual. There are many different ways of living and many kinds of people. They also agree that it is the therapist's responsibility to initiate what happens during therapy and to design a particular approach for solving each of the client's problems (Haley, 1973, 1987, 1990, 1996; Madanes, 1981, 1991). Being highly practical, they deem it appropriate for the therapist to borrow any useful technique from other therapy models to address the presenting problem. They moreover espouse the epistemology of structuralism and a systemic perspective. The epistemology of structuralism attempts to identify the objective truth of universals and structures and principles underlying and governing human behavior; it holds that symptoms result from some underlying psychic or structural problem, such as an enmeshed family boundary, incongruous family hierarchies, or psychotic family games (Haley, 1987, 1990; Madanes, 1981, 1990; Minuchin, 1974; Minuchin & Fishman, 1981; Selvini-Palazzoli, 1986; Selvini-Palazzoli, Boscolo, Cecchin, & Prata, 1978). A systemic perspective assumes recursiveness or circular causality that views people and events in the context of mutual interaction and mutual influence. Instead of examining individuals and events in isolation, a systemic perspective examines the relationships between individuals and events, how each interacts with and influences the other. In other words, according to the systemic perspective, meaning is derived from the relationship between individuals and events, *where* each defines the other.

Therapeutic Content, Process, and Techniques

Haley (1987) states:

> No simple ideas about how a marriage should be can provide a map for the therapist today. There must be great tolerance of all the different ways couples find to live together or apart. A more sensible focus would seem to be on the particular problem a couple is having within their type of marriage. The nature of the marriage might not be changed at the end of therapy, but ideally there will be a change in the problems they came in with that were distressing them. (pp. 164–165)

He furthermore asserts that there are three main ways that couples arrive to present a problem: through a symptom of an individual, through a child problem, or through a direct request for marital counseling. Each of these requires a different therapeutic approach (Haley, 1987, pp. 165–173).

SYMPTOMS AS PRESENTING PROBLEMS

Haley (1987) posits that it is more expedient to bring in the spouse when an individual presents with a severe symptom because a directive given to a couple is more likely followed than one given only to the individual. Like other systemic therapists, Haley assumes that a symptom can serve some interpersonal function in a couple's relationship. For example, a wife becomes anxious whenever her husband becomes depressed. Her husband comes out of his depression to help her when she is anxious. While some therapists prefer to convince the couple that their real problem is their marriage, Haley proposes that the therapist focus on the presenting symptom/problem when dealing with the marital problem. That is, the therapist helps the couple improve the presenting symptom while attempting to indirectly improve the marital relationship. When there is an obvious improvement in the presenting symptom, the couple is more likely to trust the therapist to help them work together on their marriage.

A CHILD AS THE PRESENTING PROBLEM

Some couples can fight with each other without involving their children, while others center their marital struggle on the child. Rather than dealing with their particular difficulties with each other, they disagree with each other on how to parent. Consequently, their child may cooperate by developing symptoms to distract the parents from their marital conflict, unite them to focus on the child's problems, and so hold the family together. One of the treatment strategies is to unite the parents as a parental team to deal with the child's problems, and at the same time improve the marital relationship. Another way is to detriangulate the child from the marital dyad and advise the child to leave the responsibility of helping the parents' marriage to the therapist.

THE MARRIAGE AS THE PRESENTING PROBLEM

Haley maintains that because marital difficulties stem from lack of flexibility, one aim of couples therapy is to enlarge the possibilities of the two partners so they have a wider range of behavior. When doing therapy with a couple, it is prudent for the therapist to consider that whatever the partners do in relating to each other, they also do in relating to the therapist. For instance, a comment by the therapist is not merely a comment, but also a coalition with one spouse in relation to the other or with the unit against a larger group. In a nutshell:

> The marital therapist must take problems seriously, focus on specific issues, form deliberate coalitions to tip balances, not allow free expression of ideas that might cause irreversible harm, formulate goals, and not always require that couples talk explicitly about problems. Most important, the marital therapist should not assume that one couple or one problem is identical with another. (Haley, 1987, p. 179)

In addition, Madanes (1991) specifies six dimensions to conceptualize couples/family problems: involuntary versus voluntary behavior; helplessness versus power; metaphorical versus literal sequences; hierarchy versus equality; hostility versus love; and personal gain versus altruism (pp. 398–401). The dimensions of helplessness versus power, hierarchy versus equality, hostility versus love, and personal gain versus altruism seem to be easily applied to common couple difficulties. For example, when a spouse develops a symptom, two incongruous hierarchies are simultaneously defined in the marriage. In one hierarchy, the symptomatic person is in an inferior position because of helpless and disturbed behavior, and the other spouse is in the superior position of helper. Yet, at the same time, in another hierarchy the symptomatic spouse is in a superior position by not being influenced and helped, while the nonsymptomatic spouse is in the inferior position of being an unsuccessful helper whose efforts fail and whose life can be organized around the symptomatic spouse's needs and problems (Madanes, 1981, 1991).

To be effective and efficient, Haley and Madanes formulate hypotheses about the problems presented before the therapy sessions:

> By hypothesizing we refer to the formulation by the therapist of a hypothesis based upon the information he possesses regarding the family he is interviewing. The hypothesis establishes a starting point for his investigation

as well as his verification of the validity of the hypothesis based upon specific methods and skills. If the hypothesis is proven false, the therapist must form a second hypothesis based upon the information gathered during the testing of the first. (Selvini-Palazzoli, Boscolo, Cecchin, & Prata, 1980, p. 4)

There are no right or wrong hypotheses; there are only more or less useful hypotheses. A therapist may be guided by one or more factors to the more useful hypothesis with which to conceptualize a problem. These factors include what appeals most to the therapist, what elicits the therapist's sympathy for the couple, and what elicits the therapist's interest in the couple. Flowing logically from the assessment, therapeutic interventions are usually delivered in the form of an in-session question, and/or an end-of-session assignment or directive. They are selected on the basis of how the therapist thinks about the presenting problem as well as the specific characteristics of the problem itself or of the people who present it (Haley, 1987, 1990, 1996; Madanes, 1981, 1990, 1991).

SOLUTION-FOCUSED THERAPY

Solution-focused therapy (SFT) has been one of the most popular current approaches because of its emphasis on a nonpathological view of individuals, the focus on brief treatment, its pragmatic nature, and its easily teachable techniques (Becvar & Becvar, 2003; Nichols & Schwartz, 2004). The solution-focused orientation descends from the Mental Research Institute (MRI) Brief Therapy model and yet departs from the latter. It stays away from the focus on problems. Solution-focused therapists help clients concentrate exclusively on solutions that have worked in the past or will work in the future, while MRI therapists zoom in on the interactional context of the presenting problems with an eye on discovering problematic attempted solutions.

Albeit immensely effective with individual clients, SFT cannot be blindly applied to couples and the family. There are some problems with blind application of SFT to couples therapy. For instance, when applying SFT to a couple, the therapist may still maintain an individual focus. She may interview each person sequentially and lack knowledge and skills to facilitate the interactions between the couple. Moreover, the therapist may not have the proficiency to help the couple negotiate and resolve their differences. Consequently, SFT must be tailored or modified to be used effectively in couples therapy. The specific details of how SFT can be tailored for effective couples therapy are beyond the scope of this discussion. Nonetheless, suffice it to say that the following caveat and warning should be heeded. SFT can be applied to couples and families, only if the therapist constantly maintains a balanced view of each person's needs, resources, and characteristics in the family system, and promotes the use of their resources for the well-being of all the persons involved.

Underlying Assumptions and Key Concepts

The SFT approach begins with some refreshing assumptions. Individuals are healthy and competent. They have the capability to construct solutions that can enhance their lives, but have lost sight of these abilities because their problems emerge so large to them that their strengths are crowded out of the picture. They do not resist change; they in fact want to change. The solution-focused therapist ardently adheres to the belief that a simple shift in focus from what is not going well to what the clients are already doing that works can remind them of, and expand their use of, their resources (Berg & Miller, 1992; de Shazer, 1985, 1988, 1991, 1994; O'Hanlon & Weiner-Davis, 1989).

Like the Constructivists who believe in the notion of no true reality, solution-focused therapists believe that they should not impose what they think is normal on their clients. They disagree with the Structuralists' claims that symptoms are a sign of some underlying problem (e.g., covert parental conflicts, maladaptive communication). They focus only on the complaints clients themselves present, and help the clients reexamine the ways they describe themselves and their problems. Due to individual differences, therapy is highly individualized (Berg & de Shazer, 1993; Berg & Miller, 1992; de Shazer, 1994; O'Hanlon & Weiner-Davis, 1989).

Therapeutic Content, Process, and Techniques

The goals and contents of therapy revolve around resolution of the client's presenting complaints. To do that:

> Efforts are made to create an atmosphere in therapy where the individuals are helped to reorient themselves from focusing on their problems to recognizing and utilizing their strengths to resolve their problems. (O'Hanlon & Weiner-Davis, 1989, p. 34)

Solution-focused therapists contend that you cannot change your past, but you can change your goals. Better goals can get you out of your stuck places and can lead you into a more fulfilling future. Much of the work for SFT lies in the negotiation of an achievable goal (Berg & de Shazer, 1993; Berg & Miller, 1992). Instead of changing personality and psychopathology types, SFT therapists help clients construct well-defined goals (Berg & Miller, 1992; de Shazer, 1991; Walter & Peller, 1992).

Effective therapeutic goals have the following characteristics:

- *Positive.* Instead of having negative goals such as "I will get rid of my depression," the goals should be positive. A solution-focused therapist may ask, "*Instead* of being depressed, what will you be doing?" The emphasis is "What are you going to do *instead*?"

- *Present.* Change happens not yesterday, nor tomorrow, but *now.* A simple question to ask is "As you leave my office *today,* and you are *on track,* what will you be doing or saying differently to yourself?" Today, and not tomorrow, is the emphasis.
- *Process.* The key word is *how.* "*How* will you be doing this healthier and happier thing?"
- *Practical.* Ask the question "How *attainable* is this goal?" to help the client set realistic and attainable goals. In so doing, the therapist empowers the client to succeed and avoid disappointment.
- *Concrete and specific.* To help the client put his or her global, abstract, and ambiguous goals in specific, concrete, and objectively measurable terms, questions such as "How *specifically* will you be doing this?" or "How many times a week will you be working out?" or "What would you say *specifically* to him?" are asked.
- *Client control.* The question is "What will *you* be doing?" because it is assumed that the client has the competency, responsibility, and control to make better things happen.
- *Client language.* Use the client's words for formulating goals rather than the therapist's theoretical jargon (Prochaska & Norcross, 2003, pp. 461–462).

After the goal for therapy is set, solution-focused therapists play an active role in shifting the focus as quickly as possible from problem talk to solution talk. To attain this aim, they employ several techniques. These techniques can utilize questions or assignments:

1. *The question that highlights presession changes.* To capitalize on the client's existing strengths and resources, a question like this is asked:

   > It is our experience that many people notice that things are better between the time they set up an appointment and the time they come in for the first session. Have you noticed such changes in your situation? (Berg & Miller, 1992, p. 72)

   This sets up an expectation and assumption that it is quite normal and expected that their serious problems may be eased a bit since they made the appointment. Rather than rigidly adhering to the format of immediately asking a direct question about any presession changes in the beginning of the first session, this question, like any useful question, should be asked in a timely fashion.

2. *The formula first session task.* This is the standard assignment given clients at the end of the first session. The task goes like this:

   > Between now and the next time we meet, I would like you to observe, so you can describe to me next time, what happens in your (pick one:

family, life, marriage, relationship) that you want to continue to have happen. (de Shazer, 1985, p. 137)

This task is used to help clients reorient from a focus on bad things in their lives to thinking about and expecting the good; this shift in perspective is thought to build on itself.

3. *The exception-finding question.* This question prevents clients' global and persistent perception of their problems and directs their attention to times in the past or present when they did not have the problem, when ordinarily they would have:

   Can you think of a time when you didn't have the problem? What was different? What were you doing then? (Berg & Miller, 1992, pp. 75–76)

   The therapist explores with the client what was different about these times and finds ways to expand the number of exceptions to the problem.

4. *Miracle question.* This is an example of such a question: "Suppose one night, while you were asleep, there was a miracle and this problem was solved. How would you know? What would be different?" (de Shazer, 1988, p. 5). The question is used to activate a positive problem-solving mind-set as well as to steer the client to articulate a clear vision of the goal in treatment. It further helps the client look beyond his or her problem to what the solution would look like (Berg & Miller, 1992).

5. *Scaling question.* "On a scale of 0 to 10 with 0 being how depressed you felt when you called me, and 10 being how you feel the day after the miracle, how do you feel right now?" Such a question is used to identify concrete behavioral changes and goals, and nurture small changes toward treatment goals (Berg & Miller, 1992).

6. *Coping question.* "Given how bad that was, how were you able to cope?" This question is used to recognize the client's strengths to cope with the adverse situation, heighten his or her awareness of success, and motivate him or her to do more of what seems to work (Berg & Miller, 1992).

7. *Indirect compliments.* "Wow, how did you manage to do that?" is used instead of direct compliments or reinforcement. Indirect compliments trigger more self-observation or self-introspection and can unleash more resiliency, creativity, and strength to discover, consolidate, and expand successful solutions (Berg & Miller, 1992).

Solution-focused therapists also come up with five practical guides to therapeutic choices for the therapist and the client:

1. If it works, don't fix it. Choose to do more of it.
2. If nothing seems to be working, choose to experiment, including imagining miracles.

3. Keep the intervention simple.
4. Choose to approach each session as if it were the last. Change starts now, not next week.
5. There is no failure, only feedback (Walter & Peller, 1992, pp. 37–41).

RATIONALE OF SSCT AND GUIDELINES FOR SELECTIVELY INTEGRATING TECHNIQUES FROM SCT AND SFT

At first glance, especially to a novice practitioner, there appears to be an incompatibility between strategic couples therapy (SCT) and solution-focused therapy (SFT). We may raise the question of how these two distinct approaches to therapy can be integrated. This is especially so, since they espouse two diametrically opposed epistemologies. However, on careful study and consideration, the utility of SSCT's integration of selected techniques from each school of therapy is readily appreciated. Once understood, there are several compelling, though not obvious, reasons for such integration.

First, both approaches are brief in duration. Second, combining the two approaches can provide the therapist with a more comprehensive and balanced view of an issue than either one alone. Just as there are always two valid sides to a story or conflict between a couple, so a dialectical approach utilized by SSCT to selectively integrate principles from two apparently opposite therapy models is isomorphic to the couple and is a sound alternative for couples therapy. SSCT utilizes SCT, which espouses the Structuralist epistemology, to provide normative information from our family life cycle knowledge in order to help certain couples realize the normalcy and validity of their dilemmas and difficulties in life (Carter & McGoldrick, 1999; Haley, 1973). With recursiveness or circular causality as an integral part of its conceptualization, SCT also aims at improving relationship problems. In short, SSCT utilizes techniques from SCT to provide a macro view, or a high-level view of the issues facing the couple. Furthermore, strategic couples therapists are willing to offer education, directives, and guidance to certain couples who may need them at their stage of development and therapy.

On the other hand, SSCT utilizes SFT, which is informed by Social Constructionism; SFT focuses on the individual's phenomenological field and his or her constructed reality through language, our common social medium. It emphasizes the empowerment of the client to defer to the client's knowledge and ability to resolve his or her issues. This approach helps the client by shifting the focus of treatment to specific goal setting and solution talk. In brief, SSCT utilizes techniques from SFT to provide a micro view, or a close-up view of particular issues facing each person in the couple. Solution-focused therapists, in addition, aim at an egalitarian relationship between the therapist and the client from the very beginning of therapy and can fit perfectly with a lot of clients. It is evident that perceiving and conceptualizing an issue from these diagonally opposite viewpoints can offer the therapist a balanced and enhanced view of maintaining the normative/collective and individualistic foci at the same time.

Third, both approaches have made unique contributions in effectively and efficiently conceptualizing human dilemmas, engaging clients, organizing the therapeutic process, asking questions of impact, and facilitating changes. This integration provides the therapist more flexibility and versatility to draw on a broader range of knowledge and skills to accommodate a myriad of needs, motivations, and expectations of clients and their problems. By selectively integrating principles and techniques from SCT and SFT, SSCT provides the therapist the ability and framework to serve a wider range of clientele with a wider range of problems than a therapist armed with only SCT or SFT.

The guidelines for integration are as follows: First and foremost, begin where your client is. Because most clients come with a distressing problem with the hope of some removal of or relief from it, the therapist starts with the problem-solving emphasis of SCT by exploring with the client the presenting problem, offering emotional validation of his or her attempted solution, and instilling realistic hope for change in order to combat the client's demoralization and despair. Second, specific therapy goals are set and the ways to reach the goals are explored. Depending on the couple's cultural expectations of therapy, problems, and interpersonal styles, the therapist may stay problem focused for a while, because a premature shift from problem talk to solution talk may be construed as a lack of empathy for, or an utter disrespect of, the client's suffering. Third, when the client is connected to the therapist and the therapeutic process, the therapist skillfully uses the various solution-focused questions and interventions to highlight current and past successes, and tap into the client's internal and external resources to generate creative and effective solutions to his or her problems.

CASE STUDY

The following case of an individual demonstrates one of the most common ways a couple comes for therapy as Haley observes. A combination of individual and couples therapy sessions was offered to meet the intrapersonal and interpersonal needs of the situation.

Cathy, a 24-year-old Caucasian single female, was referred for treatment of bulimia of eight years' duration. She admitted to bingeing once a day and purging from three to four times a day to no purging for several days. Her weight was 110 pounds and her height five-foot three inches. She denied any interruption of her menstrual cycle. She was an administrative assistant in a small wholesale company. She was cohabiting with her fiance David, who had proposed that they get married within a year; nevertheless, her father was strongly against their relationship. Recently, David's information technology business had required much more of his time in traveling (that is, he spent three to four days a week away from home). Cathy had lately realized the deterioration of her condition resulting from the aggravation of her bulimic problems and decided to seek help.

Ever since her parents' divorce when she was 10 years old, she had been reared by her paternal grandmother. She had very little contact with her mother, who had remarried shortly after the divorce and moved out of the country. She remained close to her father, who in her eyes was a perfectionist and whom she strove to please. After her grandmother died, she moved to a boarding school at age 16. Within the year, at the suggestion of her friends, she experimented with different dieting methods, including the use of laxatives and self-induced vomiting. Since then she has used purging to regulate her weight.

David was invited to all the sessions, but due to his schedule he began attending the couple sessions only after Cathy had completed three individual sessions. Before Cathy's first session, the therapist formulated the following systemic hypotheses:

1. The decompensation of Cathy's bulimic symptoms was used to deal with her loss, stress, and loneliness.
2. She might have used her bulimic symptoms to take a one-down position in relation to David and to delay her decision to marry him against her father's wishes.
3. She had been exerting her independence from her perfectionistic father, which she experienced as disloyal to him, and she seemed to deal with her guilt with her self-handicapping symptoms.

In the first session, efforts were made to establish rapport, clarify the presenting problems, and set treatment goals. Cathy admitted to feeling distraught especially when she was alone at home after work. She reported that bingeing and purging had been her usual attempted solution and requested that a quick fix be prescribed. The therapist used the hypotheses above to guide his systemic information gathering about the specific nature and severity of the problem, and the attempted solutions and their efficacy so as to confirm and disconfirm the hypotheses. Because Cathy insisted that she obtain a fast relief from her problem and asked for solutions from the therapist, he respected Cathy and began where she was by employing a strategic model to ascertain what *had predisposed, precipitated, and perpetuated* the problem. Empathy and emotional validation and support were offered throughout the session to establish a good working relationship. While realistic hope was instilled, appropriate psychoeducation was provided. There was some preliminary information from the initial session to support the three hypotheses to varying degrees: that is, Cathy's symptoms serve the function of managing her feelings of loss, loneliness, and stress on the one hand, and balancing her relationship with David and her father on the other. At the end of the session, assignments were given in the form of filling out a dietary log and completing some psychoeducational reading material (Cash & Pruzinsky, 2004; Fairburn, 1995; Fairburn & Brownell, 2001; Fairburn, Marcus, & Wilson, 1993; Garner, 1997; Garner & Garfinkel, 1997). The purpose of the dietary log was to create baseline data of the client's eating problems and to serve as a springboard for highlighting and monitoring her current and future successes. The psychoeducational reading material was to give some education and explanation for Cathy's problem, which she required from the therapist.

In the second session, she reported that she binged about two times and purged four times in seven days, which corresponded to David's absence that week. She indicated that she initiated a binge or a purge after she had had negative interactions with her father or David earlier. She admitted that she felt unaccepted and unsupported by them when they criticized her for what she did, or did not praise her for her accomplishments. She felt sad, frustrated, and lonely; her feelings were empathized and validated. It followed smoothly that the Miracle Question be asked. She replied that on the day of the Miracle she will be free of bingeing and purging, and she will have no conflict with David or with her father. When asked what she will be doing differently then, she said she will feel content despite her father's critical comments and will be able to ask for support directly from both David and her father. She was then asked what she did to binge and purge *only* a few times that week so as to highlight her improvement. She reported that she had become more aware of what she was doing and thinking, and made an effort to call or be with someone, including her friends and David, when feeling most vulnerable. To zoom in on more of her successful efforts and solutions, she was further asked how she managed to make such an effort to reduce the frequency of her bingeing and purging. In the next two sessions, Cathy continued to indicate less and less bingeing and purging until in the fifth session she reported no symptoms at all. All along, she was helped to focus on what she was doing that worked and was given indirect compliments.

David and Cathy came in for conjoint sessions after the first three individual sessions with Cathy alone. Due to David's work schedule, the frequency for the conjoint couple session ranged from once every four weeks to every six or eight weeks. The focus of the couple sessions was to elicit David's understanding and support of Cathy's bulimic symptoms and help the couple manage Cathy's symptoms and their relationship issues. David and Cathy were motivated to deal with Cathy's symptoms and the relationship issues not only between the two of them but also between Cathy's father and them. They worked well as a team and were helped to stay solution focused with indirect compliments. In the third conjoint session, they realized how the disapproval of Cathy's father had an impact on Cathy's symptoms and the couple relationship. They decided that it was desirable to have the praise and blessing from Cathy's father on Cathy's accomplishments and their relationship. However, they also realized that they could not change her father's perceptions and actions toward them, but only their own. Cathy initially had a difficult time accepting this, but through open communication with David and her father in the coming weeks, she was able to accept this reality. Since the second month of treatment, Cathy had been symptom-free and had been increasingly assertive with David and her father in her opinions and needs. As the majority of the treatment was provided from a solution-focused perspective, it was logical to attribute the couple's success to themselves. The sessions were spaced out shortly after Cathy reported no bulimic symptoms in the fifth individual session. There were a total of six couple's sessions and six individual sessions over a span of six months.

DISCUSSION

In accordance with Cathy's needs, the therapist integrated SCT with SFT quite smoothly. First, the presenting problem was explored, and the initial psychoeducation and assignment were given in the spirit of the strategic model in which the therapist took charge of the session, made in-session interventions via circular questioning and psychoeducation, and offered directives in the form of assignments. The focus on the exploration of feelings and relationship building and maintenance, though not explicitly emphasized in either the strategic or solution-focused models, was paramount to facilitating rapport building and client improvement and growth. Only when Cathy and David were comfortable with the therapist and therapeutic processes, did the therapist doggedly remain solution focused. The solution-focused approach focusing on strengths and possibilities brought about positive changes and growth, which could easily be attributed to David and Cathy's efforts.

CONSIDERATION OF ETHNIC DIVERSITY ISSUES

As illustrated above, the integrated approach of SSCT can be applied to most situations that bring a couple in for therapy.

The examination and discussion of how SSCT can be specifically tailored to suit the cultural expectations of an ethnic group is beyond the scope of this discussion (Cheung, 2001). Nevertheless, it is noted that the efficacy of SSCT can be enhanced by ethnic and cultural sensitivity to and awareness of a couple's background.

For example, both approaches are relationship focused and are therefore congruent with most ethnically diverse client populations with a collective culture (i.e., Asian American, African American, Latino American, and Native American; Ho, 1997; Hong & Ham, 2001; Kim, 1985; Lee, 1982, 1996, 1997; Sue & Sue, 2003). Because these ethnic groups tend to look up to the therapist for some structure for treatment and expect to receive some kind of expert advice and directives, a strategic model will be consonant with the client's cultural expectation of therapy. In other words, with couples whose cultural identity is with one of these ethnic groups, case conceptualization and interventions from a strategic model will expediently be employed in the beginning stage of treatment. Not until the client is ready to explore his or her strengths and feels comfortable with a more egalitarian relationship with the therapist will a solution-focused approach be used (Cheung, 2001).

It should also be noted that for some Asian American cultures, the primary relationship in a family is not between a husband and a wife, but between parents and their children. Therefore, therapists do not see a lot of direct requests for couples therapy; instead, they may encounter quite a lot of child referrals that require interventions in the parenting and parent-child relationship domains. In these referrals, the therapist often detects some marital discord that may contribute to the child problem, or parent-child relational problem. The best way to handle the referral is to stay with the presenting problem to help the parents deal with the issue without focusing on the marital issues directly. Only when the couple see improvement in the presenting problem and trust the therapist and the therapeutic process will they ask for help in their marriage. Only then will the therapist have permission to look into the marriage. In many cases, the couples stop therapy when the presenting problem is resolved. This is acceptable to the therapist if he or she truly respects the clients' self-determination. Also, for the family that has had a good therapy experience, there is a greater likelihood that they will return later for other problems including marital issues.

SUMMARY

As discussed, human suffering is ubiquitous, complex, multidimensional, and multidetermined; therefore, no one single therapy approach can be effective with all people with all types of problems at all times. Ineffective couples therapy likely results from a mismatch between a conglomerate of factors such as client factors (e.g., inner resources, motivation, and interpersonal styles), therapist factors (including therapy styles and approaches), problem factors (i.e., the nature and chronicity of the problem), and relational factors. Therapists, who employ SSCT, enhance their treatment flexibility and efficacy by judiciously integrating and applying the theories and techniques from both SCT and SFT. They utilize the accumulated knowledge and skills of *both* approaches. On the one hand, SSCT utilizes SCT, which incorporates Structuralism and Systems thinking. In the spirit of Structuralism, SCT searches for the underlying causes of presenting problems, and uses the existing family developmental normative data from the human and medical sciences to understand, empathize, validate, and normalize the person's suffering. With recursiveness as a seminal part of its Systemic perspective, SCT accentuates the person's family context and circular causality to conceptualize his or her life tasks and challenges. It also employs the principles of change from SCT to effect rapid changes by giving directives or assigning between-session tasks. On the other hand, SSCT uses SFT, informed by Social Constructionism. It emphasizes the person's phenomenological field and his or her constructed reality through language. It provides a positive, empowering, and person-centered approach to help the clients focus less on the effects of the problems, but more on generating successful solutions. By employing SSCT, therapists increase their versatility and flexibility to conceptualize and intervene effectively with a wide variety of clientele burdened with a myriad of problems and challenges. Certainly, cultural competence in applying the SSCT model will only increase the therapist's effectiveness.

REFERENCES

Becvar, D. S., & Becvar, R. J. (2003). *Family therapy: A systemic integration* (5th ed.). Needham Heights, MA: Allyn & Bacon.

Berg, I. K., & de Shazer, S. (1993). Making numbers talk: Language in therapy. In S. Friedman (Ed.), *The new language of change* (pp. 5–24). New York: Guilford Press.

Berg, I. K., & Miller, S. D. (1992). *Working with the problem drinker.* New York: Norton.

Carter, B., & McGoldrick, M. (Eds.). (1999). *The expanded family life cycle: Individual, family, and social perspectives* (3rd ed.). Needham Heights, MA: Allyn & Bacon.

Cash, T. F., & Pruzinsky, T. (Eds.). (2004). *Body image: A handbook of theory, research, and clinical practice.* New York: Guilford Press.

Cheung, S. (2001). Problem-solving and Solution-focused therapy for Chinese: Recent developments. *Asian Journal of Counselling, 8*(2), 111–128.

Corey, G. (2004). *Theory and practice of counseling and psychotherapy* (7th ed.). Pacific Grove, CA: Brooks/Cole.

de Shazer, S. (1985). *Keys to solutions in brief therapy.* New York: Norton.

de Shazer, S. (1988). *Clues: Investigating solutions in brief therapy.* New York: Norton.

de Shazer, S. (1991). *Putting difference to work.* New York: Norton.

de Shazer, S. (1994). *Words are originally magic.* New York: Norton.

Fairburn, C. G. (1995). *Overcoming binge eating.* New York: Guilford Press.

Fairburn, C. G., & Brownell, K. D. (Eds.). (2001). *Eating disorders and obesity: A comprehensive handbook* (2nd ed.). New York: Guilford Press.

Fairburn, C. G., Marcus, M. D., & Wilson, G. T. (1993). Cognitive-behavioral therapy for binge eating and bulimia nervosa: A comprehensive treatment manual. In C. G. Fairburn & G. T. Wilson (Eds.), *Binge eating: Nature, assessment, and treatment* (pp. 361–404). New York: Guilford Press.

Garner, D. M. (1997). Psychoeducational principles in treatment. In D. M. Garner & P. E. Garfinkel (Eds.), *Handbook of treatment for eating disorders* (2nd ed., pp. 145–177). New York: Guilford Press.

Garner, D. M., & Garfinkel, P. E. (Eds.). (1997). *Handbook of treatment for eating disorders* (2nd ed.). New York: Guilford Press.

Haley, J. (1973). *Uncommon therapy: The psychiatric techniques of Milton H. Erickson, M.D.* New York: Norton.

Haley, J. (1987). *Problem-solving therapy* (2nd ed.). San Francisco: Jossey-Bass.

Haley, J. (1990). *Strategies of psychotherapy* (2nd ed.). Rockville, MA: Triangle Press.

Haley, J. (1996). *Learning and teaching therapy.* New York: Guilford Press.

Ho, M. K. (1997). *Family therapy with ethnic minorities* (2nd ed.). Thousand Oaks, CA: Sage.

Hong, G. K., & Ham, M. D. (2001). *Psychotherapy and counseling with Asian American clients: A practical guide.* Thousand Oaks, CA: Sage.

Ivey, A. E., D'Andrea, M., Ivey, M. B., & Simek-Morgan, L. (2002). *Theories of counseling and psychotherapy: A multicultural perspective* (5th ed.). Boston: Allyn & Bacon.

Kim, S. (1985). Family therapy for Asian Americans: A strategic-structural framework. *Psychotherapy, 22*(2), 342–348.

Lee, E. (1982). A social systems approach to assessment and treatment for Chinese American families. In M. McGoldrick, J. K. Pearce, & J. Giordano (Eds.), *Ethnicity and family therapy* (pp. 527–551). New York: Guilford Press.

Lee, E. (1996). Asian American families: An overview. In M. McGoldrick, J. Giordano, & J. K. Pearce (Eds.), *Ethnicity and family therapy* (2nd ed., pp. 227–248). New York: Guilford Press.

Lee, E. (Ed.). (1997). *Working with Asian Americans: A guide for clinicians.* New York: Guilford Press.

Madanes, C. (1981). *Strategic family therapy.* San Francisco: Jossey-Bass.

Madanes, C. (1990). *Sex, love, and violence: Strategies for transformation.* New York: Norton.

Madanes, C. (1991). Strategic family therapy. In A. S. Gurman & D. P. Kniskern (Eds.), *Handbook of family therapy* (Vol. 2, pp. 396–416). New York: Brunner/Mazel.

Minuchin, S. (1974). *Families and family therapy.* Cambridge, MA: Harvard University Press.

Minuchin, S., & Fishman, H. C. (1981). *Family therapy techniques.* Cambridge, MA: Harvard University Press.

Nichols, M. P., & Schwartz, R. C. (2004). *Family therapy: Concepts and methods* (6th ed.). Boston: Allyn & Bacon.

O'Hanlon, W. H., & Weiner-Davis, M. (1989). *In search of solutions: A new direction in psychotherapy.* New York: Norton.

Prochaska, J. O., & Norcross, J. C. (2003). *Systems of psychotherapy: A transtheoretical analysis* (5th ed.). Pacific Grove, CA: Brooks/Cole.

Selvini-Palazzoli, M. (1986). Towards a general model of psychotic family games. *Journal of Marital and Family Therapy, 12,* 339–349.

Selvini-Palazzoli, M., Boscolo, L., Cecchin, G., & Prata, G. (1978). *Paradox and counter-paradox: A new model in the therapy of the family in Schizophrenic transaction.* Northvale, NJ: Aronson.

Selvini-Palazzoli, M., Boscolo, L., Cecchin, G., & Prata, G. (1980). Hypothesizing—circularity—neutrality: Three guidelines for the conductor of the session. *Family Process, 19*(1), 3–12.

Sue, D. W., & Sue, D. (2003). *Counseling the culturally diverse: Theory and practice* (4th ed.). Hoboken, NJ: Wiley.

Walter, J., & Peller, J. (1992). *Becoming solution-focused in brief therapy.* New York: Brunner/Mazel.

CHAPTER 13

Integrative Healing Couples Therapy: A Search for the Self and Each Other

Patricia Pitta

THEORETICAL ROOTS OF INTEGRATIVE HEALING COUPLES THERAPY

PSYCHOANALYTIC AND PSYCHODYNAMIC APPROACHES

THE FIELD OF couples therapy had its beginnings in psychoanalytic and psychodynamic theories where marital problems are viewed as the result of individual problems stemming from childhood experiences, innate drives, and unconscious forces. A psychodynamically oriented therapist assumes that partners choose each other based on unconscious needs and that their problems are a reenactment of intrapsychic conflict (Pine, 1963). With these therapies, treatment is rather long, and a focus on the individual is primary. It has been reported that while the individual is learning about the self and his or her unconscious drives and repetitions, many marriages and families fall apart (Guerin, Fay, Burden, & Kautto, 1987).

FAMILY THERAPY APPROACHES

In the late 1940s and the early 1950s, family therapy began to examine how people relate and how individual and family functioning provide the tapestry for overall family function and dysfunction. The early contributors to the field of family therapy, Haley (1963), Jackson (1967), Bowen (1985), and Satir (1964) set the stage for future family therapists to look systemically (see also Chapters 7 and 12) at how families interact. This approach enables family therapists to evaluate the effect of intergenerational influences on couples relations and to teach clients how to improve everyday living skills, particularly communication, conflict resolution, and coping skills (Bowen, 1985; Fogarty, 1983; Guerin et al., 1987; Papero, 1990). One of the complaints regarding family therapy approaches is that the individual's differentiation is compromised and made secondary to the growth of the family system (Pine, 1963).

By contrast, behavioral schools of thought offer ways to improve marital interactions based on observing client behaviors. Aberrant behaviors are seen as learned rather than stemming from unconscious unresolved trauma of childhood. The behavior therapist works in the here and now to change the obvious causes of problematic behaviors and to provide solutions. Many see behavior therapy as a technology rather than a coherent therapy because it focuses on the outcomes of behaviors (Becvar & Becvar, 1988). Cognitive behavior therapy (Beck, 1976; Dryden & DiGiuseppe, 1990; Goldfried & Davison, 1994) has integrated social learning theory (Bandura, 1963) and cognitive processing (Mahoney, 1974; Meichenbaum, 1974). Cognitive behavior therapy enables clients to change their irrational perceptions and beliefs, and replace them with realistic perceptions, leading to behavior change and emotional well-being.

OBJECT RELATIONS APPROACH

Another way of looking at the marital interaction is offered by object relations theory (Scharff & Scharff, 1992), which views spouses' interactions by examining the internal object world of individuals and how each partner contains or projects his or her negative or positive feelings to promote healthier interactions or further dysfunction (see also Scharff and de Varela, Chapter 9, this volume). This approach was the first to integrate the individual's functioning, unconscious processes, and the marital interaction. This approach sets the stage for new ways to think about treating the couple interaction through the blending of several theories.

COMMUNICATION APPROACHES

Communication theories promote the use of skills such as the collaborative dialogue (Heitler, 1990, 1997) and a variety of more effective communication strategies that enable couples to share, explore, and problem solve (Gottman, 1999; Gottman, Notarius, Gonso, & Markman, 1976; Guerney, 1977). Better communication in turn promotes more intimate interactions and less conflict. The role of communication in couples who function well provides another theoretical avenue to include as part of integrative theories of couple treatment.

INTEGRATIVE APPROACHES

In the 1980s, integrative therapy became a means to explore the use of many theories simultaneously and in many different contexts (McDaniel, Lusterman, & Philpot, 2001; Mikesell, Lusterman, & McDaniel, 1995; Norcross & Goldfried, 1992; Striker, 1994; Striker & Gold, 1993; Wachtel, 1994). Proponents of integrative approaches include Pinsof (1995) whose couples therapy integrates behavioral, biobehavioral, experimental, family of origin, psychodynamic, and self-psychological family interventions, and Pitta (1995, 1996a, 1996b, 1996c, 1996d, 1996e, 1997, 1999, 2003) whose approach integrates psychodynamic, behavioral, communication, and systemic theories to view the growth of the individual within the system, while at the same time working on furthering system differentiation and integration.

Utilizing integrative healing couples therapy enables a therapist to integrate a basic ideology and philosophy of treatment with other theoretical approaches. The resulting therapy helps individuals to change their thoughts, perceptions, and behaviors. It also enables the system to shift toward higher levels of differentiation and cohesion in functioning. Integrative healing couples therapy enables a therapist to teach couples to grow without unduly compromising their relationship. This therapy provides therapists with the flexibility to utilize a wide variety of approaches, tools, and techniques to explore changes in the system in order to facilitate individual intrapsychic shifts and explorations, and to learn how to make changes at a behavioral level (e.g., learning specific communication skills). Integrative healing couples therapy is an effective therapeutic strategy because of the richness of theories that can be applied to promote growth in patients' overall functioning, thinking, and behavior.

While working with couples, it is essential that therapists be sensitive to gender issues, power, control, money, and cultural backgrounds as determinants of how couples function and organize their lives, both individually and together. This chapter delineates for the therapist how to use integrative healing therapy to help couples change their perceptions, actions, and reactions to each other while further differentiating themselves.

CONTEXTUAL VARIABLES

To assist patients in differentiating and growing both as individuals and as members of a couple, we need to be respectful of the many contextual variables that affect their lives and therefore influence treatment. Contextual variables include race, ethnic background, cultural background, religion, gender, life cycle stage, socioeconomic background, and sexual preference. It is essential that therapists be comfortable with messages from their own cultural or ethnic background in order to appreciate patients' differences in thinking, acting, and beliefs, without assuming that their own cultural experience is the norm. Ho (1987) indicates that ethnicity is more than race, religion, national origin, and geography. Ethnicity includes conscious and unconscious processes that fulfill a deep psychological need for identity, security, and historical continuity. It is essential that a therapist be a cultural broker helping family members to reorganize their thinking about ethnic values and resolve conflicts that evolve out of different perceptions and experiences (McGoldrick, Giordano, & Pearce, 1996). Pinderhughes (1989) further notes that a therapist in relation to cultural and ethnic variables needs to be a teacher, advocate, coach, group leader, consultant, researcher, and organizer. A patient's ethnic and cultural identity can foster positive or negative self-esteem, self-worth, and identity. Identity, communication styles, family connectedness, and spiritual and communal sharing are highly linked to ethnicity and cultural issues. Many conflicts that couples experience can be dictated by culturally and ethnically stated or unspoken roles. Also, relatedness to extended family, as defined by culture and ethnicity, can contribute to the formation of conflict, leaving the couple struggling with anger, deprivation, and hunger for something different. Later in this chapter, issues of culture are revisited in a case that illustrates aspects of integrative healing couples therapy.

ROLES OF THE COUPLE—ACHIEVEMENT OF GOALS OF TREATMENT

Couples entering therapy often cite their desire for increased intimacy as one of their goals for therapy. Some of the criteria for intimacy to develop include:

- Providing a safe emotional place where the individual is free to be who he or she is without negative consequences.
- Establishing equality of power between men and women. Among other aspects, equal power means equal access to money regardless of which partner makes the money.
- Enhancing emotional equality between men and women (by helping them identify and express feelings enabling them to participate equally within a relationship (Brooks, 1995, 1998).

INTEGRATIVE HEALING COUPLES THERAPY—THE TREATMENT OF CHOICE

My work is an integration of psychodynamically oriented therapy, looking at the individual, and systemic-oriented therapy looking at the individuals within the system. Communication and behavioral skills are taught and applied when needed.

Integrative healing couples therapy is ideal for couples because it allows focus on individual issues while treating the couple together. In contrast, when a married couple goes for treatment with individual therapists, the likelihood of the marriage ending is 50% greater than if the couple went to joint treatment (Guerin, Fay, Burden, & Kuatto, 1987). Good marital therapy focuses on the individual's growth and differentiation, deals with the system's interactions (nuclear and extended family), and respects timing. Good therapy deals with problems so the relationship does not become unduly compromised or ridden with overwhelming anxiety or acting out, which leads to premature breakup. In integrative healing couples therapy, four types of conflicted couples have been identified:

1. Couples with underlying depression and use of primitive defenses, such as addictions (alcohol, drugs, gambling, work, alcoholism, and affairs) as presenting symptoms, without obvious extreme conflict.
2. Couples with extreme conflict, with borderline and psychotic defenses impairing their ability to define selves and attempts to maintain appropriate boundaries and interactions.
3. Couples with overt anxiety or depression with enmeshed families of origin.
4. Couples dealing with multiple marriages or relationships and their unresolved enmeshments.

EVALUATING THE COUPLES' AND SYSTEM'S LEVEL OF FUNCTION

In integrative healing couples therapy, it is essential to evaluate both the individuals' and the system's level of functioning before treatment begins so that the therapist can map out where to put the focus in treatment. The road map (see Table 13.1) provides a description of the process to be implemented in therapy (including the underlying theoretical approach). In drawing the road map, the therapist determines whether to begin with the individual or the system in the evaluation phase by assessing whether the environment is safe enough for the therapist to go right into individual work. Table 13.1 is the road map for the case described in detail in this chapter. When the environment is more combative and intense, a system's intergenerational approach enables the couple to realize that what is happening in their relationship is a pattern that began in previous generations. Therapy provides an opportunity to change history. For some couples, dealing directly with behavioral change may be a good place to start the work.

How to Evaluate and Treat a Couple's System

It is essential for the therapist to evaluate each individual's levels of integration and differentiation, and to assess how each person negotiates satisfaction in the world. At the same time, it is important for the therapist to observe how the members of the couple interact with each other, with their nuclear family, the families of origin, and the extended family. Part of the

Table 13.1

Road Map: Marital Couple with Depression Intergenerational Enmeshment

Process	Outcome
1. Systemic and individual evaluation	Create genogram-pictorial presentation.
2. Psychodynamic individual work with wife	Decreasing anxiety and depression.
3. Systemic extended family work	Limit setting and differentiation with wife's nuclear family.
4. Psychodynamic individual work	Husband's passivity and depression reduction.
5. Communication enhancement	Working on listening, validating, and negotiation in couple interaction.
6. Object relations	Husband worked on changing process of taking projections of wife.
7. Intergenerational work	Worked with husband's family of origin including joint session with nuclear family.
8. Communication enhancement	Members of the intergenerational families learn to listen, validate, and negotiate.
9. Object relations and psychodynamic individual work	Husband working through splitting defenses.
10. Cognitive behavioral skills	Husband changing perceptions as to what it means to be a man.
11. Systemic work strategies	Working with pursuit and distance.
12. Communication and individual psychodynamic work	Working with sexual problems from an individual and communication perspective.
13. Object relations work	Wife taking responsibility for splitting around money and using defenses of fear.

goal of the evaluation is to help the couple define the process they use to relate to each other and to others in their system. It is also important for growth and change for the individuals to own their own behaviors and to decide if they want to change patterns that no longer work for them.

In integrative healing couples therapy, joint sessions are ideal but are not always the norm, depending on the extent of conflict in the relationship. When the levels of conflict are high (Guerin et al., 1987), levels of safety are usually compromised, and little if any communication takes place, other than attempts at expressing anger and disdain. In very conflictual relationships, many individual sessions may be needed to lower the level of anxiety and hostility before couples can meet and discuss issues and feelings.

FREQUENCY AND TYPE OF SESSIONS

Ideally, couples are seen together for several sessions while we evaluate, decide on the goals, and devise a treatment plan. By contrast, joint sessions to clear the air can become quite destructive, since the session becomes a place to berate and put the other down. The person with the gift of gab or with uncontrollable anger proceeds to attempt to control the session and to intimidate the other partner. In integrative healing couples therapy, the individual is a major focus with the eventual goal of joining in therapy of the couples to negotiate the more differentiated and integrated selves.

When couples are more disorganized, chaotic, and anxious; when the safety factor is less; and when the ability to discuss feelings together is limited; individuals are seen alone with the goal of joining them later. This is accomplished once they can come together with self-control and less anxiety, to discuss issues and negotiate terms of the relationship.

The goals of the couple therapist are different from those of the individual therapist. The couples therapist must ensure that the couples differentiate their personalities within short periods of time, so that the marital bond does not get compromised. The couples therapist must also teach people to listen to each other, letting go of the defenses each has spent a lifetime developing. Helping each to become an empathic partner is essential for mutual respect. In order to be effective in working with couples, therapists must maintain emotional stability, connect with both partners, surface and neutralize toxic issues leading to decreased anxiety, define positions and then renegotiate them if possible, remain detriangulated as a therapist (considering all parties as equals and not taking sides), considering the impact of contextual variables on the couple and individual functioning, model appropriate interactions for the couple and individuals, and maintain a sense of humor. (Humor is an important ingredient in all therapy; it brings relief to the situation and helps reality to be worked with more calmly.)

INDIVIDUAL PERSPECTIVE

When looking at the individuals comprising the couple from a psychodynamic perspective, I consider basic drives such as sex, hunger, and aggression, and how they influence behavior. I consider how the individual can attain fulfillment and balance these drives so as to achieve integrated psychological functioning (Freud, 1959). Object relations theory provides a helpful cognitive map to identify how patients use defenses such as splitting, cutting off, projection, and projective identification to further impede their relating (Scharff & Scharff, 1992; see also Scharff and de Varela, Chapter 9, this volume). As a result of focusing on defenses, patients are able to own their split-off feelings, take responsibility for them, and then decide if they want to keep or give up their dysfunctions and accept responsibility for their behaviors. Acceptance of this new reality, leads the patient to take a more mature stance at levels of both individual and mutual functioning. Identification and introjection are explored as to their role in the patient's self-concept, view of reality, personality structure, and individual functioning. Reparenting skills (Kirschner & Kirschner, 1986) are utilized to enable patients to experience corrective emotional experiences. Cognitive behavioral strategies are utilized, which enable patients to bring both perceptions and behaviors to a healthier level of functioning. Cognitive relabeling, assertiveness training, role modeling, relaxation, and reinforcement scheduling are useful interventions, which may lead to learning new skills and changing behaviors, perceptions, and feelings (Goldfried & Davison, 1994). The improvement of communication skills is also emphasized through which couples can explore their newly acquired understanding and emotional expression within the marital bond (Gottman, 1999; Guerney, 1977; Heitler, 1990, 1997).

INDIVIDUAL WORK APPLIED TO THE SYSTEM

When working with the couple systemically, the goal is to help the couple, as well as the individuals who comprise it, to evaluate their specific actions and the effect of their actions on their partners, themselves, and their extended family members. I tell patients, "Remember every action gets a reaction; particularly, negative behaviors get reactions with interest (compounded geometrically)."

It is also important to guide individuals and couples to identify the origins of this behavior as stemming from the nuclear family, family of origin, or extended family. Behavior and belief patterns that may be transmitted include such things as addictions, or emotional disorders, which can usually be traced back to previous generations. That is why it is essential to take a history through the use of a genogram going back at least three generations. Creating a genogram normalizes people's perceptions when they realize dysfunctional behavior has been happening for generations and that they are repeating the patterns without being aware of what they are doing. Also, this process gives the couple and therapist an appreciation of ethnic and cultural influences that have been transmitted through the generations. Learning about the family through the genogram takes the stigma out of the couple's problems and enables patients to become empowered with information that enables them to change their behaviors and feelings.

CASE STUDY: OVERT ANXIETY AND DEPRESSION— ENMESHMENT WITH FAMILY OF ORIGIN

The family described represents not only a religion, but a culture with its own set of rules, norms, beliefs, and rituals that determine people's relationships, how they connect, and what is valued. The couple's extended families were survivors of the Holocaust. Both extended families were traumatized and robbed by this experience. The couple became aware that their parents and grandparents were involved in survival rather than relating. Both families lived in a state of dysfunction filled with fears and loss. The couple realized that their parents did not know how to parent, since they had not been parented themselves. Also, the couple's Jewish culture did not support divorce as an alternative thus supplying reinforcement for the patients to continue to work together rather than separate and deal with, as they said, "outside judgment and persecution."

BACKGROUND

At the first session, Harry, a 44-year-old male, from the Jewish middle class (a radiologist) and Suzanne, a 38-year-old female, also from the Jewish middle class (a housewife and tutor) presented with the complaint that Suzanne was demonstrating symptoms of overwhelming anxiety and anger, and was having fits of rage with her parents, husband, and husband's family. She was also having difficulty parenting their children, particularly her eldest child (age 10) whom she felt to be an emotional burden. Suzanne was also experiencing severe conflict with the members of her family of origin and her husband's family. She demonstrated outward emotionality for the family system, while Harry appeared as the cool detached nice guy. Harry appeared dazed, cut off, and emotionally dead. He attempted to pacify Suzanne's outbursts. This marital relationship could be described as an enmeshed conflicted system with underlying depression and anxiety. Harry's relationships with his family of origin were distant. He was cut off from contact with them except for the rituals of holidays and family milestone gatherings. He spent a great deal of time working, and he also devoted time in the evenings to his children. The couple's interactions were limited to attempting to solve problems with which Suzanne was overwhelmed. They had very little if any intimate time when they could be alone to experience emotional and physical intimacy.

WORKING ON THE INDIVIDUAL IN THE SYSTEM

We worked on Suzanne's level of anger and anxiety. She was a time bomb waiting to explode. She was furious that the majority of her friends who were economically and culturally similar had parents who lived locally and who lent a good deal of emotional and financial support. Her parents' behaviors were not typical of "Jewish families" that she knew. She felt not understood, ignored, and left alone. As a result, she felt paralyzed by paranoid feelings of being persecuted by her family. Suzanne had felt traumatized and abandoned at 20 years of age when her parents moved to Arizona and stopped all financial and emotional support. This abandonment was a repeat of earlier abandonment in her formative years. She was working at the time, but couldn't meet all of the expenses to live on her own. She was left in a terror, which reinforced her earlier childhood terror. The emotional and financial terror was not new to the patient, since in her family of origin money was pulled away and given at the whim of an inconsistent, self-centered, and immature father. Her mother sat by passively watching her husband's torment of herself and the family. Suzanne's self-image and gender identity was one filled with fear and passivity and uncontrolled emotionality, which was outwardly demonstrated by her actual fear of thinking, dealing, or handling money (repetition compulsion). She worked on separating herself from her parents. She was able to identify parts of her parents (passivity and anger) that she had introjected that no longer worked for her. She began to take responsibility for the feelings and emotions that she did not own and projected onto others (separation and differentiation). She needed to explore her cultural expectations of what a "Jewish family" meant and what her family was willing and able to give.

TREATMENT

We worked 90% of the time in joint sessions, in which Harry stood by while Suzanne worked on extended family issues. As a result of Suzanne's rebellion against her parents, her mother began therapy, and her father joined her mother at a later time in joint and individual sessions (intergenerational transmission process influencing family of origin). Suzanne's anxiety decreased to levels that she could comfortably attempt to work on her individuation from her parents. She began to draw clear boundaries between herself and her mother. She mourned her parents' abandonment and the cultural expectations she had of the role of parents and grandparents (differentiation). She presented limits and boundaries to her family of origin of what would be acceptable behaviors or interactions for all. She stated her needs and desires, even though they could not be met initially (assertiveness training). She was no longer allowing herself to be a confidante to her mother about issues with her father (differentiation). In many ways, she was parenting her mother rather than being parented. She began to set realistic expectations of what her parents could give her and what she could give to them emotionally (more differentiated stance). As Suzanne gained strength, so did her mother in her treatment; they eventually joined in a healthier coalition in a mother-daughter relationship. They even had a mother-daughter weekend to connect without tension and to function on a more differentiated level.

While I worked actively with Suzanne, Harry sat supportively through her growth. Harry was learning to listen (communication skills enhancement) and obtain access to his feelings through Suzanne's growth. We worked on improving communication and on an overall level of connectedness between the couple.

What was Harry's role in contributing to the dysfunction in the marriage? He married or rescued his wife when she felt abandoned by her parents as a result of their move. He took on the role of Suzanne's negative projections of men (projective identification) on one hand, and on the other hand, rescued her from her turmoil, while at the same time depriving her of access to a nurturing emotional connection because he was not connected to himself. As Suzanne's anxiety and functioning improved, the focus of treatment transferred to Harry's lack of connectedness to himself and others. He had no relationship with his family. He was an emotional escape artist, and as soon as he sensed tension, he left (exploring defensive structure). He came from a divorced family in which his father was an alcoholic and risk taker who left the family when Harry was 2 years old. Harry was left in a household with an overwhelmed, distraught, and distracted mother, and two brothers. The older brother took over the responsibility of nurturing the family. The middle brother was the one who carried the anger for the family, while Harry escaped and was allowed the freedom that the other siblings did not experience. In his family of origin, Harry learned few skills for dealing with feelings and expressing feelings and words (see Table 13.1). In the marriage, he remained silent, a good provider, and deprived his wife of a mutual interaction. We worked on how Harry, like his father, left the family emotionally, leaving the emotional work for the others (repetition compulsion). We also discovered that when his emotional distress and anxiety increased, he would think about his patients and business ventures. To further relieve his stress, he would leave Suzanne emotionally, even though he was physically present in the home. We discussed cultural expectations that Harry interpreted as providing money for the family. He was not aware that emotional support, understanding, and communication were also requirements for a healthy husband.

When Suzanne felt sufficiently strong and the relationship with her parents had improved, we had a joint session where the parents came to treatment when in town (intergenerational work). I spoke with the parents' therapist several times to compare progress and to exchange suggestions. Both therapists were working for the present and future integration of the systems (therapists working to enable further intergenerational differentiation). When I met with the couple and Suzanne's parents, we discussed mutual problems in the intergenerational systems. I made suggestions to both of them on how communication and interactions could become more effective and growth producing. We discussed old and present hurts, disappointments, and angers (relieving the bitter bank of anger and hurts). We explored expectations about coming from a "Jewish family" plagued with sadness from loss (both emotional and financial) stemming from the Holocaust. We discussed the effects of these atrocities on the lives of their grandparents and parents as well as their own. It became apparent that Suzanne's parents' expectations of their own parents were very limited. This set the stage for not meeting the daughter's expectations of so-called "modern American Jewish parents." Suzanne realized that her parents had limitations based not only on their personalities but based on the cultural messages and experiences transmitted from previous generations. As Harry listened, he became aware of the impact of the Holocaust on his family as well. His grandparents and parents had been survivors of the Holocaust. He came to realize that his parents, like Suzanne's parents, received little if any nurturing in their formative years. He became aware of the high level of depression and sadness in his family of origin and extended family, acted out as silence and avoidance. The couple became aware that the sadness and depression in both families of origin and extended families were acted out in abandonment, verbal abuse, and money control. As a result of this realization, the couple was able to make a shift in their thinking and adjust their expectations of their parents. As the couple became more secure with themselves and each other, they changed their expectations of what they wanted and expected from each other.

When Suzanne's parents felt their relationship with their daughter became stuck, I spoke with them on the phone, after obtaining Suzanne's permission. At times, they did not agree with my view of the problems, but it appeared that these conversations relieved their anxieties and enabled them to stay in positive contact with Suzanne. Suzanne's anger, anxiety, and overall functioning improved within nine months of our work together. The couple and I decided jointly that Harry's emotional growth was crucial to enable the couple to reach more intimacy and growth. We agreed that I would see Harry individually for a while, because in the joint sessions Suzanne took over, judged, criticized, and became anxious in dealing with or hearing about her husband's problems. Her self-centeredness and level of agitation (even though improved) got in the way of Harry's work. Therefore, I worked with Harry alone to enhance his ability to feel his and other's feelings, and to work through his defensive structure of splitting and cutting off. He utilized these defenses when issues were explored with which he did not want to deal. He needed the safety and one-on-one experience to work through these issues and to enable him to develop a new bonding. For about eight months, we worked weekly, and Harry's level of consciousness, ability to feel, and level of interaction improved remarkably (more differentiated and assertive). He became assertive as a "man" with his wife. He worked on becoming more connected and assertive with his family of origin. He invited his family to a session, and his brothers attended, which was a breakthrough for him. He was able to share his feelings about his passive behaviors, his siblings' actions, and how these interactions affected his life. The brothers talked about their parents, their culture, and their individual perceptions of their life histories. Harry also discussed his realization about the effect of the Holocaust on his family of origin. At this point in the treatment, Harry requested that Suzanne come back to treatment so they could work on their "stuckness" concerning money and sex in the relationship. Money was an issue that Suzanne refused to deal with because of the anxiety it caused within her and the re-running of the old tapes from her family of origin. Also, Harry wanted more intimacy from Suzanne both emotionally and sexually.

We worked jointly for three months discussing issues related to money and sexuality. Suzanne was interested and committed to overcoming her anxieties and fears in dealing with money. She worked with Harry in paying the bills, taking responsibility for paying some bills, where previously she had worked and kept the money she earned for herself. She started to learn about their investments and began to face her fears of "not having money"(cognitive behavioral strategies). At the same time, the couple's sexual relationship became more satisfying to both. The couple decided to end treatment at this point because they felt they had attained the level of emotional and physical interaction they both wanted with each other. In addition, they felt they had made essential changes in their interactions with their families of origin. As a result, both members were empowered to be emotional and financial equals sharing life in a more meaningful way. They were able to have romance and repair the past inherited from their families of origin (resolution and changing the repetition). Through successful family therapy, not only does the individual grow and differentiate, but the individuals within the systems grow (see how relationships have changed within their nuclear family and family of origin), supporting the maintenance of the family structure and individuation of the members.

As mentioned earlier (evaluation of the couple and their system), it is essential for a therapist to set a road map of treatment enabling the setting of goals and ways to reach them. The road map offers a written and visual tool to enable effective and efficient growth for the couple in relationship to their presenting and evolving issues. The road map evolves as the couple grows in treatment similarly to the way that roads progress in life's journey. As shown in Table 13.1, the process starts from a systemic and individual evaluation (Step 1), followed by individual work with Suzanne (Step 2), which extends to exploring extended family work with Suzanne's family (Step 3). The extended family work was an outcome of the individual work and Suzanne's readiness to deal with family patterns and interactions. In Step 4, Harry's individual work begins to give him some understanding of why he acts and reacts as he does. Since the couple has a better understanding of where they begin and end as individuals and within the system (differentiation), the couple is able to begin improving their communication (Step 5). As a result of communication improving, more intergenerational work can be done with Harry's family (Step 6), allowing him to grow further and differentiate himself. As a result of improved communication within the couple, Harry was able to see how he accepted unwarranted projections from Suzanne, which enabled him to further differentiate his functioning and create a more solid self. Harry was able to realize that he needed to do joint work with his family of origin to further free himself of old roles and patterns of behavior (Step 7). Within the context of Harry's intergenerational work, communication enhancement between the generations became a focus (Step 8).

In integrative healing couples therapy, the growth of one individual enables the system. As a consequence, members of the system interact with the ability to grow and differentiate as long as the individual maintains his or her new, healthier functioning (solid self). When working with Harry's extended family, Harry's use of splitting when dealing with toxic issues became apparent. This realization lent itself to work on Harry's individual issues through understanding the concept of splitting and its application to himself and interactions with others (Step 9). After working with the extended family and after focusing on Harry's use of the defense of splitting, he no longer saw himself as "the boy who runs," but as a capable man. He was able to change his cognitions about self and then act as the mature man he was becoming (Step 10). When he felt more manly and in charge of self, he began to pursue Suzanne in the way she really wanted from the beginning of treatment. We discussed pursuit and distance strategies, which enabled him to change his behaviors (Step 11). As he began to pursue his wife through verbal communication, sexual issues came to the forefront. Through the use of improved communication skills and individual work, looking at feelings and beliefs about sexuality, the couples' sexual functioning improved (Step 12).

The last step in the couple's work was for Suzanne to own her fears around dealing with money issues. We explored her internalized images of being a woman and how they relate to making, spending, and sharing money. As Suzanne was able to act more appropriately, more mutual sharing with money, respect, and sexuality ensued (Step 13). The couple felt that concerns about the relationship were resolved at this point and they were ready to leave therapy and to enjoy the new life they had created. See Table 13.1 for the integrative road map for this case.

Table 13.2 offers a description of steps in outline form for therapists to follow when working with couples to resolve conflict (Steps 1 through 9).

Table 13.2
Steps in Resolving Couple Conflict

1. Calming the system—reducing anger and anxiety in the couple
2. Taking responsibility—enabling partners to take responsibility for their parts in the dysfunction
3. Remediate and heal wounds—work toward self-healing and forgiveness, which will lead to self nurturing enabling mutual healing to occur
4. Defining individual's needs and wants
5. Meeting one's needs and wants
6. Defining couples' needs and wants
7. Meeting each other's needs and wants
8. Developing a more differentiated self
9. Developing a more mature connection and relationship with intimacy and friendship at the core intertwined with passion

It is most essential to calm the anxiety in the system and in the couple (Step 1). The therapist needs to focus on either the individual's anxiety reduction or on the couple's interactions (around issues of abandonment, money, sex, children, etc.). The less anxiety the couple demonstrates, the more the therapist is able to focus on the couple's interactions. Steps 2 and 3 can be worked on simultaneously. For some couples, healing the hurt and reaching forgiveness needs to be the focus before each can "own responsibility." Some couples (especially those who have been in previous therapies) come to session and ask, "What is it I need to own (or what can I do) to take responsibility for a change in the quality of our relationship?" Steps 4 and 5 enable individuals who have stopped blaming the other for their problems to define what they perceive they really need at this time in their relationship. The therapy also emphasizes how to get these needs met. Steps 6 and 7 help the couple to allow for themselves what they expect from the relationship. There is also a focus on how to meet these expectations. Steps 8 and 9 are the results of previous steps whereby individuals have developed a more differentiated and mature self. As a result, their relationship will function at a more mature level. They will also enjoy intimacy and friendship intertwined with passion.

The therapist can check progress after each session in following the steps outlined in Table 13.2.

REFERENCES

Bandura, A. (1963). *Social learning and personality development.* New York: Holt, Rinehart and Winston.

Beck, A. (1976). *Cognitive therapy and emotional disorders.* New York: International Universities Press.

Becvar, D. S., & Becvar, R. J. (1988). *Family therapy: A systemic integration.* Boston: Allyn & Bacon.

Bowen, M. (1985). *Family therapy in clinical practice.* Northvale, NJ: Aronson.

Brooks, G. (1995). *The centerfold syndrome.* New York: Jossey-Bass.

Brooks, G. (1998). *New psychotherapy for traditional men.* New York: Jossey-Bass.

Dryden, W., & DiGiuseppe, R. (1990). *A primer on rational emotive therapy.* Champaign, IL: Research Press.

Fogarty, T. (1983). On emptiness and closeness: Part 1 & Part 2. *The Best of the Family 1973–1978* (Vol. 1, pp. 70–90). New Rochelle, NY: Center for Family Learning.

Freud, S. (1959). The instincts and their vicissitudes. In J. Strachey (Ed.), *The standard edition of the complete psychological works of Sigmund Freud* (Vol. 14, pp. 60–84). London: Hogarth Press. (Original work published 1915)

Goldfried, M., & Davison, G. (1994). *Clinical behavior therapy.* New York: Wiley.

Gottman, J. M. (1999). *The marriage clinic.* New York: Norton.

Gottman, J. M., Notarius, C. I., Gonso, J., & Markman, H. (1976). *A couple's guide to communication.* Champaign, IL: Research Press.

Guerin, P., Fay, L., Burden, S., & Kautto, J. (1987). *The evaluation and treatment of marital conflict.* New York: Basic Books.

Guerney, B. (1977). *Relationship enhancement.* New York: Jossey Bass.

Haley, J. (1963). *Strategies of psychotherapy.* New York: Grune & Stratton.

Heitler, S. (1990). *From conflict to resolution.* New York: Norton.

Heitler, S. (1997). *The power of two.* Oakland, CA: New Harbinger.

Ho, M. (1987). *Family therapy with ethnic minorities.* Beverly Hills, CA: Sage.

Jackson, D. (1967). *Therapy, communication and change.* Palo Alto, CA: Science and Behavior Books.

Kirschner, D., & Kirschner, S. (1986). *Comprehensive family therapy.* New York: Brunner/Mazel.

Mahoney, M. J. (1974). *Cognition and behavior modification.* Cambridge, MA: Ballinger.

McDaniel, S. H., Lusterman, D.-D., & Philpot, C. L. (2001). *Casebook for integrating family therapy: An ecosystemic approach.* Washington, DC: American Psychological Association.

McGoldrick, M., Giordano, J., & Pearce, J. K. (1996). *Ethnicity and family therapy* (2nd ed.). New York: Guilford Press.

Meichenbaum, D. H. (1974). *Cognitive behavior modification.* Morristown, NJ: General Learning Press.

Mikesell, R. H., Lusterman, D.-D., & McDaniel, S. H. (1995). *Integrating family therapy: Handbook of family psychology and systems theory.* Washington, DC: American Psychological Association.

Norcross, J., & Goldfried, M. (1992). *Handbook of psychotherapy integration.* New York: Basic Books.

Papero, D. (1990). *Bowen family systems theory.* Boston: Allyn & Bacon.

Pinderhughes, E. (1989). *Understanding race, ethnicity and power in clinical practice.* Glencoe, IL: Free Press.

Pine, F. (1963). *Development theory and clinical process.* New Haven, CT: Yale University Press.

Pinsoff, W. (1995). *Integrative problem-centered therapy.* New York: Basic Books.

Pitta, P. (1995, Spring). Adolescent centered family integrated philosophy and treatment. *Psychotherapy, 3*(1).

Pitta, P. (1996a, Summer). Family therapy treatment issues—Family therapy integration. *Independent Practitioner, 6*(3).

Pitta, P. (1996b, Winter). An integrated supervisory model. *Family Psychologist, 12*(1).

Pitta, P. (1996c, Fall). Marital therapy—A search for the self and each other—A systemic psychodynamic integrated approach. *Psychotherapy Bulletin, 31*(4).

Pitta, P. (1996d, Fall/Winter). *Psychodynamic-systemic integration in family therapy.* New York: Family Matters, New York Association of Marriage and Family Therapy.

Pitta, P. (1996e, Summer). Psychodynamic and systemic integration theory: Application to the individual. *Psychotherapy Bulletin, 31*(3).

Pitta, P. (1997, Winter). Marital therapy: A systemic psychodynamic integrated approach: A case study. *Psychotherapy Bulletin, 32*(1).

Pitta, P. (1999). Marital therapy. *Practice Information Clearinghouse of Knowledge.*

Pitta, P. (2003). *Parenting your elderly parents.* Washington, DC: American Psychological Association.

Satir, U. M. (1964). Conjoint marital therapy. In B. L. Green (Ed.), *Psychotherapies of martial disharmony.* New York: Free Press.

Scharff, J. S., & Scharff, D. E. (1992). *Scharff notes: A primer of object relations therapy.* Northvale, NJ: Aronson.

Stricker, G. (1994). *Reflections on psychotherapy integration* (Vol. d12, pp. 3–12). Washington, DC: American Psychological Association.

Stricker, G., & Gold, J. (Eds.). (1993). *Comprehensive handbook of psychotherapy integration.* New York: Praeger.

Wachtel, P. (1991). From eclecticism to synthesis: Toward a more seamless psychotherapy integration. *Journal of Psychotherapy Integration, 1,* 43–53.

CHAPTER 14

Feminist and Contextual Work

Roberta L. Nutt

MANY APPROACHES TO psychotherapy and counseling emphasize the importance of context to understanding the life circumstances of clients. Counseling psychology has historically stressed the importance of person-environment interactions (Gelso & Fretz, 1992, 2001). Family psychology is based on the premise that one cannot understand an individual without information regarding the family system and the larger systemic context in which the individual was reared and exists (Liddle, 1992; Sexton, Alexander, & Mease, 2004; Weeks & Nixon, 1991). Feminist psychology emphasizes the role that social, political, cultural, and economic circumstances play in client problems and solutions (Gergen & Davis, 1997; Greenspan, 1983; Sturdivant, 1980; Worell & Remer, 1992, 2003). Cross-cultural psychology holds that no counseling can be competent if it does not accept, understand, and value cultural backgrounds and issues (Arredondo, 2002; Hall, 1997; Sue, Ivey, & Pederson, 1996; Sue & Sue, 2003).

This chapter focuses on feminist approaches to couples therapy. However, to truly understand context in its broadest sense, feminist therapy must include attention to issues of family, relationships, and culture, as well as issues of gender (Worell & Johnson, 1997).

OVERVIEW

There is a long history of evidence of gender bias in therapy and psychology. As the women's movement flourished in the 1970s, researchers and theoreticians began to question gender bias in psychological theories and therapeutic interventions.

Early developmental theorists (Erikson, 1964, 1968; Freud, 1953) postulated that a woman could not independently form a stable and mature identity. An important part of her identity depended on her husband and children. The public and professional stance at the time suggested that a woman was incomplete without a male partner (Dowling, 1982; Horney, 1973; Kolbenschlag, 1981; Russianoff, 1981). In contrast, men were to develop an identity through autonomy and the absence of significant connection to others (Mahalik, 1999; Mahalik, Cournoyer, DeFranc, Cherry, & Napolitano, 1998; Mintz & Mahalik, 1996; Pollack, 1995, 1998), thereby forfeiting the strength women gain from intimate relationships (Jordan, Kaplan, Miller, Stiver, & Surrey, 1991; Miller, 1986). Similarly, Gilligan (1982) criticized Kohlberg's (1981) theory of moral development as making male-as-normative assumptions that emphasize decision making by autonomy at the expense of attachment.

Other personality theories have been criticized for describing women as innately passive, masochistic, dependent, and hysterical (Belote, 1981; Carmen, Russo, & Miller, 1981; Chesler, 1972; Lerner, 1981, 1984) while describing men as innately stoic, achievement oriented, aggressive, and unemotional (David & Brannon, 1976; Levant et al., 1992; O'Neil, 1982; E. Pleck & Pleck, 1980; J. H. Pleck & Sawyer, 1980). Theories of career development have also exhibited male model bias (Fitzgerald & Crites, 1980; Osipow & Fitzgerald, 1996) and discrimination against women (Betz & Fitzgerald, 1987) and men (Robertson & Fitzgerald, 1990) with nontraditional interests. Similarly, family psychology theories have been criticized as being based on patriarchal models that disadvantage women, foster traditional roles, and blame women for family pathology (Ault-Riche, 1986; Avis, 1985; Goldner, 1985a, 1985b; Goodrich, Rampage, Ellman, & Halstead, 1988; Hare-Mustin, 1978, 1987; McGoldrick, Anderson, & Walsh, 1989; Pittman, 1985; Walters, Carter, Papp, & Silverstein, 1988).

In the 1970s and 1980s, a plethora of research demonstrated widespread gender discrimination and bias in the practice of psychotherapy. In 1980, Sherman presented an extensive review of the evidence that therapists stereotype their clients by gender, by assuming a double standard of mental health (Broverman, Broverman, Clarkson, Rosenkrantz, & Vogel, 1970), having differing standards for or expectations of female versus male clients (Abramowitz, Abramowitz, Jackson, & Gomes, 1973; Billingsley, 1977; Fabrikant, Landau, & Rollenhagen, 1973; Gingras-Baker, 1976; Nutt, 1992), differentially diagnosing women and men with pathologies that fit their gender-role stereotyping (Belote, 1981; L. S. Brown, 1992a; Caplan, 1985, 1991, 1995; Chesler, 1972; Cook, Warnke, & Dupuy, 1993; Kaplan, 1983; Kutchins & Kirk, 1997; Lerner, 1981; J. H. Pleck, 1995; Sobel & Russo, 1981; Tavris, 1992), and devaluing and abusing, including sexually abusing, women clients (Bates & Brodsky, 1989; Bouhoutsos, Holroyd, Lerman, Forer, & Greenberg, 1983; Holroyd & Brodsky, 1977; Pope, 1990; Task Force on Sex Bias and Sex Role Stereotyping in Psychotherapeutic Practice, 1975).

Research in family and couples therapy practice also demonstrated a pattern of sex-role stereotyping and devaluing of women. Therapists have encouraged men to bear the burden of being the breadwinner (David & Brannon, 1976; Goldner, 1985a; Goodrich et al., 1988; Hare-Mustin, 1978; Pittman, 1985) while expecting women to excel at domestic tasks and emotional support of the family (Friedan, 1963; Goldner, 1985b; Hare-Mustin, 1983). Mothers have been labeled as overinvolved or enmeshed with their children and thereby blamed for family pathology, and boundaries have been overemphasized with a strictness that devalues connection and family intimacy (Hare-Mustin, 1978; Miller, 1986; Walters et al., 1988). Therapist neutrality has served to support the status quo of gender power differentials that oppress women and stress men (Goldner, 1985b; Hare-Mustin, 1987; O'Neil, 1982; J. H. Pleck & Sawyer, 1980). This power differential encourages what Gottman (1999; Driver, Tabares, Shapiro, Nahm, & Gottman, 2003) termed the "Four Horsemen of the Apocalypse" that destroy marriage: criticism, contempt, defensiveness, and stonewalling. Contempt is the most damaging because it conveys disrespect, hostility, and disgust. Additional problems are caused by emotional disengagement because issues are never addressed, and both partners become less of themselves as they hide parts of their personalities. Gottman defines some problems as solvable and others as not solvable. For unsolvable problems, "successful couples try to understand what is at the foundation of the differences that are causing conflicts and use this understanding to communicate amusement and affection while learning to cope with their perpetual issue" (Driver et al., 2003, p. 500). They find a point of agreement in each other's position by "understand[ing] the meaning of the other's perspective" (p. 501).

In more recent times, gender bias in psychological practice has been demonstrated to be sometimes more subtle, but still actively present. One particular area of concern has been the continuing biased use of diagnostic labels and the presence of gender bias within diagnostic criteria (Caplan, 1995; De Barona & Dutton, 1997; Hartung & Widiger, 1998; Marecek, 2001; Ross, Frances, & Widiger, 1997). Women's and girls' gender role socialization may contribute to the ongoing overdiagnosis of certain disorders such as histrionic and borderline personality disorders, depression, and agoraphobia (Becker & Lamb, 1994; Bekker, 1996; L. S. Brown, 1992a; Garb, 1997; Hartung & Widiger, 1998; Klonoff, Landrine, & Campbell, 2000). Many symptoms associated with the aforementioned disorders may be seen as exaggerations of traditional femininity.

Other recent research has demonstrated that some therapists and trainees expect a more positive prognosis with male clients, still stereotype women as expressive, and take an instrumental "let's-fix-it" approach with men (Klonoff et al., 2000; Rudman & Glick, 2001; Seem & Johnson, 1998). Practitioners also may not perceive the specific external stresses and context of women's and girls' lives, but instead still emphasize intrapsychic factors inappropriately and/or detrimentally (Boston Women's Health Book Collective, 1998; L. S. Brown & Ballou, 1992; McBride, 1990; Porter, 2002). As summarized by Worell (2001), "interventions based on medical models that are designed to reduce the observed symptoms of specific disorders may bring short-term relief but may also inadvertently return women in distress to the toxic environments from which their problems originated" (p. 336). Inattention to contextual factors may contribute to the lack of recognition of women's and girls' problems such as battering and other forms of victimization (Hansen & Harway, 1993; Harway & Hansen, 1994; Porter, 2002), the double standard about problems such as alcohol abuse (Brooks & Silverstein, 1995; Greenfield, 2002; Toneatto, Sobell, & Sobell, 1992), the overuse or inappropriate use of labels such as premenstrual dysphoric disorder (Chrisler & Johnston-Robledo, 2002), and inattention to the ways in which culture and ethnicity influence women's and girls' problems such as depression and schizophrenia (C. Brown, Abe-Kim, & Barrio, 2003; Sparks, 2002) and men's and boys' problems such as violence, risk taking, sexual addiction, and substance abuse (Brooks & Silverstein, 1995; Hoyenga & Hoyenga, 1993). Power abuses, including sexual relationships, still occur in therapy and training (Gilbert, 1999; Pope, 1994). Additional research has demonstrated therapist insensitivity to racial stereotypes, the interaction of race and gender (Davenport & Yurich, 1991; Reid, 2002; Robinson & Howard-Hamilton, 2000), and social and economic conditions that have an impact on women and girls who live in poverty and women and girls and men and boys of color (Bernal & Scharro-del-Rio, 2001; C. Brown et al., 2003; Fischer, Jome, & Atkinson, 1998; Gil, 1996; Greene, 1996; Helms & Cook, 1999; Herring, 1999; Hong & Ham, 2001; Horne & Kiselica, 1999; Kim, Atkinson, & Umemoto, 2001; Klonoff, Landrine, & Scott, 1995; Sparks, 2002). Lesbian relationships and partnerships have also been pathologized through the description of lesbian relationships using terms such as "merged," "fused," or "enmeshed" (Morton, 1998; Pardie & Herb, 1997). Even though many psychologists believe that women's issues in psychology were dealt with and resolved in the 1970s and 1980s, recent research indicates a continuing need for professional guidance to avoid harm in psychological practice with girls and women. Many psychologists do not recognize the harmful aspects of male gender role socialization.

Hence, for couples' counseling, a critical issue of context is the sex-role stereotype expectations of any given culture. This sex or gender role context is further complicated by issues of socioeconomic status, ethnicity, acculturation, sexual orientation, and ability/disability (L. S. Brown, 1992b; L. S. Brown & Root, 1990; Clunis & Green, 1988; Comas-Diaz & Greene, 1994; Lijtmaer, 1998; Matsuyuki, 1998; Prilleltensky, 1996; Wyche, 1993).

This chapter begins by describing the theory and practice of feminist therapy. Feminist therapy is then applied to the issues that couples bring to therapists. A case illustration is provided to further the understanding of feminist therapy applications. Numerous issues of interacting diversity are addressed as are future needs for theory development and research.

FEMINIST THERAPY THEORY AND PRACTICE

Principles of feminist therapy have been described by a number of authors (L. S. Brown, 1994; L. S. Brown & Brodsky, 1992; Enns, 1997; Espin, 1994; Gilbert, 1980; Greenspan, 1983; Morrow & Hawxhurst, 1998; Szymanski, Baird, & Kornman, 2002; Worell & Johnson, 1997; Worell & Remer, 1992, 2003; Wyche & Rice, 1997). Feminist therapy assumes that all voices are valued—women's and men's, girls' and boys'. The principle that "the personal is political" reflects the fact that all persons live in a political and social climate and that differences in power cause differences in socialization and personality development. Therefore, client problems may be caused more by external messages and limitations than by intrapsychic factors. Feminist therapy credits clients as coping with their lives to the best of their current abilities and views symptoms as ways to cope with problems if one understands context and gender role expectations. Clients are viewed as competent and experts on themselves.

Feminist therapists attempt to demystify therapy and seek as egalitarian a therapeutic relationship as possible. Since client empowerment is a goal of feminist therapy, informed consent and equalizing power are necessary. Pittman (1985) labeled therapists as gender brokers who help clients examine their gender role socialization to decide what parts to discard and which to keep. Feminist therapists challenge both women and men to incorporate instrumental and expressive behaviors into their repertoires and help the clients own and nurture their own needs. Worell and Remer (1992) summarized some of the goals of feminist therapy as helping clients "become aware of their own sex-role socialization process, identify their internalized sex-role messages/beliefs, [and] develop a full range of behaviors that are freely chosen, not dictated" (p. 94). It is also important to learn to balance independence and dependence (interdependence) in one's relationships and to cultivate a broad range of interpersonal and life skills for work, family, and social areas. Owning personal strengths, recognizing and utilizing anger appropriately, and developing skills for assertive but compassionate conflict management are also desirable outcomes. Female skills, perspectives, and value systems are also valued for both women and men.

Worell and Remer (1992, 2003) also described a number of techniques of feminist therapy. Sex-role analysis increases client awareness of gender-role expectations and consequences and how they differ for women and men by helping the client "identify how societal structures and expectations related to traditional gender arrangements have influenced their lives" (1992, p. 23). Power analysis identifies the power differential that exists between men and women in a variety of arenas, assists clients "in understanding both the destructive and effective uses of power" (1992, p. 23), and empowers them to impact external institutions and individuals and systems around them. Assertiveness training allows clients to own both their anger and their passivity and teaches them to express their needs and viewpoints assertively.

Consciousness-raising groups support clients by giving them a forum to discuss their lives. Clients may be encouraged to read relevant books and articles in bibliotherapy. Shifting the focus of client issues from the intrapsychic to the external may utilize the family therapy strategy of reframing or relabeling. Therapy is demystified by therapists sharing information regarding the therapy process and their theoretical orientation, mutually developing a contract and goals, teaching new life skills to clients, and processing the progress of therapy together. Therapists may also teach clients how women and men may use language differently based on their gender-role socialization (Lakoff, 1975, 1990; Spender, 1985; Tannen, 1990).

FEMINIST THERAPY FOR COUPLES

How are feminist therapy principles applied to couples therapy? Although any therapy that utilizes principles such as power analysis, analysis of gender-role socialization, or empowerment might be termed feminist, feminist couples therapists assume that a significant proportion of problems for couples, particularly heterosexual couples, are due to differences in and misunderstandings about gender-role socialization and expectations (Philpot, Brooks, Lusterman, & Nutt, 1997). Therapists suggest that men and women carry nearly archetypal expectations of relationships that are often not in awareness, so they are not shared and therefore create conflicts. "Heterosexual marriages and relationships often seem to be formed between two persons who come from different worlds, each bringing very different expectations and skills to the relationship" (p. 106). One important role for the therapist is to bring these expectations into awareness and act as a translator between the couple, helping them to understand each other's worldview, gender-role socialization, relationship expectations, and language usage. Therefore, it is essential that feminist couples' therapists have a thorough grounding in the gender role development of both sexes (Gilbert & Scher, 1999; Jolliff & Horne, 1999) and their own gender role journey (O'Neil & Egan, 1992; O'Neil & Roberts-Carroll, 1988).

Feminist couples therapists must help clients stop seeing each other as "the enemy" and help them understand that they have both been negatively affected by stereotyped gender socialization. This gender-sensitive therapy must be sensitive to both women's and men's issues and be able to impart, model, and teach a nonblaming, flexible, and empathic attitude toward each gender. "Clients must first be educated regarding the different gender messages they have been taught and come to understand that both genders have valuable skills and attributes" (Philpot et al., 1997, p. 166). Both must appreciate "affiliation and autonomy, cooperation and competition, control and nurturance, and reason and emotion" (p. 166). The overlap between women and men can aid their mutual understanding of the differences.

The therapeutic goal is empathic knowing, which allows for trust and resulting commitment in relationships. Understanding the personal struggles of others allows greater acceptance. Partners need to gain knowledge of the systemic nature of gender socialization and appreciate the plight and pain of both genders. The therapist must create an environment of safety in which clients can discard their defensiveness and entitlement and develop true empathy for their partner. This safe environment necessitates that both partners must feel heard, understood, and valued.

It is best at first to avoid toxic and emotionally laden topics on which the couple disagree and that have caused interpersonal stress. One helpful way to gain distance from current pain and problems is to focus on the past to discuss gender messages they received from parents, extended family, teachers, peers, media, and others from childhood, with the goal to connect these old messages and expectations to present behaviors and attitudes. The focus on the past can avert the present-day blaming and attempts to change the partner. Understanding the background of a partner's behaviors and values and often the pain associated with gender-role expectations leads the partners to understand the origin of their problems. Partners can learn to unite against the gendered system in which they have been reared rather than blame each other. As stated earlier, the role of the therapist is that of gender broker (Pittman, 1985), translator, reframer, or decoder to explain the female code to men and the male code to women. The therapist provides intragender and cross-gender consciousness raising while supporting women's empowerment and men's expression of emotions. Empathy is engendered for the other gender through the insight obtained by understanding gender messages and how the messages are both part of the larger culture and transmitted across families and generations. Additional work on understanding gender-based use of language can also be helpful (Lakoff, 1975, 1990; Tannen, 1990).

As a final goal, in the spirit of the feminist principles of demystifying therapy and giving clients the tools for their own growth, the therapist teaches the couple to interview one another to create greater acceptance and mutual understanding. This technique, called *gender inquiry* (Lusterman, 1989; Philpot et al., 1997), teaches that the source of many couple misunderstandings and dissatisfactions has its origins in the larger system of gender expectations, that gender-role messages are interrelated and mutually influencing, and that cognitive change is possible.

In effect, the therapist teaches the couple Interviewing Skills 101, by showing the couple how to mutually use open-ended questions to learn about each other; develop active listening skills to better hear one another; learn to reflect what they hear to check the accuracy of what they heard and understood; paraphrase and summarize what they heard; avoid interrupting the partner or reacting defensively to what is said; and validate the concerns, hopes, and needs of the partner. When the couple learns to deeply understand the experience of the other, a major cognitive-affective shift occurs, which can lead to a reduction in conflict, more effective decision making and problem solving, and increased emotional intimacy.

Lusterman (Philpot et al., 1997) has developed a set of guidelines to help clients interview one another productively and to produce empathy. These principles include the following: listen attentively to both content and feeling; look directly at your partner while speaking and listening; be aware of body posture and nonverbal communication; avoid comparing each person's feelings and thoughts; speak in "I" language, since "you" language can sound blaming; and don't criticize, interrupt, interpret, attack, or say "you're wrong."

Specific topics that might provide useful beginning questions include those regarding parents' teaching and expectations, relationships with siblings, activities encouraged or forbidden because of gender, treatment by peers at different ages, life transitions such as puberty and dating, school achievements and social activities, work experience, and relationship and/or marital dreams and expectations. One source of possible issues can be found in Adler's (1927, 1931) strategies for examining the family constellation through early recollections.

CASE STUDY

Martin and Martha are a couple in their forties with two teenage children, Alison, 17 and Andrew, 14. Martin and Martha married 19 years ago, at which time Martin was beginning a career as an electrical engineer in a major corporation and Martha was looking forward to starting a family and running a household to support Martin's career.

During the first 10 years of the marriage, Martin worked hard and received several promotions in his company. Martha got pregnant the second year of marriage, had Alison and then Andrew. For the first eight years of marriage, she stayed home with the children, decorated their two homes, volunteered at their church in the nursery, and took gourmet cooking lessons. As Andrew started school, Martha began to feel more and more worthless and unimportant. She was diagnosed with depression and put on medication by their family physician.

The stresses and competitiveness in Martin's corporation began to wear on him. Although he was financially successful, enabling them to move into a third, larger, and more luxurious suburban home in the twelfth year of the marriage, his drinking also increased. He traveled often and spent little time with Martha and their children. He felt less and less like a person and more and more like a paycheck to his family.

As Martha felt more and more lonely, she decided to go back to school, completed her BA degree in business, followed by an MBA. She stopped her antidepressant medications, purchased a new business wardrobe, and took a position with a fast-growing marketing company. She enjoyed her work and felt appreciated by her boss and coworkers.

Approximately a year before entering couples therapy, Martin lost his job because of his out-of-control drinking. After three months in rehab, he announced to the family that he was tired of the corporate rat race and had decided to sell their home and move the family to a small town and begin a hardware business. Martha, Alison, and Andrew refused. The children were unwilling to leave their friends, their schools, and their lifestyles. They resented their father's loss of income and the advantages it provided. Martha was unwilling to leave her new career. Her newfound independence and identity were bringing her exciting new satisfactions in her life, and she refused to leave her own personal growth behind one more time. Martha and Martin came to counseling/therapy in great distress fearing there was no solution short of divorce. Neither felt comfortable with the idea of divorce, so they were stuck.

Therapy began by getting an overview of current functioning and problems. Then, because it was obvious that their current "stuckness" in their entrenched positions was overly emotional laden and toxic for a beginning point, the therapist began to inquire into their histories, both separately and together.

Martin reported growing up in what he termed a normal family. His father worked long hours in the family car repair business. His mother cared for the home and reared Martin and his younger brother and two sisters. From time to time, the family struggled financially and his parents argued frequently and loudly. His mother constantly put down his father for his lack of earning ability. Her father had been an attorney. Martin learned from that experience that his worth as a man was tied to his ability to support his family. Martin's father died at the age of 49 of a heart attack brought on by high blood pressure and stress. Martin always feared he too would die young. He realized in therapy that he had used alcohol to medicate and dull his fears of death.

Being fired was a wake-up call for Martin. He realized that if he did not want to end up like his father, he needed to reduce his stress. He began questioning the gender role he had been taught—that a man worked hard, supported his family, hid his pain, and never complained. He was able to get in touch with and share his fears with Martha.

On the other hand, Martha had grown up in a family of divorce. Her father had left his wife and two daughters when Martha was six. He was seldom in contact with the family and only infrequently paid child support. Martha's mother struggled to support herself and her two daughters, and regularly borrowed money from her own parents. Martha vowed to marry a man who would be reliable and allow her to be at home with her children. As a teenager, when asked about her career goals, Martha would answer "Mother."

As Martha realized her dream of a lovely home, two children, and a dog, she began to feel depressed. At first, she felt guilty about her sadness. What was wrong with her? She had everything she had ever wanted, but it did not seem like enough. She was bored. On the encouragement of a woman friend from church, she tried a class at the local community college and loved it.

She wanted more, felt like she was doing something important, and at that point, she decided to pursue earning a degree. That was followed by a second degree and a job she loved. Martha had been feeling fulfilled, valued, and happy. She was doing and accomplishing things she'd never believed were possible. She never wanted to return to her old lifestyle.

Therapy consisted of helping Martin and Martha hear each other's stories. Both were encouraged to include both content and emotions in their narratives. The goal was for them to gain a deep emotional understanding of each other and their gender-role journeys. They were encouraged to ask each other open-ended questions that allowed the partners to further explore their histories. The therapist acted as a coach and teacher.

Martha began to realize how driven Martin had felt and how unhappy he had been in the competitive corporate world. She learned how much of his identity was caught up in his job title and earning power—to the exclusion of other important aspects of himself. She conveyed her understanding to him and let him know that she welcomed his becoming a more involved family member.

Martin realized how bright and ambitious Martha really was and how frustrating it had been for her to follow her stereotyped stay-at-home-mom script. He understood how as a young person, she was also discouraged from questioning the traditional roles that she had been taught. He felt her excitement at discovering she had something to offer the business world, where she was appreciated for her talents and accomplishments.

With increased understanding, Martin and Martha were better able to appreciate their individual backgrounds and needs. Their caring for each other increased. They were able to negotiate a win-win solution to their current struggle by moving the family into a suburb of their current city, which had enough of a small town feel to allow Martin to open his hardware store but was still commutable for Martha. Their children were also able to commute to their familiar schools and stay connected with their friends. Martin and Martha bought Alison a car so she could help with the carpooling for Andrew.

DIVERSITY ISSUES

Additional layers of analysis of socialization and family transmission of values would have been necessary if this couple had come from a different ethnic background or if they had been a lesbian or gay couple. The additional messages related to their ethnic group, their acculturation, the meaning of family, their family-of-origin socioeconomic status, and homophobia would have increased the complexity of the gender-role messages (Carter, 1995; Comas-Diaz, 2000; Falicov, 1998; Fischer et al., 1998; Fukuyama & Ferguson, 2000; Ponterotto, Casas, Suzuki, & Alexander, 1995).

For example, in an Hispanic couple, the gender-role messages might have been even more rigid because of machismo for men (Arcaya, 1999; Lazur &

Majors, 1995; Niemann, 2001) and *marianisma* for women. The couple might have had even greater difficulty examining their gender roles because of additional feelings of being disloyal to their families and culture.

In an African American family, it would have been less likely that Martha had dreamed of staying home with her children. Typically, African American women do not suffer from the home-career conflict that afflicts many white middle-class women because they have always expected both to work and rear children (Collins, 1994; Lazur & Majors, 1995; Leonard, Lee, & Kiselica, 1999; Sparks, 1996).

In a lesbian or gay couple, there are two persons who may have similar gender-role socialization. It is crucial to examine this similarity carefully, however, and not assume similarity that is not there. In lesbian couples, there may be two persons socialized to seek and nurture relationships. If stereotypically socialized, both could give too much to the detriment of self-development (Clunis & Green, 1988; Falco, 1991; Slater, 1995). A gay couple in which both men have been traditionally socialized may struggle with intimacy and commitment (Harrison, 1995). Both types of couples would have the additional layers of cultural discrimination and homophobia complicating their relational issues. Ethnic diversity would add further complexity (Greene, 2000; Lowe & Mascher, 2001).

RESEARCH

Research on feminist therapy in general is in its infancy. Worell and Remer (1992, 2003) have extrapolated from counseling and psychotherapy outcome studies in general to feminist therapy results by noting common successful characteristics. Process variables that have been found to be effective in therapy (Beutler et al., 2004; Orlinsky & Howard, 1986; Orlinsky, Ronnestad, & Willutzki, 2004) that are compatible with feminist therapy include therapist warmth and credibility, empathy, affirmation, expressiveness, and a good therapeutic bond. Other variables related to successful outcomes (Beutler, Crago, & Arizmendi, 1986; Beutler et al., 2004; Brehm & Smith, 1986; Orlinsky & Howard, 1986; Orlinsky et al., 2004) that are compatible with feminist therapy include the implementation of a therapeutic contract; collaborative roles between therapists and clients; the experiencing and processing of negative affect such as hostility and anger; the viewing of the therapist by the client/patient as positively engaged; the therapeutic use of empathy; a focus on client strengths and resources; and affirmation and empowerment.

Beutler and colleagues (2004) reviewed literature that suggested good outcomes were related to positive therapist behaviors (p. 240), complementarity and collaboration and topic agreement between therapist and client, lack of internalized dominance or dogmatism in the therapist, and interventions that involved emotional arousal early in therapy. There also appears to be a clinically weak but significant positive effect of therapist's self-disclosure on therapy outcome.

Specific research "into the process of marital therapy and its relationship to outcomes [was termed] still in its infancy" by Alexander, Holtzworth-Munroe, and Jameson in 1994 (p. 606). Research in marital and couples therapy has grown significantly in recent years, and literature reviews including meta-analyses have demonstrated that couples therapy in general is an effective treatment. However, research comparing specific approaches and models has been sparse (Sexton et al., 2004). In addition, there are questions concerning the long-term effect of some couples therapies.

One study (Johnson & Greenberg, 1988) reported more successful outcomes when partners became more affectionate with more softened feelings toward each other. Other important factors leading to successful outcome included the perception by the couple that the therapist and interventions were personal and helpful; a strong therapeutic alliance, which was often higher for more experienced therapists; the teaching of problem-solving and communication skills to increase expressions of caring and resolve problems constructively; the uncovering and resolution of negative relational patterns and hurt feelings; and the normalization of their problems as a couple. All of these factors fit well with a feminist approach that emphasizes a collaborative and helpful therapeutic alliance, an examination of gender roles and resulting differences in communication styles and expectations, and a teaching of gender inquiry so the partners can continue to learn about each other and develop a stronger emotional connection.

Beutler and colleagues (2004) report several studies that found that therapists who identify as feminists may be better at establishing good therapeutic relationships (Cantor, 1991), and that female clients demonstrate more satisfaction when working with therapists who hold nontraditional gender-role viewpoints (Banikiotes & Merluzzi, 1981; Enns & Hackett, 1990; Hart, 1981; Moradi, Fischer, Hill, Jome, & Blum, 2000). However, Beutler and colleagues stated while there was a plethora of literature on sexist bias in therapy on the part of either the therapist or the client, there were as yet no outcome studies of feminist therapy. The challenge for feminist therapy researchers is "to translate the broad goal of empowerment into its conceptual and measurable components" (Worell, 2001, pp. 339–340). The following measurable goals that have been suggested by a research team at the University of Kentucky (Worell, 1996, 2001) include positive self-evaluation, comfort rather than distress in daily functioning, awareness of the impact of gender and culture, self-efficacy and resilience, self-nurturance and avoidance of abuse, problem-solving skills, flexibility, assertiveness, access to personal and community resources, and activities aimed toward social justice change. These goals are, however, difficult to reach in a toxic or unsupportive environment. Outcome research will need to address both.

The future for research on feminist therapy is bright, because the need is great to better evaluate its success. Preliminary results are promising. Research in feminist and contextual couples therapy needs to assess efficacy and effectiveness of feminist interventions and their helpfulness to couples in conflict. In addition to symptom relief, personal growth in life satisfaction and empowerment need to be addressed. Current literature suggests some common processes between feminist therapy and some other types of therapy, therefore, it is also important to examine the efficacy and effectiveness of combining feminist therapy with other types of interventions. Which work well together, and which do not? As culture and therapeutic professions grow in awareness of the importance of gender-role socialization and expectations, the relevance of this research and its impact on therapy will increase in significance and impact.

REFERENCES

Abramowitz, S. I., Abramowitz, C. V., Jackson, C., & Gomes, B. (1973). The politics of clinical judgment: What nonliberal examiners infer about women who do not stifle themselves. *Journal of Consulting and Clinical Psychology, 41*, 385–391.

Adler, A. (1927). *Practice and theory of individual psychology.* New York: Harcourt, Brace & World.

Adler, A. (1931). *What life should mean to you.* Boston: Little, Brown.

Alexander, J. F., Holtzworth-Munroe, A., & Jameson, P. (1994). The process and outcome of marital and family therapy: Research review and evaluation. In A. E. Bergin & S. L. Garfield (Eds.), *Handbook of psychotherapy and behavior change* (pp. 594–630). New York: Wiley.

Arcaya, J. (1999). Hispanic American boys and adolescent males. In A. M. Horne & M. S. Kiselica (Eds.), *Handbook of counseling boys and adolescent males* (pp. 101–116). Thousand Oaks, CA: Sage.

Arredondo, P. (2002). Counseling individuals from specialized, marginalized and underserved groups. In P. Pederson, J. G. Draguns, W. J. Louver, & J. E. Trimble (Eds.), *Counseling across cultures* (5th ed., pp. 241–250). Thousand Oaks, CA: Sage.

Ault-Riche, M. (Ed.). (1986). *Women and family therapy.* Gaithersburg, MD: Aspen.

Avis, J. M. (1985). The politics of functional family therapy: A feminist critique. *Journal of Marital and Family Therapy, 11*, 145–148.

Banikiotes, P. G., & Merluzzi, T. V. (1981). Impact of counselor gender and counselor sex-role orientation on perceived counselor characteristics. *Journal of Counseling Psychology, 28*, 342–348.

Bates, C., & Brodsky, A. (1989). *Sex in the therapy hour: A case of professional incest.* New York: Guilford Press.

Becker, D., & Lamb, S. (1994). Sex bias in the diagnosis of borderline personality disorder and post traumatic stress disorder. *Professional Psychology: Research and Practice, 25*, 56–61.

Bekker, M. H. J. (1996). Agoraphobia and gender; A review. *Clinical Psychology Review, 16*, 129–146.

Belote, B. (1981). Masochistic syndrome, hysterical personality, and the illusion of a healthy woman. In S. Cox (Ed.), *Female psychology: The emerging self* (2nd ed.). New York: St. Martin's Press.

Bernal, G., & Scharro-del-Rio, M. R. (2001). Are empirically supported treatments valid for ethnic minorities? Toward an alternative approach for treatment research. *Cultural Diversity and Ethnic Minority Psychology, 7,* 328–342.

Betz, N. E., & Fitzgerald, L. F. (1987). *The career psychology of women.* Orlando, FL: Harcourt Brace Jovanovich.

Beutler, L. E., Crago, M., & Arizmendi, T. G. (1986). Research on therapist variables in psychotherapy. In S. L. Garfield & A. E. Bergin (Eds.), *Handbook of psychotherapy and behavior change* (pp. 257–310). New York: Wiley.

Beutler, L. E., Malik, M., Alimohamed, S., Harwood, T. M., Talebi, H., Noble, S., et al. (2004). Therapist variables. In M. J. Lambert (Ed.), *Bergin and Garfield's handbook of psychotherapy and behavior change* (5th ed., pp. 227–306). Hoboken, NJ: Wiley.

Billingsley, D. (1977). Sex bias in psychotherapy: An examination of the effects of client sex, client pathology, and therapist sex on treatment planning. *Journal of Consulting and Clinical Psychology, 45,* 250–256.

Boston Women's Health Book Collective. (1998). *Our bodies, ourselves for the new century: A book by and for women.* New York: Touchstone.

Bouhoutsos, J., Holroyd, J., Lerman, H., Forer, B., & Greenberg, M. (1983). Sexual intimacy between psychotherapists and patients. *Professional Psychology: Research and Practice, 14,* 185–196.

Brehm, S. S., & Smith, W. T. (1986). Social psychological approaches to psychotherapy and behavior change. In S. L. Garfield & A. E. Bergin (Eds.), *Handbook of psychotherapy and behavior change* (pp. 69–116). New York: Wiley.

Brooks, G. R., & Silverstein, L. B. (1995). Understanding the dark side of masculinity: An interactive systems model. In R. F. Levant & W. S. Pollack (Eds.), *A new psychology of men* (pp. 280–333). New York: Basic Books.

Broverman, I. K., Broverman, D. M., Clarkson, F. E., Rosenkrantz, P. A., & Vogel, S. R. (1970). Sex-role stereotypes and clinical judgments of mental health. *Journal of Consulting and Clinical Psychology, 34,* 1–7.

Brown, C., Abe-Kim, J. S., & Barrio, C. (2003). Depression in ethnically diverse women: Implications for treatment in primary care settings. *Professional Psychology: Research and Practice, 34,* 10–19.

Brown, L. S. (1992a). A feminist critique of personality disorders. In L. S. Brown & M. Ballou (Eds.), *Personality and psychopathology: Feminist reappraisals* (pp. 206–228). New York: Guilford Press.

Brown, L. S. (1992b). While waiting for the revolution: The case for a lesbian feminist psychotherapy. *Feminism and Psychology, 2,* 139–253.

Brown, L. S. (1994). *Subversive dialogues: Theory in feminist therapy.* New York: Basic Books.

Brown, L. S., & Ballou, M. (Eds.). (1992). *Personality and psychotherapy: Feminist reappraisals.* New York: Guilford Press.

Brown, L. S., & Brodsky, A. M. (1992). The future of feminist therapy [Special issue: The future of psychotherapy]. *Psychotherapy, 29,* 51–57.

Brown, L. S., & Root, M. P. P. (Eds.). (1990). *Diversity and complexity in feminist therapy.* New York: Harrington Park Press.

Cantor, D. W. (1991). Women as therapists: What we already know. In D. W. Cantor (Ed.), *Women as therapists: A multitheoretical casebook* (pp. 3–19). New York: Springer.

Caplan, P. J. (1985). *The myth of women's masochism.* New York: Signet.

Caplan, P. J. (1991). Delusional dominating personality disorder (DDPD). *Feminism and Psychology, 1,* 171–174.

Caplan, P. J. (1995). *They say you're crazy: How the world's most powerful psychiatrists decide who's normal.* Reading, MA: Addison-Wesley.

Carmen, E. H., Russo, N. F., & Miller, J. B. (1981). Inequality and women's mental health: An overview. *American Journal of Psychiatry, 138,* 1319–1330.

Carter, R. T. (1995). *The influence of race and racial identity in psychotherapy.* New York: Wiley.

Chesler, P. (1972). *Women and madness.* Garden City, NY: Doubleday.

Chrisler, J. C., & Johnston-Robledo, I. (2002). Raging hormones?: Feminist perspectives on premenstrual syndrome and postpartum depression. In M. Ballou & L. S. Brown (Eds.), *Rethinking mental health and disorder: Feminist perspectives* (pp. 174–197). New York: Guilford Press.

Clunis, D. M., & Green, G. D. (1988). *Lesbian couples.* Seattle, WA: Seal Press.

Collins, P. H. (1994). The meaning of motherhood in Black culture. In R. Staples (Ed.), *The Black family* (5th ed.). Belmont, CA: Wadsworth.

Comas-Diaz, L. (2000). An ethnopolitical approach to working with people of color. *American Psychologist, 55,* 1319–1325.

Comas-Diaz, L., & Greene, B. (1994). *Women of color: Integrating ethnic and gender identities in psychotherapy.* New York: Guilford Press.

Cook, E. P., Warnke, M., & Dupuy, P. (1993). Gender bias and the *DSM-III-R. Counselor Education and Supervision, 32,* 311–322.

Davenport, D. S., & Yurich, J. M. (1991). Multicultural gender issues. *Journal of Counseling and Development, 70,* 64–71.

David, D. S., & Brannon, R. (1976). *The forty-nine percent majority: The male sex role.* Reading, MA: Addison-Wesley.

De Barona, M. S., & Dutton, M. A. (1997). Feminist perspectives on assessment. In J. Worell & N. G. Johnson (Eds.), *Shaping the future of feminist psychology: Education, research, and practice* (pp. 37–56). Washington, DC: American Psychological Association.

Dowling, C. (1982). *The Cinderella complex.* New York: Pocket Books.

Driver, J., Tabares, A., Shapiro, A. N., Nahm, E. Y., & Gottman, J. M. (2003). Interactive partners in marital success and failure. In F. Walsh (Ed.), *Normal family processes: Growing diversity and complexity* (3rd ed., pp. 493–513). New York: Guilford Press.

Enns, C. Z. (1997). *Feminist theories and feminist psychotherapies: Origins, themes, and variations.* New York: Haworth Press.

Enns, C. Z., & Hackett, G. (1990). Comparison of feminist and non-feminist women's reactions to variants of non-sexist and feminist counseling. *Journal of Counseling Psychology, 37,* 33–40.

Erikson, E. H. (1964). The inner and outer self: Reflections on womanhood. *Daedalus, 93,* 582–606.

Erikson, E. H. (1968). *Identity, youth and crisis.* New York: Norton.

Espin, O. (1994). Feminist approaches. In L. Comas-Diaz & B. Greene (Eds.), *Women of color: Integrating ethnic and gender identities in psychotherapy* (pp. 265–286). New York: Guilford Press.

Fabrikant, B., Landau, D., & Rollenhagen, J. (1973). Perceived female sex role attributes and psychotherapists' sex role expectations for female patients. *New Jersey Psychologist, 23,* 13–16.

Falco, K. L. (1991). *Psychotherapy with lesbian clients: Theory into practice.* New York: Brunner/Mazel.

Falicov, C. J. (1998). *Latino families in therapy: A guide to multicultural practice.* New York: Guilford Press.

Fischer, A. R., Jome, L. M., & Atkinson, D. R. (1998). Reconceptualizing multicultural counseling: Universal healing conditions in a culturally specific context. *Counseling Psychologist, 26,* 525–588.

Fitzgerald, L. F., & Crites, J. O. (1980). Toward a career psychology of women: What do we know? *Journal of Counseling Psychology, 27,* 44–62.

Freud, S. (1953). Some psychological consequences of the anatomical distinctions between the sexes. In J. Strachey (Ed. & Trans.). *Collected papers* (Vol. 5). London: Hogarth Press.

Friedan, B. (1963). *The feminine mystique.* New York: Norton.

Fukuyama, M. A., & Ferguson, A. D. (2000). Lesbian, gay, and bisexual people of color: Understanding cultural complexity and managing multiple oppressions. In R. M. Perez, K. A. DeBord, & K. J. Bieschke (Eds.), *Handbook of counseling and psychotherapy with lesbian, gay and bisexual clients* (pp. 81–106). Washington, DC: American Psychological Association.

Garb, H. N. (1997). Race bias, social class bias, and gender bias in clinical judgment. *Clinical Psychology: Science and Practice, 4*(2), 99–120.

Gelso, C. J., & Fretz, B. R. (1992). *Counseling psychology.* San Diego, CA: Harcourt Brace Jovanovich.

Gelso, C. J., & Fretz, B. R. (2001). *Counseling psychology* (2nd ed.). Orlando, FL: Holt, Rinehart and Winston.

Gergen, M., & Davis, S. (Eds.). (1997). *Toward a new psychology of gender.* New York: Routledge.

Gil, R. M. (1996). Hispanic women and mental health. *Women and Mental Health: Annals of the New York Academic of Sciences, 789,* 147–159.

Gilbert, L. A. (1980). Feminist therapy. In A. Brodsky & R. T. Hare-Mustin (Eds.), *Women and psychotherapy* (pp. 245–265). New York: Guilford Press.

Gilbert, L. A. (1999). Reproducing gender in counseling and psychotherapy: Understanding the problem and changing the practice. *Applied and Preventive Psychology, 8*(2), 119–127.

Gilbert, L. A., & Scher, M. (1999). *Gender and sex in counseling and therapy.* Boston: Allyn & Bacon.

Gilligan, C. (1982). *In a different voice.* Cambridge, MA: Harvard University Press.

Gingras-Baker, S. (1976). Sex role stereotyping and marriage counseling. *Journal of Marriage and Family Counseling, 2,* 355–366.

Goldner, V. (1985a). Feminism and family therapy. *Family Process, 24,* 31–47.

Goldner, V. (1985b). Warning: Family therapy may be hazardous to your health. *Family Therapy Networker, 9,* 9–23.

Goodrich, T. J., Rampage, C., Ellman, B., & Halstead, K. (1988). *Feminist family therapy: A casebook.* New York: Norton.

Goodrich, T. J., & Silverstein, L. B. (Eds.). (2003). *Feminist family therapy: Empowerment in social context.* Washington, DC: American Psychological Association.

Gottman, J. M. (1999). *The seven principles of making marriage work.* New York: Crown.

Greene, B. (1996). African-American women: Considering diverse identities and societal barriers in psychotherapy. *Women and Mental Health: Annals of the New York Academy of Sciences, 789,* 191–209.

Greene, B. (2000). African American lesbian and bisexual women. *Journal of Social Issues, 56,* 239–249.

Greenfield, S. F. (2002). Women and alcohol use disorders. *Harvard Review of Psychiatry, 10*(2), 76–85.

Greenspan, M. (1983). *A new approach to women and therapy.* New York: McGraw-Hill.

Hall, C. C. I. (1997). Cultural malpractice: The growing obsolescence of psychology with the changing U.S. population. *American Psychologist, 52,* 642–651.

Hansen, M., & Harway, M. (Eds.). (1993). *Battering and family therapy: A feminist perspective.* Newbury Park, CA: Sage.

Hare-Mustin, R. T. (1978). A feminist approach to family therapy. *Family Process, 17,* 181–194.

Hare-Mustin, R. T. (1983). An appraisal of the relationship between women and psychotherapy: 80 years after the case of Dora. *American Psychologist, 38,* 593–601.

Hare-Mustin, R. T. (1987). The problem of gender in family therapy theory. *Family Process, 26,* 15–27.

Harrison, J. (1995). Roles, identities, and sexual orientation: Homosexuality, heterosexuality, and bisexuality. In R. F. Levant & W. S. Pollack (Eds.), *A new psychology of men* (pp. 359–382). New York: Basic Books.

Hart, L. E. (1981). An investigation of the effect of male therapists' views of women on the process and outcome of therapy with women. *Dissertation Abstracts International, 42,* 2529B.

Hartung, C. M., & Widiger, T. A. (1998). Gender differences in the diagnosis of mental disorders: Conclusions and controversies of the *DSM-IV. Psychological Bulletin, 213,* 260–278.

Harway, M., & Hansen, M. (1994). *Spouse abuse: Treating battered women, batterers and their children.* Sarasota, FL: Professional Resource Press.

Helms, J. E., & Cook, D. A. (1999). *Using race and culture in counseling and psychotherapy: Theory and process.* Boston: Allyn & Bacon.

Herring, R. D. (1999). *Counseling with Native American Indians and Alaska Natives: Strategies for helping professionals.* Thousand Oaks, CA: Sage.

Holroyd, J. C., & Brodsky, A. M. (1977). Psychologists' attitudes and practices regarding erotic and nonerotic physical contact with patients. *American Psychologist, 32,* 843–849.

Hong, G. K., & Ham, M. D. C. (2001). *Psychotherapy and counseling with Asian American clients.* Thousand Oaks, CA: Sage.

Horne, A. M., & Kiselica, M. S. (1999). *Handbook of counseling boys and adolescent males: A practitioner's guide.* Thousand Oaks, CA: Sage.

Horney, K. (1973). *Feminine psychology.* New York: Norton.

Hoyenga, K. B., & Hoyenga, K. T. (1993). *Gender-related differences: Origins and outcomes.* Boston: Allyn & Bacon.

Johnson, S. M., & Greenberg, L. S. (1988). Relating process to outcome in marital therapy. *Journal of Marital and Family Therapy, 14,* 175–183.

Johnson, S. M., & Lebow, J. (2000). The "coming of age" of couple therapy: A decade review. *Journal of Marital and Family Therapy, 26,* 23–38.

Jolliff, D., & Horne, A. M. (1999). Growing up male: The development of mature masculinity. In A. M. Horne & M. S. Kiselica (Eds.), *Handbook of counseling boys and adolescent males: A practitioner's guide* (pp. 3–23). Thousand Oaks, CA: Sage.

Jordan, J. V., Kaplan, A. G., Miller, J. B., Stiver, I. P., & Surrey, J. L. (1991). *Women's growth in connection.* New York: Guilford Press.

Kaplan, M. (1983). A woman's view of the *DSM-III. American Psychologist, 38,* 786–792.

Kim, B. S. K., Atkinson, D. R., & Umemoto, D. (2001). Asian cultural values and the counseling process: Current knowledge and directions for future research. *Counseling Psychologist, 29,* 570–603.

Klonoff, E. A., Landrine, H., & Campbell, R. (2000). Sexist discrimination may account for well-known gender differences in psychiatric symptoms. *Psychology of Women Quarterly, 24,* 93–99.

Klonoff, E. A., Landrine, H., & Scott, J. (1995). Double jeopardy: Ethnicity and gender in health research. In H. Landrine (Ed.), *Bringing cultural diversity to feminist psychology: Theory, research, and practice* (pp. 335–360). Washington, DC: American Psychological Association.

Kohlberg, L. (1981). *The philosophy of moral development: Essays on moral development.* (Vols. I & II). San Francisco: Harper & Row.

Kolbenschlag, M. (1981). *Kiss Sleeping Beauty good-bye.* Toronto, Ontario, Canada: Bantam Books.

Kutchins, H., & Kirk, S. A. (1997). *Making us crazy: DSM the psychiatric bible and the creation of mental disorders.* New York: Free Press.

Lakoff, R. T. (1975). *Language and women's place.* New York: Harper & Row.

Lakoff, R. T. (1990). *Taking power: The politics of language.* New York: Basic Books.

Lazur, R. F., & Majors, R. (1995). Men of color: Ethnocultural variations of male gender role strain. In R. F. Levant & W. S. Pollack (Eds.), *A new psychology of men* (pp. 337–358). New York: Basic Books.

Leonard, S., Lee, C., & Kiselica, M. S. (1999). Counseling African American male youth. In A. M. Horne & M. S. Kisebica (Eds.), *Handbook of counseling boys and adolescent males* (pp. 75–86). Thousand Oaks, CA: Sage.

Lerner, H. E. (1981). The hysterical personality: A "woman's" disease. In E. Howell & M. Bayes (Eds.), *Women and mental health.* New York: Basic Books.

Lerner, H. E. (1984). Female dependency in context: Some theoretical and technical considerations. In P. P. Rieker & E. H. Carmen (Eds.), *The gender gap in psychotherapy: Social realities and psychological processes.* New York: Plenum Press.

Levant, R. F., Hirsch, L., Celentano, E., Cozza, T., Hill, S., MacEachern, M., et al. (1992). The male role: An investigation of norms and stereotypes. *Journal of Mental Health Counseling, 14,* 325–377.

Liddle, H. A. (1992). Family psychology: Progress and prospects of a maturing discipline. *Journal of Family Psychology, 5,* 249–263.

Lijtmaer, R. M. (1998). Psychotherapy with Latina women. *Feminism and Psychology, 8,* 538–543.

Lowe, S. M., & Mascher, J. (2001). The role of sexual orientation in multicultural counseling: Integrating bodies of knowledge. In J. G. Ponterotto, J. M. Casas, L. A. Suzuki, & C. M. Alexander (Eds.), *Handbook of multicultural counseling* (2nd ed., pp. 775–778). Thousand Oaks, CA: Sage.

Lusterman, D.-D. (1989). Empathic interviewing. In G. Brooks, D.-D. Lusterman, R. Nutt, & C. Philpot (Chairs), *Men and women relating: The carrot or the stick?* Symposium presented at the annual conference of the American Association of Marriage and Family Therapy, San Francisco.

Mahalik, J. R. (1999). Interpersonal psychotherapy with men who experience gender role conflict. *Professional Psychology: Research and Practice, 30,* 5–13.

Mahalik, J. R., Cournoyer, R. J., DeFranc, W., Cherry, M., & Napolitano, J. M. (1998). Men's gender role conflict and use of psychological defenses. *Journal of Counseling Psychology, 45,* 247–255.

Maracek, J. (2001). Disorderly constructs: Feminist frameworks for clinical psychology. In R. K. Unger (Ed.), *Handbook of the psychology of women and gender* (pp. 303–316). New York: Wiley.

Matsuyuki, M. (1998). Japanese feminist counseling as a political act. *Women and Therapy, 21,* 65–77.

McBride, A. B. (1990). Mental health effects of women's multiple roles. *American Psychologist, 45,* 381–384.

McGoldrick, M., Anderson, C. M., & Walsh, F. (Eds.). (1989). *Women in families: A framework for family therapy.* New York: Norton.

Miller, J. B. (1986). *Toward a new psychology of women* (2nd ed.). Boston: Beacon Press.

Mintz, L. B., & Mahalik, J. R. (1996). Gender role orientation and conflict as predictors of family roles for men. *Sex Roles, 34,* 805–821.

Moradi, B., Fischer, A. R., Hill, M. S., Jome, L. M., & Blum, S. A. (2000). Does "feminist" plus "therapist" equal "feminist therapist"?: An empirical investigation of the link between self-labeling and behavior. *Psychology of Women Quarterly, 24,* 285–296.

Morrow, S. L., & Hawxhurst, D. M. (1998). Feminist therapy: Integrating political analysis in counseling and psychotherapy. *Women and Therapy, 21,* 37–50.

Morton, S. B. (1998). Lesbian divorce. *American Journal of Orthopsychiatry, 68,* 410–419.

Niemann, Y. F. (2001). Stereotypes about Chicanas and Chicanos: Implications for counseling. *Counseling Psychologist, 29,* 55–90.

Nutt, R. L. (1992). Feminist family therapy: A review of the literature. *Topics in Family Psychology and Counseling, 1,* 13–23.

O'Neil, J. M. (1982). Gender-role conflict and strain in men's lives. In K. Solomon & N. Levy (Eds.), *Men in transition: Theory and therapy* (pp. 5–44). New York: Plenum Press.

O'Neil, J. M., & Egan, J. (1992). Men's and women's gender role journeys: A metaphor for healing, transition, and transformation. In B. R. Wainrib (Ed.), *Gender issues across the life cycle* (pp. 107–123). New York: Springer.

O'Neil, J. M., & Roberts-Carroll, M. (1988). A gender role journey. *Journal of Counseling and Development, 67,* 193–197.

Orlinsky, D. E., & Howard, K. I. (1986). Process and outcome in psychotherapy. In S. L. Garfield & A. E. Bergin (Eds.), *Handbook of psychotherapy and behavior change* (pp. 311–384). New York: Wiley.

Orlinsky, D. E., Ronnestad, M. H., & Willutzki, V. (2004). Fifty years of psychotherapy process-outcome research: Continuity and change. In M. J. Lambert (Ed.), *Bergin and Garfield's handbook of psychotherapy and behavior change* (5th ed., pp. 307–389). Hoboken, NJ: Wiley.

Osipow, S. H., & Fitzgerald, L. F. (1996). *Theories of career development* (4th ed.). Englewood Cliffs, NJ: Prentice-Hall.

Pardie, L., & Herb, C. R. (1997). Merger and fusion in lesbian relationships: A problem of diagnosing what's wrong in terms of what's right. *Women and Therapy, 20*(3), 51–61.

Philpot, C. L., Brooks, G. R., Lusterman, D.-D., & Nutt, R. L. (1997). *Bridging separate gender worlds: Why men and women clash and how therapists can bring them together.* Washington, DC: American Psychological Association.

Pittman, F. (1985). Gender myths: When does gender become pathology? *Family Therapy Networker, 9,* 25–33.

Pleck, E., & Pleck, J. H. (Eds.). (1980). *The American man.* Englewood Cliffs, NJ: Prentice-Hall.

Pleck, J. H. (1995). The gender role strain paradigm: An update. In R. F. Levant & W. S. Pollack (Eds.), *A new psychology of men* (pp. 11–32). New York: Basic Books.

Pleck, J. H., & Sawyer, J. (1980). *Men and masculinity.* Englewood Cliffs, NJ: Prentice-Hall.

Pollack, W. S. (1995). No man is an island: Toward a new psychoanalytic psychology of men. In R. F. Levant & W. S. Pollack (Eds.), *A new psychology of men* (pp. 33–67). New York: Basic Books.

Pollack, W. S. (1998). *Real boys: Rescuing our sons from the myths of boyhood.* New York: Random House.

Ponterotto, J. G., Casas, J. M., Suzuki, L. A., & Alexander, C. M. (Eds.). (1995). *Handbook of multicultural counseling.* Thousand Oaks, CA: Sage.

Pope, K. S. (1990). Therapist-patient sex as sex abuse: Six scientific, professional, and practical dilemmas in addressing victimization and rehabilitation. *Professional Psychology: Research and Practice, 21,* 277–289.

Pope, K. S. (1994). *Sexual involvement with therapists: Patient assessment, subsequent therapy, forensics.* Washington, DC: American Psychological Association.

Porter, N. (2002). Contextual and developmental frameworks in diagnosing children and adolescents. In M. Ballou & L. S. Brown (Eds.), *Rethinking mental health and disorder: Feminist perspectives* (pp. 262–278). New York: Guilford Press.

Prilleltensky, O. (1996). Women with disabilities and feminist therapy. *Women and Therapy, 18,* 87–97.

Reid, P. T. (2002). Multicultural psychology: Bringing together gender and ethnicity. *Cultural Diversity and Ethnic Minority Psychology, 8,* 103–114.

Robertson, J., & Fitzgerald, L. F. (1990). The (mis)treatment of men: Effects of client gender role and life-style on diagnosis and attribution of pathology. *Journal of Counseling Psychology, 37,* 3–9.

Robinson, T. L., & Howard-Hamilton, M. (2000). *The convergence of race, ethnicity, and gender.* Upper Saddle River, NJ: Prentice-Hall.

Ross, R., Frances, A., & Widiger, T. A. (1997). Gender issues in *DSM-IV.* In M. R. Walsh (Ed.), *Women, men, and gender: Ongoing debates* (pp. 348–357). New Haven, CT: Yale.

Rudman, L. A., & Glick, P. (2001). Prescriptive gender stereotypes and backlash toward agentic women. *Journal of Social Issues, 57,* 743–762.

Russianoff, P. (1981). *Why do I think I am nothing without a man?* Toronto, Ontario, Canada: Bantam Books.

Seem, S. R., & Johnson, E. (1998). Gender bias among counseling trainees: A study of case conceptualization. *Counselor Education and Supervision, 37,* 257–268.

Sexton, T. L., Alexander, J. F., & Mease, A. L. (2004). Levels of evidence for the models of mechanisms of therapeutic change in family and couples therapy. In M. J. Lambert (Ed.), *Bergin and Garfield's handbook of psychotherapy and behavior change* (5th ed., pp. 590–646). Hoboken, NJ: Wiley.

Slater, S. (1995). *The lesbian family life cycle.* New York: Simon & Schuster.

Sobel, S. B., & Russo, N. F. (1981). Sex roles, equality, and mental health. *Professional Psychology, 12,* 1–5.

Sparks, E. E. (1996). Overcoming stereotypes of mothers in the African American context. In K. F. Wyche & F. J. Crosby (Eds.), *Women's ethnicities: Journeys through psychology* (pp. 67–86). Boulder, CO: Westview.

Sparks, E. E. (2002). Depression and schizophrenia in women: The intersection of gender, race/ethnicity, and class. In M. Ballou & L. S. Brown (Eds.), *Rethinking mental health and disorder: Feminist perspectives* (pp. 279–305). New York: Guilford Press.

Spender, D. (1985). *Man made language* (2nd ed.). London: Routledge & Kegan Paul.

Sturdivant, S. (1980). *Therapy with women: A feminist philosophy of treatment.* New York: Springer.

Sue, D. W., Ivey, A. E., & Pederson, P. B. (Eds.). (1996). *A theory of multicultural counseling and therapy.* Pacific Grove, CA: Brooks/Cole.

Sue, D. W., & Sue, D. (2003). *Counseling the culturally diverse: Theory and practice* (4th ed.). Hoboken, NJ: Wiley.

Szymanski, D. M., Baird, M. K., & Kornman, C. L. (2002). The feminist male therapist: Attitudes and practices of the 21st century. *Psychology of Men and Masculinity, 3,* 22–27.

Tannen, D. (1990). *You just don't understand: Women and men in conversation.* New York: Ballantine Books.

Task Force on Sex Bias and Sex Role Stereotyping in Psychotherapeutic Practice. (1975). Report. *American Psychologist, 30*(1), 169–171, 175.

Tavris, C. (1992). *The mismeasure of woman.* New York: Simon & Schuster.

Toneatto, A., Sobell, L. C., & Sobell, M. B. (1992). Gender issues in the treatment of abusers of alcohol, nicotine, and other drugs. *Journal of Substance Abuse, 4,* 209–218.

Walters, M., Carter, B., Papp, P., & Silverstein, O. (1988). *The invisible web: Gender patterns in family relationships.* New York: Guilford Press.

Weeks, G. R., & Nixon, G. F. (1991, Fall). Family psychology: The specialty statement of an evolving field. *Family Psychologist,* 9–18.

Worell, J. (1996). Opening doors to feminist research. *Psychology of Women Quarterly, 20,* 469–485.

Worell, J. (2001). Feminist interventions: Accountability beyond symptom reduction. *Psychology of Women Quarterly, 25,* 335–343.

Worell, J., & Johnson, N. G. (Eds.). (1997). *Shaping the future of feminist psychology: Education, research, and practice.* Washington, DC: American Psychological Association.

Worell, J., & Remer, P. (1992). *Feminist perspectives in therapy: An empowerment model.* New York: Wiley.

Worell, J., & Remer, P. (2003). *Feminist perspectives in therapy: Empowering diverse women* (2nd ed.). Hoboken, NJ: Wiley.

Wyche, K. F. (1993). Psychology and African-American women: Findings from applied research. *Applied and Preventive Psychology, 2,* 135–141.

Wyche, K. F., & Rice, J. K. (1997). Feminist therapy: From dialogue to tenets. In J. Worell & N. G. Johnson (Eds.), *Shaping the future of feminist psychology: Education, research, and practice* (pp. 57–71). Washington, DC: American Psychological Association.

SPECIAL ISSUES FACED BY COUPLES

CHAPTER 15

Managing Emotional Reactivity in Couples Facing Illness: Smoothing Out the Emotional Roller Coaster

William H. Watson and Susan H. McDaniel

TED: "We haven't slept together in two years. Ever since her back problems and fibromyalgia got really bad."

DIANE: "I have a very difficult time sleeping with all the pain I'm in, so Ted decided it might be better if he slept in the other bedroom. Ever since this happened, we've grown more and more distant. Can you help? I have to manage my pain AND my marriage"

As psychotherapists, we can forget that our clients are biological creatures, that they have bodies as well as minds, and that body and mind are intimately connected. How our bodies function impacts not only our emotional lives but also the emotional lives of those with whom we are close. And, conversely, our emotional lives and the interpersonal contexts in which we live affect our physical and biological functioning. Since illness is considered to be the domain of medicine, therapists often are untrained and uninterested in dealing with these issues, despite their prevalence in the general population. Biomedical illness often is viewed as ancillary to the "real" issues of therapy. Yet the emotional and relational dynamics that are of interest to therapists play a critical role in determining how individuals and couples cope with illness, and the presence of illness in the family often has a profound impact on the individual and relational functioning. Therapist reluctance to address medical illness in couples can also be compounded by countertransference issues. Confronting serious illness in patients can arouse therapists' own fears of mortality and feelings of impotence in the face of overwhelming pain, loss, and disability.

Nonetheless, illness or disability can strike at any time and can complicate couple and family relationships in significant ways. Illness in one family member can have not only emotional but physical repercussions for other
family members, especially spouses. Recent studies have supported the contention that chronic stress—especially the stress of caring for a chronically
ill spouse—weakens the immune system and makes one more susceptible to
becoming physically ill. Kiecolt-Glaser et al. (2003) found that caregivers of
spouses with Alzheimer's and other long-term illnesses show elevated levels of the stress hormone Interleukin-6 (associated with increased rates of
heart disease, arthritis, diabetes, osteoporosis, and cancer) more than three
years after their stressful tasks ended.

Physicians and other health professionals are increasingly recognizing
the need that couples and families have for assistance in dealing with the
psychosocial impact of illness, from infertility and epilepsy to cancer and
heart disease. It behooves us in the mental health professions to equip ourselves to deal with these needs. This chapter discusses how illness affects
couples, reviews the basics of medical family therapy, and presents a technique for addressing emotional roadblocks in the marital or couple relationship that can emerge as couples deal with the particular challenges that
illness presents.

A REVIEW OF THE LITERATURE ON
PSYCHOTHERAPY WITH COUPLES FACING ILLNESS

A significant body of research examines the impact of couple relationships
on health, and the impact that chronic illness or disability has on the couple
(Campbell, 2003; Kiecolt-Glaser & Newton, 2001; Osterman et al., 2003;
Schmaling & Sher, 1997). Very few studies, however, focus on couple interventions that might inform psychotherapeutic treatment. We review two
cases here and then turn to the clinical literature on couple interventions
with medically ill patients that provides guidance for therapists working
with this population.

Early research focused on couple interventions to improve disease management, medical compliance, quality of life, and mortality for patients with
chronic illness. Morisky et al. (1980) found that home visits to counsel the
spouses of hypertensive patients significantly improved treatment compliance and lowered both blood pressure and overall mortality, compared with
controls. In another controlled study (Taylor, Bandura, Ewart, Miller, & De-
Busk, 1985), wives of heart attack patients were asked either to observe their
spouse take a treadmill stress test or to take the test with their spouse, three
weeks after the heart attack. Wives who walked the treadmill and directly
experienced what their husbands were capable of were significantly more
confident and less anxious about their husbands' health and capability than
the wives who only observed the test. They were also less overprotective of
their husbands, which may relate to the finding that their husbands showed
improved cardiac functioning at 11 and 26 weeks after the heart attack.

Although there is a significant body of clinical literature that addresses psychotherapy with families facing illness (see McDaniel, Hepworth, & Doherty, 1992), literature that focuses on helping couples in particular is still relatively scarce—usually found either in textbooks on couples therapy with illness treated as a special issue (e.g., Bobes & Rothman, 1998; Gurman & Jacobson, 2002; Snyder & Whisman, 2003); in textbooks on families and illness with the couple relationship treated as a special issue (e.g., McDaniel, Hepworth, & Doherty, 1997; Rolland, 1994); or in literature that addresses the psychosocial impact of specific illnesses or disabilities, such as Alzheimer's, spinal cord injury, diabetes, or HIV (e.g., Burgoyne, 1994; Mohr et al., 2003; Rait, Ross, & Rao, 1997; Webster, 1992). There are few books devoted to the topic of couples and physical illness (e.g., d'Ardenne & Morrod, 2003).

A wide variety of specific approaches have been offered on the subject of couples and illness, including behavioral (Schmaling & Sher, 2000), existential (Lantz, 1996), and interpersonal (Lyons, Sullivan, Ritvo, & Coyne, 1995). Many of these approaches delineate key issues that couples must confront when illness strikes and offer strategies, drawn from their particular theoretical framework, to help couples negotiate these issues.

Rolland (1994) addresses the impact of illness on intimacy in the couple relationship, focusing in particular on the need for the therapist to assist the couple in addressing the relationship imbalances (skews) that can emerge as a result of illness in one member. Differences in ability that derive from the health status of each member of the couple can translate into differences in power and control between them, leading to tension, resentment, guilt, distance, and discouragement. Rolland recommends that the couple redefine the illness as "our" problem, rather than "your" or "my" problem, and work as partners to manage the challenges they both face as a result of the illness. Rolland also suggests that therapists assist the couple to resist the tendency of illness to dominate the family identity by drawing a boundary around the illness. This can be done by, for example, establishing protected time in which illness talk is off limits as well as by maintaining their pre-illness family and social routines as much as possible.

Kowal, Johnson, & Lee (2003) have applied the tenets of Emotionally Focused Therapy (EFT) to working with couples and illness; EFT is an integration of experiential and systemic approaches to therapy that understands couple conflict as relating to behaviors and emotions that express underlying attachment needs. They argue that since attachment style has been shown to be related to the onset and exacerbation of chronic illness as well as to a variety of health-related behaviors, then addressing attachment needs and the emotions they generate by use of EFT is a promising avenue for assisting couples dealing with chronic illness. They go on to note that "the goals of EFT in working with chronic illness in couples are to normalize and validate each partner's experience, to help partners process their emotional experiences, to externalize negative interaction cycles, and to help partners seek safety, security, and comfort from each other (i.e., create a more secure attachment bond," p. 304).

COUPLES AND ILLNESS—STATEMENT OF THE PROBLEM

Factors that influence how illness affects a couple include the nature and severity of the illness; individual variables such as age, gender, ethnicity, general coping style, and previous experience with illness; and relationship variables such as degree of conflict, stability, and trust, communication and problem-solving styles, and relationship satisfaction. Issues facing couples dealing with illness include loss—of ability, of a sense of normalcy, of expectations for the future, and possibly loss of life; identity changes precipitated by the presence of the illness; relationship imbalances deriving from the loss of function in the ill spouse; the need to communicate about difficult subjects; establishing the meaning of the illness; the legacy of transgenerational family experiences with illness, vulnerability, and loss; gender issues; caregiver burden and burnout; and the ill spouse's feelings of guilt and uselessness.

Literature about helping couples deal with the impact of illness generally addresses the emotional and pragmatic impact of illness on the couple relationship, including loss of function and identity, reassignment of roles, learning to communicate about difficult issues, and so on. What has received less attention is how to understand and address complicated emotional reactions to illness—reactions that seem to go beyond what would be expected, even given the extremely difficult nature of the challenges that illness can present.

For some couples, illness presents an opportunity to put things in perspective, resulting in increased intimacy and relationship satisfaction in the face of challenge. For other couples, the challenge of illness may derail previously adequate coping mechanisms and plunge a formerly stable relationship into a terrifying tailspin. A strain of serious illness can exacerbate prior relationship difficulties and accelerate the deterioration of a couple relationship. The emotional processes underlying such problematic reactions to the difficult challenges of illness are rooted in the premorbid levels of functioning in each spouse and in the couple relationship. Bowen family systems concepts (Bowen, 1985)—especially emotional reactivity and differentiation—offer a way to understand how to assess and assist couples experiencing particularly problematic reactions to physical illness.

BACKGROUND AND KEY PRINCIPLES OF THE APPROACH—MEDICAL FAMILY THERAPY

Medical family therapy is a metaframework for psychotherapy; it provides overarching principles within which any form of psychotherapy can be practiced (McDaniel et al., 1992, 1997). Medical family therapy is based on a biopsychosocial systems theory (Engel, 1980; McDaniel et al., 1992). This theory, unlike traditional biotechnical medicine, is expressly systemic and sensitive to the effects on health and illness of context, including such variables as gender, race, culture, and class. The goals of medical family therapy are to optimize agency and communion for the patient, the family, and the health professionals involved (Bakan, 1966). Agency refers to a sense of self-efficacy in the face of challenge. Communion refers to a sense of connection—with family, friends, health professionals, community, and spiritual communionity. Taken together, agency and communion are the foundations of individual effectiveness within a relational context. Vicki Hegelson (1994), in a review of the research on agency and communion, concludes that both agency and communion are required for optimal health, but that the effects on health are curvilinear. She found that both unmitigated agency and unmitigated communion are associated with negative health outcomes. The goal is to find a balance between these extremes.

Medical family therapy emphasizes the development of a collaborative (rather than hierarchical) relationship between the health professional, the patient, and the spouse or partner; this is a necessary corrective to the well-described power problems that can occur in the doctor-patient relationship (McDaniel & Hepworth, 2004; McDaniel et al., 1992). This collaborative stance involves respecting the patient's and family's agendas, supporting their goals, and providing care from a consultative rather than authoritarian position.

Techniques for helping couples and families in medical family therapy include the following: (1) recognize the biological dimension along with the psychological, (2) solicit the illness story, (3) respect defenses, (4) remove blame and accept unacceptable feelings, (5) attend to developmental issues, (6) increase sense of agency, (7) facilitate communication, and (8) remain available.

The first technique is to *attend to the biological dimension* of any problem. This is fundamental to a biopsychosocial approach. Historically, various approaches to family therapy have looked askance on biological explanations of human functioning, in part out of an understandable concern with the reductionism of traditional biomedical approaches. In working with couples facing illness, however, it is critical to recognize the importance of biology and its profound impact on the life of the couple. It is often helpful, when possible, to sit with the couple and their physician or other member of their health care team to demystify the illness by discussing their questions, concerns, and reactions to it and to the treatment recommendations.

In the context of an ambiguous diagnosis or course of illness, it is important to be open to many possible explanations for the patient's symptomatology (Ruddy & McDaniel, 2002). Illness is virtually always both biological and psychological, or at least involves aspects of each. Tolerance for ambiguity in the therapist helps avoid the temptation to attribute the patient's symptoms definitively to either psychological or biological causes. Particularly in cases where the diagnosis is unclear (e.g., fibromyalgia, subtle neurological impairments, chronic fatigue syndrome), overemphasis on psychological causes risks invalidating the patient and even exacerbating the need to "prove" that the illness has a genuine biomedical cause. On the other hand, a clinician's overemphasis on biological explanations risks encouraging the patient to avoid looking at the relationship between emotions and symptom expression. We do well to maintain a certain humility about our knowledge of illness. It certainly happens that an illness diagnosed as psychological at one point is later found to have a bona fide biomedical cause as the illness progresses or a new diagnostic approach is taken. It can sometimes be helpful to focus on the fact that stress has been shown to exacerbate virtually all illnesses, whether the etiology be psychological or biological, and that working to reduce stress through enhancing coping strategies is likely to be beneficial, regardless of ultimate cause.

The second technique, *soliciting the illness story*, involves asking about the patient and couples' experience with the illness from the time of diagnosis to the present, including the associated feelings. Understanding the emotional and family context of the illness is facilitated through inquiry about family illness history, illness meanings, and transgenerational health beliefs and coping strategies. A respectful collaborative relationship greatly facilitates the eliciting of the illness story from the patient and spouse or partner, and lays the foundation for developing a successful partnership for care.

Views of illness and of the relationship with health care providers varies by cultural group, and often by gender. These views can present special challenges to the health professional and the psychotherapist. Because of the power differential, women may need to develop a trusting relationship with their health care provider before being able to share their illness story. For men, sharing their experience of illness may conflict with American male socialization that discourages expression or acknowledgment of vulnerability; patient, supportive questioning by the therapist may therefore be required.

The development of an effective therapeutic relationship in medical family therapy requires *respecting the patient and partner's defenses, diminishing blame and guilt, and accepting unacceptable feelings in reaction to illness.* An overfunctioning spouse who falls ill will be prone to feel guilt and self-blame about not being able to maintain previous levels of functioning. The stress and anxiety that accompanies illness can generate irritability and blame toward the sick (or toward the healthy) spouse or partner. Gender roles can compound the difficulty of adjusting to the demands of illness—for example, unacceptable feelings may arise related to ways in which men or women respond to illness that run counter to their gender script. A man who is weepy or a woman who is angry in response to a new diagnosis may feel the additional burden of criticism from others. Medical family therapy works to counteract the dehumanizing experience of these gender scripts (McDaniel & Cole-Kelly, 2003).

It is important to *understand developmental issues* at the individual, couple, and family levels as they interact with the demands of the illness or disability (Rolland, 1994). For example, breast cancer in a woman of child-bearing age will have different psychosocial implications than at other stages of development as she struggles with the need for treatment (e.g., mastectomy; chemotherapy during pregnancy) versus the biological and emotional needs of her children, born and unborn. The development of a serious illness in a member of a couple entering retirement may provide unique challenges around adjustment to a life filled with patienthood and caregiving in contrast to the active retirement they had planned for themselves.

Increasing agency is accomplished through providing psychoeducation and information for men and women, encouraging the patient, couple, and family to maintain individual, couple, and family identities, developing flexible roles in caring for the illness, and drawing out individual and family strengths and resources. Connection (or communion) between the patient and the family, and the patient and the health care team, is strengthened through ongoing attention to clear *communication*. This technique often involves understanding idiosyncratic styles of communication regarding illness and treatment. With one couple, for example, therapy focused on negotiating a balance between the wife's need to discuss her fears regarding her husband's heart attack and her husband's desire to avoid the subject and focus on the future. They were able to resolve the impasse by allowing each other equal time within specific parameters—alternating half-hour conversations, twice a week. As their anxiety lessened, their ability to actively support each other reemerged.

REMAIN AVAILABLE

Finally, medical family therapy recognizes that chronic illness has a natural life course of its own, independent of the family's adaptation to the illness. Consequently, it is helpful to have a flexible approach regarding the time-line of therapy to accommodate to the shifting need of the family as new medical crises erupt or the shifting demands of the developmental life cycle interact with the demands of chronic illness. It is also helpful to have a flexible approach to the nature of the therapeutic relationship, understanding it to be part of the broader health care team rather than an independent domain. It is useful to remain involved and available, both through encouraging the family to consult with the therapist on an as-needed basis and through remaining connected over time through periodic contacts with the family, the physician, or other members of the health care team.

ADDRESSING EMOTIONAL REACTIVITY IN ILLNESS: FACILITATING AGENCY AND COMMUNION THROUGH INCREASING DIFFERENTIATION

Illness can precipitate a crisis with regard to the need to change roles, as the ill person often can no longer fulfill all the roles in the family that he or she previously held, or can fulfill them in only a limited fashion. There is a need to assist couples with negotiating these role changes and with both the loss associated with being unable to carry out one's roles, and the stress and strain of shifting roles. For example, the husband may now need to take a different kind of role with regard to parenting the children and managing daily life—jobs that previously were done by his wife, now ill with cancer and the effects of chemotherapy. Therapists can be helpful by assisting couples in determining how they might best maintain a sense of agency in the face of these losses and stresses—helping the husband recognize, for example, the importance of supporting his disabled wife's desire to maintain some semblance of contributing to the parenting or household management. Likewise, a sense of connection to others (communion) helps to make the experience of loss more bearable. Interaction with emotionally significant others can generate new ideas about management of the challenges at hand. Therapists need to track how the couple is dealing with their needs for contact and for space—with each other and in their wider family and social network.

An aspect of agency and communion that has not been commented on in the medical family therapy literature to date is the importance of attending to the couples' level of differentiation (Bowen, 1985). Increasing one's level of differentiation, according to Bowen, is a lifelong project in which each individual seeks to become more fully aware of self and able to maintain a clear sense of self while in emotionally significant contact with others. Increasing one's level of differentiation increases the ability to recognize when one's internal responses are being driven by emotional reactivity and are out of proportion to external circumstances. This ability is in contrast to the natural tendency to assume that our anger, say, is a reasonable response to the annoyances inflicted on us by others. Differentiation impels us and enables us to instead ask, "In what way is my reaction to this situation being fueled by my own vulnerabilities, by my own fears, by my own unresolved issues that are so painful or confusing that I am not fully aware of them?"

This perspective can become particularly important when helping couples address the meaning of the illness and the meaning of the various losses and changes that illness requires of them. In examining each family member's vulnerabilities concerning not only issues pertaining to illness, health, and their relationship to their bodies, but also to loss, intimacy, closeness, and identity, the therapist lays the groundwork for a deeper understanding of the reasons for the impact of the illness on the life of the couple. For example, a woman who has experienced repeated abuse from parents may be prone to experience her cancer as one more instance of abuse, whereas a man who has felt plagued by a chronic sense of failure and inadequacy may experience his cancer as further confirmation that something is fatally flawed in him, and still another individual with a history of controlling and intrusive parenting may experience his cancer as an invading force that destroys his autonomy and leaves him feeling helpless and resentful. This perspective can also illuminate reasons for reactions that a patient or family member has to not only the illness itself but also to health care providers and to family members. The woman with the history of abuse may be prone to see her harried, terse physician as abusive and exploitative, the man with fears of inadequacy may become resentful of his wife's taking over the management of the family finances or even resentful of her health, and the man sensitive to issues of control and autonomy may experience hospital stays as unbearable exercises in humiliation.

A SEVEN-STEP APPROACH FOR ADDRESSING EMOTIONAL REACTIVITY TRIGGERED BY ILLNESS CONCERNS

In working with couples dealing with chronic or terminal illness, one useful way of working with the impact and meaning of the illness is by using the following seven-step process to clarify areas of reactivity in the couple interaction triggered by illness concerns and to increase their ability to manage it: (1) explore the impact of the illness at both the pragmatic and the emotional levels, (2) determine which areas of impact are most colored by emotional reactivity, (3) redirect attention from the outer reality of the illness to the inner response and meaning of the illness, (4) draw out and intensify the associated affects, (5) connect these affects to each person's particular vulnerabilities and previous injuries, (6) facilitate separation of past from present and increase awareness of emotional reactivity, and (7) facilitate development of alternative responses to both past and present stressors and injuries.

Step 1: Explore the Impact of the Illness at Both the Pragmatic and the Emotional Levels

Illness impacts couples at numerous levels in profound and subtle ways, from the obvious and concrete—for example, the ill spouse becoming unable to drive or to earn an income—to the less obvious and more indirect—for example, the sense of helplessness of the healthy spouse that leads him or her to become irritable or to become emotionally distant out of reluctance to burden the ill partner with his or her own concerns. It can be useful to ask the couple to detail every way they can think of that the illness has impacted their lives, or, conversely, how they imagine life would be different if the illness were to suddenly be cured. The therapist should write these down, preferably on an easel so the couple can track the flow of the discussion. Exploration should attend not only to the pragmatic aspects of the changes in their daily routine necessitated by the illness, but also to changes that have been brought about to their self image and their image of their relationship, to how they interpret and manage the normal developmental changes in their children in light of the illness, to how they parent, to their sense of time, to how they think about the future and how they reflect on the past, to their spiritual and religious life, to their relationship to God or a higher power.

It is important to remember that in this process the therapist should be not only listening for, and asking about, the challenges or difficulties brought about by the illness, but also for areas of positive change, of enhanced functioning, or of benefit brought about by the presence of the illness or their adaptation to it. It is not uncommon for patients and family members to report closer relationships as a result of illness, or a deeper appreciation for life, or the discovery of an authentic spirituality or a greater sense of God's closeness and care, or a valued shift in priorities and focus. Yet even such positive changes can be a source of relationship stress if they are not mutual or at least mutually understood and respected.

Step 2: Determine Which Areas of Impact Are Most Colored by Emotional Reactivity

As the list of changes brought about by the illness is detailed, it often becomes clear that some seem to the couple to be fairly manageable and under control, while others cause considerable distress and anxiety. It is the latter that are typically the focus of therapy. Among the changes that are most distressing, some will seem more straightforward and amenable to empathic support or problem solving—fear of death and loss, financial anxieties— while others will seem more complicated and entrenched—resentment of the ill spouse for being sick, denial of the illness (by patient or family member), depression over loss of identity or loss of function.

Illness often creates isolation, which in turn is a hothouse in which problems grow and thrive. Often, the process of talking about formerly unvoiced concerns in therapy is healing in and of itself. But in some cases, decreasing the isolation of the patient and couple from each other, from their extended family and community, and from their health care providers is not sufficient. This may be an indication of an emotional complication arising from unresolved issues that antedate the illness. It is probably always true that a person's reaction to an external stressor like an illness is colored, at least in some degree, by one's history and particular vulnerabilities, and by the history of the present relationship. But for some issues this is far truer than for others.

Even though she knew it wasn't his fault, Emily couldn't help being furious with Charles for having seizures. The referring neurologist and her nurse commented on Emily's lack of support when they made the referral. In recent years, Charles's epilepsy had grown increasingly unresponsive to medication, and he was now having several grand mal seizures a week. He was unable to work and was on disability. He was also limited in his ability to care for their young children, since he could neither carry them for fear of dropping them were he to have a sudden seizure, nor could he be left alone with them lest a seizure render him unconscious or impaired for a period of time. Cooking, climbing, working with power tools, or using sharp implements were likewise off limits. The situation was admittedly dire and created a tremendous burden on Emily. But in addition to her exhaustion and anxiety, she was furious with Charles for not being able to work or help out more with the demands of family life. Charles was devastated. He would plead with her that he didn't like the situation any more than she did. He struggled to do all he could between seizures to maintain the household, but his efforts seemed, if anything, to only increase her anger and disgust. Their marriage was in dire straits when they came to see me (WHW). Emily's response to her husband was puzzling and distressing at first, until she shared her history. She was the oldest of five. Her father was alcoholic and abusive of their mother, although not to the children. Her mother had become severely depressed and anxious, and largely unable to function around the house. From an early age, Emily had found that taking the role of housekeeper and caretaker of the younger children had lessened her mother's depression and given Emily some sense of safety and value in an otherwise bleak situation. She both felt sorry for her mother and resented her.

Because chronic illness can have such a profound impact on the life of the patient and his or her family, it is easy to forget that emotional factors unrelated to the illness can have an equally profound impact on how the couple manages the illness and the changes it requires. In the case of Charles and Emily, it was clear that the emotional reactions to the situation were being fueled by factors external to the illness and the stress and isolation it brings. It is not always so clear, however, how emotional reactivity is contributing to the difficulties couples face in dealing with illness. The signs can be subtle, and masked by the realities of the illness.

The term *emotional reactivity* refers to the tendency to get caught up in emotional reactions, which then drive behavior, in contrast to being able to be aware of when one's responses are out of proportion to the situation and limit the extent to which these responses drive behavior.

Indications that emotional reactivity is complicating adjustment to illness include reactions that appear especially intrusive and out of proportion to the situation, problems that do not respond to the couples' usual coping strategies, or conflicts or concerns that have a sticky quality—that repeat endlessly and with a level of anxiety or intensity that is not easily calmed or soothed, even temporarily. When these signs are present, it is helpful to explore what else might be going on internally that is driving the response, in addition to the real challenges presented by the illness.

STEP 3: REDIRECT ATTENTION FROM THE OUTER REALITY OF THE ILLNESS TO THE INNER RESPONSE AND MEANING OF THE ILLNESS

Having determined which areas of concern are most likely to be colored by emotional reactivity, it can then be useful to explore the underlying meanings associated with those areas of concern. The goal is to begin to clarify the sources of the emotional reactivity. The first step in the process is to highlight the emotions or reactions that are elicited by the particular circumstance or conflict. As a first approach, each member of the couple can be asked why he or she imagines he or she is having such a reaction:

> To the healthy spouse: "Of course this illness is devastating, but do you have any idea about the reasons for the depth of your frustration about your husband's illness?" To the ill spouse: "What is the meaning for you of no longer being able to drive [. . . coach the kids' baseball team, work two jobs . . .]?"

More indirectly, each member can be asked about what he or she experiences internally when confronted with a given difficult issue:

> "What feelings come up for you when . . . you see him struggle with the walker . . . hear her complain about the medication side effects . . . you need his assistance with the kids but he can't because of the pain . . . ?" "What does it mean to you when X happens, or when you think Y is true?" "It's as if he or she were saying what to you when that happens? What's the message you hear?" "How do you wind up feeling about yourself then?"

Step 4: Draw Out and Intensify the Associated Emotions

The goal here is to shift the person's awareness and focus from the external circumstances to the internal reaction to them. Having begun this process in the previous step, each individual is now asked to further describe his or her reactions. In the process of description, the speakers elaborate on their internal processes. The therapist responds empathically, underlining the emotions or attitudes hinted at in the speaker's statement and asking questions to help the speaker continue to elaborate, subtly directing attention to his or her inner experience. As this process continues, the focus shifts from the external difficulty to the speaker's reaction to it. For example:

- The patient begins with an external focus:
  PATIENT: "This endless treadmill of doctor's appointments is running us into the ground."
- Therapist shifts the focus to the patient's inner experience:
  THERAPIST: "It is a lot! What's happening to you in the midst of all that?"
  PATIENT: "I'm exhausted with all this running around."
- Therapist helps patient to elaborate the inner experience:
  THERAPIST: "What emotions do you find coming up in you as your exhaustion grows?"
  PATIENT: "I feel I have no life left, I feel so discouraged, there's all these demands that I can't manage, I feel incompetent and angry,

furious really, like what I need doesn't matter and all I'm allowed to do is be the nurse no matter what."

With the third of these elaborations, some sense begins to emerge of the speaker's deeper feelings about the situation, feelings that suggest roots of emotional reactivity in areas of particular vulnerability for the speaker.

STEP 5: CONNECT THESE EMOTIONS TO EACH PERSON'S PARTICULAR VULNERABILITIES AND PREVIOUS INJURIES

With the speaker now more clearly in contact with the internal feeling state elicited by the external conflict or challenge, the therapist can ask when, under what circumstances, or with whom he or she may have felt such feelings before. "It's as if your feelings don't matter, you just have to do what is demanded of you, and it's too much and you feel you can't do it all, and you get furious and resentful. Have you ever had these kind of feelings before? Was there ever a time when you were younger that anyone interacted with you in a way that left you feeling like your feelings don't matter and you just have to do what's demanded of you?" The speaker might respond with "Why, yes! That was the way I felt constantly growing up. My mother was so controlling, I wasn't even allowed to have an opinion about what flavor ice cream I wanted. She'd really make you pay if you didn't do what she expected!"

However, at times the speaker may quickly say "no" to such a question. The spouse often jumps in at this point with a revealing comment about the speaker's childhood experiences. The husband in one couple I (WHW) saw would feel enraged when his wife asked him questions about the management of the house when she was laid up with her illness. "She's criticizing me! Like I'm some kind of idiot who can't do anything right" he protested. His wife convincingly explained that he had this reaction to the most innocent and gentle of questions she might ask. I asked him if he had ever had a similar feeling or reaction before with anyone else. "No, sure haven't," he shrugged. His wife exclaimed, "What about your mother!?" "Oh," he responded, "I've learned to ignore her." He then went on to describe, rather dismissively at first and then with increasing distress, the particularly hostile and denigrating scapegoating to which his mother had subjected him throughout his childhood.

STEP 6: FACILITATE SEPARATION OF PAST FROM PRESENT AND INCREASE AWARENESS OF EMOTIONAL REACTIVITY

As the speaker describes these previous injuries, the therapist listens to ensure that the speaker is emotionally connected to what he or she is describing and not reporting in a detached or distant manner. This emotional connection usually happens automatically as the story is shared in more detail. If the speaker remains detached throughout the telling, the therapist might comment about this, and ask what it is like to describe these difficult issues, or empathize about how it is difficult to permit oneself to remember how painful it was.

Emotional connection to these prior injuries often facilitates awareness of how similar these old feelings are to the feelings in the current situation. This awareness, in turn, often clarifies the extent to which the speaker's emotional reactions to the current stressor are out of proportion to it, as well as how the peculiar intensity behind the feelings derives from unresolved feelings about old injuries and issues. The very reason for the sense of hopeless futility and chronic misunderstanding associated with the couple's previous attempts to address these intense reactions in their relationship is the emotional engine driving the issue, and is not something they have access to. The couple is being guided by their reactivity to seek a solution in the present when the key issue in need of attention lies in the past. This awareness often comes as a surprise to the speaker, who is typically convinced that his or her feelings are completely reasonable responses to the current conflict and entirely unrelated to any personal issues or sensitivities. Indeed, it is a hallmark of emotional reactivity that the more convinced one is that one's responses are entirely justified and objective, the more likely they are not.

Sometimes, it is useful for the therapist to explicate these connections for the speaker and spouse or partner:

> When you are told you have to increase your meds, it feels like it's your fault, like it's proof of your father's oft-repeated saying that you screw up whatever you touch. And when your wife gets anxious and impatient that you're avoiding your meds, you scream at her the way you never could at your father. Sure, her criticism about this is a problem, though it's a relatively minor one—but because it hits a sore point for you, it *feels* like a huge one. The *depth* of the pain you feel about this isn't about your wife, it's about your dad, which is why you haven't been able to feel any better about it by trying to address it with her. We need to start by taking this intensity to where it belongs, by talking through this issue about you and your dad, and how you've handled that in the past and how it affects you in the present, and how you can begin to feel some relief on *that* front.

STEP 7: ENCOURAGE DEVELOPMENT OF ALTERNATIVE RESPONSES TO BOTH PAST INJURIES AND CURRENT STRESSORS

As above, it can be helpful to provide some explicit psychoeducation about how emotional reactivity works—how a current crisis precipitated by illness can seem much bigger if it happens to touch on a sore point—an area of particular vulnerability or sensitivity; and conversely, how the interpretation of, and response to, that upset changes once the reactivity it triggers is addressed. The task then becomes to solve the proper problem—unresolved issues from the past cannot be resolved by focus on a current illness concern. This misdirected energy is why conflicts that are driven by emotional reactivity have such a sticky, endlessly repeating, and intractable quality. The intensity of the reaction to the current illness needs instead to be directed toward the underlying issue or vulnerability that is being triggered.

As is often the case, once the couple has gained some appreciation that their responses to the illness do not just stem from the particular challenges it presents, but are also colored by emotional reactivity, their stance toward the current conflict or issue often softens. The intensity and polarization of their responses lessens, allowing new perspectives and new solutions to emerge in the current illness situation. Sometimes, however, this softening is not possible (or is fleeting) until the unresolved issues from the past are more directly addressed and worked through. Doing such work in couples therapy has the advantage of allowing each member of the couple to function as a resource to the other in the process. In addition, the therapist as part of the health care team is able to collaborate with the couple's other care providers to prevent the kind of judgments or stereotypes that can be common among professionals when a spouse or parent has difficulty being supportive in the face of illness.

The resulting increase in maturity (or self-differentiation in Bowen's terms) greatly facilitates adaptive coping with the pragmatic and relational stresses of illness. A sense of agency is increased through enhanced ability to observe self and be increasingly responsible for one's own emotional functioning. A sense of communion is increased through an improved ability to be more fully present to self while also being more fully present to others. This ability to be present to self and others is an especially important factor in establishing meaning and experiencing support in the context of the many challenges that illness presents.

COUPLES, ILLNESS, AND CULTURE

In working with couples facing a serious physical or chronic illness, understanding the cultural context in which the illness occurs is as important as understanding the couple's particular illness story and the family history of experience with illness. There are wide cultural variations in how illness is expressed, in the meaning attributed to illness and disability, in the definition of the role of the patient, in the understanding of the patient-provider relationship, and in the role expectations for the family and community caring for the patient (Kleiman, Eisenberg, & Good, 1978; Loustaunau & Sobo, 1997; Mechanic, 1986). Filipino women, for example, have been found more likely to attribute the cause of illnesses to spiritual-social explanations than American women (Edman & Kameoka, 1997). Pantilat (1996) describes how patients from different ethnic groups have differing attitudes toward autonomy and medical decision making, including whether and how the patient (or family) should be given news of illness.

These issues highlight the need for the therapist to be sensitive to the wider ethnic and sociocultural factors influencing emotional reactivity, in addition to the more immediate "culture" of a particular family group. This will be particularly germane when the members of a couple come from different cultural or ethnic backgrounds. In such cases, spouses or partners may misinterpret culturally based behavior as personal attack, setting off a cycle of intensifying reactivity. It can be helpful to clarify such dynamics by asking the couple about how their respective cultures would view the concerns they present. Where relevant, it can be useful to explore their cultures' concepts about the meaning of illness, how sick people are to behave, and the role expectations for family members.

The relationship each member of the couple has with his or her own cultural background may shed light on the impasses that illness has created for them. For example, a couple who has moved to the United States from another country five years ago may be experiencing different rates of assimilation, which in turn leaves them speaking a different language from each other (Landau-Stanton, 1982). In such a context, the development of a serious illness in one spouse may cause a smoldering resentment to burst into open conflict as they struggle with their now-different expectations for management of the illness. These differences, in turn, may bring up complicated feelings relating to immigration and the dilemma of assimilation to the new culture versus maintenance of traditional values. Unresolved family of origin issues may serve to further intensify the struggle with cultural transition. For example, if one partner has significant guilt about leaving family in the home country, significant unresolved and unexpressed guilt about betrayal of family and cultural loyalties may function as a source of emotional reactivity in their current conflict over management of illness (McDaniel, Harkness, & Epstein, 2001).

BOWEN THEORY AND CULTURE

Western culture places particular stress on the individual over the group, on self-assertion over self-sacrifice, nonconformity over conformity, intellect over affect, novelty over tradition, youth over age, and doing over being. Many other cultures, especially those with collectivist traditions, emphasize the opposite of each of these polarities. Bowen theory has been criticized from a feminist perspective for valuing thinking and devaluing feeling, and emphasizing the differentiation side of the differentiation-togetherness pole in emotional functioning (Bograd, 1988; Lerner, 1985; Luepnitz, 1988).

Cautions regarding Bowen theory and its implementation have also been offered from a cultural perspective for similar reasons. For example,

Tamura and Lau (1992), note that "the preferred direction of change for Japanese families in therapy is toward a process of *integration*—how a person can be effectively integrated into the given system—rather than a process of *differentiation*. (p. 319)" While they agree that systemic thinking is valid for all families regardless of cultural differences, they caution that culture will influence how relational health is defined: "In Japan, the 'right' balance of separateness/connectedness is defined much more toward the connected side of the continuum than in Britain" (p. 329).

This discussion of differentiation from the perspective of Japanese culture illustrates that the interpretation of healthy relatedness is heavily influenced by cultural values. As therapists, it is important to be mindful of our own cultural biases and the cultural values of the couples with whom we work, just as it is important to be aware of our own areas of reactivity as we help couples address theirs.

SUMMARY

From a holistic approach, all couples therapy should include a careful analysis of the impact of health concerns on relational functioning, and vice versa. Medical family therapy, with a special focus on managing emotional reactivity and facilitating differentiation, can provide valuable support and treatment to patients and partners facing illness challenges. Couples therapists can also provide valuable consultation to other health professionals by actively becoming part of the patient's larger team.

REFERENCES

Bakan, D. (1966). *The duality of human existence: An essay on psychology and religion.* Chicago: Rand McNally.

Bobes, T., & Rothman, B. (1998). *The crowded bed: An effective framework for doing couple therapy.* New York: Norton.

Bograd, M. (1988). Power, gender, and the family: Feminist perspectives on family systems theory. In M. A. Dutton-Douglas & L. E. A. Walker (Eds.), *Feminist psychotherapies: Integration of therapeutic and feminist systems* (pp. 118–133). Norwood, NJ: Ablex.

Bowen, M. (1985). *Family therapy in clinical practice.* Northvale, NJ: Aronson.

Burgoyne, R. (1994). Counselling gay male couples living with HIV. *Canadian Journal of Human Sexuality, 3,* 1–14.

Campbell, T. L. (2003). The effectiveness of family interventions for physical disorders. *Journal of Marital and Family Therapy, 29,* 263–281.

d'Ardenne, P., & Morrod, D. (2003). *The counselling of couples in healthcare settings: A handbook for clinicians.* London: Whurr.

Edman, J., & Kameoka, V. (1997). Cultural differences in illness schemas: An analysis of Filipino and American illness attributions. *Journal of Cross-Cultural Psychology, 28,* 252–265.

Engel, G. L. (1980). The clinical application of the biopsychosocial model. *American Journal of Psychiatry, 137*, 535–543.

Gurman, A., & Jacobson, N. (2002). *Clinical handbook of couple therapy* (3rd ed.). New York: Guilford Press.

Hegelson, V. S. (1994). Relation of agency and communion to well-being: Evidence and potential explanations. *Psychological Bulletin, 116*, 412–428.

Kiecolt-Glaser, J. K., & Newton, T. L. (2001). Marriage and health: His and hers. *Psychological Bulletin, 127*, 472–503.

Kiecolt-Glaser, J. K., Preacher, K. J., MacCallum, R. C., Atkinson, C., Malarkey, W. B., & Glaser, R. (2003). Chronic stress and age-related increases in the proinflammatory cytokine IL-6. *Proceedings of the National Academy of Sciences, USA, 100*, 9090–9095.

Kleiman, A., Eisenberg, L., & Good, B. (1978). Culture, illness, and care: Clinical lessons from anthropologic and cross-cultural research. *Annals of Internal Medicine, 88*, 251–258.

Kowal, J., Johnson, S., & Lee, A. (2003). Chronic illness in couples: A case for emotionally focused therapy. *Journal of Marital and Family Therapy, 29*, 299–310.

Landau-Stanton, J. (1982). Therapy with families in cultural transition. In M. McGoldrick, J. K. Pearce, & J. Giordano (Eds.), *Ethnicity and family therapy* (pp. 552–572). New York: Guilford Press.

Lantz, J. (1996). Existential psychotherapy with chronic illness couples. *Contemporary Family Therapy, 18*, 197–208.

Lerner, H. G. (1985). Dianna and Lillie: Can a feminist still like Murray Bowen? *Family Therapy Networker, 9*, 36–39.

Loustaunau, M. O., & Sobo, E. J. (1997). *The cultural context of health, illness, and medicine.* Westport, CT: Bergin & Garvey.

Luepnitz, D. A. (1988). *The family interpreted: Feminist theory in clinical practice.* New York: Basic Books.

Lyons, R. F., Sullivan, M. J. L., Ritvo, P. G., & Coyne, J. C. (1995). *Relationships in chronic illness and disability.* Thousand Oaks, CA: Sage.

McDaniel, S. H., & Cole-Kelly, K. (2003). Gender, couples, and illness: A feminist analysis of medical family therapy. In L. B. Silverstein & T. J. Goodrich (Eds.), *Feminist family therapy: Empowerment in social context* (pp. 267–280). Washington, DC: American Psychological Association.

McDaniel, S. H., Harkness, J., & Epstein, R. (2001). Differentiation before death: Medical family therapy for a woman with end-stage Crohn's disease and her son. In S. McDaniel, D. Lusterman, & C. L. Philpot (Eds.), *Casebook for integrating family therapy: An ecosystemic approach* (pp. 232–336). Washington, DC: American Psychological Association.

McDaniel, S. H., & Hepworth, J. (2004). Family psychology in primary care: Managing issues of power and dependency through collaboration. In R. G. Frank & S. H. McDaniel (Eds.), *Primary care psychology* (pp. 113–132). Washington, DC: American Psychological Association.

McDaniel, S. H., Hepworth, J., & Doherty, W. J. (1992). *Medical family therapy: A biopsychosocial approach to families with health problems.* New York: Basic Books.

McDaniel, S. H., Hepworth, J., & Doherty, W. J. (1997). *The shared experience of illness: Stories of patients, families, and their therapists.* New York: Basic Books.

Mechanic, D. (1986). The concept of illness behaviour: Culture, situation and personal predisposition (First International Conference on Clinical and Social Aspects of Illness Behaviour, 1984, Adelaide, Australia). *Psychological Medicine, 16,* 1–7.

Mohr, D., Moran, P., Kohn, C., Hart, S., Armstrong, K., Dias, R., et al. (2003). Couples therapy at end of life. *Psycho-Oncology, 12,* 620–627.

Morisky, D. E., Levine, D. M., Green, L. W., Russell, R. P., Smith, C., Benson, P., et al. (1980). The relative impact of health education for low- and high-risk patients with hypertension. *Preventive Medicine, 9,* 550–558.

Osterman, G. P., Sher, T. G., Hales, G., Canar, W. J., Singla, R., & Tilton, T. (2003). Treating difficult couples: Helping clients with coexisting mental and relationship disorders. In D. K. Snyder & M. A. Whisman (Eds.), *Treating difficult couples: Helping clients with coexisting mental and relationship disorders* (pp. 350–369). New York: Guilford Press.

Pantilat, S. (1996). Patient-physician communication: Respect for culture, religion, and autonomy. *Journal of the American Medical Association, 275,* 107.

Rait, D., Ross, J., & Rao, S. (1997). Treating couples and families with HIV: A systemic approach. In M. F. O'Connor & I. D. Yalom (Eds.), *Treating the psychological consequences of HIV.* (pp. 225–268). New York: Jossey-Bass.

Rolland, J. S. (1994). *Families, illness, and disability: An integrative treatment model.* New York: Basic Books.

Ruddy, N., & McDaniel, S. H. (2002). Couple therapy and medical issues: Working with couples facing illness. In A. S. Gurman & N. S. Jacobson (Eds.), *Clinical handbook of couple therapy* (pp. 699–716). New York: Guilford Press.

Schmaling, K., & Sher, T. (1997). Physical health and relationships. In W. K. Halford & H. J. Markman (Eds.), *Clinical handbook of marriage and couples interventions* (pp. 323–345). New York: Wiley.

Schmaling, K., & Sher, T. (2000). *The psychology of couples and illness: Theory, research, and practice.* Washington, DC: American Psychological Association.

Snyder, D. K., & Whisman, M. A. (2003). *Treating difficult couples: Helping clients with coexisting mental and relationship disorders.* New York: Guilford Press.

Tamura, T., & Lau, A. (1992). Connectedness versus separateness: Applicability of family therapy to Japanese families. *Family Process, 31,* 319–340.

Taylor, C. B., Bandura, A., Ewart, C. K., Miller, N. H., & DeBusk, R. F. (1985). Exercise testing to enhance wives' confidence in their husbands' cardiac capability soon after clinically uncomplicated acute myocardial infarction. *American Journal of Cardiology, 55,* 635–638.

Webster, L. (1992). Working with couples in a diabetes clinic: The role of the therapist in a medical setting. *Sexual and Marital Therapy, 7,* 189–196.

CHAPTER 16

Treating Couples with Sexual Abuse Issues

Michele Harway and Ellen Faulk

MARIA ELENA (35) AND Jose (37) have been married for 10 years and have two children, Rob (9) and Sylvia (7). Maria Elena is an elementary school teacher and Jose is a state government employee in a managerial position. Jose complains that Maria Elena has not enjoyed sex during the entire time they have been married. He has tried to be patient but he is really tired of it. Maria Elena says she is always busy with her work and the children and sex just is not that important to her. During an early session, Jose admits that lately he has been having problems with premature ejaculation, commenting that before marriage "I could go all night." Jose states that he thinks his problem is due to the fact that Maria Elena always has to have things her way, including when, where, and how they have sex.

If you are the therapist who is treating Maria Elena and Jose, what is your initial assessment of the presenting problem? Do you focus on treating Jose's sexual dysfunction? Do you instead consider the couple's issues around control? Or do you determine that the best course of treatment would be to focus on the couple's mismatched sexual drives?

In each instance, without an appropriate exploration of the possibility of sexual abuse, the treatment would most likely NOT focus on the most important issue that is affecting Jose and Maria Elena—the fact that Maria Elena was sexually abused when she was 9, and how it has impacted her individually and in her relationships with others. While most psychotherapists do receive training on child abuse, the focus of such training is on the identification of currently occurring abuse in families with children (and the consequent legal/ethical and treatment issues this raises). Psychotherapists are seldom trained to identify adults who were molested as children, particularly when they present with relationship problems.

The focus of this chapter is on couples who present for psychotherapy, where one member of the couple has experienced sexual abuse as a child. Working with these couples requires special understanding of the impact of sexual abuse on the survivor and consideration of how the coping mechanisms the survivor develops to live through her abuse experience might impact her relationship with her partner.

Because the issue of sexual abuse is extremely complex, this chapter necessarily is limited to certain types of sexual abuse. Thus, although as many as 16% of men are sexually abused (Wurtele & Miller Perrin, 1992), this chapter focuses on couples where the abuse survivor is female (studies summarized by the same authors indicate 7% to 62% of women have a sexual abuse history). The impact of sexual abuse on men is as deleterious as it is on women and some would say that it impacts men's relationships at least as much as it does those of women. Others, however, would argue that given the importance of relationships to women's sense of self, sexual abuse is likely to have a greater impact on women's relationships than on men's. Gilligan (1982) and Erikson (1968) suggest that in gaining a sense of themselves, young women rely more on interpersonal relationships than do young men, thus women who were abused by someone of a close familial nature may have difficulties developing a healthy self-identity. In either case, however, a focus on male survivors and their partners is beyond the scope of this chapter. Female survivors of sexual abuse can be in same sex or other sex relationships. Because most perpetrators of sexual abuse are likely to be men, the impact of having been sexually abused on a later romantic relationship is different when the partner is female (as in a lesbian relationship) than when the partner is male. However, to limit the scope of issues to be considered in this chapter, we focus exclusively on heterosexual relationships.

Prior to discussing how couples therapists might proceed in treating a couple such as Maria Elena and Jose, and before meeting other couples with similar histories, this chapter includes an overview of the impact and nature of sexual abuse and considers the experience of the sexual abuse survivor's partner. We next discuss assessment issues looking at the case of Maria Elena and Jose in more detail. We conclude the chapter with the cases of Sharon and Luke, and Glenda and James, illustrating key issues in the treatment of these couples.

NATURE AND IMPACT OF SEXUAL ABUSE

Sexual abuse by a family member or by someone outside of the family may involve a child or adolescent. This abuse can include a variety of forms of sexual violations ranging from fondling, to sexual intercourse, to more unusual forms of sexual behavior. The form of the sexual abuse, how long it lasted, whether it encompassed a single violation or multiple violations, whether there was a single or multiple perpetrators, the nature of the relationship between perpetrator and victim (e.g., when the perpetrator is a father-figure, Ketring & Feinauer, 1999), the age of the victim, her developmental stage at the time of the violation, the manner of disclosure and how family members reacted, all contribute to the nature and severity of the sequelae. Females are more likely to be abused by a family member (Finkelhor, Hotaling, Lewis, & Smith, 1990), and those sexually abused by a father figure exhibit the most long-lasting effects and the worst adjustment outcomes (Finkelhor, 1979; Herman, Russell, & Trocki, 1986; Russell, 1986; Tsai, Feldman-Summers, & Edgar, 1979).

Briere (1992), in describing the long-term impacts of child abuse, indicates that these reflect "(a) the impacts of initial reactions and abuse-related accommodations on the individual's later psychological development and (b) the survivor's ongoing coping responses to abuse-related dysphoria" (p. 18). Of particular interest here, will be the way in which those individual reactions in turn impact the couple relationship.

Recent thinking suggests that experiencing sexual abuse (or any type of trauma) may actually impact the biological processes of brain development. According to Siegel (1999), ". . . traumatic experiences at the beginning of life may have more profound effects on the 'deeper' structures of the brain, which are responsible for basic regulatory capacities and enable the mind to respond later to stress" (p. 13). Further, early severe trauma may give rise to "a form of divided attention (such as entering a state of intense imagination or trance)" and explicit (conscious) memory for the trauma may be impaired. Implicit (unconscious) memory may encode the more frightening aspects of the trauma that can later be "automatically reactivated, intruding on the traumatized individual's internal experience and external behaviors without the person's conscious sense of recollection or knowledge of the source of these intrusions" (pp. 295–296). This is supported by early research (Hebb, 1949). "Neurons that fire together at one time will tend to fire together in the future" (p. 70). Memories are biologically encoded then stored, and when repeatedly active at the same time become associated so that they facilitate each other.

The varieties of symptomology displayed by survivors of childhood sexual abuse are impressive. Stein, Golding, Siegel, Burnam, and Sorensen's (1988) study of more than 3,000 Los Angeles adults, identified a subgroup that had been sexually abused as children and studied the lifetime prevalence of emotional reactions. Seventy six percent of those abused developed some type of symptom, with 83% of women and 66% of men becoming symptomatic. Eighty-six percent of Hispanics and 73% of non-Hispanic whites, respectively, developed some symptom. For the group as a whole, 50% developed symptoms of anxiety, 48% had difficulty with anger, 48% felt guilty, 45% were depressed. Thirty three percent were fearful, and 24% to 28% experienced behavioral restrictions, diminished sexual interest, fear of sex, diminished sexual pleasure or insomnia. Among women, the above symptoms were experienced by as many as 10% more participants in each category. The type of symptoms described in the above-cited study are consistent with those reported by others (for example, Briere & Conte, 1993; Browne & Finkelhor, 1986; Chu & Dill, 1990; D. M. Elliott & Briere, 1992; E. Elliott, 1994; Springs & Friedrich, 1992; Steiger & Zanko, 1990). In regard to symptoms that manifest themselves in the sexual arena, Becker, Skinner, Gene, Axelrod, and Cichon (1984) suggest that the survivor's inhibition of sexual feelings leads to avoidance behavior and allows the negative attitude toward sex to endure. While the fear or avoidance of sex may exist for women with a history of sexual abuse, women survivors may also present with histories of high-risk sex, promiscuity, and prostitution (Maltz, 2002) in an effort to resolve intrapsychic conflicts (Scharff & Scharff, 1994), factors that may further confound their sense of self and sexuality and impact their relationships with a spouse or partner. Browne and Finkelhor (1986) conclude that about 20% of adults who were sexually abused as children evidence *serious* psychopathology as adults. Other researchers (Kessler, Abelson, & Zhao, 1998) found that lifetime depression for women survivors of sexual abuse was 39.1% compared with 21.3% in the general population. The incidence of any mood, anxiety, or substance disorder was 78% compared to 48.5% of women in the general population. Briere, Cotman, Harris, and Smiljanich (1992) indicate that intrusive, avoidant, and arousal symptoms of posttraumatic stress disorder (PTSD) are experienced by both clinical and nonclinical groups of individuals who experienced childhood sexual abuse. Intrusive symptoms are often quite disturbing. They include flashbacks of the perpetrators, or of the abuse; and, they may be experienced as visual, auditory, olfactory, or other sensory memories (Briere, 1992). They are experienced as bizarre in content and seem outside of the control of the victims who often describe their apparitions as "out of the blue," although they are usually triggered by a variety of real-time stimuli such as sexual interaction, vicarious experience of others' abuse, or perceived or actual abusive behaviors by other adults (also reported by Briere, 1992).

Briere (1992) also indicates that intrusive thoughts or memories of past victimization may interfere with concentration and normal cognitive functioning. Abuse-related nightmares (either graphic or symbolic representations of victimization) may also plague the survivor.

Avoidant symptoms may include a wide range of dissociative phenomena that in their extreme form may lead to Dissociative Identity Disorder (*DSM-IV*). Briere (1992) defines dissociation as "defensive disruption in the normally occurring connections among feelings, thoughts, behaviors, and memories, consciously or unconsciously invoked in order to reduce psychological distress" (p. 36). Putnam (1989) suggests that dissociation allows the survivor to "(1) escape from the constraints of reality; (2) [contain] . . . traumatic memories and affects outside of normal conscious awareness; (3) [alter or detach] ... [a] sense of self (so that the trauma happens to someone else or to a depersonalized self); and (4) [serve as] analgesia" (p. 53). Dissociation may include disengagement, detachment or numbing, and observation (Briere, 1989). Disengagement (described as spacing out by survivors) lasts for a few seconds to a few minutes and is a relatively shallow form of dissociation that allows the survivor to separate herself cognitively from her surrounds during a time of stress. This cognitive separation is sometimes under conscious control of the survivor, more often it is outside of her awareness. Detachment or numbing involves the shutting down of affect so as to be able to complete necessary activities without being incapacitated by psychic pain. Observation or spectatoring is a form of depersonalization when the survivor reports experiences that are occurring to her from the perspective of an uninvolved third-person observer. The resulting calm experienced by the survivor also allows her to accomplish what she needs to without being incapacitated by her pain.

Finally, arousal symptoms include anxiety or fearfulness. Root (1992) has written about how the worldview of the trauma survivor shifts, as a result of the trauma, from a belief in the world as a safe place to one in which everything and everyone represents potential danger. Consequently, elevated anxiety is a common sequel to sexual abuse. Briere (1992) notes that "adults and adolescents with childhood histories of abuse frequently present with cognitive, classically conditioned, or somatic components of anxiety" (p. 33). Some of the presenting behaviors, therefore, include hypervigilence, preoccupation with control, and misinterpretation of interpersonal overtures as evidence of danger.

Because the perpetrator is often known to the victim and the relationship between the two prior to the abuse may have involved dependence and some form of attachment, disrupted attachments are often the result. In adulthood, attachment patterns learned during childhood and adolescence may result in significantly impaired relational functioning. Attachment theory (Hazan & Shaver, 1987, 1990) suggests that individuals who experienced a positive and trusting relationship with an adult attachment figure in childhood grow up expecting similar trustworthy relationships with others. Likewise, those who were unable to trust the adult attachment figures in their childhoods may later avoid close relationships with others or may behave in close relationships in a way to perpetuate their belief about the unreliability of others. These expectations, in particular, may substantially disrupt couples relationships.

Siegel (1999) suggests that understanding the attachment histories of each member of a couple can be essential in clarifying how "micromoments of misattunement can be blown up into major battles and interlocking, dysregulated dyadic states of despair and distancing" (p. 292) and these repeated patterns reinforce the historical mental models of relationships and keep the partners continually reexperiencing lack of attunement, misattunements, and repeated verification of the lessons learned from their own individual attachment histories. Siegel also suggests that survivors of child sexual abuse are particularly susceptible to feeling as if they are not believed, a factor that must be considered by both the therapist and her partner. Indications for treatment include helping the survivor develop conscious awareness of her automatic responses to past abuse and helping the couple to reduce "primitive, nonproductive defenses and to develop mature, 'socially helpful' ones . . ." (p. 292).

The Partner's Experience

While an extensive literature has developed around the impact of sexual abuse on the survivor, much less has been written about how the family reacts, in particular the partner.

Landry (1991) describes the special challenges that face sexual abuse survivors' partners, particularly when the survivor has begun individual therapy to confront the abuse. Initially, the partner may feel compassion for the survivor's pain and may be willing to emotionally support her in many different ways. However, as treatment continues and because the process is usually a lengthy one, the partner may become increasingly discouraged with the lack of rapid progress. Moreover, during treatment, survivors often are unable to function at the level of competence they once demonstrated. As a result, the partner may have to take on additional tasks and he may come to resent the increased load. Resentment may in turn alter his feelings about his partner. Some men experience frustration at their own powerlessness in being able to relieve the pain of the survivor—their male upbringing has convinced many men that "fixing things" is part of their responsibilities and that includes fixing their partner. This is particularly difficult in some relationships as the men may experience their partners' needs as overwhelming. Their frustration and powerlessness may make it difficult for them to listen empathically, to give comfort, or simply to witness their partner's pain. Acknowledging this inability is important, as is seeking therapeutic support. Partners of sexual abuse survivors need a great deal of education about the impact of the abuse on women's adult functioning and on the lengthy process of recovery that is required.

Sexual intimacy, one area that remains strong in many troubled relationships, is often an early area of dyadic functioning that is impacted when one member of the couple experienced sexual abuse. Because the violation was a sexual one, it is likely that during sexual intimacy many of the survivor's symptoms will be activated. Sexual intercourse may bring flashbacks, dissociation, or extreme fear. During their recovery process, some survivors regress to the age they were when abused and thus may prefer holding and nurturing that is both nonsexual and nonadult in nature, to the great frustration of the nonabused partner. Sexual abstinence may be a necessity in some cases. Recovery may also require the survivor to experience many areas of early developmental stages, missed because of the abuse. This may manifest, for example, as an abnormal amount of dependency on the partner, fearing he will leave. However, it is important to educate the partner that this is a necessary developmental stage that the survivor must experience and is not mental illness. He must be guided to validate his partner's needs and to reassure her of his commitment to the relationship and to the process (Maltz, 2002).

The survivor may experience or express other painful emotional states that may make it difficult for her partner to continue to emotionally support her. For example, she may suddenly express a great deal of fear toward her partner, even if he is gentle. Or, she may become angry with him and all men because of what the perpetrator did to her. Painter and Howell (1999) suggest that unexpressed anger from the past becomes distorted into rage and is often pushed into the unconscious of women survivors of sexual abuse, thus the partner may experience her as distant and cold. Societal constraint further negates the expression of anger. When working through her childhood abuse, the survivor may begin to experience her rage as overpowering her entire body and manifesting itself in unexpected and uncontrollable ways. However, it is important to emphasize that anger and rage of both survivor and partner are important parts of the recovery process. Finding creative and safe ways to express the rage that both are feeling is a challenge that must be confronted. Examples include hitting a pillow, dialoguing about the anger in a journal, or role-playing it in a contained individual therapy session. His own anger may be related to her new unavailability to be a full partner in the relationship. Or, he may be angry at the cost of treatment to help his partner reclaim what the abuser stole. He may, in fact, be angry at the abuser and want to seek revenge. At the same time, her recovery process may stir up his own dormant issues (Oz, 2001).

Some men, initially attracted to the survivor because of her prerecovery behavior, may find that as she gets better he becomes symptomatic. As the sexual abuse issues are worked through, other issues in the relationship masked until now by the sexual abuse, come to the forefront. Choice of partner by both survivor and spouse is important to helping the couple understand their initial attraction to each other and their unconscious expectations about the relationship. Future research may reveal that the marriage in which one spouse is a survivor of child sexual abuse actually involves a *dual trauma couple,* where the husband has also experienced some type of trauma or neglect, such as combat exposure, leading to the development of posttraumatic stress disorder (Oz, 2001). The therapist can help the couple to understand the relational impact of their dual trauma status and ensure that the sexual abuse survivor is not perceived as the more dysfunctional spouse.

ASSESSMENT ISSUES

How do you make the assessment with couples who present for couples therapy to rule out the possibility that one member was sexually abused?

Because many family dynamics and familial factors are related to a history of child sexual abuse (adverse family conditions: Fergusson, Lynskey, & Horwood, 1996; Fleming, Mullen, & Bammer, 1997; poverty and parental maladjustment: Svedin, Back, & Söderback, 2002) a complete family-of-origin history must be obtained from each spouse upon the initiation of couples therapy. In the course of history taking, the therapist inquires of each partner whether he or she has a history of any type of abuse or trauma. Because a direct question may not yield useful information, especially if the partner is not aware of the abuse history, a good way to introduce the subject is to ask, "In what ways have you been hurt in your life?" If sexual abuse is ruled out at intake, the standard clinical assessment protocol for couples may be implemented. If, on the other hand, this question elicits information about sexual abuse that is new information to the partner, he may feel betrayed and angry that such an important part of his loved one's history has been kept from him. The therapist must acknowledge his feelings and educate the couple about the secrecy and concealment that usually accompany sexual abuse, while simultaneously attending to the acute emotion likely to be experienced by the survivor at her acknowledgment. If this is the first time that the survivor has spoken about her abuse, there is likely to be a maelstrom of emotions and needs that must get high priority in treatment. The delicate nature of the issues that underlie this couple seeking therapy requires that individual therapy take precedence over the couples therapy. The competent therapist is likely to refer the survivor to a highly skilled clinician who specializes in working with this population and to defer couples work until a later time (Oz, 2001). The therapist may also want to recommend a support group or individual therapy for the partner who is likely to develop many needs during the course of the survivor's therapy. In some cases, her admission of abuse may stimulate a parallel admission on his part. In all cases, couples therapy can only proceed once the survivor has achieved a level of stability that will allow her to explore other issues in her relationship.

CASE STUDY

Recall Maria Elena and Jose whom we met at the beginning of the chapter. In our intake with the couple, we learn about Maria Elena's sexual molestation by her stepfather at age 9. Jose had been privy to this information for some time. This is a key element in Marie Elena and Jose's presentation. Although Maria Elena has been in ongoing individual therapy to work on her incest issues, it will be important for her to continue to do so while the couples therapy is undertaken. The couples therapy is important because, even though she has been working on her abuse issues in individual therapy, the couples issues have persisted. Nonetheless, while working in a couples modality, issues related to the sexual abuse must be seen as primary and other issues must often take a back seat.

An understanding of Maria Elena's history of molestation can tell us a great deal about what kinds of issues we can expect to surface in the couple's relationship. Models such as TRIAD provide a framework for understanding Maria Elena's molestation. TRIAD is a trauma assessment tool developed by Ann Burgess (Burgess, Hartman, & Kelley, 1990), which allows identification of key aspects of Maria Elena's molestation experience. The "T" in TRIAD refers to the type of abuse experienced, with sexual abuse having more serious emotional consequences than either physical or psychological abuse. "R" has to do with the role relationship between the victim and the perpetrator: for example, symptoms are expected to be more acute when the perpetrator is a family member, in particular, a father, stepfather, or father figure. "I" stands for intensity including the number of acts and offenders. Whether the molestation consisted of a single episode or multiple ones over time will inform us as to the amount of damage we can expect. The nature of the perpetration and whether vaginal penetration was involved is also related to severity of symptoms. "A" relates to the affective state of the survivor, whether she expresses her feelings freely or demonstrates a controlled demeanor. Sexual abuse survivors can look highly functional on the outside—most are very competent but focused on controlling their environment—and that makes it more difficult to identify it and to counter their denial. "D" is duration. As with the intensity of the perpetration, the period of time over which molestation occurred will also relate to the severity of symptoms one can expect.

In this case, the apparent sexual dysfunction that Maria Elena and Jose bring to couples therapy is symptomatic of the underlying sexual abuse issues. Maria Elena's behavior in compensating for her abuse and Jose's reactions to Maria Elena's behavior are reflective of the circular interactions that become problematic in some couples and these become the focus of couples therapy.

Cultural issues must also be considered by the couples therapist. In the case of Maria Elena and Jose, both Latino, the therapist is wise to consider the traditional family structure of their culture. According to Sue and Sue (2003), "traditional Hispanic families are hierarchical in form with special authority given to the elderly, the parents, and males. Within the family, the father assumes the role of primary authority figure" (p. 247). Also, the therapist must consider the role of machismo, Jose's reactions to Maria Elena's lack of sexual interest and the importance of Jose's sexual functioning on the couple's interaction.

Other interactional issues that are common in couples where childhood sexual abuse is a factor include: difficulties with trust, emotional expressiveness and intimacy, communication, substance abuse, eating disorders or other addictions, and issues related to household, money, time management, and parenting (Oz, 2001). Although these issues are common in many types of couples, when they occur in the context of sexual abuse, the etiology of these problematic relational patterns and their impact on the relationship can be decidedly different than in other couples. The assessment includes identifying which of these relational issues are operating but looking at them through the context of sexual abuse.

The TRIADS model helps the therapist to better understand Maria Elena. In the context of couples therapy, it may be a useful tool to identify areas of the relationship that are most likely to be impacted. For example, the "R" in TRIADS refers to the relationship between victim and perpetrator. As we have learned, Maria Elena's perpetrator was her stepfather. Attachment theory would suggest that the rupture of this primary relationship (between father/father figure and young daughter) is likely to impact adult attachments. Therefore, the possibility of trust issues within Jose and Maria Elena's relationship must be explored. Even though Maria Elena's stepfather was her only abuser, the fact that the abuse continued until she was 16 suggests that the degree of damage to her sense of self may be great and that her identity as a competent adult has been impaired. Even though she was highly functional both at home and at work, when she began her individual therapy, she regressed to an earlier stage of development. Jose comments that he was attracted to her strength and is distressed at having to take over many of the household and parenting chores.

In assessing Maria Elena's affective state (the "A" of TRIADS), it is obvious that she is highly emotional but she indicates that early in her individual therapy she was largely cut off from her feelings. She indicates that now she is acutely aware and intensely reactive in ways that differ from her previous demeanor. Jose just shakes his head and wonders where the Maria Elena he married has gone.

TREATMENT CONSIDERATIONS

In exploring Maria Elena's control issues with respect to the time, location, and means of their sexual interaction, it is clear that she does so in an attempt to protect herself from the memories of the abuse and to prevent any recurrence of the aversive sexual interactions. As Jose understands the dynamics of their sexual interaction (that is, that she is not rejecting him but attempting to keep herself safe), his concern about his sexual performance diminishes. At the same time, it would be unrealistic to assume that the issues in their sexual relationship have been resolved. More work will need to be done in this area.

CASE STUDY

Shannon and Luke are another couple who reflect different areas in which couple relationships can be impacted by sexual abuse. Shannon (32) and Luke (32) have been dating for two years. They recently moved in together and have been discussing marriage. Luke states that he loves Shannon very much but he's concerned about her angry outbursts that occur without warning. Luke says he doesn't understand it and Shannon says she doesn't understand it either and she feels terrible about the outbursts. She's a nurse and people tell her that she does things that she denies doing. For example, another nurse found a used syringe on the lunch tray of one of Shannon's patients. Shannon denies having left it there. Luke is a mechanic and a veteran of the 1991 Gulf War.

Like Maria Elena, Shannon has been in individual therapy for some time. Not surprisingly, she presents with clear features of posttraumatic stress disorder (PTSD). Her angry outbursts, which further exploration suggests may be based on flashbacks, are consistent with PTSD. There is the possibility of some type of dissociative disorder given the response of Shannon's coworkers who notice her forgetfulness at work and Shannon's inability to remember these incidents. Her individual therapist is already attending to the safety issues of Shannon's patients. In relation to the dissociative behaviors, what concerns the couples therapist, however, is how these may impact the relationship. According to Luke, "Shannon seems to be spaced out a lot of the time. I talk to her and she doesn't even hear what I say. I am starting to feel like she doesn't even care about me anymore."

In addition, Luke's withdrawal from Shannon suggests that he may also be suffering from PTSD. We assess this by using a number of psychological inventories including the Impact of Events Scale (Horowitz, Wilner, & Alvarez, 1979), the Trauma Symptom Checklist (Briere, 1996), and the PTSD subscale from the MMPI (Keane, Malloy, & Fairbank, 1984). Luke may also require individual treatment related to his own trauma and this may retard the onset of the couples therapy.

Shannon and Luke represent a dual-trauma couple and their dynamic appears to be a cycle of angry outbursts (Shannon) and retreat (Luke), leaving the couple feeling confused. The therapist will need to be alert to a possible additional diagnosis of substance abuse in either or both persons.

Throughout the couples therapy, Shannon and Luke need to develop conscious awareness of those moments when Shannon experiences angry outbursts or dissociation. Shannon tells us in therapy that she finds Luke "insensitive and uncaring" as he continues to become more withdrawn from her and "leaves the house for hours" after her outbursts. Luke states that Shannon's angry outbursts "scare me" and he leaves because, "I don't know what to do when she's like that." The couples therapist can help Shannon and Luke recognize that these behaviors may relate to their trauma histories. Shannon's outbursts may be triggered by environmental cues (the smell of alcohol and tobacco during sex with Luke). This likely stimulates thoughts and feelings from the past that intrude on her present reality, causing Shannon to believe that she is in danger. As Siegel (1999) describes it, the brain is an anticipation machine and Shannon's sense of anticipation is heightened due to her traumatic experience of the past. Shannon's dissociative behavior at work suggests that she may also be dissociating when she is with Luke. Luke's withdrawal from Shannon may rekindle feelings of abandonment related to her earlier abuse. Knowing that Shannon's mother was aware of but did not stop the sexual abuse, helps the therapist understand Shannon's feelings of abandonment and her vulnerability to her stepfather's victimization. The therapist can help her separate memories of these early attachment failures from the interpersonal workings of the relationship with Luke. This in turn will reduce the personalization and reactivity that is taking place within the context of the current relationship. Educating the couple about the etiology of dissociation, helping them understand that it is a protective measure, is a first step to mitigating this issue. The couples therapist can reframe each of Shannon and Luke's behaviors as providing protection in moments of fear and can help them find alternative methods to communicate their fears to each other. Shannon's rage can also be explained as a normal response to her abuse and its expression as a part of her healing process. The therapist must help Shannon become aware of the triggers that cause her outbursts and help her develop the conscious awareness of her fear, so as to better communicate her fear with Luke and ease her distress. Somatic cues that precede problematic behaviors (for example, muscle tension and stomach upset) can serve as early warning signals of these reactive behaviors. For example, Shannon's reactions to the smells of alcohol and tobacco may now be associated with traumatic memories of her abuse and these surface when she is having sexual contact with Luke. In addition to olfactory memories, other somatic memories might include body, tactile, and visual ones and should be explored with the couple. Learning communication skills and practicing them through role playing in session provides the couple with alternatives to problematic behaviors and can instill a sense of competence in each of them. Role playing in session allows the therapist to help the couple refine their responses to each other. As treatment continues, the therapist can support the couple in communicating their fears, particularly as issues of trust, intimacy, and sexuality surface. Identification of cognitive distortions that are common in trauma survivors can be changed from "I am damaged goods" (Sgroi, 1982) to statements of empowerment such as, "I am strong for having survived this pain" or "I will not allow what others have done to me to stop me from having a happy life." The aforementioned issues may take considerable education and time for resolution, and the therapist's patience during this process is important.

CASE STUDY

In contrast to the other couples we have described, both of whom have been comprised of relatively high-functioning individuals, Glenda and James reflect a different picture.

Glenda (45) is unemployed and on a government social assistance program. She has been married four times and presents for couple's therapy with her fifth husband, James (58), who was a construction worker until his accident two years ago. He now receives a small disability payment. Glenda is chronically unemployed, she does not concentrate well, has poor follow through, and is chronically depressed. Glenda's brothers and sisters are all gainfully employed and property owners; one brother is even on the city council. Early in their relationship, James was attracted to Glenda because she was sensitive and seemed to need him so much. But now no matter what he does, she just does not respond to him anymore. James is also getting upset because she just doesn't seem to be able to hold down a job and his meager disability check can't support them both.

During intake, we learn that Glenda is a multiple abuse survivor. After an early molestation by an uncle, Glenda was raped at age 13, and sexually abused in the immediate aftermath by her older brother. While some years ago Glenda was in individual therapy for her abuse issues, she has not been able to afford treatment in some time. A referral to a low-fee counseling clinic has allowed her to resume individual therapy. After six months in this therapy, she returned with James for adjunctive therapy to explore their issues as a couple, paid for by state assistance.

Glenda and James represent a couple with multiple layers of concerns. The first is their socioeconomic status. Persons with economic challenges must often cope with day-to-day survival in addition to the abuse issues presented here. James's relatively recent physical disability further complicates the presentation. Glenda's chronic unemployment, poor concentration, and follow-through have led to the diagnosis of a depressive disorder and the prescription of an antidepressant medication. James has suffered a physical loss due to his accident and a significant loss in his ability to provide financially. James is angry that Glenda cannot hold down a job and that she has retreated emotionally from him.

Part of the assessment in cases of couples with sexual abuse includes assessing for domestic violence and substance abuse. Harway and Hansen (1994, 2004) detail how to do an assessment for domestic violence. Holtzworth-Munroe, Clements, and Farris (Chapter 17, this volume) further detail interventions with this population. Substance abuse assessment is described by Stanton (Chapter 18, this volume). While James denies any substance use, he does admit to having hit Glenda because he is "just so frustrated sometimes that I can't help it." In contrast to the other couples we have met in this chapter, Glenda and James present a pattern of a man rescuing an abuse survivor and gradually becoming another perpetrator in the survivor's life.

Treatment for this couple starts with a batterer's group for James. As James's abusive behavior curtails, the slow building of trust between Glenda and him begins. Glenda has said to James, "Every man in my life has betrayed me sooner or later, so what's the use of trusting you or letting you into my life." Glenda's statement reflects her broken trust in relationships relative to her multiple abuse history and the subsequent misattunement in her current relationship with James. The couples therapist can utilize Glenda's sense of betrayal and distrust to help her understand that she has the power to modify her thoughts and feelings relative to this issue and that she is capable of communicating her needs in a relationship. This is something that abuse survivors rarely consider, since in the past they have had choices taken from them.

As James and Glenda learn to resolve their interpersonal issues, the couple becomes willing to discuss the estrangement in their sexual relationship, which began shortly after their marriage. Glenda relates that during intercourse with James, she sometimes has "flashes" of her uncle who molested her and wants to "scream" and "get away" from James, but forces herself to complete sexual intercourse so James is not disappointed with her. She further states that during the abuse by her brother, she sometimes experienced an orgasm and has felt deep shame since that time. The therapist can take this opportunity to educate the couple about Glenda's flashbacks as well as her physical response during the molestation by her brother. The therapist can teach Glenda that the human body is programmed to respond to sexual stimulation with sexual arousal regardless of the circumstances and that her arousal does not in any way mean that she wanted to be sexually violated. Glenda's symptomology and her shame relative to sexual pleasure might necessitate a cessation of sexual contact while Glenda is able to address these feelings in her individual therapy. Over the long term, a program of sex therapy might be initiated to gradually ease the couple from nonsexual touch to increasingly more intimate forms of touch, as they both feel comfortable. When Glenda feels safe to resume intercourse with James, the therapist can teach behavioral methods, such as relaxation and thought stopping, to minimize the chance of flashbacks. Communication between the couple during sex can be encouraged so that Glenda can let James know if she becomes frightened, allowing her to regain a sense of control over her body. Should she choose to stop during intercourse, other sexual stimulation techniques can be substituted. This process over time also helps to engender mutual trust and care within the couple relationship.

SUMMARY

The complexities of treating couples where one partner has experienced childhood sexual abuse have been explored through three cases demonstrating different aspects of the long-term impact of this abuse. Specific symptoms and a wide variety of disparate presenting problems, which may not in themselves be identified by the couple as related to child sexual abuse, may be the motivators for starting couples therapy. The well-trained clinician will do an assessment that includes identifying or ruling out sexual abuse whenever couples present for psychotherapy. Because the survivor and her partner have reacted to her sexual abuse history in a variety of ways, a one-size-fits-all approach has been difficult to document here, therefore several approaches are suggested. Knowledge of the impacts of sexual abuse on the survivor and on her partner are critical for appropriate treatment. Finally, couples therapy with these couples is ancillary to individual therapy for the survivor and in some cases for the partner as well. Couples therapy may need to be deferred until the survivor has made sufficient progress in her individual therapy to allow her to shift her focus and her emotional energy to the more interpersonally difficult work required in couples therapy.

REFERENCES

Becker, J. V., Skinner, L. J., Gene, G. A., Axelrod, R., & Cichon, J. (1984). Sexual problems of sexual assault survivors. *Women and Health, 9,* 5–20.

Briere, J. N. (1989). *Therapy for adults molested as children: Beyond survival.* New York: Springer.

Briere, J. N. (1992). *Child abuse trauma: Theory and treatment of the lasting effects.* Newbury Park, CA: Sage.

Briere, J. N. (1996). Psychometric review of the Trauma Symptom Checklist-40. In B. H. Stamm (Ed.), *Measurement of stress, trauma, and adaptation.* Lutherville, MD: Sidran Press.

Briere, J. N., & Conte, J. (1993). Self-reported amnesia for abuse in adults molested as children. *Journal of Traumatic Stress, 6,* 21–31.

Briere, J. N., Cotman, A., Harris, K., & Smiljanich, K. (1992, August). *The Trauma Symptom Inventory: Preliminary data on reliability and validity.* Paper presented at the annual meeting of the American Psychological Association, Washington, DC.

Browne, A., & Finkelhor, D. (1986). Impact of child sexual abuse: A review of the research. *Psychological Bulletin, 99,* 66–77.

Burgess, A. W., Hartman, C. R., & Kelley, S. (1990). Assessing child abuse: The TRIADS checklist. *Psycho-Social Nursing, 28*(4), 7–14.

Chu, J. A., & Dill, D. L. (1990). Dissociative symptoms in relation to childhood physical and sexual abuse. *American Journal of Psychiatry, 147,* 887–892.

Elliott, D. M., & Briere, J. (1992). Sexual abuse trauma among professional women: Validating the Trauma Symptom Checklist-40 (TSC-40). *Child Abuse and Neglect, 16,* 391–398.

Elliott, M. (1994). Impaired object relations in professional women molested as children. *Psychotherapy, 31,* 79–86.

Erikson, E. H. (1968). *Identity, youth and crisis.* New York: Norton.

Fergusson, D. M., Lynskey, M. T., & Horwood, L. J. (1996). Child sexual abuse and psychiatric disorder in young adulthood: 1. Prevalence of sexual abuse and factors associated with sexual abuse. *Journal of American Adolescent Psychiatry, 35,* 1355–1364.

Finkelhor, D. (1979). *Sexually victimized children.* New York: Free Press/Guilford Press.

Finkelhor, D., Hotaling, G., Lewis, I. C., & Smith, C. (1990). Sexual abuse in a national survey of adult men and women: Prevalence, characteristics, and risk factors. *Child Abuse and Neglect, 10,* 5–15.

Fleming, J., Mullen, P., & Bammer, G. (1997). A study of potential risk factors for sexual abuse in childhood. *Child Abuse and Neglect, 21,* 49–58.

Gilligan, C. (1982). *In a different voice.* Cambridge, MA: Harvard University Press.

Harway, M., & Hansen, M. (1994). *Spouse abuse: Assessing and treating battered women, batterers, and their children.* Sarasota, FL: Professional Resource Press.

Harway, M., & Hansen, M. (2004). *Spouse abuse: Assessing and treating battered women, batterers, and their children (2nd ed.).* Sarasota, FL: Professional Resource Press.

Hazan, C., & Shaver, P. R. (1987). Romantic love conceptualized as an attachment process. *Journal of Personality and Social Psychology, 52,* 511–524.

Hazan, C., & Shaver, P. R. (1990). Love and work: An attachment-theoretical perspective. *Journal of Personality and Social Psychology, 59,* 270–280.

Hebb, D. O. (1949). *The organization of behavior: A neuropsychological theory.* New York: Wiley.

Herman, J., Russell, D., & Trocki, K. (1986). Long-term effects of incestuous abuse in childhood. *American Journal of Psychiatry, 143,* 1293–1296.

Horowitz, M., Wilner, M., & Alvarez, W. (1979). Impact of Event Scale: A measure of subjective stress. *Psychosomatic Medicine, 41,* 209–218.

Keane, T. M., Malloy, P. F., & Fairbank, J. A. (1984). Empirical development of an MMPI subscale for the assessment of combat-related posttraumatic stress disorders. *Journal of Consulting and Clinical Psychology, 52,* 888–891.

Kessler, R. C., Abelson, J. M., & Zhao, S. (1998). The epidemiology of mental disorders. In J. B. W. Williams & K. Ell (Eds.), *Advances in mental health research: Implications for practice* (pp. 3–24). Washington, DC: National Association of Social Workers.

Ketring, S. A., & Feinauer, L. L. (1999). Perpetrator-victim relationship: Long-term effects of sexual abuse for men and women. *American Journal of Family Therapy, 27*(2), 109–121.

Landry, D. B. (1991). *Family fallout: A handbook for families of sexual abuse survivors.* Brandon, VT: Safer Society Press.

Maltz, W. (2002). Treating the sexual intimacy concerns of sexual abuse survivors. *Sexual and Relationship Therapy, 17*(4), 321–328.

Oz, S. (2001). When the wife was sexually abused as a child: Marital relations before and during her therapy for abuse. *Sexual and Relationship Therapy, 16*(3), 287–298.

Painter, S. G., & Howell, C. C. (1999). Rage and women's sexuality after childhood sexual abuse: A phenomenological study. *Perspectives in Psychiatric Care, 35*(1), 5–18.

Putnam, F. W. (1989). *Diagnosis and treatment of multiple personality disorder.* New York: Guilford Press.

Root, M. P. P. (1992). Reconstructing the impact of trauma on personality. In L. S. Brown & M. S. Ballou (Eds.), *Personality and psychopathology: Feminist reappraisals* (pp. 229–265). New York: Guilford Press.

Russell, D. (1986). *The secret trauma: Incest in the lives of girls and women.* New York: Basic Books.

Scharff, J. S., & Scharff, D. E. (1994). *Object relations therapy of physical and sexual trauma.* Northvale, NJ: Aronson.

Sgroi, S. M. (1982). *Handbook of clinical intervention in child sexual abuse.* Lexington, MA: Lexington books.

Siegel, D. J. (1999). *The developing mind: How relationships and the brain interact to shape who we are.* New York: Guilford Press.

Springs, F. E., & Friedrich, W. N. (1992). Health risk behaviors and medical sequelae of childhood sexual abuse. *Mayo Clinic Proceedings, 67,* 527–532.

Steiger, H., & Zanko, M. (1990). Sexual traumata among eating disordered, psychiatric, and normal female groups: Comparison of prevalence and defensive styles. *Journal of Interpersonal Violence, 5,* 74–86.

Stein, J. A., Golding, J. M., Siegel, J. M., Burnam, M. A., & Sorensen, S. B. (1988). Long-term psychological sequelae of child sexual abuse: The Los Angeles Epidemiologic Catchment Area Study. In G. E. Wyatt & G. J. Powell (Eds.), *Lasting effects of child sexual abuse* (pp. 135–154). Newbury Park, CA: Sage.

Sue, D. W., & Sue, D. (2003). *Counseling the culturally diverse: Theory and practice* (4th ed.). Hoboken, NJ: Wiley.

Svedin, C. G., Back, C., & Söderback, S. B. (2002). Family relations, family climate and sexual abuse. *Nordic Journal of Psychiatry, 56*(5), 355–363.

Tsai, M., Feldman-Summers, S., & Edgar, M. (1979). Childhood molestation: Variables related to differential impact on psychosexual functioning in adult women. *Journal of Abnormal Psychology, 88,* 407–417.

Wurtele, S. K., & Miller-Perrin, C. L. (1992). *Preventing child sexual abuse: Sharing the responsibility.* Lincoln: University of Nebraska Press.

CHAPTER 17

Working with Couples Who Have Experienced Physical Aggression

Amy Holtzworth-Munroe, Kahni Clements, and Coreen Farris

T HE QUESTION OF whether or not conjoint couples therapy is an appropriate intervention for couples experiencing physical aggression is a controversial one. For reasons outlined later in this chapter, some experts believe that it is never appropriate to offer violent couples conjoint therapy. In contrast, other experts, including ourselves, are willing to try such interventions cautiously and have experienced some clinical advantages in doing so. Despite this debate, almost all experts in this area can agree on some points. First, although many couples seeking couples therapy have experienced physical aggression, most will not report this aggression during the therapy intake unless they are explicitly asked about it; thus, therapists should assess every couple for the possible occurrence of physical aggression. In doing so, they should use methods likely to increase the reporting of aggression (e.g., a behavioral checklist) and in ways that protect the safety of a potentially battered woman (e.g., individual interviews). Second, couples therapy is not recommended for all violent couples and should be denied to some (e.g., when the wife is fearful of the husband or wants to end the relationship, or when a risk of lethality exists). Third, even when a violent couple is offered conjoint treatment, that treatment should not be traditional couples therapy; instead, it must have the elimination of violence as a major treatment goal and must include interventions to help the couple achieve this goal (e.g., anger management). Fourth, couples therapists should be aware of resources for violent couples in their communities (e.g., batterer intervention programs, shelters and support groups for battered women). Fifth, therapists working with couples should try to keep abreast of the rapidly burgeoning research literature on marital violence, as our understanding of relationship violence is constantly changing and expanding. This chapter is designed to address these issues, providing therapists with a brief overview of the research on violent couples and of the issues to be considered when assessing couples, deciding whether or not to offer conjoint therapy, and working with couples who have experienced physical aggression.

DIFFERING LEVELS OF RELATIONSHIP AGGRESSION

When considering marital violence, one often thinks of battery, assault, and severe male-to-female aggression. One imagines men arrested for domestic violence and women seeking refuge at shelters. Such violence has been called battering, severe physical aggression (O'Leary, 1993), and patriarchal terrorism (Johnson, 1995), and the types of men who perpetrate such violence have been divided into subtypes such as generally violent/antisocial men and borderline/dysphoric batterers (Holtzworth-Munroe, Meehan, Herron, Rehman, & Stuart, 2000). This level of male violence is, unfortunately, all too common. National surveys suggest that, in the United States, 1.5 to 2 million women per year are severely assaulted by their male partners (Straus & Gelles, 1990). Some experts have suggested that severe male-to-female violence is used by men to control and dominate women (Johnson, 1995). Clearly, this level of violence has negative consequences. Wives who experience severe husband abuse are at risk for physical injury, health problems, and psychological symptoms, including fear, lowered self-esteem, and symptoms of depression and posttraumatic stress disorder (PTSD). As discussed below, most experts believe that conjoint couples treatment for couples experiencing this level of husband violence is inappropriate. Thus, such couples will not be the focus of this chapter, and we will refrain from reviewing research involving samples clearly experiencing more severe male partner violence (e.g., samples of men in domestic violence treatment programs or women in shelters).

Unfortunately, however, lower levels of physical aggression (e.g., pushing, shoving, or grabbing), that may not fit the stereotypical images of battering, are also quite common in intimate relationships. National surveys suggest that, each year, one in eight men will engage in physical aggression against his wife (Straus & Gelles, 1990). Approximately half of all newlywed couples experience physical aggression early in marriage (e.g., Lawrence & Bradbury, 2001; O'Leary et al., 1989), and the proportion of couples seeking marital therapy who have experienced such aggression approaches two-thirds or more (e.g., Cascardi, Langhinrichsen, & Vivian, 1992). Studies of such samples suggest that, in the majority of cases, both partners engage in physical aggression (e.g., 85% of couples in Cascardi et al., 1992). Such aggression has been labeled mild physical aggression (O'Leary, 1993), common couple violence (Johnson, 1995), or bidirectional aggression (Cascardi et al., 1992), and the men involved in such relationship have been called "family only violent men" (Holtzworth-Munroe, Meehan, et al., 2000). In our experience, couples who have experienced lower levels of physical aggression are the most likely to seek help from a couples therapist. As reviewed next, existing research suggests that conjoint couples therapy with such couples may not be unsafe and may not differ in the level of effectiveness from other therapy approaches (e.g., sending the male to a batterer intervention group). Thus, given the focus of this book, our chapter focuses on this type of physically aggressive couple. In doing so, we limit our research review to studies of samples that might experience lower levels of aggression (e.g., newlywed, community, and marital therapy samples).

NEGATIVE CONSEQUENCES OF COUPLES' PHYSICAL AGGRESSION

Although the prevalence rates of male and female physical aggression against an intimate partner are comparable, the consequences of partner violence differ for men and women (Archer, 2000). Women suffer more fear and physical injury. In a nationally representative sample, Stets and Straus (1989) found that 3% of women reported having needed medical attention as a result of marital violence, compared with only 0.4% of men. Among couples seeking marital therapy, Cascardi and colleagues (1992) found that, relative to husbands, wives rated the impact of marital violence as more negative and were more likely to sustain serious injuries. Women are also more likely to report experiencing fear in response to partner violence (e.g., Cantos, Neidig, & O'Leary, 1993). Relative to husbands, wives are also more likely to experience negative psychological consequences as a result of partner physical aggression. For example, studies of couples seeking marital therapy demonstrate that wives in violent marriages are at risk for depression (e.g., Christian, O'Leary, & Vivian, 1994). Quigley and Leonard (1996) found that newlywed wives experiencing husband physical aggression had higher levels of depressive symptomatology in the first three years of marriage than wives whose husbands had ceased physical aggression or wives in nonviolent marriages.

Research findings similarly suggest that children who reside in maritally violent households are at risk for internalizing and externalizing problems and impaired social and academic functioning. Again, however, the data suggest that fewer differences are found between children in violent and nonviolent homes when community samples are studied (i.e., likely to be lower levels of violence) than when children from nonviolent homes are compared to children in shelters or clinical samples (see review by Margolin, 1998).

Marital distress and dissolution are other consequences of marital aggression. O'Leary and colleagues (1989) found that among newlyweds, the reported occurrence of spouses' physical aggression at more than one time point (over a 30-month period) led to lower marital satisfaction, compared with nonaggressive relationships. In this same sample, wives whose husbands were physically aggressive premaritally were more likely to take steps toward a divorce than wives who had not experienced physical aggression (Heyman, O'Leary, & Jouriles, 1995). Quigley and Leonard (1996) found that husbands' stable physical aggression was associated with a decline in wives' marital satisfaction in the first three years of marriage. In a longitudinal study of bidirectionally aggressive newlyweds, Rogge and Bradbury (1999) found that marital dissolution was predicted by interspousal aggression.

STABILITY OF AGGRESSION

Early research, based on interviews with battered women, suggested that husband violence, once begun, would inevitably escalate in severity and frequency (e.g., Walker, 1979). However, findings from newer studies of couples experiencing lower levels of aggression suggest that, although there is stability in the perpetration of physical aggression, not all men who engage in marital violence continue to be violent over time. In particular, men who engage in low levels of aggression are less likely to escalate and more likely to desist than more severely violent men (e.g., Aldarondo, 1996; Quigley & Leonard, 1996). Yet, even among less violent couples, perhaps only one-quarter to one-half will desist from violence (e.g., approximately 25% over two years in Quigley & Leonard, 1996; approximately 40% over three years in Holtzworth-Munroe, Meehan, et al., 2000). In a longitudinal study of engaged and newlywed couples, O'Leary and colleagues (1989) found that the conditional probability of marital violence 30 months after marriage was 0.72 for women and 0.59 for men among couples who were physically aggressive before marriage and 18 months after marriage.

It is important to begin trying to predict which men will consistently be violent toward their wives and which will cease their physical aggression. For example, in a longitudinal study of subtypes of maritally violent men, we found differences between men who were likely to desist from violence over a three-year period and those who were not. Men who also engaged in violence outside the home and other antisocial behavior (e.g., arrest record, substance abuse), who had criminal friends, who were impulsive and jealous, and who had positive attitudes toward violence and negative attitudes toward women were more likely to continue their marital violence than men who did not have such risk factors (Holtzworth-Munroe, Meehan, Herron, Rehman, & Stuart, in press). Until such risk factors are firmly established, we recommend that clinicians assume that any physical aggression has the potential to escalate, so that the cessation of any marital violence must be made a priority even for couples experiencing only low levels of physical aggression.

CONJOINT TREATMENT FOR MARITAL AGGRESSION

WHETHER AND WHEN CONJOINT TREATMENT IS APPROPRIATE

Research examining the efficacy of conjoint treatment for physically aggressive couples has been limited, perhaps due to controversy surrounding the issue of whether such couples should be offered conjoint therapy. There is concern that seeing both partners in therapy and focusing on issues such as the couple's communication patterns may imply that the husband's violence is caused by both partners, becoming a form of victim blaming. An additional concern is that the wife may not be able to be honest about the level of violence she experiences, her fear, or her desire to end the relationship, as she may fear further violence from her partner if she discusses such issues. Also, there is concern that addressing relationship problems in therapy could increase anger and marital conflict, such that therapy would increase the risk of husband violence (for further discussion of such issues see Bograd, 1984; O'Leary, Heyman, & Neidig, 1999).

In contrast, there are potential advantages to conjoint treatment. One is the ability to obtain a more accurate picture of the violence (i.e., husband and wife reports often differ considerably). In addition, the therapist can ensure that both spouses understand the therapist's conceptualization of violence and how techniques should be implemented. Some interventions seem to be more successful when both spouses are present to hear the rationale and procedures (e.g., both partners understand what an appropriate time-out from conflict involves), and a husband may be less likely to use therapy to further abuse his wife when his wife has also heard what the therapist says (e.g., he can't go home and say "my therapist told me that I wouldn't be violent if you'd stop complaining about my behavior")! Conjoint therapy also allows couples to postpone volatile discussions until therapy sessions, thus helping them to avoid escalating arguments at home until they are better trained to handle such discussions.

There are theoretical rationales for using conjoint treatment. Physical aggression often occurs in the context of an argument between partners (O'Leary et al., 1999). Therefore, decreasing negative communication in conjoint treatment may decrease violence by changing the interactional patterns that precede it. Also, as many couples presenting for marital therapy have experienced bidirectional violence, and self-defense accounts for less than 20% of these cases (Cascardi & Vivian, 1995), both partners may benefit from learning to control their use of physical aggression. Although husband violence often can have severe physical and psychological effects, many women seeking marital therapy are not experiencing such a high level of violence, nor are they fearful of participating in treatment with their husbands (O'Leary et al., 1999). Indeed, in many cases, these wives are seeking conjoint therapy and wish to remain in their relationships.

Unfortunately, no available research provides empirically tested rules for deciding whether conjoint treatment is appropriate. However, three studies have examined the efficacy of conjoint couples therapy with physically aggressive couples (each is reviewed in more detail later). An examination of the subject exclusion criteria used in these studies provides suggestions for guidelines, along with ideas about procedures that can be implemented to protect wife safety.

Harris, Savage, Jones, and Brooke (1988) examined conjoint treatment for aggressive couples. For a couple to be eligible for this study, during an individual interview, the wife had to indicate that she wanted to remain in the relationship and that she did not feel endangered by her partner's knowledge that she had discussed his violence with a counselor. Additionally, the husband had to exhibit no psychotic symptoms, serious brain injury, psychopathic disturbance, or substance abuse that was not being treated. Intake workers helped the wives construct individualized safety plans and provided them with information about community resources for battered women.

O'Leary and colleagues (1999) conducted a study that included couples therapy as one treatment condition. To protect the safety of the wives, they included couples in the study only if they met the following criteria: the wife did not report sustaining injuries that required medical attention; the wife reported, during a private interview, feeling comfortable being assigned to conjoint treatment; the wife was not afraid of living with her husband; the husband did not meet criteria for alcohol dependence; and neither spouse reported psychotic symptoms nor met criteria for psychopathology severe enough to interfere with participation. Also, the man had to admit the perpetration of at least one act of physical aggression.

Brannen and Rubin (1996) also included a conjoint therapy condition for husband violent couples. They did not exclude couples based on the severity of husband violence or alcohol abuse. However, precautions were taken to ensure the wives' safety. A separate orientation was provided for the wives, in which wives were provided a 24-hour emergency phone number, and phone numbers for law enforcement officials and shelters. In addition, husbands and wives completed weekly reports concerning the use of psychological and physical abuse or threats. If any indication of a threatening situation existed, follow-up calls and additional help were provided for the wife.

Based on clinical experience, others have suggested guidelines for determining when conjoint therapy is inappropriate for violent couples (e.g., Holtzworth-Munroe, Beatty, & Anglin, 1995; O'Leary, 1996). Most agree that conjoint treatment is only appropriate for low to moderate levels of aggression and only if the wife is not perceived to be in danger of imminent physical harm. Related to this, the wife must not fear the husband, must feel comfortable in therapy with him, and must not feel so intimidated by him that she can't be honest in therapy. Both partners must be interested in staying in the relationship. A conjoint format is inappropriate if one spouse does not acknowledge the existence or problematic nature of violence in the relationship or is not willing to take steps to reduce the violence.

DATA REGARDING THE EFFICACY OF CONJOINT COUPLES TREATMENT

It is standard to review the research data regarding treatment efficacy at the end of a chapter. However, given the strong political controversy concerning the question of whether conjoint treatment is ever appropriate for physically aggressive couples, we believe that a review of the research should be presented before discussing possible conjoint interventions. Thus, we here review the only three published studies we know of that have examined the effectiveness of conjoint therapy with couples experiencing husband violence. All three compared conjoint treatment with gender-specific treatment (GST—in which men are seen in a men's treatment group and women are seen in a women's support group).

In the earliest study, Harris and colleagues (1988) recruited over 70 couples who had experienced husband violence and were requesting therapy at a family service agency. Using random assignment, some couples were assigned to a couples counseling program that explicitly addressed violence as the primary relationship problem. The other treatment condition involved a combination of gender-specific and couples groups (i.e., after the gender-specific group meeting, a couples meeting was held each week). Subject attrition from the study was significant. Across both treatment conditions, 35% of the sample never began treatment. A large number of couples who began treatment did not complete it, particularly among the couples counseling condition (i.e., attrition was 67% in the couples conditions and 16% in the gender-specific condition). Attrition continued after treatment; by follow-up (i.e., 6 to 12 months after therapy), only 28 women could be interviewed. These attrition problems pose severe limitations on interpretation of the data. Nonetheless, the follow-up data indicated that the two treatment conditions were equally effective in reducing the husbands' physical violence (based on wife report) and in improving the subjects' sense of psychological well-being.

Brannen and Rubin (1996) recruited a sample of couples who were referred to batterer treatment by the court system and who indicated a desire to remain in their current relationship. Couples were randomly assigned to either a couples group treatment (i.e., several couples jointly attended group meetings) or a GST group intervention. The conjoint therapy was designed to address husband violence as a primary problem. Forty-two of the 49 couples who began treatment completed it. In contrast to the study conducted by Harris and colleagues (1988), six of the seven batterers who dropped out of treatment were in the gender-specific intervention condition. Follow-up data, collected six months after the completion of treatment, showed no significant differences between the two groups in levels of recidivism; in both therapy conditions, just over 90% of the subjects reported that they were violence free. These researchers also examined the concern that couples treatment may endanger the victim. Specifically, weekly data were gathered to assess for any ongoing physical and psychological abuse. Over the course of treatment, six instances of physical and emotional abuse were reported; two involved couples assigned to the conjoint treatment, while four were among couples assigned to gender-specific treatments, suggesting that women in couples treatment were not in more danger than women in GST.

In the final study, O'Leary and colleagues (1999) randomly assigned couples to participate in either group conjoint therapy or gender-specific group therapy. Study participants responded to a newspaper ad offering free therapy to couples experiencing low levels of physical aggression. As discussed above, screening criteria were used to select a group of couples in which it was believed that the wife would be safe in conjoint therapy. As in the other studies, the conjoint therapy employed was not standard marital therapy but rather focused directly on the problem of marital violence (Heyman & Neidig, 1997). A total of 75 couples were randomly assigned to one treatment condition or the other, but only 37 couples completed treatment; dropout rates did not differ significantly across the two treatment conditions. Although both treatment approaches resulted in statistically significant changes in men's violence and psychological abuse, neither appears to have been particularly clinically effective (i.e., over 70% of the men engaged in some physical aggression during follow-up). Comparing the conjoint and GST groups, there were no differences in rates of physical aggression outcome, nor did the treatment condition have any differential impact on husbands' psychological aggression, wives' depressive symptomatology, or wives' marital adjustment; husbands' marital satisfaction was higher at follow-up for husbands in the conjoint therapy condition. Finally, based on regular safety checks, it was found that women in the conjoint treatment did not report fear of their husbands during therapy and did not report that therapy discussions led to physical aggression.

In summary, across the three available studies, no difference in outcome favored either gender-specific or conjoint therapy. Given that the studies involved couples who were interested in remaining together and willing to enter conjoint therapy, these samples may resemble couples seen by marital therapists. However, the couples in these studies were seeking help for husband violence, although many couples seeking marital therapy do not report husband violence as a presenting problem (see later). In addition, in all of the studies, a specialized couples treatment, addressing the man's violence directly, was used. In two of the studies (Brannen & Rubin, 1996; O'Leary et al., 1999), a group format was used. Thus, these data do not support the use of standard marital therapy, applied to individual couples, in reducing male violence. Rather, the data suggest that for carefully screened couples, conjoint treatment will be as effective as the more widely used GST approach.

ASSESSMENT ISSUES AND IMPORTANT CORRELATES OF RELATIONSHIP AGGRESSION

NEED TO DIRECTLY ASSESS PHYSICAL AGGRESSION

Given the known negative impact of violence in marital relationships, it might be expected that couples seeking therapy would spontaneously volunteer information about their aggression. Unfortunately, this is not the case. In a sample of couples seeking marital therapy, only 11% of individuals who later reported violence on a questionnaire had spontaneously mentioned their violence to the clinician as a presenting concern. Similarly, among couples who later reported, on a questionnaire, that they had engaged in mild physical aggression, only half had replied affirmatively when directly asked by a clinician if they had engaged in "physical aggression" in their marriage. The most common reasons couples gave for not reporting marital aggression were that they did not define the aggression as a problem, they considered it unstable (e.g., unlikely to reoccur), and they considered it to be secondary to their presenting problems, assuming that the violence would end with treatment of the presenting problem (Ehrensaft & Vivian, 1996).

For these reasons, we recommend the routine administration of a written, self-report questionnaire measure of marital violence to all potential clients, given that this was the method most likely to result in self-disclosure of marital aggression (Ehrensaft & Vivian, 1996). Single-item questions, such as "Have you ever engaged in physical aggression against your partner?" seem to lead to underreporting. Thus, more specifically, we recommend the use of a behavioral checklist such as the Conflict Tactics Scale (Straus, 1979) that lists multiple aggressive acts.

Ideally, a complete measure of all forms of violent behaviors would be included in the assessment. However, given concerns about length of assessment, existing scales can be shortened to include the initial questions, assessing minor violence, as almost all couples engaging in severe violence answer affirmatively to questions assessing minor violence as well. If either partner reports the occurrence of any physical aggression, we recommend that the clinician conduct a more thorough follow-up assessment.

FURTHER ASSESSING AGGRESSION

The follow-up assessment should be conducted individually so that each partner, particularly the wife, can be candid. These sessions can correct for the shortcomings of paper measures by asking questions beyond specific behaviors (e.g., precipitating events to the violence, the intent of the perpetrator, the response of the victim, and the consequences of the violence). The clinician should use these individual sessions to gather information necessary to determine whether conjoint therapy is safe and appropriate for the couple, as outlined earlier.

In cases of moderate to severe aggression, lethality must be assessed immediately. Recent escalation of violence, access to weapons, direct or indirect threats of lethality, significant fear of the perpetrator, victim steps toward separation, and the involvement of alcohol or drugs should all be considered. If the clinician has concerns about lethality, he or she must conduct safety planning immediately with each spouse. For perpetrators, this must include stressing the potential dangerousness of the violence and developing plans to prevent future violence (e.g., using time-outs, accessing emergency crisis lines, removing weapons from the home). Planning with the victim must include developing a comprehensive safety plan to respond to future dangerous situations. Information should be provided on legal options, such as obtaining a restraining order, and local resources (e.g., battered women's shelters and social service agencies). Also, a plan should be developed that will allow the woman and her children to exit a violent situation as safely as possible (e.g., keeping car keys, important documents, and money in a place that is easily accessible in case she needs to leave hurriedly).

ASSESSING CORRELATES OF PHYSICAL AGGRESSION

Information gathered during an assessment will guide the therapist in making a judgment about the appropriateness of conjoint therapy. In addition, it is important to assess other issues that have been linked to marital violence in past research. Such issues may need additional attention in therapy or may lead the therapist to refer the spouses elsewhere for more specialized help.

Women's Symptomatology   As reviewed briefly earlier, aggression in intimate relationships has been linked with deleterious consequences for women, their children, and the partners' relationship. For women, victimization may increase risk for psychiatric symptomatology, such as depressive or PTSD symptoms, although in samples of women seeking marital therapy, the rates of psychological symptomatology do not always differ significantly between abused and nonabused women (Cascardi et al., 1992; Vivian & Malone, 1997). Nonetheless, we would recommend that clinicians screen for psychological problems prior to treatment and provide referrals to appropriate individual treatment in the case of potentially dangerous symptoms (e.g., suicidality).

In addition, as noted previously, we believe that women in a violent relationship should be given information on local resources for battered women and on their legal options. Providing such information makes it clear to the couple that the therapist views the violence as a problem and is willing to help the woman take whatever steps are necessary to be free of violence.

Husbands' Psychological Symptoms   For husbands, perpetration of marital violence is associated with psychological symptoms such as depression and anxiety (Hamberger & Hastings, 1991; Pan, Neidig, & O'Leary, 1994). There also is evidence that men who are aggressive within their marriages experience higher levels of trait and state anger and hostility than other men (e.g., Eckhardt, Barbour, & Stuart, 1997; Holtzworth-Munroe, Rehman, & Herron, 2000; Leonard & Blane, 1992). As with wives, differences in rates of these symptoms are most robust when comparing severely violent with nonviolent husbands (e.g., Holtzworth-Munroe, Rehman, et al., 2000), so that differences, across violent and nonviolent husbands in marital therapy clinics may be less clear (Cascardi et al., 1992).

One of the psychological problems most consistently linked to husband violence is that of alcohol use disorders. Alcohol dependence and heavy drinking by the husband predict both concurrent and future marital violence (e.g., Heyman et al., 1995; Kaufman Kantor & Straus, 1987; Leonard & Blane, 1992; Leonard & Senchak, 1993; Quigley & Leonard, 2000). Among severely violent men, daily reports demonstrate that the risk of husband violence perpetration is significantly higher on days of husband alcohol consumption than on days of abstinence (Fals-Stewart, 2003). Similarly, there is an association between illicit drug use and marital violence, although this may be less apparent for couples engaging in low-level aggression. For example, in a nonclinical sample, after controlling for demographic factors, Pan and colleagues (1994) failed to show that the use of illicit substances substantially increased the risk of mild marital aggression; however, drug use was significantly associated with severe aggression. Thus, clinicians who have detected the occurrence of marital violence should screen for alcohol and drug. For clients with substance use disorders, it is generally recommended that they seek concurrent substance abuse treatment. This may be of particular importance because following couples treatment, alcoholics who relapse are more likely to engage in marital violence than alcoholics who remain abstinent (O'Farrell & Murphy, 1995).

Violent husbands also may have higher than expected personality disorder symptoms and diagnoses. Research by Dutton (1998) has called attention to similarities in behavior between maritally violent men and individuals with borderline personality disorder and has demonstrated that violent husbands are likely to self-report related problems such as high interpersonal dependency, jealousy, fear of abandonment, and trauma symptoms (also see Holtzworth-Munroe, Stuart, & Hutchinson, 1997). Another personality disorder commonly linked to marital violence is antisociality (Magdol et al., 1997). Holtzworth-Munroe, Meehan, et al. (2000) have suggested that distinct subtypes of violent husbands may be partially defined by presence or absence of symptoms of these two personality disorders (i.e., generally violent/antisocial and borderline/dysphoric are two subtypes of more severely violent men). Clinicians should understand that some maritally violent men will present with personality disorders and should be aware that treatment efficacy may be negatively affected by this intervening variable.

Husbands' Skills and Cognitions Relative to nonviolent men, violent husbands have been found to show deficits in social skills such as communication, problem solving, and spouse-specific assertiveness (e.g., Holtzworth-Munroe & Anglin, 1991; O'Leary & Curley, 1986). They also have been found to evidence particular cognitive patterns, including attributing hostile intent to their wives' behaviors (e.g., Holtzworth-Munroe & Hutchinson, 1993) and expressing attitudes supportive of violence and hostility toward women (see review in Holtzworth-Munroe, Bates, Smutzler, & Sandin, 1997). Again, most of these studies have included more severely violent men and differences between men engaging in low levels of aggression and nonviolent men are harder to find (e.g., Holtzworth-Munroe, Meehan, et al., 2000). However, during intake sessions, clinicians should assess for the presence of these problematic attitudes and interaction styles.

Psychological Aggression An important correlate of husband violence is psychological aggression. In laboratory-based discussions of marital problems, physically aggressive husbands are more likely than nonviolent husbands to engage in psychologically aggressive behavior (e.g., threatening gestures; angry or accusatory voice tones; hostile affect, such as contempt or belligerence; demanding behavior; Burman, Margolin, & John, 1993; Holtzworth-Munroe, Smutzler, & Stuart, 1998; Jacobson et al., 1994; Margolin, John, & Gleberman, 1988). Of particular importance, longitudinal research has shown that psychological aggression predicts future onset of physical aggression (Murphy & O'Leary, 1989). Thus, even for couples who are not currently engaging in physical aggression, it is important to assess psychological aggression not only for the direct negative consequences of this behavior, but also as a warning sign for potential future physical violence.

SENSITIVITY TO DIFFERING GROUPS OF COUPLES

Cross-Cultural Issues Nationally representative surveys demonstrate differences in the prevalence of marital violence across African American, Latino, and Caucasian couples, with a higher proportion of African American and Latino couples engaging in marital violence in a given year. However, this relationship may be mediated by other factors such as social class or family income, as it appears that the relationship is significantly attenuated when including socioeconomic variables in the model (see Holtzworth-Munroe, Smutzler, & Bates, 1997, for review).

Clinicians should be sensitive to the fact that different belief systems may be used by different ethnic groups to explain violence and should be ready to examine these beliefs in a culturally sensitive manner. They also should be aware of particular issues for different ethnic groups (e.g., an African American man's dismissal of the seriousness of his arrest for domestic violence, given his belief that the police are racially prejudiced; the stressors faced by an immigrant in a move to this country). However, the basic goal of therapy—violence desistance—will remain the same for couples of all ethnic backgrounds, as all individuals have the right to live in a violence-free relationship.

Same-Sex Couples To our knowledge no studies of physical aggression in same-sex relationships have included randomly selected, representative samples of gay or lesbian couples. Thus, although our understanding of this phenomenon is limited, research examining convenience samples suggests that rates of physical aggression are very similar to those in heterosexual relationships (Turell, 2000; Waldner-Haugrud & Gratch, 1997; West, 2002).

There may be some issues specific to same-sex couples. For example, some same-sex couples have described one partners' threats of outing the other partner as a means of psychological abuse or to prevent an abused partner from leaving the relationship (Freedner, Freed, Yang, & Austin, 2002). As another example, some abused partners describe the lack of police response to their pleas for help, given the incorrect assumption that two same-sex partners must have equal power and physical strength and thus one cannot abuse the other (Renzetti, 1992). Although the clinician must be sensitive to such issues, we again believe that the therapy goal (i.e., cessation of violence) will be the same for same-sex and heterosexual couples and that the basic therapy interventions will be similar.

CASE STUDY

Consider the case of Joan and Michael. Both were in their late twenties; they met during college. They had been married for five years and had a three-year old and a new baby. Joan was staying home with their children, having quit her job when pregnant with their second child. Michael had not finished college. He had a house painting business and was also in the process of establishing a karaoke business on weekends. The couple reported that they were seeking therapy because they "just couldn't talk anymore," couldn't "solve their problems without fighting," and "argued about everything." Joan was particularly concerned because they had begun fighting in front of the children, and she didn't want their children exposed to yelling and swearing. They fought about almost any issue, but frequent topics were finances, household responsibilities, and how much time to spend with their families (both of whom lived in town).

During their first appointment, the couple mentioned "bad fights." When the therapist asked them to describe their worst fight, they mentioned "yelling, swearing, name calling . . . it got pretty bad." The therapist then asked if their fights had ever escalated to the point of physical contact, such as pushing, grabbing, or slapping. They admitted that it had. On several occasions, Joan had tried to storm out of the room but Michael had grabbed her, to prevent her from leaving. On one occasion, she had slapped and pushed him, to get him to let go of her, and both had sustained scratches or bruises. They also reported having thrown objects (e.g., a picture, a pen, and a clipboard) at one another on several occasions. When asked, they said that they'd had one such fight early in their relationship, then none until about a year ago, but had "several" physical fights in the past year.

The next session, they each completed the Conflict Tactics Scale. This revealed one other violent behavior, with Joan reporting that Michael had slapped her once. In individual interviews, both spouses stated that they were committed to their marriage and wanted to stay together. Joan said that she was not afraid of Michael but might become so if his violence got worse. She believed that she could take the children and go to her parents should she ever feel endangered. In his interview, Michael initially minimized the violence but was willing to work on the problem, as he admitted that he felt guilty about losing his temper and knew that "these fights can't be good for anyone." He said that he was willing to let Joan take the children and go to her parents, without following her there, should she feel the need to remove herself and the children to a safer place. There were no weapons in the home. Neither spouse had other major psychopathology, although both were experiencing some depressive symptoms.

SETTING OF GOALS AND THERAPY CONTRACTS FOR CONJOINT TREATMENT

Before beginning conjoint treatment with a couple experiencing husband violence, the therapist must make clear his or her expectations and goals for treatment. Specifically, couples should be informed that cessation of physical aggression is one of the primary goals of treatment. We have found that, despite our careful assessment of aggression during intake procedures, many couples are surprised by our concern regarding their aggression and wish to dismiss it as excessive.

Thus, to help motivate couples to change, we review the reasons for our concern, including the following. Although the current level of aggression may be low, any level of physical aggression carries with it a risk of injury. We provide examples of relevant cases (e.g., a man who pushed his wife with no intent to hurt her, but she happened to fall into the water heater, breaking it and spewing hot water over them). Although some couples cease their aggression or maintain low levels of aggression, research also demonstrates that many couples continue or even escalate their aggression. Unfortunately, given a lack of available data to use in predicting which couples are at risk for continuing or escalating aggression, we must conservatively assume that every aggressive couple we work with is at risk for escalating violence. In addition, if the assessment revealed the presence of specific risk factors for violence (e.g., psychological aggression, excessive substance use, violence in the family of origin), we cite the relevant research to explain that these factors make us concerned that the aggression may escalate. We also discuss any possible negative consequences of the aggression that has occurred (e.g., couples often wish to model better conflict resolution for their children). Finally, we explain that without a direct focus on ending the aggression, there is a risk that the therapy itself may escalate the aggression, as the couple will be asked to discuss difficult topics likely to engender anger.

We then explain that treatment will take a two-pronged approach. In the first prong, the therapy will help the spouses to control their behavior when angry. Once anger management skills are learned, the couple will be in a safer position to engage in the second prong of therapy—problem solving regarding their major presenting problems. We find that following such a discussion, most couples are willing to agree to a treatment plan that will initially focus on anger management and controlling aggression.

In cases in which both spouses have used physical aggression, we acknowledge that both spouses must take responsibility for their own aggression and any consequences of it. We discuss the notion that violence is a learned behavior and a choice, and accordingly, that both spouses must take responsibility for stopping their physical aggression. In most cases, however, we also emphasize that because husband violence carries greater risk (e.g., physical injury, negative psychological effects), it will be a particular target of treatment. We ask both spouses to make a no-violence contract, either written or verbal, with the therapist. As part of the contract, the couple also should agree to report any incidents of physical aggression to the therapist. To remove the burden on spouses to bring up such events, the therapist explains that he or she will regularly ask about the occurrence of any physical aggression. Further occurrences of aggression will lead to a reexamination of the level of danger, the reasons the treatment plan is not working, and the appropriateness of the treatment plan. In some cases, continuing or worsening violence will be grounds for termination of conjoint treatment and referral of the spouses to gender-specific treatments specializing in relationship violence. This message helps to emphasize how concerned the therapist is about their aggression.

If not already been done, it is important to consider safety plans with both spouses. Among couples accepted for conjoint therapy (e.g., less severe violence), detailed planning may not be necessary. There still, however, should be a conversation with the woman about her safety (e.g., safe places to go if a fight is escalating; information regarding local resources). In addition, both spouses should be asked to consider steps they could take to prevent their further perpetration of physical aggression (e.g., discussing heated issues only in public or in therapy sessions) and to lessen the danger of any injury (e.g., removing guns from the home).

In the case of Joan and Michael, the establishment of the therapy goal of violence elimination went smoothly, as most aspects of this issue had already been discussed in their individual interviews. Joan was relieved to hear that Michael would agree to let her take the children and go to her parents house if she believed that she needed to; they negotiated this (e.g., whether he could call her there, how long she might stay). They both agreed to a no-violence contract. They understood the idea behind our two-pronged approach and were interested in learning anger management. In fact, in the course of discussing this, Michael brought up a new concern—that they might be using spanking too often, particularly when angry, as a way to discipline their older child. This issue was assessed and although no child abuse was detected, the couple were thrilled to add parent training to the therapy plan and could see how anger management might be useful when interacting with their children.

We use a behavioral-cognitive approach to conjoint treatment, focusing first on anger management and then on communication skills training. Our approach parallels, to a large extent, the treatment protocols for other existing conjoint treatment programs for husband violence and relationship aggression (e.g., Geffner, Mantooth, Franks, & Rao, 1989; Heyman & Neidig, 1997).

Anger Management

As intimate aggression frequently occurs during an argument, we usually begin treatment with anger management modules. The term *anger management* is a misnomer, as anger is a natural emotion that will continue to occur once therapy is over. Instead, we actually are trying to help spouses manage their behavior (i.e., aggression or abuse) when angry. In most cases, given the lower levels of aggression among the couples we accept into conjoint therapy, we find that one to three full therapy sessions devoted to anger management, followed by attention to these skills in subsequent therapy sessions, provides adequate coverage of anger management. Our procedures are borrowed from existing programs for anger management (e.g., Novaco, 1975, 1976), batterer treatment (e.g., Hamberger & Hastings, 1988; Saunders, 1989; Sonkin, Martin, & Walker, 1985), and conjoint therapy for relationship aggression (e.g., Heyman & Neidig, 1997).

Recognition of Anger   To adequately manage and control their anger, spouses must first be able to identify anger. Thus, the therapist helps each spouse to describe how they experience anger, identifying their personal physical (e.g., flushing, tenseness, rapid heart beat, sweating), cognitive (e.g., "hot thoughts" or "anger up statements"), and behavioral (e.g., tapping fingers, slamming doors, violence) anger cues. Next, the therapist asks each spouse to construct a personalized anger continuum, from the least to most extreme anger they experience, using a line marked from 1 to 10. To help spouses understand different intensities of anger, the clients label key anchor points along the line (e.g., "frustrated," "angry," "furious") and list physical, cognitive, and behavioral signs of anger for each key point. For example, Michael reported that he knew he was angry when he became flushed and tense and that his anger level became "dangerous" when he "stopped thinking" and just felt "steaming." In contrast,

Joan reported feeling nauseated and alternating between self-blame and blaming Michael as her anger increased.

Anger logs are also introduced. On an anger log, a spouse reports the details of one or more episodes when he or she felt angry. The client records the situation; the intensity of the anger (on the 1 to 10 scale); and the physical, cognitive, and behavioral anger cues experienced. Spouses are instructed to keep these anger logs for homework and to look for patterns in their anger (e.g., when, and with whom, they are angry; how they know they are angry), perhaps helping them to identify high risk situations for arguments and aggression. In the case of Michael and Joan, five weeks of anger logs revealed that many of their arguments occurred in the evenings, after Michael came home from work. At this time, Michael was tired and expected to be allowed to relax, while Joan expected him to help her take care of the children, after her day home alone with them. They decided to add the issue of how to handle this time of day to the list of problems they would address in problem-solving sessions.

Time-Outs   We teach couples to take time-outs to avoid engaging in aggression during conflicts. Many couples have difficulty accepting time-outs, as this procedure (i.e., leaving a fight) runs counter to many common cultural beliefs (e.g., that one should never walk away from a fight, that it is better to hash out an issue until some insight or resolution is reached). Thus, it often is important for the therapist to help the couple weigh the risk of continued aggression against the temporary suspension of the discussion of a heated issue. In some cases, one spouse may have avoided discussing issues for years, and his or her partner may be concerned that time-outs will become a therapy-sanctioned method of continuing this pattern. In all cases, it is important that both spouses understand that a time-out does not permanently end discussion of the problem. They will be asked to discuss the issues, calmly, after the time-out or to bring the issue to therapy for eventual discussion. We also have found that many couples initially respond negatively to the term *time-out*, having heard it applied to the discipline of children. In contrast, we introduce the procedures using analogies to time-outs taken in sports (e.g., to regroup and collect yourself before making a costly mistake).

Time-outs have several components. First, a spouse must recognize his or her anger and take responsibility for acknowledging the anger and taking a time-out. Thus, they are to state, "I am beginning to feel angry and I need to take a time-out." Each part of that statement is discussed in detail—using an "I statement" to take responsibility for one's feelings, acknowledging the anger without blaming the spouse, calmly announcing a time-out rather than just leaving the discussion. We have implemented a rule that neither spouse can tell the other when to take a time-out, because this quickly becomes another form of abuse (e.g., "you need to take a time-out"). However, because some women report that they fear their husbands' anger when he refuses to take a time-out, we have implemented another version of time-out, in which either spouse can take a time-out for any negative feeling that is likely to make further discussion of an issue unproductive (e.g., "I am beginning to feel upset and I need to take a time-out"). The time-out statement also includes another important component—notifying the spouse when one will return. With couples in marital therapy, we usually ask spouses to try a half-hour initially, and then to adjust this time period as they learn whether it is too long or too short. Thus, the initial time-out statement becomes "I am beginning to feel angry and I need to take a half-hour time-out."

After announcing the time-out, the spouse is to leave the area where the argument was occurring, as we have found spouses may get more angry as they listen to their partner in another room. Couples should be asked to consider how they would take time-outs in various problematic situations (e.g., a fight in the car or in public). During a time-out, spouses are encouraged to engage in techniques aimed at decreasing anger. Meditation and relaxation techniques can be used, as can physical exercise. It is also helpful to have each spouse develop a personalized list of "cool thoughts" or "anger down statements" to de-escalate angry thoughts. Activities to be avoided during a time-out include things that may further escalate the anger or be dangerous, such as alcohol and drug use, aggressive exercising (e.g., chopping wood), driving, and ruminating about the argument.

At the end of the specified time, the spouse taking the time-out must either return or contact the partner and take another time-out (e.g., "I am still angry and need to take another half-hour time-out"). After the time-out is over, the angry spouse should continue discussing the problem with his or her partner. The couple is encouraged to take another time-out if needed or to suggest another time (including therapy) in which to continue discussing the problem.

As with the learning of any new skill, it is helpful to have couples practice taking time-outs in session and at home. Using a time-out log, clients should write down incidents in which they used a time-out, including the argument that led to the time-out, how the time-out was implemented, and what happened after the time-out. Therapist debriefing of these incidents often can pinpoint problems in the use of time-outs. We also have found it useful to ask couples to take a time-out during any therapy sessions in which they are becoming angry. In such cases, usually the therapist suggests that they take a time-out (a short one). One spouse makes the time-out statement and leaves the room. The therapist also leaves, so as not to get drawn into an alliance with the spouse left in the therapy room. Both the spouse and the therapist return at the agreed-on time. At that point, the therapist can help review the time-out from both partners' perspectives. Such discussions often help to elucidate potential problems with time-out, allowing the couple and therapist to brainstorm methods for handling such issues.

Despite repeated reminders, Michael and Joan never took a practice time-out at home. However, in three early therapy sessions, they began to argue and the therapist asked them to take a time-out. (Actually, by the third occasion, the therapist simply said, "You both are becoming noncollaborative, so this might be a good time to . . ." and was interrupted by Michael saying, "to take a time-out"!) The couple found that just a 10-minute break was very useful to them, and they were able to continue the session after such a break. Following these in-session experiences, they began to take time-outs at home when their arguments were escalating.

Other Anger Management Skills   Although many methods of managing anger are covered in the time-out procedure, it is often necessary to develop these skills further. Such discussions focus on learning methods to manage the three components of anger discussed during anger recognition—physical (e.g., relaxation, slow breathing, exercise), cognitive (e.g., self-statements), and behavioral (e.g., communication skills). Once these skills are taught, the weekly anger logs should be modified to include a section regarding what steps the spouse took to manage each of the three components of anger. Anger logs and time-out logs can be combined and should be monitored weekly.

COMMUNICATION AND PROBLEM-SOLVING SKILLS

Once couples are managing their anger more appropriately and have not engaged in further aggression, it is appropriate to begin training in communication and problem-solving skills. The spouses usually are very eager to do so, as attention to their presenting problems may have been delayed for the few weeks of anger management training. At this point, we generally use techniques derived from behavioral marital therapy (BMT; e.g., Jacobson & Margolin, 1979) to teach good listening skills (i.e., nonverbal and verbal paraphrasing), expression of feelings, behavioral descriptions of problems, and problem-solving skills (e.g., a behavioral definition of the problem, brainstorming and discussion of possible solutions, a written contract incorporating agreed-on solutions). Given that such methods are well outlined in other publications, and are probably familiar to most couples therapists, we do not present them here.

Michael and Joan were very excited to begin the sessions on communication training and problem solving. They learned these skills over the course of three sessions. They then applied them to each of their major presenting problems, usually solving one major problem per week. They used problem solving to write contracts for several financial problems, the issue of how to handle household tasks, and the problem of how much time to spend with each of their families. One particularly sensitive issue (how to say no to Joan's families frequent invitations) took several sessions and had to be revised twice, following their discovery of problems with their initial contract on its implementation. Nonetheless, overall, they were happy with their progress. They found that as they began implementing these contracts, the frequency of their arguments declined, lowering the risk of aggression.

OTHER THERAPEUTIC INTERVENTIONS

Other interventions may be considered to address additional problems. For example, many aggressive couples benefit from some sessions of parent training, learning to discipline their children in nonaggressive ways. On a regular basis (e.g., every four to five sessions), the therapist and couple jointly review the progress they have made on presenting problems and new problems identified during the course of therapy. They adjust the therapy plan to make sure that all of these problems are addressed. Once violence has been eliminated, the major presenting issues have been addressed, and the skills taught are being successfully applied, the therapist moves to less frequent meetings, serving as a consultant to a couple who is now managing their problems on their own and helping them to anticipate upcoming stressors or major life changes.

In the case of Michael and Joan, several sessions were spent on parent training. Much of what they had already learned (e.g., anger management, time-outs, communication skills, contracting) was readily translated to this new topic. They made good progress and learned a variety of nonphysical methods of punishment. As part of this process, they agreed to no longer use spanking as a method of discipline.

SUMMARY

Physical aggression is a common problem among couples seeking marital therapy. Indeed, once couples therapists begin to screen for violence, they may find that 50% to 75% of couples seeking their help report the occurrence of aggression in the past year. Familiarity with research on marital aggression, particularly on the correlates of such aggression, will help therapists assess potentially important aspects of the problem. In addition, a thorough assessment will help therapists decide whether or not conjoint treatment is appropriate for a particular couple. Current data suggest that conjoint therapy with a direct focus on eliminating husband violence may be as effective as the more widely utilized gender-specific treatments, although the current data are mixed regarding how effective such interventions will be. In general, we suggest a cautious approach, focusing on anger management and communication skills, to help couples end the violence in their relationship.

REFERENCES

Aldarondo, E. (1996). Cessation and persistence of wife assault: A longitudinal analysis. *American Journal of Orthopsychiatry, 66,* 141–151.

Archer, J. (2000). Sex difference in physical aggression to partners: A reply to Frieze (2000), O'Leary (2000), and White, Smith, Koss, and Figueredo (2000). *Psychological Bulletin, 126,* 697–702.

Bograd, M. (1984). Family systems approaches to wife battering: A feminist critique. *American Journal of Orthopsychiatry, 54,* 558–568.

Brannen, S. J., & Rubin, A. (1996). Comparing the effectiveness of gender-specific and couples groups in a court-mandated spouse abuse treatment program. *Research on Social Work Practice, 6,* 405–424.

Burman, B., Margolin, G., & John, R. S. (1993). America's angriest home videos: Behavioral contingencies observed in home reenactments of marital conflict. *Journal of Consulting and Clinical Psychology, 61,* 28–39.

Cantos, A. L., Neidig, P. H., & O'Leary, K. D. (1993). Men's and women's attributions of blame for domestic violence. *Journal of Family Violence, 8,* 289–303.

Cascardi, M., Langhinrichsen, J., & Vivian, D. (1992). Marital aggression: Impact, injury, and health correlates for husbands and wives. *Archives of Internal Medicine, 152,* 1178–1184.

Cascardi, M., & Vivian, D. (1995). Context for specific episodes of marital violence: Gender and severity of violence differences. *Journal of Family Violence, 10,* 265–293.

Christian, J. L., O'Leary, K. D., & Vivian, D. (1994). Depressive symptomatology in maritally discordant women and men: The role of individual and relationship variables. *Journal of Family Psychology, 8,* 32–42.

Dutton, D. G. (1998). *The abusive personality: Violence and control in intimate relationships.* New York: Guilford Press.

Eckhardt, C. I., Barbour, K. A., & Stuart, G. L. (1997). Anger and hostility in maritally violent men: Conceptual distinctions, measurement issues, and literature review. *Clinical Psychology Review, 17,* 333–358.

Ehrensaft, M. K., & Vivian, D. (1996). Spouses' reasons for not reporting existing physical aggression as a marital problem. *Journal of Family Psychology, 10,* 443–453.

Fals-Stewart, W. (2003). The occurrence of partner physical aggression on days of alcohol consumption: A longitudinal diary study. *Journal of Consulting and Clinical Psychology, 71,* 41–52.

Freedner, N., Freed, L. H., Yang, Y. W., & Austin, S. B. (2002). Dating violence among gay, lesbian, and bisexual adolescents. *Journal of Adolescent Health, 31,* 469–474.

Geffner, R., Mantooth, C., Franks, D., & Rao, L. (1989). A psychoeducational conjoint therapy approach to reducing family violence. In P. L. Caesar & L. K. Hamberger (Eds.), *Therapeutic interventions with batterers: Theory and practice* (pp. 103–133). New York: Springer.

Hamberger, L. K., & Hastings, J. E. (1988). Skills training for treatment of spouse abusers: An outcome study. *Journal of Family Violence, 3,* 121–130.

Hamberger, L. K., & Hastings, J. E. (1991). Personality correlates of men who batter and nonviolent men: Some continuities and discontinuities. *Journal of Family Violence, 6,* 131–147.

Harris, R., Savage, S., Jones, T., & Brooke, W. (1988). A comparison of treatments for abusive men and their partners within a family-service agency. *Canadian Journal of Community Mental Health, 7,* 147–155.

Heyman, R. E., & Neidig, P. H. (1997). Physical aggression couples treatment. In W. K. Halford & H. J. Markman (Eds.), *Clinical handbook of marriage and couples interventions* (pp. 589–617). Chichester, England: Wiley.

Heyman, R. E., O'Leary, K. D., & Jouriles, E. N. (1995). Alcohol and aggressive personality styles: Potentiators of serious physical aggression against wives? *Journal of Family Psychology, 9,* 44–57.

Holtzworth-Munroe, A., & Anglin, K. (1991). The competency of responses given by maritally violent versus nonviolent men to problematic marital situations. *Clinical Psychology Review, 12,* 605–617.

Holtzworth-Munroe, A., Bates, L., Smutzler, N., & Sandin, E. (1997). A brief review of the research on husband violence: Part I. Maritally violence versus nonviolent men. *Aggression and Violent Behavior, 2,* 65–99.

Holtzworth-Munroe, A., Beatty, S. B., & Anglin, K. (1995). The assessment and treatment of marital violence: An introduction for the marital therapist. In N. S. Jacobson & A. S. Gurman (Eds.), *Clinical handbook of marital therapy* (2nd ed., pp. 317–339). New York: Guilford Press.

Holtzworth-Munroe, A., & Hutchinson, G. (1993). Attributing negative intent to wife behavior: The attributions of maritally violent versus nonviolent men. *Journal of Abnormal Psychology, 102,* 206–211.

Holtzworth-Munroe, A., Meehan, J. C., Herron, K., Rehman, U., & Stuart, G. L. (2000). Testing the Holtzworth-Munroe and Stuart batterer typology. *Journal of Consulting and Clinical Psychology, 68,* 1000–1019.

Holtzworth-Munroe, A., Meehan, J. C., Herron, K., Rehman, U., & Stuart, G. L. (in press). Do subtypes of maritally violent men continue to differ over time? *Journal of Consulting and Clinical Psychology.*

Holtzworth-Munroe, A., Rehman, U., & Herron, K. (2000). General and spouse specific anger and hostility in subtypes of martially violence men and nonviolent men. *Behavior Therapy, 31,* 603–630.

Holtzworth-Munroe, A., Smutzler, N., & Bates, L. (1997). A brief review of the research on husband violence: Part III. Sociodemographic factors, relationship factors, and differing consequences of husband and wife violence. *Aggression and Violent Behavior, 2,* 285–307.

Holtzworth-Munroe, A., Smutzler, N., & Stuart, G. L. (1998). Demand and withdraw communication among couples experiencing husband violence. *Journal of Consulting and Clinical Psychology, 66,* 731–743.

Holtzworth-Munroe, A., Stuart, G. L., & Hutchinson, G. (1997). Violent versus nonviolent husbands: Differences in attachment patterns, dependency, and jealousy. *Journal of Family Psychology, 11,* 314–331.

Jacobson, N. S., Gottman, J. M., Waltz, J., Rushe, R., Babcock, J., & Holtzworth-Munroe, A. (1994). Affect, verbal content, and psychophysiology in the arguments of couples with a violent husband. *Journal of Consulting and Clinical Psychology, 62,* 982–988.

Jacobson, N. S., & Margolin, G. (1979). *Marital therapy: Strategies based on social learning and behavior exchange principles.* New York: Brunner/Mazel.

Johnson, M. P. (1995). Patriarchal terrorism and common couple violence: Two forms of violence against women. *Journal of Marriage and the Family, 57,* 283–294.

Kaufman Kantor, G., & Straus, M. A. (1987). The "drunken bum" theory of wife beating. *Social Problems, 34,* 213–230.

Lawrence, E., & Bradbury, T. N. (2001). Physical aggression and marital dysfunction: A longitudinal analysis. *Journal of Family Psychology, 15,* 135–154.

Leonard, K. E., & Blane, H. T. (1992). Alcohol and marital aggression in a national sample of young men. *Journal of Interpersonal Violence, 7,* 19–30.

Leonard, K. E., & Senchak, M. (1993). Alcohol and premarital aggression among newlywed couples. *Journal of Studies on Alcohol, 11,* 96–108.

Magdol, L., Moffitt, T. E., Caspi, A., Newman, D. L., Fagan, J., & Silva, P. A. (1997). Gender differences in rates of partner violence in a birth cohort of 21-year-olds: Bridging the gap between clinical and epidemiological approaches. *Journal of Consulting and Clinical Psychology, 65,* 68–78.

Margolin, G. (1998). Effects of domestic violence on children. In P. K. Trickett & C. J. Schellenbach (Eds.), *Violence against children in the family and the communication* (pp. 57–101). Washington, DC: American Psychological Association.

Margolin, G., John, R. S., & Gleberman, L. (1988). Affective responses to conflictual discussions in violent and nonviolent couples. *Journal of Consulting and Clinical Psychology, 56,* 24–33.

Murphy, C. M., & O'Leary, K. D. (1989). Psychological aggression predicts physical aggression in early marriage. *Journal of Consulting and Clinical Psychology, 57,* 579–582.

Novaco, R. W. (1975). *Anger control: The development and evaluation of an experimental treatment.* Lexington, MA: Lexington Books.

Novaco, R. W. (1976). Treatment of chronic anger through cognitive and relaxation controls. *Journal of Consulting and Clinical Psychology, 44,* 681.

O'Farrell, T. J., & Murphy, C. M. (1995). Marital violence before and after alcoholism treatment. *Journal of Consulting and Clinical Psychology, 63,* 256–262.

O'Leary, K. D. (1993). Through a psychological lens: Personality traits, personality disorders, and levels of violence. In R. J. Gelles & D. R. Ioseke (Eds.), *Current controversies in family violence* (pp. 7–29). Newbury Park, CA: Sage.

O'Leary, K. D. (1996). Physical aggression in intimate relationships can be treated within a marital context under certain circumstances. *Journal of Interpersonal Violence, 11,* 450–452.

O'Leary, K. D., Barling, J., Arias, I., Rosenbaum, A., Malone, J., & Tyree, A. (1989). Prevalence and stability of marital aggression between spouses: A longitudinal analysis. *Journal of Consulting and Clinical Psychology, 57,* 263–268.

O'Leary, K. D., & Curley, A. D. (1986). Assertion and family violence: Correlates of spouse abuse. *Journal of Marital and Family Therapy, 12,* 281–289.

O'Leary, K. D., Heyman, R. E., & Neidig, P. H. (1999). Treatment of wife abuse: A comparison of gender-specific and couples approaches. *Behavior Therapy, 30,* 475–505.

Pan, H., Neidig, P. H., & O'Leary, K. D. (1994). Predicting mild and severe husband-to-wife physical aggression. *Journal of Consulting and Clinical Psychology, 62,* 975–981.

Quigley, B. M., & Leonard, K. E. (1996). Desistance of husband aggression in the early years of marriage. *Violence and Victims, 11,* 355–370.

Quigley, B. M., & Leonard, K. E. (2000). Alcohol and the continuation of early marital aggression. *Alcoholism: Clinical and Experimental Research, 24,* 1003–1010.

Renzetti, C. (1992). *Violent betrayal: Partner abuse in lesbian relationships.* Newbury Park, CA: Sage.

Rogge, R. D., & Bradbury, T. N. (1999). Till violence does us part: The differing roles of communication and aggression in predicting adverse marital outcomes. *Journal of Consulting and Clinical Psychology, 67,* 340–351.

Saunders, D. G. (1989). Cognitive and behavioral interventions with men who batter: Application and outcome. In P. L. Caesar & L. K. Hamberger (Eds.), *Treating men who batter: Theory, practice and programs* (pp. 77–98). New York: Springer.

Sonkin, D. J., Martin, D., & Walker, L. E. A. (1985). *The male batterer: A treatment approach.* New York: Springer.

Stets, J. E., & Straus, M. (1989). The marriage license as a hitting license: A comparison of assaults in dating, cohabiting, and married couples. *Journal of Family Violence, 4,* 161–180.

Straus, M. A. (1979). Measuring intra family conflict and violence: The Conflict Tactics (CT) scales. *Journal of Marriage and the Family, 41,* 75–88.

Straus, M. A., & Gelles, R. J. (1990). *Physical violence in American families: Risk factors and adaptations to violence in families.* New Brunswick, NJ: Transaction.

Turell, S. C. (2000). A descriptive analysis of same-sex relationship violence for a diverse sample. *Journal of Family Violence, 15,* 281–293.

Vivian, D., & Malone, J. (1997). Relationship factors and depressive symptomatology associated with mild and severe husband-to-wife physical aggression. *Violence and Victims, 12,* 3–18.

Waldner-Haugrud, L., & Gratch, L. (1997). Sexual coercion in gay/lesbian relationships: Descriptives and gender differences. *Violence and Victims, 12,* 87–98.

Walker, L. (1979). *The battered woman.* New York: Harper & Row.

West, C. M. (2002). Lesbian intimate partner violence: Prevalence and dynamics. *Journal of Lesbian Studies, 6,* 121–127.

CHAPTER 18

Couples and Addiction

Mark Stanton

ADDICTIVE BEHAVIORS OCCUR in the context of real-life relationships. Many addicts have a significant other, but treatment may exclude that person from the process or relegate him* to an occasional family night group session. A national survey of substance abuse treatment programs indicated that only 27% used any type of couples therapy, and that those that did conduct couples therapy averaged only 3.1 sessions. This is despite the fact that some couple therapies have outcomes more positive than individual treatment, including fewer days of drug use, greater abstinence, fewer arrests and hospitalizations due to drug use, reduced domestic violence, and more relationship satisfaction (Fals-Stewart & Birchler, 2001). The standards of the Joint Commission on Accreditation of Health Care Organizations currently requires that a family member be included in substance abuse treatment, when possible, for at least the initial assessment. Seventy percent of the programs not using couples therapy indicated that staff were not trained to provide it (Fals-Stewart & Birchler).

Current models of addictive behavior recognize the systemic relationship between the addiction and the social context of the addict. Couple functioning interacts with substance abuse in reciprocal fashion (Epstein & McCrady, 2002). Couple interventions for addictive behaviors have considerable support in the clinical research literature, as we see in this chapter.

OVERVIEW OF THE CHAPTER

This chapter provides key elements of couples therapy for the treatment of addictive behaviors. The model presented follows the therapeutic process,

---

*We have used the male pronoun as a convention but are well aware that addicts are both male and female.

from initiation of treatment, to assessment and diagnosis, to utilization of evidence-based treatments, to methods to avoid relapse. Several intervention models for addiction psychotherapy that have been adapted for use within the systemic dynamic of couple relationships are reviewed in light of a case presentation. The case presentation is an amalgam of real-life cases meshed together to provide an overview of issues and therapeutic processes found relevant for couples with addiction. It reflects the somewhat optimistic evidence for couples treatment of addiction; actual individual cases often have complications at one stage or another. The role of personality factors, as they interact with addictive behaviors, and a process for relationship restoration following sobriety are considered. Finally, specific features that impact some couples, but not others (e.g., domestic violence, ethnic identity, addiction by both partners), are included to illustrate the many faces of addiction in couples.

INITIAL CASE PRESENTATION

Rick was a 35-year-old Caucasian manager in a technology company. He was a strong, popular boss who attracted a great deal of admiration at work. He was married to Liz, a 33-year-old Latina he had met in college and married shortly after graduation. They had two children, Richard Jr., called Ricky, and Martina, ages 8 and 6, respectively. Rick made good money and Liz worked part-time while the kids were in school. They had all the trappings of an upper-middle-class family, but things were starting to fall apart because Rick had a drinking and drug abuse problem.

INITIATION OF CHANGE BY THE PARTNER

Addictive behaviors may plague a couple's relationship for some time before treatment is sought. It is common knowledge that denial of the problem is characteristic of addicts. Partners are often stuck between conflicting reactions of enabling and confronting. Enabling reflects the powerlessness experienced by some partners and their desire not to rock the boat with the addict. They believe that if they can manage or control the consequences of the addictive behavior, things will eventually improve. Although it is not their intent, by minimizing negative consequences and keeping the family on track despite the addictive behavior, they may actually perpetuate the problem. On the other hand, partners will sometimes become so hurt by the addictive behavior that they react in anger to confront the addict with demands for change. Intense encounters may lead to promises of change, but when the anger of the partner diminishes, so does the addict's commitment to change. Alternatively, some addicts will defend themselves or simply pull away during confrontational episodes; this has been termed the demand-withdraw interaction, and it may predict poor retention in treatment that is similar in making demands for abstinence of the addict (Shoham, Rohrbaugh, Stickle, & Jacob, 1998). Over time, some partners begin to alternate between enabling and confronting, resulting in a contradictory and confused relationship (Yoshioka, Thomas, & Ager, 1992).

Eventually, the partner may initiate an attempt to change by entering psychotherapy. This is a crucial time in the process, because the recommendations of the therapist are central to the direction of the intervention.

A friend who had been in treatment two years previously referred Liz to me for psychotherapy. When she called, she was hesitant and uncertain how to proceed. She knew she needed help because she was "overwhelmed" by her husband's long-term drug and alcohol problem. She reported that her son was having problems at school and her daughter appeared nervous and tense. She agreed to meet for an initial appointment to consider how to proceed.

STAGES OF CHANGE

The transtheoretical model of intentional human behavior change provides a framework for understanding that behavior change occurs in progressive stages, from precontemplation to the contemplation stage, to preparation for action, to the action stage, to maintenance and/or relapse and recycling (see DiClemente & Velasquez, 2002, for a review of the model). This model has been utilized in substance abuse treatment to conceptualize engagement in treatment and progression toward improvement. Although addicts are often characterized as resistant or in denial of their problem, this model suggests that understanding of the addict's current stage of change may facilitate use of the most appropriate therapeutic method for that stage. For instance, DiClemente and Velasquez argue that motivational interviewing is an "excellent counseling style to use with clients who are in the early stages" (p. 202). They note that people in the precontemplation stage dislike lectures and resist action ideas because they are not yet ready to change. Even those who are contemplating change (Stage 2) may resist confrontational methods that push them when they are not yet ready to commit to change. Understanding the stages of change ensures that treatment does not get ahead of the addict in the change process. Miller and Tonigan (1996) have created an assessment instrument that quickly determines the level of motivation to change according to these stages.

THE ROLE OF THE PARTNER IN INITIATING THERAPY

Partners play a significant role in the initiation of therapy for the addictive behavior (Cunningham, Sobell, Sobell, & Kapur, 1995; Meyers, Miller, Smith, & Tonigan, 2002). One study of the sources of motivation to seek treatment for male alcoholics found that 53% were motivated by their spouse or family (Steinberg, Epstein, McCrady, & Hirsch, 1997). Sometimes, they take strong measures after months or years of enduring negative consequences of the addiction. One patient brought her husband into therapy after she grew tired of cleaning up the vomit and excrement he left in their bed following his alcoholic binges. She videotaped him throughout the binge and forced him to watch the video, pushing him toward action. Another stopped covering for her husband with his employer, refusing to call in sick for him when he was unable to go to work after doing drugs throughout the weekend. His employment problems moved him to consider therapy.

There are three well-known approaches that therapists recommend for partners who are uncertain how to proceed. Al-Anon is a primary, popular source of assistance. It is focused exclusively on the nonaddict partner and disavows any intent to change the behavior of the addict. It may be effective for improvement in the nonaddict partner on some dimensions (reduced depression, anger, and family conflict; increased cohesion and relationship happiness), but it is less effective than other means for engaging the addict in treatment (Meyers et al., 2002; Miller, Meyers, & Tonigan, 1999). The primary difficulty with this approach is that it does not address the addictive behavior; it detaches from it or manages it better. Before therapists refer a partner patient to Al-Anon exclusively for the addiction issue, it is important to recognize that this referral is unlikely to result in addict engagement in the change process.

Confrontational interventions are another means to initiate treatment for addictions. Interventions have been popularized by portrayal in the entertainment media. The partner is often the person who initiates this process, which involves gathering the social network of the addict for preparation and training to conduct a meeting with the addict in which the addict is confronted regarding the negative impact of his addictive behavior. Uncontrolled research for this method shows some positive outcome (i.e., engagement in treatment), but the greatest difficulty appears to be the tendency for the partner to discontinue the process prior to conducting the intervention; as many as 70% of those who begin the preparation do not proceed to intervention (Miller, Meyers, & Tonigan, 1999). Anecdotal experience indicates that interventions require significant personal strength by the participants, because they must face the addict in a confrontational context, and maintenance of clear agreement with high cohesion in the group.

An alternative model adopts elements of motivational interviewing to provide the partner with coping skills and methods to encourage motivation to change in the addict. Known as the community reinforcement approach, it is especially appropriate to the one-on-one therapy that may occur when a partner contacts a therapist for treatment before the addict is willing to participate. It focuses on eliminating positive reinforcement for substance use and provision of positive reinforcement for sobriety. In the early stages of treatment, this model involves the following: (1) raising awareness of the positive benefits of treatment for the partner and the addict, (2) reinforcement mechanisms to reduce or eliminate drug use, (3) couple's communication training, (4) means to address dangerous situations, (5) creation of activities that could replace substance use activities, and (6) preparation of the partner to suggest counseling when the addict seems ready to receive the suggestion (Miller, Meyers, & Tonigan, 1999). This model was found in random assignment comparison studies to result in significantly higher engagement of unmotivated problem drinkers (approximately two-thirds of unmotivated addicts; Miller, Meyers, & Tonigan, 1999) and unmotivated drug addicts (Meyers et al., 2002) in treatment than Al-Anon facilitation or intervention methods. It is effective in the most common treatment format of weekly psychotherapy sessions in an outpatient setting, and it may result in engagement of the addict in treatment within as few as five sessions (Miller, Meyers, Hiller-Sturmhöfel, 1999).

Clinical experience and some research indicate that the majority of non-substance-abusing partners who initiate psychotherapy for a drug-abusing partner are female (Miller, Meyers, & Tonigan, 1999; Winters, Fals-Stewart, O'Farrell, Birchler, & Kelley, 2002). This does not mitigate the reality of initiation by some males for their partners, but it is more rare.

During the in-take session, Liz reported feelings of hopelessness and exhaustion at dealing with her husband's addictive behaviors. Rick had begun using marijuana in junior high school, and he had progressed to alcohol and methamphetamine use in high school. When they met in college, she was enthralled by his self-confidence and energy. Once they were married, however, she found that he was unwilling to adjust his life to her needs. He expected her to accommodate to him, and he ignored her reactions to his drug and alcohol use. The birth of two children had not changed things for the better, and Rick's drug and alcohol use was increasing. He had a good job, but he was starting to have problems at work. Sexual relations were an area of tension, as Rick was more aggressive about sex when he was using drugs. Recently, Rick was arrested for driving under the influence of drugs, and he spent five days in jail. Liz had thought about divorce, but she really did not want to break up the family. She was concerned that the children were being exposed to behavior that might influence them to use drugs in the future.

Noting her desire to address these concerns, I suggested that we work initially on helping her to manage her reactions to Rick's substance use and on developing techniques for her to use to influence him to decrease his use. A second goal would focus on helping her to increase his motivation to change and to enter couples therapy.

We spent the next four sessions decreasing her hopelessness by developing ideas for her to implement at home to change the dynamics in the marriage. She would stop harassing Rick about his use and begin to engage him in fun activities that did not include drugs. We developed techniques for Liz to use so that neither she nor the children would ride in the car with him when he was driving under the influence (e.g., assertive refusal instead of begrudging compliance; carrying taxicab money to use if Rick refused to let her drive; not leaving the children alone with him in high-risk situations). Finally, we practiced ways to invite Rick to participate in therapy without pressuring him and techniques she might use if we transitioned to couples therapy. Liz presented in a more positive manner as these sessions progressed and she demonstrated some hope that things could improve. Rick noticed the change in her behavior, and he began to question her about what was happening in therapy. In addition, his attorney had indicated that voluntary participation in therapy might benefit him at trial for his DUI offense. Finally, an opportune moment arose, and Liz asked Rick to consider participating in the therapeutic process. With some misgivings, he agreed to attend at least one session.

MOTIVATIONAL INTERVIEWING WITH COUPLES

Traditional approaches to engaging addicts in the recovery process have emphasized confrontation and challenge, and readiness to change has required acceptance of the addict label (Handmaker & Walters, 2002). Motivational interviewing (MI) takes a very different approach. It accepts people wherever they are in the stages of change and helps them to move forward (Miller & Rollnick, 2002); MI was one of three treatment protocols used in Project MATCH, the large multisite, multimethod study matching particular patients to specific treatments hypothesized to suit them best (Project MATCH, 1997). Although the hypotheses regarding matching were not supported in the study, MI was demonstrated to have substantial effect on alcoholic participants in only four sessions with outcomes comparable to the other forms of treatment. A thorough review of the research evidence for various adaptations of MI may be found in Burke, Arkowitz, and Dunn (2002).

The essence of MI is a collaborative therapeutic relationship that avoids authoritarian approaches in order to emphasize exploration and support instead of confrontation or argument (Miller & Rollnick, 2002). In essence, MI is based on a view of human nature that seeks to elicit the best within a person. It draws out the motivation existing within the addict to facilitate change. The therapist does not try to force a label or a diagnosis on the addict in order to compel consideration of the problem; the therapist does not argue with the addict about the reality of the problem. Responsibility for change remains entirely with the addict.

There are four principles that guide the transition from general approach to specific clinical practice: (1) express empathy, (2) develop discrepancy, (3) roll with resistance, and (4) support self-efficacy (Miller & Rollnick, 2002, p. 36). Empathy involves acceptance through careful reflective listening and recognition that ambivalence about change is common. Developing discrepancy includes increasing awareness of the difference between the current conditions and the person's desires or goals; MI is focused and directed, it does not simply follow the addict anywhere, but it brings him or her back to consideration of the addictive behaviors that brought the person to therapy. Rolling with resistance means that the therapist must not be the one pushing for change while the addict adopts the resistance or withdrawal position. The therapist avoids becoming the problem solver in order to facilitate problem solving by the addict. Supporting self-efficacy suggests that the therapist plays a significant role by believing that the person is capable of change and communicating that belief to the addict.

In fact, MI has been adapted for use in couples therapy because research has indicated that inclusion of a partner improves retention in treatment and overall treatment outcomes (Burke, Vassilev, Kantchelov, & Zweben, 2002; Zweben, 1991). Burke, Vassilev, et al. suggest that traditional MI often does not take the social context into account. They note that the positive effects of an MI session may be canceled out if the person returns home to a partner who is confronting and demanding. Inclusion of the partner enhances the implementation of MI factors in the clinical hour and extends the MI factors into the real world. In therapy, for instance, a partner may assist the therapist in developing discrepancy by providing information unavailable to the therapist about the behavior of the addict and its impact on marital and family relations. Later, the partner may encourage self-efficacy with supportive, positive comments about incidents that the addict has handled well. This approach recognizes the systemic nature of resistance and change, and utilizes the system to influence movement toward change. Often, a pattern develops in a couple's relationship that serves to reinforce the addictive behavior; MI may turn that around to create an interpersonal dynamic that facilitates change by helping the couple to utilize MI concepts in their relationship (Burke, Vassilev, et al.). The version of MI used in Project MATCH included the partner or significant other in at least one-half of the intervention sessions (Project MATCH, 1997).

Harm reduction is an approach that meshes well with MI. It avoids the typical focus in substance abuse treatment on all-or-nothing goals (abstinence or relapse) and treatment outcome assessments (any substance use may be considered treatment failure). Although abstinence may be an appropriate goal for some, others may not be ready or able to maintain abstinence if it is advocated as the only acceptable outcome (Barrett & Marlatt, 1999). Inability to reduce use may convince some of the need for abstinence. Harm reduction accepts the person, wherever he is in the stages of change, and seeks to assist him through the process. It includes the biopsychosocial context of the addictive behavior and seeks to help the addict understand the interactions between the addictive behavior and other life problems.

When Rick came for the initial couples session, I used techniques from MI to engage him in the process. He reported that he knew he had a problem with drugs and alcohol, but he didn't think it was a "big deal." He indicated that he didn't really use "that much." We discussed his reasons for identifying use as a problem, and one of the things he mentioned was the impact on his wife and children. I asked Liz to comment on her perspective of the problem, knowing that we had practiced how to do so in our earlier, individual sessions. She recounted positive times with Rick when he was clean and sober, and then gave a couple of examples of times that his use had been difficult for her. She did not demand that he stop using. Rick seemed to receive her input well. I asked him if there were other reasons he thought his substance use was a problem, and he discussed some problems at work and his DUI incident. To avoid conflict at home about prior substance use, I asked Rick and Liz to use therapy sessions as a controlled environment for any further discussion of past use.

ASSESSMENT AND DIAGNOSIS

When partners participate in treatment, they can be a helpful source of information about the amount of substance consumed, the topographical characteristics of consumption (rapidity, frequency, presentation of the drug for consumption), the social context, and typical locations of use. Meyers et al. (2002) uniformly found significant correlation between partner reports of addict drug use and employment attendance, as well as other factors, and addict self-report after entering treatment. For reports to be accurate, it is necessary that the partner have regular contact with the addict for the period reported (typically they are living together and the partner regularly observes the behavior of the addict). If the couple is separated and does not have consistent contact, reports may not reflect actual behavior (Miller, Meyers, & Tonigan, 1999). The presence of the partner provides a collateral report on use, to balance any desire by the addict to conceal or minimize use. For instance, when asked how much alcohol he drank on a typical Saturday, one man indicated that he consumed "a couple." When his wife reacted in disbelief, he clarified that he drank "a couple of 12 packs." Another man indicated that he would have one or two drinks each night when he came home from work. His wife clarified that he mixed his own drinks and that he poured alcohol from the bottle into a tumbler, so that each drink actually contained three to four shots of alcohol. The primary caution regarding partner collateral reports arises when marital separation or divorce is at hand, or a partner is preparing for a child custody contest and wants to clearly identify the substance abuse problems of the spouse for legal benefit.

Traditional psychological assessment instruments may be useful at the initiation of treatment of the addict for evidence of addictive behavior or addictive potential. The results of addict assessment assist the therapist in determination of the intensity of the problem and they may facilitate treatment discussion of standardized results that suggest admission of behavior more extreme than that of most people. When discussed in a friendly, explanatory manner, the addict may begin to recognize that his behavior is not in the normal range.

For example, the Millon Clinical Multiaxial Inventory (MCMI-III) has alcohol and drug scales that are based on the substance use disorder criteria in the *Diagnostic and Statistical Manual of Mental Disorders* (*DSM-IV-TR;* American Psychiatric Association, 2000) and personality characteristics that have been found associated with substance use disorders (Millon,

Davis, & Millon; 1997). Questions contain obvious substance use content, so responses usually indicate admission of the behavior. Questions regarding relationship functioning are included (e.g., "My use of so-called illegal drugs has led to family arguments" and "I have an alcohol problem that has made difficulties for me and my family"). The Minnesota Multiphasic Personality Inventory-2 (MMPI-2) has three scales that specifically assess addiction issues, the MacAndrew Alcoholism-Revised (MAC-R) Scale (one of the most researched addiction measures that was originally intended to assess alcoholism but is now understood to assess more general addiction elements), the Addiction Potential Scale, and the Addiction Admission Scale (Weed, Butcher, McKenna, & Ben-Porath, 1992). Although each of these measures has limitations and qualifications (e.g., the MAC-R has an extremely high false positive rate for women in some groups and African American men; Greene, 2000), they do provide standardized information that can be combined with partner report and addict report to determine the intensity of the substance use problem. In addition, when administered to both partners, they provide other information that can be useful in couples therapy (e.g., personality factors). I have found that addicts and partners are usually willing to complete psychological assessments if they are introduced in a nonthreatening manner.

   Once an addict has admitted a problem with substance use and indicated a desire to improve, completion of a thorough substance use history can facilitate accurate assessment of the problem. The history notes date of earliest use, historical and current frequency of use, route of administration, environmental circumstances (i.e., solitary or social use, locations), and *DSM* criteria questions. A genogram and family history of substance use provide a systemic context. The addict and the partner can contribute information to the history to ensure accuracy. This information helps identify factors that are important in relapse prevention once reduced usage or sobriety is achieved. For the therapist, complete information may allow establishment of a *DSM-IV-TR* diagnosis, even if that diagnosis is not used to confront or pressure the addict. Diagnosis facilitates an understanding of the difference in intensity and the implications for treatment prognosis across the spectrum from social or habitual use to substance abuse and substance dependence. Although MI advocates often eschew labels, I have found that *DSM* terminology can be used to help addicts explore the problem in light of established standards for designation of a problem, when they are ready for such information (i.e., contemplation stage or change state). It is also helpful to distinguish the level of problematic behavior between different drugs used to focus treatment (e.g., it is common for a person to use multiple drugs, although only meeting *DSM* criteria for select drugs; alternatively, it is possible to diagnose more severe dependence on one drug and less severe abuse on another). The key issue appears to be therapist behavior; if the therapist uses the information in a demanding, confrontational manner, he may elicit the same addict withdrawal pattern found in some couples relationships (Shoham et al., 1998). If the therapist uses the substance history and the *DSM* diagnostic criteria as information for understanding, he may facilitate addict motivation. This type of feedback is similar to an MI technique called the "Drinker's Check-Up" that has been found to be effective in motivating addicts to change (Handmaker & Walters, 2002).

Physiological assessment of substance use is often employed in substance abuse treatment. If the addict accepts random screening as part of a movement toward sobriety, it can provide additional incentive to the addict and reassurance to the partner. Medical laboratories may be utilized, but there are also inexpensive screening kits that can be used at home or in the treatment office to provide basic clean or dirty results when use is suspected. The addict may agree, in advance, to allow the partner to request a screen whenever the partner suspects use. Therapist introduction of screening only after the addict has entered the action stage of change may avoid addict resistance. The couple can role-play the transaction in therapy to avoid unnecessary implementation problems. Refusal to complete the screen is agreed, in advance as a ground rule, as admission of use.

In the first session, I asked Rick if we could review his lifetime use of alcohol and drugs to get the big picture. He was open to this, and I used a drug use history form I had developed to detail his use over the years and currently. Liz jumped in several times to provide information. I asked questions that reflected the *DSM* criteria for abuse and dependence, but I didn't talk about any diagnosis at this point. Instead, we discussed the social, employment, and legal complications he noted when responding to the questions. It was clear from his comments that gathering the information raised his consciousness regarding the problem. He mentioned that he might try to "cut down," and I reflected this movement toward change back to him by saying, "So you're thinking that it might be a good idea to reduce your use to address some of these difficulties we've been talking about," and he agreed. Toward the end of the first session, I introduced the idea of psychological assessment, suggesting that it might help me help them. Both partners agreed to complete the MCMI-III immediately after the session, since it only takes about 30 minutes to complete. Rick agreed to return the following week and "see how it goes" after that. I explained my policy requiring sobriety at the time of the session, and Rick agreed to submit to screening on demand and to assume financial responsibility for sessions that could not be billed to insurance if cancelled due to substance use on the day of sessions.

BEHAVIORAL COUPLES THERAPY

One model of couples therapy for addiction that has demonstrated effectiveness is behavioral couples therapy (BCT; Epstein & McCrady, 1998; O'Farrell & Fals-Stewart, 2000). The term BCT is somewhat of a misnomer, in that although the focus is on behavior modification, BCT includes cognitive and relationship (affective) elements to improve initiation and maintenance of behavioral change; BCT seeks to improve relationship factors that increase the likelihood of abstinence, including partner rewards for improvement in the addict and improved relationship communication skills that decrease the risk of relapse. O'Farrell and Fals-Stewart review the typical elements of the treatment, including a daily sobriety contract (stated by the addict, supported and recorded by the partner, "one day at a time"), several assignments that develop positive interaction and relationship factors that enhance sobriety (e.g., shared rewarding activities, "catch your partner doing something nice," caring day), and relapse prevention. Communication skills training include listening, reflection, accurate empathy, and recognition that understanding does not require agreement. A common communication assignment involves three to four 15-minute sessions per week, each addressing a specific problem in the relationship. Couples agree not to threaten divorce when in conflict, and they commit to complete the assignments designed to incorporate skills into daily life (Rotunda, Alter, & O'Farrell, 2001; Rotunda & O'Farrell, 1997).

Research has shown this intervention to be more effective than individual treatment in reducing use, increasing abstinence, improving relationships, benefiting psychosocial functioning of children in the home, and lowering risk of divorce in couples facing the challenges of an addictive behavior (Epstein & McCrady, 1998; Kelley & Fals-Stewart, 2002; O'Farrell & Fals-Stewart, 2000). In addition, cost outcomes analysis studies have demonstrated that BCT evidenced substantially lower social costs, and it was more cost-effective per $100 spent on treatment than an individual model of treatment (Fals-Stewart, O'Farrell, & Birchler, 1997).

In addition, BCT is amenable to treatment positioning subsequent to motivational interviewing. For instance, MI may be utilized to engage the couple in treatment for the addictive behavior and to provide an underlying approach that locates responsibility for change in the addict and the partner. When the addict enters the preparation for action and/or the action stages, BCT steps in. It provides a framework of tried and true methods that the therapist may present to the couple for consideration and implementation.

When Rick and Liz came for the next session, it was clear that he was ready to consider ways to change his addictive behavior. The problems at work and an upcoming court date for his DUI incident convinced him he needed to do something. We discussed the idea of a daily sobriety commitment and how to structure the relationship interaction around it. Liz was excited to learn that Rick would ask her to express her fears and concerns about his possible use as part of the daily sobriety commitment, and that he would try to reassure her. Rick was willing to try this plan, although he was not yet willing to commit to complete abstinence in the future.

Because it had been a long time since they had gone out together, I introduced the idea of finding mutually satisfactory activities that they would do as a couple, and we began to develop a list of things they might do in the coming weeks. It was clarified that these activities should not include substances, and Liz volunteered not to consume any alcohol herself in order to help Rick maintain his sobriety. Rick and Liz had a history of arguing a lot, so we spent the last few minutes of the session discussing the idea of trying to understand the other person's ideas without necessarily agreeing with them. Two recent issues were raised in session, and we used those issues to model this type of communication.

Over the next few sessions, I worked to establish a positive therapeutic alliance with this couple through open and supportive interaction. It was clear that they felt the need for a safe environment in which to process some of the challenges of the week.

DOMESTIC VIOLENCE AND ADDICTION

Domestic violence (DV) is regularly linked with substance abuse, especially in couples where the addict is the male. In two studies, approximately 60% of alcoholics had been violent toward their female partner in the year prior to treatment (O'Farrell & Fals-Stewart, 2000). Substances often lower inhibitory mechanisms and increase volatility, so interpersonal relations are more likely to contain violence. Prevalence of DV has been found to be twice as much in addiction treatment groups than in the general population (Fals-Stewart, Kashdan, O'Farrell, & Birchler, 2002). The likelihood of violence increases substantially on days when the male is using substances; one study found that for men entering a DV treatment program, male physical aggression toward the partner was "more than 8 times higher on days when men drank than on days of no alcohol consumption" and 11 times more likely in similar circumstances for men entering an alcoholism treatment program (p. 87). A national DV survey found that male partner drug use was the most significant variable separating female victims of DV from women who had not been victimized, and another study reported greater than 80% experience of at least one DV episode in the prior year when a polysubstance abusing male entered treatment (see Fals-Stewart et al., 2002). Epstein and McCrady (1998) note the connection between aggression and sexual functioning in alcoholic couples, suggesting that these two areas should be included in couples therapy for addiction.

The high coincidence of substance abuse and DV suggests that treatment for addictive behaviors should include treatment for DV. Research on BCT (see above) indicates that couples therapy for addictive behaviors that targets substance abuse and relationship dynamics can have a significant effect on decreasing male aggression against the female partner. In the two studies that had found about 60% incidence of DV in the year prior to treatment, male-to-female violence was significantly lower for all couples in the two years after BCT treatment (19% to 28%) and nearly eliminated for those couples when the addict was abstinent during that period (O'Farrell & Fals-Stewart, 2000). A subsequent study compared BCT to individual treatment for substance abuse and found that BCT significantly reduced the percentage of couples who reported DV from 43% pretreatment to 18% at one year after treatment, while there was no significant pretreatment-post-treatment difference in DV for the individual treatment couples. This study also found that the key variables that mediated reduction in DV were relationship improvement and decreased frequency of severe use (Fals-Stewart et al., 2002). These findings suggest that BCT, as a couples treatment that focuses not only on reduction of substance use but on relationship factors as well, addresses factors that reduce DV.

Several sessions later, we discussed the sensitive issue of sexual relations, and Liz explained that she still had resentment about Rick's behavior toward her while using. His level of aggression in the initiation of sex had left Liz feeling that she had to engage when she really wanted nothing to do with him. Rick had a difficult time with this discussion, because he did not recollect that his behavior was problematic. He was upset that Liz did not seem interested in sex now that he was in therapy. I tried to facilitate his understanding of her feelings by asking Rick to think about how he feels when someone forces him to do something, but it was hard for him to empathize with her. Finally, he indicated that he would not initiate sex if he was using or drinking, and we discussed how Liz might maintain her boundaries when he used. It was clear that this area would need more work.

COUPLE INTERACTION WITH TWELVE-STEP GROUPS

Participation in a twelve-step (TS) group for addictive behavior is a well-known stand-alone treatment and a common adjunct to other interventions (Rotunda & O'Farrell, 1997). I have found Alcoholics Anonymous, Cocaine Anonymous, Narcotics Anonymous, and the other drug-specific manifestations of the program to be a helpful ancillary support to couples therapy for addiction. Twelve-step facilitation (TSF) is an intervention designed to encourage participation in TS meetings, abstinence, and change in the social context of use for the addict. It was one of three treatments included in Project MATCH, and it was found to be more effective than motivation enhancement and cognitive-behavior therapy for addicts who had lower levels of psychopathology (no dual diagnosis; TS groups focus exclusively on substance abuse) and more effective than motivational enhancement for addicts in social contexts that supported use, because TS groups provide a replacement network of new friends who are working the program and conduct clean and sober social events (Humphreys, 1999; Nowinski, 2002). TSF is a structured approach to guiding an addict into involvement in the program. It requires therapist awareness of TS program practices and distinctives. The therapist prepares the addict for participation by encouraging acceptance of the substance problem, developing a lifestyle contract that delineates people and circumstances that support recovery or create a risk for relapse, surrender to the need for assistance from others and the possibility of recovery, and action steps in the TS program (attending meetings, working the steps, and finding a sponsor; see Nowinski for a thorough review of TSF). Other research provided initial indication that participation in TS groups increases a variety of common therapeutic factors found in other models to reduce substance use (active coping, increased self-efficacy) and that TS affiliation predicted commitment to abstinence (Morgenstern, Labouvie, McCrady, Kahler, & Frey, 1997).

Twelve-step groups welcome the newcomer and provide substantial support for people in the early stages of recovery. "Keep coming back" is a common refrain and encouragement to give the program a chance. However, two concerns may impact referral to TS meetings: commitment to abstinence and acceptance of the addict label. Several of the treatment models we have introduced recognize the benefit of engaging the addict in a non-threatening and encouraging manner that does not require abstinence in order to initiate therapy or as a certain goal of therapy. Most TS groups, on the other hand, are quite explicit in the ultimate expectation of abstinence. Meetings are geared around those who have found themselves to be "powerless" over the substance and cannot control their use; anything less is considered a failure to work the program, because the groups are designed around sobriety, including statement of a sobriety date and recognition of sobriety milestones (one month, two months, one year, and so on). In addition, clear personal identification as an alcoholic or addict is fundamental to the TS and incorporated into the familiar personal introduction at meetings. Individuals who continue to use will be welcomed for a while, and those who relapse but return to state a desire for sobriety are welcomed, but those who want to cut back only are likely to find that their sponsor will "fire them" until they are ready for abstinence. In clinical practice, those who have met the criteria for substance abuse, but not substance dependence, may be able to reduce their use to a subclinical level without abstinence. These individuals are probably not appropriate for referral to TS groups, certainly not without adequate preparation for the reaction they are likely to receive, because it may undermine therapy.

Individuals who are abstinent and cognizant of their addiction may benefit from the features of TS groups. The groups provide peer support, testimonials, one-on-one sponsors, substance-free activities (e.g., sober New Year's Eve parties), and a worldwide network of meetings. These features can augment couples therapy.

The inclusion of spirituality is a central feature to TS groups that originated from Alcoholics Anonymous (AA; Nowinski, 2002). Steps 2 and 3 specifically refer to God and the need to turn one's will over to a "higher power" as part of the recovery process (AA, 1976). Recognition of a higher power reduces one's individualism and provides an awakening to resources beyond oneself to assist in the recovery process. Although, for some, the higher power may be the TS group, for many it reflects more traditional religious perspectives on God and spirituality. The therapist needs to be willing to interact around spirituality with the addict (Nowinski). However, many therapists are not religious and are disinclined to include spirituality or religion in psychotherapy. Pargament (1997) provides substantial evidence for the role of religion in coping with difficult life challenges in order to encourage therapists to include spirituality in treatment. It is possible to refer nonreligious addicts to Rational Recovery, a comparable program that deliberately excludes the spirituality in most TS groups.

One final aspect of TS programs may interfere with couples therapy. There is sometimes a strong attitude that only the addict can work his or her program, and some sponsors may mandate practices that have negative consequences for couple and family relationships ("it's a selfish program"). I have found that it is important to balance the focus on recovery with an awareness that the addict lives in a system that also impacts potential relapse and recovery.

Rick initially resisted the idea of going to a TS meeting. "I'm not like those losers" was his reaction to sitting with a group of addicts in a meeting. We spent time in therapy discussing the program and preparing him for possible participation. One crucial factor involved determination of his addiction. He met the criteria for methamphetamine dependence and alcohol abuse; as we discussed his history, it was clear that his life became unmanageable when speed entered the picture. Narcotics Anonymous seemed like the right fit for Rick, and he eventually agreed to visit some meetings in hope of finding a "home meeting" (one where he would go regularly to build relationships) in which he felt comfortable. I explained the different types of meetings (speaker's meetings, participation meetings, step meetings, etc.) and encouraged him to identify himself as a newcomer and to interact with others at the coffee break.

Rick was actually excited when he returned a week later to announce that after two "bad" meetings, he had found a "great" meeting and that he met two men who were upper managers for their companies. He identified with them and they were not "losers" at all. One had several years of sobriety, and he agreed to sponsor Rick while he got involved in the program. The sponsor and his wife hosted a couples meeting and Liz was glad that Rick wanted to attend. She liked the spirituality in the program, because it matched her heritage of growing up with the Catholic church in her Latino family. We discussed the possible role of spirituality in recovery.

PERSONALITY FACTORS IN COUPLES ADDICTION THERAPY

Personality style or disorder can impact couples therapy for substance abuse. Rounsaville et al. (1998) found that 57% of substance abuse patients had a dual diagnosis personality disorder, usually from Cluster B (Antisocial, Borderline, Histrionic, or Narcissistic). On the MMPI-2, high scorers on the Addiction Potential Scale are likely to be "angry, resentful, upset, and generally distressed" (Greene, 2000, p. 255), common features in these personality disorders. On the MCMI-III, certain personality scales tend to be elevated when the B (alcohol) or T (drugs) scales are the highest clinical elevations, including Cluster B disorders as well as Avoidant, Schizoid, Compulsive, Aggressive/Sadistic, and Passive-Aggressive (Choca & Van Denburg, 1997).

Referral to TS meetings is especially appropriate to narcissistic and antisocial addicts, because these individuals struggle to admit that they are powerless or that they need any higher power than themselves. On the other hand, dependent personalities often manifest the first three steps before they ever attend a TS meeting.

Strong personality style or personality disorders may manifest themselves systemically in a couple. In my experience, an addict with a Narcissistic or Antisocial personality disorder is likely to be attracted to a partner with Histrionic, Dependent, or Borderline personality, because these styles are complementary to the addict's style. In couple's therapy, these dynamics impact the application of interventions and may need individual or couples treatment to keep the addiction therapy on track.

Rick had an elevated score on the MCMI-III Narcissism Scale, and Liz had an elevated score on the Dependent and Histrionic Scales. My clinical impressions and clinical history confirmed these scores, although both individuals had only moderate characteristics of the disorders. Rick had been attracted to Liz because of her gregarious style, and her willingness to go along with his desires. Liz liked it when Rick took charge and made her feel special. After marriage, though, they had settled into a pattern where Rick did what he wanted, and expected Liz to accommodate. Liz felt neglected, and she disliked Rick's increasing drug use, but she felt powerless to stop him. In therapy, I found that I needed to challenge Rick to empathize with Liz, and I had to factor his narcissistic reactions into planned interventions. Liz needed substantial support to state her real feelings and concerns to Rick. I met separately, on occasion, with each of them to address personality issues so that we could keep couples therapy for the addictive behavior on track.

FORGIVENESS AND RECONCILIATION

Couples therapy for addiction often requires relationship reconciliation once the addictive behavior is reduced or eliminated for a time. The idea of addiction recovery as a panacea for the relationship is a myth. Partners may have focused so much on the substance abuse or dependence that they begin to believe that if it could only be removed or resolved, everything would be wonderful. In my experience, significant reduction in substance use or sobriety and participation in a recovery process may exacerbate tensions in the couples' relationship after the honeymoon period ends.

A primary factor that increases tension is the need to clean up the past. Addicts often commit various errors of commission and omission while using. Any therapist working regularly with addicts has heard numerous horror stories of situations in which the addict's behavior negatively impacted his or her partner and others. Often, addicts have little or no recollection of these events because they were under the influence of drugs. Partners may have stored up memories and emotions over a period of years, with no way to discuss these incidents with the addict. Now, as the addictive behavior improves, partners may need or desire to address the past. They are usually looking for understanding of the hurt inflicted and an apology by the addict in order to restore trust in the relationship. One wife described a holiday extended family meal at a restaurant and the loud and obnoxious behavior of her husband as he interacted with her relatives. The husband drank excessively and eventually, after an agitated encounter with another family member, vomited on the table. She was mortified, and she was reminded of that incident every year at that holiday. Her husband did not even remember the occasion and had little tolerance for her strong sentiment ("When is she going to get over this? It happened a long time ago."). Conflict over past incidents may trigger relapse if not handled properly, so couple interactions about the past are best contained in psychotherapy sessions that facilitate address of the issues with limits and mediation between the partner and the addict (O'Farrell & Fals-Stewart, 2000).

Therapeutic facilitation of forgiveness and reconciliation for these past events is an important part of couples therapy for addiction. Smedes (1984) suggests that forgiveness that leads to relationship reconciliation is multifaceted, involving an admission of the behavior that caused harm to the other, sincere apology for the harm, and commitment not to harm the other in the same manner again. These steps are important for relationship reconciliation when there is a history of problems due to substance abuse.

Eventually the relationship was stable enough to process Liz's feelings about Rick's aggression during sex when he was using. Rick was far enough along in his recovery process that he was more open to hearing her feelings and trying to empathize with them. Although he had apologized before, he had been cursory, and Liz felt he had lacked real recognition of the hurt inflicted. Now, things were different, for Rick seemed to really get it, and he made a commitment not to ever coerce her into sexual relations again. Liz was able to release some of her resentment, and they noted they had a positive sexual encounter when they came back the next week. More work on the relationship would be needed to strengthen this area of interaction.

RELAPSE PREVENTION FROM A COUPLES PERSPECTIVE

Relapse prevention (RP; Marlatt & Gordon, 1985) treatment involves strategies to prevent relapse to an addictive behavior. It may be situated in the action and maintenance stages of change because it seeks to reinforce behavioral change and prevent minor lapses in the recovery process from becoming full-blown relapses (Irvin, Bowers, Dunn, & Wang, 1999; Rawson, Obert, McCann, & Marinelli-Casey, 1993). In addition, RP includes identification of high-risk situations, recognition of warning signs for impending relapse, increasing self-efficacy by development of coping responses to high-risk situations, and avoiding the abstinence violation effect (decreased self-efficacy after relapse) by focusing on return to prevention (Rawson et al., 1993). This treatment has demonstrated effectiveness; McCrady (2000) indicates that it now meets the criteria for efficacious treatments established by an APA Division 12 task force and a meta-analysis (Irvin et al.) supports the overall effectiveness of RP in decreasing substance use (especially alcohol and polysubstance abuse) and increasing psychosocial functioning. The meta-analysis found RP in couples therapy for alcohol was effective, but there were only two studies in this format, so further research is needed. However, initial results indicated that RP was effective in all types of treatment modalities.

The presence of a partner can assist in identification of high-risk situations, because often the partner recognizes cues and attitude changes before the addict. However, it is important for the addict to give permission to the partner to point out these warning signs; this avoids any perception of criticism or demand. In addition, the partner may support the self-efficacy of the addict by complimenting and supporting him as a sober companion in real-life situations that involve risk. On the other hand, perceived criticism from the partner may undermine self-efficacy and lead to relapse (Fals-Stewart, O'Farrell, & Hooley, 2001), so it is important to coach the partner in supportive behaviors in the RP process.

Rick had cut down significantly on alcohol, and he was abstinent for methamphetamine after about four months in couples therapy. However, as we discussed relapse prevention, it was clear that he was more vulnerable to using speed when he was drinking because he had often mixed use of the two drugs. We discussed the potential danger of drinking alcohol and identified it as a risk factor. This was a tough one for Rick, because he truly enjoyed an occasional drink, and the idea of total abstinence was hard to handle. Liz suggested that perhaps it would be okay for him to have one or two only when around her, because he had agreed not to use drugs in her presence. This seemed like a good compromise for the present, and one that Rick eagerly accepted.

I asked Rick and Liz to identify other people, places, and circumstances that raised temptation to use speed. Together, they constructed a list of about 15 entries and we spent time discussing how to avoid or manage each person or situation. Rick decided that there were a couple of guys that he simply could not associate with any longer, much to Liz's delight. New Year's Eve was coming up, and they decided together to attend a Narcotics Anonymous party being held at a regional attraction.

Liz noticed that when Rick had to interact with his father he became stressed and often used drugs soon after those interactions. We spent considerable time role-playing interaction with his father, until Rick felt he could handle it and not let his father get to him. Finally, we discussed what to do if Rick did use, and how to avoid a full relapse. Rick had collected 10 phone numbers of NA people to call if he was facing any temptation (a common practice), and I clarified that although we wanted to avoid a lapse, if it occurred, we would use it as a learning experience. This is a delicate issue, because I did not want to appear to endorse lapses, but it is important to avoid a major break in therapy if one occurs.

SPECIAL POPULATION ISSUES

ETHNIC DIVERSITY: VARIATIONS IN ASSESSMENT AND TREATMENT

Increased research attention is being given to the evidence of substance abuse intervention effectiveness with ethnic minority populations (Mercado, 2000; Rotunda et al., 2001). Several initial findings relate to interventions reviewed here.

Project MATCH results have been analyzed by self-reported Hispanic/ Latino identification. In general, Latino participant outcomes paralleled non-Latino outcomes with CBT and MET interventions, but had lower outcomes for the TSF intervention (primarily more drinking per occasion than non-Hispanic Whites). Results confirmed existing findings that Latino treatment-seeking alcoholics are less likely to attend AA than similar non-Latinos, but found that those Latino participants who did attend TS groups reported higher involvement in the groups (Arroyo, Miller, & Tonigan, 2003). They attribute higher participation to the influence of Latino spirituality and religiosity, a component of the culture, and suggest that the inclusion of religion should be explored further for Latino interventions. Referral to TS groups may require more sophisticated mechanisms that reduce barriers to Latino participation (Tonigan, Connors, & Miller, 1998).

A review by Tonigan et al. (1998) suggests that studies vary in estimates of Latino and African American selection of TS treatment. One study of general populations found that 12% of Latinos are likely to attend AA, versus 5% for African American and European Americans; another found no ethnic preference for AA or other treatment among alcoholics. Latino membership in AA is about 4%, and African American about 5%.

The community reinforcement model has been adapted for use in New Mexico with a Native American tribe. The model is capable of inclusion of clan ties and traditional or religious practices in this community. Early results are promising (Miller, Meyers, & Hiller-Sturmhöfel, 1999).

BCT research at the Harvard Families and Addiction Program is currently developing a sufficient sample to assess the relationship of minority group status to outcome variables (Rotunda et al., 2001).

Mercado (2000) reviews substance abuse and treatment among Asian Americans. She notes that substance abuse is increasing in this stereotyped "model minority" population, but that little research has been done, and they disappear within the "other" demographic category in many studies. She suggests that systemic models that value marital and family dynamics are best for this group, but little clear research demonstrating evidence of effectiveness exists.

Gay, Lesbian, and Bisexual Couples

There are a variety of issues that differentiate gay, lesbian, bisexual, or transgender (GLBT) couples from heterosexual couples in substance abuse treatment. Although GLBT addicts have many of the same issues as other addicts, they often face many additional concerns (e.g., societal stigmas, discrimination, coming out dynamics). *A Provider's Introduction to Substance Abuse Treatment for Lesbian, Gay, Bisexual, and Transgender Individuals* (U.S. Department of Health and Human Services, 2001) surveys many issues, including therapist competence in treating GLBT clients, treatment accessibility, and specific clinical issues with each group. Further research is needed to determine the effectiveness of the couple interventions reviewed here for GLBT couples and possible treatment modifications that may be beneficial.

Dual Addiction: Both Partners in Recovery

The most common relationship pattern is for couples to contain a substance-abusing male and a nonabusing female partner. If the female abuses substances, it is likely that her partner does as well. Couples in which the female abuses substances, but the male partner does not, are a minority (Winters et al., 2002). Because many research projects exclude couples in which both are addicts, there is little evidence for treatment effectiveness with such couples.

When both partners are addicts, the dynamics are intensified, and the therapeutic process is complicated. At each stage of the change process, both partners must be considered and the different motivating factors addressed. Treatment may be longer and differences in motivation, support system, and both providing and receiving support have to be navigated (Epstein & McCrady, 2002). Couples therapy provides a context that allows the unique interaction of factors between the two addicts to be considered in concert.

SUMMARY

This chapter presents a process model of couples therapy for addiction that includes assistance for the addict's partner designed to help the partner and encourage addict participation in therapy, motivational techniques to engage the addict in the change process, assessment of the addictive behavior to facilitate change, behavioral couples therapy to improve the relationship and reduce or eliminate the addictive behavior, and relapse prevention to maintain change. Therapists who provide treatment for addictions may utilize these interventions to augment or replace existing individual treatments, based on research effectiveness outcomes. The case study presented here demonstrated outcomes comparable to the research outcomes, but interventions do not always go smoothly or obtain positive outcomes at each stage of the process. In some cases, more intensive out-patient or in-patient treatment for the addictive behavior may be needed.

Rick now had six months of sobriety for methamphetamine and his alcohol consumption was minimal. Rick and Liz were communicating better, and major resentment from past behaviors no longer clouded their interaction. Liz was behaving more assertively, and Rick was trying to understand her feelings more, although it was clear that he still dominated the relationship. Rick attended Narcotics Anonymous at least once a week, and he talked to his sponsor regularly. Both parents indicated that Ricky was demonstrating fewer behavior problems at school, and Martina was less anxious at home. Rick and Liz plan to come to therapy every other week for a while to support the changes they have made.

REFERENCES

Alcoholics Anonymous. (1976). *Alcoholics Anonymous* (3rd ed.). New York: Author.

American Psychiatric Association. (2000). *Diagnostic and statistical manual of mental disorders* (4th ed., text rev.). Washington, DC: Author.

Arroyo, J., Miller, W. R., & Tonigan, J. S. (2003). The influence of Hispanic ethnicity on long-term outcome in three alcohol treatment modalities. *Journal of Studies on Alcohol, 64*, 98.

Barrett, K., & Marlatt, G. A. (1999). Relapse prevention and harm reduction in the treatment of co-occurring addiction and mental health problems. In E. T. Dowd & L. Rugle (Eds.), *Comparative treatments of substance abuse* (pp. 176–192). New York: Springer.

Burke, B. L., Arkowitz, H., & Dunn, C. (2002). The efficacy of motivational interviewing and its adaptations: What we know so far. In W. R. Miller & S. Rollnick (Eds.), *Motivational interviewing* (2nd ed., pp. 217–250). New York: Guilford Press.

Burke, B. L., Vassilev, G., Kantchelov, A., & Zweben, A. (2002). Motivational interviewing with couples. In W. R. Miller & S. Rollnick (Eds.), *Motivational interviewing* (2nd ed., pp. 347–361). New York: Guilford Press.

Choca, J. P., & Van Denburg, E. (1997). *Interpretive guide to the Millon Clinical Multiaxial Inventory.* Washington, DC: American Psychological Association.

Cunningham, J. A., Sobell, L. C., Sobell, M. B., & Kapur, G. (1995). Resolution from alcohol treatment problems with and without treatment: Reasons for change. *Journal of Substance Abuse, 7*(3), 365–372.

DiClemente, C. C., & Velasquez, M. M. (2002). Motivational interviewing and the stages of change. In W. R. Miller & S. Rollnick (Eds.), *Motivational interviewing* (2nd ed., pp. 201–216). New York: Guilford Press.

Epstein, E. E., & McCrady, B. S. (1998). Behavioral couples treatment of alcohol and drug use disorders: Current status and innovations. *Clinical Psychology Review, 18,* 689–711.

Epstein, E. E., & McCrady, B. S. (2002). Couple therapy in the treatment of alcohol problems. In A. S. Gurman & N. S. Jacobson (Eds.), *Clinical handbook of couple therapy* (pp. 597–628). New York: Guilford Press.

Fals-Stewart, W., & Birchler, G. R. (2001). A national survey of the use of couples therapy in substance abuse treatment. *Journal of Substance Abuse Treatment, 20,* 277–283.

Fals-Stewart, W., Kashdan, T. B., O'Farrell, T. J., & Birchler, G. R. (2002). Behavioral couples therapy for drug-abusing patients: Effects on partner violence. *Journal of Substance Abuse Treatment, 22,* 87–96.

Fals-Stewart, W., O'Farrell, T. J., & Birchler, G. R. (1997). Behavioral couples therapy for male substance-abusing patients: A cost outcomes analysis. *Journal of Consulting and Clinical Psychology, 65,* 789–802.

Fals-Stewart, W., O'Farrell, T. J., & Hooley, J. M. (2001). Relapse among married or cohabitating substance-abusing patients: The role of perceived criticism. *Behavior Therapy, 32,* 787–801.

Greene, R. L. (2000). *The MMPI-2: An interpretive manual.* Needham Heights, MA: Allyn & Bacon.

Handmaker, N. S., & Walters, S. T. (2002). Motivational interviewing for initiating change in problem drinking and drug use. In S. G. Hofmann & M. C. Tompson (Eds.), *Treating chronic and severe mental disorders: A handbook of empirically supported interventions* (pp. 215–233). New York: Guilford Press.

Humphreys, K. (1999). Professional interventions that facilitate 12-step self-help group involvement. *Alcohol Research and Health, 23,* 93–98.

Irvin, J. E., Bowers, C. A., Dunn, M. E., & Wang, M. C. (1999). Efficacy of relapse prevention: A meta-analytic review. *Journal of Consulting and Clinical Psychology, 67,* 563–570.

Kelley, M. L., & Fals-Stewart, W. (2002). Couples versus individual-based therapy for alcohol and drug abuse: Effects on children's psychosocial functioning. *Journal of Consulting and Clinical Psychology, 70,* 417–427.

Marlatt, G. A., & Gordon, J. R. (Eds.). (1985). *Relapse prevention: Maintenance strategies in the treatment of addictive behaviors.* New York: Guilford Press.

McCrady, B. S. (2000). Alcohol use disorders and the Division 12 task force of the American Psychological Association. *Psychology of Addictive Behaviors, 14,* 267–276.

Mercado, M. M. (2000). The invisible family: Counseling Asian American substance abusers and their families. *Family Journal: Counseling and Therapy for Couples and Families, 8,* 267–272.

Meyers, R. J., Miller, W. R., Smith, J. E., & Tonigan, J. S. (2002). A randomized trial of two methods for engaging treatment-refusing drug users through concerned significant others. *Journal of Consulting and Clinical Psychology, 70,* 1182–1185.

Miller, W. R., Meyers, R. J., & Hiller-Sturmhöfel, S. (1999). The community-reinforcement approach. *Alcohol Research and Health, 23,* 116–121.

Miller, W. R., Meyers, R. J., & Tonigan, J. S. (1999). Engaging the unmotivated in treatment for alcohol problems: A comparison of three strategies for intervention through family members. *Journal of Consulting and Clinical Psychology, 67,* 688–697.

Miller, W. R., & Rollnick, S. (2002). *Motivational interviewing: Preparing people for change* (2nd ed.). New York: Guilford Press.

Miller, W. R., & Tonigan, J. S. (1996). Assessing drinkers' motivation for change: The stages of change readiness and treatment eagerness scale (SOCRATES). *Psychology of Addictive Behaviors, 10,* 81–89.

Millon, T., Davis, R., & Millon, C. (1997). *MCMI-III manual* (2nd ed.). Minneapolis, MN: National Computer System.

Morgenstern, J., Labouvie, E., McCrady, B. S., Kahler, C. W., & Frey, R. M. (1997). Affiliation with Alcoholics Anonymous after treatment: A study of its therapeutic effects and mechanisms of action. *Journal of Consulting and Clinical Psychology, 65,* 768–777.

Nowinski, J. (2002). Twelve-step facilitation therapy for alcohol problems. In S. G. Hofmann & M. C. Tompson (Eds.), *Treating chronic and severe mental disorders: A handbook of empirically supported interventions* (pp. 258–276). New York: Guilford Press.

O'Farrell, T. J., & Fals-Stewart, W. (2000). Behavioral couples therapy for alcoholism and drug abuse. *Behavior Therapist, 23*(3), 49–54, 70.

Pargament, K. I. (1997). *The psychology of religion and coping: Theory, research, practice.* New York: Guilford Press.

Project MATCH Research Group. (1997). Matching alcoholism treatments to client heterogeneity: Project MATCH posttreatment drinking outcomes. *Journal of Studies on Alcohol, 58,* 7–29.

Rawson, R. A., Obert, J. L., McCann, M. J., & Marinelli-Casey, P. (1993). Relapse prevention strategies in outpatient substance abuse treatment. *Psychology of Addictive Behaviors, 7,* 85–95.

Rotunda, R. J., Alter, J. G., & O'Farrell, T. J. (2001). Behavioral couples therapy for comorbid substance abuse and psychiatric problems. In M. M. MacFarlane (Ed.), *Family therapy and mental health: Innovations in theory and practice* (pp. 289–309). New York: Haworth Clinical Practice Press.

Rotunda, R. J., & O'Farrell, T. J. (1997). Marital and family therapy of alcohol use disorders: Bridging the gap between research and practice. *Professional Psychology: Research and Practice, 28,* 246–252.

Rounsaville, B. J., Kranzler, H. R., Ball, S., Tennen, H., Poling, J., & Triffleman, E. (1998). Personality disorders in substance abusers: Relation to substance abuse. *Journal of Nervous and Mental Diseases, 186,* 78–95.

Shoham, V., Rohrbaugh, M. J., Stickle, T. R., & Jacob, T. (1998). Demand-withdraw couple interaction moderates retention in cognitive-behavioral versus family-systems treatments for alcoholism. *Journal of Family Psychology, 12,* 557–577.

Smedes, L. (1984). *Forgive and forget: Healing the hurts we don't deserve.* San Francisco: Harper & Row.

Steinberg, M. L., Epstein, E. E., McCrady, B. S., & Hirsch, L. S. (1997). Sources of motivation in a couples outpatient alcoholism treatment program. *American Journal of Drug and Alcohol Abuse, 23,* 191–205.

Tonigan, J. S., Connors, G., & Miller, W. R. (1998). Special populations in alcoholics anonymous. *Alcohol Health and Research World, 22,* 281–305.

U.S. Department of Health and Human Services. (2001). *A provider's introduction to substance abuse treatment for lesbian, gay, bisexual, and transgender individuals* (Publication No. 01-3498). Rockville, MD: Author.

Weed, N., Butcher, S., McKenna, T., & Ben-Porath, Y. (1992). New measures for assessing alcohol and drug abuse problems with the MMPI-2: The APS and AAS. *Journal of Personality Assessment, 58,* 389–404.

Winters, J., Fals-Stewart, W., O'Farrell, T. J., Birchler, G. R., & Kelley, M. L. (2002). Behavioral couples therapy for female substance-abusing patients: Effects on substance use and relationship adjustment. *Journal of Consulting and Clinical Psychology, 70,* 344–355.

Yoshioka, M. R., Thomas, E. J., & Ager, R. D. (1992). Nagging and other drinking control efforts of spouses of uncooperative alcohol abusers: Assessment and modification. *Journal of Substance Abuse, 4,* 309–318.

Zweben, A. (1991). Motivational counseling with alcoholic couples. In W. R. Miller & S. Rollnick (Eds.), *Motivational interviewing* (pp. 225–235). New York: Guilford Press.

CHAPTER 19

Infidelity: Theory and Treatment

Don-David Lusterman

LTHOUGH THERE MAY be disagreement about the accuracy of statistical evaluations of the occurrence of infidelity during the course of marriage, there is no doubt that, at least in Western cultures, marriage is based on a contract that pledges both members to be faithful to one another. Marital infidelity occurs when one member of the couple continues to believe that the commitment to monogamy obtains, while the other *secretly* violates it. Many unmarried couples, whether heterosexual, gay, or lesbian, also endorse monogamy as a central relationship value. To the degree that a pledge of faithfulness is the bedrock of a relationship, the discovery of infidelity is a profoundly traumatic event, certainly for the discoverer, and often for the discovered person as well. This chapter focuses on various sorts of long-term extramarital behavior, and excludes very brief involvements, such as one-night stands.

It should be noted that the issue of secrecy lies at the heart of infidelity and that the discovery of the act of infidelity is invariably intensified by the knowledge that one's partner has lied. Perhaps the most frequently asked question following the act of discovery is "Will I ever again be able to trust this person?" Not only is the discoverer's faith in the partner damaged, confidence in the discoverer's ability to perceive untruth is also shaken. For this reason, one barrier to recovery following discovery is the fear that improvement in the relationship may prove, in time, to be a nothing more than a set-up for still more hurt. "What if I come to believe that things are really better, and then discover that my partner is still extramaritally involved?"

There are still other sources of the discoverer's pain. Marriage has a proprietary quality. Many couples feel that they own certain parts of their marriage. For this reason, discoverers report that they feel profoundly violated when they learn that their husband or wife has shared private information about their parents or siblings, their children or themselves. A couple may appear to be in the process of recovery from a discovered infidelity, until the discoverer becomes aware that their song has been shared with someone else by the offending partner.

The discovered partner may also experience trauma. Although some extramarital involvements are nothing more than a final chapter in a marriage that is irreparably broken, many are not, and the ambivalence that the discovered partner has suppressed is thrust into prominence by the act of discovery, or even the fear of impending discovery. When an extramaritally involved individual comes to therapy voluntarily to explore the infidelity, it is often because of the fear that discovery is imminent. This impending crisis may force the affair-involved person to face the ambivalence that often underlies affairs. It is not unusual for the patient to say something like "I thought I had found my soul mate, and my marriage was over. Now I'm just not sure. I don't know what I want now." It is important for the therapist to point out how often, in the throes of an affair, people imagine qualities in their affair partner that are not so much a reality as they are a projection of needs and wishes that they have felt were unfulfilled in their marriages. When people end affairs, they often report later that they can now see how illusory the affair was. It is also important that the affair-involved person understand that there is no way to appraise the real potential of the marriage while the affair continues.

FREQUENCY OF MARITAL INFIDELITY

Popular literature would lead one to believe that everybody does it. For this reason, some authorities (Finzi, 1989) find it hard to understand why discovery is reported to cause such pain. Kinsey's studies (Kinsey, Pomeroy, & Martin, 1948; Kinsey, Pomeroy, Martin, & Gebhard, 1953) estimated that 50% of husbands and 26% of wives engaged in extramarital sex (EMS) at some point in their marriage. Glass and Wright (1992) found that 41% of men and 25% of women had at least one EMS experience. Greeley (1991), however, estimates that fewer than 10% of all marriage partners have been unfaithful. Smith conducts an annual full-probability survey through the National Opinion Research Center. In 1993, he reported that roughly 15% of individuals had sexual relations with a person other than their spouse, including 21% of men and 12% of women. His 2002 survey supports the earlier findings (T. Smith, personal communication, September 11, 2003). Because this statistic is part of a full-probability study with a very large sample (over 1,200 respondents), and has been replicated often, it appears to be a particularly robust finding.

It should be noted that, regardless of the estimated frequency of EMS, almost all studies find that men are considerably more likely to engage in EMS than are women. One possible explanation is that many of the men's EMS may have been with prostitutes. It is well known that many more men than women frequent prostitutes and that each prostitute services many clients per day. There is anecdotal evidence that many more women seek treatment about their partners' infidelity than do men, although there is also anecdotal evidence that the ratio is beginning to equalize. Chances are that this is a function of a gender-based power inequality and that the change in the ratio is still another evidence of changes in gender roles.

TYPOLOGY

Humphrey (1987) proposed a schema for the description of infidelity, using six criteria. I have added a seventh, and also suggest that it is more useful to conceptualize infidelity in terms of EMI (extramarital involvement) rather than the more specific EMS (extramarital sex). Here are Humphrey's somewhat modified descriptors:

1. Time
2. Degree of emotional involvement
3. Sexual intercourse or abstinence
4. Secret or not
5. Single or bilateral EMS (or EMI)
6. Heterosexual or homosexual
7. Number of EMS (or EMI) partners (Lusterman, 1995)

An assessment of the responses to these questions may help the clinician both to make clear to patients the need for all concerned (therapist, discoverer, and discovered partner) to understand and agree on the facts attendant to the infidelity. This may also help to determine the mode of treatment.

Glass and Wright (1992) describe three categories of EMI: *primarily sexual, primarily emotional,* and *combined-type involvement.* Other typologies include brief sexual encounters (one-night stands); lengthy relationships that may be emotionally intense and erotically charged, but are not necessarily sexual; and arrangements (in which a couple agrees that they will maintain their existing relationship, but that each is free to date others). It should be noted that arrangements are not comparable to any other type of EMI, because they are not secret.

Internet EMI is an increasing issue, and its discovery often evokes the same traumatic reaction that other EMI causes. Cooper, Scherer, Boies, and Gordon (1999) studied the anonymous responses of over 9,000 subjects to a 59-item questionnaire that he posted on the MSNBC web site. The study revealed that 86% of male respondents and 14% of females visited sexually explicit sites. Forty-nine percent of females and 23% of males surveyed favored chat rooms. Sixty-four percent of those surveyed were either married or in a committed relationship. Although the study did not examine how many respondents developed ongoing EMIs with their Internet contacts, it is reasonable to assume that a good number did. There is little question that the disparity between men's preference for sexually explicit sites as compared to women's preference for chat rooms supports the concept of significant gender differences in EMI.

Infidelity can also be examined by exploring the function that it serves for the unfaithful partner. *Pursuit* behavior is the result of a deep-seated personality disorder and takes the form of womanizing. It is, for the most part, planned behavior. It is a compulsive search for a woman to "find, bed, and forget" with the greatest possible efficiency. (See Table 19.1.)

The woman sought by a womanizer is invariably perceived as an object, while his wife may be idealized ("wonderful mother, good person, great cook and homemaker," etc.). In my experience, most married womanizers have little desire to end their marriages. They like the package of home, wife, and children. Pursuit behavior fills emotional emptiness, as is the case with most addictions. Social factors, particularly those of power and privilege, make this addiction a particularly male behavior. As the power differential changes as a function of gender, we may expect an increase in "Donna Juanas," and, at least in my practice, I have noted a slight increase in such behavior, particularly when the wife has a high-powered job.

People involved in affairs, by comparison, usually believe that they have fallen out of love with their partner and fallen in love with someone else. For the most part, affairs are not sought—they simply occur. (For a

Table 19.1
A Comparison of Affair and Pursuit Behavior According to Humphrey's Typology

Humphrey's Typology	Affair	Pursuit
Time	Extended	Brief
Degree of emotional involvement	Generally strong, even when the dominant element is thought to be sexual	None
Sexual intercourse or abstinence	Either	Usually although not invariably sexual
Secret or not	Secret	Secret
Single or bilateral EMS (or EMI)	Either	Either, but usually single
Heterosexual or homosexual	Either, but more often heterosexual	Generally heterosexual
Number of EMS partners	One, although over time there may be serial involvements	Many

comparison of the range of affair behaviors in comparison with pursuit behaviors, see Table 19.1.)

TREATMENT ISSUES

CONFIDENTIALITY

Patients enter therapy in several different ways. The EMI partner may come in alone. The discoverer may come in alone. The couple may come in after discovery has occurred. They may come in about what appears to be an unrelated issue, but it may soon become apparent that some sort of EMI is involved. It is important to establish confidentiality procedures during this first meeting. There is a compelling reason to establish confidentiality rules early. Gottlieb (1995) reminds us that traditionally, psychotherapy was seen as a relationship between patient and therapist. Ethical principles "were relatively unambiguous. . . . [A] psychologist's primary obligation is to his or her client, whose autonomy and welfare he or she is expected to promote" (American Psychological Association, 1990). He points out that Margolin (1982) proposed four issues that are unique to systems therapy: (1) Who is the client? (2) If there is more than one, how does the therapist maintain a posture of therapeutic neutrality, and under what circumstances must this position be abandoned in favor of an individual family member? (3) How is confidentiality to be managed? and (4) How does the therapist handle issues of informed consent? Gottlieb informs us that, in this same article, Margolin coined the term "change of format." She noted that an ethical dilemma arose when a therapist who had been treating an individual changed the format to work conjointly, but she did not make any procedural suggestions.

Change of format is almost invariably an element in the treatment of infidelity. The therapist may begin with any of the combinations noted above, but there is a strong probability that, at some point, there will be a change of format. Therapists must carefully examine their own convictions concerning their role in the preservation of confidentiality. Pittman (1989) offers no guarantee of confidentiality. He makes it quite clear that he will hold no secrets and that it is appropriate and necessary that he convey to the partner whatever has been reported to him. My position is quite the opposite. I believe that, during the course of any therapy, there may be changes of format, therefore, my informed consent procedure includes a statement defining how confidentiality will be handled. I explain that at times a person may have an individual session. Unless I am legally required to share a confidence, I will regard the content of any individual session as confidential. I explain that when I meet with a couple or a family, my job is to help them to hear each other better and to work toward change. When I see an individual, I explain that my task is to help that person to clarify issues that he or she may not yet be ready to share with the marital partner. My only requirement is that the partner be informed that such a meeting will take place. The person may choose to share the session. I will not, and I ask the other person not to pry for details.

There are other clinical reasons that dictate this course of action. There are three elements to couplehood: two individual members, and one relational entity. If I see only the couple, I may be missing underlying issues that are profoundly significant. If I see a member of the couple alone without a clear agreement about confidentiality, there is little reason to believe that the person will square with me. After all, if he is ready to explore the problem, but knows that I will reveal whatever I have been told, what would be the point of seeing me alone? Of course, the burden this course of action places on me as a therapist is that I must never reveal the contents of the individual meetings. For that reason, the next time I see either the couple or the other partner, I once again remind them about the confidentiality agreement. In my close to 30 years of working in this manner, I have never been accused of dishonesty or withholding important information from the other.

Still another reason for operating this way is strategic. One of my aims if the EMI partner is continuing the infidelity is to attempt to arrange a moratorium on the affair, so that the couple's full attention may be devoted to the marital issues. If I see the involved partner and he is unready to do this, I will continue to see the partner alone until the issue is resolved. Generally speaking, this leads to either an admission that the affair is still going on (thus ending the secrecy issue) or the person agrees that a moratorium is in order. I may see that partner alone for several meetings. This often raises tension for the couple because the other partner begins to wonder why there have been so many individual sessions.

CASE STUDY

In about the fourth month of therapy following the discovery of an affair, Bill, the husband, requested a session alone. In that session, he revealed that he continued to feel very confused. The marital sessions had helped him to see that there were many good things in his marriage, but he couldn't seem to break the relationship with the other person. Several individual sessions followed, in which his ambivalence was deeply explored. At the third individual session, he announced that his wife had told him that she too was going to ask for an individual session. She told him it seemed only fair, given his three sessions. He asked what I would do if she voiced her suspicions to me. I explained that I would treat her as I would anyone who suspected the possibility that his or her mate was involved in an affair. I would explore what she was feeling, and ask her if she had spoken clearly with her husband about her concerns. I would not, I reminded him, deliver his message for him. A few days later, I received a call from the wife, indicating that, although she had considered coming in alone, it was no longer necessary, since her husband had revealed some important information to her. The following session dealt with his revelation, and at that point a moratorium was successfully started.

Janine and Arthur came to therapy about a year after he had discovered his wife's infidelity. He remained enraged. "I caught her with her hand in the cookie jar," he said, "but even now, after a year, she's still lying. I must work 15 hours a day. I'm killing myself with work. And what does it do—it gives her time to cheat." I pointed out to him that therapy was not a criminal court proceeding, but he pressed for detail after detail, and Janine produced denial after denial. At the third session, she said, "Look, a little something happened. It's long over, and it's not nearly as bad as you think." He jumped out of his chair and slammed out of the room. When he returned, she said, "This is the kind of rage I've always faced. How do you expect me to tell you every little detail? You'll only get angrier." During the week, she called to ask for an individual session. I reminded her about the rules of confidentiality, and that, if she wished, a session would be arranged, but, of course, she must tell Arthur that the meeting had been arranged. At the meeting, she told me that there was more to the affair than she had so far admitted, but that she was terrified of his rage. She also said that during the affair she had been in individual therapy and that her therapist had urged her to keep the affair a secret. We explored the risks of maintaining secrecy (that it would further increase his anxiety and anger) as opposed to openness (and the fear that he would immediately end the marriage). With this new information, I was able to devote the next meeting to an examination of how anger was managed in the marriage and how she had often hidden thoughts and feelings from him, long before the affair, because of her fear. For two sessions, the focus remained on anger and fear issues. She then requested a second session alone, in which we role-played how she would give him a truthful account of the affair. Knowing the history of anger, I was able to get them to agree at the next session that she would give a full account, but only on the condition that there be no further talk about it until the next meeting. Both agreed. Once the issue of anger and honesty were linked, the chain of anger and fear was loosened. The affair was laid to rest, and the issue of anger received the necessary attention.

POSTTRAUMATIC ISSUES

Following the informed consent procedure concerning confidentiality, it is usually important to examine the degree of trauma and posttraumatic reaction that the discoverer has experienced. Most discoverers are profoundly shocked at the time of discovery. Most report that, whatever the problems in their marriages, they never expected this. The degree of trauma is not gender-related. Men are as traumatized as women. Unfortunately, a strict reading of the *DSM-IV* diagnostic criteria for PTSD does not exactly cover this trauma. For that reason, it is generally advisable to report the treatment under the *DSM-IV* code for Adjustment Disorder with Mixed Anxiety and Depressive Mood. Nonetheless, it is valuable for both partners to understand that trauma has occurred and that changes in their relationship will entail the examination and treatment of its sequelae. These may include:

- Difficulty staying or falling asleep
- Irritability or outbursts of anger
- Difficulty concentrating
- Hypervigilance
- Exaggerated startle response
- Physiological reactivity upon exposure to events that symbolize or resemble an aspect of the traumatic event (e.g., being unable to watch a TV show or movie about infidelity)

It is important to explain to the individual or the couple at the outset that the responses that the discoverer exhibits are *normal* and not pathological, but that they need to be understood, and that there are precise ways of helping the discoverer to recover. It is almost invariable that discoverers at first see themselves as the victims of their partner's behavior. If the therapist does not acknowledge the sense of victimhood, it is difficult to appropriately join with him or her. By the same token, if the patient continues to feel victimized following treatment, little has been accomplished. It is the therapist's responsibility to help the couple to understand that trauma creates a sense of victimhood, and that there are prescribed ways of helping the discoverer to transcend this dangerous and helpless feeling. Therefore, the therapeutic approach, although sensitive to the affective issues, also includes a psychoeducational element. Couples report that clearly defined information produces a sense of relief, and often helps to improve marital communication. I explain that the posttraumatic reaction is at this point both understandable and useful. If the discoverer passively accepted the infidelity, he or she would feel totally undefended against a possible recurrence. I explain that PTSD is very much like recombinant DNA. A tiny reminder, the occurrence of any thought or feeling or action connected with the discovered infidelity, immediately recreates all of the overwhelming feelings that occurred during discovery.

Many patients will finally admit the infidelity, but demand that there be no further discussion of it. I point out that this is impossible for the discoverer, whose antennae, at this point, are always alert for more danger. Since avoidance, silence, and lying were aspects of the act of infidelity, each is a part of this DNA, and recreates the pain of discovery. Avoiding may bring some immediate relief, but, over time, will cause more problems. Both partners want to know when and whether the trauma will be relieved. It is important to point out that, working together, the couple can begin a process of recovery.

The therapist should explain to the discovered mate that he or she can play a crucial role in helping the discoverer, who needs to express grief, shock, and anger directly to the mate, and requires honest answers to his or her questions. This process is crucial to the restoration of trust (Lusterman, 1989).

TREATMENT OF WOMANIZERS

The treatment of couples where there has been womanizing differs from that of couples whose marriage has included an affair. Chronic womanizing may be seen as a type of personality disorder. *DSM-IV* describes a personality disorder as "An enduring pattern of inner experience and behavior that differs markedly from the expectations of the individual's culture." This pattern is manifested in two (or more) of the following areas: (1) cognition (i.e., ways of perceiving and interpreting self, other people, and events); (2) affectivity (i.e., the range, intensity lability, and appropriateness of emotional response); (3) interpersonal functioning; and (4) impulse control. The diagnostic criteria for Narcissistic Personality Disorder, particularly the qualities of grandiosity or self-importance, a belief in the person's "specialness," need for excessive admiration, entitlement, exploitativeness, and lack of empathy are often present in chronic womanizers.

Unlike an affair, whose roots may lie in problems within the marriage, womanizing is a quality that, for the most part, long precedes the marriage. As indicated earlier, womanizing is a planful behavior, in contrast with most (although not all) affair behavior. Many womanizers experienced narcissistic deprivation in their childhood, and because of it develop a great need for something that creates a sense of self-importance and of being desired. Some womanizers come from an environment that provided a surfeit of attention (for example, a first-born male in a family with a large number of female children, who may have felt idolized growing up). Some begin as deficit narcissists, but their careers, for example, sports or entertainment figures, governmental officials, strongly inflame the tendency toward womanizing, because they experience some social approval in this context.

Couples where womanizing has been discovered require a very different mix of individual and conjoint sessions than do those in which there has been an affair. The diagnosis of womanizing may be made by using the Humphrey schema as a checklist. It is urgent that the initial meeting include some consideration of the possibility that womanizing, rather than an affair, is the problem. If there is agreement that the problem is womanizing, it is important to clarify for the couple the differences between womanizing and affairs, and the consequent differences in treatment. Although it is hard to believe that the wife of a womanizer is consciously unaware of the womanizing, it is often the case, and for this reason, the trauma of discovery is a significant factor in treatment, and is in no way different from the treatment of discoverers of affairs.

CASE STUDY

Clarissa, a 50-year-old retired businesswoman, brought her husband, an airline pilot, aged 52, to therapy because she discovered that he had had a string of alliances with female flight attendants. John, who said that he was in what he saw as a happy marriage, came only because she had threatened him with divorce. He at first vehemently denied her accusations, but she produced enough proof that he finally confirmed her suspicions. He pointed out that many pilots did this and that, since he did not love any of these women, he saw his actions as "victimless crimes." I pointed out to him that there were two issues for his wife, and that they were, for her, of equal importance. One was that he had endangered her physical health, because he may have contracted or transmitted a sexually transmitted disease to her. The second was that she had, until then, believed that their marriage was monogamous, and that he had hurt her deeply by secretly violating what she saw as the privacy of marriage. Despite her anger and tears, he continued to deny that he had hurt her and seemed genuinely unable to experience any empathy for her. Her threat to terminate the marriage if he did not "seek help," however, caused him a great deal of anxiety, which impelled him to accept therapy.

Therapy consisted of couples work, combined with many individual meetings with him, and occasionally with her as well. It was explained at the outset that it was each person's responsibility to report to the other if there were individual meetings, but that the content of individual meetings would be considered confidential.

THE TRAUMA OF DISCOVERY

The first issue in couples therapy was to deal with her posttraumatic reaction to the discovery of his infidelity. A major task was helping John to grasp why the discovery was so painful for her and beginning the task of sensitizing him to her feelings. I encouraged Clarissa to seek John's help when she was having a "bad day." Her tendency, like many discoverers, was to attack him each time she made a new discovery of one of his many lies. In one session, she screamed at him as he once again told her it was a "victimless crime." "*I* am the victim," she shouted, "and if you can't get that, there's no hope for us." His response was "I'm not going to do it any more, so why bring up the past?" I suggested that Clarissa talk about "having a bad day" rather than attacking him, and try to enlist him in helping her through her difficulty. This enabled John to accept some coaching about how to comfort her, instead of responding defensively to what he saw as her attacks on him. Over several sessions, and with much coaching, he became more aware and supportive of her feelings. As his ability to assure her that he heard her increased, she reported fewer bad days.

In another session, he accepted her demand that he stop any involvement with other women beyond normal social pleasantries, including his constant flirtatious behavior, both at work, and in their social interactions at home. The nature of his employment entitled her to free air travel, and she began to accompany him on many of his flights, in an attempt to regain some sense of order in her own life, and to see for herself whether John could control his seductive actions toward women.

As the immediate issues were attended to and produced an increased stability in the marriage, it became possible to begin to investigate what caused John to feel the need for and the entitlement to this behavior. In his first individual sessions, he presented his family of origin as comfortable and normal, and denied any problems growing up. Family history questions were repeated in a joint session with Clarissa, with very different results. She reminded him that his mother had been, on the one hand, extremely overprotective, and on the other, very demeaning toward him. His father had been very critical of him because he was a sensitive boy who did not engage in athletics and did not date during high school. His father clearly favored John's older brother, who was a successful athlete at school, and who always "played the field" with girls, much to his father's vicarious satisfaction. Both his brother and father constantly taunted John. Although John acknowledged Clarissa's perceptions in the couples meeting, he denied them in the following individual session. Alternation of individual and couples meetings helped me to begin a thoughtful examination of the issues with his family of origin. This process helped him to become aware of what he had really experienced, and, for the first time, to experience long-dormant feelings of hurt and anger. As he became more conscious of his own feelings, there was some increase in his empathy for Clarissa. It was only at this point that work could begin on the issue of womanizing and how it had negated the possibility of marital intimacy. There were many individual sessions. One of the advantages of these private meetings was that they provided an opportunity to learn how successful John was in stopping further womanizing or flirtatious behavior. Despite the importance of maintaining a good ratio of individual and conjoint meetings, the following description of the phases of treatment is applicable to both pursuit and affair behavior.

PHASES OF TREATMENT

There are three phases in the treatment of infidelity (Lusterman, 1989, 1995). Although each stage focuses on specific therapeutic issues, it is unlikely that there will be a smooth continuity. Even after the therapist feels that Phase 1 issues have been fully dealt with, they frequently erupt during the second and third phases. A key to successful treatment is the ability to interrupt Phases 2 and 3 and return to the posttraumatic issues until the couple has sufficient competency to deal with these issues on their own.

PHASE 1: RESTORING TRUST

The initial trauma of betrayal of trust is explored. The discovered partner is encouraged to validate and support the discoverer. The three phases of the work are clearly outlined, so that the couple has some sense of the task ahead. It is important to make clear that this work is not a promise that the marriage will be saved. Rather, it is a time to explore change. I define a successful outcome as either a better marriage or a better divorce.

The process of moderating the discoverer's hurt and anger to usable proportions is difficult for both the couple and the therapist, because it generates high levels of anxiety. The system that includes the discovered and the discoverer is by its nature tension-filled. Developing theory around "expressed emotion" (EE) is helpful in conceptualizing treatment in this phase. Although the concept was originally explored in the context of the systemic aspects of schizophrenia, research now indicates that it is relevant to many other systemic issues, including diabetes (Liakopoulou et al., 2000), children's behavioral problems (Lam, Giles, & Lavander, 2003), and affective illness (Coiro & Gottesman, 1996). An understanding of the EE phenomenon and its relevance to infidelity-related PTSD is often an important psychoeducational aspect of treatment. Discoverers almost invariably go through at least a period of very high EE, even if it has never been part of their personality structure. Some discovered partners are also very high in EE. Discoverers must learn to express rather than emote their feelings. For this reason, is not unusual for Phase 1 to be the most lengthy element of treatment. Periods of trust often increase feelings of vulnerability, so that the conclusion of a good week may at first be a predictor of a period of increased hypervigilance on the part of the discoverer. The discovered person, often still suffering his or her own guilt (and sometimes depression due to the loss of the affair partner) requires therapeutic support so that he or she can provide the emotional support that the discoverer requires. As mentioned earlier, Phase 1 issues often reappear as the two other phases are entered.

PHASE 2: EXAMINATION OF PREDISPOSING FACTORS

This work is familiar to any systems-oriented therapist. A review of courtship and marriage, with particular attention to conflicts and how they were (or were not) resolved is important, as is a review of issues involving the family of origin. It is not unusual for couples in which there has been an affair to report that there were no conflicts. Careful examination usually reveals that each member of the couple had thoughts and feelings about important issues, but that these were never revealed, and therefore, never resolved. Often, it is impossible to help the couple discover and process these issues until family-of-origin issues are explored. For example, one couple reported that the events surrounding their wedding and its planning had gone very well. It was only as the wife described her family of origin, and her mother's hypercritical behavior, that it became evident that her mother had strongly opposed the wedding. Her husband was unaware that his fiancée had been under such pressure. This difficulty in self-disclosure is often a significant precursor of infidelity. Because couples dealing with infidelity are often exquisitely aware of the possibility of being blamed, it is important that the patients not feel that the therapist's choice of which family of origin to begin with implies therapeutic finger pointing. One way to avoid this worry is through the use of gentle humor. It is my practice, for example, to ask the couple to toss a coin when I am ready to explore these issues. As this exploration continues, the theme of poor self-disclosure tends to become more apparent, and issues that have lain dormant, often for years, now find a context for a safe exploration.

It is important to remember that Phase 1 issues are often triggered by issues that are discussed in Phase 2. The therapist should be strongly aware of this possibility. If there is not sufficient therapeutic flexibility during this phase, the couple may terminate prematurely.

PHASE 3: RAPPROCHEMENT

The couple is reminded that the purpose of the work has been change and that the object of therapy has been the possibility of moving toward a better marriage or a better divorce. By now, it is hoped, the blaming that characterizes Phase 1 has subsided, and the couple has come to understand the factors that predisposed the couple to a possible infidelity. The issue of Phase 3 is to improve their self-disclosure and problem-solving skills. With a clearer understanding of the issues that have complicated their marriage, they are now able to consider whether they can develop a more satisfying marriage, or need to consider the possibility of a good divorce. The advantages of a better marriage are obvious. A better divorce creates the groundwork for good coparenting and may help each member of the couple to make better decisions about future relationships, both in the matter of partner choice and personal conduct.

SUMMARY

A major focus of this chapter has been the traumatic reaction that almost invariably follows the discovery of infidelity. Therapists who do not respect and honor this reaction, but treat it instead as a form of pathology, may cause great harm to both parties. Unfaithful partners almost never had the intention of harming their marital partner. For this reason, knowing that they can help to begin the process of healing is often as important to unfaithful partners as it is to their discoverers. If the couple begins a mutual act of healing, there is little reason to believe that they will not then undertake a cooperative reexamination of their marriage. For many couples, the outcome of this reexamination is more than a return to the marriage that was. Rather, it provides the opportunity to build on this new understanding in order to reinvent their marriage. When couples find that there is no meaningful continuation of their marriage, they are more likely to end their marriages with a minimum of acrimony. If there are children, they can only benefit from a dignified end to their parents' marriage. Such an ending helps children to trust that, even if a marriage must end, parents will always remain parents, and maybe, do a better job as mother and father than they did as husband and wife. Whether or not there are children, couples who must divorce will benefit from a review of their courtship and marriage, because it increases the probability that they will do better in a subsequent relationship.

REFERENCES

American Psychological Association. (1990). Ethical principals of psychologists. *American Psychologist, 45,* 390–395.

Coiro, M., & Gottesman, I. (1996). The diathesis and/or stressor role of expressed emotion in affective illness. *Clinical Psychology: Science and Practice, 3,* 310–322.

Cooper, A., Scherer, C., Boies, J., & Gordon, B. (1999). Sexuality on the internet: From sexual exploration to pathological expression. *Professional Psychology: Research and Practice, 30,* 154–164.

Finzi, S. (1989, May/June). Cosi fan tutti. *Family Therapy Networker, 13,* 31–33.

Glass, S., & Wright, T. (1992). Justifications for extramarital relationships: The association between attitudes, behaviors and gender. *Journal of Sex Research, 29,* 361–387.

Gottlieb, M. C. (1995). Ethical dilemmas in change of format and live supervision. In R. H. Mikesell, D.-D. Lusterman, & S. H. McDaniel (Eds.), *Integrating family therapy: Handbook of family psychology and systems theory* (pp. 561–569). Washington, DC: American Psychological Association.

Greeley, A. (1991). *Faithful attraction: Discovering intimacy, love and fidelity in American marriage.* New York: Tom Doherty Associates.

Humphrey, F. (1987). Treating extramarital sexual relationships in sex and couples therapy. In G. Weeks & L. Hof (Eds.), *Integrating sex and marital therapy: A clinical guide* (pp. 149–170). New York: Brunner/Mazel.

Kinsey, A., Pomeroy, W., & Martin, C. (1948). *Sexual behavior in the human male.* Philadelphia: Saunders.

Kinsey, A., Pomeroy, W., Martin, C., & Gebhard, P. (1953). *Sexual behavior in the human female.* Philadelphia: Saunders.

Lam, D., Giles, A., & Lavander, A. (2003). Carers' expressed emotion, appraisal of behavioural problems and stress in children attending schools for learning disabilities. *Journal of Intellectual Disability Research, 47,* 456–463.

Liakopoulou, M. (2001). Maternal expressed emotion and metabolic control of children and adolescents with diabetes mellitus. *Psychotherapy and Psychosomatics, 70,* 78–85.

Lusterman, D.-D. (1989, May/June). Marriage at the turning point. *Family Therapy Networker, 13,* 44–51.

Lusterman, D.-D. (1995). Treating marital infidelity. In R. Mikesell, D.-D. Lusterman, & S. McDaniel. *Integrating family therapy: Handbook of family psychology and systems theory* (pp. 561–569). Washington, DC: American Psychological Association.

Margolin, G. (1982). Ethical and legal considerations in marital and family therapy. *American Psychologist, 37,* 788–801.

Pittman, F. (1989). *Private lies: Infidelity and the betrayal of intimacy.* New York: Norton.

Smith, T. (1993). *American sexual behavior: Trends, sociodemographic differences, and risk behavior* (Version 1.2). Chicago: University of Chicago, National Opinion Research Center.

CHAPTER 20

Religious and Spiritual Issues in Couples Therapy

Ilene Serlin

Love's mysteries in soules doe grow.

—John Donne

GIVEN THE EFFECTS of increased mobility and globalization, many couples are facing unprecedented issues as they combine their families' cultural backgrounds and traditions. Although research is beginning to track the impact of multicultural couples, there is relatively little on the effect of spiritual or religious combinations. Spiritual and religious differences may show up in "conflicts between love and tradition" (Crohn, 1995, p. 9), such as child-rearing, family traditions, in-law issues, and personal versus traditional religious or spiritual paths. Because of the mix of places and the loss of community, people increasingly need to create their own personal paths, new combinations of beliefs, practices, and support systems. However, they lack the role models and support necessary to create these new ones. Couples are left on their own to figure out how to create shared meanings and traditions.

A community used to provide a stable sense of identity about oneself, one's place in the universe, and a set of values and beliefs by which to live. Behavioral norms of moral behavior regulated relationships during courtship and marriage and provided a connection to the ancestors and continuity through time. Many individuals today are disconnected from that source of identity and stability (Serlin, 1989a, 1989b, 2001). They may find the task of personally constructing a worldview of purpose and meaning too great and become confused and depressed. In traditional communities, they would have sought help from priests or other religious figures; today, they come to psychologists' offices with *crises of meaning:*

> One client told me that she was having a difficult time putting together her own forms of spiritual practice. Her mother was a Southern Baptist and her father Catholic. She has memories of being in both churches, but doesn't have a church of her own. In fact, she describes her lack of roots in any one community as a source of psychological pain.

Psychologists should be competent to deal with these issues (Vaughan, 1987), yet most are trained to be rational and may in fact have a bias against religion. They report themselves as poorly prepared to deal with clients' religious and spiritual issues (Shafranske & Maloney, 1990), or the psychological effects of globalization (Arnett, 2002). They may overmedicate or overpathologize their clients, missing an opportunity to help them discover the meaning of their symptoms and construct new identities. Just beginning to acknowledge religious issues in psychotherapy, psychologists are now discovering spirituality (Crohn, 1995). In fact, the American Psychological Association's (APA) ethics code requires that psychologists keep up with the primary issues of their patients. At the APA's 1999 National Multicultural Conference and Summit, one of the three major themes was about "spirituality as a basic dimension of the human condition" (Sue, Bingham, Porche-Burke, & Vasquez, 1999, p. 1065). The conference organizers stated that "psychology must break away from being a unidimensional science, that it must recognize the multifaceted layers of existence, that spirituality and meaning in the life context are important, and that psychology must balance its reductionistic tendencies with the knowledge that the whole is greater than the sum of its parts. Understanding that people are cultural and spiritual beings is a necessary condition for a psychology of human existence" (Sue et al., 1999, p. 1065).

What is the difference between spirituality and religion? How is spirituality both a problem and a helpful framework for couples therapy? This chapter proposes that all psychologists need to have a clinical proficiency in religious and spiritual diversity issues, and that training programs have an "ethical responsibility" to teach it (Shafranske, 1996).

This chapter, therefore, addresses issues of religion and spirituality in relationships by (1) providing a review of the psychotherapeutic approaches that do address spiritual issues in couples therapy and (2) making recommendations for principles and practices to help psychologists address issues of religious and spiritual differences in couples therapy.

THEORETICAL BACKGROUND

The reemergence of an interest in spirituality in psychotherapy can be understood in one sense as a commentary on the limitations of modern psychiatry, which has positioned itself in the realm of science, aiming to liberate humankind from religion (Needleman, 1983, p. 6). Psychology, once linked with philosophy, theology, and the arts, has followed medical psychiatry into science. It has focused on assessment, control and prediction, and symptom reduction, to the exclusion of the experience of the soul. It no longer meets the needs of many people, who are struggling to find meaning and purpose in their lives. By contrast, a national survey showed that 92% of all Americans felt that "my religious faith is the most important influence in my life" (Bergin & Jensen, 1990, p. 5), Most Americans report that they believe in God and 75% identify themselves as religious (Cadwallader, 1991), while more than 40% admitted to a mystical experience or communication with transpersonal beings (Gallup & Castelli, 1989). Many people today are attracted to Zen and Tibetan Buddhism, Sufism, Hinduism, and contemplative or mystical branches of Christianity and Judaism. Nine out of 10 Americans say they pray, and 97% believe that their prayers are heard (Steere, 1997). Spiritually based rituals have been shown to be effective coping strategies for dealing with life stresses (Pargament, 1997). The importance of religion is growing among married couples and is identified as an "essential ingredient" in long-term satisfying marriages (Kaslow & Robinson, 1996). Other individuals today choose new forms of religion or spirituality, or even more esoteric practices such as witchcraft and neopaganism, while some develop a strictly personal form of spirituality.

DEFINITION OF TERMS

One problem with understanding the role of religion and spirituality in psychotherapy is the lack of clear definition of these terms. The literature in psychology shows a confusion about what extent experiences of religion or spirituality include a divine power, a set of beliefs or practices, or a cultural context. Religion is usually associated with structured rituals or practices, while spirituality can be defined as a personal and direct experience of the sacred (R. Walsh, 1999). For example, the experience of spirituality in family therapy practice has been defined as: "a relationship with a Transcendent Being that fosters a sense of meaning, purpose, and mission in life" (Hodge, 2000, pp. 218–219). Definitions of spirituality have also included an ecological and moral dimension, such as the sense of connectedness that spreads out to a compassionate concern for all beings (Elkins, Hedstrom, Hughes, Leaf, & Saunders, 1988) and "living in a manner consistent with their interior value framework" (Genia, 1990). Whatever definitions are used to describe the dimensions of meaning and self-knowledge that individuals are seeking, however, these have been significantly left out of a valuefree scientific psychology. Further, although individuals may seek help in counseling, many are reporting that they feel fragmented by having to consult both psychotherapists and pastors (Griffith & Griffith, 1992) to address both relationship and spiritual issues.

SPIRITUALITY AND PSYCHOLOGY

Recently, however, there has been a new understanding among mental health professionals about the reality of this crisis of meaning, as demonstrated in the creation of a new diagnostic category called "Religious or Spiritual Problems" in the American Psychiatric Association's *Diagnostic and Statistical Manual of Mental Disorders* (*DSM-IV*). The role of spirituality is gaining notice in psychology (Richards & Bergin, 1997; Tan, 2003; R. Walsh, 1999) and family therapy and couples counseling (Anderson & Worthen, 1997; Moules, 2000; Prest & Keller, 1993; Richards & Bergin, 1997; Rotz, Russell, & Wright, 1993). Some psychospiritual interventions have been empirically validated (Jacobs, 1992; Pargament, 1997; Worthington, Kurusu, McCullough, & Sandage, 1996), and correlated with religious attitudes of the therapist (Diblasio, 1993; Moon, Willis, Bailey, & Kwansy, 1993). Crises of meaning can occur at any point in the life cycle, but are particularly apt to hit during times of transition like graduation from high school, marriage, birth of a child, loss of a loved one, and living with a life-threatening illness. A few organizations, like the Spiritual Emergency Network in Palo Alto, California, specially train counselors to recognize and help with "spiritual emergencies." Some graduate programs, like the MFCC program at the University of San Diego, offer graduate level courses on "Spiritual Issues in Family Therapy" (Patterson, Hayworth, Turner, & Raskin, 2000). Graduate programs in psychology that are explicitly Christian include Brigham Young University and the Graduate School of Psychology at Fuller Theological Seminary, while others have an East-West perspective on spirituality and psychology, like the Naropa Institute in Colorado, the California Institute of Integral Studies, and the Institute of Transpersonal Psychology.

Many crises of meaning, however, do not present floridly as spiritual or religious emergencies, but show up in the everyday descriptions of inner emptiness and despair. Some clients describe the vague feeling of wanting to connect to something "beyond themselves," others want to connect to a sense of meaning in their work. These spiritual crises are not psychiatric disorders that require treatment. They are existential and spiritual afflictions of the psyche.

For example, in my office I see young people working for high-tech or prestigious companies who find no meaning in their lives. They have arrived; in their prime years of late twenties or early thirties, they are making large salaries, and feel that they should be enjoying their lives. Instead, many are lonely, feel that what they are doing every day is pointless, and have trouble motivating themselves. Their life has lost its meaning.

A crisis of meaning occurs also in relationships. Why should they marry today? No longer a guarantee of security, relationships need a new reason for being. Some couples come to therapy to find more meaning in their lives together. Or they may discover that a relationship does not guarantee intimacy or stop their loneliness. Many couples find their religious organizations more concerned with outer appearances than with the truth of experience. New studies have shown that intramarriage does not bring more intimacy than intermarriage. Marrying someone of the same religion does not necessarily bring shared experiences (Heller & Wood, 2000, p. 245). What couples miss is a sense of communion and connection, which is often described as spiritual. The need for "reclaiming connection" to the basic web of relationships and life is a basic human right (Spretnak, 1991, p. 22).

Finally, relationships no longer provide a sense of home. Couples are transient, few have the traditional family homes left. Many young couples in my practice are desperate to make homes, but cannot afford the high urban prices. Not only do they not have a literal home, but they also lack the neighborhood and web of family responsibilities to create a sense of place. Consequently, they are disoriented, flighty, agitated. Spiritual practices teach them how to ground themselves, as they find their sense of place in all other aspects of their lives.

SCHOOLS OF PSYCHOTHERAPY WITH RELIGIOUS OR SPIRITUAL ELEMENTS

A growing number of psychotherapeutic approaches integrate spirituality into their theory and practices. To build a proficiency in religious and spiritual elements of psychotherapy, this chapter summarizes some of the major East-West schools of psychotherapy that have addressed these issues in couples therapy and illustrates them with case vignettes.

JUNGIAN PSYCHOLOGY

Jungian psychology contains a spiritual perspective on psychology (Jung, 1954, 1958, 1963). For the past several decades, there has been a new interest in Jungian psychology from a nondogmatic approach. People sense that something is missing in modern life, in everyday life and relationships. Some call it the quality of "soul," by which they mean the anima or animating principle of life (Hillman, 1972).

According to Jungian analyst, Robert Johnson, the basic principles of an in-depth perspective on relationships are:

- The soul manifests in symbols and myths.
- For the man, the woman is the symbol of the soul (anima). The task of psychotherapy is to help the man see what qualities he has projected onto the woman, his muse, when he falls in love. He must then withdraw them and discover them in himself. The woman must learn how to carry the projection but not get lost in it. Both partners must eventually break the spell and see each other as they really are.

- Marriage is considered to be a sacred vessel, allowing the couple to pass through difficult moments. It creates a strong holding environment for the heat needed for an alchemical transformation of the psyche.
- Psychotherapy helps the couple see romantic love as a stage in their psychological evolution, converting romantic love to real love. Romantic love and passion are directed at our projections, although real love involves appreciation of the other person as a real person. Real love involves friendship and *agape,* or disinterested lovingkindness. Wholeness comes once the projections are analyzed and withdrawn, and the love is internalized as a marriage between inner aspects of the self: the inner king and queen, the yin and the yang.

SACRED PSYCHOLOGY

A sacred psychological approach to couples therapy understands love between human beings is a path to love of the Divine: the "Beloved" is the object of our deepest longing. It is by most profoundly surrendering to this longing that we, paradoxically, most become ourselves. The mystical vision of divine marriage was driven underground by the Christian church during the Crusades, and emerged in its secular form as "courtly love" and its *myth of romantic love.* This myth can be read psychologically as a story of the drive for wholeness (Houston, 1982).

Jungian therapist Thomas Moore in, *Soul Mates* (1994), spoke to a generation yearning for connection and laid out principles and descriptions of a soul perspective on couples therapy. A soulmate is defined as "someone to whom we feel profoundly connected, as though the communicating and communing that take place between us were not the product of intentional efforts, but rather a divine grace" (p. xvii). The term "soulmates" can refer to actual couples, but is also a metaphorical term for the quality of soul in all our relationships, including ones with family and coworkers. The presence of the sacred does not take place as a result of religious dogma, but is personal.

The qualities of a soulful relationship are:

- *Individualistic.* Since the soul favors the individual and idiosyncratic rather than the general or categorical, a soulful relationship will be unique. Each couple will find its own healthy balance between the individual and the community.
- *Intimate.* The soul loves the intimate details of domestic life, the vernacular (p. viii). Soul love is marked by Eros; it is messy, sometimes uncontrollable. Soul love is not made of abstract principles or quick fixes, but dwells in the intimate moments.

A couple who complained of lack of intimacy, finally touched at night. His answer to her query about how it felt was general, and deflated her feeling of closeness. In therapy, she was able to ask for a comment more specific to her, such as the feeling of her skin.

- *The language of the soul is poetry and image, not technical jargon.* There- fore, a psychology of couples therapy from a soul perspective would not have treatment goals, outcome measures, or try to make the rela- tionship work. Instead, a soul perspective would be about intimacy, about deepening and appreciating the relationship. Instead of seeing love problems as a disorder to be fixed, sacred psychology sees falling in love as an awakening to a longing for connection: an initiatory ex- perience. The psychological question would explore the phenomenon of longing and would ask: "What is this longing for deeper love, and why does it never seem to be satisfied?"
- *Perspective.* A soulful relationship is marked by a shift in perspective from narcissistic dwelling on one's mistakes or imperfections to see- ing oneself in context of life's larger mysteries. The language of soul is cyclic rather than linear. A soul perspective on couples therapy would understand the natural ebbing and flowing of energy, passion, and closeness.

A young woman came to me worried about her new boyfriend. The initial passion had already cooled, and she had crashed. The imagery of fusion versus crashing suggested no alternative but to bounce back and forth from relationship encounter to encounter. The therapeutic task here, therefore, was to help her find a new and more flexible image for her relationships. We ended with a guided imagery exercise in which she envisioned herself surfing the ebbs and flows of her relationship. In her imagination, she danced between fusion and separateness at the boundary of contact be- tween herself and the other. The ability to tolerate ambiguity left her feel- ing empowered with increased stamina at staying present in a relationship.

- *Love's pathologies. Pathos,* used by the early Greeks to mean "emotion or the impact of the divine on human life," is more than the modern dictionary definition of "suffering." A soul perspective on couples therapy would see a "malady of love" such as obsessive love or the suf- fering of Saint Teresa of Avila as an initiation into deeper truths and communions. Love has a dark side; it is a trickster, a demon bringing the madness of melancholy, jealousy, and heartache.

Partnership Model

Anthropologist Riane Eisler's (1987) model of the *hieros gamos* (sacred mar- riage) is based on discoveries of partnership models of egalitarian relation- ships that purportedly existed in places like Minoan Crete before the male dominator model swept over Europe in the form of invading warriors.

Psychotherapeutic practices include finding images for dysfunctional role models in relationships like the "Inner Suffering Heroine," the masochistic or self-sacrificing part of the self that includes Sleeping Beauty, the Dumb Blonde, the romantic madwoman, and then developing more functional images of egalitarian partnerships. Clients bring in images of the women in their families, for example, to see which archetypes run in their families, and to search for more empowering images. In a lending library, some read about suffering Ophelia in *Hamlet,* or identify with figures like the Fallen Woman, the Scarlet A, the Dying Heroine, or Carmen in *La Traviata.* Others examine their internalized images of saintliness or virginity. Further images include the Scheming Bitch and the Seductive Temptress. Making the unconscious conscious in terms of imagery will help them avoid habitual pitfalls in relationships, but more importantly it will help them to begin constructing newer and more functional ones. One client would get overwhelmed with insecurity in a relationship. Since her only role model was a passive, suffering mother, she would instead ask herself: "What would Catherine Deneuve do?"

Men can also examine their relationship archetypes relative to the way they partner in relationships. One young man came from an extended Italian family. As he approached age 30, he faced new pressures about being a man and establishing himself in the eyes of the community. Through imagery exercises, he began to visualize himself taking his place among the men of his tribe. He visualized the strengths that he inherited from the father he never saw to strengths from his uncles, grandfather, and other role models. He was able to deal with his pending marriage and issues like how to discover his own unique way of becoming a man in his new partnership.

Another man replaced images of "Hero as Conquerer" with images like "Hero as Healer" and Martin Luther King.

PASTORAL COUNSELING

The Emmanuel Movement in Boston was one of the clergy's first "attempts to help the sick through mental, moral, and spiritual methods" (Cabot, in Vande Kemp, 1996, p. 87). After this movement faded, the clinical pastoral education (CPE) and pastoral counseling movements emerged. Current organizations include the American Association of Pastoral Counselors and the Association of Mental Health Clergy. Christian psychiatric hospitals and psychology internship sites are available at the Fuller Theological Seminary's Psychological Center, the Mennonite mental hospital, and the New Life Christian psychiatric hospital (p. 89).

JEWISH MYSTICISM

Sex, although commanded to occur only within the sacred covenant of marriage, was not a sin in the Old Testament (Patai, 1978). In fact, the cleaving together of husband and wife was meant to heal the "primal wound of separation" (Gen. 2:23 to 24; in Bloch & Bloch, 1995, p. 11) and they were commanded to "be fruitful and multiply" (Gen. 1:28). The Song of Songs is a text associated with King Solomon in the tenth century B.C.E. containing erotic, sensuous descriptions of love, which some Biblical scholars interpret as metaphors for the relationship between humans and the divine.

SUFI PSYCHOLOGY

The most famous Sufi poet of devotional love, Rumi, taught that love is a madness that is not an illness to be fixed:

> This that is tormented and very tired.
> tortured with restraints like a madman,
> this heart.
> Still you keep breaking the shell
> to get the taste of its kernel.

TRANSPERSONAL PSYCHOLOGY

Abraham Maslow, president of the American Psychological Association in 1967–1968, helped establish transpersonal psychology in the United States. He theorized that human beings need to first satisfy their basic needs for food and shelter, but then experience a drive for higher states of consciousness (Maslow, 1971). Maslow identified such extraordinary states of mind as metavalues of "wholeness, perfection, completion, justice, aliveness, richness, simplicity, beauty, goodness, uniqueness, effortlessness, playfulness, truth, and self-sufficiency" (Hastings, 1999, p. 193).

In 1969, Maslow and Sutich founded the *Journal of Transpersonal Psychology* and the Association for Transpersonal Psychology to explore "the farther reaches of human nature." The first issue of the *Journal of Transpersonal Psychology* defined it as: "Transpersonal (or 'fourth force') Psychology is the title given to an emerging force in the psychology field by a group of psychologists and professional men and women from other fields who are interested in those *ultimate* human capacities and potentialities that have no systematic place in positivistic or behavioristic theory ('first force'), classical psychoanalytic theory ('second force'), or humanistic psychology ('third force')" (Sutich, 1969, p. 15). The early transpersonal theorists believed that consciousness exists as a phenomenon that can be systematically studied by science and used clinical and experiential methods such as meditation to study inner states (Wilbur, 1981).

Transpersonal psychologists critique Western psychology for not going far enough. Western psychology can help us recognize dysfunctional patterns and free ourselves from our pasts, but it lacks theory or practices to help us move beyond these patterns. Western psychology has a well-developed taxonomy of mental disorders, but almost nothing about mental "order" or, as the Buddhists say, "basic sanity." Tibetan teacher Chogyam Trungpa's term for the Western psychological approach that reduces everything to categories of internal disorder is "psychological materialism" (Trungpa, 1969, p. 126). Through 2,000 years of intense introspection, Buddhist monks and scholars have developed an extraordinarily sophisticated taxonomy of normal, as well as abnormal, states of mind called the *Abidharma* (Welwood, 1983, p. 205). Most important, they developed a road map to go beyond normal to extraordinary states of mind.

BUDDHIST PSYCHOLOGY

Because the Buddhist method of inquiry into the phenomenology of mind is experiential, it includes the bodily experience of mind: namely, emotions (Trungpa, 1983). A Buddhist approach to psychotherapy, therefore, integrates body and mind through meditation and cultivation of the mind. In Sanskrit, for example, the words for "heart" and "mind" are part of the same reality or *citta* (Welwood, 1983, p. viii). The expanded mind brings expanded awareness, which lets us see things in perspective as they truly are, and with expanded compassion. The essence of Buddhist psychotherapy is the cultivation of compassion, or *maitri.* In the encounter between client and therapist, both hearts awaken. The awakened heart is called *bodhicitta* (p. 159), and the awakened state is called "Buddha nature."

A commitment to relationship from a Buddhist point of view is a commitment to using the relationship as a "path" for awakening two hearts together in a *conscious relationship.* What is awakened in conscious relationship is "the goodness and strength already present in us" (Welwood, 1990b, p. 13). Rather than staying in habitual patterns of flight-or-fight response, a "warrior of the heart" cultivates the three aspects of warriorship: "awareness, courage, and gentleness" (p. 22). A spiritual approach to psychotherapy helps couples harness this desire to grow and views intimacy as an opportunity to "awaken and bring forth our finest human qualities, such as awareness, compassion, humor, wisdom, and a fearless dedication to truth" (pp. 1–2). Couples are committed to change, seeing relationships as teachers that show us where we need to grow. The act of falling in love is understood as an expression of the desire to realize the fullness of one's own being. Psychotherapy for conscious relationships consists of transformative practices to foster compassion, courage, and awareness.

CASE STUDY

A young woman was dating two people, and her head was literally spinning with choices. She couldn't think her way through them any more.

I asked her if she would like to close her eyes, feel her breath, her weight, and her spine. As her breath became slow and steady, she felt her own rhythm. She was able to sense her interiority, and feel at home in herself. She felt less panicked, and could assess the situation more clearly, feeling a newly internalized locus of control.

A well-developed observing ego brings balance and stability to relationships.

RELIGION AND SPIRITUALITY IN PSYCHOTHERAPY PRACTICE

What would proficiency in religious and spiritual issues in psychotherapy look like? The following section presents some basic principles of a religious and spiritual approach to couples therapy distilled from across Western and Eastern approaches to couples therapy. They will then be applied to two case histories.

The following elements characterize a spiritual approach to psychotherapy:

- *Here-and-now.* Buddhism teaches about the truth of impermanence. Facing our mortality allows us to live more fully in the moment; a spiritual approach to psychotherapy emphasizes the present moment, and the development of presence (Suzuki, 1949). We learn that we are always home in ourselves. Spiritual practices teach concentration and ways to calm the mind. Spiritually oriented psychotherapy practices emphasize the importance of fit in clinical work rather than using pre-structured sessions (Maturana & Varela, 1992). These practices build on strengths and help people find their own voices, similar to postmodern, feminist, and narrative therapies (Saleebey, 1997). Therapy is discovery-oriented, and the therapist is not an authority figure. The therapeutic reality is coconstructed, in line with a collaborative approach to therapy (Kok & Leskela, 1996).
- *Identity.* Most people normally identify with their bundle of personality traits and neuroses, jobs, or roles as their identity; a spiritual approach knows that we can be more. A spiritual approach teaches that even if these things change, we have a deeper identity. Beyond the narrow perspective of our insecure egos, or the "self" with a small "s" as Jung observed, lies a larger egolessness and panoramic awareness, or "vipassana," which Jung called the "Self with a large 'S'." (Jung, 1958). Developing a larger awareness helps us get perspective on ourselves and our problems, and provides space for change to occur (Welwood, 1983).
- *Transcendence.* Most psychological histories and diagnoses start with a history of symptoms; "transpersonal therapists assume that one goal of therapy is to facilitate growth of the self toward these higher levels of experience" and that "there is a natural, spontaneous movement toward

wholeness" (Hastings, 1999, p. 203). Behind the confusion of the neurosis is usually a deeper level of clarity that is available to most human beings. This wakefulness goes beyond the usual Western dichotomies of good and evil, of images of human nature as either basically good or positive, or else teeming with conflicting drives seeking tension reduction. Instead, a spiritual approach to psychotherapy embraces paradox (Schneider, 1990), and the ability to stay present in the midst of life's inevitable challenges.

- *Meaning.* The search for meaning is an essentially human activity, but life may often feel meaningless. Victor Frankl (1959), coming out of a concentration camp, developed an approach, which he called "Logotherapy," that showed how the search for the meaning of even these events can overcome despair. Spiritual practices also help us face the void (Buddhist *sunyata*) and discover new meanings in the new spaces or emptiness.
- *Compassion.* Seeing and accepting ourselves as we truly are allows us to develop compassion toward ourselves, and then extend that compassion to others. A spiritual practice trains the mind, which develops the discipline and courage to face life squarely. Through spiritual practices such as "active love" (Spretnak, 1991), we can honor our kinship with other human beings. Through the crucible of our own suffering, we transform passion into compassion.
- *Home.* Seeing a larger context than the self, we rediscover our larger connection to community and the universe. We find our sense of place: we belong. Some family therapists have developed practices such as spiritual genograms (Frame, 2000) and spiritual ecomaps (Hodge, 2000) to help couples perceive these connections in their own families and extended families.

A spiritual approach to psychotherapy can bring what has been called "psychological maturity" to couples in therapy. A spiritual approach to psychotherapy has been positively correlated with decreased anxiety and conflict (Murphy & Donovan, 1997), enhanced creativity, increased health and longevity, deeper empathy, and greater marital satisfaction and resiliency (F. Walsh, 1998, 1999).

CASE STUDIES

The following two case studies illustrate how elements of religion and spirituality can be integrated into psychotherapy practice.

The first case is of a highly competent professional man who found himself in an affair. Waking up to the need to revitalize his marriage, he wanted to avoid his previous dysfunctional patterns of coping. Instead of being passive-aggressive and withdrawn, he longed to speak with his own authentic voice, and meet his wife with power and presence.

His usual posture of anxiety and despair was of a sunken chest and constricted body. Relaxation and meditation suggestions included the following:

- *Relaxation.* Learning to sit upright, he could sense his weight and
  breath. As he let tension out with the exhalation, he was able to release
  some of the claustrophobic struggle. Letting go of familiar inner critical voices and depressing scenarios, he was able to let himself experience new possibilities in the situation.
- *Breathing.* Slowing down the breath slowed down his whole body
  physiology and calmed his anxiety. As he felt his breath travelling up
  his spine, it expanded his lungs, opened his chest and heart. He began
  to experience his heart and listen to its voice.
- *Imagery.* Opening his heart and lungs, he opened his arms. He experienced this as a basket, with the strands of his life holding all the tumultuous experience. He had created a holding container, so that he
  could experience and contain his emotions. Carrying this gesture and
  image through the next week gave him a physical touchstone that
  helped him stay strong and present in his interactions.
- *Communication.* Feeling his heart, he was able to experience more emotion. Slowing his breath, he was able to slow down the overwhelming
  feelings and take space to sort them out. Once sorted out, he could address them one at a time. With time, he was able to know more clearly
  what he needed to say and to whom.

Over time, this man began to feel more centered, was able to trust his
perceptions, speak his truth, and act more responsibly and compassion-
ately. He is rebuilding trust and intimacy with his wife, while taking steps
to resolve the affair.

The second case involved a couple who had been married for over 25
years and had four children. They were becoming estranged and had been
referred by a divorce lawyer. Part of the presenting problem was that "she is
interested in spiritual things and he is not" and she was worried about
their children "growing up with two different points of view on spirituality and religion." This configuration has familiar gender roles: The wife is
increasingly attracted to spiritual studies and meditative quiet, while her
husband is a very rational, successful scientist. She wants more depth in
their communication. When she doesn't find it, she withdraws. When she
withdraws, he experiences her as cold and sexually unresponsive. She says:
"It's a little hall of mirrors—he wants me to be more sexual, and I want him
to be more spiritual." He doesn't understand what "more" she wants; she
thinks they don't speak the same language anymore.

DIAGNOSIS

The initial stages of the therapy process, therefore, focused on collaborating
on defining the problem and establishing treatment goals.

The wife tried to explain what she meant by spirituality:

If spirituality is more than the material world of essences, then how is our relationship going to proceed? How comfortable am I having a household that is not concerned about waste products . . . in so many little details during the day we rub a little. It adds up.

The husband described himself as "tolerant" but "not engaged" with spirituality. The problem for him is that he felt her criticism, and a sense of "rejection," "intolerance," and "lack of understanding." He doesn't understand the need to bring spirituality into the relationship; things could be dealt with squarely and practically on their own. For example, he could understand the rationale behind recycling simply as good practice, not because there was "some spirit" involved.

COURSE OF THERAPY

By more clearly identifying what they were missing, the partners were able to describe it in language that both could understand. Through careful clinical observation and description, the problem came into focus. The issue was primarily about a loss of intimacy in their relationship. Since what they both missed was intimacy, their words had previously intellectualized away their experience. By focusing on the here and now of their nonverbal experience, they were able to let themselves slow down, feel each other's presence, and communicate the language of feeling.

Learning how to just "be" together was essential for this couple. When habits set in, couples can make assumptions about who the other person is or used to be. Structuring time together and creating rituals for closeness is part of a spiritual perspective. A soul perspective on couples therapy would help them rediscover each other in the living reality of their lives.

Through the intense period of childrearing, this couple had become used to spending their time together checking in during the day on their travel plans, the children. I noticed that when they greeted each other in my office after a separation, their conversation was immediately about schedules. Not even acknowledging that they missed each other, their conversation lacked intimacy.

Therapy therefore consisted of various ways to rediscover intimacy. It combined communication skills training, sitting in silence together, with new rituals that create shared space like reading to each other before bed. Part of the therapy, therefore, consisted in carving out a time of day when they would both leave their very active work lives behind and practice simply being together. Their conversation was not to be instrumental about work or arrangements. They designed a bedtime ritual of lighting a candle and sharing new and old poetry and music favorites. After the first week, they came in with a renewed interest in rediscovering each other.

OUTCOME

The couple reported an improved overall sense of closeness and intimacy. Although they still struggle to find time together, they continue to understand and open to each other. Their understanding of the issue of spirituality in their relationship had now shifted to include new complexities and similarities and differences. Instead of being used to separate them, the exploration of spirituality brought them closer. She explained what it meant to her:

> I go back to hunger again. Spirituality is a hunger for a connection to the spirit, or a desire to feel that my purpose here is not just set to what I feel are the small needs, but a larger picture that I can't decide what that is. It has to be giving myself over to what life is going to bring.

Looking at her husband, she said, "When we spoke about spirituality, I can't believe you don't have strong spirituality because you hold such values of integrity with other people." He described their differences: "I think that there is destiny and a path for her, a quest. I don't think there is a path for me. I think you have to bushwack and when it's over it's over—no beyond. If there is no destiny, you come back to what are your choices at the moment. I think for her my view would be a profoundly empty existence." She continued: "I wouldn't use the term 'profoundly empty,' but for you the intellect is the pinnacle and for me there is something that is more profound than the intellect." Through this discussion, a bridge was built. He said: "I think what she describes as 'spirit' I have as much as anyone else. Sometimes, in nature or walking with people, I experience a loss of individuality or a merging of consciousness. I don't know if I experience as much as others do, but I certainly experience the joy of that. I don't know if I attach the word 'spirit,' nor is it a religious construction, but it is a dropping of boundaries. Whether this is about God or spirit, I don't think it makes it any less profound. That's one of the things I've been trying to think about in trying to explore this life with my wife and in the work that we do here."

SUMMARY

Given the scattering effects of globalization on the religious and spiritual aspects of couples today, psychologists should be prepared to help their clients confront new issues of meaning and purpose, identity and family rituals. Although psychologists are not trained to deal with religious and spiritual issues, this chapter lays out a series of questions, reviews existing related literature, and describes clinical principles to help psychologists confront religious and spiritual issues in couples therapy. It is hoped that training in religious and spiritual issues in psychotherapy will become part of new cultural proficiencies for training psychologists.

REFERENCES

American Psychiatric Association. (1994). *Diagnostic and statistical manual of mental disorders* (4th ed.). Washington, DC: Author.

Anderson, D. A., & Worthen, D. (1997). Exploring a fourth dimension: Spirituality as a resource for the couple therapist. *Journal of Marital and Family Therapy, 23,* 3–12.

Arnett, J. J. (2002). The psychology of globalization. *American Psychologist, 57*(10), 774–783.

Barks, C. (Trans.). (1995). *The essential Rumi.* New York: HarperCollins.

Bergin, A. E., & Jensen, J. P. (1990). Religiosity of psychotherapists: A national survey. *Psychotherapy, 27*(1), 3–7.

Bloch, A., & Bloch, C. (1995). *The song of songs.* New York: Random House.

Cadwallader, E. (1991). Depression and religion: Realities, perspectives, and directions. *Counseling and Values, 35,* 83–92.

Crohn, J. (1995). *Mixed matches.* New York: Ballantine Books.

Diblasio, F. A. (1993). The role of social workers' religious beliefs in helping family members forgive. *Families in Society, 74,* 163–170.

Eisler, R. T. (1987). *The chalice and the blade: Our history, our future.* San Francisco: Harper & Row.

Elkins, D. N., Hedstrom, L. J., Hughes, L. L., Leaf, J. A., & Saunders, C. (1988). Toward a humanistic-phenomenological spirituality: Definition, description and measurement. *Journal of humanistic Psychology, 28*(4), 5–18.

Frame, M. W. (2000). The spiritual genogram in family therapy. *Journal of Marital and Family Therapy, 26*(2), 211–216.

Frankl, V. (1959). *Man's search for meaning.* New York: Praeger.

Gallup, G. J., & Castelli, J. (1989). *The people's religion: American faith in the 90's.* New York: Macmillan.

Genia, V. (1990). Religious development: A synthesis and reformulation. *Journal of Religion and Health, 29*(2), 85–99.

Griffith, J. L., & Griffith, M. E. (1992). Therapeutic change in religious families: Working with the God construct. In L. Burton (Ed.), *Religion and the family* (pp. 63–86). Binghamton, NY: Haworth Press.

Hastings, A. (1999). Transpersonal psychology: The 4th force. In D. Moss (Ed.), *Humanistic and transpersonal psychology: A historical biographical sourcebook* (pp. 192–209). Westport, CT: Greenwood Press.

Heller, P., & Wood, B. (2000). The influence of religious and ethnic differences on marital intimacy: Intermarriage versus intramarriage. *Journal of Marital and Family Therapy, 26*(2), 241–252.

Hillman, J. (1972). *The myth of analysis: Three essays in archetypal psychology.* New York: Harper & Row.

Hodge, D. (2000). Spiritual ecomaps: A new diagrammatic tool for assessing marital and family spirituality. *Journal of Marital and Family Therapy, 26*(2), 217–228.

Houston, J. (1982). *The search for the beloved: Journeys in sacred psychology.* Los Angeles: Tarcher.

Jacobs, J. L. (1992). Religious ritual and mental health. In J. Schumacher (Ed.), *Religion and mental health* (pp. 291–299). New York: Oxford University Press.

Jung, C. G. (1954). Marriage as a psychological relationship (R. F. C. Hull Trans.). *Collected works* (Vol. 17, Bollingen Series 20). Princeton, NJ: Princeton University Press.

Jung, C. G. (1958). Psychology and religion: West and East (R. F. C. Hull Trans.). *Collected works* (Vol. 2, Bollingen Series 30). New York: Pantheon Books.

Jung, C. G. (1963). Mysterium coniunctionis (R. F. C. Hull, Trans.). In *Collected works* (Vol. 14, Bollingen Series 20). Princeton, NJ: Princeton University Press.

Kaslow, F., & Robinson, J. A. (1996). Long-term satisfying marriages: Perceptions contributing factors. *American Journal of Family Therapy, 24*(2), 153–170.

Kok, C. J., & Leskela, J. (1996). Solution-focused therapy in a psychiatric hospital. *Journal of Marital and Family Therapy, 22,* 397–406.

Maslow, A. (1971). *The farther reaches of human nature.* New York: Viking.

Maturana, H. R., & Varela, F. J. (1992). *The tree of knowledge: The biological roots of human understanding* (Rev. ed., R. Paolucci, Trans.). Boston: Shambhala.

Moon, G., Willis, D., Bailey, J., & Kwansy, J. (1993). Self-reported use of Christian spiritual guidance techniques by Christian psychotherapists, pastoral counselors, and spiritual directors. *Journal of Psychology and Christianity, 12,* 24–37.

Moore, T. (1994). *Soul mates.* New York: HarperCollins.

Moules, N. (2000). Postmodernism and the sacred: Reclaiming connection in our greater-than-human worlds. *Journal of Marital and Family Therapy, 26*(2), 229–240.

Murphy, M., & Donovan, S. (1997). *The physical and psychological effects of meditation* (2nd ed.). Sausalito, CA: Institute of Noetic Sciences.

Needleman, J. (1983). Psychiatry and the sacred. In J. Welwood (Ed.), *Awakening the heart: East/West approaches to psychotherapy and the healing relationship* (pp. 4–17). Boston: Shambhala.

Pargament, K. I. (1997). *The psychology of religion and coping.* New York: Guilford Press.

Patai, R. (1978). *The Hebrew goddess.* New York: Arno Press.

Patterson, J., Hayworth, M., Turner, C., & Raskin, M. (2000). Spiritual issues in family therapy: A graduate-level course. *Journal of Marital and Family Therapy, 26*(2), 199–210.

Prest, L. A., & Keller, J. F. (1993). Spirituality and family therapy: Spiritual beliefs, myths, and metaphors. *Journal of Marital and Family Therapy, 21,* 60–77.

Richards, P. S., & Bergin, A. E. (1997). *A spiritual strategy for counseling and psychotherapy.* Washington, DC: American Psychological Association.

Rotz, E., Russell, C. S., & Wright, D. W. (1993). The therapist who is perceived as "spiritually correct": Strategies for avoiding collusion with the "spiritually one-up" spouse. *Journal of Marital and Family Therapy, 19,* 369–375.

Saleebey, D. (Ed.). (1997). *The strengths perspective* (2nd ed.). New York: Longman.

Schneider, K. (1990). *The paradoxical self: Toward an understanding of our contradictory nature.* New York: Plenum Press.

Serlin, I. A. (1989a, Fall). From Buddhism and back. *Lilith Magazine, 21,* 23–24.

Serlin, I. A. (1989b). A psycho-spiritual body approach to a residential treatment of Catholic religious. *Journal of Transpersonal Psychology, 21*(2), 177–191.

Serlin, I. A. (2001). Book review: Berman, Morris. (2000). [Review of the book *Wandering God: A study in nomadic spirituality.*] *Journal of Transpersonal Psychology, 33*(1), 72–74.

Shafranske, E. P. (Ed.). (1996). *Religion and the clinical practice of psychology.* Washington, DC: American Psychological Association.

Shafranske, E. P., & Maloney, H. N. (1990). Clinical psychologists' religious and spiritual orientations and their practice of psychotherapy. *Psychotherapy, 27,* 72–78.

Spretnak, C. (1991). *States of grace: The recovery of meaning in the postmodern age.* New York: HarperCollins.

Steere, D. A. (1997). *Spiritual presence in psychotherapy: A guide for caregivers.* New York: Brunner/Mazel.

Sue, D. W., Bingham, R. P., Porche-Burke, L., & Vasquez, M. (1999). The diversification of psychology: A multicultural revolution. *American Psychologist, 54*(12), 1061–1069.

Sutich, A. (1969). Some considerations regarding transpersonal psychology. *Journal of Transpersonal Psychology, 1,* 11–20.

Suzuki, D. T. (1949). *Introduction to Zen Buddhism.* London: Rider.

Tan, S. Y. (2003). Integrating spiritual direction into psychotherapy: Ethical issues and guidelines. *Journal of Psychology and Theology, 31,* 14–23.

Trungpa, C. (1969). *Meditation in action.* Boulder, CO: Shambhala.

Trungpa, C. (1983). Becoming a full human being. In J. Welwood (Ed.), *East/West approaches to psychotherapy and the healing relationship* (pp. 126–131). Boston: Shambhala.

Vande Kemp, H. (1996). Historical perspective: Religion and clinical psychology in America. In E. P. Shafranske (Ed.), *Religion and the clinical practice of psychology* (pp. 71–113). Washington, DC: American Psychological Association.

Vaughan, F. (1987). A question of balance: Health and pathology in new religious movements. In D. Anthony, B. Ecker, & K. Wilbur (Eds.), *Spiritual choices: The problem of recognizing authentic pathos to inner transformation* (pp. 265–282). New York: Paragon House.

Walsh, F. (1998). Beliefs, spirituality, and transcendence. In M. McGoldrick (Ed.), *Re-visioning family therapy: Race, culture, and transcendence in clinical practice* (pp. 62–77). New York: Guilford Press.

Walsh, F. (Ed.). (1999). *Spiritual resources in family therapy.* New York: Guilford Press.

Walsh, R. (1999). *Essential spirituality.* New York: Wiley.

Welwood, J. (1983). *Awakening the heart: East/West approaches to psychotherapy and the healing relationship.* Boston: Shambhala.

Welwood, J. (1990a). Intimate relationship as path. *Journal of Transpersonal Psychology, 22*(1), 51–58.

Welwood, J. (1990b). *Journey of the heart.* New York: HarperCollins.

Wilbur, K. (1981). *No boundary.* Boston: Shambhala.

Worthington, E. L., Jr., Kurusu, T., McCullough, M. E., & Sandage, S. (1996). Empirical research on religion and psychotherapeutic processes and outcomes: A ten-year review and research prospectus. *Psychological Bulletin, 119,* 448–487.

CHAPTER 21

Working with Same-Sex Couples

Daniel J. Alonzo

ARIO, A 35-YEAR-OLD Mexican American male, and Kevin, a 33-year-old Euro-American male, enter couple therapy because, in Mario's words, "We argue over the smallest things and criticize each other constantly." Mario, who works as a county social worker, reports that he grew up the eldest of seven children, "and I learned that you have to get along and take care of each other or nothing gets accomplished." In a moment of vulnerability, he confesses that he feels extremely fortunate to have met Kevin, whom he sees as very good-looking, intelligent, and self-assured. He admits that he has always had a secret fear that one day Kevin would leave him, and he wonders what he would tell his family, who love Kevin very much. Kevin, a general contractor who is closeted at work, grew up the younger of two in a fairly disengaged family. He complains that after seven years he and Mario do everything together, and now he wants more time to himself. Yes, he reassures Mario, he does enjoy all the time they spend with Mario's family, but he says he has been plagued by worries that he may have settled down too soon. Mario asks, "Do you want to talk about sex?" and Kevin answers yes, but in this first session the men seem to hold back and talk only in generalities. Kevin wonders aloud if they should explore the possibility of an open relationship, and Mario reacts quickly, asking, "Why would you want to put us in danger, what with AIDS and everything out there?" Kevin says nothing and looks quietly down at his hands.

This brief case example reminds us that working with same-sex couples has its challenges and surprising twists. Clinicians must bring all their expertise in relational dynamics to the consultation room in working with gay and lesbian couples. Gay, lesbian, bisexual, and transgender (GLBT) clients deserve the same level of skilled attention that heterosexual clients receive. However, there are several obstacles in the current therapeutic world that interfere with the acquisition of these important skills.

One such obstacle is the common dismissal of differences between same-sex and heterosexual couples. Frequently, both beginning and experienced clinicians state, "All people are the same, people are just people, and at the end of the day, relationships are all alike." These assumptions are based on well-intentioned efforts to be accepting, but they also discount the sociocultural realities that shape the psychologies of sexual minorities.

Another obstacle is seemingly the opposite of the first. Many heterosexual clinicians feel that same-sex relationship problems are too different or too complicated to treat. There can be an assumption that such couples require a highly specialized expertise that only GLBT therapists can provide. It is not uncommon to hear colleagues say, "But wouldn't a gay couple want to see a gay therapist?" Although some GLBT people do feel safer with a therapist who is similar along several demographic lines, many others are more interested in choosing a good, validating therapist of any sexual orientation. Also, such an assumption relieves the therapist of the responsibility to learn more about same-sex relationships. Unfortunately, some of the most troubling research in the past decade shows that almost half of all members of the American Association for Marriage and Family Therapy report not feeling competent treating sexual minorities (Doherty & Simmons, 1996). And yet, a large majority (72%) of these therapists report that one out of every 10 of the cases in their practices involves lesbians or gay men (S. K. Green & Bobele, 1994)!

GLBT therapists face different obstacles. It is common for GLBT therapists to over-identify with their clients and perhaps steer their clients toward the "solutions" that they applied to their own relationship "problems." Understandably, GLBT therapists who have done the difficult work of coming out and relationship exploration would want to "transfer" this knowledge to those who are still struggling. Nevertheless, it is important for GLBT therapists to expand their professional knowledge of dynamics in same-sex couples so that they can offer the most balanced treatment possible.

Yet another obstacle is the lack of a broad base of professional literature on the subject of same-sex couples. A recent survey found that an extremely small number of articles in family therapy journals examined gay and lesbian issues (Clark & Serovich, 1997). R.-J. Green, Bettinger, and Zacks (1996) point out that much of the literature on couples has focused on the concept of gay male "disengagement" and lesbian "fusion." Are these valid concepts? What about discussions of other relational dynamics necessary for the couples therapist? There is an overwhelming need for more research in this field.

This chapter examines some of the more prominent forces in same-sex relationships. After a review of the opportunities and challenges for creating relationships, we look more closely at special issues for male couples and female couples. A second case example illustrates therapeutic considerations involved in this work, including considerations of cultural diversity. It is beyond the scope of this chapter to discuss the host of issues associated with relationships where at least one partner is transgendered. Perhaps this chapter will stimulate the reader to consider other sources for a full discussion of that topic.

HOMOPHOBIA AND HETEROSEXISM

It is impossible to underestimate the pervasive effects of societal discomfort and disapproval of same-sex coupling. *Homophobia,* the irrational fear and hatred of homosexual behavior and the individuals who engage in it (Weinberg, 1972), and *heterosexism,* the term that describes the dominant cultural assumption that heterosexuality is the preferred sexual orientation (Okun, 1996), are the two foundational forces that shape the lives of same-sex couples on a daily basis. The very real threat of anti-gay violence, the omnipresent possibility of disapproving attitudes from others, and the fear of discovery in a potentially hostile environment lead gay and lesbian couples to disguise, minimize, or deny their relationships. Couples develop an automatic vigilance for prejudice and discrimination—not an exaggerated response when we consider the regulatory, legislative, judicial, and religious frameworks that still do not recognize the reality, validity, or sanctity of their partnerships.

It is not uncommon for therapists to hear that some of their same-sex couples have never expressed affection outside the walls of their homes. Many same-sex couples learn to be discreet, to be unnoticeable, and to hide, except within certain "gay" neighborhoods or areas where the probabilities for censure or attack are minimal. Furthermore, although increasing numbers of GLBT people are featured in television and films, very few stable, well-adjusted same-sex couples receive any kind of accurate media portrayal. The gay commercial media often focuses on the "single" lifestyle, using youth and sex to sell products and services. As a result of all of this, same-sex couples are essentially invisible in both the dominant culture and the gay subculture. Same-sex couples have trouble locating the relational role models that can demonstrate resilience, longevity, and humor in the face of oppression (Greenan & Tunnell, 2003). Therapists hear frequently from gay and lesbian couples that they have difficulty finding other couples with whom to socialize. Many partnerships feel isolated from a network of other couples that would provide a sense of predictable lifespan development. They report loneliness as a result, increasing the pressure on partners to meet every need of their mates. Our opening case, Kevin and Mario may be dealing with these very pressures. Furthermore, Mario may find himself feeling even more isolated because of his double-minority status as a gay man and a Mexican American. This couple will deal with both the oppression by the dominant culture and the oppression by the most visible and privileged part of the gay community—the segment that is White and male (Greene, 1997).

Internalized homophobia and heterosexism also interact with other intrapsychic forces in same-sex couples. Self-psychology and attachment theory remind us that sexual minority clients may not have had their basic psychological needs met as children because of the differences between themselves and parental figures (Baker & Baker, 1987; Johnson, 1996; Josephson, 2003; Mohr, 1999; Wolf, 1988). Caretakers may not be able to meet the mirroring needs of GLBT youth, either because they are ignorant of or threatened by the differences they see in their children, or because the children hesitate in revealing their true selves. GLBT children perceive their families as different from them, and they perceive themselves as being different from the other children in their environment. As a result, some GLBT people learn to distrust their impulses to be close to others, especially those of the same sex. They may carry this hesitance and relational ambivalence into their adult relationships. At the same time, having experienced loneliness and isolation as children, some GLBT adults may come to their relationships desperate to bond with others. Attachment styles may appear to be ambivalent or avoidant (Mohr, 1999). It is important that clinicians not pathologize these relationships but instead help clients understand that they are attempting to repair injuries in their early relational histories.

The effect of internalized cultural attitudes on self-esteem has been well-documented (Forstein, 1986; Malyon, 1982; Ritter & Terndrup, 2002). Internalized homophobia and heterosexism can lead GLBT people to sabotage their relationships in countless, often subtle ways: They doubt the viability of their relationships, as perhaps Mario is doing when he talks about his on-going fear that Kevin will leave him; they feel guilty as they experience closeness; they inhibit displays of affection; they interrupt intimacy and sexuality, as perhaps Kevin is doing as he withdraws from Mario; they choose not to have children when they secretly want them; they collude with families, friends, and work environments that doubt the viability of their partnerships; they sometimes hastily end relationships before alternatives have been explored, and we have to wonder if Kevin is headed in this direction. In some cases, internalized homophobia can create enough shame and self-doubt to have more serious consequences: GLBT people can become anxious and depressed; they can become involved in addictive behaviors as frustrated attempts to deal with helplessness and hopelessness; they can abuse partners as a means of acting out feelings of powerlessness. Therapists should not automatically assume that all couples are caught in the tangle of unconscious, self-destructive webs. However, working with same-sex couples requires an ongoing, careful assessment of internalized beliefs, and, if necessary, a primary treatment plan of helping partners deconstruct relationship dynamics influenced by society's prejudicial attitudes. Using a multicultural lens and framework—that is, a culturally sensitive approach that affirms diversity, validates differences, and discusses privilege and oppression—can help the clinician guide couples to examine the social stigmatization that has probably affected the integrity of their relationships (Israel & Selvidge, 2003).

CREATING RELATIONSHIPS: OPPORTUNITIES AND CHALLENGES

Given the numerous vulnerabilities that same-sex relationships experience, you might wonder if such relationships ever do succeed in providing satisfaction. The answer is a resounding "Yes!" Despite all the external and internal obstacles discussed thus far, GLBT people do find ways to create satisfying, committed, and loving relationships. This statement might strike some as being obvious and elementary, but it is easy for clinicians to develop a skewed perspective as they regularly counsel people with relationship problems. Forgetting the viability of healthy GLBT relationships creates a fertile ground for a therapist's unconscious heterosexism to take root.

Thanks to the pioneering work of investigators like Letitia Peplau and Lawrence Kurdek, we now have 20 years of solid research that supports the proposition that sexual minorities have the same capacities to create satisfying relationships as do their heterosexual counterparts (Haas & Stafford, 1998; Kurdek, 1988; Kurdek & Schmitt, 1987; Means-Christensen, Snyder, & Negy, 2003; Peplau & Cochran, 1990). On almost every variable tested— intimacy, partner similarity, attachment, trust, liking, use of maintenance behaviors, to name a few—lesbians and gay men are as satisfied with their relationships as heterosexuals. Gay men and lesbians do report more autonomy and fewer barriers to leaving (Kurdek, 1998), but this would be expected given the lack of societal and religious validation given to same-sex couples. This research reminds us that same-sex couples persevere in the face of difficult odds. This research does not invalidate the previously stated point that same-sex couples are under tremendous stress. What the research does support is the idea that there is nothing innate in gay, lesbian, and bisexual people that would make their relationships impossible or dysfunctional.

We must consider the special stressors that GLBT people face in creating intimate relationships without the use of culturally approved guidelines. First, where will GLBT people meet and find partners? As discussed earlier, because homosexuality is often hidden and invisible, GLBT people often cannot take for granted that they will meet potential dating partners in the weekly course of their lives. Larger cities in the United States, especially along the coasts, have higher concentrations of sexual minorities and larger GLBT communities, but even there gay people must "dichotomize" their worlds. That is, how often should they shun the heterosexual world to spend time in gay neighborhoods, frequent gay establishments, join gay organizations, and so forth—all in the service of finding possible dates? Today, GLBT bars and night/dance clubs remain prime gathering places. Of course, alcohol has the potential to mix dangerously with internalized homophobia to create further adjustment problems.

Due to the lack of social validation, guidelines, and structures for GLBT couples, same-sex partners often have to negotiate boundaries in their relationships. Therapists may hear couples struggling with any of the following questions: What type of relationship is this? Is this just a friendship? Can we just be sex buddies? Can we maintain a primary partnership even if we are not having sex anymore? Is it okay with you if I spend lots of time with my ex who is still my best friend? R.-J. Green and Mitchell (2002) assert that "commitment ambiguity," where one partner is not sure about his or her place in the relationship, is prevalent in same-sex couples that find their way to therapy, perhaps due to the lack of social and legal recognition of these partnerships. In the opening case example, Kevin may be experiencing this commitment ambiguity. It is also likely that such ambiguity is common because GLBT people experience a delayed adolescence (Malyon, 1982), attempting to experiment with dating while at the same time resisting pressures to create adult relationships common for someone at their chronological age. When Kevin wonders if he settled down too early, he may be grieving an adolescence that was not fully, satisfactorily experienced.

Gender role socialization provides other challenges. GLBT men and women experienced the same socialization forces in childhood that their heterosexual counterparts did, even if they could not easily conform or even if they actively rebelled. The probability is high that lesbians and gay men will have some values, attitudes, and cognitive/emotional frameworks that are typical for their gender. In areas of division of labor, negotiation of power, patterns of communication, cooperation and competition, initiation of sexuality, sexual activity, and reciprocity, to name a few, two members of the same sex must create patterns that work for them rather than trying to adhere to traditional male-female roles. Such a task often creates tension and confusion, leading a couple to mislabel a challenge as a hopeless dilemma. Gender role socialization also creates guilt and shame, as some partners experience anxiety and depression around violation of learned social norms (Bepko & Johnson, 2000).

Finally, where does the couple find social support? Many same-sex couples do not find loving support from families-of-origin who are all-too-often disappointed, confused, grieving, or rejecting. No wonder Mario feels fortunate to have the support of his family; no wonder he thinks about their disappointment should he and Kevin separate. Many GLBT people have to create new families to fill the void left by embarrassed or hostile blood relatives. These families-of-choice include friendship networks, other same-sex couples, affirming heterosexual individuals/couples, and even ex-partners (R.-J. Green & Mitchell, 2002). Even those fortunate enough to have supportive blood relatives have usually had to travel a lengthy psychological distance to reach a place of healthy differentiation: They may naturally turn toward chosen friends who have also experienced similar journeys. Some heterosexual therapists are incredulous that GLBT people frequently maintain ties with previous partners. Perhaps having witnessed some ugly and brutal child custody wars in heterosexual break-ups, some therapists expect that all ex-relationships will be fraught with anger, bitterness, and contempt. Although that might be true in some cases, therapists must remember to appreciate the resilience of same-sex couples who have learned to value the gifts that previous relationships have provided them. Many GLBT people have learned to cultivate a nurturance, reciprocity, and affection with the people who have been witnesses to their personal struggles over the years.

SPECIAL ISSUES FOR GAY MALE COUPLES

Having considered some of the general dynamics in same-sex relationships, it might now be useful to look at special issues for male and female couples separately. Much of the literature on male couples has traditionally focused on "male disengagement" and "difficulty with intimacy." Bepko and Johnson (2000) persuasively argue that there is little empirical validity to the idea that there is widespread disengagement among male couples. Couples that present for therapy, especially couples where one or both of the partners have been raised in families where traditional gender role socialization took place, will experience more difficulty with intimacy and commitment than healthy couples where this is not the case. However, as we discussed earlier, it is fair to say that most gay men did grow up acutely aware of their differences from the majority of boys, that they could not talk to their parents about these differences, and that internalized homophobia may make men more likely to struggle unconsciously to fit into society's expectations of manhood. These strong forces might affect a gay man's ability to show vulnerability to his partner, tolerate his partner's emotionality rather than fix it, or quickly give up on a relationship rather than experience an extended process of indecision that might lead to dissolution anyway—an outcome that might create a sense of "failure," a difficult feeling of guilt for many men socialized in the dominant culture.

An additional component to this dilemma is what I refer to as "the masculine imperative": That is, the pressure within larger gay male communities for men to adhere to a rigid attitudinal and physical presentation to the world. Similar to the pressures that women feel to conform to the unrealistic body type presented in the mass media, gay men are inundated with images exhorting them to develop "hypermasculine" physical qualities—gym-created biceps, "cut" chests, defined abdominal muscles—perhaps as an invitation to fight stereotypes of weakness and perhaps a way of celebrating man-to-man sexuality openly. And perhaps these images are prevalent because, as everywhere, sex sells. The problem lies in the danger of further reinforcement of narrow gender guidelines and a shaming of feminine or androgynous qualities, thus making it even more difficult to show emotions to one's partner. Vulnerability, receptiveness, and surrender of control are states of mind necessary for satisfying and passionate sex, and male partners who are invested in maintaining narrow hypermasculine stances might encounter more difficulty in maintaining long-term intimacy in relationships.

In their groundbreaking, six-stage model of male couple development, McWhirter and Mattison (1984) note that at each level men must accomplish tasks to manage the tension between closeness and autonomy, avoiding the extremes of fusion and withdrawal. "Stage discrepancy," when one partner is moving into the next stage and the other partner is not, may be a key to conflict in these relationships. After seven years, Kevin and Mario are likely working with appropriate developmental tasks of reestablishing independence while also remaining emotionally faithful.

McWhirter and Mattison (1984) found that all the couples in their study that had been together at least five years had a conversation about sexual exclusivity, even if they ultimately decided to keep the arrangement monogamous. Kevin and Mario are struggling with this issue. There may be no topic that arouses greater countertransference in working with male couples than the issue of monogamy. Almost every male couple at some point will grapple with this question, and therapists must be careful not to avoid the difficult conversation out of fear or uncertainty. Admittedly, much of the research on this topic was completed less than 10 years after the first wave of AIDS-related deaths swept through gay communities (e.g., Blumstein & Schwartz, 1983; Kurdek & Schmitt, 1986). As a result, it is difficult to obtain a current, accurate estimate of prevalence of open relationships among gay men, although some recent research does discuss sexual risk taking and the use of rule making in open relationships (Hickson, Davies, Weatherburn, Coxon, & McManus, 1992; Paul, Stall, Crosby, Barrett, & Midanik, 1994; Wagner, Remien, & Carballo-Dieguez, 2000). There is great variance in the way that gay men conduct their relationships because, as mentioned before, they create their relationships outside the context of accepted societal norms, and also because men are socialized to separate sex and emotion. Research does show that many male couples maintain closed relationships. Others develop mutually agreeable guidelines to keep the emotional primacy of the relationship intact while allowing for extradyadic sex (e.g., not having outside sex with the same person twice, only having sex when away on a business trip, never with a friend, never in our house; Hickson et al., 1992). The bulk of the research shows that nonmonogamous couples do not experience less satisfaction than their monogamous counterparts. Therapists must carefully examine their biases that might interrupt a couple's negotiation of a workable and affirming relationship.

Finally, it is important to note that there will not be a single male couple that enters treatment who is not somehow affected by HIV and AIDS. Whether or not one or both of the partners is HIV-positive, the lives of gay men have been profoundly affected by this epidemic. In the dating process, gay men struggle with questions of when to test, whom to date, when to disclose one's HIV status, and how to have sex. Almost all gay men know others who are positive; men over 30 most probably know someone who died. The use of condoms is a huge issue, with larger numbers of younger men taking risks that their older counterparts would not, and some older gay men longing for their earlier days when sex seemed more carefree and spontaneous. Male partners in their forties and beyond may have lost a previous mate to AIDS, and processes of comparison, grief, and letting go become important. The question of whether to open the relationship, and the type of sex that will be allowed outside the relationship, raises strong issues of honesty and trust. If Kevin and Mario decide to open their relationship, they will face these issues. Also, if at least one partner of a male couple is HIV positive, the couple must grapple with questions of medication adherence, safer sex, and fear of the future. Even today with the advent of miraculous combination drug therapies, side effects of medication can still be severe, and people do still die. It is incumbent on every therapist to explore with every couple, in empathic and nonjudgmental ways, the realities of HIV in the world and the inescapable effects on their relationship.

SPECIAL ISSUES FOR FEMALE COUPLES

If much of the professional literature on male couples has focused on disengagement, it is also true that literature on female couples has focused on the opposite—"fusion." The earliest writings on the subject proposed that women, socialized to attend to the needs of others, would tend to lose their boundaries and enter a state of "undifferentiation" (Krestan & Bepko, 1980). Sometimes this merger was explained in terms of the female couple turning inward as a response to a hostile, homophobic environment (Vargo, 1988). Nevertheless, the discussion seemed to hint at a pathological nature to this arrangement. Perhaps some of the discourse that followed from this early literature was founded on assumptions that two women in a couple cannot possibly be happy together, that the male model of independence and individuation is the preferable state, and that two people attending closely to each other's needs will naturally produce dysfunctional relationships. Recently, there has been a reevaluation of this assessment. In fact, research shows that female couples are not struggling to achieve a demonstrated male ideal. In their influential research, R.-J. Green et al. (1996) report that lesbian couples are more flexible and cohesive than heterosexual and gay male relationships, that less flexible and cohesive female couples are more likely to break up in the first two years, and that lesbian partners are actually quite satisfied with their relationships. Perhaps women enjoy their relationships more because female socialization actually produces benefits. Perhaps women are able to leave behind patriarchal assumptions and use their relational abilities to produce empathy and intimacy, making possible both closeness and independence (Marvin & Miller, 2000).

Similarly, therapists must be careful not to assume that all female couples are suffering from "lesbian bed death," the frequently used term to indicate the lack of sexuality in lesbian relationships. Iasenza (1999) persuasively argues that this myth may have come from a hasty reading of Blumstein and Schwartz's *American Couples* (1983), where empirical evidence found that lesbian couples had less sex than the other three types examined—gay male couples, heterosexually cohabiting couples, and heterosexually married couples. Part of the problem, Iasenza argues, is how we define sexuality. If sex is defined in terms of genital acts leading to orgasm, then we are adhering to sexist and heterosexist assumptions. In a review of the research, Iasenza reports that lesbians "are found to be more sexually assertive; sexually arousable; verbally and nonverbally communicative about sexual needs, desires, pleasures, and distractions; and more satisfied with the quality of their sexual lives than are heterosexual women" (p. 10). If they prefer, two women together are able to enjoy many ways of relating sexually that do not fit traditional notions of intercourse, penetration, and climax.

This is not to say that some lesbian couples are not vulnerable to particular pressures in their intimate relationships. Nichols (1987a, 1987b, 2000) asserts that women may develop sexual patterns that do not mimic patriarchal models, but this can also interfere in individual sexual pleasure; women may be trapped in egalitarian models that do not allow for playful domination and submission; and having internalized the cultural messages that suppress female sexuality, lesbians may not have the language for discussing sexual difficulties with their partners or with their therapists. In their clinically based, six-stage model of the development of lesbian relationships, Clunis and Green (1988) explain that couples may naturally experience tension in their sexual relationships as they enter the stage of conflict management and struggle for power, especially after the early periods of "prerelationship" acquaintanceship and romantic immersion. Women do not seem to grapple with questions of sexual exclusivity in the same predictable way that gay men do, most likely due to female socialization, and research shows that most female couples are monogamous (Ritter & Terndrup, 2002). Slater's model of lesbian lifespan development (1995) also explains that as women confront the necessary "middle years" (a period where partners must deepen the investment) and the stage of "generativity" (when partners must create something larger than themselves to deal with their mortality), avoidance and tension can also interfere with sexual communication. Slater (1994) cautions that some partners may avoid the work of their relationship's "middle years" by engaging in outside attractions, perhaps to deal with menopause, symbolize an act of individuation, revive early attachment affects, or rebel against oppressive cultural narratives.

Other dynamics may increase conflict in lesbian relationships. Differences in lesbian identity acquisition may interfere with intimacy. Some partners who enter a same-sex relationship directly out of a heterosexual marriage may have mixed feelings about being with another woman. Some partners self-identify as bisexual, and this can frustrate a feminist partner who proudly identifies as lesbian. Also, lesbians may have children from a previous heterosexual marriage, creating challenges for a successful blended family. Women who have not had children but want them must prepare themselves for a time-consuming, often expensive process in a medical establishment that often does not value alternative families. Another dynamic that might create conflict relates to recovery from sexual abuse. Because rates of sexual abuse of female children are very high, the odds are doubled that one of the women in a lesbian partnership may be dealing with recovery from such trauma (Kerewsky & Miller, 1996). Finally, power differentials, isolation from other couples, female socialization that cultivates dependency, and heterosexist oppression may all contribute to high rates of domestic violence (Waldner-Haugrud, Gratch, & Magruder, 1997). A brief case study illustrates some of these therapeutic issues facing female couples.

CASE STUDY

Sarah, 44, and Chris, 29, together for two years, come to therapy at Sarah's insistence because "we are not getting our needs met." Sarah, Euro-American, sober and attending AA for the past 15 years, is a local realtor in a middle-class, identifiably gay neighborhood, and Chris, African American, is a first-grade teacher in an economically depressed part of the city. They live together in a house that Sarah owned when she met Chris. Sarah feels proud of her independence, having worked hard for the quality of her present life. Sarah looks forward to spending time with their friends, most of whom are older Caucasian lesbian individuals and couples. She has had three serious relationships with women, two of whom remain close friends. Sarah is frustrated, asking for more "intimacy," afraid that once again she will not be satisfied in a relationship. Chris, on the other hand, a survivor of childhood sexual abuse, says that she enjoys their current level of intimacy: "I just like it when we're warm and close." This is Chris's first cohabiting relationship with a woman, and Chris refers to herself as "bisexual." Chris was married briefly to a man, and she only dated one other woman before she met Sarah at a lesbian discussion group. She and her husband did not have children. She would like to have one, but Sarah says, "I don't know if I want to tackle that at this point in my life." Chris likes Sarah's friends, but she also likes to spend generous amounts of time with her family-of-origin. She enjoys her work in the public schools, but she is acutely conscious that she makes much less than Sarah does in real estate.

First, it is important to note, just as we did with Kevin and Mario, the intersection of issues around same-sex coupling and cultural diversity. An African American woman like Chris may struggle to integrate different identities—member of the Black community, member of her family-of-origin, woman, and bisexual (Bridges, Selvidge, & Matthews, 2003). African American lesbian and bisexual women have also been shown to maintain stronger ties to families, children, and community than their Caucasian counterparts (Greene, 1997). Chris knows that an important part of her history is tied to her family. For Sarah, whose AA-related recovery is a sign of her strength and perseverance, the concept of family is symbolized in the close relationships with women she has cultivated over the years. The therapist will have to facilitate a conversation in which the two women compare and contrast their different family systems and explore how each side of the relationship can contribute to the richness of their lives together. Their racial difference may also be a part of the unstated power dynamics in the relationship. While the therapist must recognize Sarah's determination and diligence, the therapist must sensitively address the privileges that Sarah has that Chris does not—higher discretionary income, ownership of property, established professional status in the community, ability to be "out" at work, and Caucasian status.

All of these factors—in addition to the fact that Sarah is older, more comfortable in the lesbian world, and "insists" that the couple come to therapy—may be upsetting the balance of power in the relationship. The couple definitely could be struggling with Clunis and Greene's (1988) stage of relationship conflict, a sometimes challenging task when the two female partners have been socialized to value nonassertion. The therapist might see if each partner can balance hearing each other's needs while also holding on to a strong sense of self. Each woman might indeed have very different life-goals. Chris wants children, and the therapist can discuss with the partners how institutionalized heterosexism and the lack of social support for same-sex parents makes their decision a more difficult one—how it might, in fact, even fuel Sarah's ambivalence.

Before giving in to the idea that this couple is another casualty of "lesbian bed death," the therapist must probe each partner's definition of "intimacy." Perhaps the sexual issue is how the couple system deals with conflict—that is, how Chris works to get more leverage and power in the relationship. The therapist must be sensitive to each woman's sexual script; however, since lesbian sexuality is largely invisible in our culture, the therapist must help the clients bravely voice their specific needs, fears, and fantasies. Certainly, the therapist must explore how Chris's childhood sexual abuse affects them, but there may be other factors affecting their sexual pleasure. Where is Chris in her acquisition of an identity as a woman who loves another woman? Does she exercise some pride and ownership in her bisexuality, or does she cling to the label as a way of avoiding a lesbian identity, which may not carry much currency in her African American culture-of-origin (Greene, 1997)? How does Chris feel about two of Sarah's ex-partners being a part of their life? Fortunately, the therapist and the couple have multiple places to begin a discussion about reducing conflict in their relationship.

SUMMARY

Sarah and Chris, as well as Mario and Kevin, are seeking professional help from a knowledgeable therapist who validates and affirms one of the most intensely personal and revealing parts of their lives—a loving union with another person. What is the therapist's job here? The therapist's job is to identify relationship patterns of the couple and how those patterns may be affected by societal prejudice and oppression. The therapist needs to help the partners gain a clear understanding of the remnants of their internalized homophobia and heterosexism and how it affects their relationships. The therapist needs to bravely call the partners on their avoidance and denial, and the therapist needs to do this with empathy and compassion. The therapist needs to help the couple find support in both the gay and heterosexual worlds, but the therapist also need to help the partners find the courage to create their own relationships when those worlds demand rigid compliance and conformity. The therapist must help Mario and Kevin discover ways to celebrate their male sexuality while allowing themselves to be vulnerable and intimate. The therapist must help Sarah and Chris discover ways to treasure the bonds of female intimacy while finding ways to balance the power in their relationship. If the therapist can do all this, then the therapist will have helped these four partners develop new stories for themselves as couples—new narratives that acknowledge hard-earned lessons from the past, emphasize flexible strengths of the present, and identify budding dreams for the future.

REFERENCES

Baker, H. S., & Baker, M. N. (1987). Heinz Kohut's self psychology: An overview. *American Journal of Psychiatry, 144*(1), 1–9.

Bepko, C. S., & Johnson, T. (2000). Gay and lesbian couples in therapy: Perspectives for the contemporary therapist. *Journal of Marital and Family Therapy, 26*(4), 409–419.

Blumstein, P., & Schwartz, P. (1983). *American couples: Money, work, and sex.* New York: Morrow.

Bridges, S. K., Selvidge, M. M. D., & Matthews, C. R. (2003). Lesbian women of color: Therapeutic issues and challenges. *Journal of Multicultural Counseling and Development, 31*(2), 113–130.

Clark, W. M., & Serovich, J. M. (1997). Twenty years and still in the dark? Content analysis of articles pertaining to gay, lesbian, and bisexual issues in marriage and family journals. *Journal of Marital and Family Therapy, 23*(3), 239–253.

Clunis, D. M., & Green, G. D. (1988). *Lesbian couples.* Seattle, WA: Seal Press.

Doherty, W. J., & Simmons, D. S. (1996). Clinical practice patterns of marriage and family therapists: A national survey of therapists and their clients. *Journal of Marital and Family Therapy, 22*(1), 9–25.

Forstein, M. (1986). Psychodynamic psychotherapy with gay male couples. In T. S. Stein & J. Cohen (Eds.), *Contemporary perspectives on psychotherapy with lesbians and gay men* (pp. 103–137). New York: Plenum Press.

Green, R.-J., Bettinger, M., & Zacks, E. (1996). Are lesbian couples fused and gay male couples disengaged? Questioning gender straightjackets. In J. Laird & R.-J. Green (Eds.), *Lesbians and gays in couples and families: A handbook for therapists* (pp. 185–230). San Francisco: Jossey-Bass.

Green, R.-J., & Mitchell, V. (2002). Gay and lesbian couples in therapy: Homophobia, relational ambiguity, and social support. In A. S. Gurman & N. S. Jacobson (Eds.), *Clinical handbook of couple therapy* (pp. 546–568). New York: Guilford Press.

Green, S. K., & Bobele, M. (1994). Family therapists' response to AIDS: An examination of attitudes, knowledge, and contact. *Journal of Marital and Family Therapy, 20*(4), 349–367.

Greenan, D. E., & Tunnell, G. (2003). *Couple therapy with gay men.* New York: Guilford Press.

Greene, B. (1997). Ethnic minority lesbians and gay men: Mental health and treatment issues. In B. Greene (Ed.), *Ethnic and cultural diversity among lesbians and gay men* (pp. 216–239). Thousand Oaks, CA: Sage.

Haas, S. M., & Stafford, L. (1998). An initial examination of maintenance behaviors in and lesbian relationships. *Journal of Social and Personal Relationships, 15*(6), 846–855.

Hickson, F. C. I., Davies, P. M., Weatherburn, P., Coxon, A. P. M., & McManus, T. J. (1992). Maintenance of open gay relationships: Some strategies for protection against HIV. *AIDS Care, 4*(4), 409–419.

Iasenza, S. (1999). The big lie: Debunking lesbian bed death. *In the Family, 4*(4), 8–11, 20, 25.

Israel, T., & Selvidge, M. M. D. (2003). Contributions of multicultural counseling to counselor competence with lesbian, gay, and bisexual clients. *Journal of Multicultural Counseling and Development, 31*(2), 84–98.

Johnson, S. M. (1996). *The practice of emotionally focused marital therapy: Creating connection.* New York: Brunner/Mazel.

Josephson, G. J. (2003). Using an attachment-based intervention with same-sex couples. In S. M. Johnson & V. E. Whiffen (Eds.), *Attachment processes in couple and family therapy* (pp. 300–317). New York: Guilford Press.

Kerewsky, S. D., & Miller, D. (1996). Lesbian couples and childhood trauma. In J. Laird & R.-J. Green (Eds.), *Lesbians and gays in couples and families: A handbook for therapists* (pp. 298–315). San Francisco: Jossey-Bass.

Krestan, J., & Bepko, C. S. (1980). The problem of fusion in the lesbian relationship. *Family Process, 19*(3), 277–289.

Kurdek, L. A. (1988). Relationship quality of gay and lesbian cohabiting couples. *Journal of Homosexuality, 15*(3/4), 93–118.

Kurdek, L. A. (1998). Relationship outcomes and their predictors: Longitudinal evidence from heterosexual married, gay cohabiting, and lesbian cohabiting couples. *Journal of Marriage and the Family, 60*(3), 553–568.

Kurdek, L. A., & Schmitt, J. P. (1986). Relationship quality of gay men in closed or open relationships. *Journal of Homosexuality, 12*(2), 85–99.

Kurdek, L. A., & Schmitt, J. P. (1987). Partner homogamy in married, heterosexual cohabiting gay and lesbian couples. *Journal of Sex Research, 23*(2), 212–232.

Malyon, A. (1982). Psychotherapeutic implications of internalized homophobia. In J. Gonsiorek (Ed.), *Homosexuality and psychotherapy: A practitioner's handbook of affirmative models* (pp. 59–69). New York: Haworth Press.

Marvin, C., & Miller, D. (2000). Lesbian couples entering the 21st century. In P. Papp (Ed.), *Couples on the fault line: New directions for therapists* (pp. 257–283). New York: Guilford Press.

McWhirter, D. P., & Mattison, A. M. (1984). *The male couple: How relationships develop.* Englewood Cliffs, NJ: Prentice-Hall.

Means-Christensen, A. J., Snyder, D. K., & Negy, C. (2003). Assessing nontraditional couples: Validity of the Marital Satisfaction Inventory—Revised with gay, lesbian, and cohabiting heterosexual couples. *Journal of Marital and Family Therapy, 29*(1), 69–83.

Mohr, J. J. (1999). Same-sex romantic attachment. In J. Cassidy & P. R. Shaver (Eds.), *Handbook of attachment: Theory, research, and clinical applications* (pp. 378–393). New York: Guilford Press.

Nichols, M. (1987a). Doing sex therapy with lesbians: Bending a heterosexual paradigm to fit a gay lifestyle. In Boston Lesbian Psychologies Collective (Ed.), *Lesbian psychologies: Explorations and challenges* (pp. 242–260). Urbana: University of Illinois Press.

Nichols, M. (1987b). Lesbian sexuality: Issues and developing theory. In Boston Lesbian Psychologies Collective (Ed.), *Lesbian psychologies: Explorations and challenges* (pp. 97–125). Urbana: University of Illinois Press.

Nichols, M. (2000). Therapy with sexual minorities. In S. R. Leiblum & R. C. Rosen (Eds.), *Principles and practice of sex therapy* (3rd ed., pp. 335–367). New York: Guilford Press.

Okun, B. F. (1996). *Understanding diverse families: What practitioners need to know.* New York: Guilford Press.

Paul, J. P., Stall, R. D., Crosby, G. M., Barrett, D. C., & Midanik, L. T. (1994). Correlates of sexual risk-taking among gay male substance abusers. *Addiction, 89*(8), 971–983.

Peplau, L. A., & Cochran, S. D. (1990). A relational perspective on homosexuality. In D. P. McWhirter, S. A. Sanders, & J. M. Reinisch (Eds.), *Homosexuality/heterosexuality* (pp. 321–349). New York: Oxford University Press.

Ritter, K. Y., & Terndrup, A. I. (2002). *Handbook of affirmative psychotherapy with lesbians and gay men.* New York: Guilford Press.

Slater, S. (1994). Approaching and avoiding the work of the middle years: Affairs in committed lesbian relationships. *Women and Therapy, 15*(2), 19–34.

Slater, S. (1995). *The lesbian family life cycle.* New York: Free Press.

Vargo, S. (1988). The effect of women's socialization on lesbian couples. In Boston Lesbian Psychologies Collective (Ed.), *Lesbian psychologies: Explorations and challenges* (pp. 161–173). Urbana: University of IL Press.

Wagner, G. J., Remien, R. H., & Carballo-Dieguez, A. (2000). Prevalence of extra-dyadic sex in male couples of mixed HIV status and its relationship to psychological distress and relationship quality. *Journal of Homosexuality, 39*(2), 31–46.

Waldner-Haugrud, L. K., Gratch, L. V., & Magruder, B. (1997). Victimization and perpetration rates of violence in gay and lesbian relationships: Gender issues explored. *Violence and Victims, 12*(2), 173–184.

Weinberg, G. (1972). *Society and healthy homosexual.* New York: St. Martin's Press.

Wolf, E. S. (1988). *Treating the self: Elements of clinical self psychology.* New York: Guilford Press.

CHAPTER 22

Treating Couples across the Socioeconomic Spectrum

Florence W. Kaslow

WHY THIS TOPIC NEEDS INCLUSION—RATIONALE

IN THE FIRST decade of the twenty-first century, family psychologists/ therapists around the world are seeing couples who range financially from very poor to very rich. Most articles and books on this topic have been geared to couples (and families) who cluster at one specific rung of the socioeconomic ladder, such as poor, inner-city families, in books such as the now classic S. Minuchin, Montalvo, Guerney, Rosman, and Schumer volume, *Families of the Slums* (1967), and Sharlin and Shamai's (1999) treatise on intervening with poor and disorganized families, which is based on an Israeli population. Some clinicians specialize in working with a particular population segment and find this specificity of focus very relevant. Yet, many other clinicians treat people who fall along different rungs of the socioeconomic ladder, ranging from their pro bono patients, who are worried about surviving at a bare subsistence level, through those who are middle class, working diligently and trying to make their lives meaningful and to find time to be together, to the fabulously wealthy, who superficially seem to have it all.

Talking and writing about money and economic status seems to make many therapists and psychology researchers uncomfortable, and so this topic frequently is avoided in our professional literature. One rarely sees copies of *Money Magazine* or *Forbes* in therapists' waiting rooms. In fact, Krueger (1986) called talking about money "The Last Taboo." This is strange in light of the changing demographics of the American family (Teachman,

Polonko, & Scanzoni, 1999), attributable in part to the feminist revolution and to the entry of so many women into the paid labor force, after receiving their high school or college degree, seeking to be a wage earner because *money does matter.* The revolution has had reverberations in many other countries also. Being paid and recognized for one's contributions increases one's motivation, enhances one's self-esteem and confidence, and is conducive to a stronger sense of self-sufficiency and independence. In dual wage earner/career couples, this has changed some of the marital dynamics irrevocably. It has decreased a woman's dire need to stay married if her husband is abusive or unfaithful. When a woman can support herself, and her children if necessary, her desire for a husband shifts away from mainly needing him as a source of support to wanting her husband to be a lover, friend, good conversationalist, fine companion, as well as a person who is competent in the career or money earning dimensions of life.

Interestingly, some women who have chosen to remain financially dependent may resent the career woman for all of her achievements, which make them look lazy or inadequate by comparison, for creating a different kind of role model that they do not wish to follow, or because their husbands refuse to "allow" them to work and they are jealous of the freedoms working and earning an income can bring. Still others, after working a while, may envy their nonworking counterparts whose partners give them everything, including nannies to watch the children while the moms play (McLaughlin & Kraus, 2002) and closets full of fashionable clothes, and fabulous jewelry. It doesn't seem fair! And these differences in the covert and overt desires of women regarding whether they wish to work or be totally taken care of financially by a husband or sugar daddy must be kept in the foreground when there are discussions about what women want in general, and in specific, what does this particular woman want who is part of a dyad in couple therapy.

Then, too, the female lawyer, engineer, or psychologist who wanted desperately to acquire an advanced degree and pursue her dreamed-of career and break through the glass ceiling is in a very different stratum from the lower-class woman who works because she has no choice, when the family is poor, the husband is unemployable, unemployed, alcoholic, severely impaired, or nonexistent, and she is responsible for providing for her daily subsistence needs and those of her children. Low-paying or low-status work, such as being someone else's house cleaner or a waitress in a fast-food restaurant, may be boring, routine, demeaning, and unexciting, but the money is essential. For some, having any job is better than being on welfare; for others, it supplements the welfare or other social relief program checks, or replaces benefits when they expire. Thus, money has a multiplicity of meanings from providing for survival to purchasing luxury items, to ascending to positions and circles of power and prestige. Perhaps this chapter will represent a giant step forward in shattering the taboo about discussing money, particularly before many couples get married, except in global economic terms and college economics courses, which may raise such concepts as Veblen's theory of the leisure class and their *Conspicuous Consumption* (1899/1994), which is quite apparent with many well-to-do patients.

Money does matter! Financial concerns and disagreements over who should earn the money; to whom the money belongs; and how it should be saved, spent, or disbursed often surface in treatment.

Obviously, there are substantial differences in terms of the financial issues of concern to couples in therapy who are lower class, middle class, and upper class (and who fall in the subdivisions of each category), and how these issues are lived with, played out, and resolved or allowed to remain an area of submerged resentment or overt continuous contention. The use of the classification system of lower, middle, and upper is generally accepted in economic classification schema, and is in no way meant to be pejorative. No specific cutoff points are utilized herein to differentiate the three major classes, given that this book is intended for a multicultural and international audience, and various ethnic and cultural groups define poor, rich, and in-between quite differently. (See Sharlin, Kaslow, & Hammerschmidt, 2000, for further elaboration on this.) Money, and all of its attendant meanings and usages, affect the couple's relationship; their perception of self and other and those in their social and family networks; who their friends and neighbors are; what kind of residence(s) and car(s) they can or cannot afford to rent or buy; what kind of education they want to, and are able to, provide for their children; what kind of therapy they seek and with whom; and how they view health insurance and/or fee-for-service therapists; and a multitude of other daily concerns. The meaning and usage of money is also an expression of one's personality pattern, with thriftiness and withholding styles of dealing with money (when objectively this is unnecessary) being seen psychodynamically as being typical of anal retentive or compulsive individuals, and excessive spending being an expression or characteristic of the anal explosive (Abraham, 1921) or impulsive personality. It is also a characteristic of many with addictive personality disorders who squander money to satisfy their addiction of choice, unconcerned about the consequences of their spending binge, and of some individuals during a manic phase of an affective disorder (American Psychiatric Association, 1994). Thus, a chapter on socioeconomic strata and money issues was deemed useful for inclusion in this volume on couples therapy.

If a couple is contemplating divorce (Schwartz & Kaslow, 1997) and they are rich, issues arise about division of assets, including what constitutes premarital assets that are exempt, whether jewelry and family heirlooms were gifts to one or both, whether inheritances belong to both, and what claims are or are not legitimate on either one's trust funds or pension plans. Conversely, if the couple is poor or lower middle-class, there may be almost nothing to divide. It is impossible to divide one car. If they have been barely able to pay rent on an apartment, a serious dilemma confronting them is how they can possibly afford two places to live and essential clothing and food

(Weitzman, 1985). Frequently, one or both see no alternative but going back to live with their parent(s) in a home that may already be overcrowded. There may be woefully inadequate space there for him or her—plus for several children to live or visit. Some senior-generation parents respond to the breakup and request to return home with the reply, "We're all family and will do whatever we need to for each other in times of crisis." Others say, "You're an adult, and you'll have to manage on your own. It's not our problem." This may leave people emotionally desolate and financially desperate, and they turn to shelters, public welfare, and other relief programs to keep themselves alive. By contrast, in a rich couple there are sufficient funds for the partner who is moving out to rent or buy a condominium or house, or to stay in a friend's guest house until he or she has decided where to live and what direction he or she wishes to pursue. Middle-class couples fall in between; they are not destitute, but each will have to manage with considerably less than they did when married.

PREVIEW AND OVERVIEW OF CHAPTER CONTENTS

A bevy of issues have already been mentioned and will be addressed further in the following pages. These include:

- *Love, marriage, and money.* Is there ever enough, and the many shades of meaning of money—from poverty and a sense of failure, being middle class and always running short for unseen expenses, to having wealth and the power and prestige that often accompany it.
- *Socioeconomic status (SES) and marriages in lower and middle-class couples.* Typical and atypical problems, therapeutic issues, despair versus hope, confronting weaknesses and building on strengths.
- Marriages and other unions of the rich and famous.
- Treatment issues and implications emanating from financial status and personal values about money of both patients and therapists.
- Does being wealthy (or famous) ensure greater marital bliss and less conflict? Does it bring about a greater sense of well-being, of responsibility to, and helping of those less fortunate?

Given the page limit set for this chapter, it is not possible to explore each of these issues in depth; nonetheless, every effort will be made to provide a succinct discussion.

RELEVANT THEORETICAL FORMULATIONS

Maslow's hierarchy of needs (1962, 1968) seems a useful conceptualization that in some ways ties in with one's socioeconomic status. He posited that at *Level 1* people are concerned about meeting basic subsistence needs for food, clothing, and shelter. Meeting these needs is the motivation that drives poor couples to work extra hard, sometimes at two or three menial jobs each. Striving to make ends meet often leaves them depleted at the end of the day and without time or energy on the weekends for relaxation and fun. They are often frustrated in their efforts to pay the rent, have enough to eat, and keep from becoming homeless. When they use drugs or alcohol to assuage the pain of feeling like a failure or to drown sorrows caused by too many early losses of loved ones, the problems of poverty, marital discontent, and sometimes physical abuse may become exacerbated, leading to trouble with the police and soon the legal system. When these severe difficulties are further complicated because someone is African American (Boyd-Franklin, 1989), Native American, or Hispanic (Latino; Sue & Sue, 1999) and has been subjected to prejudice and discrimination in school, in the work world, or in the community, the stresses this places on a couple's sense of safety and security (also characteristics of Maslow's Level 1 Basic Needs) and well-being may seem so insurmountable that the marriage cannot survive.

POVERTY AND COUPLEHOOD

There have been several excellent books written about poor, lower-class families (see for examples Lindblad-Goldberg, Dore, & Stern's [1998] volume on home-based services for chaotic families; and P. Minuchin, Colapinto, & Minuchin's [1998] descriptive volume on *Working with families of the poor* plus the two books on this topic mentioned earlier and many chapters such as Boyd-Franklin's, 1995) on therapy with African American inner-city families. The poor and underclass everywhere frequently include struggling refugee and immigrant couples, the unemployed, and the homeless.

In brief, treatment, which may include home-based services for those who cannot or will not come to an agency, must be reality-oriented and nonjudgmental. People need to have their stories heard and accepted, and their strengths as well as their crises and weaknesses assessed. It is their strengths and resiliencies that will provide the foundation for improving their life situation and engendering hope (Beavers & Kaslow, 1981). Since their daily problems in living may be huge, solution-focused problem-solving efforts may constitute the treatment of choice (de Shazer, 1988). Often, such people need to be connected to an array of community resources, and the therapist may need to intervene to see that the recipient referral sources, like hospitals and employment training agencies, are receptive to these clients' requests for service. The therapist may need to stay with the client to teach follow-up and follow-through skills, and compliment them when an agreed upon course of action is taken. Helping the partners appreciate and support each other is vital if the marriage is to last. And helping the couple rebuild relationships with or tap into their extended family and community support system, often including the church, is central to countering their sense of alienation, isolation, and loneliness. Sometimes, guidance needs to be given about budgeting and how to begin saving, when money becomes less scarce.

It is essential that the therapist be optimistic and believe that her clients can improve their life circumstances and are entitled to a sense of well-being, security, and happiness—whatever that means for them.

MIDDLE-CLASS COUPLES

Much of the couples literature has tended to focus predominantly on White, middle-class couples. There is a great deal available that is drawn from clinical experience based on typical agency or private practice case loads. Although socioeconomic status and money rarely are mentioned as variables (Waring, 1988; Wile, 1993), descriptions of the couples' lifestyles would seem to place them mostly in the vast middle class (Paul & Paul, 1986; Sager, 1976). Willi (1982) discusses the collusive nature of many marital patterns that represent the unconscious interplay between partners who maintain their repetitive battles. Writing from a psychoanalytic perspective, he elucidates how troubled couples triangulate their relationship to stabilize it (Bowen, 1978, 1988), and develop psychosomatic illnesses to serve as neutralizers to the conflict or as a joint defense system. The latter tends to elicit sympathy from extended family members and friends.

In *The Good Marriage: How and Why Love Lasts,* Wallerstein and Blakeslee (1995) describe four types of marriage and the tasks associated with each:

1. Romantic
   - Separating from family of origin
   - Building togetherness and creating autonomy
   - Becoming parents
2. Rescue
   - Coping with crises
   - Making a safe place for conflict
3. Companionate
   - Exploring sexual love and intimacy
   - Sharing laughter and keeping interests alive
4. Traditional
   - Providing emotional nurturance

Some of the tasks cut across several of the types of marriages, rather than typifying only one. This classification schema is useful and is quite applicable for the vast array of middle-class couples. Those who are poor have the more basic tasks of survival to contend with, which often entail coping with crises these authors associate with the rescue marriage. Either or both partners in lower- and middle-class couples may need huge amounts of emotional nurturance—in traditional and nontraditional cohabiting and marital relationships.

Most of the literature on understanding and counseling the "culturally different," that is, those who are not White Catholics or Anglo-Saxon Protestants, is either about individuals (Sue & Sue, 1999), or families (McGoldrick, Giordano, & Pearce, 1996). However, since couples are the architects of families, these two volumes are informative about couples from enormously diverse ethnic, racial, and religious backgrounds—most of whom, on a bell-shaped curve, would fall in the broad middle-income range.

Returning to the paradigm articulated by Maslow, the majority of middle-class couples are able to provide their Level 1 basic needs for food, clothing, shelter, safety, security, and protection. They will want to, and will be able to, fulfill their Level 2 needs for belongingness to family, community groups, their tribe, business or professional organizations, special interest groups, and so on—some of these separately, and many of them together as a couple. The more financially and emotionally secure they feel, the more they are likely to want to ascend up to Level 3 on the hierarchy of needs scale—seeking to gain approval and respect from others, and having good self-esteem. They crave friendship, affection, and love from one another and from others close to them.

Financially, they value having a home and may move from renting to owning, or from owning a small house to purchasing a larger one. In therapy, they may argue because there is never enough money for all they want to do, and they may need help in prioritizing and taking turns getting what they want and in determining what they most value in life. If they are postponing having a first or second child because they believe "we can't afford it yet," time in treatment may be spent on how much is enough, how long do you wish to delay parenting, and are money worries camouflaging other doubts and problems. Often, they quarrel over how much should be spent versus what percentage should be saved. Frequently, one partner is a here-and-now, pleasure-oriented person, and the other is more conservative and future-oriented. The therapist may strive to help them find a way to enjoy both, and not to continue arguing over the polarities of either/or. They may also disagree about whether or not the woman will continue working after they have children, and it is important to discuss what her working and the income this produces means for both of them. Often middle-class couples share traditional values emphasizing fidelity, the importance of the extended family system, being very involved with their children, obtaining a good education, and striving for upward mobility.

THE RICH AND FAMOUS

Because there is a dearth of literature on treating couples who are rich or famous, the rest of this chapter highlights this realm of therapy. The case illustration is based on a composite of various cases having similar themes and dynamics, drawn from the author's private practice in affluent Palm Beach County, Florida. It seeks to analyze this specific patient population as typified in this prototypical case. (Commentaries appear in parenthesis.)

CASE STUDY

The A-List Billionaires: Power, Prestige, Privilege, and Philanthropy: So Why Is/Are He/They in Therapy?*

The Referral and Phone Intake

In the winter of 2001, Mr. A called me, based on a referral from his highly esteemed and expensive divorce lawyer. The attorney, who has, as if by osmosis, taken on many of the mannerisms of his wealthy clients, had not apprised me of the pending referral. He assumed I would feel fortunate to have the opportunity to treat someone of the stature of Mr. A, and so decided no direct referral was needed. During the telephone intake, Mr. A told me his name and that his attorney, Mr. C, had just handled his much-publicized divorce. Mr. C thought there were some important issues concerning his children, his postdivorce adjustment, and his relationships with women about which he should consult me. I indicated that I would not have an opening for about two weeks, but we could set an appointment in advance. He sounded miffed and said, "You don't recognize my name, do you?" Since I rarely read the society pages of our local newspaper and don't read *Fortune* magazine regularly, I did not. He hastened to let me know *who* he is, his various claims to fame and fortune, and the size of the monumental settlement that wife number 3 had been awarded; it was substantially over $10 million. I realized that his assets had to be of staggering proportions. (Secretly I wondered if I should immediately double the fee I was going to quote him, but I did not; I just increased it slightly. This actually was a wise decision, since the fabulously rich do not think anything inexpensive can be very valuable or worthwhile. Also, they expect to be seen immediately, at their convenience, and sometimes ask why you can't change someone else's appointment to suit their schedule. It is crucial to politely refuse and to stay in charge of structuring the therapy; Napier & Whitaker, 1978.)

Therapy Process and Content

In the first session, as in most subsequent sessions, he presented as a pleasant, affable man. He is Caucasian and considers himself very much a WASP. He looks younger than his real age (mid-sixties) and keeps himself in good shape physically. Like many of his Palm Beach peers, he owns a large yacht, a private jet, and a mansion on the ocean (or it could be the intercoastal waterway). He owns one other large residence, in this case in Newport (but it could be the Hamptons, the Berkshires, or Cape Cod). There are nannies for the children (sometimes one for each child) and

---

*The case presented is an amalgamation of several cases. Camouflage has been used to protect the identity of the several individuals/families used to develop this prototypical case. But the essence of the substance and issues has been retained to render an accurate kaleidoscopic portrait.

ample staff to take care of the homes and grounds. Either the chauffeur or a nanny (usually) takes the children to and from the private schools they attend (until they go off, quite young, to proper Northeastern or Swiss boarding schools). The chauffeur or nanny also do sundry errands. It had become obvious to him that the cost of supporting such a staff is staggering and that frequently they slough off doing their chores unless they are carefully supervised by a house manager. He prefers not to worry about such details and about being short-changed, but is not always able to ignore staff machinations. He knows that he relies heavily on his staff at home, as well as in his businesses, just as he relies on his several attorneys, to manage his affairs and make his complicated life run as efficiently as possible. Nonetheless, he remains very much in charge, and all around him know this. In this era of cost cutting to offset huge losses attributable to the major stock market decline experienced from 2000 to 2003, he feels pressured to do substantial cost cutting, but without sacrificing the luxuries of life to which he is accustomed.

Mr. A had five children who ranged in age from 2 years to 30 years when he commenced treatment with me. The 30-year-old son was married and living in Palm Beach with his wife and a child about the same age as Dad's youngest son. Todd was born during Dad's first marriage and was now involved in one of Dad's thriving businesses, which he hopes to take over when Dad retires. He has resented Dad's involvements in the past decade with women in their thirties, whom he sees as being in his generation and not in Dad's, and he perceives them to be gold diggers. Dad likes his son Todd, but doesn't believe he is smart enough, or ambitious and hardworking enough, to become president or CEO of the business he is currently engaged in, or any of Mr. A's other numerous enterprises. (Over time we have gotten into many issues about seeing his enterprises as a family business and have broached succession issues, but he, like many of his peers, is not yet ready to consider his own mortality.) He revealed he is disappointed in his first-born offspring. He believes his son is jealous of his lavish lifestyle and the beautiful women he escorts and has married, while his son lives a more stable and sedentary lifestyle. This eldest son was not as indulged as the younger children have been because Mr. A was not as wealthy when this child was in his formative years, and his first wife was more conservative—until it came to putting forth her demands for alimony and child support when he sued for divorce to end the boredom and stuckness he felt. Wife number 1 continued to reside in Philadelphia and had had primary custody of Todd. Mr. A had visited monthly, had flown his son down to visit him in Palm Beach whenever possible, and gladly taken him during agreed-upon vacations. He had paid child support willingly and been generous with presents. Whenever he thought his ex-wife was contentious about matters pertaining to their son, like visitation, which private school he should attend, and later—which colleges were suitable to apply to, he would threaten to take the matter to court to have it settled. She usually succumbed to his wishes to avoid such a battle and to not jeopardize the generous monthly allotment, that she was slated to get as long as Mr. A lived—that is, she had been awarded permanent alimony. (This is quite commonly demanded and received, since the judges are privy to knowledge of the amount of the man's assets.) She had kept his name as hers after the divorce, as did his two subsequent wives, since the name provided instant recognition for getting hard-to-come-by reservations in toney restaurants, coveted theater tickets for hit Broadway shows, and for opening certain social doors for themselves and their children. Prager (2001) indicates that wives and girlfriends of the ultrarich often continue to have a "seductive package of perks" even when the love affair (or marriage) is over. It appears that some of them plan their strategy for this to be part of the aftermath.

His threats of resorting to legal action whenever an ex-wife challenged him or disobeyed his wishes about a child continued as a major ploy in his repertoire with wives number 2 and number 3. His children from his second marriage were Bart, age 14, and Bettina, age 12. Lonnie, his mistress for several years after his divorce, had assured him she did not want children but that she was using birth control nevertheless, so he had nothing to worry about. When she decided she didn't want to risk losing him if and when he became bored or disenchanted with her, as he had with her predecessors, she decided not to tell him she had stopped taking the pill. He recounted to me that when she announced to him that she was pregnant, he had experienced multiple mixed emotions, including shock, annoyance, pride (at being able to again create a human life and propagate an expanding family), and excited anticipation. Her ruse worked. She had figured out, correctly, that he would not want a child of his aborted and that his code of honor was such that he would marry her under these circumstances. He did.

Lonnie came from a lower middle-class split family and was brassy, crass, overtly seductive, and not well versed in social graces. She had been fun to date, but he never intended the relationship to move beyond fun and games. But Mr. A doted on being a dad and adored the son she gave birth to, so he overlooked Lonnie's shortcomings and had a member of his staff attempt to teach her how to become a better, more appropriate stepmother and partner for him. Lonnie was enthralled with her new social standing and extravagant lifestyle and decided, secretly, to become pregnant again quickly to ensure that Mr. A would not leave her.

Numerous times in therapy we have probed how he (and many of his compatriots), who is so shrewd, brilliant, and tough in business, can be so easily bedazzled by women whom he is aware are not potentially good partners for him, and how once having become involved because they are fun and offer great sex, he can then be tricked into fatherhood and marriage. It took many months before we were able to break through his denial and he could see the pattern well enough to ponder the kind of choices he has made and how gullible he has been (Kaslow & Magnavita, 2002). Despite his love for Bart and his infatuation with their second child, Bettina, his first and only daughter, he had reached a point in this marriage where he could not tolerate Lonnie's crudeness and chicanery. When Bettina was 2 years old, he opted for a second divorce. He had insisted on joint and fully shared custody, which Florida law permits, and which Lonnie willingly granted, since she had no burning desire to raise the children alone and wanted at least half of her time free to "do her own thing." To her friends, she had allegedly added "and not be saddled with his two brats." She insisted on a huge settlement, and knowing how much he dislikes negative publicity, she threatened to "tell all to the tabloids" unless he agreed to her astronomical demands. He did, unwillingly and angrily, and vowed to never marry again unless an airtight and very restrictive prenuptial agreement was signed (Kaslow, 2000; Spencer, 1997). He entered therapy several years later, still harboring much animosity and resentment toward Lonnie, and he wanted to continue retaliating whenever possible.

After his divorce from Lonnie, he dated all kinds of women, from young, never-married party girls, to more mature and successful career women who had achieved high stature in their own right. Although he had convinced himself that he now preferred an independent and self-supporting career woman as a partner, he continued to be drawn to statuesque and lively single moms, some divorced, some never married, some with a child out of wedlock. (Not an unusual occurrence in this social set; this doesn't seem to meet with much disapproval.) He reported never having "done drugs," but he participates readily in the heavy drinking that is a major part of the party scene he frequents, and he admits that he imbibes quite a bit. He only likes the best vintage wines and considers himself a connoisseur of gourmet cuisine. (Many of this social set treasure their large wine collections. Alcohol is served liberally at dinner parties in private homes, at country clubs and pricey restaurants, and at the highly fashionable charity balls they all attend.)

Following several years of dating (in various countries around the world) while juggling his far-flung and diverse business empire and seeing his three children as often as possible, he again began to yearn for a slightly more settled lifestyle. At that time, around 1998, he saw a gorgeous, early-thirties woman at a local soiree. He immediately found her so alluring that the night matched the lyrics of "Some Enchanted Evening." He introduced himself and found her very responsive to his overtures to dance and then to be his partner at dinner. As local legend has it, she was out on a proverbial big game hunt (not unusual here), and he qualified. In addition to his well-publicized fortune, he is good looking and has a casual, nonarrogant charm and versatility, so it was easy for her to be, or act, smitten by him. He reported that they had had an idyllic whirlwind courtship, and he was enthralled by her. She treated his children well—which meant a great deal to him—but this only lasted until about six months after they got married.

Dawn's beauty, and what turned out to be her superficial sweetness and kindness also captivated his friends. Initially, she was affectionate and appreciative, flattered him skillfully and frequently, and appeared to be genuinely in love with him. He considered himself to be "the luckiest guy in the world" to have met her and to have his intense attraction to her reciprocated. Despite protests from his oldest son, and some warnings from several friends who thought the age difference (over 25 years) was too great and that it was really his bank account and other assets she desired, he was in a great hurry to "make her my own." They were married within five months of having met, after a very romantic, storybook courtship. She received a "dowry" of sorts from him a week before the wedding; that is, a gift of $2 million put in her name only, a gift he made at her request when he was deliriously in love with her, because she wanted to feel "really secure."

Once they were married, Dawn told him how much she wanted to bear his children. As his business enterprises were growing, he envisioned creating a dynasty that would carry his name for decades to come, with each child ultimately running some branch of the vast family empire. He also relished recreating his image in the children he sired and thought they would be superbeautiful with Dawn as their biological mother. So her declaration of intent to have several A-babies pleased him enormously. Once again, he totally failed to recognize that this was her way of ensuring her continuing wealth, whether or not the marriage lasted. Although she had signed a very generous prenuptial agreement, she was reasonably certain from the first that she could retain an attorney who would be able to find loopholes, which is what she did several years and two children later (*Rider* v. *Rider*, 1995; *Ritz* v. *Ritz*, 1995). (This is not an infrequent occurrence in communities like Palm Beach.)

According to Mr. A, during her pregnancies she was irritable, demanding, and totally self-centered. Whenever his other children came to visit, she no longer was nurturing and welcoming; she had turned into the wicked stepmother. She told him stories about their obnoxious and disrespectful behavior, most of which turned out to be fabricated. But she did succeed in driving a wedge between Mr. A and his three children, who had predated her in his life and to whom he had always felt strong love, loyalty, and a deep sense of commitment, which now became highly tinged with guilt (Boszormenyi-Nagy & Spark, 1973/1984). He now saw them less often. In therapy, he finally recognized that her primary motive had been to alienate him from his other children so the ones he had with her would be the only heirs to inherit his throne (and his multitudinous assets). By the time their adorable daughter was 4 years old and their mischievous son was 2, he was totally disenchanted with Dawn. Her vanity, deceitfulness, manipulative ways, and unscrupulousness could no longer be overlooked, and he had ceased to see her as beautiful now that he found her character to be despicable. He also had learned, from several reliable sources, that she had been cheating on him. Thus, he embarked on his third divorce, and an ugly, bitter, protracted battle began. Both hired top-notch, high-profile, combative attorneys who fought valiantly on their client's behalf in this high-stakes litigated break-up and division of tangible and intangible assets case (Schwartz & Kaslow, 1997; Wallerstein & Kelly, 1980). Mr. A resented having to pay a settlement of $10 million in violation of the prenuptial agreement. Dawn's sense of entitlement (very typical) and her greed (again the "there is never enough" theme), overwhelmed and repelled him. He wanted to retaliate and "destroy her" for her deceit and all of the disillusionment she caused him. As the legal contest was drawing to a close, it became obvious to his warrior attorney that Mr. A was emotionally depleted, disillusioned, stripped of confidence in his judgment about women, and a very angry man. It was at this juncture that he had referred him for therapy.

Over the years that he has been in treatment, we have shifted back and forth, exploring these interlocking themes and the knots they have caused in his psyche and soma (many aches and pains with no apparent physiological cause). He has proven capable of forming a strong, positive therapeutic alliance. He seems to welcome the knowledge that I am available by phone as necessary and on time when we have an appointment; that I am tuned in, listening with the third ear (Reik, 1948), and that I am observant of his body language (Birdwhistle, 1962) and interpret the cues I am picking up back to him and ask that he confirm or disconfirm what he is feeling and unknowingly communicating. He is extremely bright and is fascinated by the process of learning more about himself, why he does what he does, and how to create a happier, less conflict-ridden present and future. He realizes how often he has felt abandoned, rejected, unloved, and unappreciated for himself, and is determined to break the pattern of choosing beautiful, narcissistic, demanding, sexy, manipulative yet dependent partners.

During the several years since he started treatment, he has been seen an average of once every other week. Like many of my other Palm Beach patients, he prefers to pay a large sum up front, have me keep a record until that amount is used up, and then give him the receipts in a packet and let him know that the next payment is due. When he is out of town for any length of time, we do sessions by telephone. Like many of the other men in this locale, his appointments are often made by and cancelled through his secretaries. It is the secretary who keeps his schedule and reminds him of appointments. I have gone over confidentiality issues carefully with him and have given him the HIPAA privacy regulations and had him sign for this, but the secretaries remain the point people. Refusal to accept this as part of his (and others like him) modus operandi would be the death knoll to therapy. (This is part and parcel of dealing with the rich and famous. So my secretary converses with his secretary—keeps the secretary's name on the patient's file card and follows strict guidelines on what can and cannot be said.)

In treatment, we have focused on various themes episodically. These include:

- His fear of being abandoned as he was emotionally in childhood by both parents, which is reflected alternately in his desire to strike back and his desire to please—so that any love and attention, even if contingent on his wealth, is better than no love at all.

- How he contributes to setting himself up to be exploited financially.
- Why he seeks recourse through the courts to settle his interpersonal and intrafamilial disputes instead of trying to negotiate solutions more peacefully through one-on-one discourse or with the help of a therapist or mediator.
- What clinging to old slights and hurts and internalized anger do to his ability to let go and become healthier and capable of developing mutual and reciprocal caring relationships in the here and now.
- Why he craves retribution and being exonerated from responsibility for his choices, which later boomerang.
- Why he gravitates toward the type of woman he still prefers, knowing that their lack of good breeding, their narrow range of interests, their self-absorption, and their lust for material possessions ultimately alienate his affections (partially Wallerstein & Blakeslee's rescue marriage).
- His children and what he wants to instill in them regarding values, responsibility, acceptable behavior, a work ethic, goals for the future, and the importance of being philanthropic.
- His parenting style and the necessity of setting reasonable limits and insisting these be adhered to.
- Not overindulging the children with things—the big and costly items the wealthy give their children, often as a substitute for love.
- His desire to be well respected in the community, which has led to our devising a plan through which he has achieved this by acting in an exemplary fashion at social events; by contributing to local and national charities in a leadership role as well as with huge contributions, and through hiring a publicist to improve his image in the press.

Currently, he is on the brink of another involvement, but has moved more slowly. He has joint-shared custody of the four younger children and delights in being with them and is much more hands-on in their child-rearing than he was with his oldest son, Todd. He has sought out relationships that have somewhat more substance and depth. He realizes that being a billionaire can buy big toys, but not happiness or physical or emotional health, even if he has access to the best doctors.

Frequently, he has discussed complex business affairs with me, primarily about possible mergers and acquisitions and about problems with staff. He knows that I do family business consultation and am conversant with the issues he raises (Kaslow, 1993). One time, when I queried why he was discussing a possible risky new acquisition with me instead of with his attorney or accountant, he answered, "You are quite knowledgable and more objective, honest, and trustworthy, since you have no personal gain at stake, because you would not be an investor or receive a percentage cut of any deal." He has also commented on how refreshing and enlightening it has been to work with a female therapist whom he sees as an equal.

Periodically, he has brought in one of the women he is dating for therapy sessions with him. Currently, he is being seen conjointly with the woman with whom he is involved. This relationship seems a little less tumultuous. But she too is about 25 years younger than he is and has not worked since graduating from college—except at her hobbies—tennis and skiing.

COMMENTARY ON THE RICH AND FAMOUS

My theoretical and therapeutic approach throughout has been integrative (Kaslow & Lebow, 2002), comprehensive (Kirschner & Kirschner, 1986), and multimodal (Lazarus, 1981). I have tried to work judiciously from whatever theoretical set of assumptions most illuminates what he is sharing and what is transpiring—always within a family systems perspective so that what we discuss and what he decides to do have a beneficial impact on his significant others. My basic psychodynamic view of personality structure and diagnosis (Brenner, 1992) undergirds how I interpret what I see and hear. Sometimes, I use a narrative approach (White & Epston, 1990); other times my work veers toward cognitive behavioral (Kaslow & Patterson, 2002), or humanistic and existential (Kaslow, Massey, & Massey, 2002; Maslow, 1968).

What has become glaringly apparent in my treatment of dozens of rich and famous couples or families is the sense of privilege and entitlement they have. For example, they start out by expecting the therapist to be at their beck and call regarding appointment times and to accept their cancellations when something comes up at the last minute—be it a business meeting or a tennis or fishing engagement (and they often resent being charged for this). Extreme narcissism and impulsivity is manifested in "I want what I want whenever I want it" and *it* should be bigger and better than what anyone else has, whether it be a canary, diamond ring, or a yacht. The conspicuous consumption first described over a century ago by Veblen (1899/1994) is rampant and unabashed.

Many of these couples treat *au pairs* and nannies as modern-day slaves, often underpaid and expected to be available for extra hours and tasks whenever requested (really demanded) without additional compensation. The portrait presented in *The Nanny Diaries* (McLaughlin & Kraus, 2002) is all too typical—nannies have very little leverage for bargaining, and since they often become devoted to the children they care for and have few other job options or time off to go on interviews, they are easily, and at times, heartlessly exploited.

The affluent are sought as board members for boards of directors of corporations, hospitals, philanthropic organizations in the health and welfare arena, and by cultural organizations. They bring prestige to the role, are expected to make sizeable contributions and to convince their acquaintances to do so also. Some, like Mr. A, bring plenty of experience and know-how to the table.

Returning to Maslow's hierarchy of needs, we would expect the basic survival requirements of Level 1 would have been fulfilled, but this is not always the case. Despite all of the material possessions, some of the rich feel emotionally deprived, empty, and insecure. This is particularly true of those who have had everything given to them financially by their parents while growing up, even if they were not available emotionally. They have never really acquired the kind of self-esteem and sense of self-worth (Level 3) that come from working to achieve mastery, making mistakes, losing out in competitions, and then trying again. When status is ascribed and not achieved, people are uncertain about their own capabilities. This is true of many of the women who circulate in this social scene and worry about what might happen if they became divorced single moms at age 40 and had no one to support them in style. They know their attractiveness for rich, older men may wane soon.

Many of the trust fund babies I see grew up living off inheritances, scoffing at those who work, partying to excess, and being supercilious on the outside, while feeling worthless underneath. I often see couples in which one or both members suffer from eating disorders, substance abuse disorders, and poor self-concept. They often lack a framework that gives a sense of purpose and meaning to life, and they may be plagued by uncertainties about whether their friends are true friends who would stand by them in times of financial and emotional crisis. With them, therapy may focus on issues such as: "Who am I, who are we, what do I want to do and be, what values do I hold and want to transmit to my children, how much do I want to raise them versus turning their care over to a nanny?"

Some are able to attain Maslow's Level 4—Self-Actualization. They become free, through therapy, to pursue their dreams, fulfill their potential—vocationally or avocationally—and to be philanthropic in the fullest sense of altruism and humanism. When they reach this level and have developed true self-confidence based on real achievements and contributions, their D (deficiency) needs have been replaced by their B (being) needs and therapy is terminated—by mutual agreement (Maslow, 1968). When couples achieve this plateau, they radiate health. Clearly, it is easier to become self-actualizing without being narcissistically self-absorbed when people have the financial resources to embark on any undertaking they want and to be beneficent in many different ways.

Treating the wealthy is challenging. They expect a great deal from the therapist and won't settle for less. Like poor and middle-class clients, they need to feel accepted and respected and to know that the therapist understands their values and lifestyle, and appreciates the fact that being wealthy does not preclude having problems—including uncertainties, jealousies, affairs, addictions, anxieties, and depressions. They just may be better able to mask their doubts, fears and hurts, and it may be harder to penetrate their defenses, since putting on a good act is an art in which many of the well-to-do are quite proficient. But once they do form a therapeutic alliance and like the changes they see in themselves, they stay in treatment until they feel and function substantially better, They often refer their friends.

SUMMARY

People across the socioeconomic scale need our services and we must tailor these to the needs of the specific patients and populations we are privileged to serve, treat, coach, and consult with. To enhance the efficiency and effectiveness of treatment, the therapist must be comfortable discussing money and financial concerns and knowledgable about the values, behaviors, and needs of people of all social classes. He or she should be able to be empathic with their interpretation of their life story in order to enable them to be willing to shift their view of the world, to becoming more optimistic and self-directing; able to utilize available resources or reestablish severed family connections; willing to take more responsibility for their own behavior and attempting to make the changes they want instead of expecting others to do so for them; able to reevaluate their needs and goals in terms of an evolving clearer sense of what gives meaning and purpose to their life; overcome their pervasive sense of isolation, emptiness, or anger; and able to earn the money they need or access what is available from community resource funds to live decently; or to be generous and charitable if they have the financial wherewithal to give for the benefit of others.

REFERENCES

Abraham, K. (1921). Contributions to the theory of the anal character. In K. Abraham (Ed.), *Selected papers on psychoanalysis* (pp. 370–392). New York: Brunner/Mazel.

American Psychiatric Association. (1994). *Diagnostic and statistical manual of mental disorders* (4th ed.). Washington, DC: Author.

Beaver, W. R., & Kaslow, F. W. (1981). The anatomy of hope. *Journal of Marital and Family Therapy, 7*(2), 119–126.

Birdwhistle, R. L. (1962). An approach to communications. *Family Process, 1*(2), 194–201.

Boszormenyi-Nagy, I., & Spark, G. (1984). *Invisible loyalties: Reciprocity in intergenerational family therapy.* New York: Brunner/Mazel. (Original work published 1973)

Bowen, M. (1978,). *Family therapy in clinical practice.* Northvale, NJ: Aronson.

Bowen, M. (1988). *Family therapy in clinical practice* (2nd ed.). Northvale, NJ: Aronson.

Boyd-Franklin, N. (1989). *Black families in therapy.* New York: Guilford Press.

Boyd-Franklin, N. (1995). Therapy with African-American inner city families. In R. H. Mikesell, D.-D. Lusterman, & S. H. McDaniel (Eds.), *Integrating family therapy: Handbook of family psychology and systems theory* (pp. 357–371). Washington, DC: American Psychological Association.

Brenner, C. (1992). *An elementary textbook of psychoanalysis* (Rev. ed.). New York: International Universities Press.

de Shazer, S. (1988). *Clues: Investigating solutions in brief therapy.* New York: Norton.

Hollingshead, A., & Redlich, F. C. (1958). *Social class and mental illness: A community study.* New York: Wiley.

Kaslow, F. W. (1993). The lore and lure of family business. *American Journal of Family Therapy, 21*(1), 3–16.

Kaslow, F. W. (2000). Prenuptial and postnuptial agreements: Sunny or stormy bellwethers to marriage or remarriage. In F. W. Kaslow (Ed.), *Handbook of couple and family forensics* (pp. 3–22). New York: Wiley.

Kaslow, F. W., & Lebow, J. (2002). *Comprehensive handbook of psychotherapy: Vol. 4. Integrative/eclectic.* New York: Wiley.

Kaslow, F. W., & Magnavita, J. (2002). *Comprehensive handbook of psychotherapy: Vol. 1. Psychodynamic/object relations.* New York: Wiley.

Kaslow, F. W., Massey, R. F., & Massey, S. D. (2002). *Comprehensive handbook of psychotherapy: Vol. 3. Interpersonal, humanistic and existential.* New York: Wiley.

Kaslow, F. W., & Patterson, T. (2002). *Comprehensive handbook of psychotherapy: Vol. 2. Cognitive-behavioral approaches.* New York: Wiley.

Kirschner, D. A., & Kirschner, S. (1986). *Comprehensive family therapy.* New York: Brunner/Mazel.

Krueger, D. W. (1986). *The last taboo.* New York: Brunner/Mazel.

Lazarus, A. (1981). *The practice of multi-modal therapy.* New York: Springer.

Lindblad-Goldberg, M., Dore, M., & Stern, L. (1998). *Creating competence from chaos: A comprehensive guide to home-based services.* New York: Norton.

Maslow, A. (1968). *Toward a psychology of being.* New York: Van Nostrand.

McGoldrick, M., Giordano, J., & Pearce, J. K. (Eds.). (1996). *Ethnicity and family therapy* (2nd ed.). New York: Guilford Press.

McLaughlin, E., & Kraus, N. (2002). *The nanny diaries.* New York: St. Martin's Griffin.

Minuchin, P., Colapinto, J., & Minuchin, S. (1998). *Working with families of the poor.* New York: Guilford Press.

Minuchin, S., Montalvo, B., Guerney, B. G., Rosman, B. L., & Schumer, F. (1967). *Families of the slums.* New York: Basic Books.

Napier, A. Y., & Whitaker, C. A. (1978). *The family crucible.* New York: Harper & Row.

Paul, N. L., & Paul, B. B. (1986). *A marital puzzle.* New York: Gardner Press.

Prager, E. (2001, November). Who's got pulling power? *Harper's Bazaar* (Magazine), pp. 204, 206.

Reik, T. (1948). *Listening with the third ear.* New York: Grove Press.

Rider v. Rider. (1995). 648 N. E. 2d 661 (Ind. Ct. App.).

Ritz v. Ritz. (1995). 666 So. 2d 1181 (La. Ct. App.).

Sager, C. J. (1976). *Marriage contracts and couple therapy: Hidden forces in intimate relations.* New York: Brunner/Mazel.

Schwartz, L. L., & Kaslow, F. W. (1997). *Painful partings: Divorce and its aftermath.* New York: Wiley.

Sharlin, S. A., Kaslow, F. W., & Hammerschmidt, H. (Eds.). (2000). *Together through thick and thin: A multinational picture of long-term marriages.* Binghamton, NY: Haworth Press.

Sharlin, S. A., & Shamai, M. (1999). *From distress to hope: Intervening with poor and disorganized families.* New York: Haworth Press.

Spencer, G. (1997, May 9). Nuptial agreement invalidated on appeal, from *New York Law Journal.* In Lexus-Nexis Universe summary (pp. 1–2).

Sue, D. W., & Sue, D. (1999). *Counseling the culturally different: Theory and practice* (3rd ed.). New York: Wiley.

Teachman, J. D., Polonko, K. S., & Scanzoni, J. (1999). Demography and families. In M. B. Sussman, S. K. Steinmetz & G. W. Peterson (Eds.), *Handbook of marriage and the family* (2nd ed., pp. 39–76). New York: Plenum Press.

Veblen, T. (1994). *The theory of the leisure class.* Mineola, NY: Dover. (Original work published 1899)

Wallerstein, J. S., & Blakeslee, S. (1995). *The good marriage: How and why love lasts.* New York: Houghton Mifflin.

Wallerstein, J. S., & Kelly, J. B. (1980). *Surviving the breakup: How children and parents cope with divorce.* New York: Basic Books.

Waring, E. M. (1988). *Enhancing marital intimacy through facilitating cognitive self disclosure.* New York: Brunner/Mazel.

Weitzman, L. J. (1985). *The divorce revolution: The unexpected social and economic consequences for women and children in America.* New York: Free Press.

White, M., & Epstom, D. (1990). *Narrative means to therapeutic ends.* New York: Norton.

Willi, J. (1982). *Couples in collusion.* New York: Aronson.

CHAPTER 23

Divorcing Couples

Joy K. Rice

Almost all marital and couple therapy involves some consideration of divorce, whether or not it becomes a reality for the couple. The boundaries between marital therapy and divorce therapy are often overlapping and unclear. This will become readily apparent in a later discussion of the goals and therapeutic strategies of divorce therapy. It is also important to include a discussion of divorce therapy in a book on couples therapy because divorce is a global phenomenon and now a common event in the marital and family life cycle, especially in the United States. International comparisons of divorce rates for the past four decades reveal that the United States continues to have a significantly higher rate of divorce than other nations (J. K. Rice, 2000). Although the U.S. divorce rate has stabilized since the 1980s, half of all marriages still end in divorce (U.S. Census Bureau, 1999). Nearly one out of every three children is living in a single-parent family. As a result of divorce (as well as cohabitation), family forms are increasingly complicated, diverse, and continually evolving (J. K. Rice, 2001). Thus, marital therapists need to have knowledge about the realities of divorce; an understanding of the dramatic changes in expected individual, family, and marital life cycle in the last decades of the twentieth century; and the theoretical tools and practical clinical strategies to help clients get through and adjust to the difficult personal and familial problems and challenges that most divorces engender. This chapter discusses these issues and presents relevant research underpinning our information. First, however, is a brief summary of key information on the cultural and social aspects of divorce and the ongoing debates about its causes and impact that dramatically affect our clinical perspectives and strategies.

THE CAUSES AND EFFECTS OF DIVORCE

Global rising divorce rates have been attributed to a multitude of causes, including changing religious, legal, economic, and social factors, and prior psychological dysfunction. Certain factors appear repeatedly in the divorce literature, such as the liberalization of laws permitting marital dissolution (Glenn, 1999), increasing secularization, the greater acceptance of alternative families, and increased social and economic freedom for women. Male violence has been found to significantly increase the likelihood of marital disruption (DeMaris, 2000). Women are more likely to initiate divorce today than are men, being more financially able and willing to leave unhappy, inequitable, or abusive marriages than in the past, and divorce can be interpreted as a form of gender resistance to oppression (J. K. Rice, 2003). Economists also note that the opportunity costs of marriage have decreased, resulting in lower marital rates and a greater willingness to divorce and explore other choices and opportunities. Another line of research considers prior psychological dysfunction or a marital selectivity hypothesis (Amato, 2000). Prior psychiatric disorders have been found to be associated with a substantially higher risk of divorce, but these associations cannot be interpreted unequivocally as causal (Kessler, Walters, & Forthofer, 1998). Divorce must also be understood in relation to the culture of which it is a part. Western cultures such as ours increasingly emphasize individualism, emotional self-fulfillment, and autonomy. It seems likely that divorce will continue to be a frequent event and painful process in American culture, which strongly values emotional bonding between spouses and increasingly downplays and devalues economic and religious ties.

There is a large body of research now that also documents the costs of divorce. Early research has been widely disseminated to the public with fearful admonitions about how children of divorce are irrevocably scarred (Wallerstein, Lewis, & Blakeslee, 2000). This research, however, was seriously flawed and, as Dreman summarized, "suffers not only from temporal confounds and failure to employ control groups of intact families, but also from the fact that it is of a mainly descriptive, clinical and non-quantitative nature employing a small nonrepresentative sample of 60 divorced families from an affluent community in northern California" (pp. 153–154). Other earlier research on divorce outcomes have been criticized for a reliance on static, cross-sectional assessments, personal accounts, small, unrepresentative samples, no comparison or control groups, and a lack of consideration of mediating and confounding variables such as length of the divorce and marriage, locale, socioeconomic status (SES), income, and the significant effects of family dysfunction before the divorce (Hetherington & Kelly, 2002; Kesner & McKenry, 2001; Swartz & Kaslow, 1997). Fortunately, we now have other longitudinal research based on decades of meticulous, multivariable study with broad-based national samples that gives us a much clearer picture of the outcomes of divorce and length of recovery. In their landmark, comprehensive study of 1,400 families over a period of three decades of research, Hetherington and her colleagues present a more balanced summary of the problems and challenges of divorcing families (Hetherington, Bridges, & Insabella, 1998; Hetherington & Kelly, 2002). They find that most adults and children go through a very difficult period of crisis and may often experience traumalike feelings and adjustments. Very young children of both sexes are likely to exhibit behavior problems, and boys may show problems for longer periods than girls. Problems for adolescents tend to center on depression, low self-esteem, and antisocial behaviors. Adolescent girls may have problems with precocious sexual behavior and adolescent boys with defiant, aggressive behaviors. There is less agreement on the magnitude of these effects. It usually takes from two to five years of adjustment to stabilize to more normal positive feelings and behaviors, but the good news is that most people, including children, are remarkably resilient, suffering no long-term psychopathology as a result of divorce. Divorce is certainly painful for children, and the effects are not to be taken lightly, but six years after a divorce, the vast majority of children emerge, without permanent scars or significant diminution of trust in others, and are functioning within the normal range of adjustment (Braver & Cookston, in press; Hetherington & Kelly, 2002; King, 2002).

A key consistent factor that emerges for children's adjustment is the degree to which the divorcing parties cooperate and avoid involving the children in the divorce conflict (Baum, 2003; Gilman, Kawachi, Fitzmaurice, & Buka, 2003; Hetherington et al., 1998; King, 2002). This latter finding has tremendous implications for clinicians helping divorcing parents and will be discussed at length in the section on clinical strategies. In a very careful review of the past two decades of divorce research, Amato (2000) concludes that both perspectives—divorce as lingering disaster for individuals, families, and society versus divorce as a benign force for change and growth—are one-sided representations of reality. Divorce benefits some individuals, leads others to experience temporary psychological detriments, and exacerbates the problems of others, who experience a downward decline from which they never recover. Women and children still bear the economic brunt of divorce, and their subsequent incomes are 56% that of their former husbands (Bianchi, Subaiya, & Kahn, 1999). An increasing number of men, especially lower-income men also suffer a reduced standard of living following separation (McManus & DiPrete, 2001). Children suffer the loss of fathers, because fathers still are less likely to receive custody and are frequently less involved in their children's lives. Men suffer also from that parental loss. Remarriage rates after divorce continue to be higher for men (75%) than for women (66%; Hetherington et al., 1998).

DIVERSITY AND DIVORCE

The divorce rate is 20% to 30% higher among African Americans, even when controlling for socioeconomic status (McKenry & McKelvey, 2003;

U.S. Census Bureau, 1999). College-educated Black women, like their White counterparts, are more likely to divorce (Kposowa, 1998). Black mothers are not only less likely to remarry, but also to receive less alimony and child support. They are more likely to have full custody, to live in poverty, and to face economic and social oppression than White divorcees (Amato, 2000). The higher divorce rates among Blacks have been explained in both economic and cultural terms. There is less of a social taboo on separation and single-parent living among African Americans. Multigenerational parenting is normative, and cooperative kinship networks and sharing represent a traditional strength of African American society (Hetherington, 1999). Cultural patterns and economic trends are linked, however, and the choices of Black families have been made under conditions of economic hardship (Cherlin, 1998). Any social or cultural advantage for Black women in initially coping with marital dissolution is diminished in the long term, and longitudinal research indicates five years after a divorce White women evidence greater personal mastery, informal and overall happiness, as well as the economic advantages of a higher probability of remarriage. Marriage is a temporary state for most Black women, lasting about 22 years, and is followed by increasingly longer periods of single status, before and after marriage (McKenry & McKelvey, 2003). As they age, Black women also may have to raise grandchildren alone on limited incomes and with significantly lower retirement benefits than older White women (Butricia & Iams, 2003; Ruiz, Zhu, & Crowther, 2003).

Although gay marriages have not yet been widely sanctioned legally, children and adults in these marriages have few benefits of the protection of the law nor from public scrutiny. There are varying estimates of from 6 to 14 million children being raised by lesbian or gay male parents (Laird, 1993). No studies have found that children of gay and lesbian parents are disadvantaged in any important respect compared to children of heterosexual parents (American Psychological Association, 1995). Legal recognition of these marriages, however, would be very beneficial to these children in terms of protecting their economic interests and guaranteeing custody and stability of caretaking in the event of a death or divorce (Wald, 2000).

THEORETICAL FOUNDATIONS: DIVORCE AND SELF-ESTEEM

There is an almost total absence of writing that outlines and analyzes the theoretical underpinnings of divorce therapy from related disciplines and other interventions strategies. A brief summary is presented here that should help marital therapists who are seeking to understand the foundations of the strategies employed in doing divorce work with couples and clients. However, for an in-depth discussion of the theoretical origins and debts of divorce therapy, the reader is referred to our earlier book (J. K. Rice & Rice, 1986). Divorce therapy is still in its early stages of defining itself as a specialized form of therapy, but most marital therapists find themselves employing some strategies of divorce therapy as they help their clients work through the decision about divorce and the adjustment to divorce, once it is clear that the marriage is going to be dissolved. Sprenkle (1989) has written that divorce therapy can be described as relationship treatment whose goal is to diminish and eventually dissolve the marital bonds, in contrast to marital therapy that seeks to enhance and preserve the marital bond. Of course, such a dichotomy is rarely apparent in clinical practice. More often, the therapist finds himself or herself in a period that may be lengthy and ambiguous of alternating back and forth between exploring preservation and uncoupling, reflecting the normal ambivalence of the separating partners. Couples may present with goals of saving the marriage, when, in actuality, at least one partner is fairly certain and committed to dissolution. The opposite may also be the case. The point is that the distinction between divorce therapy and marital therapy is not tidy, and the therapist must continue to help clients assert their real desires and must sensitively monitor the goals and commitments of the clients, and be flexible to changing strategies appropriate to those goals.

There are essentially five areas from which divorce therapy, as currently conceived and practiced, has derived: (1) marital and family therapy, including both psychodynamic systems and behavioral approaches; (2) crisis-intervention treatment; (3) grief and bereavement counseling; (4) educational-supportive counseling; and (5) developmental psychology (J. K. Rice & Rice, 1986). My approach incorporates elements of all these areas, but I find it most valuable to work with divorcing clients from a family life cycle perspective that will be elaborated later in greater detail.

Psychoanalytic Approaches

A basic premise of most psychodynamic approaches in treating marital and family conflict is that partner and family difficulties are often seen as symptoms of unresolved childhood conflicts. These conflicts may be repeated across generations, paralleling the idea of fixation or regression to earlier less mature developmental levels. The idea of the intergenerational transmission of divorce is also predicated on the assumption that unresolved personal, relational, and familial conflicts get played out in succeeding generations of the family. Much of the initial phases of treatment in working with divorcing clients focuses on ameliorating the crisis and traumatic aspects of the divorce decision and adjustments. Later in treatment, a careful exploration of the history and patterns of individual and family dysfunction is critical in helping clients understand the dynamics of the problems and in gaining insights and tools to break old patterns and to make healthier choices. Thus, both practical problem solving and dynamic exploration need to be part of the divorce process in therapy.

A tenet of psychodynamic couple therapy is that the root of most couple problems can be found in the failure of one or both partners to individuate and master the developmental task of separation and differentiation. This concept has had a great impact on the theory and practice of divorce therapy, requiring that client and therapist explore the person's history of separations, to work through and master the most difficult separation of all, the loss of the partner. The underlying theme of these therapeutic strategies revolves around understanding how earlier conflicts are manifested in the marriage and later in the divorce (Alvin & Pearson, 1998). The therapist, however, also takes into account that marital conflict and dissolution may occur in the absence of significant individual psychopathology and may be the result of the cultural and situational constraints on the partners and the interaction between the partners. Such a view respects a family systems approach.

FAMILY SYSTEMS APPROACHES

Divorce can be treated as part of a larger family system problem. It is often unproductive to work on a marital relationship in individual therapy without the actual presence and contributions of both partners. Similarly, in working with divorcing couples, it is often most advantageous to work through and understand the "marital autopsy" history as well as the divorce decision and postdivorce adjustments involving the welfare of children with both individuals present. Since each member of the family interacts within a system of operation, during divorce therapy the children or extended family members may also be brought into treatment as appropriate. This contextual system (the use of conjoint, individual, or family therapy at appropriate stages of the divorce) helps the therapist to make more informed, realistic assessments and to better ensure the goal of positive lasting change within the individual family members and within any future blended family.

Divorce has the power to alter radically the individual and familial relationships of people within a system and thus to change the nature of the system itself. This is readily apparent in continually evolving new family forms and kinship structures (J. K. Rice, 2001). Conversely, if ex-spouses continue to repeat old games and dyadic stratagems and never divorce emotionally, then the family system itself may not be altered significantly, except to replay versions of the old dysfunctional patterns. Triangulating and "parenting" the children offers many opportunities for maintenance of the old family system.

BEHAVIOR THERAPY CONTRIBUTIONS

The behavioral models applied to marital therapy have had considerable impact on the practice of divorce therapy and mediation, particularly in managing and resolving the often intense relational conflict engendered by the decision to divorce and by the divorce itself. Most therapists helping divorcing couples utilize behavior management techniques to control con-flict within the divorce process and to de-escalate postdivorce conflict. The divorce mediation movement developed in reaction to the adversarial nature of the legal system. Despite no fault divorce, the legal system works toward specifying the winner and loser in divorces. Divorce mediation borrowed heavily from conflict management techniques largely based on behavioral change approaches (she gets the house if she agrees that he gets to keep his retirement). Divorce mediation, although not therapy per se, may be therapeutic for both parties involved, and a marital therapist can often effectively refer a divorcing couple to a divorce mediation specialist when they both agree to keep the legal adversarial process to a minimum. A behavioral exchange framework can also be applied in deciding whether to divorce and recognize the point of no return, when the disadvantages of the marriage heavily outweigh the advantages.

STRUCTURED EDUCATIONAL INTERVENTION

The trauma of postdivorce adjustment also can be effectively eased by using structured educational group interventions. Parent education programs and school-based divorce intervention programs for children have become commonplace and are often very helpful in both facilitating effective co-parenting and helping children adjust (Emery & Sbarra, 2002). Other divorce adjustment groups aim to help participants understand the practical adjustments necessary to heal from divorce and to develop interpersonal, communication, and social skills facilitating the recovery of self-esteem and the building of a new social network. Role playing, nonverbal exercises, directed reading, writing, keeping a journal, problem-solving and decision-making exercises, and referrals to other educational and community resources may be involved. An advantage of the group approach is that participants gain validation for their disturbing feelings and supportive opportunities for mutual problem solving with peers who may become friends. The author has found that such groups can be a very effective adjunct to postdivorce psychotherapy.

CRISIS INTERVENTION

The decision and process of divorce often engender such acute anxiety in clients that they may temporarily lose their bearings and ability to function on a daily basis. A client may voice that he feels he is going crazy. Thus, some therapists in the field have viewed divorce as primarily a crisis, that is, an event or circumstance that the person feels requires accommodations or solutions beyond his or her capacities (Granvold, 2002). Certainly, events that may precipitate or accompany a divorce like the escalation of violence or alcoholism, the discovery of an affair or gross financial irresponsibility, or a child's reactive problems may contribute to intense acute anxiety and disorganization. There may be an immediate need to employ crisis management techniques and an intervention plan that ensures the safety and well-being of the family members. This would involve an assessment of initial risk for suicide or homicide, problem definition, the clients' strengths and resilience and prior coping strategies, de-escalating intense emotion, a possible referral for medication, and an action plan with the concrete steps agreed to by all parties involved. It is also important, however, for marital therapists not to mistake the acute grief, personal stress, and disorganization accompanying the decision to divorce as indicative of more serious underlying psychopathology or endogenous depression. A period of reactive depression and intense grief is normative in the divorce process, and a task of the therapist is to give repeated reassurances to clients that time to heal from losses is necessary and beneficial.

GRIEF COUNSELING

Because divorce involves *object loss* and intense *ego injury* (J. K. Rice & Rice, 1986) that leads to depression and mourning, some investigators in the field have used elements of grief theory to define the stages of divorce. The four-phase sequence of grief behavior (denial, protest, despair, and detachment) that follows separation is derived from attachment theory (Bowlby, 1982). Love and passion may erode or die, but attachments may still persist and resist dissolution despite anger, betrayal, and hurt. This is a common pattern in divorce and makes emotional divorce harder to achieve than legal divorce. Denying or abridging the necessary initial grief work may only perpetuate unrealistic attachment to the ex-spouse, and therapists must be very patient in working with such clients.

DIVORCE AND STAGE THEORY

Less a theory and more a convenient description based on the usual sequence of events, stage theory categorizes common phases of divorce, employing both actual events (e.g., decision to divorce, separation) or the psychological sequel and practical tasks (psychic divorce, co-parental divorce) to describe the process of divorce. The conceptualization of the divorce process may be simple like Sprenkle's three stages (1989) and Glick and Patel's four stages (2000) or more complex like Swartz and Kaslow's seven stages (1997). Despite the differences in the number and labeling of the stages, basically all these conceptions refer to three phases: (1) a predivorce period (shock, denial, disillusionment, decision to divorce); (2) a restructuring transition period (separation, negotiations, restructuring); and (3) a postdivorce recovery period (reorientation, stability, equilibrium). Although presenting the therapist with some convenient markers in the divorce therapy process, stage theory, to this author's mind, suffers from an oversimplification of the divorce process. Being linear and assuming predictability of process, stage theory can also be very misleading to the marital and divorce therapist who wishes to do effective therapy. To understand effective divorce therapy, one must go beyond the discrete, fairly predictable tasks and adjustments defined by the legal system and society to a consideration of the underlying psychological issues and processes. The important psychic processes in divorce are better conceptualized as developmental in nature and therefore continuous and multileveled.

DIVORCE AND THE LIFE CYCLE: A DEVELOPMENTAL APPROACH

If therapy for divorcing couples is defined as involving the mediation of interpersonal conflict, the management of crisis, or the working through of grief, one has basically only a first-order change situation. That is, surface issues have changed, for example, economic and custody issues are presumably settled. Yet, no significant change in the person's level of personal and interpersonal functioning and development may have been accomplished. The individuals are often still struggling with a particular developmental task of individuation or intimacy and are likely to reenact the developmental struggle in future relationships. When a marriage comes apart because two people do not or cannot grow together or are frozen in the status quo, then divorce can be a powerful and positive release of energy and development. In the case of significant interlocking developmental blocks, the decision to divorce is more problematic unless the individual and dyad dysfunction is explored and carefully worked through.

Although almost all marital therapists understandably share a promarriage bias, separation and divorce can be more realistically viewed by the therapist as increasingly common milestones in adult development that bring potential for both stress and growth. When half of the people in a society experience a significant personal and interpersonal life event, there is an obvious need to integrate that event into our thinking about what is normative experience in the individual, marital, and family life cycle. Two decades ago, Carter and McGoldrick (1980) discussed divorce as a paranormative event in the family life cycle. A basic reader on marital and family therapy published in 2000 described the stages of normative marital life cycle as courtship and marriage, and defined the stages of the family life cycle entirely by the presence of children and the state of the child's development, for example, "child raising" with no mention of divorce or remarriage or even cohabitation (Glick, 2000). These traditional models presume one major lifetime relationship, one marriage, one commitment. They are also predicated on the view that the individual and marital tasks of establishing autonomy and intimacy are defined mainly through bonding, rather than through an actual cycle of bonding, separating, and rebonding.

Intimacy and Identity   A more useful approach to conceptualizing a marital/family life cycle model applicable to all people, married or divorced, in alternative or emerging family forms, and from different cultures and ethnicities, is to employ general concepts of development (instead of marriage and child raising) that all family members must accomplish at various points in their (multiple) marriages and families. David Rice and I earlier published this model in greater detail (J. K. Rice & Rice, 1986). In sum, a parsimonious model of life cycle development is based on the assumption that there are but two key tasks of all human development. These key tasks may recur and need to be reworked and redefined over the course of a lifetime of passage through perhaps several significant relationships. The first is *intimacy* in which one works to achieve *communion,* that is, closeness with another person; and the second, *identity,* in which one works to achieve successful *separation* or differentiation of self from others. These two tasks are basic to all human development. They are also interlocking: "The goal is to be close, yet separate; to be intimate, yet autonomous; to find the self, yet to merge with the other" (p. 84).

The basic themes of *intimacy/communion* and *identity/separation* recur over and over again in the life cycle, but with different meanings in each period of life, necessitating redefinition and transformation. The adaptive solution for one period of life may not be the best one for the next.

Unlike traditional marital and family life cycle conceptions, the proposed model is nonlinear and multileveled, and the sequence is not rigid or necessarily predictable. Key marker events like marriage and divorce have the potential for impeding individual development in intimacy and identity and conversely to stimulating further growth in these tasks. Paradoxically, in divorce it is the very breakdown of intimacy, of the task of communion with a significant partner, that has the potential to lead to a better-defined individual identity and differentiation of self, yet also involves the danger of permanently blocking growth in intimacy if other issues are not resolved. Table 23.1 provides a conceptualization of this model as applied to divorce, noting the developmental tasks, dangers, and opportunities for the divorcing adult or child of divorce—and the corresponding goals for therapy. The model does not seek to oversimplify the complexities of human development over the lifespan. The concepts of intimacy and identity have enormously rich complexity and interaction. Nonetheless, a basic understanding of these concepts helps us see individual development as a continuous unfolding of basic themes that have always had historical, cultural, and interpersonal meaning.

A further advantage is that the model can be easily applied to a multicultural context. Lyle and Faure (2000) have taken the model and used it very effectively to integrate concerns about ethnicity and divorce, incorporating the parallel elements of acculturation and enculturation. In multicultural counseling with Hispanic families, they note that using a recursive, nonlinear developmental model has many benefits and shifts attention away from the completion of a particular stage toward the process of development.

Table 23.1
Effects of Divorce on Key Developmental Tasks of
Intimacy and Identity and Therapeutic Goals

Childhood		
	Intimacy	Identity
Developmental task	Receiving love and attachment to parents.	Explore outside world; test boundaries aided by positive parental communion.
Divorce danger	Intimacy/communion with parent jeopardized leading to anxiety and/or depression. Parental alienation. Intimacy/communion with step-parent(s) problematic.	Premature parental separation. Parentification of child. Overprotection or overindulgence.
Developmental opportunity	Cessation of conflict permits unrestricted bonding with parents. Experience love from another parental figure. More open kinship networks.	Learning resilience. Appropriate greater independence and self-sufficiency.
Therapeutic goals	Reassure continuing parental love and bond. Ensure cooperative co-parenting. Set realistic expectations for blended family relationships.	Ensure regular visitation/contact with both parents. Support mutual expectations of child's responsibilities.

Adolescence/Young Adult		
	Intimacy	Identity
Developmental task	Intimacy/communion redefined by closeness to peers and others outside family.	Increasing self-differentiation and identification with peers and others outside family.
Divorce danger	Mistrust of others. Reluctance to trust, bond.	Over-identification with a parent. Rejection of parent or stepparent.
Developmental opportunity	Peer attachment is buffer to parental conflict. Development of empathy for parent(s).	Role model of parent achieving healthy separation/individuation. Appropriate familial responsibility.
Therapeutic goals	Affectionate, authoritative co-parenting. Rebuild trust and respect.	Support parental patience, perspective, and constancy. Aid conflict de-escalation and management.

(continued)

Table 23.1   *Continued*

| | **Adulthood** | |
	Intimacy	Identity
Developmental task	Loving and committing to a person outside family of origin. Achievement of autonomous intimacy.	Strong sense of self through personal and economic self-sufficiency. Commitment to work and goals within and outside the family.
Divorce danger	Retreat from or inability to be intimate and to commit. Narcissistic love predominant.	Incomplete self-differentiation and search for new person to complete identity. Identity exclusively defined by intimacy with partner. Identity exclusively defined by work achievement leading to intimacy erosion.
Developmental opportunity	Compassionate concern for self and others. Forgiveness and peace with ex-spouse, self, and family. Achievement of reciprocal and autonomous intimacy with a new person.	New or enhanced sense of self and self-sufficiency. Balance of communion and separation in work and relationships. Understanding and alleviation of irrational guilt.
Therapeutic goals	Understand personal contribution to divorce and projection of blame. Work through blocks to intimacy. Develop realistic expectations of a partner permitting compromise, trust, and communion.	Understand and change pattern of seeking another to complete identity. Separate self from spouse and parent(s). Positively assume responsibility for personal happiness. Balance relationships with work and other interests, pursuits.

Divorce has a primary impact on both the central developmental tasks of intimacy and identity. Divorce affects intimacy through *object or person loss* and ego injury. Divorce primarily affects identity through *role loss* and role disorientation (J. K. Rice & Rice, 1986). Both person loss and role loss lead to a loss of self-esteem. Thus, the primary goals of helping adults and children transcend and adjust to divorce are to work through the losses of person and role, thereby restoring, rebuilding, and increasing self-esteem. The following section explores the specific strategies and issues in divorce that therapists can apply to achieve these goals.

THERAPEUTIC ISSUES AND STRATEGIES IN DIVORCE

THERAPIST BIAS AND ORIENTATION

It is important in working with divorcing couples to have a realistic understanding of one's own attitude and possible bias toward marriage, divorce, and alternative families. One must ask oneself about one's own beliefs about divorce when children are involved, about one's own religious values, family history, and marital/divorce experience. A therapist should be willing to refer a couple to another therapist if he or she is uncomfortable in making the transition from marital to divorce therapy. A related issue is the therapist's own feelings of failure if marital therapy has not been effective in saving a marriage. A therapist who measures success rate by how many couples stay together may feel like a failure much of the time. Thus, it is important to come to terms with such feelings and to appreciate that helping a couple to divorce more comfortably and with less emotional sequelae for themselves and their children is a worthy goal. Feelings of dissatisfaction, disappointment, or impatience are likely to compound the clients' existing feelings of failure and rejection. Several issues and value judgments also arise in conjunction with vested interests in one member of the couple. Usually, it is very difficult to remain neutral toward either party when one spouse has been the victim of abuse and violence, and the therapist must carefully explore whether he or she is projecting personal anger and judgment that could influence the decision to separate or divorce.

More commonly, vested interests are a key issue when, after a decision to divorce is made, the therapist also worked individually with one of the spouses, usually during the separation period. Unless the therapist has previously established rapport and trust with both parties and has carefully and openly discussed the rules and parameters of confidentiality in the individual versus the couple therapy, it can be difficult to get the other spouse back into treatment to explore divorce and postdivorce issues. It may be necessary to see the other spouse at least once or twice in individual therapy to reestablish the therapeutic alliance. Another related issue is pressure for the therapist to take sides in the divorce when difficult legal and custody issues are involved, or a party's lawyer feels the therapist has critical information to support his client's position. In this case, it is fortunate when the therapist has continued to see both parties, can maintain that both are clients, and that choosing sides is not fair or ethical (D. G. Rice, 1989). All these strategic issues underscore the importance of seeing both individuals in the divorce process and divorce therapy. This may not always be easy when during marital therapy the hidden agenda has been divorce all along, and once a decision to divorce is made, usually by the initiator, the initiator wants to leave therapy. The initiator may also want to hand over the ex-spouse to the therapist, who becomes the substitute spouse. Often, when it is clear there will be a divorce, clients abruptly terminate treatment.

CASE STUDY

This was Laura's (43) second marriage and Michael's (45) first. Laura's first marriage occurred at age 26 and ended in divorce two years later. Laura and Michael had been married for 15 years and had two children, Caitlyn (14) and Josh (8). The marriage began to falter seriously after the birth of Josh. Laura returned to work full-time, taking the night shift as a nurse on an emergency ward. A crisis occurred when Michael discovered that Laura had a short-lived affair with a doctor with whom she worked. She also revealed that she had been unhappy in the marriage for some time and was considering separation. They came into marital therapy with different goals. Michael was extremely anxious, distraught, and unsure that he could even forgive or transcend the affair. Nonetheless, he felt he still loved Laura and wanted to save the marriage. The affair had made Laura much more aware of how deeply dissatisfied she was with the lack of intimacy in the marriage and what she characterized as Michael's passivity and emotional unavailability. They had one brief separation early in the marriage and two sessions of couple counseling at that time, which they felt helped their communication, but didn't resolve their basic personality and value differences. Having divorced once, Laura felt she could manage on her own, but was very ambivalent about declaring she wanted a divorce, since she was fearful of hurting Michael and their children. She wanted the options for separation and divorce to be a part of the marital therapy. Unlike Michael, she did not feel she was still in love with her spouse. She cared for him, but was very dubious about their resolving their differences.

Their children were doing well and were relatively unaware of the depth of their parents' problems. The couple avoided displaying any overt conflict or anger. The first four sessions involved taking a detailed individual, marital, and familial history in which it was learned that Laura felt smothered and overprotected as an only child. To the consternation of her family, at age 20 she moved to Las Vegas to cohabit with and marry an older man. He was a pilot and impressed her with his attentiveness and energy. His gambling addiction debts precipitated the divorce as well as her realization that she had married too young, essentially to escape her family. She moved back to her hometown, met Michael at work, and dated for a year before marrying. She saw Michael as stable and attractive, and her parents liked him immensely. Michael, a quiet man and a contrast to Laura's first husband, was attracted to her outgoing personality and ability to make friends easily.

THE DECISION TO DIVORCE

The transition to divorce therapy is not as clear as a therapist might like, often involving a fairly lengthy period in which the clients go back and forth about whether to stay together. Finally, a time comes when the therapist can offer the observation that the issue the couple is discussing has been repeatedly addressed without resolution and that neither party has desired to or been capable of making necessary changes and accommodations to preserve the marriage. The implicit question is whether the marriage is ended and there is a need to make a decision to move forward. Often, this point of no return occurs after clients see a continuous pattern, a marital flip-flop, sometimes over months, sometimes over years, of repetitious emotional partings, bondings, and partings again. If the couple has gone to therapy and tried to conscientiously do what they feel they could to preserve the relationship, then subsequent postdivorce guilt and regret may be lessened. Thus, it behooves the therapist not to abort this process, but also to be a realistic observer and reporter about when a couple is simply repeating patterns and is locked into a status quo that is hurting themselves and perhaps their children. What unhappy, dissatisfied couple doesn't actively fight or manifest dysfunction in front of their children? Recent research has shown that children do better when parents divorce in high-conflict marriages, but stay married in low-conflict, unhappy marriages. This is, of course, a dilemma for the therapist: whose interest to put first. Whatever your personal bias, the therapist should conscientiously help the couple discuss the consequences of a decision to divorce for the children as well as for themselves. Sometimes, the decision will be to wait until the children are older, but more often in today's milieu of high expectations for personal fulfillment, individual needs are put first. "Rarely is there anything anyone can do to dissuade a spouse who is determined to sever the marital ties . . . the therapist can suggest a trial separation, which can serve as cooling-off period during which to make more rational choices" (Kaslow, 1995, p. 274).

Structured Separation   The likelihood is high that a divorcing couple will experience a period of separation. This separation can serve several functions. It can be a conflict management tool—a means of de-escalating anger and irrational decision making, and a protection against escalating physical or emotional violence. It can be a temporary vacation from the dispute. It can afford a structured, time-limited period for decision making or breaking an impasse, and it can be a period for new learning and value clarification in which to explore other options in relationships, work, and living independently and to acknowledge there are choices. Most importantly, the therapist needs to help the couple openly acknowledge whether the separation is really a dress rehearsal for divorce, in which the partners are buying some time to make the emotional and behavioral adjustments necessary for divorce. Conversely, it can be agreed that the separation is a tool to continue to work on preserving the marriage by reformulating the marital contract, breaking old perceptions, and working on independence and personal growth conducive to helping the marriage. The latter case involves a structured separation with counseling. Both parties agree they will continue couple therapy on a regular basis while physically separated. Most often, the couple agrees that financial arrangements stay in place and no big life changes (change of residence, jobs, placement of children) will occur except for one spouse's moving out. Sometimes, an arrangement can be made where the spouses take turns living in the house or other temporary housing. If the parties agree not to bring in lawyers right away, the process is far more likely to remain nonadversarial, and the therapist can better help the couple to maintain or achieve a nonblame attitude that is far more conducive to personal and familial healing. The therapist basically continues to do couple counseling. The couple should be informed that more than half of couples who decide to physically separate do go on to divorce. Knowing this, the noninitiator may strongly oppose a separation, fearing it signals the reality of a divorce.

Mixed messages about separating may be given by both parties, and the therapist needs to help the couple not only sort out those messages, but to explore the advantages and disadvantages of a separation. A legal separation involves essentially all the financial and custodial decisions of a divorce, but may be preferred by couples who feel there need to be very clear guidelines in these areas and who want the relief and security of having these decisions in place. Whether a separation is a dress rehearsal or acknowledged prelude to divorce or an alternative attempt to change perceptions and save a marriage, it is important for the therapist and clients to go over the ground rules of the separation. In this author's experience, amazingly few couples openly talk about all the practical ramifications and decisions of a separation, other perhaps than to discuss what happens with the children.

Issues that must be decided include length of initial separation, time of evaluation and follow-up, continuing counseling, placement and visitation, child support and finances, whether to involve lawyers, how to tell the children, which individuals outside the family will be told about the separation and by whom and how, and whether the couple will see other people or remain monogamous. The latter decisions can be the cause of much conflict and misunderstanding, and damage control can be prevented in therapy by clear ground rules. These areas, of course, must also be addressed if and when the parties go on to a final divorce. In this author's experience, a structured separation with counseling needs a minimum period of three months and is often six months to one year in length.

CASE STUDY

After 10 sessions of marital therapy focused on efforts to explore their differences and to solve their conflicts, Laura declared that she was tired of their repeated, unsuccessful efforts to fix the marriage. She declared she wanted to separate and asked Michael to move out. Michael was very reluctant and feared it would hasten a divorce, but tentatively agreed to a three-month separation with the proviso that neither would date or see other people. At this point, the therapist initiated a discussion of the meaning and purpose of the separation. Their homework was to discuss and outline the ground rules of their separation. Before the next scheduled session, the therapist received a phone call from a very anxious Laura who said that

Michael was extremely depressed, couldn't sleep or work, and was making suicidal threats. She didn't trust him with the children and was threatening to take them to her parents' house. An individual therapy session and medication referral helped stabilize Michael, and he gradually realized, if not totally accepted, the reality of the separation. He indicated that he still did not understand why Laura had the affair and wanted to end the marriage. He said that his ego was badly wounded.

In the next several conjoint sessions, the therapist explored with the couple how to cope with the several pressing needs of the situation, including deescalating the conflict, informing the children and ensuring their welfare, and agreeing to the ground rules of the separation. The therapist recommended that they continue in conjoint therapy, explaining that it was important in helping them to make decisions regarding their parting, especially about the children. It was also important to co-parent cooperatively as well as to unravel and understand the demise of their relationship. Michael and Laura came in together for two more sessions in which they discussed how to tell their children about the separation. The therapist emphasized that, if possible, they should sit down with Caitlyn and Josh together and briefly and calmly explain that although they no longer could live together and be married, that they deeply loved them and would still be actively there for them as mom and dad. The therapist explained how it was critical to stress continuing love, presence, and security with their children, emphasizing that the children were not to blame for the separation and that their lives and home would not change. They also agreed to suspend negative comments about each other to their children as well as to their friends and family. Michael knew he would have a difficult time living up to this agreement, alternating between seeing Laura as the evil adulteress who betrayed him, and himself as culpable, unworthy, and sexually inadequate. He was encouraged to maintain regular contact with his children and to establish an attractive alternative residence for them. This would help him heal and to feel some sense of home and competence instead of loneliness and uprootedness. The therapist also encouraged him to reach out to his family and friends, emphasizing the importance of a network of support. It was agreed that Michael would start individual therapy with another therapist to help him with his depression, hostility, and blame mentality. Laura's correspondingly difficult task was to avoid assuming that Michael could not be an effective parent because he was despondent and angry. Laura said that she did not want to continue in conjoint divorce therapy after the practical agreements about temporary dissolution were made, but that she also would like to have some occasional individual visits with the therapist.

RESTRUCTURING

After a decision to divorce has been made, the therapist's initial job is to help the couple, and particularly the one who was not the initiator (Michael in the previous case) stabilize emotionally and accept the reality of the divorce.

Some individual therapy and medication may be necessary if emotions are disturbing or as in a minority of cases, there are symptoms of acute break-down or possible violence. Normalizing the feelings of dysfunction, disbelief, and disorientation helps clients realize they are experiencing a temporary, albeit intense, crisis for themselves and their families. If there is significant anger or acting out, using crisis management tools as discussed in the prior section is useful to de-escalate the conflict and stabilize emotions.

Ego Reparation   Even couples who manage to negotiate feasible divorce agreements and amicable postdivorce relations must first overcome an initially hostile, oppositional dynamic (Hooper, 2001). This conflict stems from many sources that all lead to ego loss. There may be resource or power differentials affecting separation decisions. The adversarial legal system may generate more conflict. Conflict is also engendered by feelings of being hurt, humiliated, abused, or betrayed by a divorcing spouse or shamed and stigmatized by divorce. The sacred is coming undone, and the dream/fantasy one had about the partner and what he or she would do for one is hard to give up. Thus, the symbolic dimension in divorce is also useful to explore in helping parties understand their strong reactions and resistance to divorce.

   Ego reparation is a primary goal of divorce therapy and a need stemming from the *ego loss* or *object loss* in divorce leading to narcissistic wounding. Ego reparation is more easily achieved if the person gives up not only the blame mentality, but the unrealistic ideas and symbols of what the partner and marriage unconsciously represented. Narcissistic repair of self-esteem can become maladaptive to the degree that a person must distort reality to regain a sense of equilibrium. This dynamic work is not typically achieved in the divorce therapy sessions with both partners. These sessions are generally brief and more focused on practical readjustments. Repairing self-esteem is more readily explored in postdivorce individual therapy (discussed in the next section). In the middle of divorce, however, both parties need to realize they must accept the inevitable and make some necessary plans to move on. Here is where the therapist can help clients in making necessary personal and pragmatic adjustments to being single and living alone.

Role Restructuring   The practical tasks necessary during and after divorce directly relate to the second primary goal of divorce therapy, helping clients with *role restructuring* stemming from the multiple *role losses* in divorce, all of which can lead to disorientation. Role loss after divorce involves more than losing the marital role as husband or wife. The client realizes that there is the potential for loss of extended family, family of origin (if disapproving), a partner in parenting, couple and personal friends, and the societal status of being married. The latter involves both financial and social status. Taking on the single-adult role, although certainly an adjustment, is easier than assuming the single-parent role. For many fathers, it may be the first time they are solely responsible for their children, although for mothers it may be the first time they cannot be in an overseeing role of the father's parenting behaviors. Another look at Table 23.1 in the "Therapeutic Tasks" category shows how so much of good divorce adjustment for children involves cooperative co-parenting, parenting that is both affectionate and authoritative by both parents, and that does not "parentify" the child (Amato & Gilbreth, 1999; Hetherington et al., 1998; Holloway & Machida, 1991; Koerner, Jacobs, & Raymond, 2000). When parents cannot achieve this goal, referral to preventive intervention divorce groups for children can be highly effective and lead to less substance abuse, mental health problems, and social maladaptation in later years (Wolchik, Sandler, Millsap, & Plummer, 2002).

The therapist also needs to strongly encourage fathers to stay involved with their children and needs to work with the couple in accepting this necessity and implementing its reality. This may also involve reeducation work with mothers, particularly gatekeeper mothers. Some research has found that the degree of parental support from the former spouse is the most important predictor of continued involvement in a father's co-parental involvement and interaction, since 70% of mothers retain custody (Madden & Leonard, 2000). Mothers may feel greater security and be more cooperative in custody arrangements when there is adequate, regular child support from fathers. In the past 30 years, however, there has been no change in the proportion of eligible children receiving child support, hovering at only 30% in the United States (Lin & McLanahan, 2003). Therapy discussion can include the fact that children's well-being has been found to be significantly associated with fathers' payment of child support (Amato & Gilbreth, 1999).

Relationships with same-sex parents may be particularly vulnerable in the event of parental separation, such as when boys experience father loss. Opposite-sex parents constitute a significant influence on adolescents' depression, leading most clinicians to work toward involving both parents in joint custody (Videon, 2002). Exceptions occur when there is violence, mental instability, parental abuse or rejection, substance abuse, or problems with relocation. The advice to clients is that their adjustment to separation and divorce and that of their children depends in large part on how the divorce is positively managed. This advice bears frequent repeating in therapy. Parents can be reminded that despite the dissolving of the marriage, they still have one common goal: the welfare of their children. I find it makes an impact in divorce therapy when I tell parents that we have solid research demonstrating that children fare better when (1) they maintain a good relationship with preferably both parents; (2) when they are kept out of the middle of parental conflicts; (3) when there are fewer disruptions in their lives, including economic ones (Emery & Sbarra, 2002); and (4) when there are flexible and adaptable custody and child support arrangements that can be easily modified as the life and financial situations of the parents change (Thompson & Amato, 1999).

CASE STUDY (CONTINUATION)

After five months of separation, Laura and Michael came in together to see the therapist again. Laura had filed for divorce. She had received a promotion at work and was feeling more secure financially as well as relieved emotionally. They came in to discuss their son, Josh, who was reacting poorly to the divorce. He was wetting the bed and acting aggressively with his peers. Their daughter appeared to be adjusting well, although her semester grades had taken a dip as she spent increasing amounts of time with her peers. Laura worried that Michael turned to their daughter too much for emotional support, and Michael complained that Laura was too lenient with the children, perhaps in response to her own parents' strictness. The session was spent exploring appropriate boundaries with the children and the need to establish and maintain consistent, authoritative parenting by both. They finally agreed to a therapeutic referral for their son and also to investigate a school program for kids going through divorce.

A final couple session discussed additional parenting issues. A beginning understanding of their mutual interlocking problems with intimacy and identity, which were unresolved when they went into the marriage, was also addressed. Michael had made some progress in individual therapy in understanding the causes for his passivity and inability to show his feelings, his anger at his parents' stoicism, and his emotional constriction in the marriage. He had hoped to get the unconditional love he never received from his parents from Laura, yet he could not reciprocate that love. Laura, however, was reluctant to explore the roots of her unsuccessful marital partnerships and the pattern of problems that she had replicated in her first and second marriages. She was more content to simply say she had made mistakes and to focus on the present.

Postdivorce Adjustment

Following key tasks of restructuring and adjustment engendered by divorce, therapy can focus more on ego reparation tasks: regaining self-esteem and confidence, coping with loneliness and aloneness, and building a social support network of friends and intimates. These tasks are immeasurably helped if the person has gained a realistic understanding of the causes of the divorce, his or her contributions, and unraveling the patterns of unconscious childhood strivings in the marriage and other relationships as well as family of origin issues. This is the so-called marital autopsy. Alvin and Pearson (1998) further point out that the relationship system before the divorce is likely to continue to be perpetuated in the divorce, which may lead to continuing painful conflict for all parties involved. Thus, an ambitious second-order goal of postdivorce therapy is to change this pattern of dysfunctional relating and to resolve old narcissistic wounding. Such goals can improve the likelihood of better co-parenting and family relationships. The general goal is to help the person use the trauma and changes wrought by the divorce to effect further developmental change and growth.

A minority of individuals appear in postdivorce therapy many years after the divorce, still obsessed and stuck in the divorce trauma. They may have had severe psychopathology prior to their divorce or have become severely depressed and dysfunctional postdivorce. They cannot resolve their rage, projection of blame, and desire for retaliation. They are nowhere near completing the emotional and psychic divorce necessary for adjustment and healthy development. This type of high-conflict family and parent who cannot empathize with the other parent is often damaging to children's long-term adjustment. Reviewing a large body of research and the mediating variables in postdivorce adjustment, Hetherington et al. (1998) concludes that family process emerges as the key variable. It is largely negative, continuing dysfunction in family relationships between parents, children, and siblings that accounts for differences in children's adjustment. Pathological adjustments to divorce-related ego wounding can involve a perceptual distortion of reality and being rigidly stuck in childhood conflicts. Thus, the child within the parent is perceived and projected onto the real child. Any assault on one's self is perceived as an assault on the child. Furthermore, the person projects his own anger with the ex-spouse onto the ex-spouse, maintaining instead that the ex-spouse is the angry person (Baris, 2001). The perception of the ex-spouse's anger acts to justify continuing retaliation, sometimes to the point where no differing opinion can be accepted, leading to a stalemate in therapy. Fortunately, such high-conflict families and individuals represent a minority of postdivorce therapy clients, but they are memorable enough to warrant careful screening before the therapist becomes involved in an essentially intractable dispute. When clients, through the help of therapy, can finally realize how damaging this continuing blame, projection, and conflict are *to themselves,* they are better able to give up the secondary gains of maintaining the delusion and conflict. Such realization brings relief, forward movement, and the breaking of the developmental impasse.

Postdivorce adjustment changes may involve *role restructuring* tasks as well as *ego reparation,* particularly if one spouse remarries. Kinship structures and roles within blended or binuclear families are often ambiguous and fraught with ambivalent expectations and uncertainties (Simpson, 1998). Consider the 57-year-old man with two children and four grandchildren who marries a 35-year-old woman with two young children, one of whom is adopted. He may be a grandfather, a new husband, and a new father simultaneously, but his role is even more undefined with his new children, his old in-laws, and his new in-laws. Yet, he may want his in-laws, wife, and ex-wife to recognize all these children as members of their families, although each of these people draw their kinship webs somewhat differently from his. Thus, postdivorce therapy often focuses on mediating the ambivalence and conflicts produced when previously mapped-out relationships of the nuclear and extended family are transformed by divorce, producing competing and contradictory depictions and expectations of kinship.

Well-known protective factors in postdivorce adjustment and resilience include not only a supportive new partner, but higher education, satisfying, stable employment, financial security, and supportive social networks (Amato, 2000). Goals in therapy often include helping the client initiate new friendships with single friends, repair old friendship and family relationships, join various clubs or groups, and explore new interests and hobbies. The person may question previously held beliefs about his or her talents and work goals. A change of job or a return to school for new tools and skills may be very beneficial in raising self-esteem and confidence as well as in providing necessary financial security postdivorce. Men may have to be encouraged to learn child rearing, cooking, and housekeeping skills to make a comfortable home for themselves and their children. Women may have to learn new skills in financial management, car repair and maintenance, or other areas that a former spouse controlled. Children may have to become more responsible and share in household tasks. The potential for challenge and growth is obvious.

Transitional Relationship   At some point, sometimes early in the postdivorce adjustment process, the client may become involved in a new relationship. Sometimes, this person is waiting in the wings prior to the divorce. The person often represents a contrast to the old partner. Superficial personal, physical, or situational characteristics draw the divorced person in. The opportunity for some ego repair and regaining of confidence in one's attractiveness and worthiness can be valuable in these relationships, but often they are transitory and do not represent a real change of direction or pattern in the person's development of intimacy and identity. It is useful to explain to clients the dynamics of the transitional relationship, even though they may want to bask in the feeling of temporary love and security without analyzing their motives or the similar variables in that relationship and the unsuccessful marriage. It takes many clients a while to understand that they need a period of being alone, of introspection and change after a divorce, to successfully transcend old patterns of choice and unresolved strivings. The primary losses in divorce, *ego/object loss* and *role loss* result in major challenges to the clients' self-esteem, identity, and the capacity to be intimate. Ultimately, a therapist must help the person get to the point where he or she can say, "I love myself without the love of that other" and "I can love myself without being the spouse of that other" (J. K. Rice & Rice, 1986, p. 108).

CASE STUDY (CONTINUATION)

One year later, after the divorce was final, Laura returned to individual therapy. Although there were small, ongoing disputes with Michael over expenditures, for the most part they were cooperatively co-parenting. Michael had stopped blaming her for leaving him when he became seriously involved with another woman. He told Laura that he was able to express his feelings more fully for the first time with his new fiancée. Laura's mother's diagnosis of incurable cancer was the precipitant for her return to therapy. Having experienced a lifetime of running away from her mother's strictures and criticisms, now as an only child, she was faced with having to take care of her mother on a daily basis. She felt anxious, angry, and unhappy and even questioned whether she had made a mistake in divorcing Michael. Therapy focused on grief work and helping her to accept her mother's illness and death, but also on finishing the uncompleted emotional work of the divorce. Painfully, she began to see how she had continued to replicate an unsatisfactory parent-child relationship in her first marriage, looking for a father, but instead taking on the responsible parent role with her older, gambling husband. With Michael, Laura believed she had finally found a stable man who would be an equal partner and good provider, but found herself again in a position of unrequited emotional dependency. When Laura understood and made peace with her marital decisions as well as with her mother, she also found more contentment in being alone and being a single parent. As Michael prepared to remarry, Laura expressed the sentiment that she would probably never marry again, being happy with her work, parenting, and the companionship of several close women and men friends.

REFERENCES

Alvin, P., & Pearson, J. (1998). *Enmeshment and estrangement in the process of divorce.* New York: Guilford Press.

Amato, P. (2000). The consequences of divorce for adults and children. *Journal of Marriage and the Family, 62,* 1269–1287.

Amato, P., & Gilbreth, J. G. (1999). Nonresident fathers and children's well-being: A meta-analysis. *Journal of Marriage and the Family, 61,* 557–573.

American Psychological Association. (1995). *Lesbian and gay parenting: A resource for psychologists.* Available from http://www.apa.org/pi/parent.html.

Baris, M. A. (2001). *Working with high conflict families of divorce: A guide for professionals.* Northvale, NJ: Aronson.

Baum, N. (2003). Divorce process variables and the co-parental relationship and parental role fulfillment of divorced parents. *Family Process, 42,* 117–131.

Bianchi, S. M., Subaiya, L., & Kahn, J. R. (1999). The gender gap in the economic well-being of non-resident fathers and custodial mothers. *Demography, 36,* 196–203.

Bowlby, J. (1982). *Attachment and loss: Volume I. Attachment* (2nd ed.). New York: Basic Books.

Braver, J., & Cookston, J. (in press). The legacy of divorce: Controversies, clarifications and consequences. *Family Relations.*

Butricia, B. A., & Iams, H. M. (2003). The impact of minority group status on the projected retirement income of divorced women in the baby boomer cohort. In C. L. Jenkins (Ed.), *Widows and divorcees in later life: On their own again* (pp. 67–88). New York: Haworth Press.

Carter, E. A., & McGoldrick, M. (Eds.). (1980). *The family life cycle: A framework for therapy.* New York: Gardner Press.

Cherlin, A. J. (1998). Marriage and marriage dissolution among black Americans. *Journal of Comparative Family Studies, 29,* 147–158.

DeMaris, A. (2000). Till discord do us part: The role of physical and verbal conflict in union disruption. *Journal of Marriage and the Family, 62,* 683–692.

Dreman, S. (1999). The experience of divorce and separation in the family: A dynamic systems perspective. In E. Frydenbery (Ed.), *Learning to cope: Developing as a person in complex societies* (pp. 150–171). London: Oxford University Press.

Emery, R. E., & Sbarra, D. A. (2002). Addressing separation and divorce during and after couple therapy. In A. S. Gurman & N. S. Jacobson (Eds.), *Clinical handbook of couple therapy* (pp. 508–530). New York: Guilford Press.

Gilman, S. E., Kawachi, I., Fitzmaurice, F. M., & Buka, S. (2003). Family disruption in childhood and risk of adult depression. *American Journal of Psychiatry, 160,* 939–946.

Glenn, N. D. (1999). Further discussion of the effects of no-fault divorce. *Journal of Marriage and the Family, 61,* 800–802.

Glick, I. D. (2000). Understanding the functional family. In I. D. Glick (Ed.), *Marital and family therapy* (pp. 57–81). Washington, DC: American Psychiatric Press.

Glick, I. D., & Patel, R. M. (2000). Understanding the Functional Family: Alternative Family Forms. In I. D. Glick (Ed.), *Marital and family therapy* (pp. 86–105). Washington, DC: American Psychiatric Press.

Granvold, D. K. (2002). The crisis of divorce: Cognitive-behavioral and constructivist assessment and treatment. In A. Roberts (Ed.), *Crisis intervention handbook: Assessment, treatment and research* (pp. 307–336). London: Oxford University Press.

Hetherington, E. M. (1999). *Coping with divorce, single parenting and remarriage: A risk and resiliency perspective.* Mahwah, NJ: Erlbaum.

Hetherington, E. M., Bridges, M., & Insabella, G. (1998). What matters, what doesn't: Five perspectives on the association between divorce and remarriage and children's adjustment. *American Psychologist, 53,* 167–183.

Hetherington, E. M., & Kelly, J. (2002). *For better or for worse: Divorce reconsidered.* New York: Norton.

Holloway, S. D., & Machida, S. (1991). Child-rearing effectiveness of divorced mothers: Relationship to coping strategies and social support. *Journal of Divorce and Remarriage, 14,* 179–184.

Hooper, J. (2001). The symbolic origins of conflict in divorce. *Journal of Marriage and Family, 62,* 430–445.

Kaslow, F. W. (1995). The dynamics of divorce therapy. In R. H. Mikesell, D.-D. Lusterman, & S. H. McDaniel (Eds.), *Integrating family therapy: Handbook of family psychology and systems theory* (pp. 271–284). Washington, DC: American Psychological Association.

Kesner, J. E., & McKenry, P. C. (2001). Single parenthood and social competence in children of color. *Families in Society, 82,* 136–144.

Kessler, R. C., Walters, E. E., & Forthofer, M. S. (1998). The social consequences of psychiatric Disorders: 3. Probability of marital stability. *American Journal of Psychiatry, 155,* 1092–1096.

King, V. (2002). Parental divorce and interpersonal trust in adult offspring. *Journal of Marriage and Family, 64,* 642–656.

Koerner, S. S., Jacobs, S. L., & Raymond, M. (2000). When mothers turn to their adolescent daughters: Predicting daughters' vulnerability to negative adjustment outcomes. *Family Relations, 49,* 301–308.

Kposowa, A. J. (1998). The impact of race on divorce in the United States. *Journal of Comparative Family Studies, 29,* 529–548.

Laird, I. (1993). Lesbian and gay families. In F. Walsh (Ed.), *Normal family process* (pp. 282–328). New York: Guilford Press.

Lin, I.-F., & McLanahan, S. S. (2003). Explaining trends in child support: Economic, demographic, and policy effects. *Demography, 40,* 171–189.

Lyle, R. R., & Faure, F. (2000). Life cycle development, divorce and the Hispanic family. In M. T. Flores & B. Carey (Eds.), *Family therapy with Hispanics: Toward appreciating diversity* (pp. 185–203). Boston: Allyn & Bacon.

Madden, D. A., & Leonard, S. A. (2000). Parental role identity and fathers' involvement in co-parental interaction after divorce: Fathers' perspectives. *Family Relations, 49,* 311–318.

McKenry, P. C., & McKelvey, M. W. (2003). The psychosocial well-being of black and white mothers following marital dissolution: A brief report of a follow-up study. *Psychology of Women Quarterly, 27,* 31–36.

McManus, P. A., & DiPrete, T. A. (2001). Losers and winners: The financial consequences of separation and divorce for men. *American Sociological Review, 66,* 246–268.

Rice, D. G. (1989). Marital therapy and the divorcing family. In M. Textor (Ed.), *The divorce and divorce therapy handbook* (pp. 151–169). Northvale, NJ: Aronson.

Rice, J. K. (1994). Reconsidering research on divorce, family life cycle, and the meaning of family. *Psychology of Women Quarterly, 18,* 559–584. (Reprinted from D. Anselmi & A. Law, Eds., *Psychology and gender: An annotated reader,* 1998, New York: McGraw-Hill)

Rice, J. K. (2000, August). *Cross-cultural perspectives on divorce and family life cycle* (Invited address). Washington, DC: American Psychological Association.

Rice, J. K. (2001). Contemporary trends in family patterns and forms. In J. Worell (Ed.), *Encyclopedia of women and gender* (pp. 411–423). San Diego, CA: Academic Press.

Rice, J. K. (2003). I can't go back: Divorce as resistance. In L. Silverstein & T. Goodrich (Eds.), *Feminist family therapy: Empowerment in social context* (pp. 51–63). Washington, DC: American Psychological Association.

Rice, J. K., & Rice, D. G. (1986). The origins of divorce therapy. In J. K. Rice & D. G. Rice (Eds.), *Living through divorce: A developmental perspective to divorce therapy* (pp. 35–69). New York: Guilford Press.

Ruiz, D. S., Zhu, C. W., & Crowther, M. R. (2003). Not on their own again: Psychological, social and health characteristics of custodial African American grandmothers. In C. L. Jenkins (Ed.), *Widows and divorcees in later life: On their own again* (pp. 167–184). New York: Haworth Press.

Simpson, B. (1998). *Changing families: An ethnographic approach to divorce and separation*. New York: Berg.

Sprenkle, D. H. (1989). The clinical practice of divorce therapy. In M. Textor (Ed.), *The divorce and divorce therapy handbook* (pp. 171–191). Northvale, NJ: Aronson.

Swartz, L., & Kaslow, F. (1997). *Painful partings: Divorce and its aftermath*. New York: Wiley.

Thompson, R. A., & Amato, P. R. (1999). *The postdivorce family: Children, parenting, and society*. Thousand Oaks, CA: Sage.

U.S. Census Bureau. (1999). *Selected social characteristics of the population by region and race*. Washington, DC: Author.

Videon, R. M. (2002). The effects of parent-adolescent relationships and parental separation on adolescent well-being. *Journal of Marriage and Family, 64*, 489–503.

Wald, M. S. (2000). *Same sex couples: Marriage, families and children, an analysis of Proposition 22, the Knight initiative*. Palo Alto, CA: Stanford Institute for Research on Women and Gender.

Wallerstein, J., Lewis, J., & Blakeslee, S. (2000). *The unexpected legacy of divorce*. New York: Hyperion.

Wolchik, S. A., Sandler, I. N., Millsap, R. E., & Plummer, B. A. (2002). Six-year follow-up of preventive interventions for children of divorce: A randomized controlled trial. *Journal of the American Medical Association, 288*, 1874–1881.

CHAPTER 24

What the Research Tells Us

Sally D. Stabb

W HY INCLUDE A chapter on research in a book that is dedicated to the practice of couples' therapy? Because systematic, scientific inquiry is the gold standard by which our therapeutic efforts are judged. Research is needed to inform practice, to test our theories and models of couples intervention, and to expand our knowledge base about the very nature of couples' functioning. Furthermore, the managed care environment continues to make pressing demands on practitioners to use empirically validated/supported treatments (EVTs/ESTs). Thus, practitioners' livelihoods are increasingly dependent on their ability to demonstrate the efficacy and effectiveness of their work. As McCollum and Stith (2002) cogently note, "no therapy model can be judged successful if frontline therapists are not able to use it, if it costs too much, or if it cannot be delivered within the confines of our existing health care delivery system" (p. 5).

OVERVIEW

This chapter summarizes the empirical literature in two major domains: (1) what we know about the nature of well-functioning and dysfunctional couples and (2) what we know about what contributes to successful couples therapy outcomes. Specific inclusion and exclusion criteria were used to narrow down the massive amount of recent research in the field.

Studies conducted between the years 2000 to 2003 were included if they involved the use of real couples and real therapists, with the focus of the study being the couple per se (versus children or whole family). Both qualitative and quantitative studies were included, as long as the sample sizes were over one. Reviews of research and meta-analyses were used, as well as articles relevant to the efficacy or effectiveness of couples' therapy as it relates to managed care. Relationship quality/satisfaction, relationship stability, therapy outcome, and therapy process investigations were key targets. Excluded were analog studies, training issues, pure theoretical articles, clinical advice without an empirical study, single-case studies, or case studies used to illustrate a theory or method. Assessment and measurement issues, and investigations where children or the entire family were the focus, were likewise excluded.

The choice to use only materials published since the year 2000 is based on the fact that a number of excellent reviews and metaanalyses had been conducted prior to that time. Most notable among these are the founding metaanalytic work of Shadish and colleagues (1993) as well as the more recent reviews of empirically supported interventions by Pinsof and Wynne (1995) and Baucom, Shoham, Mueser, Daiuto, and Stickle (1998). It is assumed that studies published in the new millennium have included any previous, relevant work.

REVIEW OF THE EMPIRICAL LITERATURE

WHAT MAKES OR BREAKS COUPLES' RELATIONSHIPS?

OBJECTIVE CHARACTERISTICS OF THE COUPLE   It has been long assumed that similarity on a variety of variables such as personality, age, socioeconomic status, education, values, religious beliefs, ethnicity, and so on is conducive to relational satisfaction and stability (see Lykken, 2002 for a brief review). However, the recent research in these domains is mixed.

Religion   Regarding religious similarity, Heller and Wood (2000) found no differences in levels of intimacy between intramarried Jewish couples and intermarried couples with one Jewish partner. Interestingly, when interviewed, the intramarried couples saw their ethnic/religious bond as a source of mutual understanding, while intermarried couples found that the negotiation of their differences deepened intimacy for them. Also studying inter- and intramarried Jewish couples, Chinitz and Brown (2001) discovered that disagreement on religious issues, versus a couple's status as inter- or intramarried, predicted marital dissatisfaction.

Ethnicity   Recent research on interethnic couples challenges the stereotype that these relationships are doomed to instability. Gaines and Brennan (2001) provide evidence that interethnic couples can be successful when differences are appreciated rather than just tolerated, when partners actively create their own unique relationship culture, and when each partner views the other as contributing to her or his personal growth via their cultural differences. For example, no differences in marital satisfaction were found between Mexican American couples, White American couples, and couples with one Mexican American and one White American partner (Negy & Snyder, 2000), interracial White/Asian and intraracial Asian couples (Asidao, 2002), or among interethnic African American/White couples in comparison to both monoethnic African American and monoethnic White couples (La Taillade, 2000).

Regarding monoethnic couples, Allen and Olson (2001) developed a five-category typology of African American marriages, and tested their associations with marital satisfaction and stability. Each of the five types had unique profiles. Santisteban, Muir-Malcolm, Mitrani, and Szapocznik (2002) address variation within an ethnic or cultural group in terms of acculturation. Instability in a couples' relationship is likely to occur when partners move through the acculturation process at varying rates. They note, "an abrupt and accelerated reconfiguration of a couple's egalitarian versus complementary relations dimension . . . cannot help but disrupt family functioning and affect their ability to reach joint decisions and set clear and consistent rules and consequences" (p. 343). Kelly and Floyd (2001) discovered that racial perspectives were key predictors of Black couple adjustment; again, conflicting attitudes held by Afrocentric Black men were associated with deterioration in Black couple relationships.

Psychopathology Individual differences in levels of psychopathology, including trauma history, have been related to couple functioning. Regarding trauma, Nelson and Wampler (2000) compared clinic couples in which one or both partners had a history of childhood abuse with couples in which neither partner had a trauma history. Those couples in which one or both partners experienced early trauma reported lower levels of marital satisfaction and family cohesion. Similarly, Lev-Wiesel and Amir (2001) find that in couples where one member has been a Holocaust survivor with a posttraumatic stress disorder (PTSD) diagnosis, spouses report declines in marital quality, especially when the traumatized partner shares reminiscences or displays hostile behavior. In a study of over 1,300 Palestinian women, Haj-Yahia (2002) found that all forms of abuse (physical, emotional, sexual, and economic) were associated with lower levels of marital commitment, satisfaction, affection, happiness, and harmony. In a slightly different vein, Watt (2002) confirms that couples who come from alcoholic families report more marital instability and dissatisfaction.

A great deal of attention has been given in the couples literature to the relationship between depression and couple functioning; recent studies continue to support this link in a variety of ways (for a review, see O'Mahen, Beach, & Banawan, 2001). In couples where one partner is depressed and the other is not, Benzon and Coyne (2000) identified spousal burden (emotional strain, constant worrying, concern over relapse, partner's feelings of worthlessness and lack of energy) as key elements in the nondepressed partner's mood. When the depressed partner was male, both patient and spouse had higher levels of depression. Katz, Monnier, Libet, Shaw, and Beach (2000) found that medical students' depression was related to increased levels of depression in their spouses, as well as to reduced marital satisfaction. In an examination of women who had experienced a severe marital stressor (infidelity, abuse, or threat of divorce), Cano, Christian-Herman, O'Leary, and Avery-Leaf (2002) determined that 16 months after the event, levels of marital discord, depression, and relationship dissolution were elevated.

Children   Another variable of interest is presence or absence of children in couples' lives. Recent research confirms that marital intimacy declines between one month and three years after children are born (O'Brien & Peyton, 2002), regardless of whether or not it is a first child. Differences in attitudes toward child rearing were associated with drop-offs in marital intimacy as well. In a review of the research on families with young children, Demo and Cox (2000) indicate that after a period of initial adjustment, most couples regain satisfactory levels of marital quality. This is more likely when the marital bond was strong to begin with, when neither partner was depressed, when solid problem-solving communication skills were in place, when parenting expectations were realistic, and when fathers played an active role in caregiving. Negative relationships with in-laws have also been shown to erode marital satisfaction and stability (Bryant, Conger, & Meehan, 2001).

Relationship Status   The status of a couple as married or cohabiting has also been examined in terms of relational happiness (Moore, McCabe, & Brink, 2001). These investigators compared dating, cohabiting, and married couples on indices of intimacy and dyadic adjustment. Married couples had lower levels of affectional expression and engagement in comparison to cohabiting or dating couples. However, levels of intimacy were similar across all three groups. Both married and cohabiting couples had high levels of agreement regarding intimacy and relational adjustment factors in comparison to dating couples.

Gender   Gender is a complex and multifaceted construction, and its influence on intimate relationships has been very widely studied. It would be impossible to comprehensively review this literature in this chapter (but for a concise overview, see Levant & Philpot, 2002); thus, only select studies relating to couples' relationship quality and stability will be included. For example, Acitelli (2001) finds that women see relationship talk as a routine way of maintaining relationships, while men only value such discussions when problems arise. Men may see the need to share activities as more important to relationship maintenance than women. She views the key to relationship duration as agreement on what it takes for each partner to maintain the relationship. Kiecolt-Glaser and Newton (2001) note that men and women's experiences of conflicted versus well-functioning relationships have differential effects on health. Although both men and women experience negative health effects in conjunction with poor marital quality, in general, the associations between relational dysfunction and poor health outcomes are stronger for women than for men. Kiecolt-Glaser and Newton found this to be true in regard to cancer, heart disease, acute and chronic pain, and general rates of morbidity and mortality. Marital conflict/ hostility has been linked to higher levels of physiological arousal and more sustained arousal for women than for men; this may be a factor in women's suppressed immune functioning when marital functioning is poor. Broadly speaking, both men and women benefit from supportive couple relationships, which facilitate both health-promoting behaviors and health itself. Croyle and Waltz (2002) report that women had higher levels of emotional awareness in their relationships than did men, and this higher awareness was associated with less marital satisfaction. In particular, women were aware of hard emotions (anger, resentment). When partners had differing levels of emotional awareness, lower relational satisfaction was evident for both men and women. Soft emotions such as fear and sadness showed no relationship to marital satisfaction for either gender.

Sexual Orientation Like gender, sexual orientation and sexual identities are intricate biopsychosocial constructions. The literature on the nature of well-functioning gay, lesbian, and bisexual couples is small, but growing. Ossana (2000) summarized the literature from the previous decade and concluded that lesbian and gay couples have relationships that are as satisfying as those of heterosexuals (sometimes better for lesbian couples) and that the mechanisms for relational satisfaction are similar across sexual orientation. This appears to be true despite the fact that same-sex couples face unique challenges. Kurdek (2001), reports that gay and lesbian couples report higher levels of comfort with closeness than heterosexual-nonparent couples. Lesbian couples had higher levels of equality, satisfaction, positive problem solving, and dyadic cohesion in comparison to heterosexual-nonparent couples, as well as lower levels of relationship costs. Gay couples reported lower levels of relationship commitment than heterosexual-nonparent couples. In an earlier study with both gay/lesbian and opposite-sex couples, Kurdek (2000) found that the degree of commitment in close relationships over time could be predicted by individuals perceptions of their own constraints, their own attractions, and their partner's attractions. Constraints are those factors that keep people from leaving relationships, while attractions are those factors that draw people into relationships. In a qualitative study looking at the relational challenges of HIV-serodiscordant gay couples, Palmer and Bor (2001) note that partners must negotiate a series relationship of shifts regarding caregiving, boundaries, sexual behaviors, and their future—all within a context of loss and often a hostile environment. Palmer and Bor cite mutuality and openness to communication as key for couples to cope together and for their relationship to remain intact.

Intersections A recent trend in the couples' literature has been to study more than one status variable at a time. Hall and Greene (2002) investigated class differences in African American lesbian relationships. They discovered that class differences were cited as a primary cause of relational strain and dissolution. For African American gay men, McLean, Marini, and Pope (2003) found racial identity to be unrelated to relational satisfaction. Beals and Peplau (2001) determined that lesbians who were mismatched on levels of political activism were less satisfied in their relationships; those who had similar and moderate levels of political activity were most satisfied. Jordan and Deluty (2000) determined that when lesbian partners had discrepant levels of identity self-disclosure, they experienced lower levels of relationship quality.

Dillaway and Broman (2001) found complex relationships between gender, race, and class in their study of marital satisfaction in almost 500 dual-income couples and suggest that studying these variables in isolation is problematic. Inequalities among the structural variables they measured were related to lower levels of couple adjustment. Haddock (2002), who likewise investigated dual-income couples, found that these couples do better when divisions of labor are equitable and when they were not locked into traditional gender-role expectations.

Personality   Individuals' personalities may also contribute to couples' satisfaction and stability in relationships. Asendorpf (2002) reviews the literature showing an association between higher levels of neuroticism and lower levels of marital quality. Lykken (2002) makes an argument for the heritability of negative personality traits, noting that when one member of a pair of identical twins divorces, the chance that the other twin will do so as well is extremely high. Trait hostility is also reliably linked to poor relational functioning, especially for men; men's hostility likewise influences their female partner's emotional health (Kiecolt-Glaser & Newton, 2001).

Watson, Hubbard, and Wiese (2000) examined associations between the Big Five personality traits (neuroticism, extraversion, openness, agreeableness, conscientiousness), positive and negative affectivity, and marital satisfaction. As predicted, people high in positivity rate their relationships as more satisfying and those high in negativity rate their relationships as much less satisfying. Extraversion, agreeableness, and conscientiousness were also reliable predictors of satisfaction; neuroticism was associated with dissatisfaction, and openness was unrelated to marital quality. When rating their partners, the only reliable indicator of relationship (dis)satisfaction was partner negativity. Personality and affectivity explained up to a third of the variance in marital satisfaction scores, indicating that individual personality does make a difference in the extent to which couples are happy. The work of Robins, Caspi, and Moffitt (2000) shows similar trends. Each individual in the couples they studied contributed independently to relationship outcomes. Relational happiness was associated with partner's low negative emotionality for both men and women. Women's relational happiness was also predicted by her partner's high positive emotionality and constraint (the tendency to act in a cautious manner and to conform to and endorse social norms).

AFFECTIVE PROCESSES   More than one researcher has noted that positive affect is curiously understudied in the literature on couples adjustment (Gable & Reis, 2001; Heyman, 2001); however, that is changing. Findings are converging on the discovery that relationship dissolution is not so much a function of high levels of negativity per se, but of declines in positivity over time (Gable & Reis, 2001; Gottman, Ryan, Carrère, & Erley, 2002), especially when predicting the dissolution of long-term relationships (Gottman, 2000). Gottman and colleagues have found that couples use positive affect to both soothe themselves and to deescalate conflicts; engaging in such a manner is predictive of successful relationships. The ratio of positive to negative interactions in couples' interactions is also predictive of relationship success or failure. Gottman discusses the concept of positive sentiment override (originally from the work of Weiss, 1990), in which couples make global, positive judgments regarding their relationships as well as interpreting negative messages from their partners as neutral. These processes are critical in maintaining happy relationships; similarly, the opposite process—negative sentiment override—is destructive. Gottman also cites a ratio of 5:1 positive to negative interactions as indicative of well-functioning couples. Similarly, Flora and Segrin (2000) note a positive global sense of the relationship protects couples from feeling negative affect, even during complaining interactions.

Attachment processes have been extensively studied in regard to adult romantic relationships. As noted by Scott and Cordova (2002), adult attachment has been consistently related to marital adjustment. In their particular study of adult attachment, depression, and marital adjustment, Scott and Cordova determined that depressive symptoms are more strongly related to marital distress when husbands or wives reported anxious-ambivalent attachment than when they are securely attached or when they report avoidant attachment styles. In another recent study of attachment, marital interaction, and relationship satisfaction, Feeney (2002) discovered that both greater attachment security and frequency of positive spouse behavior were related to marital satisfaction. Insecure individuals, especially those with anxious attachment, were more reactive to both positive and especially negative spousal behaviors. This pattern was also evident for those low in comfort with closeness. Secure people appear to hold more stable and global positive views of their partners, which allow them to be less reactive to day-to-day fluctuations in their partners' behaviors. Interestingly, Feeney found these patterns to hold for those in long-term (over 10 years together) marriages but not for those in shorter-term marriages.

COGNITIVE PROCESSES A variety of cognitive processes, particularly attribution, have been indicated in couples' adjustment. Perceptions, attitudes, and a number of social-cognitive biases have likewise been examined.

Over a 15-year course of research, Frank Fincham and associates (Fincham, Harold, & Gano-Phillips, 2000) have established a clear association between attributions and marital satisfaction. In summary, "locating the cause of negative relationship events in the partner, viewing the cause as more stable and global, and seeing the partner's behavior as intentional, blameworthy, and reflecting selfish motivation are more likely among distressed partners" (p. 268). However, in their recent work, these researchers found that attributions were linked to satisfaction because they influence couples' efficacy expectations (the belief that he or she can perform the actions needed to resolve marital conflicts). This suggests that therapists might do better to target efficacy versus attribution per se.

Expanding on the extensive work of Fincham and colleagues, Karney, McNulty, and Frye (2001) found that when couples make positive and global evaluations of their relationship, these broad ways of thinking about their bond can carry them through specific negative events in the course of day-to-day interactions. When couples start to see their partners as responsible for specific negative events, their global evaluations of the relationship may also decline over time. Similarly, selective attention to negative partner behaviors, as well as interpreting neutral or positive partner behavior through a negative cognitive filter, is clearly related to marital distress (Heyman, 2001).

Challenging the assumption that people have an ingrained and stable attibutional style (essentially like a personality trait), Karney and Bradbury (2000) determined in a four-year longitudinal study that spouses' attributions change over time along with fluctuations in their marital satisfaction and ongoing experiences in their relationships. This doesn't mean that attributions are irrelevant to marital satisfaction, just that they are so interrelated that one can't be said to cause the other. However, Karney and Bradbury found that if spouses started out with maladaptive attributions early on in their relationships, this did predict sharper declines in satisfaction over time.

Recent work also shows that couples have hindsight biases when reporting relationship events over the course of a week (Halford, Keefer, & Osgarby, 2002). Marital satisfaction was measured at the beginning of the week, and couples then kept diaries of positive and negative relationship events for seven days. They were then asked to talk about what they remembered over the course of the week about their relationship. Those individuals who recalled mostly negative information (negative hindsight memory bias) were the same ones who had reported lower marital satisfaction at the beginning of the study. Obviously, this finding has implications for therapists who routinely ask similar questions.

Carrère, Beuhlman, Gottman, Coan, and Ruckstuhl (2000) found that the perceptions of newlywed spouses predicted the stability of their marriages with a high degree of accuracy up to nine years after marriage. Selective attention to positive or negative aspects of one's partner, or to the marriage itself, appear to influence the course of the relationship. Using the Oral History Interview, the authors found that spouses who had strong positive perceptions of their initial marital bond ("we-ness," fondness, expansiveness) were more likely to remain together versus those who had negative perceptions (negativity, disappointment, and chaos). The authors theorize that positive perceptions of the marital bond may serve as a buffer during times of conflict or transition.

BEHAVIORAL PROCESSES AND VERBAL INTERACTIONS   A number of mutual, reciprocal processes are key in the maintenance of romantic relationships. Likewise, specific mechanisms and choices in couple interactions maintain cycles of conflict.

Positive Processes   In examining relationship-enhancing dynamics, Mills and Clark (2001) discovered that well-functioning relationships are communal relationships, which are defined as "a relationship in which each member has a concern for the welfare of the other . . . [and is] motivated to provide benefits to the other without expecting a specific benefit in return" (p. 13). This differs from basic equity or exchange relationships in which more of a keeping score mentality is the norm. Strong communal bonds include understanding each other's needs, compatibility of needs, agreement about the primacy of couple bond over other relationship connections, and benign interpretations of a partner's intentions when needs are not met (e.g., he or she wanted to be supportive, but was unable to do so).

This is not to say that equity has no role in relationship satisfaction. Equity theory (the idea that couples are more satisfied when the ratio of inputs and outputs for each party are equal; no one is over- or underbenefited in the relationship) has a long and well-substantiated history. Recently, Canary and Stafford (2001) have examined how perceptions of equity are related to specific relationship maintenance behaviors, such as openness, positivity, assurances, social networking, and sharing tasks. Well-functioning couples engage in these behaviors proactively to sustain their bond.

A similar process—preemptive relationship maintenance—has been identified by Simpson, Ickes, and Oriña (2001). Preemptive relationship tactics involve premeditated actions taken to avert problems before they develop, routinely addressing small issues so that they don't escalate into larger ones, and cognitive strategies that focus on positive inferences about one's partner and relationship.

In long-term relationships, Aron, Norman, and Aron (2001) found that when couples periodically engage in mutually agreed on "self-expanding" activities, marital quality increases. Self-expanding behaviors are novel, arousing, or exciting, rather than just being routinely pleasant; they serve to mitigate boredom and monotony. Interestingly, the opposite is also true; having established and cherished couple rituals and routines has been associated with marital satisfaction (Fiese et al., 2002).

Using interdependence theory as a base, Rusbult, Olsen, Davis, and Hannon (2001) note that people become more dependent on their relationships when their levels of satisfaction and investment are high, and when the quality of their potential alternatives is low. Higher dependence leads to increased commitment; that is, we are more motivated to stay in our relationships. This sustained level of commitment is then maintained by behavioral accommodation to one's partner, willingness to sacrifice and to forgive, as well as by cognitive mechanisms such as a focus on interdependence, positive illusions, and derogation of alternatives. When both partners engage in such activities over time, trust is enhanced, and couples' well-being results.

The negotiation of the contradictions inherent in couple relationships has been shown to have important associations with relationship commitment and quality. Sahlstein and Baxter (2001) found that the working through of such basic couple dialectics such as autonomy-connection, openness-closedness, and stability-change are part and parcel of the process of commitment—commitment is not a one-shot promise or an unchanging aspect of emotional investment. Sahlstein and Baxter suggest that "living on friendly terms with paradoxes and contradictions" (p. 125) is key in relationship maintenance. Behaviors such as denying contradictions or passively giving up in the face of contradictions leads to relationship decline. Functional strategies for handling contradictions include turn taking, compromise, integration (responding fully to both sides of the issue), recalibration (reframing contradiction so that it is no longer experienced as opposition), and reaffirmation (enjoying and celebrating differences).

In a similar vein, Whitton, Stanley, and Markman (2002) find that individuals who are successful in their intimate partnerships are willing to make sacrifices and report satisfaction about sacrificing itself. They define sacrifice as "acts in which individuals give up some immediate desire in the interest of bettering their relationship or benefiting their partner" (p. 159). Such sacrificing often takes the form of stepping back from the immediate conflict to consider actions that will have a positive long-term impact on the relationship versus being reactive in the moment, or to return negativity with neutral or even positive affect.

A number of studies find that rates of conflict are often relatively stable (Noller & Feeney, 2002) and that many couples engage in what Roloff and Johnson (2002) call serial arguments. Surprisingly, these enduring and often repetitive conflicts do not necessarily lead to relationship dissolution. In some cases they do, and in others they don't. For example, Roloff and Johnson note that the more a couple is together, the higher their investment, the fewer important issues remain unresolved, and the more partners learn to be proactive in deterring conflict in the first place or to develop ways to temper conflict with positive affect. Gottman and colleagues (2002) likewise discuss what they call perpetual problems (p. 160); these are unresolvable, longstanding disagreements that are probably based on couples' personalities. However, such perpetual problems do not contribute to relationship dissolution if they are handled with affection and amusement.

Negative Processes Couples who develop destructive conflict patterns early on are more likely to dissolve their relationships (Noller & Feeney,

2002). Heyman (2001) presents a concise summary of what these distressed couples' verbal interaction patterns look like, stating that such couples:

> (a) are more hostile, (b) start their conversations more hostilely and maintain it during the course of the conversation, (c) are more likely to reciprocate and escalate their partners' hostility, (d) are less likely to edit their behavior during conflict, resulting in longer negative reciprocity loops, (e) emit less positive behavior, (f) suffer more ill health effects from their conflicts, and (g) are more likely to show demand-withdrawal patterns. (p. 8)

Similarly, Gottman and colleagues (2002) conclude, "The most consistent discriminator between distressed and non-distressed marriages is negative affect reciprocity" (p. 158). Negative interactions identified by Gottman and associates include criticism, contempt, defensiveness, and stonewalling (avoiding, shutting down, or turning away from interaction). Both the perpetual problems noted earlier and potentially resolvable problems do become predictive of relationship failure when couples choose to handle them in the unproductive ways noted above.

Additional support for the idea that initial negative views of one's relationship can distort the perception of later interaction comes from Flora and Segrin (2000). Individuals who began interactions with negative sentiment override did not respond to changes in the topic (compliments versus complaints) of conversation with their spouses. Not surprisingly, both spouses in this study reported declines in marital satisfaction with increased complaining; this was especially true for husbands. Relationships were happier when spouses could talk through complaints with more gazing behavior, less negative emotion, less wife talk time, and more husband talk time.

The trends noted in the section above, both in terms of positive and negative interactions, were recently supported by Stanley, Markman, and Whitton (2002) in a creative study using a national random sample of over 900 participants and a phone survey. Through this atypical method, the researchers confirmed that "[n]egative interaction was negatively associated with every index of relationship quality and positively associated with thoughts and talk of divorce" (p. 670). Their work also gives credence to the idea that for men, negative interaction is more predictive of divorce than for women; for women, lack of positive interaction is more predictive of divorce. Men also withdrew from interaction more often than did women, and for both genders, withdrawal was related to loss of connection and increased negativity.

Furthermore, Stanley and colleagues (2002) conclude that conversational process is more important than conversational topic. However, Sanford (2003) found that topic difficulty did make a difference in couples' communication, although indirectly. He suggests that difficult conflicts (topics) decrease relational satisfaction, which then leads to poor communication styles. For both members of the couple, discussions of their most difficult issues were accompanied by more negative forms of talk (criticism, contempt, defensiveness); husbands also showed poor listening when discussing the couple's most difficult topics.

SEX   Reviews of the literature on the association between sexual satisfaction and relational satisfaction generally support the expected positive link between these two aspects of couples' lives (e.g., Christopher & Sprecher, 2000). In a more recent study, Sprecher (2002) notes that most of the previous work has been cross-sectional, so changes in sexual satisfaction and relational satisfaction cannot be tracked across time.

Sprecher's 2002 study investigated sexual and relational satisfaction over a five-year period, allowing for more predictive tests. Although Sprecher continued to find that sexual satisfaction and relationship satisfaction were related for both genders and across both dating and married couples, predictive analyses failed to provide useful information because "sexual satisfaction and relationship quality may influence each other almost simultaneously" (p. 197). Regarding staying together or breaking up, sexually dissatisfied couples broke up more often and sexually satisfied couples had longer-lasting relationships. Associations between relational and sexual satisfaction were stronger for men than for women; Sprecher states, "I would speculate that men are more likely than women to use the quality of their sexual relationship as a barometer for the quality of the entire relationship" (p. 197).

SYNTHESIS AND THERAPEUTIC IMPLICATIONS   It is the opinion of this reviewer that affective processes are emerging as *the* central organizing element in understanding successful and unsuccessful coupling. How couples choose to react to discrepancies, demographic differences, or inequities in their relationships, the ways in which harmfully toned perceptions and cognitions influence couple judgments, and cycles of poor communication and conflict all seem to share a common link in the generation and maintenance of negative affect. Likewise, consistent positive affect appears to buffer couples against temporary fluctuations in their relationships and to maintain vital connections through its interrelationship with both cognitive processes (such as positive illusion and focus on a global sense of "we-ness") and with pleasing behaviors. So it is not simply differences in personality, ethnicity, acculturation, values, religion, or what have you that matters; it is what each couple does with their differences that matters. Although it is no doubt true that all behavior, cognition, and affect interact in complex ways, emotion appears to provide a conceptual and practical starting point that is eminently useful.

WHAT MAKES OR BREAKS COUPLES THERAPY?

OUTCOME LITERATURE   A series of recent reviews continue to find that couples therapy is modestly effective, although concerns remain regarding both the proportion of couples who make progress and the duration of changes (Sexton, Alexander, & Mease, 2003). A number of specific treatment modalities have enough replicated support to be designated as EVTs/ESTs. Behavioral marital therapy (BMT) and emotionally focused therapy (EFT) have the strongest current research base, and have been accepted as empirically validated (Denton, Burleson, Clark, Rodriguez, & Hobbs, 2000; Gollan & Jacobson, 2002; Johnson, 2003; Johnson & Boisvert, 2002; Johnson & Lebow, 2000; Lebow, 2000; Sexton et al., 2003; Shadish & Baldwin, 2003).

A newer therapy that is gaining empirical support is integrative behavioral couples therapy (IBCT; Jacobson, Christensen, Prince, Cordova, & Eldridge, 2000; Jones, Doss, & Christensen, 2001; Wheeler & Christensen, 2002). Also called just integrative couples therapy (ICT; Gollan & Jacobson, 2002), IBCT goals are both emotional acceptance and behavior change. The first is brought about via the revelation of vulnerable feelings, which enhances empathy. The second is accomplished by identifying problems as externalized situations couples "get into with each other" versus blaming each other for "the bad things you do to me" (Jones et al., 2001, p. 324). This allows the couple to more objectively identify the specific triggers for their cycles of negative interaction and to then intervene.

The scientifically based marital therapy developed by John Gottman and colleagues (e.g., Gottman, 2001; Gottman et al., 2002) deserves inclusion on any list of effective couples therapies. Based on his sound marital house theory and well-executed in-house clinical research over the past decade, Gottman's work has garnered substantial support.

Reviewers (Gollan & Jacobson, 2002; Johnson, 2003; Sexton et al., 2003) list IBCT along with cognitive-behavioral marital therapy (CBMT), strategic therapy, and insight-oriented marital therapy (IOMT) as being better than no treatment for couple distress, although these four therapies do not have the degree of empirical support that BMT and EFT do. Epstein (2001) offers additional support for cognitive-behavioral approaches.

Marital and premarital enrichment/enhancement programs, including couple communication (CC), relationship enhancement (RE), the prevention and relationship enhancement program (PREP), and PAIRS (DeMaria & Hannah, 2002) continue to enjoy empirical support as well (Accordino & Guerney, 2002; Halford, Sanders, & Behrens, 2001; Johnson & Boisvert, 2002; Johnson & Lebow, 2000; Silliman, Stanley, Coffin, Markman, & Jordan, 2002; Sullivan & Goldschmidt, 2000). Couples participating in these programs, especially those with a strong skills base, report satisfaction with relationship education as well as gains in communication, quality of relationship, and changes in the way they handle conflict over time. As with couples' therapy per se, effects of these interventions past the 6- to 12-month mark are less well-documented, with the strongest support for PREP (Halford, Markman, Kline, & Stanley, 2003). A recent metaanalysis (Carroll & Doherty, 2003), provides support for premarital enhancement programs as well. Overall effect sizes were moderately large (.80), indicating that couples who participated in such programs were better off than 79% of those who do not. Premarital enrichment leads to immediate and short-term gains in relationship quality and interpersonal skills.

Two recent additions to the prevention/enhancement ranks were found. One, called the Marriage Checkup (MC; Gee, Scott, Castellani, & Cordova, 2002) gives couples a two-session motivational interview consisting of assessment and feedback (p. 399). Even two years after participation, MC resulted in moderate changes for the better in couples' relationships, and increased levels of therapy-seeking by wives. The second, Couples' Coping Enhancement Training (CCET; Bodenmann, Charvoz, Cina, & Widmer, 2001), takes a cognitive-behavioral and couples' coping skills approach. Couples who completed the 18-hour course maintained gains in marital adjustment at one-year follow-up.

Couples therapy has been shown to be helpful in the treatment of a host of mental health disorders and difficulties (Johnson & Lebow, 2000). For example, in the treatment of depression, Kung (2000) notes that couples therapies that attend to four dimensions—marital stress, support, role expectations, and interactional dynamics—are likely to be the most effective. In particular, Kung recommends Teichman and Teichman's (1990) cognitive marital therapy (CMT). Mead (2002) finds the strongest empirical support for BMT in the treatment of co-occurring marital distress and depression. Denton, Golden, and Walsh (2003) note that although couples and individual therapies seem equally effective in treating depression, couples therapy is typically superior in enhancing relational adjustment.

In special sections of the *Journal of Marital and Family Therapy* devoted to MFT effectiveness, support is noted for the treatment of schizophrenia (McFarlane, Dixon, Lukens, & Lucksted, 2003), substance abuse (Rowe & Liddle, 2003), alcohol abuse (O'Farrell & Fals-Stewart, 2003), and affective disorders (Beach, 2003), with mixed results in studies of couple counseling for adult chronic illnesses (Campbell, 2003). In a related vein, Cloutier, Manion, Walker, and Johnson (2002) found EFT to be effective over the course of two years in helping couples cope with the marital distress generated by caring for chronically ill children. In a multicase qualitative study, Trute, Docking, and Hiebert-Murphy (2001) found brief conjoint therapy helpful for couples in which the female partners were both recovering addicts and survivors of childhood sexual abuse. A review by Sexton and colleagues (2003) supports the effectiveness of couples therapy in the treatment of depression, substance abuse (up to one year, after which individual therapy is found to be equally effective), and to a modest degree for sexual disorders. Johnson (2003) adds agoraphobia and obsessive-compulsive disorders to the list. Lantz and Gregoire (2000) report that traumatized Vietnam veteran couples responded well to existential couples therapy, with treatment gains maintained at one-year follow-up.

From a cultural perspective, Santisteban and colleagues (2002) emphasize that it is important to match relationship patterns to treatments. Couples who embrace cultural patterns of symmetrical and egalitarian relationships are likely to do well in therapies that emphasize direct negotiation. In contrast, couples who organize their relationships along complementary lines may do better with more indirect interventions such as those promoted in strategic models or in therapies that focus on acceptance.

PROCESS LITERATURE Couples therapy process research looks at what happens inside therapy sessions that makes a difference to outcome. Frielander, Wildman, Heatherington, and Skowron conducted a seminal review of this literature in 1994. These authors concluded that important processes in couples work should include an active therapist; client changes in cognition, behavior, and especially affective states; the therapeutic bond as experienced by the client; and client's level of engagement in therapy. At the turn of the millennium, Lebow (2000) concluded that the therapeutic alliance was the primary empirically supported change process in couples therapy. More recently, authors such as Diamond and Diamond (2002) have suggested that from a transtheoretical approach, common key tasks in the process of couples therapy would include building alliances, reattribution/reframing, reattachment, and for those couples with children, attention to parenting practices.

However, Sexton and colleagues (2003) caution: "In its present state, the trends and specific findings of couples therapy process research provide no more than provocative possibilities" (p. 607). They do identify three empirically supported change mechanisms, including the reduction of negative communication/blame, the therapeutic alliance, and a therapy structure in which the couple is allowed substantial responsibility in guiding their sessions. Factors such as clients' level of distress or psychopathology and therapist experience (skill) may moderate the effects of couples therapy.

Getting more specific, Heyman (2001), in his impressive review of approximately 200 studies on couples' observation research, concludes that critical interventions are based on teaching couples how to monitor and then exit their poor communication cycles. Core processes that need to be assessed in therapy include:

> How does the conversation start? Does the level of anger escalate? What happens when it does? Do they enter repetitive negative loops? Do they indicate afterward that what occurred during the conversation is typical? Is their behavior stable between . . . discussions? Do their behaviors differ when it is her topic rather than his? Do they label the other person or the communication process as the problem? (p. 16)

Using concepts derived from the sound marital house theory, Gottman and colleagues (2002) note that building positive affect is a crucial task in the process of therapy. Telling partners to just be nice to each other doesn't work; Gottman and colleagues recommend rebuilding the couple's friendship in three ways. The first is through deeply knowing one's partner (love maps). The second is expressing fondness and admiration for one's partner. The third is to turn toward (p. 157) one's partner in everyday interactions, rather than ignoring or discounting. It is important that these processes be carried out in nonconflictual contexts. Additionally, couples must be helped to exit negative cycles of interaction. This can be accomplished in four ways: "(a) softened startup, (b) accepting influence, (c) repair and deescalation, and (d) compromise" (p. 160). If couples become gridlocked in negative sentiment override and eventual emotional detachment, Gottman recommends techniques such as "creating shared symbolic meaning and honoring life dreams" (p. 161) to reconnect the partners. Such reengagement is accomplished through exploring "each person's experience history with the basic emotions . . . the meaning of everyday rituals, as well as the meaning of fundamental roles in their family of origin and their own marriage and family" (p. 161).

Johnson (2003), from the perspective of EFT, has identified a number of key therapy processes related to successful outcomes. Clients in EFT report that crucial sessions involve deep experiencing and positive self-focused statements, which tend to allow their partners to come closer and to respond with reciprocal self-disclosure. Johnson refers to such moments as "softening," which "refers to a previously hostile and blaming spouse's asking for an affiliative response from the other in a vulnerable and congruent fashion. The other spouse, previously withdrawn, is then able to be accessible and responsive, thus creating emotional engagement" (p. 809).

A recent qualitative study by Helmeke and Sprenkle (2000) examined pivotal change moments in couples therapy. They found that these moments were characterized by being highly individualized, personal, and private, "[r]ather than being emotionally charged moments that were shared by or at least evident to all the participants" (p. 479). Pivotal moments in early sessions often gave hope, clarified, or reframed couple problems. Additionally, therapists often needed to revisit core emotional themes across a number of sessions before pivotal moments occurred later in therapy. This study is noteworthy for its focus on couples' immediate postsession reports of important changes experienced from their own perspectives.

SUMMARY/SYNTHESIS   It should be clear at this point that many forms of couples therapy are effective modes of intervention. In keeping with the idea that affective processes are key in couple relationships, attention to both interrupting cycles of negative emotion and to rebuilding emotional connections in therapy seem pivotal in all effective therapies. Evidence for this can clearly be seen in EFT, and in the recent modifications of BMT to include more focus on emotion (IBCT), and in Gottman's approach. However, it should be noted that certain types of couples do better in therapy; those who are younger and who don't have children, those who start therapy with less negative affect, those who are less gender-traditional, those with less individual psychopathology, those who are not yet seriously disengaged from each other, and those who are economically advantaged (Gollan & Jacobson, 2002; Gottman et al., 2002; Johnson, 2003).

Another indicator of overall effectiveness is that couples therapy has been shown to reduce the utilization of other health care services (Law & Crane, 2000). However, although couples therapy has now clearly demonstrated a basic level of success, some cautionary notes are in order. As Johnson and Lebow (2000) note, most client couples are White and middle class; thus, so is most of the research on couples therapy. Although diversity issues are beginning to be addressed in the basic literature regarding couples' adjustment, relational satisfaction, and relational stability, the field of couples therapy research has lagged behind. Some studies have started to address the particular personal/therapist qualities and skills needed to deliver effective couples therapy to specific populations, such as rural couples (Hovestadt, Fenell, & Canfield, 2002), ethnically diverse couples (Bean, Perry, & Bedell, 2001; Constantine, Juby, & Liang, 2001), and gay, lesbian, or bisexual couples (Bepko & Johnson, 2000; Bieschke, McClanahan, Tozer, Grzegorek, & Park, 2000; Laird, 2000).

Additionally, more research linking process and outcome would be helpful. Newer, complex models and statistical techniques are allowing for more sophisticated work to emerge in this area. Likewise, creating (and then documenting) sustained changes in couples therapy remains a challenge.

CASE STUDY: A THERAPEUTIC FAILURE

DESCRIPTION OF THE CASE

A White, middle-class, childless, dual-income couple, Amanda (28) and Roger (31) presented for therapy to resolve issues regarding infidelity and poor communication. They had been dating for two and half years and had been married for one year. Amanda brought a history of childhood and adolescent sexual abuse, as well as current problems with alcohol abuse. She initiated a short-term affair that was the crisis that brought the two to counseling. Roger used both alcohol and marijuana when stressed, and self-identified as wanting to avoid conflicts. Roger desperately wanted to stay in the relationship, but reported feeling helpless and ineffectual. Both expressed a wish for more closeness and affection, although Amanda had no sexual desire for Roger and also talked about ending the relationship. Amanda had been in individual therapy previously working on her sexual abuse concerns.

In the first session, the therapist, a relatively inexperienced clinician, conducted a half-hour interview to get the history behind the couple's presenting concerns. They reported difficulty for the past six months, with Amanda attending classes part-time in a nearby city and Roger working 12-hour days to make ends meet. Roger admitted resentment over Amanda's new interests and friends at school; Amanda complained about Roger's lack of responsiveness to her in the evening. Roger felt unappreciated for all his hard work. Amanda would try to engage Roger, usually in angry ways, which would be followed by Roger's shutting down and withdrawing. Amanda would then withdraw as well, and eventually chose to turn to an extra-marital relationship for support. Amanda had stopped the affair before the couple entered therapy and expressed anger and impatience that Roger did not appear to be "over it" yet. The therapist made no specific interventions in the initial session.

In four following sessions, the therapist taught and coached the couple on communications skills and had them practice using the skills in session to discuss something positive in their relationship and then to discuss more difficult issues. The therapist helped the couple to identify negative patterns of interaction and reframed or challenged dichotomous thinking and dysfunctional relationship beliefs. For homework, the therapist asked the couple to come up with a time they could do something fun together at least one time during the week and made a concrete and specific plan tailored to their preferences and schedules. The couple was also asked to have check-in conversations with each other each evening, with each partner alternating the initiation of that conversation. Amanda and Roger complied with all assignments, but remained hostile and frustrated in sessions. The therapist constructed a genogram with the couple in their fourth session to explore family-of-origin patterns that might be related to their own relationship. The couple failed to attend the next two sessions and appeared to have quit with their core issues unresolved.

APPLICATION OF THE RESEARCH: WHAT COULD THE THERAPIST HAVE DONE DIFFERENTLY?

The main therapeutic mistake here would seem to be the therapist's failure to attend to the negative affect that continued to be actively expressed between the couple. Therapy remained at a largely cognitive level, without the opportunity for the couple to access or experience their deep feelings of vulnerability and missed connection with each other. Although attempts were made to increase positive interactions, these interventions were probably premature, given that the couple remained engaged in a cycle of mutual resentment, blame, and fear. Any number of techniques based on BMT, EFT, IBCT, or Gottman's sound marital house (all described earlier) could have been applied here.

SUMMARY

It would appear that we are drawing nearer to a science of couple relationships in which converging themes regarding verbal/behavioral interactions, cognition, and especially affective processes are recognizable. Similarly, common processes that underlie successful and sustainable couples therapy outcomes are being identified. Work remains to be done in determining how these basic processes interrelate, as well as how they may be influenced by the intersections of gender, race, class, sexual orientation, ethnicity, acculturation, cultural values, and so on. Programmatic and practical research efforts, building on the promising initial base that has already been established, should lead clinicians to well-informed and successful couples therapies.

REFERENCES

Accordino, M. P., & Guerney, B. G. (2002). The empirical validation of relationship enhancement couple and family therapy. In D. J. Cain & J. Seeman (Eds.), *Humanistic psychotherapies: Handbook of research and practice* (pp. 403–442). Washington, DC: American Psychological Association.

Acitelli, L. K. (2001). Maintaining and enhancing a relationship by attending to it. In J. H. Harvey & A. Wenzel (Eds.), *Close romantic relationships: Maintenance and enhancement* (pp. 153–168). Mahwah, NJ: Erlbaum.

Allen, W. D., & Olson, D. H. (2001). Five types of African-American marriages. *Journal of Marital and Family Therapy, 27,* 301–314.

Aron, A., Norman, C. C., & Aron, E. N. (2001). Shared self-expanding activities as a means of maintaining and enhancing close romantic relationships. In J. H. Harvey & A. Wenzel (Eds.), *Close romantic relationships: Maintenance and enhancement* (pp. 47–66). Mahwah, NJ: Erlbaum.

Asendorpf, J. B. (2002). Personality effects on personal relationships over the life span. In A. L. Vangelisti, H. T. Reis, & M. A. Fitzpatrick (Eds.), *Stability and change in relationships* (pp. 35–56). Cambridge, England Cambridge University Press.

Asidao, C. S. (2002). Exploring variables associated with interracial and intraracial couples' relationship satisfaction. *Dissertation Abstracts International, 63(2-B),* 1085.

Baucom, D. H., Shoham, V., Mueser, K. T., Daiuto, A. D., & Stickle, T. R. (1998). Empirically supported couple and family interventions for marital distress and adult mental health problems. *Journal of Consulting and Clinical Psychology, 66,* 53–88.

Beach, S. (2003). Affective disorders. *Journal of Marital and Family Therapy, 29,* 247–262.

Beals, K. P., & Peplau, L. A. (2001). Social involvement, disclosure of sexual orientation, and the quality of lesbian relationships. *Psychology of Women Quarterly, 25,* 10–19.

Bean, R. A., Perry, B. J., & Bedell, T. M. (2001). Developing culturally competent marriage and family therapists: Guidelines for working with Hispanic families. *Journal of Marital and Family Therapy, 27,* 43–54.

Benzon, N. R., & Coyne, J. C. (2000). Living with a depressed spouse. *Journal of Family Psychology, 14,* 71–79.

Bepko, C., & Johnson, T. (2000). Gay and lesbian couples in therapy: Perspectives for the contemporary family therapist. *Journal of Marital and Family Therapy, 26,* 409–419.

Bieschke, K. J., McClanahan, M., Tozer, E., Grzegorek, J. L., & Park, J. (2000). Programmatic research on the treatment of lesbian, gay, and bisexual clients: The past, the present, and the course for the future. In R. M. Perez, K. A. DeBord, & K. J. Bieschke (Eds.), *Handbook of counseling and psychotherapy with lesbian, gay, and bisexual clients* (pp. 309–335). Washington, DC: American Psychological Association.

Bodenmann, G., Charvoz, L., Cina, A., & Widmer, K. (2001). Prevention of marital distress by enhancing the coping skills of couples: 1-year follow-up-study. *Swiss Journal of Psychology, 60,* 3–10.

Bryant, C. M., Conger, R. D., & Meehan, J. M. (2001). The influence of in-laws on change in marital success. *Journal of Marriage and the Family, 63,* 614–626.

Campbell, T. L. (2003). The effectiveness of family interventions for physical disorders. *Journal of Marital and Family Therapy, 29,* 263–282.

Canary, D. J., & Stafford, L. (2001). Equity in the preservation of personal relationships. In J. H. Harvey & A. Wenzel (Eds.), *Close romantic relationships: Maintenance and enhancement* (pp. 133–152). Mahwah, NJ: Erlbaum.

Cano, A., Christian-Herman, J., O'Leary, K. D., & Avery-Leaf, S. (2002). Antecedents and consequences of negative marital stressors. *Journal of Marital and Family Therapy, 28,* 145–151.

Carrère, S., Beuhlman, K. T., Gottman, J. M., Coan, J. A., & Ruckstuhl, L. (2000). Predicting marital stability and divorce in newlywed couples. *Journal of Family Psychology, 14,* 42–58.

Carroll, J. S., & Doherty, W. J. (2003). Evaluating the effectiveness of premarital prevention programs: A meta-analytic review of outcome research. *Family Relations: Interdisciplinary Journal of Applied Family Studies, 52,* 105–118.

Chinitz, J. G., & Brown, R. A. (2001). Religious homogamy, marital conflict, and stability in same-faith and interfaith Jewish marriages. *Journal for the Scientific Study of Religion, 40,* 723–733.

Christopher, E. S., & Sprecher, S. (2000). Sexuality in marriage, dating and other relationships: A decade review. *Journal of Marriage and the Family, 62,* 999–1017.

Cloutier, P. F., Manion, I. G., Walker, J. G., & Johnson, S. M. (2002). Emotion focused interventions for couples with chronically ill children: A 2-year follow-up. *Journal of Marital and Family Therapy, 28,* 391–398.

Constantine, M. G., Juby, H. L., & Liang, J. J.-C. (2001). Examining multicultural counseling competence and race-related attitudes among white marital and family therapists. *Journal of Marital and Family Therapy, 27,* 353–362.

Croyle, K. L., & Waltz, J. (2002). Emotional awareness and couples' relationship satisfaction. *Journal of Marital and Family Therapy, 28,* 435–444.

DeMaria, R., & Hannah, M. (2002). *Building intimate relationships: Bridging treatment, education and enrichment through the PAIRS program.* New York: Brunner-Routledge.

Demo, D. H., & Cox, M. J. (2000). Families with young children: A review of the research in the 1990s. *Journal of Marriage and the Family, 62,* 876–896.

Denton, W. H., Burleson, B. R., Clark, T. E., Rodriguez, C. P., & Hobbs, B. V. (2000). A randomized trial of emotion-focused therapy for couples in a training clinic. *Journal of Marital and Family Therapy, 26,* 65–78.

Denton, W. H., Golden, R. N., & Walsh, S. R. (2003). Depression, marital discord, and couple therapy. *Current Opinion in Psychiatry, 16,* 29–34.

Diamond, G. S., & Diamond, G. M. (2002). Studying a matrix of change mechanisms: An agenda for family-based process research. In H. A. Liddle, D. A. Santisteban, R. F. Levant, & J. H. Bray (Eds.), *Family psychology: Science-based interventions* (pp. 41–66). Washington, DC: American Psychological Association.

Dillaway, H., & Broman, C. (2001). Race, class and gender differences in marital satisfaction and divisions of household labor among dual-earner couples. *Journal of Family Issues, 22,* 309–327.

Epstein, N. (2001). Cognitive-behavioral therapy with couples: Empirical status. *Journal of Cognitive Psychotherapy: An International Quarterly, 15,* 299–310.

Feeney, J. A. (2002). Attachment, marital interaction, and relationship satisfaction: A diary study. *Personal Relationships, 9,* 39–55.

Fiese, B. H., Tomcho, T. J., Douglas, M., Josephs, K., Poltrock, S., & Baker, T. (2002). A review of 50 years of research on naturally occurring family routines and rituals: Cause for celebration? *Journal of Family Psychology, 16,* 381–390.

Fincham, F. D., Harold, G. T., & Gano-Phillips, S. (2000). The longitudinal association between attributions and marital satisfaction: Direction of effects and role of efficacy expectations. *Journal of Family Psychology, 14,* 267–285.

Flora, J., & Segrin, C. (2000). Affect and behavioral involvement in spousal complaints and compliments. *Journal of Family Psychology, 14,* 641–657.

Friedlander, M. L., Wildman, J., Heatherington, L., & Skowron, E. A. (1994). What we do and don't know about the process of family therapy. *Journal of Family Psychology, 8,* 390–416.

Gable, S. L., & Reis, H. T. (2001). Appetitive and aversive social interaction. In J. H. Harvey & A. Wenzel (Eds.), *Close romantic relationships: Maintenance and enhancement* (pp. 169–194). Mahwah, NJ: Erlbaum.

Gaines, S. O., Jr., & Brennan, K. A. (2001). Establishing and maintaining satisfaction in multicultural relationships. In J. H. Harvey & A. Wenzel (Eds.), *Close romantic relationships: Maintenance and enhancement* (pp. 237–254). Mahwah, NJ: Erlbaum.

Gee, C. B., Scott, R. L., Castellani, A. M., & Cordova, J. V. (2002). Predicting 2-year marital satisfaction from partners' discussion of their marriage checkup. *Journal of Marital and Family Therapy, 28,* 399–407.

Gollan, J. K., & Jacobson, N. S. (2002). Developments in couple therapy research. In H. A. Liddle, D. A. Santisteban, R. F. Levant, & J. H. Bray (Eds.), *Family psychology: Science-based interventions* (pp. 105–122). Washington, DC: American Psychological Association.

Gottman, J. M. (2000). The timing of divorce: Predicting when a couple will divorce over a 14-year period. *Journal of Marriage and the Family, 62,* 737–745.

Gottman, J. M. (2001). *Marital therapy: A research-based approach™ clinician's manual.* Seattle, WA: Gottman Institute.

Gottman, J. M., Ryan, K. D., Carrère, S., & Erley, A. M. (2002). Toward a scientifically based marital therapy. In H. A. Liddle, D. A. Santisteban, R. F. Levant, & J. H. Bray (Eds.), *Family psychology: Science-based interventions* (pp. 147–174). Washington, DC: American Psychological Association.

Haddock, S. (2002). A content analysis of articles pertaining to therapeutic considerations for dual-income couples (1979–1999). *American Journal of Family Therapy, 30,* 141–156.

Haj-Yahia, M. M. (2002). The impact of wife abuse on marital relationships as revealed by the second Palestinian national survey on violence against women. *Journal of Family Psychology, 16,* 273–285.

Halford, W. K., Keefer, E., & Osgarby, S. M. (2002). "How has the week been for you two?" Relationship satisfaction and hindsight memory biases in couples' reports of relationship events. *Cognitive Therapy and Research, 26,* 759–773.

Halford, W. K., Markman, H. J., Kline, G. H., & Stanley, S. M. (2003). Best practice in couple relationship education. *Journal of Marital and Family Therapy, 29,* 385–406.

Halford, W. K., Sanders, M. R., & Behrens, B. C. (2001). Can skills training prevent relationship problems in at-risk couples? Four-year effects of a behavioral relationship education program. *Journal of Family Psychology, 15,* 750–768.

Hall, R. L., & Greene, B. (2002). Not any one thing: The complex legacy of social class on African American lesbian relationships. *Journal of Lesbian Studies, 6,* 65–74.

Heller, P. E., & Wood, B. (2000). The influence of religious and ethnic differences on marital intimacy: Intermarriage versus intramarriage. *Journal of Marital and Family Therapy, 26,* 241–252.

Helmeke, K. B., & Sprenkle, D. H. (2000). Client's perceptions of pivotal moments in couples therapy: A qualitative study of change in therapy. *Journal of Marital and Family Therapy, 26,* 469–484.

Heyman, R. E. (2001). Observation of couple conflicts: Clinical assessment applications, stubborn truths, and shaky foundations. *Psychological Assessment, 13,* 5–35.

Hovestadt, A. J., Fenell, D. L., & Canfield, B. S. (2002). Characteristics of effective providers of marital and family therapy in rural mental health settings. *Journal of Marital and Family Therapy, 28,* 225–231.

Jacobson, N. S., Christensen, A., Prince, S. E., Cordova, J., & Eldridge, K. (2000). Integrative behavioral couple therapy: An acceptance-based, promising new treatment for couple discord. *Journal of Clinical and Consulting Psychology, 68,* 351–355.

Johnson, S. (2003). Couples therapy research: Status and directions. In G. P. Sholevar & L. D. Schwoeri (Eds.), *Textbook of family and couples therapy* (pp. 797–814). Washington, DC: American Psychiatric Publishing.

Johnson, S., & Boisvert, C. (2002). Treating couples and families from the humanistic perspective: More than the symptom, more than solutions. In D. J. Cain & J. Seeman (Eds.), *Humanistic psychotherapies: Handbook of research and practice* (pp. 309–337). Washington, DC: American Psychological Association.

Johnson, S., & Lebow, J. (2000). The "Coming of age" of couple therapy: A decade of review. *Journal of Marital and Family Therapy, 26,* 23–38.

Jones, J., Doss, B. D., & Christensen, A. (2001). Integrative behavioral couple therapy. In J. H. Harvey & A. Wenzel (Eds.), *Close romantic relationships: Maintenance and enhancement* (pp. 321–344). Mahwah, NJ: Erlbaum.

Jordan, K. M., & Deluty, R. H. (2000). Social support, coming out, and relationship satisfaction in lesbian couples. *Journal of Lesbian Studies, 4,* 145–164.

Karney, B. R., & Bradbury, T. N. (2000). Attributions in marriage: State or trait? A growth curve analysis. *Journal of Personality and Social Psychology, 78,* 295–309.

Karney, B. R., McNulty, J. K., & Frye, N. E. (2001). A social-cognitive perspective on the maintenance and deterioration of relationship satisfaction. In J. H. Harvey & A. Wenzel (Eds.), *Close romantic relationships: Maintenance and enhancement* (pp. 195–214). Mahwah, NJ: Erlbaum.

Katz, J., Monnier, J., Libet, J., Shaw, D., & Beach, S. R. H. (2000). Individual and crossover effects of stress on adjustment in medical student marriages. *Journal of Marital and Family Therapy, 26,* 341–351.

Kelly, S., & Floyd, F. J. (2001). The effects of negative racial stereotypes and Afrocentricity on Black couple relationships. *Journal of Family Psychology, 15,* 110–123.

Kiecolt-Glaser, J. K., & Newton, T. L. (2001). Marriage and heath: His and hers. *Psychological Bulletin, 127,* 472–503.

Kung, W. W. (2000). The intertwined relationship between depression and marital distress: Elements of marital therapy conducive to effective treatment outcome. *Journal of Marital and Family Therapy, 26,* 51–63.

Kurdek, L. A. (2000). Attractions and constraints as determinants of relationship commitment: Longitudinal evidence from gay, lesbian, and heterosexual couples. *Personal Relationships, 7,* 245–262.

Kurdek, L. A. (2001). Differences between heterosexual-nonparent couples and gay, lesbian and heterosexual-parent couples. *Journal of Family Issues, 22,* 728–755.

Laird, J. (2000). Gender in lesbian relationships: Cultural, feminist, and constructionist reflections. *Journal of Marital and Family Therapy, 26,* 455–467.

Lantz, J., & Gregoire, T. (2000). Existential psychotherapy with Vietnam veteran couples: A twenty-five year report. *Contemporary Family Therapy, 22,* 19–37.

La Taillade, J. J. (2000). Predictors of satisfaction and resiliency in African American/White interracial couples. *Dissertation Abstracts International, 60(11-B),* 5779.

Law, D. D., & Crane, D. R. (2000). The influence of marital and family therapy on health care utilization in a health-maintenance organization. *Journal of Marital and Family Therapy, 26,* 281–291.

Lebow, J. (2000). What does the research tell us about couple and family therapies? *Journal of Clinical Psychology/In Session: Psychotherapy in Practice, 56,* 1083–1094.

Levant, R. F., & Philpot, C. L. (2002). Conceptualizing gender in marital and family therapy research: The gender role strain paradigm. In H. A. Liddle, D. A. Santisteban, R. F. Levant, & J. H. Bray (Eds.), *Family psychology: Science-based interventions* (pp. 301–330). Washington, DC: American Psychological Association.

Lev-Wiesel, R., & Amir, M. (2001). Secondary traumatic stress, psychological distress, sharing of traumatic reminiscences, and marital quality among spouses of Holocaust child survivors. *Journal of Marital and Family Therapy, 27,* 422–444.

Lykken, D. T. (2002). How relationships begin and end: A genetic perspective. In A. L. Vangelisti, H. T. Reis, & M. A. Fitzpatrick (Eds.), *Stability and change in relationships* (pp. 83–106). Cambridge, England Cambridge University Press.

McCollum, E. E., & Stith, S. M. (2002). Leaving the ivory tower: An introduction to the special section on doing marriage and family therapy research in community agencies. *Journal of Marital and Family Therapy, 28,* 5–7.

McFarlane, W. R., Dixon, L. B., Lukens, E. P., & Lucksted, A. (2003). Family psychoeducation and schizophrenia: A review of the literature. *Journal of Marital and Family Therapy, 29,* 223–246.

McLean, R., Marini, I., & Pope, M. (2003). Racial identity and relationship satisfaction in African American gay men. *Counseling and Therapy for Couples and Families, 11,* 13–22.

Mead, D. E. (2002). Marital distress, co-occurring depression, and marital therapy: A review. *Journal of Marital and Family Therapy, 28,* 299–314.

Mills, J., & Clark, M. S. (2001). Viewing close relationships as communal relationships: Implications for maintenance and enhancement. In J. H. Harvey & A. Wenzel (Eds.), *Close romantic relationships: Maintenance and enhancement* (pp. 13–26). Mahwah, NJ: Erlbaum.

Moore, K. A., McCabe, M. P., & Brink, R. B. (2001). Are married couples happier in their relationships than cohabiting couples? Intimacy and relationship factors. *Sexual and Relationship Therapy, 16,* 35–46.

Negy, C., & Snyder, D. K. (2000). Relationship satisfaction of Mexican-American and non-Hispanic White-American interethnic couples: Issues of acculturation and clinical intervention. *Journal of Marital and Family Therapy, 26,* 293–304.

Nelson, B. S., & Wampler, K. S. (2000). Systemic effects of trauma in clinic couples: An exploratory study of secondary trauma resulting from childhood abuse. *Journal of Marital and Family Therapy, 26,* 171–184.

Noller, P., & Feeney, J. A. (2002). Communication, relationship concerns, and satisfaction in early marriage. In A. L. Vangelisti, H. T. Reis, & M. A. Fitzpatrick (Eds.), *Stability and change in relationships* (pp. 129–155). Cambridge, England Cambridge University Press.

O'Brien, M., & Peyton, V. (2002). Parenting attitudes and marital intimacy: A longitudinal analysis. *Journal of Family Psychology, 16,* 118–127.

O'Farrell, T. J., & Fals-Stewart, W. (2003). Alcohol abuse. *Journal of Marital and Family Therapy, 29,* 121–146.

O'Mahen, H. A., Beach, S. R. H., & Banawan, S. F. (2001). Depression in marriage. In J. H. Harvey & A. Wenzel (Eds.), *Close romantic relationships: Maintenance and enhancement* (pp. 299–320). Mahwah, NJ: Erlbaum.

Ossana, S. M. (2000). Relationship and couples counseling. In R. M. Perez, K. A. DeBord, & K. J. Bieschke (Eds.), *Handbook of counseling and psychotherapy with lesbian, gay, and bisexual clients* (pp. 275–302). Washington, DC: American Psychological Association.

Palmer, R., & Bor, R. (2001). The challenges to intimacy and sexual relationships for gay men in HIV-serodiscordant relationships: A pilot study. *Journal of Marital and Family Therapy, 27,* 419–432.

Pinsof, W., & Wynne, L. (1995). The effectiveness of marital and family therapy [Special issue]. *Journal of Martial and Family Therapy, 21.*

Robins, R. W., Caspi, A., & Moffitt, T. E. (2000). Two personalities, one relationship: Both partners' personality traits shape the quality of their relationship. *Journal of Personality and Social Psychology, 79,* 251–259.

Roloff, M. E., & Johnson, K. L. (2002). Serial arguing over the relational life course: Antecedents and consequences. In A. L. Vangelisti, H. T. Reis, & M. A. Fitzpatrick (Eds.), *Stability and change in relationships* (pp. 107–128). Cambridge, England Cambridge University Press.

Rowe, C. L., & Liddle, H. A. (2003). Substance abuse. *Journal of Marital and Family Therapy, 29,* 97–120.

Rusbult, C. E., Olsen, N., Davis, J. L., & Hannon, P. A. (2001). Commitment and relationship maintenance mechanisms. In J. H. Harvey & A. Wenzel (Eds.), *Close romantic relationships: Maintenance and enhancement* (pp. 87–114). Mahwah, NJ: Erlbaum.

Sahlstein, E. M., & Baxter, L. A. (2001). Improvising commitment in close relationships: A relational dialectics perspective. In J. H. Harvey & A. Wenzel (Eds.), *Close romantic relationships: Maintenance and enhancement* (pp. 115–132). Mahwah, NJ: Erlbaum.

Sanford, K. (2003). Problem-solving conversations in marriage: Does it matter what topics couples discuss? *Personal Relationships, 10,* 97–112.

Santisteban, D. A., Muir-Malcolm, J. A., Mitrani, V. B., & Szapocznik, J. (2002). Integrating the study of ethnic culture and family psychology intervention science. In H. A. Liddle, D. A. Santisteban, R. F. Levant, & J. H. Bray (Eds.), *Family psychology: Science-based interventions* (pp. 331–352). Washington, DC: American Psychological Association.

Scott, R. L., & Cordova, J. V. (2002). The influence of adult attachment styles on the association between marital adjustment and depressive symptoms. *Journal of Family Psychology, 16,* 199–208.

Sexton, T. L., Alexander, J. F., & Mease, A. L. (2004). Levels of evidence for the models and mechanisms of therapeutic change in family and couple therapy. In M. J. Lambert (Ed.), *Bergin and Garfield's handbook of psychotherapy and behavior change* (5th ed., pp. 590–646). Hoboken, NJ: Wiley.

Shadish, W. R., & Baldwin, S. A. (2003). Meta-analysis of MFT interventions. *Journal of Marital and Family Therapy, 29,* 547–570.

Shadish, W. R., Montgomery, L., Wilson, P., Wilson, M., Bright, I., & Okwumabua, T. (1993). The effects of family and marital psychotherapies: A meta-analysis. *Journal of Consulting and Clinical Psychology, 61,* 992–1002.

Silliman, B., Stanley, S., Coffin, W., Markman, H. J., & Jordan, P. L. (2002). Preventative interventions for couples. In H. A. Liddle, D. A. Santisteban, R. F. Levant, & J. H. Bray (Eds.), *Family psychology: Science-based interventions* (pp. 123–146). Washington, DC: American Psychological Association.

Simpson, J. A., Ickes, W., & Oriña, M. (2001). Empathic accuracy and preemptive relationship maintenance. In J. H. Harvey & A. Wenzel (Eds.), *Close romantic relationships: Maintenance and enhancement* (pp. 27–46). Mahwah, NJ: Erlbaum.

Sprecher, S. (2002). Sexual satisfaction in premarital relationships: Associations with satisfaction, love, commitment, and stability. *Journal of Sex Research, 2002,* 190–197.

Stanley, S. M., Markman, H. J., & Whitton, S. W. (2002). Communication, conflict, and commitment: Insights on the foundations of relationship success from a national survey. *Family Process, 41,* 659–675.

Sullivan, K. T., & Goldschmidt, D. (2000). Implementation of empirically validated interventions in managed-care settings: The prevention and relationship enhancement program. *Professional Psychology: Research and Practice, 31,* 216–220.

Teichman, Y., & Teichman, M. (1990). Interpersonal view of depression: Review and integration. *Journal of Family Psychology, 3,* 349–367.

Trute, B., Docking, B., & Hiebert-Murphy, D. (2001). Couples therapy for women survivors of child sexual abuse who are in addictions recovery: A comparative case study of treatment process and outcome. *Journal of Marital and Family Therapy, 27,* 99–110.

Watson, D., Hubbard, B., & Wiese, D. (2000). General traits of personality and affectivity as predictors of satisfaction in intimate relationships: Evidence from self- and partner-ratings. *Journal of Personality, 68,* 413–449.

Watt, T. T. (2002). Marital and cohabiting relationships of adult children of alcoholics: Evidence from the National Survey of Family and Households. *Journal of Family Issues, 23,* 246–265.

Weiss, R. L. (1990). Strategic behavioral marital therapy: Toward a model for assessment and intervention. In J. P. Vincent (Ed.), *Advances in family intervention, assessment, and theory* (Vol. 1, pp. 229–271). Greenwich: CT: JAI Press.

Wheeler, J., & Christensen, A. (2002). Creating a context for change: Integrative couple therapy. In A. L. Vangelisti, H. T. Reis, & M. A. Fitzpatrick (Eds.), *Stability and change in relationships* (pp. 285–305). Cambridge, England Cambridge University Press.

Whitton, S., Stanley, S., & Markman, H. (2002). Sacrifice in romantic relationships: An exploration of relevant research and theory. In A. L. Vangelisti, H. T. Reis, & M. A. Fitzpatrick (Eds.), *Stability and change in relationships* (pp. 156–181). Cambridge, England: Cambridge University Press.

CHAPTER 25

Some Concluding Thoughts about Couples and Couples Therapy

Michele Harway

WORKING ON THIS manuscript has convinced me that operating as a couple represents an extremely complex form of human interaction. Adjusting to being in a relationship with another person with a different cultural and familial background is challenging. Added to that mix are the myriad of special challenges that life brings with it. And, it is important to remember that not only are different couples different from each other but the very same couple will change as it traverses the family life cycle. It is hoped that the chapters in this book have provided you with a strong background reflecting this perspective.

Given the complexity of the issues that working with couples brings, specific training on doing this work is imperative. Many of the previous chapters have convincingly made the point that it is not sufficient to know how to do psychotherapy. Knowing how to do psychotherapy when more than one person is in the therapy room is critical. And knowing the special needs of couples is equally important. At the same time, it is important to recognize that there is also magic in doing psychotherapy that cannot be reflected in these chapters. Each clinician must spin his or her own brand of magic in working with couples.

As attested to by the number of chapters in this volume that focus on integrative approaches to working with couples, perhaps the greatest challenge to clinicians is to develop models of working with couples that involve a variety of approaches. New integrative approaches to couples therapy are desirable.

There is also much that we do not know about couples and working with couples. Some years ago, I was on the doctoral committee of a student's dissertation focused on what she called low-quality high-longevity marriages. She was fascinated with what it was about couples that allowed some to stay together for many years even though there was very little that would have predicted longevity in the relationship. She searched for some explanation of what accounted for their willingness to stay together even though happiness eluded them. Regrettably her dissertation shed little light on these kinds of couples and provided even less information about what mental health professionals can do to make their relationships good ones in addition to lasting ones. Clearly, more needs to be explored empirically in this area. We also need to better understand what draws people to one another and which of those qualities make for healthy long-lasting relationships.

Similarly, the high number of divorces today attests to the fact that it has become easier to leave a difficult relationship than to work through the important issues it presents to the couple. When a couple engaged in a troubled relationship consults me, it is clear to me that instilling hope about the potential of the relationship is a critical first step. I find that some couples seem intensely relieved at the hopeful message. When I see a couple with potential who has given up, I remain troubled about the message they have given themselves as well as society. What can we, as a society, do to encourage couples to confront their relationship challenges early enough that they are still emotionally willing to work them through? Once they seek out clinical help, what can clinicians do to encourage them to see the inherent value of the couple bond that will facilitate their staying together rather than dissolving the relationship?

We are living in a time in history when the very meaning of family values is brought into question, with very different meanings attributed depending on which side of the political aisle one is located. This is also a time when gays and lesbians are openly challenging the portrayal of marriage as that where one man and one woman come together to procreate. And, opposing political and religious factions are demanding a constitutional amendment to ensure that the definition of marriage be restricted in this way. Where does that leave us as couples therapists? How do our own political views about family and about marriage affect what we see and what we do in the therapy room? In addition, it is likely that in no other arena of therapy does our worldview have such a strong impact on our work. Certainly, our views about the value of couple relationships affect our work and the subtle or overt messages we communicate to our couple clients. How does our own relational history impact the work we do with couples? How does what we have learned from our families or our ethnic or cultural group affect what we believe about couples? It is clear that I have a strong bias toward helping couples remain together. My own background of growing up in a two-parent family and of being in a long-term relationship (24 years) certainly plays a role. How often do we examine our own assumptions about the value of coupling and question the work we do from that perspective? How do our views of love permeate our attitudes about relationships and commitment? How does the cultural value of the individual affect both our own and our clients' views about ways to be in relationship?

For me, this volume and the work I do with couples forces me on a frequent basis to examine my assumptions about relationships. I expect that this is an important part of being a good couples therapist.

Author Index

Subject Index